dyddiad

SOVEREIGNTY AND THE STATELESS NATION

Gibraltar is an Overseas Territory of the UK within the EU, which has for three centuries been at the centre of a dispute between Britain and Spain, a dispute based on traditional perceptions of sovereignty. Hitherto the dispute has been managed in a predominantly bilateral way, but this has prevented the people of Gibraltar having an equal say on the issue of Gibraltar's sovereignty and decolonisation. It has produced a paradox of governance and constitutionalism that encases the Gibraltar people. This book considers the effects of sovereignty and the culture of bilateralism on the dispute, and examines the resulting deficits of governance and democracy. In assessing the evolution of the themes underlying the dispute it asks how its resolution might be facilitated by the application of ideas drawn from the modern legal context of late sovereignty, pluralism and stateless nationalism, suggesting that a productive trilateral approach and recognition of the legal and societal context could enable an enduring settlement.

The author marries theories from international relations, constitutional law and public international law in the context of modern literature on sovereignty and nationalism, applying these theories to the case-study of Gibraltar with emphasis on constitutionalism in its international and EU context to produce a ground-breaking addition to the literature on stateless nationalism, late sovereignty and constitutional pluralism. As such it also complements recent studies of sub-state societies, regions or nations within Europe and elsewhere, including Catalunya, the Basque Country and Scotland and Wales, and in the broader Commonwealth context, other British overseas territories.

This book will be of interest to lawyers, political scientists, constitutional historians and constitutionalists.

Studies in International Law: Volume 24

Studies in International Law

Volume 1: Between Light and Shadow: The World Bank, the International Monetary Fund and International Human Rights Law *Mac Darrow*

Volume 2: Toxics and Transnational Law: International and European Regulation of Toxic Substances as Legal Symbolism *Marc Pallemaerts*

Volume 3: The Chapter VII Powers of the United Nations Security Council *Erika de Wet*

Volume 4: Enforcing International Law Norms Against Terrorism *Edited by Andrea Bianchi*

Volume 5: The Permanent International Criminal Court *Edited by Dominic McGoldrick, Peter Rowe and Eric Donnelly.*

Volume 6: Regional Organisations and the Development of Collective Security *Ademola Abass*

Volume 7: Islamic State Practices, International Law and the Threat from Terrorism: A Critique of the 'Clash of Civilizations' in the New World Order *Javaid Rehman*

Volume 8: Predictablity and Flexibility in the Law of Maritime Delimitation *Yoshifumi Tanaka*

Volume 9: Biotechnology and International Law *Edited by Francesco Francioni and Tullio Scovazzi*

Volume 10: The Development of Human Rights Law by the Judges of the International Court of Justice *Shiv Bedi*

Volume 11: The Environmental Accountability of the World Bank to Third Party Non-State Actors *Alix Gowlland-Gualtieri*

Volume 12: Transnational Corporations and Human Rights *Edited by Olivier De Schutter*

Volume 13: Biotechnologies and International Human Rights *Edited by Francesco Francioni*

Volume 14: Human Security and International Law: Prospects and Problems *Barbara Von Tigerstrom*

Volume 15: The Arms Trade and International Law *Zeray Yihdego*

Volume 16: Africa: Mapping New Boundaries in International Law *Edited by Jeremy Levitt*

Volume 17: Forced Migration, Human Rights and Security *Edited by Jane McAdam*

Volume 18: The Use of Nuclear Weapons and the Protection of the Environment during International Armed Conflict *Erik Koppe*

Volume 19: The Shifting Allocation of Authority in International Law: Considering Sovereignty, Supremacy and Subsidiarity *Edited by Tomer Broude and Yuval Shany*

Volume 20: Counterterrorism: Democracy's Challenge *Edited by Andrea Bianchi and Alexis Keller*

Volume 21: Amnesty, Human Rights and Political Transitions *Louise Mallinder*

Volume 22: Property Rights and Natural Resources *Richard Barnes*

Volume 23: Human Dignity and the Foundations of International Law *Patrick Capps*

Sovereignty and the Stateless Nation

Gibraltar in the Modern Legal Context

Keith Azopardi
BA, PhD, Barrister

•HART•
PUBLISHING

OXFORD AND PORTLAND, OREGON
2009

Published in North America (US and Canada) by
Hart Publishing
c/o International Specialized Book Services
920 NE 58th Avenue, Suite 300
Portland, OR 97213-3786
USA
Tel: +1-503-287-3093 or toll-free: (1)-800-944-6190
Fax: +1 503 280 8832
E-mail: orders@isbs.com
Website: www.isbs.com

Hart Publishing Ltd, 16C Worcester Place, Oxford, OX1 2JW
Telephone: +44 (0)1865 517530 Fax: +44 (0)1865 510710
E-mail: mail@hartpub.co.uk
Website: http://www.hartpub.co.uk

British Library Cataloguing in Publication Data
Data Available

ISBN: 978-1-84113-916-6

Typeset by Hope Services, Abingdon, Oxon
Printed and bound in Great Britain by
TJ International Ltd, Padstow, Cornwall

To Asta, Zita and Zoe

Foreword

The issue of state sovereignty has been a point of focus for constitutional theorists over the past two decades, with particular attention centred upon the relationship between states on the one hand and international law and supranational organisations on the other. A recent turn, however, has been to address the challenges to established patterns of normative authority from below the level of the state. Keith Azopardi enters this debate addressing the fascinating case of Gibraltar. In doing so he offers, to my knowledge, the first systematic study of the constitutional status of Gibraltar in the context of inter-state relations, international law and European Community law.

The image of Gibraltar 'between three flags' captures how a small but politically sophisticated polity has learned to adapt its constitutional aspirations in the context of two powerful states whose own sovereign claims fall against the backdrop of the inchoate constitutional context of the European Union. Dr Azopardi offers us a study that is very wide-ranging in its scope, addressing the pertinent issues of law and legal theory across a number of normative sites of purported legal authority. His is a rich account of the historical development of Gibraltar's constitutional status and an authoritative excursus into international and European law to explain Gibraltar's location within a complex multi-level Europe. But more than this, Gibraltar is also deployed as a case study with which to interrogate the fuzzy nature of legal authority at the interstices between sub-state, state and supra-state level in contemporary Europe. The study of a small territory thereby becomes nothing less than an important book about Europe's legal self. The innovative techniques used by Gibraltarian political actors to find constitutional space for a small self-governing entity offers insights into how states need to understand sub-state constituent power more broadly as a challenge to assumptions about the unitary nature of legal authority. It also demonstrates how states within Europe, facing sovereign challenges from beyond and finding their own sovereignty increasingly attenuated, need to respond by developing similarly imaginative tools with which to move beyond the Westphalian paradigm. Dr Azopardi is to be commended for such an enlightening study and one which uses Gibraltar as a mirror with which to view more clearly Europe as a complex and in many ways messy legal space. The literature on the constitutional management of sub-state nationalism is advanced in this book, but beyond this so too is our understanding of the nature of legal sovereignty in our time.

Stephen Tierney
Professor of Constitutional Theory
University of Edinburgh

Acknowledgements

In the autumn of 1998 I was asked by the Chief Minister of Gibraltar to open exploratory talks with the British Government on constitutional reform. Relations with Spain were not good and, while there were expectations of progress, it was clear enough that it would be tough going. In the event the negotiations took eight years to complete. They could easily have taken eight minutes, for, during the opening discussions, a senior British official handed me a list in response to the detailed paper with draft constitution annexed that had been sent from Gibraltar. It contained just a few headings and was apparently the limits and parameters of what Her Majesty's Government in the United Kingdom was prepared to negotiate. Our package of reform was said to be 'maximalist' and impossible. It was clear that there was much nervousness in British official circles of the possible reaction from Spain. There followed some minutes of tension and what diplomats would call 'full and frank' exchanges. Eventually, on the strength of written assurances that had been given by the then Foreign Secretary to consider all proposals received, it was decided to proceed. That was just another beginning of another episode in the long and complex relationship between Britain, Spain and Gibraltar.

This book is not the story of that process of constitutional reform, but it is about the dynamics of the relationship between the peoples and Governments of Gibraltar, Spain and the United Kingdom. It is about the underlying issues and themes that affect those relationships. Fundamentally, it is about sovereignty and how this affects the governance and status of Gibraltar. It is not just about the past. It is also about how the current legal context contains hopes for the future. It is, I hope, a small contribution to the possible future resolution of the Gibraltar dispute and the wider debate on sovereignty, nationalism and governance that affects many other territories and nations.

The completion of this work has been slow and for that my family has borne the brunt of my angst to scour resources and endlessly fine-tune passages. In the end there will, no doubt, still be imprecisions and inaccuracies as well as vague or polemical passages. All those deficiencies and judgments are solely mine. Equally any lapses of objectivity at any point are entirely mine.

This book would not have been possible without the helpful comments and guidance of my doctoral supervisors at the University of Nottingham, Professor David Harris and Professor Jeffrey Kenner. The latter especially endured the numerous drafts and re-drafts of my research on the commonwealth, constitutional colonial law and its interrelationship with European law. I am deeply grateful for their advice and navigation of my research when it was sailing through turbulent seas. Professor Stephen Tierney of Edinburgh University and Professor Panos Koutrakos of Bristol University commented on my doctoral thesis and gave me constructive suggestions on how to reshape my work into a more viable proposition. The result has been this book that is probably much more radically different to my initial research than I had anticipated but is hopefully the better for it. Again I am very grateful to both for their help and especially to Stephen Tierney for kindly agreeing to write a foreword for this book. A special thanks also to Richard Hart for showing such enthusiasm for this project and to the whole team at Hart Publishing in Oxford for making the publication process seamless. I am delighted to have had Hart Publishing's support for this work.

Finally and most importantly I want to thank Zoe, Zita and Asta for putting up with what must have seemed endless holidays and weekends full of constitutional law. While it has been my passion I recognise that through no fault of their own they have also had to forcibly endure volumes on decolonisation, sovereignty and constitutional theory. Their love and support for this work has been unquestioning and it is to them that this book is dedicated.

Keith Azopardi
Gibraltar
2 March 2009

Contents

Table of Cases

Australia

Canada

European Court and Commission of Human Rights

European Court of Justice and Court of First Instance

Chronological

Alphabetical

France

Germany

Gibraltar

International Court of Justice

Italy

Permanent Court of Arbitration

Pitcairn Islands

United Kingdom and Privy Council

Table of Legislation

European Union

Falkland Islands

Germany

Gibraltar

Ireland

Italy

Montserrat

St Helena

South Georgia

Spain

Turks and Caicos

United Kingdom

Statutory Instruments

Table of Conventions, Treaties, etc

Introduction: Between Three Flags— Constitution, Status, Governance and Sovereignty in Gibraltar

A constitution is not the act of a government, but of a people constituting a government; and government without a constitution is power without a right.[1]

THE MODERN DOCTRINE of sovereignty has ceased to be absolutist and territorial in nature. It has become more flexible, interdependent and capable of divisibility and sharing. It is much less exclusive and power-specific, and derives its authority from people as a constituent force. In that context, issues of historical title are much less relevant in the modern legal environment. The observation that Paine made about constitutions can equally now be made about the modern concept of sovereignty and power derived from it. In some ways it is a constitutional circle of power, with sovereignty depending on people for its source and then, in turn, empowering people to make laws or to govern themselves. Seen that way people are both the constituent power of constitutions and the locus of sovereignty.

People thus have the power of creation and of legitimisation. They have the power to make supreme laws or to bestow on or remove authority from such supreme laws. They have the power to decide to give up, divide or share powers. The first step in achieving that modern conceptual understanding is to recognise those popular powers based on legitimacy, self-determination and participatory governance. The necessary focus must be on placing people at the centre of governance. While this is the case in an analysis of modern western democracy it is especially so within pluri-national States and more so in cases of peoples forming nations vested with the right to self-determination. The latter not only raises issues of internal governance but of status. Of course this understanding is not unchallenged. In a State-centric environment where power is a valuable commodity more traditional territorial, functional and absolutist views of sovereignty clash with the more liberal people-sourced view of power and sovereignty.

[1] T Paine, *The Rights of Man* (London, Penguin Books, 1984) 185.

This is by no means an abstract question. In late October 2008 the House of Lords, by a slim 3:2 majority, held that Orders in Council preventing the Chagossians from returning to the Chagos Islands, in the Indian Ocean, were valid.[2] In so doing, the court revealed the tension between people and State. The majority took the view that, in legislating for a colony, the United Kingdom could clearly prefer its interests over those of the inhabitants of a colony.[3] In a strong dissenting judgment, Lord Mance observed that the 'Crown's constituent power to introduce a constitution for a ceded territory is a power intended to enable the proper governance of the territory, at least among other things for the benefit of the people inhabiting it.'[4] Eight weeks later, the European Court of First Instance seemed to agree with Lord Mance's view when considering Gibraltar's constitution. It firmly rooted the architecture of governance in the 'sacred trust' under the UN Charter to promote the self-government of a colonial people.[5] Though the *Bancoult* decision very much turned on the particular facts of the case, the overall debate about the clash between the interests and aspirations of a people and of the State administering the territory is of wider relevance to those many other territories that experience the same conflicts between power, sovereignty, legitimacy and constitutionalism. At the heart is the question of the extent to which the people of a territory can influence how they are governed and the future of their birthplace.[6] That question echoes with some sympathy and resonance in different parts of the world not least in the Mediterranean.

On the Southern tip of the Iberian Peninsula lies a stateless nation[7] metaphorically caught between three flags: the United Kingdom flag, the Spanish red and gold and the European Union flag. Each symbolises a particular dimension of the Gibraltar conundrum. The Union Jack is the symbol both of Gibraltar's colonial past and the desire of its people to retain a relationship with the Crown. The Spanish flag is a constant

2 *R (Bancoult) v Secretary of State for Foreign and Commonwealth Affairs* [2008] 3 WLR 955.

3 ibid [49] (Lord Hoffman), [114] (Lord Rodger), thus disagreeing with the Divisional Court, which had held the Constitution Order to be invalid because it was not in the interests of the Chagossians. Counsel for the Chagossians had accepted the UK was entitled to consider its interests: see [157].

4 ibid [157].

5 Cases T-211/04 & T-215/04 *Government of Gibraltar v Commission of the European Communities*, Judgment of the Court of First Instance, 18 December 2008 and see ch 7 for some discussion of this ruling.

6 And, importantly for Gibraltar, of the extent to which that question should be affected by a Treaty in respect of the territory.

7 This term will be used throughout this work to describe nations, like Gibraltar, that have not acquired statehood. The relationship that stateless nations have with their host State gives rise to much discussion. While Gibraltar is not constitutionally integrated within the UK and, as such, is in a different constitutional position to other stateless nations, it faces the same issues and contemplates similar, analogous solutions to these. As such comparison with these is pertinent and the classification of Gibraltar as a stateless nation is appropriate given its overall historical, political and legal context. The elements of nationhood and the basis for the claim that Gibraltar is a nation will be considered in ch 3.

reminder of the persistent claim to Gibraltar's sovereignty by Spain and the European blue flag is representative of the ever-increasing domestic influence of the Union and the hope that integrationist trends will erode both the obstacles to the achievement of governance improvements and the sharpness and emotion of the sovereignty debate.

Gibraltar is a small, largely self-governing British overseas territory. It is one of a small cluster of overseas territories[8] that are now all that remain of a once extensive British Empire. Uniquely among these it is situated on the European mainland and is part of the European Union by virtue of Article 299(4) of the Treaty establishing the European Community.[9] The following core factual elements make up the legal and political backdrop for this work. Gibraltar is:

(a) an overseas territory with much devolved powers of self government, but;
(b) still on the United Nations list of non-self-governing territories[10] (and therefore both a target for decolonisation and in search of a decolonised permanent status);
(c) an integral part of the European Union to which the Treaty establishing the Community is applicable;[11]
(d) at the centre of a sovereignty dispute between two Member States of the Union—Britain and Spain—and the focus of assertions of self-determination by its people.

The overall title of this work reflects the interrelationship of diverse subthemes, causes and effects that will be covered in the chapters that follow this introduction. These develop beneath the overriding thematic umbrella of sovereignty and the dispute which is at its heart. Gibraltar's life has been dominated by the ever-present Spanish territorial sovereignty claim that has spanned the last three centuries and has fostered the consequent struggle for power and control of the territory. The development of its people's aspirations, its institutions of governance, its constitutional framework, its legal status and its membership of supranational bodies have all been influenced by the sovereignty claim. This work examines how sovereignty affects Gibraltar, and how the evolution in its meaning provides opportunities for the future in unblocking the governance and status issues. It looks at the modern legal context[12] and

[8] There are 14, although only nine with a significant civilian population and local institutions.

[9] Gibraltar acceded to the European Community on 1 January 1973 with the UK. Art 299(4) makes the Treaty of Rome applicable to such European territories for whose external relations a Member State is responsible.

[10] Also a dwindling list of some 16 territories.

[11] Subject to a handful of exemptions which are detailed below and do not affect the thrust of this work.

[12] The law throughout this work is stated as at 30 December 2008.

how the forces of late sovereignty,[13] polycentric participatory governance,[14] constitutionalism, stateless nationalism,[15] pluralism[16] and self-determination can all provide the theoretical legal support for application to Gibraltar's status and governance issues. These strands can be married into a sub-State constitutionalism that can provide impetus to the legal resolution and advancement of Gibraltar's status and governance concerns. This constitutionalism is particularly important given Gibraltar's relationship with the European Union.

The overriding theme of sovereignty and the main dispute, in turn, spin off specific aspects that allow the development of various sub-themes. In the Gibraltar context it spans the status and governance arenas relatively seamlessly. As such sovereignty *qua* international law-status and sovereignty *qua* power-governance will be seen to be closely linked in the sense that they are both impacted by the deficit suffered by Gibraltar.[17] There are four broad dimensions to the sovereignty dispute that are examined in this work:

1. ***The Substance of the Dispute***: at the centre of the substantive causal issues is the conflict between three different strands of nationalism:
   (a) the sub-State nationalism of Gibraltar and aspirations of self-determination of its people;
   (b) the Spanish nationalism that puts the recovery of the territory of Gibraltar in the foreground of its objectives and;
   (c) the rather more phlegmatic strategic expediency of the United Kingdom that places primacy on its military interests in the region and its political interests in the European Union.
2. ***The Methodology of the Dispute***: this brings into sharp focus the conflict between State-centric bilateralism[18] and multi-party trilateralism[19] as competing methodologies of approach and resolution to this

[13] N Walker (ed), *Sovereignty in Transition* (Oxford, Hart Publishing, 2003).

[14] JHH Weiler and M Wind (eds), *European Constitutionalism Beyond the State* (Cambridge, CUP, 2003).

[15] M Keating, *Plurinational Democracy, Stateless Nations in a Post-Sovereignty Era* (Oxford, OUP, 2001).

[16] S Tierney, *Constitutional Law and National Pluralism* (Oxford, OUP, 2004).

[17] Indeed Tierney has noted that 'the notion that the functions municipal and international law can be discretely differentiated' in the context of sovereignty is under challenge: see S Tierney, 'The Normative Challenge in Forging an International Community' in C Warbrick and S Tierney (eds), *Towards an International Legal Community: The Sovereignty of States and the Sovereignty of International Law* (London, British Institute of International and Comparative Law, 2006) 2.

[18] Meaning the mechanical method by which Britain and Spain to the exclusion of Gibraltar sought (inter-governmentally and as between themselves exclusively) to determine Gibraltar-related issues: a pure intergovernmental approach.

[19] Meaning the conversion of discussion of Gibraltar-related issues into a tri-partite approach which included the representatives of the Gibraltar Government on behalf of its people: a multi-level approach.

dispute. It will be seen how Britain and Spain have, for much of the period, tried to maintain any dealings on a bilateral basis. Slowly, and in parallel to developments in other theatres, the people of Gibraltar have made increasing calls for a trilateralisation of the dispute—in other words, a recognition that they are also a player in this dispute with a right to fully participate in its resolution;

3. ***The Manifestations of Conflict***: the dispute results in consequences across a range of issues. The tussle for power and control between the main players to the dispute raise issues of democracy, legitimacy and governance. The backdrop for this tussle is varied and principally occurs in three theatres:

   (a) the domestic arena, where the main struggle is the search for greater devolution of power and self-government;
   (b) the international arena, where the main subject is the method of decolonisation of Gibraltar and its legal status; and
   (c) the European arena, which is influenced by integrationist trends, the evolution of the meaning of sovereignty and the greater reliance on concepts of participatory governance. Slowly, the European stage has become the primary arena of the conflict between the parties.

The by-products of the interrelationship between sovereignty, bilateralism and the inter-party struggle have been wide-ranging. From the creation of a democratic and governance deficit in Gibraltar to an effective freeze to both the process of decolonisation and the achievement of a permanent and secure status for Gibraltar. The paradox of self-governance and constitutionalism that Gibraltar has sustained, as a consequence, is that while it is a territory with more theoretical powers of self-government than other sub-State nations it has, as a result of accession to the European Community and the convergence of all the above themes onto the European stage, also experienced a deep and parallel democratic deficit.[20]

4. ***The Resolution of the Dispute***: this requires a four-layered approach that is discussed in chapters 6 and 7, and would see an analysis of the proper theoretical context of the dispute, followed by:

   (a) the tackling of the mechanical methodology issues;
   (b) the addressing of the manifestations of conflict; and
   (c) the dealing with the substantive hurdles.

These steps would be taken in that order. The dissipation of the paradox of governance, the democratic deficit and an unblockage of the efforts that seek a new status would be facilitated by a consistent and productive

[20] The paradox is outlined in some detail in subsequent chapters.

trilateralism. Central to all these themes is the interrelationship between the three players to this dispute: the administering power[21]—the United Kingdom; the third party claimant—Spain; and the stateless nation—Gibraltar. The interaction between each fuels the factual background and legal consequences produced. This work traces the historic roots of the dispute and the concept of sovereignty as traditionally seen by the parties. It sets out the main events that led to the evolution of the perspectives of the parties, especially in the post-war and decolonisation periods. These themes and sub-themes have all converged onto the European theatre over a process of decades, and this now forms the principal theatre for the overall dispute between the parties in terms of the manifestation of examples that have resulted from this overriding disagreement. The European Union is important, not only because it—slowly—became the pre-eminent stage for the parties, but also because through its own evolution it could assist in facilitating a possible resolution of the issues of contention for Gibraltar.

This book will demonstrate how the dispute could be re-focussed if the evolved meaning of the concepts of sovereignty, governance and nationalism were applied to Gibraltar. If the principles existing in the modern legal context were to be recognised and adopted then any discussion of issues would proceed on the basis of an acceptance of plurinationalism, multi-level governance, participatory democracy, trilateralism and stateless nationalism as key drivers to reform. In turn, the application of these would allow an unblockage of the traditional issues of dispute and foster the making of progress between the parties. This would necessarily impact not only on inter-governmental relations and the co-habitation of territories but would unblock issues relevant to governance and status.

The nature of this work concentrates on the official positions of Britain, Spain and Gibraltar. In doing so, it has not been possible to do justice to the various positional nuances within the States. Necessarily, therefore, when describing the 'British' or 'Spanish' views on Gibraltar, the official Government views are set out unless otherwise specified. It is accepted—especially in the complex pluri-national State that Spain is—that there will be a variety of strands of regional and political opinion on Gibraltar that will, in part, be responsive to political perspectives. It is hoped that the core concepts and points come through effectively, notwithstanding any deficiency caused by this economy of perspective.

This is not a study of title to land but rather about how people, in their interaction with territory, birthplace and rights, affect that land, its present and its future. Over the case-study of Gibraltar, it seeks to demonstrate several generic and specific points, namely:

[21] The description the United Nations uses for States that administer colonies (or, in decolonisation language, 'non-self-governing territories').

1. That sovereignty is not dead as a concept and that we are not in a period of so-called 'post-sovereignty.' Rather, what has occurred is a modification of sovereignty as a theory, and that it retains its significance and meaning to parties;
2. That sovereignty, nationalism, human rights and decolonisation are all fairly modern politico-legal concepts which have developed and continue to evolve in response to changes in the political environment;
3. That, at present, State sovereignty remains strong, but that in an interdependent era it is no contradiction to accept that more international modes of governance that involve both supra-national entities and sub-State actors are also common. While activity at inter-State level can often just involve participation of supra-State bodies and States if the interaction aspires to lay norms of governance that affect the domestic level (as the EU invariably does) then there is an inevitable trickle-down to sub-State involvement. This need to involve the sub-State level is particularly important with remaining colonial territories and 'nations' within or associated with States given their 'higher' claim to participate in governance which, in the case of non-self-governing territories, is based on the 'sacred trust' under Article 73 of the UN Charter;
4. That the tension in the political environment involves a number of different levels and a set of dynamic interplay of relationships—State v State; People(s) v State; Individuals v State; State v sub-State. Equally the relationships raise issues of modes of governance, struggles for power, territorial claims and human rights;
5. That recognition and voluntary devolution is a key to power transfer. In that context, a prior express or implied recognition of entitlement forms a necessary part of the process. This is particularly relevant to Gibraltar;
6. That as sovereignty is not dead but transformed and continues to have enduring legal and political relevance it is important to achieve an understanding of the crux of the debate in each case. This, often, is one for constitutional space—for power, territory, self-governance and international stability. It involves as many actors as necessary in a tension for inclusion and exclusion;
7. Specifically the Gibraltar issue is a territorial sovereignty struggle that is essentially a struggle for power. It involves five key actors: two States, one people[22] and two supra-State entities (the UN and EU). The dispute touches on matters of domestic and international governance, power, territory, symbolism, human rights and status. That dispute has been as much about mechanics as about philosophical approaches and consequences. In that way the dispute has been dominated by a State-centric bilateral tendency that has permeated issues of governance and status.

[22] By itself and through its sub-State Executive.

8. That, over time, a number of developments have allowed the people of Gibraltar to stake a claim to be a stateless nation and sovereignty player, and that those cumulative developments have led to a shift of sovereignty to it. In that sense a people can be sovereign when it has the right to determine its future and sufficient means and power to govern itself in the way that it wishes to without independent statehood being necessary. The essential elements would be respect, recognition, understanding and peaceful co-habitation. Achieving a higher accommodation of the conflictive aspirations is possible from a sharper contextual and conceptual understanding of the issues and aspirations. As the Gibraltar issue is at its heart a human political conundrum, there is a continual free flow of facts, events and reaction that will make the conceptual matrix constantly evolve. To adapt pragmatically to constantly changing environments it is important to move away from overly rigid formulas. This equally applies to UN decolonisation criteria that now need to be more responsive to a backdrop and group of remaining potential users that are far removed from the users of the generic template devised in the 1960s. Finally, and fundamentally, the force of people's rights cannot be ignored, and requires constitutional accommodation at some point if the politico-legal panorama is to be settled in a stable fashion.

The substance of the work is divided into seven chapters, followed by a conclusion. To make understanding of the issues easier, the chapters are organised on broad historical lines pausing at key watersheds of Gibraltar's constitutional development. Chapter 1 gives a historical overview of Gibraltar, the development of its population and its political and constitutional development to 1964, when ministerial government was acquired. Chapter 2 concentrates on developments in the period 1964–86. That year was a significant point for Gibraltar, in that it was the year Spain entered the European Community. It describes how the European stage grew in importance as the main theatre for governance developments by 1986. Chapter 3 tackles the concept of sovereignty, Gibraltar's claim to being a nation and the conflicts of methodologies and aspirations. It traces the roots of bilateralism between Britain and Spain, and how this obscures the resolution of the dispute. Chapters 4 and 5 deal with the period 1986–2004, in which the main democratic- and governance deficit of Gibraltar developed. They concentrate on the bilateralism during those years, and how this ran counter to trends that put multi-level governance and plurinationalism at the centre of developments. These chapters also examine the sub-State context of Gibraltar, with chapter 5 examining possible mechanisms for better representation, power and influence and the consequences of the current deficit. It ends in 2004, which itself was an important point, in that it saw the establishment by the parties of a more trilateral forum for specific purposes.[23] Chapter 6 outlines the possible keys to the resolution of the paradox of self-governance and constitutionalism of Gibraltar and reviews relevant developments since 2004. It recommends that the dispute be first put in its modern context in due recognition of the importance of multi-level governance, stateless nationalism, participatory democracy and the evolution of the concept of sovereignty. Chapter 7 examines how the mechanics of solution-building are important in achieving a resolution, and that securing practical self-governance would assist a long-term resolution of the dispute between the parties. This would facilitate the search by Gibraltar of a settled and decolonised legal status within the modern European legal context.

When contemplating modes of status short of independence, the interplay of sovereignty and nationalism is more closely related to concepts of governance. Issues of sovereignty arouse high emotion and continue to have significant symbolic effects for both peoples and States. While evolved in meaning, it remains a meaningful and powerful concept. The key is to recognise its continuing power, and that its power conduit and *locus* is people and not history, territorial title or State. From that point on, it is easier to make the transition to more plural, interdependent modes of governance, because the people have been recognised as having the sovereignty to give up, share or delegate power if they so wish or to be respected as retaining that sovereignty-power should they choose not to abandon it. As Bodin observed in 1576, where a people endow an individual or group of individuals with 'absolute power to manage the State and to govern freely . . . they are nothing but trustees of a power that was confided to them for a definite period of time'[24] by that people who continue to hold ultimate sovereignty. If it were ever possible to condense any book into one sentence, fundamentally, this work is about how the sovereignty of Gibraltar has shifted towards its people and the management of the relationship with the States that dance around this Mediterranean constitutional space.

[23] This has not been without its own problems, which are described later in this work.
[24] J Bodin, On Sovereignty (Cambridge, CUP, 1992) 4.

1

From Strategic Gain to Fortress Colony to 'The Right to Our Land'

INTRODUCTION

FOR THREE CENTURIES Gibraltar has been immersed in a sovereignty dispute between Britain and Spain. Caught in the headlights of the sovereignty conflict, the calls for reform by the civil population met a slow response. The issues of Gibraltar's status and its governance have been regularly impacted upon by the underlying conflict within which the two States and Gibraltar have had markedly different aims and aspirations. These proved so intractable that any progress inevitably proceeded at snail's pace. The aspirations of the parties were deeply influenced by their quite different perspectives on the overarching territorial sovereignty question. This in turn dominated not only developments on the central issues of status and governance but also the handling of day-to-day issues.

The achievement of a secure, decolonised legal status obtained in exercise of the right to self-determination, and the achievement of reforms so as to address the internal and external governance deficit that developed over the last few decades, have both been affected by the prevailing dispute.

This chapter provides a historical and political overview of Gibraltar's constitutional development over the last three centuries up to 1964. This and the following two chapters demonstrate how the people of Gibraltar became a real factor in the dispute through the growth of the population, economic success and political aspirations. Taken together they also explain the basic status and governance issues that arise and form the crux to this dispute. They trace the constitutional development gained especially over the last 90 years leading to the acquisition of the current large range of competences and self-governance. By the time of the 2006 Constitution Gibraltar had achieved almost full internal self-government. But even so the sovereignty dispute and conflict of nationalisms has hung over the process of reform and continues to have a severe effect on the dispute. The contest, which involves two States and the people of Gibraltar, raises issues of constitutional and international law, consent, legitimacy, human rights and the *locus* of sovereignty. These are as much theoretical as they are practical issues. Reduced to a number of select areas of examination, the conflict between the parties and themes spawns three questions:

1. How will Gibraltar's international legal status evolve (in the context of the right to self-determination and the process of decolonisation)?
2. How can sufficient domestic constitutional reform (the internal governance dimension) be achieved and maintained? And;
3. How can the search for greater power, representation and influence within the European context (the external governance dimension) be accommodated?

All three are impacted upon by the sovereignty dispute and the predominant bilateralism between Britain and Spain.

By 1964 the dispute with Spain over the sovereignty of Gibraltar had reached the United Nations, and tension between the parties was high. That year marked the achievement of responsible Government by Gibraltar.[1] Restrictions had been imposed on the population in the face of constitutional advances that in Spain's view undermined its own territorial claim. By then the British Prime Minister, Harold MacMillan, had pointed to the 'wind of change' running through the colonised territories of the Empire[2] and Gibraltarian leaders were claiming the 'right to our land' and emphasising the separate identity of the people of Gibraltar.

In the short space available this chapter does not pretend to provide a comprehensive historical review of all Gibraltar's social, economic and political developments over the last 300 years. Rather, it seeks to provide an overview of the main constitutional developments and of the general political and human matrix within which these evolved, to assist in understanding the themes and analysis set out in the chapters that follow. It outlines the growth and evolution of the civilian population and the relationship with colonial administrators and the British and Spanish Governments. The chapter touches on developments before 1964 with the detail in respect of constitutional changes after that date being surveyed in subsequent chapters. 1964 is simply a convenient place to pause detailed consideration of issues given the structure of this work.

[1] The Colonial Laws Validity Act 1865 s 1 defines a representative legislature as one with at least half of its members being elected. Responsible Government is generally accepted to mean a constitutional structure within which a group of Ministers are responsible for individual government departments and are accountable to the legislature for those departments. This term is to be distinguished from references to 'fully responsible status within the Commonwealth', which, in effect, describes independent status.

[2] MacMillan first used the phrase in January 1960. See R Hyam, *Britain's Declining Empire, The Road to Decolonisation 1918–68* (Cambridge, CUP, 2006) 257–61.

ACQUISITION, TITLE AND THE COMPETING CLAIMS

Gibraltar is a small peninsula bordering the mainland of southern Spain. Barely 15 kilometres opposite the North African coast, it was under Moorish occupation between 711 and 1462[3] and thereafter was in Spanish hands until 1704.[4] In that year an Anglo-Dutch force led by Sir George Rooke took the strategic Rock of Gibraltar in the War of Spanish Succession. This commenced the Crown's 300-year association with Gibraltar. The vast majority of what had been the civilian inhabitants of Gibraltar fled when military action directly affected the territory in 1704. A small residue of inhabitants remained and others returned when peace was restored. In subsequent years the level of population was directly related to the periods of peace and military activity. The British presence in Gibraltar arrived by military means and for a long time was driven by a fortress imperative. The desire to secure the fortress and sustain the garrison was put above the social and economic needs of the civilian population and their aspirations for political reform. The fortress always came first.[5] This was not unlike the experience of other colonies where there was always a 'fear . . . that the many Governors of colonies who had military backgrounds would attempt to rule their colonies as they were accustomed to rule their regiments.'[6] As Louis has noted:

> British imperialism was a catalyst for far reaching change . . . [there were] two sides to British dominion in the eighteenth century, the one evolving representative government, the other of 'enlightened' despotism in which can be found the origins of the 'White Man's burden'. Both traditions contributed to a British national commitment to Empire and sense of British identity in the nineteenth and twentieth centuries. It was an ambiguous legacy.[7]

The first two centuries of British rule in Gibraltar were firmly rooted in the latter form of governance.

The Treaty of Utrecht of 1713 confirmed British title, with Spain ceding Gibraltar to the Crown in perpetuity but retaining a 'preference' in the event that the British Crown should ever decide to alienate title over Gibraltar.[8] Article X of the Treaty stated:

[3] Save for a brief interlude between 1309 and 1333.

[4] Initially annexed to the Crown of Castile, it was then granted in 1465 to the Duke of Medina-Sidonia who returned it to the Crown of Castile in 1501.

[5] See the work by the same name by TJ Finlayson, *The Fortress Came First—The Story of the Civilian Population of Gibraltar During the Second World War* (Grendon, Gibraltar Books, 1991).

[6] N Canny, 'The Origins of Empire: An Introduction' in N Canny (ed), *The Oxford History of the British Empire—The Origins of Empire* (Oxford, OUP, 2001) 25.

[7] Wm R Louis, foreword to PJ Marshall (ed), *The Oxford History of the British Empire—the Eighteenth Century* (Oxford, OUP, 2001) viii–ix.

[8] State Papers Vol 1, 611.

> [T]he Catholic King, does hereby for himself, his heirs and successors, yield to the Crown of Great Britain the full and entire propriety of the town and castle of Gibraltar together with the port, fortifications and forts thereunto belonging: and he gives up the said propriety to be held and enjoyed absolutely with all manner of right for ever, without any exception or impediment whatsoever. But that abuses and frauds may be avoided by importing any kind of goods the Catholic King wills and takes it to be understood, that the above-named propriety be yielded to Great Britain without any territorial jurisdiction and without any open communication by land with the country round about . . . And Her Britannic Majesty, at the request of the Catholic King, does consent and agree that no leave shall be given under any pretence whatsoever either to Jews or Moors to reside or have their dwellings in the said town of Gibraltar . . . And in case it shall hereafter seem meet to the Crown of Great Britain to grant, sell or by any means alienate therefrom the propriety of the said town of Gibraltar, it is hereby agreed and concluded that the preference of having the same shall always be given to the Crown of Spain before any others.

It is well beyond the scope of this work to analyse the construction of the Treaty of Utrecht or to adequately consider the markedly different interpretations of the parties in certain areas or the competing claims to 'territorial' sovereignty in any great detail. This is in part because any strict constructionist approach that solely examines the language of the Treaty would do so in a legal vacuum that would not benefit from the application of modern legal principles. Secondly such a venture would take an unduly territorial approach devoid of consideration of the views, interests and rights of the peoples that interact in the dispute. The thrust of this work concentrates on the latter. Indeed one of the views put across in this work is that a definitive view on isolated constructionist questions would be otiose, given that the better debate depends on the rights of peoples and how these impact on the territorial rights of the States in question.

Even so and in view of the fundamental nature of the differences between the parties it is worth making some brief observations on the Treaty, its language and interpretation. First, it is important to remind ourselves that annexation, cession and bargaining over territory stemming from military conflict was commonplace in the 18th century.[9] It was not strange therefore that after the war of Spanish succession, in which one of England's objectives had been to stem the power of France, peace negotiations eventually resulted which led to territories exchanging hands. In those negotiations plenipotentiaries of England and France (not Spain) agreed the principle that Gibraltar should be ceded to England.[10] The con-

[9] Marshall (ed), n 7 above.

[10] Phillip V of Spain had allowed the French monarch to negotiate on his behalf, although the subsequent discussion as to the exact terms of cession involved Spanish negotiators. The official Spanish Government's historical contention is that Louis XIV prevented the entry into France of Spanish negotiators and had to persuade the Spanish King to accept the cession. See *Informe Sobre La Cuestion de Gibraltar, Direccion General de Politica Exterior Para Europa y*

ditions of cession and the cession itself were agreed with Phillip V of Spain. In keeping with usual practice of the times Gibraltar was not the only territory that fell within the scope of the Treaty that resulted from the aftermath of military conflict. This, for example, also dealt with the transfer and title to Minorca and Newfoundland.[11]

As Israel has noted, the British were able to reach agreement with France only after the collapse of secret Franco–Dutch peace negotiations in 1710. This allowed Britain

> to stage one of the most sensational coups in the history of the British Empire. Britain it emerged was ready to do a separate deal with France and was even willing to leave Phillip on the throne of Spain and Spanish America provided Louis granted sweeping maritime and colonial concessions to Britain.[12]

The result of the conclusion to the War of Spanish Succession and the peace negotiations was that 'Britain was now unquestionably Europe's dominant maritime and colonial power . . . with Gibraltar and (Minorca) . . . the Royal Navy was advantageously placed to control the straits of Gibraltar, dominate the southern flank of Europe and regulate the commerce of the Mediterranean.'[13]

To interpret the language of the 1713 Treaty, the principles and law of the time need to be understood[14] and considered against such modern principles as impact upon its text. The normal rules of interpretation of Treaties,[15] subsequent conduct of the parties and any modern paramount principles that have emerged would need to be assessed.[16] Any obvious ambiguity could be assisted by recourse to the *travaux preparatoires* of the Treaty.[17]

The first issue that stems from a reading of the Treaty is the nature of the cession. The word 'propriety' was used in the case of Gibraltar. However when ceding Minorca to Britain under Article XI the words used to convey title were 'all right and the most absolute dominion' over the island. At first sight, it might seem as if there was a different nature of

America del Norte, Oficina de Gibraltar (Madrid, *Ministerio de Asuntos Exteriores,* April 2007) 3. See also F Nunez Roldan, *'Los Ingleses en el Penon—el Tratado de Utrecht'* in *El Problema de Gibraltar—Tres Siglos de Reinvindicacciones, Tension y Guerras, Historia* 16 AXVI, No 187, 38–45.

11 Among other territories. Britain also gained Hudson Bay and Nova Scotia: see Marshall (ed), n 7 above, 598–99.

12 J Israel, 'The Emerging Empire: The Continental Perspective 1650–1713' in N Canny (ed), n 6 above, 443.

13 ibid 444.

14 Island of Las Palmas Case, *Netherlands v United States* [1928] 2 RIAA 829.

15 See the 1969 Vienna Convention on the Law of Treaties.

16 See the definition of norms of international law in Art 53, ibid. See also D Grieg, *Intemporality and the Law of Treaties* (London, British Institute of International and Comparative Law, 2001) as to the principles that would allow the Treaty of Utrecht to be read in the light of factual developments and current legal principles, and generally S Fatima, *Using International Law in Domestic Courts* (Oxford, Hart Publishing, 2005).

17 It is for another time and work for a more determinative view of these issues to be expressed.

cession achieved by those words but the better view would seem to be that nothing substantive turns on this, not least because when Minorca was ceded back to Spain under Article IV of the Treaty of Versailles of 1783 the British monarch was described as having agreed to 'cede (this) with all propriety'. Equally under the Treaty of Versailles it was agreed that the British Crown would retain the 'right'[18] to Newfoundland even though the original cession in Article XIII of the Treaty of Utrecht seemed to have been cast in wider terms. In general terms it is submitted that the nature of the cession was intended to and was accepted by all parties to be one of sovereignty in the way that concept was understood in the years that followed.[19] Whatever the differences in language the phrases 'propriety', 'dominion' and 'right' were all used interchangeably to generally convey 'sovereignty'. The subsequent conduct of the parties also pointed to that.[20] Britain asserted juridical, territorial and administrative control over the town and fortress without any serious contest.[21]

The second obvious issue arises as to the extent of the cession. In that context the Spanish and British positions have been markedly different. The former maintains a strict interpretation of the words 'the town and castle . . . without any territorial jurisdiction' to assert that what was ceded was land to the foot of the rock only. Side by side with that contention is the view that Gibraltar has no territorial waters and that the land referred to as 'the isthmus', which is a small strip of land adjacent to the northern end of the Rock on which the airport is situated, was not within the original grant of cession.

Title to the isthmus has been the source of controversy almost from the date of the Treaty of Utrecht itself. Sentry posts were established by Britain during the early 18th century, ostensibly as a measure to guarantee the security of the fortress. This was generally met by Spanish protests. The British position has always been that the territory ceded under the Treaty of Utrecht included a stretch of land north of the foot of the Rock as it was essential to have this land to defend what was ceded. The argument was twofold—that either this interpretation was the proper construction to the reference to 'forts' in the Treaty and/or that it was impliedly granted to give full effect to the cession.[22] The third argument fielded by Britain was

18 In the French text the '*propriété*'.

19 Meaning full power and dominion.

20 Though the demands made by British negotiators prior to the entry into force of the Treaty of Utrecht perhaps lent themselves to greater equivocation.

21 The dispute as to the territorial waters and the strip of land known as the 'isthmus' is quite different: see below.

22 For a summary of the historical arguments see on the Spanish side *Informe Sobre La Cuestion de Gibraltar, Direccion General de Politica Exterior Para Europa y America del Norte, Oficina de Gibraltar* (Madrid, *Ministerio de Asuntos Exteriores*, April 2007) cited above, and from the British perspective, House of Commons Foreign Affairs Committee, *Gibraltar: The Situation of Gibraltar and the UK Relations with Spain together with Appendices thereto* (London, HMSO, 1981) ('the 1981 FAC Report').

that it had acquired title to part of the isthmus at least by prescription having been in effective legal occupation since establishing firm lines of sentries in about 1838.[23]

This strip of land has been argued over during the last three centuries with varying degrees of intensity. Military skirmishes during the 18th century gave way to diplomatic protests during the 19th century. The British asserted their sovereignty of this land by building houses, military encampments, commercial premises and a cemetery on the land. Both the military and civil police patrolled the area.[24] Even so for some time there was controversy between the parties as to which State had legal jurisdiction over the land and should try offenders arrested there, and which system of law would apply.[25] Historically the isthmus was divided into two distinct plots that were treated differently by the parties. This area was generally referred to as the 'neutral ground'.[26] The southernmost stretch of about 1,000 yards was built on and patrolled by Britain who clearly asserted their ownership of it. To the extent that Britain has maintained its sovereign rights over this stretch for many years its description as 'British neutral ground' has been something of a misnomer. The stretch to the north of that was also commonly termed the neutral ground, behind which Spanish sentries were located. For Britain this stretch was actually 'neutral ground.' It would be impossible to set out in detail the historical events that occurred during the period 1713–1838 in respect of the isthmus, but suffice to say that the positions of the two States were markedly different and friction manifested itself as to the exertion of sovereignty, jurisdiction and control over that strip of land. The respective power of Britain and relative weakness of Spain or its distraction with internal political issues made it easier for Britain to secure its position on this issue. For example, Britain, France and Spain had the most extensive European navies by tonnage in the period 1775–1805. However, while the British navy was around 60 per cent larger by tonnage than that of Spain in 1775, by 1815 British naval capacity was 10 times that of Spain.[27] Greater military capacity allowed Britain to acquire a dominant position as the main colonising power by the early 19th century.

In 1891 Spain erected a barbed wire fence on its side of the neutral ground. In 1909 the British erected a frontier fence along the line of its

[23] As for prescription in international law see the discussion in the Kasikili-Sedudu Island case, *Botswana v Namibia* [1999] ICJ Rep 1045.

[24] In the *Las Palmas* case it was stressed that there is an important reliance on the demonstration of a 'continuous and peaceful display of State functions' in international law. See also similar comments in *Eritrea v Yemen* [1998] 114 ILR 1.

[25] TJ Finlayson, 'North Front Incidents' in *Stories from the Rock* (Gibraltar, Aquila, 1996) 73–79.

[26] The strip of land between the British sentry posts of 1838 and the Spanish lines.

[27] M Duffy, 'Worldwide War and British Expansion 1793–1815' in Canny (ed), n 6 above, 185, 204.

sentry boxes. Notification to Spain of its intentions met strong protest. During 1939–40 an airstrip was built on the British side of the isthmus with land being reclaimed from the sea in 1941 and 1945 to extend the runway. The rest of the so-called neutral ground in effect disappeared by the erection in 1954 of Spanish sentry points a few feet from the British frontier fence. Spain had thus asserted its ownership of and annexed the remaining part of the so-called 'neutral ground' even though for some years it had kept its customs post at the location of the old Spanish lines.[28] The British tabled a diplomatic protest. This drew a strong rejection by Spain, which asserted its sovereignty over the neutral ground.[29]

The issue as to whether Gibraltar had territorial waters or not has also been a regular point of dispute between the parties. Spain has argued that there was no reference to these in the Treaty, and thus that no territorial waters had been ceded. Britain's position has been that it followed from the terms of the Treaty that Gibraltar has waters, so that it could be fully defended and protected. Additionally, she argued that Gibraltar had always, before 1704, been an important port and that the country holding sovereignty had always exercised jurisdiction over these. Thirdly, it was argued that Britain had asserted her sovereignty by exercising actual control over the waters, supervising the berthing and supplies to vessels and applying its laws to these.

The extent of territorial waters has also been an issue with Britain maintaining that Gibraltar has three miles of territorial waters, as is the general position under international law, except on the north westerly side of Gibraltar, where the proximity of Spanish territory made this calculation impossible. In this case the position was maintained that the limits of territorial waters were demarcated by an imaginary line drawn through and dividing equally the waters adjacent to Spain and Gibraltar on the basis of the 1958 Geneva Convention on the Territorial Sea and Contiguous Zone.[30] Spain has maintained an argument that Gibraltar was ceded without any territorial waters and filed declarations on acceding to the 1958 Convention and the 1982 United Nations Convention on the Law of the Sea (UNCLOS) to the effect that its accession to those conventions could not be construed as recognition of territorial rights over waters around Gibraltar.[31]

[28] And left the former neutral ground to lie in a barren state.

[29] 1981 FAC Report.

[30] Extended to Gibraltar in March 1960.

[31] Art 309 of UNCLOS does not permit the entry of a reservation to the convention although Art 310 does allow the making of declarations or statements as long as these 'do not purport to exclude or modify the legal effect of the . . . convention . . . to that State.' Under UNCLOS a State may assert territorial rights of up to 12 nautical miles. In May–July 2008 a dispute arose between the Gibraltar and Spanish Governments as to the nature and effect of the declarations entered into by Spain: see the evidence of the Spanish Ambassador to London before the House of Commons Foreign Affairs Committee set out at House of Commons Foreign Affairs Committee, *Overseas Territories*, Seventh Report of Session

The third principal issue on the interpretation of the Treaty relates to the so-called first preference proviso. This made clear that in the event that Britain should decide to 'alienate' the territory Spain would get the first option. Given the terms and effect of the 1713 Treaty the only credible argument is that sovereignty was ceded to Britain. Looking forward to the eventual interplay with the people of the territory that will be central to this work it should be noted that there are a few instances of territories where sovereignty was retained by a third State where self-determination does not defeat the prior claim. Crawford considers that this may 'arguably' be the case with Gibraltar.[32] The view put forward here is that on a detailed examination of the acquisition of sovereignty by Britain under the Treaty that principle has no application to Gibraltar.

In a leasehold situation there is always a residual holding of title as a quasi-head landlord. In the Gibraltar situation the grant of sovereignty was 'for ever'. It was definitive, final and complete. There was no actual right of eventual reversion that could condition the title *ab initio* in the sense of providing for an eventual return because the grantor retained ultimate title. It was merely a right of future preference not a right of automatic transfer at a given point in time. If the day of preference never arrived there would be no reversion. So, for example, Spain's right, if it arises at all,[33] only does so if the British Crown decides to alienate the territory. If it does not, then the Crown can hold it for 'ever'. To continue the property analogy it was not a leasehold but a freehold. It follows that, if in 1723, 10 years after Utrecht, the British Crown had wanted to alienate the territory and Spain had rejected any first offer made to it, the Crown could have granted the territory absolutely to France if it had wished to. Nothing would have stood in its way then because the grant of sovereignty was absolute and indefinite subject only to the right of first preference. Otherwise the words in the first preference part of Article X that envisage the possible grant of the territory by Britain would be meaningless. The first preference right was imposed on Britain because without it the Crown could grant the territory to whomever it pleased implicitly recognising the absolute nature of the cession. That analysis makes clear that the claim cannot override the right of self-determination because title (as opposed to the right of future grant to 'another') was unconditional. Of course, it is a cornerstone of this book that what was possible in 1723 would no longer

2007–08, HC 147-I and HC 147-II (London, The Stationery Office, 2008) paras 408–10 ('the FAC Report 2008') and Gibraltar Government press release 160/2008 of 3 July 2008 (Gibraltar, Government of Gibraltar Press Office, 2008). For the nature and effect of declarations and reservations to Treaties see I Brownlie, *Principles of Public International Law*, 4th edn (Oxford, OUP, 1990) 608–11; DJ Harris, *Cases and Materials on International Law*, 6th edn (London, Sweet and Maxwell, 2004) 808–15, and A Aust, *Modern Treaty Law and Practice* (Cambridge, CUP, 2002) 100–130.

[32] J Crawford, *The Creation of States in International Law*, 2nd edn (Oxford, OUP, 2006) 642–43.

[33] Given the impact of the right to self-determination.

be possible now because of the right to self-determination. As it was a freehold, what has arisen now is that the people of the territory have acquired a supervening right to acquire the transfer themselves under the right to self-determination.

There are three plainly different ways in which the first preference provision could be construed, and all these interpretations have the potential to impact on the status and governance of Gibraltar. The first was that, for many years, Spain contended that this part of Article X prohibited any moves towards granting self-government to Gibraltar, as these, in effect, were moves towards alienation.[34] Seen in this way certain moves towards self-governance can amount to 'alienation'. Secondly, it could be argued that there is 'alienation' only on independence. An evaluation of these possibilities is heavily influenced by the interface between the Treaty and modern principles of international law that can now be said to be paramount. Centrally, the principle of self-determination has now become an accepted principle of application and would take precedence over any pre-existing international Treaty.[35] The key issue is whether the people of Gibraltar are a colonial people vested with the right of self-determination. The Government of Gibraltar and Britain contend that this is so.[36] Conversely Spain argue that the original population of Gibraltar fled at the time of occupation of the territory in 1704 and that Spanish territorial integrity is threatened by Gibraltar.[37]

As a non-self-governing territory the people of Gibraltar have the right of self-determination.[38] Accordingly any clause that purports to deny that right would either be null and void[39] or would have to be read—if possible—in manner consistent with that principle.[40] The effect of Article

[34] The position of the Spanish Socialist administration elected in 2004 has been expressed in softer terms as understanding the desire towards internal self-government in Gibraltar as long as it does not prejudice the Spanish claim to sovereignty over the territory.

[35] There is some academic debate as to whether the principle of self-determination is now *jus cogens*: see Harris n 31 above, 116 fn 1.

[36] The difference between the British and Gibraltarian positions is that Britain also contends that Art X of the Treaty constrains the right of Gibraltar to independence without Spanish consent.

[37] Without addressing the point in detail it is difficult to see how the fact that sovereignty is not held by Spain affects her territorial integrity, given that this situation arises from a voluntary cession by Treaty which was perfectly valid at the time.

[38] *The Legal Consequences for States of the Continued Presence of South Africa in Namibia (South-West Africa) Notwithstanding Security Council Resolution 276 (1970)* [1971] ICJ Reports 31, which applies that right to all non-self-governing territories.

[39] See Arts 64 and 71 of the 1969 Vienna Convention on the Law of Treaties. Even if the provision were a nullity it would not affect the sovereignty over Gibraltar because those boundaries having existed for centuries would 'have a life of its own independently of the fate of the . . . Treaty. . . . The Treaty can cease to be in force without in any way affecting the continuance of the boundary.' See *Territorial Dispute (Libyun Aruh Jamuhiriyu/Chad), Judgment,* ICJ Reports 1994 6, 37, paras 72–73. The principles are similar in the case of State succession. See also Brownlie n 31 above, 621–22.

[40] There are other parts of Art X that are obviously repugnant to modern principles, such as the requirement to exclude Jews and Moors from Gibraltar.

103 of the United Nations Charter is clear in that sense in requiring obligations under any other international agreement to be read consistently with the United Nations Charter. As such, if in a process of decolonisation the people of Gibraltar were to opt to pursue independence as their preferred option then either the restriction inherent in Article X of the Treaty of Utrecht would have to be set aside or read consistently with the principle of self-determination. There are, at least, three possible ways by which the latter would be possible.[41] First the particular phrase[42] can be read as imposing a requirement on the people of Gibraltar only to consider integration with Spain as an option side by side with any other number of options in a referendum. They would then have to be free to, without hindrance, pursue the option of their choice. This would be consonant with the right to self-determination. Secondly it may be possible to argue—if the Crown is to remain as Head of State of an independent Gibraltar—that there would be no 'alienation'.[43] The third possibility is that in fact there has already been an alienation and that nothing remains in this Article that actually stands between Gibraltar and full independence if the people were to decide to exercise their right to self-determination.

The starting point of these arguments is that the first preference provision is engaged only if there is a desire to alienate or grant the 'propriety' (meaning sovereignty) of the territory. If sovereignty can be alienated fully or partially by devolution of power then it would follow that there must already have been a large measure of 'alienation' to the Crown in right of Gibraltar by the United Kingdom Crown through the successive measures of self-governance contained in the various constitutional instruments.[44] If in fact there has been 'alienation' and, given that the steps towards self-governance have been taken in accordance with the wishes of the majority of the population, the position would only have, in a rather long-winded way, achieved consistency with the principle of self-determination. What further 'alienation' is now necessary for Gibraltar to acquire independence? The Crown in right of Gibraltar would only be required, in practice, to acquire a further range of additional responsibilities and powers given that Gibraltar has now achieved almost full internal self-government. But as long as Gibraltar does not opt to become a Republic and would retain Her Majesty as Head of State of an indepen-

[41] The permutations below are set out to describe an attempt to achieve consistency. It need not be necessary to have to consider these options in detail if the purported restriction in Art X is simply disregarded as incompatible with the right to self-determination.

[42] '[I]t is hereby agreed and concluded that the preference of having the same shall always be given to the Crown of Spain before any others.'

[43] Depending on the view that can be taken on the divisibility of the Crown and the stage at which this can be said to have occurred. In any event if this is a provision that restricts independence then there would seem to be no 'alienation' for the purposes of this Art X in a free-association Constitution.

[44] See later in this chapter and ch 6.

dent Gibraltar, she would continue to be the Queen of Gibraltar as much after independence as she was before independence. The only thing that would change is that Her Majesty would be sovereign in an independent Gibraltar not by virtue of the law of the United Kingdom but by virtue of Gibraltar law.[45]

Article X is not about independence. Indeed it could not envisage such a scenario. It was constructed during the 18th century when what was common was the bargain and transfer of territory from State to State as a result of conquest, prize or barter. The concept of democracy, rights of colonial peoples and decolonisation would have seemed a strange world to the Utrecht plenipotentiaries. What the Article was thus providing for was the event, foreseeable at the time that the subsequent cession of the territory for a military, strategic or commercial reason might be mooted. If such a situation did transpire, Spain wished to ensure it was in the driving seat of having a first offer. Nothing would have been more removed from the thinking of the Treaty's negotiators than that the people of the territory would aspire to independence, still less that this eventuality had to be catered for. Seen in its proper historical context the key words become easier to comprehend:

> [I]n case it shall hereafter seem meet to the Crown of Great Britain to grant, sell or by any means alienate therefrom the propriety of the said town of Gibraltar, it is hereby agreed and concluded that the preference of having the same shall always be given to the Crown of Spain before any others.

The Article seeks to protect Spain in the event of a grant, sale or alienation of the territory. The language of grant or sale precisely sets the context of the times. If that were not sufficiently clear, the crucial operative words are first 'therefrom' and secondly 'before any others'. This indicates that the purpose of the exercise is the protection of the Spanish Crown from the acquisition of the territory by another Crown. If, in an independence situation, Her Majesty the Queen remained Queen of Gibraltar, albeit under the authority of Gibraltar law, does this amount to alienation 'therefrom' that offends the right of the Spanish Crown to be offered Gibraltar in preference to any 'others'?

Without it being a contradiction, the United Kingdom and Overseas Territories are said to constitute an undivided realm within which the Crown is divisible in terms of the self-governance held by the representative, devolved Government of the territory.[46] It is the same sovereign that is the Head of State of both. So if alienation in the Treaty of Utrecht means that the current sovereign will be replaced by another, then the fact that the

[45] And even then as a result of the fact that under UK law she is sovereign in the UK. See *Halsbury's Laws of England*, 4th edn (London, Butterworths, 2003 reissue) vol 6, para 716. In effect this operates akin to a constitutional *renvoi*.

[46] ibid.

Queen will remain Queen of an independent Gibraltar must mean that there would be no alienation.[47] If it is argued that because Her Majesty would be 'Queen of Gibraltar' in an independence situation this would constitute alienation to 'another' Crown, the answer is that alienation has already taken place in a non-independent Gibraltar, given that Her Majesty is already 'Queen of Gibraltar' for all constitutional purposes.[48] In other words the first preference provision cannot prevent independence because in an independent Gibraltar there need not be alienation of the Crown.[49] If alienation is defined as the same sovereign constitutionally representing distinct Governments then alienation took place arguably as far back as 1957 or 1964 on the grant of a representative legislature with an elected majority, responsible Government and clear powers of self-governance.[50] Taking that argument to its logical conclusion it is not independence that triggers the first preference clause. Conversely in an independent republic of Gibraltar there are no 'others' meaning other Crowns that are being preferred so it is difficult to see a strict breach of the latter half of the Utrecht proviso.[51] Constructed as it was at a time of the rule of kings, the Treaty was plainly not an instrument that can necessarily comfortably accommodate more democratic times. To interpret it as barring other permutations of governance would give precedence to the Treaty over paramount norms of international law. If contrary to all those arguments the grant of independence would constitute alienation the basic position to which we would return is that even if 'alienation' is engaged at that point Article X could not prevent the right of independence being consummated because of the paramount nature of the right of self-determination. In either case—whether there has not been an alienation or whether the horse of alienation has bolted—nothing stands in the way of independence as an option should the people of Gibraltar decide to pursue it.

As such, three views that reach the same conclusion are possible. Either a constitutionally compliant way is found of interpreting that the concept of 'alienation' is not actually triggered in an independence situation or alternatively alienation occurred many decades ago on the grant of self-government. Finally, it can be argued that, even if 'alienation' would occur

[47] In those circumstances the right of first refusal inherent in Art X could simply be inherited by an independent Gibraltar as a condition of title. It is arguable whether that amount of consistency with Utrecht is even necessary.

[48] *R v Foreign and Commonwealth Secretary, ex p Indian Association of Alberta* [1982] 1 QB 892. The only argument against this might be that divisibility in a non-independent territory takes the form of sub-divisibility whereas in an independent situation there would be parallel and separate divisibility: see further ch 6.

[49] Quite beyond that a whole range of succession issues that would provide constitutional tension would arise in any independence scenario: see M Craven, *The Decolonisation of International Law—State Succession and the Law of Treaties* (Oxford, OUP, 2007).

[50] See below.

[51] There would arguably be a breach of the first half of the test: see the reference to 'therefrom' in the operative part of the proviso.

on independence, such 'alienation' could not be prevented, as otherwise there would be a breach of the principle of self-determination.[52] Indeed such an interpretation would also be consistent with the view expressed by the United Kingdom in the 1960s, when it made clear that 'the grant of Gibraltar to Britain under the Treaty was absolute and without any bar to constitutional changes in Gibraltar or to the acquisition by its inhabitants of a full measure of self-government as the Charter required.'[53] The United Kingdom also made clear that it 'did not accept that there was a conflict between the provisions of the Treaty of Utrecht and the application of the principle of self-determination to the people of Gibraltar.'[54]

THE OVERSEAS TERRITORIES CONTEXT

Gibraltar is one of only nine remaining populated[55] British Overseas Territories[56]—the others being Anguilla, Bermuda, British Virgin Islands, Cayman Islands, Falkland Islands, Montserrat, St Helena[57] and the Turks and Caicos Islands. There are some common characteristics to these Territories and also some unique features that distinguish Gibraltar. Of the nine territories, only Gibraltar was acquired by cession.[58] The predominant form of acquisition by the Crown of the current overseas territories was settlement. The latter fall into two groups: those that fall within the definition of the British Settlement Acts, and those falling outside of that definition.[59]

[52] It would be necessary to also have in mind consistency with the law of State succession in forming a final view of the interpretation of the first preference proviso. In that respect see Craven n 49 above.

[53] 'Gibraltar: Recent Differences with Spain' (Cmnd 2632, 1965) 6.

[54] ibid 7. The position of the UK is now different: see later.

[55] By 'populated' I mean having a significant and established local civilian population. The largely uninhabited territories of the British Antarctic Territory, South Georgia and the South Sandwich Islands, British Indian Ocean Territory, the sovereign bases in Cyprus and Pitcairn Islands are excluded from this comparison. The Pitcairn Islands, eg, have a population of approximately 43. The nine main overseas territories have civilian populations depending on the territory concerned of between about 3,000 people (Falkland Islands) to about 70,000 (Bermuda). The British Antarctic Territory was annexed by Letters Patent in 1908. It became a colony in 1962 (British Antarctic Order 1962 SI 1962/400 (amended by SI 1964/1396)). The British Indian Ocean Territory became a separate colony in 1965—see the British Indian Ocean Territory Order 1965 SI 1965/1920 (and SI 1968/111)—following discussions between Her Majesty's Government and the Mauritian Government. The administrative centre is in Diego Garcia. The South Georgia and South Sandwich Islands were part of the dependencies of the Falkland Islands until 1985.

[56] This title was first used by Foreign Secretary Robin Cook in his speech to the Dependent Territories Association conference in February 1998.

[57] And its dependencies—Ascension Island and Tristan da Cunha.

[58] There are four forms of acquisition of colonies—cession, conquest, settlement and annexation.

[59] British Settlement Act 1887 (50 and 51 Vict c 54). Under that Act a 'British Settlement' is defined as 'any British possession which has not been acquired by cession or conquest and is not for the time being within the jurisdiction of the legislature constituted otherwise than by

Only the Falkland Islands of the nine territories fall within this definition. While St Helena is outside the Acts its dependencies that were not subject to the St Helena legislature (prior to 1989) could be considered British Settlements. That would seem to be the reason why in St Helena's case the 1988 Constitution Order[60] is expressed to be made pursuant to the Government of India Act 1833 (in respect of St Helena) and the British Settlement Acts (in respect of its dependencies). The other territories acquired by settlement were all under the jurisdiction of legislatures duly constituted otherwise than under the Settlement Acts.[61]

THE NATURE OF ACQUISITION AND THE ASSERTION OF JURISDICTION

Shortly after the Treaty of Cession, conflict erupted between Britain and Spain over Gibraltar. As early as 1727 there were hostilities, with Spain pursuing her sovereignty claim to Gibraltar by military means. Several sieges ensued through the 18th century.[62] In the 20th century militarism gave way to economic and political methods as these became Spain's preferred strategy towards the prosecution of its claim. It is outside the scope of this work to trace the history of these distinct periods in any great detail. However several points stand out that are important to the themes of this work. First that the value of Gibraltar as a strategic fortress was recognised throughout the centuries, with a number of sieges aimed at taking control of the city, because it exercised great influence on maritime traffic to the Mediterranean as well as the Iberian mainland.[63] Secondly, it is worthy of note that the Spanish period has been shorter than both the British and Moorish periods. Thirdly, within those periods the larger European political dynamic influenced the attitude of sovereigns to Gibraltar. For example on a number of occasions Gibraltar was promised in exchange for

. . . virtue of this Act' (s 6). It thus also excludes territories acquired by annexation or where there is a legislature in a settled colony constituted other than under the British Settlement Act.

[60] See eg the St Helena Constitution Order 1988 SI 1988/1842.

[61] The Turks and Caicos as a result of the Turks and Caicos Act 1873, the Cayman Islands pursuant to the Cayman Islands Act 1863, Anguilla, British Virgin Islands and Montserrat because of the Leeward Islands Act 1871 and Bermuda due to it possessing an elected Assembly since 1620. Most recent legislatures existent in those territories are constituted under Orders in Council made under different Acts of Parliament.

[62] Spain has persisted with its claim even though British title to the Rock had been confirmed in the Treaties of Paris (1763) and Versailles (1783).

[63] There were ten main sieges between 1309 and 1516 and a number of other sieges in the post-1704 British period, the most important of which was the so-called Great Siege, which occurred between 1779 and 1783. See A MacMillan, *Malta and Gibraltar Illustrated* (London, Collingridge, 1915), facsimile edition (Malta, Midsea Books, 1985) 401–22, and J Drinkwater, *A History of the Siege of Gibraltar, 1779–1783* (London, 1785). For an account from a Spanish perspective, see I Lopez Ayala, *Historia de Gibraltar* (Madrid, 1782).

political concessions or territorial gains elsewhere.[64] Fourthly, the history of the various military struggles for control of Gibraltar particularly emphasises one of the points made by a number of modern authors, who remind us that the doctrine of sovereignty itself is of fairly recent predominance, having emerged as an ideological and political support for the imposition of absolutism and to counter rival claims to supremacy.[65] Fifthly, the acquisition and then cession of Gibraltar was born from 18th-century conflict between the major powers of the time—France, Spain, Holland and Britain.[66] In some ways the attitude and claims of a by-gone era have been carried over into modern times, preserved in an imperial time-warp. While it is important to set the respective positions of the parties into their historical context so as to understand and give proper weight to them, it is also a theme of this work that those historic positions of colonial conflict between super-powers cannot be seen in isolation, and that to do so would be to pay insufficient regard to modern principles of law and societal development.

Even though Gibraltar was taken by military force and it took a further nine years for there to be a Treaty ceding the territory to the Crown, it did not make the acquisition one that took place by conquest. The language of the Peace Treaty and the Crown's actions need to be scrutinised to establish when the Crown has assumed title and what the method of acquisition is.[67] Once the Crown has acted firmly as Sovereign, either by establishing a permanent civil administration or granting rights over land, it can be deemed that there is an intention to acquire.[68] In 1720 by Letters Patent the first courts under the British Crown were established in Gibraltar.[69] In 1740 a Royal Charter applying English law to Gibraltar was introduced.[70] Previously, Spanish law had applied.[71] This is a classic manifestation of the assertion of sovereignty.[72] In 1830 a Supreme Court for

[64] It was common for rival alliances to be formed between countries in Europe so as to maintain the balance of power. In that context territorial bargains were commonplace, especially during the 15th–18th centuries. During the early years of British control the exchange of Gibraltar for Florida was mooted with Spain. Indeed as Ward notes George III's cabinet agreed to exchange Gibraltar for Puerto Rico in the late 18th century but the idea was scotched by 'public outcry': see JR Ward, 'The British West Indies 1748–1815' in Marshall (ed) n 7 above, 419.

[65] This will be touched upon in ch 3.

[66] Marshall (ed), n 7 above.

[67] *Re Southern Rhodesia* [1919] AC 211.

[68] *British Honduras v Bristowe* [1880] 6 App Cas 143.

[69] These first courts applied Spanish law and the jurisdiction of these courts was relatively small restricted to debts, trespasses, contracts and personal pleas. Subsequently a Vice-Admiralty Court was established in 1739, and a 1752 Charter extended the jurisdiction of the court that had been established in 1720 to real property and probate. At that time the Governor still formed part of the Court of Sessions. In 1817 the first civil judge was appointed.

[70] 13 Geo 2d.

[71] Some dispute existed on whether certain aspects of Spanish law remained which was finally dissipated by the Privy Council in *Jephson v Riera* [1835] 3 Knapp 130.

[72] K Roberts-Wray, *Commonwealth and Colonial Law* (London, Stevens, 1966) 625–50.

Gibraltar was established with civil and criminal jurisdiction.[73] The civil judge appointed under that Charter of Justice was to be termed the Judge of the Supreme Court and appeals were to lie to the Privy Council.[74] Gibraltar was also given the status of Crown Colony. The Supreme Court's jurisdiction was progressively enlarged throughout the 19th century.

The first Gibraltar Ordinances were made in 1832.[75] By Order in Council of 1884[76] statutes of general application in force in England at December 1883 were applied to Gibraltar except as it may have been provided for by Order or local Ordinance and only so far as it was applicable to the circumstances of Gibraltar. As a number of hurdles were envisaged in that provision[77] several problems were encountered in ascertaining precisely what the law was at any given time.[78] To clarify and simplify that exercise the Legislative Council passed the English Law (Application) Ordinance 1962,[79] which provided that certain Acts of the United Kingdom Parliament specified in Schedules to the Act or applied directly by Order in Council or Act of the Gibraltar or Westminster Parliaments would apply in Gibraltar.[80] In essence the law of Gibraltar is now made up of Acts of the Gibraltar Parliament and such Acts of the Westminster Parliament as may be applied by either local legislation or Orders in Council.[81] The 1962 Act also provided that the common law and rules of equity of England would have effect as far as applicable and save to the extent as they have been modified, excluded or extended to Gibraltar by virtue of an Act of the United Kingdom Parliament, an Order in Council or an Act of the Gibraltar Parliament.[82]

[73] The Fifth Charter of Justice.

[74] Previously appeals lay to the Governor and only after his determination to the Privy Council: see J Spry, *The Gibraltar Law Reports 1812–1977* (Gibraltar, Trico Printers, 1980) vi.

[75] Previously legislation was by Order in Council, Letters Patent or by Proclamation.

[76] Application of English Law (General) Order 1883 (commenced on 27 February 1884). It replaced an Order of 1867. A similar provision was then also set out in s 23 of the Supreme Court Ordinance 1960, passed by the Legislative Council.

[77] eg first the Act had to be of general application, then there had to be a judgment as to whether it was of necessary application and finally whether there had been local Ordinance amending or affecting it.

[78] See *Legislative Council Debates*, Gibraltar, Legislative Council, Friday 25 May 1962.

[79] By virtue of the Gibraltar Constitution Order 2006, which will be referred to below, the nomenclature of primary legislation passed by the Gibraltar Parliament was changed from 'Ordinances' to 'Acts'. The rest of the work will therefore adopt that terminology. References to Acts are therefore to Acts of the Gibraltar Parliament unless the context otherwise makes clear.

[80] English Law (Application) Act 1962 ss 3, 4. About 200 Acts of the Westminster Parliament are specified in these schedules.

[81] There are also two other sources of supreme legislative authority that need to be taken into account. The first is the Constitution, which requires existing laws to be read in conformity with it and requires the Parliament to legislate subject to the Constitution's terms. Secondly, as a result of membership of the European Union, Gibraltar law is subject to compliance with European law. See ch 2 in respect of both issues.

[82] English Law (Application) Act 1962 s 2(1).

THE PEOPLE AND CONSTITUTIONAL DEVELOPMENT

The transfer of Gibraltar emerged from conflict and territorial bargain. This was the staple diet of the times. Thereafter subsequent attempts during the 18th century to discuss the transfer of the territory in exchange for other territorial or political concessions were part of the course. Powers in this regard were restricted to the States exclusively. In those early years governance of colonies was handled by Governors who 'exercised executive, judicial and legislative authority in each royal colony. The Governors represented a monarchical power that was supposedly stronger in the colonies than in England.'[83] This was to remain while the population was small and beholden to the military garrison. As the population grew and during periods of stability benefitted from economic prosperity it also led to greater political aspirations. At first these were only modest calls for participation in governance but then came louder calls for self-government to determine the future of the territory asserting thereby a claim to the right over the land of the territory. An initial step in tracing the evolution of the legal and political backdrop is to examine the development of the people of Gibraltar and their emergence as a player in the determination of that dispute. In terms of the constitutional, economic and social development of the people of Gibraltar, six phases stand out, namely 1704–1814;[84] 1815–64;[85] 1865–1945[86]; 1945–64; 1964–86 and the post-1986 period.[87]

THE PERIOD TO 1945: THE FIRST STEPS TO SELF-GOVERNMENT

Four themes marked the first three phases. First, the emphasis was on the military population above all other objectives.[88] Secondly, the British assertion of sovereignty was not immediate.[89] Thirdly, the ground was

[83] I Steele, 'The Anointed, the Appointed and the Elected: Governance of the British Empire 1689–1784' in Marshall (ed), n 7 above, 110. Though he also notes the 'relentless' rise of colonial Assemblies in certain colonies by 1784.

[84] 1814 was the first time that the population exceeded 10,000. It marked the emergence of a more stable population post military sieges and epidemic: see L Sawchuk, *Deadly Visitations in Dark Time—A Social History of Gibraltar* (Gibraltar, Gibraltar Government Heritage Division, 2001).

[85] A period of no political reform but a consolidation of British sovereignty and of the economy and population.

[86] The first period of political reform: see below.

[87] This chapter traces events up to 1964. The subsequent chapter deals with the period 1964–86.

[88] The British imperative was to safeguard the military fortress, its strategic importance and to look after the welfare of the garrison. The civilian population was secondary and what was certainly frowned upon for the better part of two centuries was any degree of political rights: see below.

[89] As stated above.

laid for the development and evolution of the civilian population but this proceeded at a very slow pace.[90] Fourthly, there were few, if any, moves towards self-government, nor were there any significant and consistent local demands for it until the 20th century.[91]

The initial absence of a significant civilian population enhanced the bilateral nature of the sovereignty dispute that emerged as early as the 18th century. This was premised on a purely territorial dispute between two States, with the population not being a material factor at the time. The population evolved dramatically during the 19th and 20th centuries. This did two things. It complicated the status issue by interposing a resident civilian population and it would eventually give rise to demands for self-government.

There has always been a clash of interests between the British garrison and the civilian inhabitants. The former viewed Gibraltar as a garrison town with the interests of the fortress being paramount. To them the civilian population was there to service the needs of the military. As the civilian population grew so did their aspirations to obtain more control over their lives and break away from this stereotype. The 18th century was a time of added instability because of the military sieges.[92] This kept the civilian population relatively low and heavily outnumbered by the garrison.[93] Military law was in place until 1753 when civilian magistrates were empowered to deal with non-military inhabitants. Even so there was a reluctance to allow civilian courts to try soldiers, with Finlayson noting that, in 1882, 50 years after the 1830 Charter of Justice, the Supreme Court had not exercised criminal jurisdiction over any soldier's case.[94] This changed shortly afterwards, although the fact that civil courts adjudicated over incidents affecting the military was not always accepted without reluctance. After a military officer had been successfully sued for damages in the civil courts in 1913 for injuring a civilian with his sword in trying to control a crowd the Governor of the time[95] observed:

[90] The civilian population was slow to grow because throughout the 18th century Gibraltar was subjected to several military sieges and because of the impact of disease. The civilian population was still only about 3,000 in 1791. The fact that civil rights were not demanded earlier was also due to the fact that this sector of the population was focusing on economic survival. The British attitude was also relevant: see below.

[91] The first real inroad came in 1865 with the appointment of Sanitary Commissioners, the function of which was to advise on municipal and health matters: see below.

[92] In 1704–05, 1727 and 1779–83.

[93] The civilian population was under 3000 just after the Great Siege. Figures for the military garrison at various times in the 19th century were 5,382 (in 1779), 2,943 (in 1821), 3,834 (in 1830) and 3,224 (in 1835). By 1807 the civilian population (7,501) was larger than the military population, with the civilian population growing steadily throughout the 19th century, being over 15,000 by 1830. See Sawchuk n 84 above, 42.

[94] 'North Front Incidents' in Finlayson above n 25, 74.

[95] Sir Archibald Hunter.

> This is not a personal matter for settlement by an individual officer. It is a matter of the rights of the Garrison of Gibraltar to carry out their duty without the illegal interference on the part of civilians who are allowed to live there.[96]

After the Great Siege (1779–83) there was a surge in the civilian population, and this exceeded 10,000 by 1814, although the numbers of service personnel still remained significant, and represented about a quarter of the total population during the early 19th century.[97] Of the civilian population of 16,394 in 1829, the three largest groups were recorded as native Christians and Jews (8,208), Spaniards (3,926) and Genoese (1,532). Already, a distinct 'native' population was larger than the military garrison and of any other ethnic group. Indeed the recognition of a so-called 'native' element by then in official records was significant in itself, by identifying the emerging distinctiveness of the growing Gibraltarian population. The civilian population grew steadily throughout the 19th and 20th centuries, although it was affected by war[98] or epidemic.[99] By 1830 there had been a significant consolidation of the population. The civilian population was to continue to grow, exceeding 20,000 by 1901. There was significant immigration from other parts of the Mediterranean—principally from Genoa in the 18th and 19th centuries and then from Malta during the 19th and early part of the 20th century.[100] Its most significant threat since its first consolidation in the 1810s was to come during the Second World War.

THE FIRST, SLOW STEPS

Albeit with official sanction from the Governor and as a reaction to a public emergency, district 'Committees of Inhabitants' were set up in 1804 to deal with an outbreak of Yellow Fever. These district committees were 'empowered to issue orders and regulations for the preservation of public health' and were then led by an overall Committee of civilians that appeared 'to have assumed responsibilities then normally the prerogative of Government.'[101] Even so this was a fledgling step that was not to be extended willingly.

[96] 'A Difficult Governor—Sir Archibald Hunter' in Finlayson above n 25, 105.

[97] Sawchuk n 84 above: in 1829, eg, there was a civilian population of 16,394 and a military garrison of 3,918 (excluding women and children).

[98] The bulk of the civilian population was temporarily evacuated during the Second World War: see below.

[99] Yellow fever and cholera were the cause of many deaths during the first part of the 19th century. See Sawchuk n 84 above, 137, 141 and also LA Sawchuk and S Benady, *Diary of an Epidemic—Yellow Fever in Gibraltar, 1828* (Gibraltar, Gibraltar Government, 2003).

[100] HW Howes, *The Gibraltarian—The Origin and Evolution of the People of Gibraltar*, 3rd edn (Gibraltar, Medsun, 1991).

[101] 'The Yellow Fever Epidemic of 1804' in Finlayson above n 25, 8–9.

The differences in treatment and access to facilities given to members of the military garrison as opposed to civilians also made the latter try to promote their own interests through sectoral organisations. In 1817 the Exchange and Commercial Library was established to provide support and resources to the civilian population who were excluded from the Garrison Library. Commonly known as the 'Exchange Committee' it soon acquired the role of lobby group and forum for the discussion of civilian concerns primarily in the area of social and economic matters.

In 1830 Gibraltar was declared a Crown Colony, ending its description as 'the city and Garrison of Gibraltar in the Kingdom of Spain.'[102] While judicial authority was also removed from the Governor in that year by a Charter of Justice that established a Supreme Court all legislative and executive power remained vested in him. The British outlook was that Gibraltar was first and foremost a fortress and that any element of self-government was undesirable and should be resisted. This belief continued to manifest itself from time to time. In 1848 the Governor, Sir George Gardiner criticised the Exchange Committee for encouraging 'notions of political rights which it has never been the intention of any British Government . . . to concede to the commercial settlers on the Rock.'[103] Subsequently meetings that had been convened in 1852 to protest about the state of civil administration in Gibraltar were banned by the Governor.[104]

The military emphasis of the administration of Gibraltar created many restrictions for the civilian population. Not only did this manifest itself in a lack of self-government but it prevented the civilian population from entering into many parts of Gibraltar and even constrained the ability to sketch or photograph in any part of Gibraltar other than for military purposes.[105] Free movement to and from Gibraltar or even within Gibraltar was not permitted, with the Attorney-General observing in 1870 that 'military exigencies . . . renders [*sic*] it impossible that it shall ever be so.'[106]

Many plots of land in Gibraltar were held by the Admiralty or by the British Government for military purposes. The transfer of these lands to the Colonial Government for civil purposes was slow and tortuous. In many respects the Governor, who was a military person and combined the role of civilian Governor with his role of Commander-in-Chief, was heavily weighted towards the military. There was a series of agreements

[102] Responsibility for Gibraltar was transferred from the War Office to the Colonial Office.

[103] J Garcia, *Gibraltar, The Making of a People—The Modern Political History of Gibraltar and its People* (Gibraltar, Medsun Publications, 1994) 8–9.

[104] In 1859 the first Colonial Secretary was appointed to assist the Governor in the civil administration of Gibraltar replacing the former post of Civil Secretary that had been created in 1749. The Colonial Secretary was the head of the civilian administration of the Government of Gibraltar and appointed by the British Government.

[105] Legislation was introduced in the 19th century regulating this activity. See Sawchuk n 84 above, 30.

[106] ibid 31.

from 1893 onwards, collectively described as the Lands Memoranda, which regulated the terms, condition and timing of the transfer of lands used for defence purposes to the colonial Government. These record the long-standing point of dispute between the Gibraltar Government[107] and the British Government as to whether lands used by the military actually belonged to it or to the Crown in right of Gibraltar. Sizable areas of Gibraltar were still being used for defence purposes or for the purposes of providing residential or leisure facilities for UK-based civilians connected with the military garrison right up to the late 1980s. The most recent of those Lands Transfer Agreements with the MOD was made in 2004.[108] The size and importance of the military garrison were also relevant. The MOD represented a contribution of around 60 per cent to the local economy as late as 1981.[109] This has now dropped significantly to the present three per cent. With major economic dominance up to the late 20th century, in occupation of much of the land and with a military man in charge of governance over a civilian population it was very difficult for Gibraltarians to make any political progress. The predominant ethos behind the British presence was to preserve imperial strategic and military interests. The mechanics of doing so was achieved by, what Lord Castlereagh described as, securing 'the keys of every great military position.'[110] Undoubtedly the major strategic fortresses of Bermuda, Gibraltar, Halifax and Malta dotted as they were in key global locations played an important part in that.[111] Mechanically this allowed the use of the navy as 'an instrument of foreign policy . . . especially in the crucial Mediterranean corridor.'[112]

The separation of the military and civilian populations was carried over into essential services with the military running its own water and power supplies and health service.[113] In many respects the local civilian and military populations developed independent of each other. As Jackson observes this divide that was 'a fault common in most British colonial societies of the 19th century (meant) that Gibraltarians no matter how eminent were not made welcome.'[114] This was not unlike the experience elsewhere.

[107] First expressed through the Colonial Secretary or Attorney-General on behalf of the Governor and after the introduction of ministerial government by Ministers.

[108] The position of the Gibraltar Government in relation to the use and ownership of crown lands was improved substantially by s 75 of the 2006 Constitution: see chs 3 and 6.

[109] FAC Report 1981, citing statements made by the Chief Minister, Sir Joshua Hassan, para 144.

[110] Cited in P Burroughs, 'Defence and Imperial Disunity' in A Porter (ed), *Oxford History of the British Empire—The Nineteenth Century* (Oxford, OUP, 2001) 323.

[111] Indeed the special position of these fortresses had long been recognised. They were excluded from the 1879 Royal Commission that reviewed the defence of British possessions: ibid 334.

[112] ibid 323.

[113] Which continues to this day, although the contraction of the military population is now making the continuation of these independent services impractical.

[114] W Jackson, *The Rock of the Gibraltarians—A History of Gibraltar* (Grendon, Gibraltar Books, 1987) 228–29.

Burroughs has noted that in several colonies British administrators often 'consciously pursued separateness and drew distinctions, whether racial, social or educational.'[115] Archer has surveyed the approximately 80 Governors that Gibraltar has had since 1704. The vast majority have been military.[116] While some have shown 'sensitivity and a desire to engage in social and political reform'[117] others 'saw the civil population as an awkward and dispensable irrelevance.'[118] Clearly in the 18th century there was no question of reform. Nor was there a desire for it. This only came with the growth of the population during the 19th century.

THE DRIVE TO SELF-GOVERNMENT

Table A—Gibraltar Population 1891–2002

Date	Total Pop[119]	Civilian Pop	Military Pop	Gibraltarians[120]	Other British	Non-British[121]
1891	25,753	19,011	5,896	14,244	2,426	2,341[122]
1901	27,460	20,355	6,266	14,761	2,939	2,568
1921	22,018	18,540	3,478	13,874	1,881	2,755
1948	28,460	23,700	4,760	18,554	2,918	2,228[123]
1951	23,232	22,284	3,196	17,847	3,196	1,241
1961	24,502	21,636	SU[124]	17,985	4,809	1,132
1970	27,965[125]	24,672	2,161[126]	18,873	3,001	2,798
1981	29,616	26,479	2,265	19,825	3,706	2,948[127]
1991	29,084	26,703	1,371	20,022	3,811	2,870
2001	31,623	27,495	745	22,882	2,627	1,986

[115] P Burroughs, 'Imperial Institutions and the Government of Empire' in Porter (ed) n 110 above, 182.

[116] Gibraltar has had three civilian governors between 1997 and 2006. All other governors from 1704–2008 have been drawn from the forces.

[117] EG Archer, *Gibraltar, Identity and Empire* (Abingdon, Routledge, 2006) 74.

[118] ibid 73.

[119] Visitor and transient figures form part of the total figures but are not detailed separately in this table.

[120] Prior to 1951 termed 'Natives of Gibraltar' in the census.

[121] Classified as 'Aliens' in some census.

[122] Of which 1,869 were Spaniards.

[123] Of which 2,079 were Spaniards.

[124] Statistics unavailable for the period.

[125] Total population on census night: it excludes the number of servicemen in the years 1970–02.

[126] 1970–02 figures are for families of servicemen: figures for servicemen are excluded from the census.

[127] Predominantly Moroccan nationals: the figures for the 1981–02 period being 2,140 (1981), 1,798 (1991) and 961 (2001). The decline in numbers being due to a Voluntary Repatriation Package Programme of the early 1990s.

Achieving participation in the governance of Gibraltar was thus arduous and problematic for the civilian population. This was primarily because of the entrenched view that the devolution of power to civilians was inappropriate in the context of the heavy military emphasis to the territory. As such, for a long time (and not unlike many other colonial territories within the Commonwealth) the Governor held plenary law-making and administrative powers. The pattern of British governance of its colonies was different to that by Spain or France. Britain displayed a more decentralised attitude that encouraged some devolution and a 'continuous interplay between mother country and colonial communities.'[128] Nevertheless while this was the case in certain territories in conquered, ceded and other settled colonies 'more authoritarian regimes were established.'[129] Here less representative forms of Government were applied 'for communities whose populations seemed unsuited to elective assemblies.'[130] The Office of the Governor was traditionally established by Orders in Council or Letters Patent and powers were then specified in Royal Instructions.[131] The authority of the Governor was limited to that set out in his Instructions or in the instrument appointing him with the courts having power to review the exercise of such powers.[132] Modern practice sets out the office of Governor and its powers in the Constitution governing the territory.[133]

The customary way of devolving power is for a representative assembly to be established and for the Governor to be required to exercise powers in a number of specified areas in consultation with the views of appointed or elected members. Gradually the areas in respect of which the Governor must consult elected politicians are increased. Eventually consultation is replaced with the need to act in accordance with the views of locally elected representatives and the introduction of responsible Government. An Executive Council with the Governor at its head is replaced by a cabinet, and a wholly elected Parliament becomes the law-making assembly for the territory.[134]

The pace towards securing civil and political rights was slow. Of course this needs to be put into historical perspective for it was only between 1850 and 1856 that Australians and New Zealanders made a 'final dash for local autonomy securing both representative institutions and responsible

[128] Burroughs in Porter (ed), n 110 above, 170.

[129] ibid 185.

[130] ibid.

[131] *Halsbury's Laws of England*, 4th edn (London, Butterworths, 1974) vol 6, para 1034. See eg the Letters Patent of 1910 or 1922 establishing the office of the Governor in Gibraltar.

[132] *Sprigg v Sigcau* [1897] AC 238. See also *Halsbury's Laws of England*, 4th edn (London, Butterworths, 1974) vol 6, para 1051.

[133] So eg the 1969 Gibraltar Constitution revoked and largely replaced the 1964 Royal Instructions: see below and ch 2.

[134] Usually the changes would be set out in constitutional provisions though the courts may also recognise conventions establishing certain practices: see *Commercial Cable Co v Government of Newfoundland* [1916] 2 AC 610.

Government in virtually one leap.'[135] Canada had taken a major step forward in the 1840s and thereafter on achieving the British North America Act 1867.[136] The constitutional picture throughout other colonial territories was generally far less enlightened. In Gibraltar the establishment of Sanitary Commissioners in 1865 was a step towards the greater participation of civilians in public administration. The Commissioners were appointed (not elected) and were responsible for public health and water. Even so there were only four Gibraltarians among the body of 12 Commissioners in 1891. In that same year the Chamber of Commerce made a request that a consultative body be formed for the discussion of all prospective legislation. The Acting Governor, Major-General Newdigate advised the Secretary of State for the Colonies that 'the formation of a Consultative Council in this Fortress is a scheme which I cannot for the moment think advisable'.[137] Later that year when a civilian ratepayers association protested against a proposed health measure the Governor, Sir Lothian Nicholson advised the British Government to

> make it clear to the inhabitants of Gibraltar that this place should primarily and properly be recognised as a Fortress and not a Colony, and that if it suits them to reside here, it must be under such conditions as will render the Government of so important a military dependency free from such attempts as that under consideration to resist the lawful acts of Her Majesty's Government.[138]

The reason for Governor Nicholson's resistance to any involvement by civilians in the civil administration of Gibraltar was motivated by the fact that

> defence must be of paramount importance and to hand over independent local self government to a Board the majority of which are to be elected from a community which is no more than quasi-alien is inexpedient and inadvisable in every way.[139]

This attitude was not unique to Gibraltar. In Malta, another historic fortress colony, the position was similar. Frendo describes how Malta was also 'governed by a succession of generals who were at the same time commanders-in-chief of the armed forces.'[140] The concern of the British was that because of its strategic value Malta could not 'be treated like an ordinary colony.'[141] To the Maltese they were treated 'not as a people but

[135] Burroughs in Porter (ed), n 110 above, 189 and also D Denoon and M Wyndham, 'Australia and the Western Pacific' in Porter (ed), n 110 above, 546 and R Dalziel, 'Southern Islands, New Zealand and Polynesia' in Porter (ed), n 110 above, 573.

[136] G Martin, 'Canada from 1815' in Porter (ed), n 110 above, 522.

[137] 'Gibraltar's First Elections' in Finlayson above n 25, 120.

[138] ibid 121

[139] Sawchuk n 84 above, 287.

[140] H Frendo, *Party Politics in a Fortress Colony: The Maltese Experience*, 2nd edn (Valetta, Medsea Publications, 1991) 5.

[141] ibid.

as the native inhabitants of a fortress.'[142] There are in fact significant parallels between Gibraltar and Malta, in terms of the interaction with the British military and official establishment, their strategic history and constitutional development. Both fortress colonies—one in the western Mediterranean and one in the eastern Mediterranean—they shared a military heritage. Home to southern peoples who struggled for political progress, they both faced thematic and practical hurdles.[143]

Generally the Edwardian era was a time of both celebration of the breadth of empire, and introspection and review of its direction.[144] 1907 was a 'decisive turning point' for the future shape of the Commonwealth, with responsible Government being achieved by the Union of South Africa shortly thereafter in 1910.[145] There would be a period of profound change after the Second World War but in the meantime, as Hyam notes, 'both before and after 1914 what was striking about the British Empire was not its slow or continuing decline but its continuing transformations and renewals.'[146]

The arrival of a more liberal Governor of Gibraltar in 1918 led to a breakthrough. In 1921 following further requests for some form of representative consultative body which could influence policy-making the Governor, Sir Horace Smith-Dorrien established a City Council of four elected and five nominated members to replace the Sanitary Commissioners.[147] The powers of the latter were to be assumed by the new City Council. In an enlightened statement the Governor explained his view 'that no Governor can legislate for the requirements of a community unless he is helped and advised by the inhabitants themselves . . . (and) that the city should govern itself with as little interference as possible.'[148] However the powers of the City Council were still to be fairly limited. The Governor was to nominate a councillor to represent each of the Government of Gibraltar, the Admiralty and the Secretary of State for War and then also appoint two other councillors.[149] The right to vote was given to male British subjects over 21 who were owners or tenants of land or premises in Gibraltar. The Workers Union made proposals before the Governor's plan was put into effect that there should be an elected civilian majority and that all males over 21 should have the right to vote. The Union was against the requirement that entitlement to vote depended on whether property was owned

[142] ibid.

[143] Some allusion to these similarities will be made in this work.

[144] R Hyam, 'The British Empire in the Edwardian Era' in J Brown and Wm R Louis (eds), *Oxford History of the British Empire—The Twentieth Century* (Oxford, OUP, 2001) 47–55.

[145] ibid 53–55.

[146] ibid 63.

[147] City Council (Constitution and Powers) Ordinance 1921. Although the proviso to the relevant sections made clear that 'no woman shall be eligible for the office of councillor' (s 3(1)) or have the right to vote (s 6). Women were given the right to vote in 1947.

[148] *Gibraltar Chronicle* (Gibraltar 1 January 1921).

[149] s 3(2).

or let as this, in effect, disenfranchised many members of the working classes. These pleas were ignored when legislation was published.[150] As such, a little over 4,600 people out of a total civilian population of about 18,000 were eligible to vote. Three of the four candidates elected had ties with the Workers Union.

By Letters Patent of 1922 an Executive Council was also established to advise the Governor in the fulfilment of his functions.[151] Royal Instructions issued the same year made clear that the Executive Council would be made up of the military officer next in seniority to the Governor,[152] the Colonial Secretary, the Attorney-General, the Treasurer and three other 'unofficial' members. The unofficial members were to be appointed from among civilians and would not always attend meetings of the Executive Council but rather be 'summon[ed] . . . only on occasions on which he [the Governor] shall deem it desirable to obtain their advice.'[153] The Executive Council was to be chaired by the Governor and he was to consult with it in all cases except those deemed too urgent or unimportant, or that in his judgment would be prejudicial to Her Majesty's service to do so.[154] In any event the Governor retained power to disregard the advice of the Executive Council.[155] Laws made could not be repugnant to the Letters Patent or Instructions[156] or be enacted without the signification of consent of the Crown through a Secretary of State except in urgent cases.[157] Additionally specific permission was required to make laws within certain subject matters.[158]

These measures did not fully satisfy the appetite for change with the Chairman of the Exchange Committee stating in 1922 that the 'natural aspirations of Gibraltar . . . (were to) assume entire control of local affairs and institutions.'[159] Further demands for reform by the Exchange Committee, Chamber of Commerce and Workers Union between 1926 and 1934 were all rejected, as was a petition signed by a vast majority of electors. These years had witnessed important developments in other territories. The First World War had 'led to an intellectual revolt against the European colonial order . . . This new worldwide discourse was to form a

[150] Finlayson above n 25, 122–23.

[151] Letters Patent of 12 September 1922, which revoked the Letters Patent of 1910: see *Laws of Gibraltar* (Gibraltar, 1935) 2502–06.

[152] Up to 1997 the post of Governor was always filled by a senior military figure of one of the armed forces.

[153] Royal Instructions of 12 September 1922, para V, cited at *Laws of Gibraltar* (Gibraltar, 1935) 2507–2516.

[154] ibid para XIII.

[155] ibid para XV.

[156] ibid para XVI(6).

[157] ibid para XVI(7) and (8). In that event if permission was not obtained subsequently then the law would automatically lapse.

[158] ibid para XVII.

[159] Finlayson above n 25, 126.

critical prelude to the struggles of decolonisation.'[160] There were troubles in various strategic locations as diverse as Ireland, the Sudan, Jamaica, India and Egypt.[161] This constituted a 'crisis of empire' that Britain survived, albeit economically weakened.[162] By 1926 the Balfour Declaration had set out that the leading self-governing dominions were

> autonomous communities within the British Empire, equal in status and in no way subordinate one to another in any aspect of their domestic or external affairs though united by a common allegiance to the Crown and freely associated as members of the British Commonwealth of nations.[163]

The 1931 Statute of Westminster that provided the necessary legal support to the political declaration had followed it.[164] Britain was preoccupied with domestic issues in the aftermath of the Wall Street crash and the Great Depression. Hyam has noted that 'for nearly ten years from 1929 the country scarcely had any foreign policy worth the name, as more and more a vague reliance was placed in the League of Nations.'[165] This was 'paralleled by the lack of a forward-looking colonial policy',[166] which 'barely existed beyond the minimum of administration and responding to local crises as they arose.'[167]

In 1941 and following the outbreak of the Second World War the City Council and Executive Council were suspended in Gibraltar and powers were assumed by the Governor because of the emergency situation created by the war. Measures to increase the level of civilian involvement in local administration remained in abeyance until the end of conflict. The inter-war suspension of moves towards constitutional development or of current powers was the norm throughout many other territories.[168]

During the Second World War the vast majority of the population was evacuated from Gibraltar as it was thought that their continued presence in the strategically important colony was too dangerous.[169] Ironically many were evacuated to London, which was, at the time, in the midst of prolonged bombing raids. The arrival of several thousands of evacuees required the prompt deployment of emergency accommodation. Controversies surrounding the accommodation of evacuees even reached

[160] Hyam above n 2, 31.
[161] ibid 32–37.
[162] ibid 33–36.
[163] J Darwin, 'The Dominion Idea in Imperial Politics' in J Brown and Wm R Louis (eds) n 144 above, 69.
[164] Described as the '*Magna Carta* of the British Empire': see D Judd, *The British Imperial Experience from 1765 to the Present* (London, Phoenix Press, 2004) 290.
[165] Hyam, above n 2, 76.
[166] ibid 84.
[167] M Thomas, B Moore and LJ Butler, *Crises of Empire—Decolonisation and Europe's Imperial States 1918–75* (London, Hodder Education, 2008) 33.
[168] ibid 38.
[169] Estimates put the number of evacuees in excess of 15,000: see Finlayson n 5 above, 147, 233.

the Court of Appeal that recorded how 12,000 Gibraltarians had been brought to England during the war.[170] In a case that turned on how long certain evacuees had in complying with notices to quit of such emergency premises Greene MR remarked:

> These people are not inhabitants of this country. Their home was in Gibraltar, and all their relationships in the matter of their way of life, their friendships and their facilities to earn their livelihood were there. They find themselves removed to this country and provision made for them by the government under a licence of this kind, and it must surely be the implied intention of the parties that, if they were turned out by the ministry, they should be given such an opportunity as strangers in the land might require, to enable them to find other accommodation. That consideration ought to be taken into account in deciding what time is to be allowed to such licensees as those in this case to comply with the notice determining their licences.[171]

In a sign of the perception of the civilian population by the military, Finlayson notes that the thousands designated for evacuation were referred to as the 'useless mouths' in exchanges between the military and officials.[172] The evacuation of the people and their repatriation to Gibraltar in the aftermath of the war were both important moments in securing the development of the population. The evacuation of large numbers of the population to places as diverse as Madeira, Northern Ireland, Jamaica and North Africa put at peril the cohesiveness of the population. In 1944 the Resettlement Board estimated the need to provide accommodation for over 16,000 returning evacuees and noted that at that point there were only 3,517 Gibraltarians present in Gibraltar. The repatriation of the evacuees in the years after 1945 proved crucial to achieve a resurgence and regeneration of the civilian population. A political grouping formed in 1942 aimed at securing political rights—the Association for the Advancement of Civil Rights[173]—was instrumental in the repatriation effort. The return of the majority of the evacuees ensured the recovery and continued development of the population.[174] As the return of evacuees depended on the provision of housing in Gibraltar it took several years for all evacuees who wanted to return to be repatriated.[175] Even so as

170 Many were then sent on to other places such as Northern Ireland, Madeira or Jamaica.

171 *Minister for Health v Bellotti* [1944] 1 KB 298.

172 Finlayson n 5 above, 3.

173 Of which a young lawyer, Joshua Hassan, was vice-president. He became the leading politician in the decades that followed and was later Chief Minister between 1972 and 1988. See F Cantos, *From Fortress to Democracy—The Political Biography of Sir Joshua Hassan* (Grendon, Gibraltar Books, 1995).

174 The most comprehensive work on the evacuation of the population and its repatriation is TJ Finlayson's *The Fortress Came First*, cited above n 5.

175 Around 14,000 returned: see Finlayson n 5 above, 234–36. The repatriation was not completed till 1951. The return of thousands of evacuees from Northern Ireland camps was particularly fraught with problems and led to acrimonious exchanges between the AACR and the colonial Government: see Finlayson n 5 above, 162–86.

Finlayson notes 'the experience gained by some evacuees in the fight for better conditions for themselves and for their compatriots gave a considerable impetus to the demand for greater self-government in the colony.'[176]

Political emancipation became a more vigorous theme after the formation in Gibraltar of the AACR. The main civilian lobbying organisations at the time were the Chamber of Commerce, Workers Union, Exchange Committee and the AACR with the latter leading on efforts to secure greater political rights. The first bone of contention was the ability to participate in the public administration of Gibraltar. The limited influence to do so via the City Council had been suspended as a result of the war. Plans had been put forward by the Governor to London in 1943 for the resumption of a City Council with an enlarged membership of equal numbers of appointed and elected members.[177] The proposal envisaged that there would also be an advisory council on which all members of the City Council, together with the colonial secretary and the Attorney-General, would sit. After input from the armed services[178] the plan was publicised on 30 December 1944. Lack of consultation with local bodies before the plan had been announced led to a generalised disappointment and a joint effort from the principal civilian lobbying groups against the proposals.[179] These considered the proposed reforms as insufficient gains. Both the Governor and the colonial secretary of the time reminded Gibraltarians that any reforms must come against the backdrop of a realisation that the interests of security and defence of the fortress were paramount.[180] Instead the demands from the civilian bodies were for the establishment of a legislative council to be composed of the members of the Executive Council under the chairmanship of the colonial secretary together with five elected members. As for the City Council, their view was that this should have an elected majority on it.

Plans to introduce the advisory council were suspended while the civilian proposals were under consideration. In the meantime legislation was introduced to lift the suspension of the City Council and convene elections to it with the colonial administration accepting that there should be seven elected seats onto the council. Elections took place in July 1945 with the AACR taking all seven seats.[181]

[176] Finlayson n 5 above, 228.

[177] There were to be six elected members.

[178] The practice of the colonial administration at the time was to place any such proposals before the military in recognition that it was necessary to obtain the military's acceptance of any proposals on internal governance.

[179] Garcia n 103 above, 27–69.

[180] Garcia n 103 above, 31.

[181] The franchise was extended to all males over 21 who had resided in Gibraltar for a period of 12 months prior to the election: see Garcia n 103 above, 30.

In 1945 the colonial administration promised that once the civilian population was returned to Gibraltar a Legislative Council composed of eight official members, six elected members and two nominated members would be introduced. When details were published it became clear that the thrust of the proposal was to fall short of giving the Council any substantial law-making powers. The main civilian representative organisations made their opposition clear to such plans. The AACR complained that the colony was governed as a conquered territory with the military having use of 80 per cent of the land with barely 20 per cent of the population and rejected the military dominance over the civilian population.[182] Garcia has noted that in an internal note in the Colonial Office the Secretary of State for the Colonies, George Hall, manifested his opposition to constitutional reform and remarked that the British Government

> should endeavour to obtain outlets for emigration . . . the ultimate ideal would be to break-up Gibraltar as a community and leave it as it was originally formed, that is as a small parasitic population hanging around the port and fortress.[183]

There was much debate and some attempt by the Colonial Office to withdraw from the position it had announced. One of the main points of concern was whether Gibraltar would be over-governed on the grant of a Legislature, given the presence of a City Council within the territory. By 1948 the City Council had powers to make contracts, bye-laws, employ persons to carry out its functions, appoint constables, undertake public works, construct or acquire houses among other functions.[184] The Governor Sir Kenneth Anderson who backed the reforms urged the Cabinet to grant a legislature because 'the people felt very strongly that they should have a wider opportunity for sharing in the administration of *their own* territory and this had not been satisfied with the establishment of a City Council with an elected majority.'[185] (emphasis added) The general consensus among representations received were that there would be no overlap of functions between the executive duties of the City Council and the legislature given that other functions of an executive nature were carried out via the Executive Council chaired by the Governor.[186] Finally a Legislative Council was agreed in 1948 composed of three official members, two nominated members and five elected members. The Governor

[182] Garcia n 103 above, 40–44.

[183] Garcia n 103 above, 43.

[184] 'OES Lloyd: Note on the Gibraltar City Council, 3 August 1948 CO 91/527/1' in F Madden (ed), *The End of Empire, Dependencies Since 1948, Part 1: The West Indies, British Honduras, Hong Kong, Fiji, Cyprus, Gibraltar and the Falklands—Select Documents on the Constitutional History of the British Empire and Commonwealth, Vol VIII* (London, Greenwood Press, 2000) 509–10.

[185] Garcia n 103 above, 57.

[186] Madden n 184 above, 513.

would preside over the Council and held a casting vote.[187] In terms of electoral system the British Government and the Governor both preferred a system of proportional representation as a method to loosen the stranglehold the AACR held over electoral results.[188] The reforms announced in 1948 did not defuse all political tension between the military establishment and representatives of the civilian population. In that year the General Secretary of the Gibraltar Confederation of Labour, Albert Fava, was deported, ostensibly not because of his trade union activities 'but because the Governor had reached a conclusion that his political activities were undesirable in the interests of the security of the Fortress.'[189] In a short time Fava had become a major force in the organisation of workers and an advocate of political rights. The latter brought him into conflict with the Governor who subsequently made clear his aim to ensure the Union did not stray into non-industrial issues.[190] Throughout the Commonwealth the British Government was alert about the small bands of 'professed communist sympathisers who might stir up discontent. Hong Kong, Gibraltar, Kenya and Guiana all needed a watchful eye in this respect.' The danger of communism lay in its 'critique of colonialism'.[191]

Military influence cast a long shadow over constitutional development with the Admiralty having put up strong representations to the Colonial Office that they should have a seat on the Executive Council.[192] This was strongly resisted by the Governor who noted that 'the most important function of an Executive Council under a Constitution which includes a Legislative Council is to serve as a liaison between the Administration and the Legislature. This aspect is likely to become obscured, it seems to me, if extraneous personalities find a place on the Executive Council.'[193] He noted that in practice the 'vast bulk of the business . . . has no interest to the naval authorities.'[194] The Governor expressed concern that the presence of a representative from the Admiralty would 'produce the impression that His Majesty's Government is fighting a kind of rather grudging rear-guard action in order to minimise the civilian control of matters civilian.'[195] Eventually the Permanent Under-Secretary of State at

[187] For a detailed recount of the period 1945–50 see Garcia n 103 above, 35–66.

[188] Madden n 184 above, 512.

[189] Letter to the National Council for Civil Liberties from the Under-Secretary of State at the Colonial Office, 2 December 1948, cited in J Jeffries and T Sibley, *The Shameful Deportation of a Trade Union Leader—The Story of Albert Fava*, Gibraltar, UNITE, 2008, 30.

[190] ibid 28. The deportation was arguably unlawful and contrary to fundamental principles of law. But see *Zabrovsky v General Officer Commanding Palestine* [1947] AC 246.

[191] Hyam above n 2, 138.

[192] One of the reasons put forward by the Admiralty was that they were the largest employers: see Madden n 184 above, 513.

[193] 'Governor Sir Kenneth Anderson to John Martin (Assistant Under-Secretary, Colonial Office), 20 May 1949, CO 91/536/6', in Madden n 184 above, 513–14.

[194] ibid 514.

[195] ibid.

the Colonial Office ruled out this possibility.[196] The Executive Council would remain as originally constituted except that the three unofficial members would come to be selected from among the elected members of the Legislative Council.

The Governor had set out that, in his view:

> the object of a new Constitution is . . . to give to Gibraltar a Constitution which is so far as possible civilian in its character and gives to the people of the place as large a share in the direction of their fortunes as the peculiar circumstances of Gibraltar permit.[197]

Finally, after some internal debate the Secretary of State for the Colonies, Creech Jones, set out the terms of the new constitutional arrangements in a Despatch to the Governor.[198] The Governor would preside the legislature with the three ex-officio members, being the Colonial Secretary, Attorney-General and Financial Secretary. As promised in 1948 there would also be five elected members and two other nominated members.[199] There were, therefore, not a majority of elected members.[200] While it would fulfil a law-making function, powers were also reserved for the Governor 'to pass into law any measure necessary in his opinion in the interests of public order, public faith or good government, including defence.'[201] The Governor would also retain wide powers of veto of bills in his discretion and specifically do so in the case of bills concerning 'external affairs, religious discrimination, military discipline and treaties.'[202] His Majesty in Council would also retain reserved powers of legislation. The Executive Council would be the body 'in which policy is crystallised and which must largely be responsible for framing the legislative programme . . . it is therefore of great importance that contact between the Executive Council and Legislative Council should be close.'[203] To ensure that and while no requirement was set it was suggested that the unofficial members of the Executive Council be drawn from the legislature. The new constitutional arrangements came into being against protests from the Spanish Government.[204]

The first elections to the Legislative Council were finally held in 1950.[205] By that time Joshua Hassan, the AACR leader was Chairman of the City

196 ibid.

197 ibid.

198 'Arthur Creech Jones to Governor Sir Kenneth Anderson, 30 July 1949, CO 91/541/3' *Gibraltar Gazette*, Extraordinary, 4 August, 1949, in Madden n 184 above, 515–16.

199 Who should be 'unconnected with any party or interest, but by character, attainment or association capable of valuable public service': ibid 515.

200 The Governor was to have a casting vote but no original vote.

201 Madden n 184 above, 515.

202 ibid.

203 ibid.

204 See CO/91/541/4 and ibid.

205 With the AACR obtaining three of the five elected seats.

Council, leader of the elected members on the Legislative Council and one of the unofficial members on the Executive Council. He was to become Gibraltar's most prominent and influential politician in the post-war effort towards internal self-government. The AACR dominated most elections in the period 1950–69 with most political rivals making little headway against it.[206] Its most serious political challenge would come with the creation in 1964 of the Integration With Britain Party (IWBP). In those early years after the war the main social concern was the house-building programme so as to ensure the provision of accommodation for returning evacuees. This was undertaken against the backdrop that the land made available for civilian use was fairly small in comparison to that occupied by the military.[207]

The renewed post-war impetus to constitutional reform was shared throughout other colonies. This 'moral regeneration of British purpose in the colonial world'[208] motivated great change and an impetus to the decolonisation process that would lead to the new Commonwealth. The stated policy of the Colonial Office in 1948 was to 'guide the colonial territories to responsible self-government.'[209] Even so, in the immediate aftermath of war there was a belief in many quarters that steps towards reform would take decades and that some territories might not be suited to independence. Indeed, this seems to have been the view of the Colonial Office and Commonwealth Relations Office, who expressed concern of a group of territories, amongst which were Gibraltar, Malta, Cyprus, Mauritius, Bermuda, Bahamas, Fiji and the Gambia, for which 'full internal self-government with the UK responsible for international and defence matters' was a more likely objective.[210] There was also substantial concern expressed about a number of African, Caribbean and Asian 'intermediate territories' and the contingent liabilities that could arise for the UK.[211] In 1951 in a wide-ranging secret report on the future of 21 smaller colonial territories a committee set up by the British Government sought to devise 'a new status short of full independence, but . . . which would satisfy the legitimate pride and aspirations of the inhabitants of those territories.'[212]

[206] The short-lived Gibraltar Commonwealth Party founded in 1954 was a good example of that: see Cantos n 173 above, 78–91.

[207] Cantos n 173 above, 75–77.

[208] WR Louis, *Imperialism at Bay 1941–45—The United States and the Decolonisation of the British Empire* (Oxford, OUP, 1977) 101–03.

[209] CO 875/24 no 8 Circular Notes on Colonial Policy, British Documents on the End of Empire Project, Part I, 327 no 71, cited in Hyam above n 2, 162.

[210] Madden n 184 above, 17.

[211] ibid.

[212] 'Report of the Committee of Enquiry into Constitutional Development in the Smaller Colonial Territories, August 1951, CO 976/146' in Madden n 184 above, 22. The point should also be made that at the time the prevalent view in the Colonial Office was that a number of colonies who subsequently became independent in a short period thereafter might never be ready to be independent or would take decades to be ready. The pace of the changing panorama took many by surprise.

It identified a number of principles to secure the consent of those territories to a non-independent relationship with the United Kingdom, amongst which it was necessary for the colonial territory to come to the view that they should 'limit their aspiration for complete independence just as the UK might surrender a degree of sovereignty in the interests of the UN and the free world.'[213] Equally the intention would be to grant the 'fullest delegation of power to and as much internal responsibility' to the people of a territory.[214] A status of 'island or City State' was devised, with three categories. The first level would be typified by a merged State Council with executive and legislative functions. The second category would envisage a legislature with the Governor having an advisory council. The third, more advanced form of Government, would envisage the Governor having an advisory council with the territory also having an elected legislature and an Executive Council of Government.[215] Three of the recommendations were: that this new status be announced as a new departure in colonial policy; that it be backed by measures encouraging territories to appoint accredited representatives in the United Kingdom, supporting education in the United Kingdom; and that a special Colonial Consultative Council be established with representatives of all non-self-governing territories.[216] The territories were all classified into these three categories. The Committee noted that 'reform had already been promised to Gibraltar—*par excellence* a candidate for Class I but now it was too late for that.'[217]

The report was sent for inter-departmental consultation and heavily criticised for its academic and apologetic approach. It was considered that to impose a strait-jacket of a fixed status would not allow for constitutional progress and be considered demoralising in certain territories. The electoral system proposed could be interpreted as less advanced as that in place in some territories and would almost certainly be considered unpopular. In terms of governance the suggested formula of executive functions being carried out through State Councils was considered possibly unworkable.[218] The report was shelved as it did not gain the backing of the new Secretary of State for the Colonies, Oliver Lyttleton. In a minute, an official within the Colonial Office stated:

> [I]t should be frankly acknowledged and on some suitable occasion authoritatively stated that the declared policy of HMG on developing territories to the point of self-government cannot be applied to certain smaller territories where HMG has vital strategic and commercial interests which it proposes to maintain

[213] Madden n 184 above, 23.
[214] ibid.
[215] Both the legislature and executive councils would have official and unofficial members.
[216] ibid 25.
[217] Madden n 184 above, 24.
[218] Madden n 184 above, 26.

> . . . and where the economic or other resources of the territories do not admit of their becoming viable States. Within these limits responsibility for self-government in local matters will be encouraged.[219]

The pace that would be generated in the period after the mid 1950s could not generally be foreseen. Additionally internal disagreements within the Colonial Office and tensions with the Foreign Office made a cohesive policy more difficult. As Hyam has noted:

> [T]he Colonial Office often felt it got no help from the Foreign Office permanent officials and often a great deal of hindrance since they seemed to regard colonial matters as rather a nuisance, especially as they appeared not to be much concerned to stand up for British rights let alone those of the inhabitants of colonial territories.[220]

The general stance was to 'bolster moderate nationalists—often through co-option into Government—as a means of preserving British economic and strategic interests' especially in the face of more radical or communist elements.[221] In the short period from 1947–57 seven countries achieved independence. From 1958–69 a further 26 countries became independent within the Commonwealth. In a number of other territories there were significant reforms, political turmoil and social unrest. The management of that process was a mammoth task. Events in Gibraltar during the period 1945–64 were a reflected microcosm of what was occurring in the global and British colonial environment.

In 1955 the Governor of Gibraltar decided, against the will of the Legislative Council, to push through a fiscal measure using his reserve legislative powers. This provoked a constitutional crisis. A demonstration of several thousand people and a request from the elected members that the British Government should intervene to withdraw such action were rejected. All elected members of the Legislative Council resigned their seats. The Secretary of State for the Colonies, Alan Lennox-Boyd, flew out from London to intervene and after agreement that the tax would be reduced and special legislative powers not exercised without prior reference to the Secretary of State the crisis was averted.[222] The case for making constitutional concessions to overcome the crisis was put by an official in an internal minute and was linked to the Spanish sovereignty claim:

> [T]he Spaniards have already made a certain amount of capital out of the fact that the Governor used his reserved power to carry through a taxation measure

[219] 'AR Thomas, 1 January 1952, CO 976/149' in Madden, 2000, 27. Thomas was Assistant Under-Secretary at the Colonial Office 1952–64.

[220] R Hyam, 'Bureaucracy and Trusteeship in the Colonial Empire' in J Brown and Wm R Louis (eds), n 144 above, 260.

[221] N White, *Decolonisation—the British Experience Since 1945* (London, Longman, 1999) 115.

[222] Garcia n 103 above, 85–94.

> against the votes of the elected members. They also of course made capital out of the light which this taxation measure threw on the success of their economic pressure on Gibraltar by restrictions at the frontier . . . [this] could only stimulate the Spaniards' further efforts.[223]

This episode made clear the strong feeling of the civilian population and the desire to manage their own affairs that was not dissimilar to other experiences around the Commonwealth. It also highlighted the interrelationship of the Spanish issue with matters of governance.

In October 1955 to coincide with the visit of the Secretary of State for the Colonies the AACR presented a Memorandum on constitutional reform, making clear its aspirations that further reform should lead to 'people being given full powers and responsibilities in civil matters.'[224] It was accepted that progress towards this goal should be 'gradual and methodical' but the AACR were clear that the composition of both the Legislative and City Councils should be changed and majorities of elected members should be achieved in both. Equally it requested the transfer of functions such as health, social welfare, education, public works, housing and town planning to the City Council. Whether these functions were held by the City Council or the Gibraltar Government was important at a time when the Governor and his officials exercised complete control over the latter. The AACR made the point that:

> [W]hen full control of all civil affairs is vested in the people through their elected representatives, it will be immaterial whether certain services are administered by the Government or by the City Council and the question of merging the City Council into the Colonial Government could then be considered.[225]

It sought that elected members of the Legislative Council should be given departmental responsibilities within the Government and that the Executive Council should be replaced by a Council of Ministers with the Governor, three official members and four elected members, styled 'Ministers'.[226] The proposal was that this organ would then be the 'principal instrument for the framing of policy and perform such functions and duties and exercise such powers as would from time to time be prescribed.' It was also requested that the Governor's reserved legislative power be subject to checks and balances and that an independent Speaker preside over the Legislative Council.

In 1956 it was announced that the elected members in the Legislative Council would be increased from five to seven and that a Speaker would be appointed in due course. Additionally a further unofficial member would be appointed onto the Executive Council. In the elections to the

[223] 'DM Smith: Minute, 3 October 1955, CO 926/281' in Madden n 184 above, 517.
[224] *Memorandum on Constitutional Reform* (Gibraltar, AACR, October 1955).
[225] ibid.
[226] With one of these being styled 'Chief Minister'.

legislature that followed the AACR made clear that the thrust of its campaign was to ensure that 'Gibraltar should be governed by the Gibraltarians.'[227] The proposals for the introduction of a ministerial system were rejected but a halfway house was introduced in 1957 with the unofficial members being associated with certain departments and termed 'Member for' the specific area.[228] This was a hybrid situation that did not give the members associated with the particular departments much specific control over policy and could only be a temporary measure. There was reluctance in official circles to introduce a ministerial form of Government until the emergence of more than one dominant political party.[229] A Speaker of the Council was first appointed in June 1958. There was concern that the members did not have executive responsibilities over their departments and consequent pressure for a review of the system. The AACR put forward a further memorandum on reform requesting demarcation of responsibilities and some executive power for those members.[230] In a letter to the Colonial Secretary Joshua Hassan called for the creation of a Council of Ministers and for complete internal self-government in internal affairs.[231] The post of Chief Member was created in 1959, being the person who commanded the greatest measure of confidence in the Legislative Council from among the unofficial members. It was also agreed that the colonial and financial secretaries would consult the Chief Member on matters of policy.[232] At that stage the prevailing view was firmly against the grant of executive responsibilities.[233]

Meanwhile in the context of the wider management of demand for reform across its colonial territories Britain was taking steps to review the macro-colonial picture. 18 days after taking office, the British Prime Minister, Harold MacMillan asked the Colonial Office to produce a 'profit and loss account for each of our colonial possessions' of the 'probable course of constitutional development in the colonies over the years ahead.'[234] The report

[227] *AACR Manifesto*, September 1956. Throughout this time the AACR also held a majority of the elected seats in elections to the City Council that were conducted separately.

[228] Six of the nine unofficial members of the legislature (seven of whom were elected) were associated in that way with Government departments in 1957. In January 1958 a further two were associated with additional departments.

[229] 'Governor Sir Harold Redman to Alan Lennox-Boyd, 17 May 1956 CO 926/280 No 291' in Madden n 184 above, 520–22.

[230] Garcia n 103 above, 114–16.

[231] 'Joshua Hassan to Darrell Bates, 26 June 1958 CO 926/768' in Madden n 184 above, 525–26.

[232] Garcia records that the ability to make these advances was due to the support of the then Colonial Secretary, Darrell Bates: see Garcia n 103 above, 117.

[233] See 'Mediterranean Department: Brief for Lennox-Boyd's Visit, 2 January 1959 CO 926/78' in Madden n 184 above, 528–29.

[234] CAB 134/1555, CPC (57)6 'Future Constitutional Development in the Colonies' Minute from Mr MacMillan to Lord Salisbury, 28 January 1957, in R Hyam and Wm R Louis (eds), *The Conservative Government and the End of Empire, 1957–64, Part 1, High Policy, Political and Constitutional Change*, British Documents on the End of Empire, Series A, Vol 4 (London, TSO, 2000) 1–2.

took five months to compile and became a major policy source for departments. In so far as Gibraltar was concerned the report noted that a withdrawal of Britain would lead to Gibraltar becoming a 'slum like parts of southern Spain.'[235] It noted that:

> Any change of status which seemed to satisfy the Spaniards' claims would momentarily increase the United Kingdom's influence with Spain but it would permanently and disastrously diminish the United Kingdom's prestige internationally. In view of the loyalty of the Gibraltarian population to the Crown and the sentimental attachment of many people in the United Kingdom to the Rock cession of Gibraltar is unthinkable. But if it were to develop into some kind of 'City-State' this would be unlikely to have any effect one way or the other on the United Kingdom's prestige and influence . . . though Spain has offered to lease Gibraltar as a base to Her Majesty's Government and our strategic requirements could theoretically be maintained without retaining sovereignty, such an arrangement in so small a territory would present practical difficulties and would become impossible if Spain became unfriendly.[236]

In a subsequent memorandum Gibraltar was listed among a group of territories which appeared 'most likely to show significant developments in internal self-government during the next ten years.'[237] The territory was listed among the seven most important colonies for military reasons.[238] In 1960 Gibraltar was considered to be on the verge of ministerial government. In an advisory minute from the Colonial Office it was noted that the factors to take into account when contemplating reforms were Britain's defence interests, economic viability and the Spanish dimension.[239] It observed that 'Gibraltar's ultimate status will for the time being have to be worked out on the basis of the Gibraltarians' own wishes and the realities of the situation.' It considered that if links with the United Kingdom were loosened too much it could increase the prospect of Spain's claim being prosecuted more vigorously. Even so it recommended that it was possible to go 'pretty far along the road to responsible Government without endangering UK interests' and that the Governor should only keep control of external affairs, defence, internal security and finance.[240] The executive business had for years been done through an Executive Council. This continued to be the case but in 1962 the British Government agreed to the

[235] CAB 134/1551, CPC (57)27, 'Future Constitutional Development in the Colonies' Report, May 1957 in Hyam and Louis (eds) n 234 above, 20.

[236] ibid.

[237] CAB 134/1556 CPC 57(30) 'Future Constitutional Development in the Colonies' Memo by Sir N Brook, 6 September 1957 in Hyam and Louis (eds), n 234 above, 30–31.

[238] ibid 35.

[239] CO 926/769 'Gibraltar: Constitutional Forward Thinking' Minute by NBJ Huijsman, CO, 1 June 1960 in Hyam and Louis (eds), n 234 above, 796–97. It was noted that Gibraltar was, at the time, much more financially dependent on defence for its economic needs than other comparative territories.

[240] ibid 797.

setting up of a Council of Members which would allow much of the work of the Executive Council to be transferred to a Council made up of the elected members who were now associated with different areas in the Legislative Council.[241] This was the beginning of the system by which executive powers were to be divided among two councils (and partially removed from the classic colonial model of the sole Executive Council). Already the role of constitutional practice developing the system of governance beyond the strict letter of statutory instruments was being alluded to. In 1962 the Governor noted in a letter to the Secretary of State for the Colonies that 'unlike most fortresses the local population have a large say in their Government, through Parliamentary institutions on British lines. In practice this goes further than a study of the constitutional instruments suggests.'[242]

This system was further formalised in 1964 when after talks held between Lord Lansdowne and the unofficial members of the Legislative Council a Constitution was introduced.[243] Gibraltar was given a ministerial system headed by a Chief Minister. There was to be an Executive Council known as the 'Gibraltar Council' made up of the Deputy Fortress Commander, the Permanent Secretary to the Government of Gibraltar,[244] the Attorney-General, the Financial Secretary and five elected members of the Legislative Council presided over by the Governor.[245] For the first time there were to be more elected members than appointed members on the Executive Council. There was also to be a Council of Ministers for the purpose of making 'recommendations to the Gibraltar Council concerning any matter for which a Minister is responsible and concerning any other matter as may be referred to it by the Gibraltar Council.'[246]

The aim of this dual council system was further clarified in the Despatch from the Foreign Secretary published simultaneously with the Constitution:

> While the Governor in Council will be free to refer to the Council of Ministers any matter on which its advice is desired, matters within the responsibility of Ministers will normally come direct to the Council of Ministers without such

[241] Garcia n 103 above, 118–27. See also 'The Constitutional Position: Note for Reginald Maudling' 31 October 1961, CO 926/1223, in Madden n 184 above, 529.

[242] 'Governor Sir Charles Keightley to Duncan Sandys' CO926/1227, 28 June 1962, in Madden n 184 above, 531.

[243] Gibraltar Constitution Order 1964, *Gibraltar Gazette* (Gibraltar 7 August 1964) (the '1964 Constitution') that also revoked the previous Letters Patent that had introduced the Legislative Council, namely the Gibraltar Letters Patent 1950, Gibraltar (Amendment) Letters Patent 1955, Gibraltar (Legislative Council) Order 1950, Gibraltar (Legislative Council) (Amendment) Order 1956, Gibraltar (Legislative Council) (Amendment No 2) Order 1956, Gibraltar (Legislative Council) (Amendment) Order 1959 and the Gibraltar (Legislative Council) (Amendment) Order 1963.

[244] The new name for the Chief Secretary that, in turn, was the name that had replaced the description 'Colonial Secretary' in 1963.

[245] 1964 Constitution ss 12–13.

[246] 1964 Constitution s 14(3).

> reference, and its recommendations on matters of purely domestic concern will as a general rule be endorsed by the Governor in Council . . . The agenda and minutes of all meetings of the Council will be sent to the Permanent Secretary, the Financial Secretary and the Attorney-General.[247]

There was to be a Legislative Council with a Speaker, two *ex officio* and 11 elected members.[248] By section 36 the Governor with the advice and consent of the Legislative Council could make laws for the peace, order and good government of the territory.[249] The effect of the Constitution was expressed to be so that

> the people of Gibraltar will enjoy fuller control of internal affairs both through increased representation in the Legislature where the Chief Minister will in future have the position of Leader of the House and be vested with the direction of Government business and by the changes in the Executive system notably the introduction of a ministerial system under which ministers will be responsible for Government departments and the establishment of the Council of Ministers, presided over by the Chief Minister.[250]

In terms of status and relationship with the British Crown the Despatch noted the view that 'no change should be made in the conduct of defence and foreign affairs and that Gibraltar should always remain in close association with Britain.'[251] The 1964 Constitution enlarged the Legislative Council and while it retained the City Council it was agreed that 'the future of the City Council should be decided early on in the life of the next Legislature.'[252] The 1964 Constitution was introduced with the accompanying Royal Instructions of the same date. Section 37 of the 1964 Constitution required the Governor and Legislative Council to conform to the Instructions 'as nearly as may be'. The Royal Instructions prescribed situations when Bills were not to be assented to without instructions from a Secretary of State, prescribed how Private Bills would be introduced, how the power of pardon in capital cases would function and generally set out other mechanical provisions in respect of legislation.

Having achieved a representative legislature in 1957 Gibraltar had now in 1964 achieved responsible Government. The post-war years to 1964 were a period of fairly rapid domestic political change. This was tempered by the continued importance of the military dimension, economic dependence and the Spanish dimension.

247 *Despatch No 253 of 31 July 1964 from the Secretary of State,* published as Government Notice No 883, *Gibraltar Gazette* (Gibraltar 8 August 1964) para 4.

248 1964 Constitution s 24.

249 The 1964 Constitution dealt with the office of Governor, the Executive Council, the Legislative Council and the procedure in the same. It did not have Parts on fundamental rights, the Judicature, Finance or the Public Service that were to be added in 1969. The City Council was also abolished in 1969.

250 Despatch 253/31 July 1964, para 2.

251 Despatch 253/31 July 1964, para 8.

252 Despatch 253/31 July 1964, para 7.

THE SPANISH DIMENSION AND CONSTITUTIONAL REFORM

Meanwhile all had not been quiet on the Spanish front. The Spanish claim to sovereignty had not only remained but had been asserted in stronger terms because of the growth of political nationalism. In 1931 the *Juntas de Ofensiva Nacional-Sindicalista* (the 'JONS'), a nationalist political movement, had been established. The initial programme of the JONS 'included a denunciation of separatism and . . . the approval of Spanish expansion to Gibraltar.'[253] This movement merged in 1934 with Primo de Rivera's *Falange* to create the right-wing ideological bedrock for the Franco regime that was to be established as a result of the Spanish civil war. In fact, the British authorities in Gibraltar viewed the start of internal Spanish hostilities in 1936 with great caution in view of its desire to safeguard its interests in Gibraltar. It was important to ensure good relations 'with whoever won the war.'[254] Britain became concerned at the possibility that Franco's Spain would join Germany and Italy in broad alliance and to obtain Gibraltar in exchange for Spanish support.[255]

> The demise of . . . Britain opened up imperial vistas which might also simplify his [Franco's] domestic problems . . . While crowds of Falangists chanted '*Gibraltar espanol*' outside the British embassy . . . Franco watched with excitement . . . [they] were impatient to seize the opportunity provided by German successes to take Gibraltar and French Morocco.[256]

In the post-war period tension still remained. Franco reacted to British lack of support to Spanish NATO membership ambitions by arranging demonstrations seeking the return of Gibraltar and by decreeing that the 4 August would be Gibraltar Day, with rallies to be held by 'the *Falange* Youth Front to mark the pain suffered by Spain as a result of foreign occupation.'[257] In late 1951 Franco offered a lease-back solution for Gibraltar to British diplomats. As part of the proposal Spain offered that the British naval base could remain and that Gibraltar could continue to be a free port.[258]

In 1954 Her Majesty the Queen had visited Gibraltar as part of her post-coronation tour. The visit incurred the 'profound displeasure' of Spain.[259] It directly led to the closure of the Spanish consulate in Gibraltar a few

[253] H Thomas, *The Spanish Civil War*, 3rd edn (London, HarperCollins, 1986) 111.
[254] ibid 392.
[255] P Preston, *Franco* (London, Fontana Press, 1995) 358.
[256] ibid 356.
[257] ibid 605.
[258] Thomas above n 253, 617.
[259] Spanish Red Book on Gibraltar (Madrid, Spanish Government, 1965) 57.

days before the visit.[260] In January 1954 the British Ambassador in Madrid had reported demonstrations and 'threats on his life by the *Falange*' if the Queen visited Gibraltar but also noted that 'more serious non-official Spaniards' had sent messages of sympathy.[261] During the years that followed Spain increased restrictions placing obstacles to the freedom of movement of Gibraltarians across the frontier.[262] In 1960 Franco appointed Fernando Maria Castiella as his Foreign minister and he was to have a significant role in the Anglo–Spanish relationship over Gibraltar during the following decade.[263] General Franco spoke of lease-back solutions to settle the Spanish claim to sovereignty and his Ministers condemned the constitutional reforms introduced by Britain as 'white-wash . . . (over) the colonial façade' so as to prevent being criticised at the United Nations.[264] Britain was concerned about Spanish reaction to the constitutional reforms of 1964 and presented these as merely intended 'to increase the efficiency of Gibraltar's internal institutions but not their powers, and Spain should not interpret this reorganisation of political life on the Rock as a continuation of that initiated . . . in 1950.'[265] Spain persisted in its objection to the reforms that it contended had 'serious international significance.'[266]

UNITED NATIONS INTEREST

Decolonisation and the development of self-determination as a principle of international law was intrinsically linked to the debate of sovereignty and legitimacy for, as Musgrave notes, 'the western European tradition of self-determination was based on the concepts of popular sovereignty, individual freedom and representative Government.'[267] The different traditions came from distinct standpoints and placed different emphasis on ethnicity questions. However there is little to distinguish the approach of

[260] Spain has not re-opened its consulate. For a summary of the events that led to the closure of the consulate on the instructions of Franco and the Spanish Council of Ministers, see F Oda-Angel, '*Gibraltar a un año de la Declaración de Córdoba: la recuperacion de la confianza*', *Real Instituto Eclano, Documento de Trabajo* 45/2007, www.realinstitutoelcano.org.

[261] Madden n 184 above, 516.

[262] Garcia n 103 above, 106–09.

[263] Castiella had been a volunteer in the *Division Azul* (Blue Division—a nationalist military force), 'had sworn allegiance to Hitler and had been awarded the iron cross': see Preston, 1995, 604.

[264] Spanish Red Book on Gibraltar (Madrid, Spanish Government, 1965) 59.

[265] Garcia n 103 above, 135.

[266] In fact as will be argued later in this book Spain was right about the significance of the constitutional reforms of 1964.

[267] T Musgrave, *Self-Determination and National Minorities* (Oxford, OUP, 2000) 13, As such this could occur within State boundaries when an 'exercise of popular sovereignty resulted in representative government'. Conversely in Eastern Europe it grew out of nationalism that stressed ethnic, linguistic or religious similarities.

States born out of the decolonising surge of the 1960s and beyond. This first grew out of nationalism and a promotion of nationhood that necessarily carried with it an awareness of common features (that might include ethnicity). The dividing line in a decolonising atmosphere is not so stark that it would force a choice between one tradition and the other. In fact a decolonising environment is not only driven by nationalism but also by desires for representative government, freedom and reform. In some ways there is a marriage of issues that form the core aspirations of a sub-State nation. This would better explain the context of Gibraltar's aspirations.

The surge in consideration of the concept of self-determination took a marked emphasis in the immediate aftermath of the First World War. As Musgrave describes this process was legitimised greatly by Bolshevik endorsement and enhanced by support from President Wilson, who stated in a speech to Congress in 1918 that:

> Peoples are not to be handed about from one sovereignty to another by an international conference or an understanding between rivals and antagonists. National aspirations must be respected . . . Self-determination is not a mere phrase, it is an imperative principle of action which statesmen will henceforth ignore at their peril.[268]

All did not endorse Wilson's adoption of the terminology of self-determination. Even senior officials within his administration thought that this phrase was 'loaded with dynamite' and would lead to 'political instability and domestic disorder.'[269] Attempts to persuade the Allies to adopt the principle and incorporate it into the Covenant of the League of Nations largely failed because of the resistance of the more generalised legal application of this principle. This became painfully obvious when Commissions of Jurists and Rapporteurs appointed to report on the Aaland Islands question in 1920 stated that self-determination was not a 'part of international law and should not normally play a role in the determination of sovereignty over certain territory.'[270] In that way it has been said 'classical international law buttressed colonialism . . . international law served as a legal tool to promulgate and justify colonial empire.'[271] The effect of that was that international law encouraged the presence of 'a relatively small group of technologically advanced sovereign States with various kinds of dependencies in their rear.'[272] The most basic consequence of 'colonial dependency was the denial of sovereignty.'[273]

[268] ibid 24
[269] ibid 30–31.
[270] ibid 35.
[271] G Kreijen, 'The Transformation of Sovereignty and African Independence: No Shortcuts to Statehood' in G Kreijen (ed), *State, Sovereignty and International Governance* (Oxford, OUP, 2004) 55, citing A Anghie, 'Finding the Peripheries, Sovereignty and Colonialism in the Nineteenth Century Law' (1999) 40 Harvard International Law Journal 1.
[272] Kreijen in Kreijen (ed), n 271 above, 55.
[273] ibid 56.

Changes in the international and European backdrop in the post-war period would progressively influence the Gibraltar issue. 'Western thought created colonialism and western thought carried the seeds of its demise.'[274] This process led western countries from a position of leading the charge on a 'sacred trust of civilisation' to being, eventually, entrusted with the 'sacred trust' to promote self-government under Article 73 of the United Nations Charter.[275] That was not an initially obvious consequence, although once anti-colonialism gathered pace it became unstoppable. This was facilitated by the markedly different approaches taken by Britain and the United States on colonialism and the support to anti-colonialism given by the latter. Slowly colonialism was transformed 'from an accepted practice to an outright illegal enterprise.'[276] It became impossible to defend and needed to be substituted for a new world order.[277] Anti-colonial pressures were global and responded as much to *realpolitik* as to advances in legal theory. Most directly for Gibraltar not only was there significant movement throughout the Commonwealth but geo-politically political unrest in North Africa was also relevant. All the European colonial powers, France, Britain, the Netherlands, Portugal and Spain were grappling with demands for reform.[278] The road to independence of Morocco in 1956 had as much to do with the acceptance of the inevitability of reform as with the need to ensure a pro-western regional balance of power.[279]

Self-determination was first set out in a multilateral Treaty in the Charter of the United Nations in 1945. But as Cassese notes the process was arduous, faced much resistance and 'States were unable to positively define' it.[280] This principle then evolved in a manner that was 'unforeseen'[281] to those that had originally drafted this when it turned its focus onto colonial peoples. 'Independence for colonial peoples . . . (was not) generally contemplated by colonial rulers until' the 1950s.[282] By this time the atmosphere at the UN was 'virulently anti-colonial' and it became impossible for colonial powers to resist the rising tide.[283] Britain that had originally 'resisted the principle of self-determination came to rely on the formula . . . as an answer' to its critics.[284] 'In the rocks, shoals and other

[274] ibid 59.
[275] ibid 57.
[276] ibid 58.
[277] ibid 58.
[278] See eg M Shipway, *Decolonisation and its Impact—A Comparative Approach to the End of the Colonial Empires* (Oxford, Blackwell, 2008).
[279] M Thomas, 'From French North Africa to Maghreb Independence: Decolonisation in Morocco, Tunisia and Algeria 1945–56' in Thomas, Moore and Butler n 167 above, 209–27.
[280] A Cassese, *Self Determination of Peoples—A Legal Appraisal* (Cambridge, CUP, 1995) 42.
[281] ibid 44.
[282] Kreijen in Kreijen (ed), n 271 above, 57.
[283] ibid 64.
[284] Wm R Louis, *Ends of British Imperialism, The Scramble for Empire, Suez and Decolonisation*, 2nd edn (London, Taurus, 2006) 691–92.

remnants of Empire what made more sense than to allow the inhabitants of Gibraltar or the Falklands to determine their own future.'[285]

The principle that colonial peoples could rely on the right of self-determination to freely determine their political status was included in two significant resolutions of the United Nations, namely 1514 (XV) and 1541 (XV), both of December 1960. These constituted 'a set of general standards specifying the principle of self-determination enshrined in the UN Charter, with special regard to colonial peoples.'[286]

The *Declaration on the Granting of Independence to Colonial Countries and Peoples*[287] forms the backbone of the decolonisation effort. It declared that 'all peoples have the right to self-determination; by virtue of that right they freely determine their political status and freely pursue their economic, social and cultural development.'[288] It called for 'immediate steps' to 'transfer all powers to the peoples of these territories . . . in accordance with their freely expressed will and desire . . . in order to enable them to enjoy complete independence and freedom.'[289] In a subsequent paragraph that would be used by Spain to argue its own case it also declared that 'any attempt aimed at the partial or total disruption of the national unity and the territorial integrity of a country is incompatible with the purposes and principles of the Charter of the United Nations.'[290] The Fourth Committee was entrusted with the responsibility of overall supervision of the decolonisation process.[291] It is assisted by a Special Committee on Decolonisation established in 1962 to monitor the implementation of GA Res 1514 and to make recommendations on its application.[292] The Committee of 24 'became famous . . . for its persistent, voluble and impassioned attacks on the western colonial powers especially Britain.'[293] While in 1945 approximately 750 million people lived in a colonial environment

285 ibid 692.

286 Cassese n 280 above, 72. Even though this is touched on here a detailed study of the applicability or otherwise of the right to self-determination is outside the scope of this work.

287 GA Res 1514 (XV), 14 December 1960. This is in the same terms as Art 1(1) of the International Covenant on Civil and Political Rights ('the ICCPR'). There is also a cross-reference in Art 1(3) to the responsibility on administering powers to promote that right in non-self-governing territories. Interestingly there is no equivalent to GA Res 1514 para 6 in the ICCPR.

288 Para 2—inadequacy or lack or preparedness is not a pretext for delaying independence (para 3).

289 Para 5.

290 Para 6.

291 Its full name is the Special Political and Decolonisation Committee and deals with political rights not dealt with by the First Committee as well as decolonisation: see www.un.org.

292 Commonly known as the Committee of 24 (its full title is the Special Committee on the Situation with regard to the Implementation of the Declaration on the Granting of Independence to Colonial Countries and Peoples). It was initially known as the Committee of 17: see Louis n 284 above, 702.

293 Louis n 284 above, 702.

at the end of 2008 there were only 16 non-self-governing territories, most of which have small populations.[294]

GA Res 1514 had tremendous moral authority and legal force having been adopted by 89 votes to zero.[295] Nine States abstained, among them the United States, Britain and Spain. By 1960 'the United Nations was a quite different organisation from the one its founders had created in 1945 . . . in its colonial guise [the UN] had become a Frankenstein's monster.'[296] The British Government was a reluctant player in all this. Initially, its stance was to maintain a studied aloofness with minimal involvement and co-operation. As Louis has noted senior British officials at the Colonial Office were adamant 'that the United Nations must not be allowed to interfere in British colonial administration.'[297] Increasingly the Afro-Asian States drove the anti-colonial agenda and deployed pressure on colonial powers. A watershed at the UN had been the Suez crisis. That had heavily influenced the perception many States had of Britain:

> [T]he British Empire was not merely in the dock but reviled as a renegade . . . denounced as being just as immoral and vicious as the Soviet Empire . . . for the next fifteen years or so Britain became Public Enemy Number One at the United Nations.[298]

It was no accident that it was during those 15 years that the main resolutions on Gibraltar were passed.

Quite different to the stance of the Colonial Office, the British UN delegation invested much time and energy to clarify Britain's colonial record in the eyes of many States. The tide of reform that swept the Commonwealth during the 1950s and 1960s led to the grant of independence to many countries.[299] The push for greater self-government became inexorable. 'The "self" in self-determination was no longer either historical or ethnic nations but artificial ex-colonial jurisdictions.'[300] In the post-war period of more intense decolonisation Gibraltar was placed on the list of non-self-governing territories of the United Nations as early as 1946. While the

[294] Ten are UK Overseas Territories. The other territories are administered by the United States (US Virgin Islands, American Samoa and Guam), New Zealand (Tokelau) and France (New Caledonia). The final territory is the Western Sahara.

[295] Kreijen in Kreijen n 271 above, 70.

[296] Louis n 284 above, 689.

[297] ibid 690.

[298] ibid 695–96.

[299] The intense period of decolonisation started with Ghana in 1957. It swept across Africa, the Caribbean, South East Asia, Europe and Asia-Pacific, eventually culminating in the present Commonwealth of 54 independent countries. A Free Association experiment was tried in the West Indies in the 1960s as a precursor to independence. The majority of the grants of independence were completed prior to 1975 but there was a small number thereafter. See S De Smith, *The New Commonwealth and its Constitutions* (London, Stevens, 1964) and Roberts-Wray n 72 above.

[300] Kreijen in Kreijen n 271 above, 72, citing RH Jackson, *Quasi-States, Sovereignty, International Relations and the Third World* (Cambridge, CUP, 1990) 77.

United Kingdom put Gibraltar forward as a non-self-governing territory in 1946 it has been noted that as the Gibraltar situation was one of cession and not colonial conquest this was slightly anomalous.[301] As pointed out in the relevant UN Resolution[302] 'the territory of a colony or Non-Self-Governing Territory has . . . a status separate and distinct' from the Administering State.[303] Four issues drove the process towards decolonisation in most Commonwealth countries: economics,[304] the people of the territory,[305] residual British interests[306] and such unique factors as arose in each case.[307] These four parameters dictated the timing, pace and extent of the demands for self-government in Gibraltar, as they did in other territories, and so are relevant to this work in explaining the context of the calls for reform and the factors that lead to their determination.[308] Analogous factors afflicted all of the remaining British overseas territories.

The form of decolonisation that each OT can opt for is governed by these shared factors and such other unique factors that reflect underlying British and local political realities that affect the process. For example, the Bermuda experience[309] clearly highlights the limits to which the United Kingdom will go in granting powers of self-government. Concerns as to contingent or residual liabilities not only set the limits for constitutional development but also set limits to secure good government that the British Government has acted on.[310] Additionally, the most basic political reality is that without the desire of the people of the territory constitutional change is impossible to achieve. The unique features of Gibraltar mean that a strict comparison with these territories is too narrow. There is a need to widen the comparison to include other Stateless nations (and self-governing regions) within State Members of the European Union for comparison on governance issues. But even such a comparison is insufficient

[301] Cassese n 280 above, 207.

[302] GA Res 2625 (XXV) of 24 October 1970, Declaration on Principles of International Law concerning Friendly Co-operation among States in accordance with the Charter of the United Nations.

[303] This separateness is also consistent with Gibraltar's EU status as a territory for 'whose external relations a Member State' is responsible.

[304] It was easier for a country that was self-sufficient or which could confidently aspire to easily become so to press for independence.

[305] The will of the people was central in each case as a driver for reform. In many countries there was agitation and social and political unrest in the campaign towards self-government.

[306] If Britain retained some national interest in the country or the region it coloured British policy on the willingness to grant such demands and on their timing.

[307] Beyond the generalisations, analogies and constitutional templates that can be drawn it is an analysis of the unique issues that arise in each case that dictated the timing, nature and extent of reform. In the case of small territories the progress towards decolonisation has been complicated by special economic issues that arise or are accentuated by the size of the country concerned. See ch 3 for further discussion. It is clear that these special factors also arise in the case of non-independent micro-territories such as the Overseas Territories.

[308] They also affect the prospect of resolution of these issues.

[309] See ch 2 pp 86–87 and below.

[310] In Montserrat and Turks and Caicos: see ch 2.

to address the status question that is not shared with any of the overseas territories or European stateless nations. While other sub-State nations also grapple with the meaning of sovereignty, conflicts of national aspirations and forms of governance, what is unique in Gibraltar's case is the juxtaposition of a third party State Claimant to its sovereignty and its European Union membership.

The first attendance by Gibraltar political leaders at the United Nations came in September 1963 when two of the elected members, Sir Joshua Hassan[311] and Peter Isola, appeared before the Special Committee on Decolonisation. Hassan made clear that full self-government was the aspiration of Gibraltarian politicians and that the stage of constitutional development reached was only an interim stage to further reform. He declared that already the influence of internal governance was such that 'nothing could be further away from the generally accepted interpretation of colonialism than the situation in present-day Gibraltar.'[312] Placing his submissions squarely within the parameters of the desire to obtain free association with Britain he observed that:

> The land in which they [the people of Gibraltar] live is their birthplace and was the birthplace of their forbearers—for no less than 250 years . . . we ask for nothing except to be allowed to live our lives the way we want to live them without interference from outside.

The British Government noted that the territory 'lives under the shadow of Spain and in view of its small size it is scarcely conceivable that it could ever become fully independent.'[313] Nonetheless it did consider that free association was a viable future status for Gibraltar and that work should be done towards achieving that.[314] After the constitutional conference that led to the 1964 Constitution (but before its commencement) the Legislative Council published a paper on their view of the future status of Gibraltar. In it the elected members made clear that 'the wishes of the people of Gibraltar are to achieve full internal self-government in a free association with Britain.'[315] It accepted that because of its size, economic constraints and political difficulties with Spain an association with another State was necessary. It made the point that the constitutional changes of 1964 'represent the last step before the formal achievement of full internal self-government which now awaits only the conclusion of an agreement between Britain and Gibraltar as to the terms and conditions of the

[311] Who had by then been knighted earlier that year. Garcia n 103 above, 128–39.

[312] *Intervention of the Petitioner from the town of Gibraltar, Sir J Hassan before the Committee of 24*, 19 September 1963.

[313] FO 371/166836 no 342 'Future Constitutional Development in the UK dependent territories', October 1962, in Hyam and Louis (eds), n 234 above, 202.

[314] FO 371/172610 no.13 'The future of British Colonial Territories' 27 September 1963 with Annex 'Likely Status' in Hyam and Louis (eds), n 234 above, 211–220.

[315] *The Future of Gibraltar*, Legislative Council, Gibraltar, May 1964.

association between them . . . it is fully expected that the final, formal achievement of self-government will take place during the life of the next legislature.' The paper added

> [W]hat Gibraltarians seek from the Committee of 24 therefore is an affirmation of their right to self-government in a free association with Britain the terms of such an association to be agreed freely between Gibraltar and Britain and fully implemented at a time to be chosen by the people of Gibraltar themselves.[316]

While making the point that the decolonisation exercise had nothing to do with the sovereignty of the territory concerned the paper acknowledged that Spain raised the issue of sovereignty in the context of debates on decolonisation by urging reliance on territorial integrity and not self-determination.[317] As such, it added that, while

> it is a matter of fact that sovereignty over Gibraltar is at present exercised by Britain . . . *the soil of Gibraltar should belong to no-one but the people of Gibraltar* . . . sovereignty over Gibraltar is not a matter for discussion between Britain and Spain. That is why Gibraltar objected to the suggestion made last September that talks to decide Gibraltar's future should be held between those two countries. The question of sovereignty over Gibraltar must be decided solely according to the wishes of the people of Gibraltar. If the people of Gibraltar wished to be associated with Spain then Britain would have to surrender Gibraltar to Spain if the principle of self-determination were not to be abused. Similarly, if the people of Gibraltar wished to be associated with Britain—as they do—then Spain's territorial claim to Gibraltar must fail, if the grant of self-government under the auspices of the Committee of 24 is not to be vitiated, nullified and made into a mockery. (emphasis added)

This statement was reflected in demonstrations of the period at which some participants carried banners asserting a 'right to our land'. By 1964 the Secretary of State for the Colonies, Duncan Sandys, was announcing 'we have no desire to prolong our colonial obligations for a day longer than is necessary.'[318] As Hyam has noted the 'wind of change' had become a 'gale force'.[319] For Gibraltar, that had willingly capitalised on the Commonwealth impetus for reform, the acquisition of responsible Government marked the high point in its development at that stage. While the global gale of decolonisation would sweep away most colonial cobwebs in the decades that followed for Gibraltar the next period in its recent history was the start of much more equivocal times.

[316] Indeed British officials considered the concept of free association as a solution to the Gibraltar issue: see no 46, CO Memo 'The Future of British Colonial Territories', 27 September 1963, R Hyam and W Louis (eds), *British Documents on the End of Empire, Conservative Government and the End of Empire, 1957–64*, Pt I (London, TSO, 2000) 211–20 and Hyam, 2006, 314–15.

[317] And that 'some members of the Committee (of 24) believe that the question of sovereignty should not be kept entirely outside the auspices of the Committee.' This is a debate that has raged for decades and was recently resuscitated in 2008: see ch 7.

[318] Cited in Hyam above n 2, 262.

[319] Hyam above n 2, 326.

2

Changing Landscapes: Sovereignty, Status and Governance by 1986, and their Convergence onto the European Stage

INTRODUCTION

THE TWO DECADES between 1964 and 1986 were years of contradiction for Gibraltar. Riding the wave of post-war decolonisation and self-determination, Gibraltar gained much in self-government during the early part of that period. The progressive force of self-government, fuelled by a redefinition of sovereignty and a climate of self-determination, led to the surge forward by 1969. Subsequently accession into the European Community with Britain in 1973 would dramatically affect issues of legislative and constitutional sovereignty. Almost in parallel, the period spanning the democratisation of Spain[1], its approximation to Britain and Spain's own accession to the Community in 1986 would see a rolling back of constitutional gains spurned on by bilateralism. It was the final episode that created the climate within which the paradox of governance sustained by Gibraltar would be fostered. By 1986 the contradiction that emerges is that in an environment that was being re-defined to boost polycentric constitutionalism there was in fact a revival of intergovernmental exclusiveness.

This chapter covers these periods of a changing legal, political and constitutional backdrop. The 1945–69 period was marked by the era of self-government, self-determination and decolonisation. By the late 1960s self-determination had emerged as a recognised principle of international law. During this initial phase Gibraltar—albeit under the political microscope and facing intense Spanish pressure—was making major constitutional gains. At the same time Britain had aspirations to join the European Community and end its exclusion from that developing entity. When Gibraltar's representatives first appeared at the United Nations in 1963

[1] That started in 1975 with the death of General Franco.

France had just vetoed the British application for membership of the EC and Spain was a dictatorship. Britain was then much firmer in its support of the right to self-determination of the people.[2] In 1969 an advanced Constitution bestowing significant self-government was granted.[3] In retaliation Spain closed its border with Gibraltar. In an unconnected but important move that would contribute to the directional shift of interests, France lifted its veto on UK membership of the EC that very same year.

During the 1969–86 period the constitutional gains dried up and were replaced by movement on the Anglo–Spanish relations front. The democratisation of Spain followed by the progressive political approximation of Britain and Spain and the culmination of Spanish accession to the Community all had a profound effect on Gibraltar. This was slowly transformed from an issue that simply divided the two countries to an obstacle to the rapprochement. By 1986 the European Community had emerged as the principal theatre of developments for Gibraltar. With the European Community taking greater prominence in day to day developments Gibraltar's governance would be impacted not only because of its own accession (with Britain) in 1973 but because of the increasing bilateralisation of its issues post Spanish accession in 1986. External/European governance came under focus and scrutiny in a much more distinct way. Conversely in the period of Anglo–Spanish gradual closeness after 1975 there was a freeze in developments on internal governance and status. Status issues took a back seat after Spanish entry to the Community with governance matters coming to the foreground of the areas affected.

In parallel, and, as self-determination gained prominence as an international legal principle of application to colonial peoples, there was a transformation in the traditional meanings of sovereignty and nationalism. These saw an evolution that placed primacy on people's rights, democracy and legitimacy. But an important nuance that was to emerge, and would so influence the supra-national (and thereafter the internal State's) governance debate, was an increasing focus on spheres of competence and control. Possessing competences or control within defined areas as an expression of 'sovereignty' or 'nationhood' did not require an assertion of complete control or secession from the State. In a world of interdependence and supra-nationalism it was possible to accommodate nationalism and sovereignty without what at one stage would have been thought to be the *sine qua non* of each concept: separatism and ultimate control. Trends emphasising multi-level governance and polycentric sub-state constitutionalism highlight how the people and the representatives of civil society are given influence, power, representation and participation at different

[2] The panorama seen at the UN of the 1960s, in which Britain forcefully argued the case for self-determination of the people of Gibraltar, would not reappear when Gibraltar's politicians returned to the UN in 1992.

[3] Gibraltar Constitution Order 1969 SI 1969 II p3602 ('the 1969 Constitution').

levels and in different ways. As such it is important as part of this work to evaluate not only the territorial sovereignty dimension but also the impact of the European Community on legislative and constitutional sovereignty. This is also related to the overall themes of the work and the deficits that flow from the dispute. This evolving environment of redefined sovereignty and stateless nationalism was emerging at the same time that Gibraltar was encountering traditional sovereignty and bilateral intergovernmentalism thus creating the first contradiction of the Gibraltar dispute.

This chapter is in three parts. In the first part it traces the state of the Constitution and the effect of decolonisation on Gibraltar's international legal status from 1964–86. The advances secured in self-governance contrast with the account provided in the second part of this chapter of how EC accession changed the governance focus of Gibraltar through its impact on constitutional and legislative sovereignty. The third part considers how Anglo–Spanish relations developed in the period 1975–86 with the democratisation of Spain and how (with a visible change of attitude by the United Kingdom) intergovernmental arrangements were entered into that affected Gibraltar. The emphasis was on a revitalisation of bilateralism.

CONSTITUTIONAL DEVELOPMENTS AND DECOLONISATION

Decolonisation and Status

By 1966 Article 1(1) of the United Nations Covenant on Civil and Political Rights declared that 'All Peoples have the right to self-determination. By virtue of that right they freely determine their political status'. State Parties to the Covenant were required to 'promote the realisation of the right to self-determination' in 'non-self-governing territories.'[4] Cassese has described the introduction of this Article as 'a major impetus to self-determination's development into a legal principle.'[5] He has also noted that:

> [I]n the era immediately after the second world war the majority of States equated the achievement of independent status by colonial countries with the final realisation of self-determination . . . Under the Covenant however the right of self-determination does not end with independence.[6]

It has as much an internal dimension that relates to domestic governance as well as an external dimension that is of greater direct relevance

[4] Art 1(3).

[5] A Cassese, *Self Determination of Peoples—A Legal Appraisal* (Cambridge, CUP, 1995) 54, and see also I Brownlie, *Principles of Public International Law*, 4th edn (Oxford, OUP, 1990) 595–98.

[6] Cassese n 5 above, 55.

to colonial peoples. Specifically in relation to Article 1(3) Cassese argues that this 'actually writes the principle of self-determination into the chapters governing dependent territories', although he concedes this cannot formally amend the Charter but merely supplement this.[7] Of some relevance to Gibraltar—though not the driving impetus behind it—the United Kingdom entered a reservation that in case of conflict between Article 73 of the Charter and the 1966 Covenant the Charter would prevail. In the *Namibia* case the International Court of Justice made clear that developments in international law had made 'the principle of self-determination applicable to all' non-self-governing territories[8] with 'the ultimate objective of the sacred trust (being) the self-determination and independence of the peoples concerned.'

Questions about the application of the principle have been steeped in controversy and complexity. The starting point in a case like Gibraltar in which Spain held historical title prior to cession to the British Crown is that questions of historical title do not stand in the way of the application of self-determination. So much was pointed out by Franck[9] and seems clear from the *Western Sahara* case.[10] A good comparative example is the *Belize* case because of the similarity of arguments between the ones fielded by Guatemala in respect of Belize and Spain in respect of Gibraltar. In Belize's case neither Guatemala's claim to sovereignty, which was prosecuted at the United Nations, the Anglo-Guatemalan Treaty nor the allegations of territorial integrity stood in the way of independence of Belize.[11] Belize sought independence in accordance with the right to self-determination which was resisted by Guatemala that asserted that this would undermine its territorial integrity. Unsuccessful talks ensued between the parties during the period 1962–75. In 1980, after securing the support of the United States and a number of Latin American countries a resolution supporting Belize's claim to independence was passed at the United Nations.[12] It was argued on behalf of Belize that the right to obtain independence should be pursued separately from the negotiations to end

[7] ibid 58.

[8] *The Legal Consequences for States of the Continued Presence of South Africa in Namibia (South-West Africa) Notwithstanding Security Council Resolutions 276 (1970)* [1971] ICJ Reports 31.

[9] T Franck and P Hoffmann, 'The Right of Self-Determination in Very Small Places' (1976) 8 *New York University Journal of International Law and Politics* 331–40.

[10] Advisory Opinion, ICJ Reports 1975 12. The Court stated that 'even if integration of a territory was demanded by an interested State it could not be had without ascertaining the freely expressed will of the people, the very *sine qua non* of all decolonization.' But see the discussion at J Crawford, *The Creation of States in International Law*, 2nd edn (Oxford, OUP, 2006) 637–47.

[11] JR MacGuire, 'The Decolonisation of Belize: Self-Determination v Territorial Integrity' (1982) 22 *Virginia Journal of International Law* 849, 853–54.

[12] In 1975 one had also been passed but without the support of either the US or any Latin American country except Cuba: see GA Res 3432 (XXX) 8 December 1975.

Guatemala's claim.[13] The similarities with Gibraltar are several. First, there was a similar self-determination versus territorial integrity contest. Secondly, the claims of the parties, like Gibraltar, stemmed from 18th century Anglo–Spanish treaties. An Anglo-Guatemalan Treaty of 1859 then replaced these. Thirdly, like Gibraltar, there was a dispute between the parties as to the extent and nature of the cession of the territory and as to its boundaries. Fourthly, Britain offered to take the claims to the International Court of Justice, but Guatemala refused. Fifthly, there were discussions between the three sides to seek to unblock the dispute. In 1981 Belize became independent with continuing talks to end Guatemala's claim to the territory and achieve a programme of co-operation.[14] It is an example of decolonisation without an end having been reached at that stage to the sovereignty claim.[15] This is relevant in Gibraltar's case where the whole of its territory is subject to a sovereignty claim. If Gibraltar were to achieve Statehood, then,

> even assuming a valid territorial claim prior to the creation of the new State, the latter's claim to Statehood is in itself a secession from that territorial claim. In such a case the continued existence of the new State as an effective territorial entity, and the protection afforded by Chapter VII of the Charter combine to defeat the previous territorial claim. Jennings' conclusion is inevitable:
>
> > If the new State . . . is established with the disputed territory or its sole authority and its Statehood is recognised, it would seem that another claim to sovereignty over the territory is defeated. In short it is only where there is room for doubt or ambiguity in the definition of a new State's territory that a claim against the territory will survive. A sufficient number of recognitions of the new State clearly implying recognition of its title to the disputed territory would presumably destroy the claim.[16]

Recognition has always been an important yardstick for an emerging State, although, as Kreijen notes, before the era of decolonisation it was based on a greater qualitative assessment of effectiveness and sustainability as a new State, among other matters.[17] From the 1960s onwards the

[13] J Sylvestre, *The Cost of Conflict: the Anglo-Belize/Guatemala Territorial Issue*, University of Chile, Institute of International Studies, Masters Programme, 1995. See also for some background SR Ashton and D Killingray, *The West Indies*, British Documents on the End of Empire, Series B, Vol 6, London, Stationery Office, 1999 and R Hyam and Wm R Louis (eds), *The Conservative Government and the End of Empire, 1957–64, Part 1, High Policy, Political and Constitutional Change*, British Documents on the End of Empire, Series A, Vol 4 (London, TSO, 2000).

[14] Sylvestre n 13 above, ch 14.

[15] Crawford n 10 above, 637–38.

[16] ibid 665–66. The latter extract in the second indented passage is from R Jennings, *The Acquisition of Territory in International Law* (Manchester, Manchester University Press, 1963) 38. A freely associated status would bestow 'substantial international personality which may in some cases approximate to Statehood': Crawford n 10 above, 633.

[17] G Kreijen in G Kreijen (ed), *State, Sovereignty and International Governance* (Oxford, OUP, 2004) 45–107.

right of self-determination transformed that by requiring an automatic recognition of any people exercising their contingent right to independence.[18] This deliberately substituted any assessment of ability to govern the State, and has in some cases been criticised as the reason that some States have failed. This 'revolution in legal thought . . . was primarily achieved by reshaping the traditional concept of sovereignty.'[19] It was fuelled by the frenetic pace of decolonisation by which two dozen colonies had become States by 1964, when their independence could scarcely be contemplated in 1950. This allowed 'entities that hardly, if at all, qualified for Statehood in the traditional sense . . . to acquire sovereignty.'[20] In effect there was 'no longer a need to demonstrate ability for self-government.'[21] It transformed the 'notion of independence from an inherently material concept based on material sovereignty to a mere formal legal condition primarily depending on external recognition.'[22] While this may have been the legal backdrop Britain continued to have concerns of the sustainability of certain territories and this affected Gibraltar. In a letter to the Foreign Secretary, George Brown, Secretary of State for Commonwealth Affairs, noted:

> We have now come practically to the end of our programme of decolonisation and we shall soon be left with territories too small and unviable to achieve independence and with a limited number of extremely difficult and delicate questions—the disputed territories of Gibraltar, Falklands, British Honduras, Fiji with its deep racial problem, Hong Kong and the New Hebrides. Each needs individual handling and we must keep clear the line of our own authority and responsibility.[23]

The criteria to enable formal decolonisation were set out in some detail during the period 1953–60. In GA Res 742 VIII[24] the UN reiterated the value of 'establishing a list of factors which should be taken into account in deciding whether a territory has or has not attained a full measure of self-government.' It approved a list annexed to the resolution as a 'guide' in making a determination as to whether 'any territory, due to changes in its constitutional status, is or is no longer within the scope of' Article 73.[25] It emphasised that each case was to be considered 'in the light of the

[18] RH Jackson, *Quasi-States, Sovereignty, International Relations and the Third World* (Cambridge, CUP, 1990).

[19] Kreijen in Kreijen (ed), n 17 above, 46–47.

[20] ibid 82.

[21] ibid 83.

[22] ibid 92.

[23] Letter from Mr Thomson to Mr Brown, 149 FCO 60/20 no 16, 8 February 1968, A Porter, SR Ashton and Wm R Louis (eds), *East of Suez and the Commonwealth, 1964–71—Europe, Rhodesia, Commonwealth*, British Documents on the End of Empire, Series A Vol 5, Pt II (London, TSO, 2004) 64–65.

[24] 27 November 1953.

[25] Para 3.

particular circumstances of that case and taking into account the right of self-determination of peoples.'[26] There was a clear bias towards independence as the option that 'primarily' enabled a territory to become fully self-governing even though 'association with another State or group of States' as an option was also recognised.[27] However it emphasised that 'the factors while serving as a guide . . . should in no way be interpreted as a hindrance to the attainment of a full measure of self-government by a non-self-governing territory.'[28] The ability to modify the list of factors 'in the light of circumstances' was expressly reserved.[29]

In terms of the factors signifying the 'attainment of independence' these were classed under the headings of 'international status' and 'internal self-government.' Under the first these included the acquisition of international responsibility,[30] eligibility for membership of the United Nations, ability to conduct international relations[31] and national defence. In relation to internal self-government this concentrated on the form of government and territorial, economic, social and cultural jurisdiction held by the territory.[32] As has been observed none of these criteria assessed actual resources or ability to govern. The second part of the Annex set out a list of 'Factors Indicative of the Attainment of Other Separate Systems of Self-Government.' This was dependent on the free expression of the population, freedom of choice between several possibilities,[33] a voluntary limitation of sovereignty, geographical,[34] cultural and ethnic considerations, some ability to conduct international relations or to change its political status, eligibility for membership in the United Nations, and an assessment of internal self-government. In relation to the latter it was dependent on the nature of its freedom to govern and the nature of the legislature, executive, judiciary, economic, social and cultural jurisdiction, and the participation of the population in governance.[35] The third part of the Annex lists 'Factors Indicative of the Free Association of a Territory on Equal Basis with the Metropolitan or Other Country as an Integral Part of that Country or in any other form.' This contains similar considerations to that set out in the second part to the Annex with modifications to reflect

[26] Para 4.
[27] Para 6.
[28] Para 7.
[29] Para 10.
[30] Responsibility for acts of external sovereignty.
[31] Power to enter into direct relations with other governments and institutions and to sign and ratify international instruments.
[32] Annex to GA Res 742 VIII, First Pt.
[33] Including independence.
[34] Extent to which the relations of a non-self-governing territory with the capital of the metropolitan government may be affected by geographical separation issues.
[35] This headings were augmented by suggested detail that would indicate that particular stages of self-government had been reached.

the fact that this was a status short of independence. It also required ability to access offices, opportunities and appointments in the metropolitan part of the country without discrimination, the convening of free elections, legislative representation in the central legislature among other issues. It was anticipated that the terms of association would be contained in a bilateral agreement or Treaty.[36] A number of questions were also suggested to assist in making the qualitative assessment necessary to establish whether this status had been attained.

In 1959 the General Assembly appointed a committee to evaluate the principles which should guide the UN as to whether a territory fell within the ambit of Article 73.[37] It then approved a set of principles annexed to GA Res 1541 XV[38] which were to be 'applied in the light of the facts and the circumstances of each case to determine whether or not an obligation exists to transmit information under Article 73e of the Charter.'[39] Principle VI sets out the classic forms of attainment of full self-government through independence, free association or integration. Free association must be the result of a 'free and voluntary choice . . . expressed through informed and democratic processes.'[40] The form of government must respect the 'individuality and characteristics of the territory' with the people having the ability to modify the 'status of the territory . . . (and) its internal Constitution without outside interference.'[41] Principles VIII and IX set out criteria for decolonising options based on integration.

Crawford records that Spain was initially quite reluctant to apply Article 73 of the UN Charter to her own territories though it eventually did.[42] In the period 1963–67 there was a flurry of activity on Gibraltar at the United Nations. The Special Committee on Decolonisation heard a number of submissions from Britain, Spain and the elected representatives of Gibraltar.

Britain's position at the United Nations was that Gibraltar was fully entitled to the application of the principle of self-determination, that sovereignty was not negotiable and that it did not even accept that there was a dispute over the status of the territory.[43] Though British and Gibraltar representatives made the case for self-determination. Spain made the case

[36] Annex, Third Pt.
[37] GA Res 1467 XIV, 12 December 1959.
[38] 15 December 1960.
[39] Para 3.
[40] Principle VII.
[41] ibid.
[42] Crawford n 10 above, 619—but not to Ceuta and Melilla (its territories in North Africa): see 756.
[43] For the British perspective during the period see 'Gibraltar: Recent Differences with Spain' (Cmnd 2632, 1965); 'Gibraltar: Talks with Spain, May–October 1966' (Cmnd 3131, 1966); 'Further Documents on Gibraltar: October 1966–June 1967' (Cmnd 3325, 1967) and 'Further Documents on Gibraltar: June 1967–June 1968' (Cmnd 3735, 1968).

for territorial integrity.[44] Thereafter the General Assembly made a string of resolutions in the late 1960s preferring aspects of the Spanish argument. While not accepted by either the United Kingdom Government or the people of Gibraltar the particular Resolutions of the General Assembly on Gibraltar[45] 'manifestly subordinated the claim by the inhabitants of Gibraltar to self-determination to the territorial claim by Spain.'[46]

In particular GA Res 2231 XXI[47] called on Britain and Spain 'to continue their negotiations taking into account the interests of the people of the Territory and asks the administering power to expedite without any hindrance and in consultation with the Government of Spain, the decolonisation of Gibraltar.' GA Res 2353 XXII considered that 'any colonial situation which partially or completely destroys the national unity and territorial integrity of a country is incompatible with the purposes and principles of the Charter of the United Nations and specifically with paragraph 6' of GA Res 1514 XV.[48] It continued that the States should 'resume without delay the negotiations provided for in [previous resolutions] . . . with a view to putting to an end the colonial situation of Gibraltar and safeguarding the interests of the population upon the termination of that situation.' Subsequently GA Res 2429 XXIII[49] requested Britain to 'terminate the colonial situation in Gibraltar by 1 October 1969.' In essence those resolutions were State-centric in nature and subordinated the people of the territory, their wishes and the right to self-determination to the progress of bilateral negotiations between the administering power and the claimant power.

Musgrave observes that the rationale of the General Assembly appeared to be based on an analysis of whether the population was indigenous to Gibraltar but then proceeds to expose the flaw in this analysis using other cases where self-determination has been applied irrespective of whether the people have been indigenous or not.[50] He also rejects that Gibraltar can be classified as a colonial enclave (that is, a territory made up of colonisers on foreign territory and having no legitimate separate identity[51]) and thus

[44] One of the central arguments used by Spain has been that Gibraltar has no distinct population and that its original (and true) population resides in San Roque (a Spanish town just a few kilometres from the border with Gibraltar). In fact over the last 300 years in the same way as the civilian community of Gibraltar has developed its separate persona the inhabitants that went to San Roque either stayed and integrated fully with that community or dispersed widely across southern Spain. In terms of length of occupation Gibraltar was Spanish for 242 years from 1462. Both the British (since 1704–13) and Moorish (711–1462) periods have been longer.

[45] Namely GA Res 2070(XX) of 16 December 1965, 2231(XXI) of 20 December 1966 and 2353(XXII) of 19 December 1967.

[46] T Musgrave, *Self-Determination and National Minorities* (Oxford, OUP, 2000) 247.

[47] 20 December 1966.

[48] For some analysis of this aspect see below.

[49] 18 December 1968.

[50] ibid 250–52.

[51] See Crawford n 10 above, 348, 647.

be an exception to the principle of self-determination.[52] These have been described as applying in very limited circumstances to territories that are 'enclaves of the claimant state which are ethnically and economically parasitic upon or derivative of that State.'[53] It is submitted that the better view of the historical, ethnic and sociological development of Gibraltar is that the colonial enclave rule has no application to Gibraltar. Whilst contending that Gibraltar is no more than a colonial enclave the same standards of analysis are not applied to the Spanish cities of Ceuta and Melilla situated in mainland North Africa. In fact as is set out in chapters one and three of this work the civilian population is largely the result of the combination of migration from diverse locations with the remnants of the original population. The growth of the population was not driven by either the military or British civilian settlers.

In 1966 the British Government faced with arguments from Spain not only on the decolonisation front but as to its legal title offered that questions concerning the title to the territory ceded under the Treaty of Utrecht and the isthmus be referred to the International Court of Justice.[54] Spain rejected this overture, inter alia, because it argued that post the principal decolonisation resolutions of 1960 the situation had changed and that examining the source of British title was now irrelevant and 'an unjustified delay in the process of Gibraltar's decolonisation.'[55] That same year the Spanish Government published the *Castiella* proposals[56] in the context of United Nations interest in Gibraltar and resolutions that urged both Britain and Spain to find a negotiated solution bearing in mind 'the interests' of the population.[57] For Spain, Gibraltar was merely 'a British military base installed in Spain'[58] and 'a foreign body in our organism.'[59] It re-stated its traditional line that the strict terms of the Treaty of Utrecht had to be adhered to. It rejected that the people of Gibraltar could decide their future, describing these as

> inhabitants (which) are a product of a British political operation aimed at successfully fabricating and refabricating the so-called population with ethnical groups uprooted from their original countries; they are inhabitants without any real political identity of their own or any real autonomy as such and they constitute a demographic group which is entirely subsidiary to a Base enclosed in a territory of two square miles almost all of it a military zone and Crown property.[60]

[52] Musgrave n 46 above, 252–54.
[53] Crawford n 10 above, 647.
[54] Further Documents on Gibraltar: October 1966–June 1967 (Cmnd 3325, 1967) 30.
[55] ibid 33.
[56] *The Spanish Proposals on Gibraltar* (Madrid, Spanish Government, 18 May 1966).
[57] GA Res 2231 XXI of 20 December 1966. See also GA Res 2070 XX of 16 December 1965.
[58] ibid 10.
[59] ibid 25.
[60] ibid 14.

Castiella left no doubt when exposing the emotional dimension to the Spanish claim that

> Gibraltar . . . has been a symbol of a series of inquiries and affronts. There is the memory of the way in which it was taken from us, the humiliations we have suffered, the intolerable political, military and economic servitudes that were imposed on us in times of national prostration. Such memories are lasting.[61]

The document set out in detail all Spain's views on why, from its perspective, Gibraltar was economically unviable and not legally or historically entitled to be treated as a people with the right to self-determination. Its essential proposals were for the 'cancellation' of Article X of the Treaty of Utrecht and for the sovereignty of Gibraltar to be passed to Spain. In that context Spain was willing to allow the continuation of a British military establishment. As for the population, it proposed:

> generous formulae . . . for the defence of [their interests] which would be fully guaranteed by an Anglo–Spanish convention registered in the United Nations according to Article 102 of the Charter.[62]

In terms of detail this would contain

> in addition to the appropriate economic and administrative formulae, a Personal Statute . . . which among other fundamental rights—such as freedom of religion—the British nationality of the present inhabitants of Gibraltar would be respected, and their right of residence would be guaranteed, as also the free exercise of their lawful activities and a guarantee of permanence in their place of work.[63]

The backdrop to the proposals and United Nations interest in Gibraltar was a programme of restrictions implemented by Spain principally targeting the freedom of movement of the population, air space restrictions or economic obstacles. In 1967 after years of escalating political tension the British Government decided to put these proposals to a referendum of the people of Gibraltar. The question put to the electorate[64] was whether they preferred to:

A Pass under Spanish sovereignty in accordance with the terms proposed by the Spanish Government to Her Majesty's Government on 18 May 1966;[65] or

B Voluntarily retain their link with Britain, with democratic local institutions and with Britain retaining its present responsibilities.

[61] ibid 24.
[62] ibid 78.
[63] ibid 82.
[64] Only registered Gibraltarians as defined under the 1962 Gibraltarian Status Act were allowed to vote.
[65] The *Castiella* proposals as described above.

In the referendum held on 10 September 1967 over 97 per cent of those voting rejected the Castiella proposals.[66] While asked to answer a limited and negatively framed question it was the first exercise of a qualified right to self-determination by the people. The United Nations rejected the referendum as a contravention of its earlier resolutions on Gibraltar.[67] This was a referendum convened by the United Kingdom. Subsequent referenda held in 2002 and 2006 on sovereignty and constitutional reform[68] were organised and convened by the Gibraltar Government. This was a key difference in the greater local assertion of control over Gibraltar's affairs during more recent years. Britain's organisation of the 1967 referendum was understandable because of the governance and sovereignty context of the time. Britain had been resolute in its support of Gibraltar at the United Nations during the 1960s and ministerial government was only three years old at the time of the 1967 referendum.

The UN resolution rejecting the outcome of the referendum ignored the wishes of the colonial people whose interests were paramount. It was a decision peculiar for its lack of legitimacy but characteristic of the engulfing State-centricity and the political lobbying strength of Spain, which benefitted both from its own influence over Latin American countries and the anti-British feeling of some Commonwealth countries. In 1967 the Prime Minister, Harold Wilson, was noted as saying:

> the Commonwealth showed little disposition to help Britain or to play a constructive part, for example, at the United Nations. Gibraltar was an eloquent example of this. The largely Afro-Asian United Nations Committee of 24 on which the Afro-Asian members of the Commonwealth should be able, if they chose to exert considerable influence was in practice supporting fascist Spain in pursuing policies directly contrary to the wishes of the inhabitants of Gibraltar.[69]

The view predominated in Whitehall that the Afro-Asian and Communist bloc of new States was reacting against any position taken by Britain irrespective of the merits and using their position on the Committee of 24 for that purpose:

> Our view of the Committee has been bitter and humiliating and no real attempt has ever been made to understand our problems. Even the more moderate members of the Committee though they often appreciate our point of view, feel obliged to vote with the extremists whatever the merits of the case . . . Our experience over Gibraltar has been particularly frustrating and has shown that

[66] By 12,138 votes to 44.

[67] GA Res 2353 XXII of 19 December 1967.

[68] See ch 3.

[69] 'Minute of Discussion AC Smith/Prime Minister', March 1967, in Porter, Ashton and Louis (eds), British Documents at the End of Empire Project, Series A, Vol 5, 2004, 416.

> decolonisation in any particular case means what the majority in the Committee decide it should mean.[70]

The British experience was not limited to Gibraltar as Louis has noted.[71] It led to a British 'revolt' against the Committee of 24.[72] The British Government was frustrated with what it perceived as the Committee's 'obsession . . . to a psychotic degree'[73] with decolonisation. It led some countries to view 'British military bases in Malta, Cyprus or Gibraltar (like) French troops in Bizerta . . . we are dealing with emotion rather than reason.'[74] Increasingly the British Government, together with the United States and Australia, gave serious consideration to entirely abandoning the Committee. Noting how the remaining colonies could be affected by the Committee, the Commonwealth Secretary, George Thomson, remarked 'our continued presence in the Committee of 24 erodes our authority and confuses responsibilities.'[75] Britain would eventually break with the Committee in January 1971.[76]

The passage of GA Res 2353 XII in 1967 was important for another reason. It included a paragraph which considers that 'any colonial situation which partially or completely destroys the national unity and territorial integrity of a country is incompatible with the purposes and principles of the Charter of the United Nations and specifically with paragraph 6 of General Assembly resolution 1514(XV).' That paragraph was built on the foundations of GA Res 1514 on the basis that paragraph 6 of the 1960 resolution was intended to cater for colonial situations. But closer scrutiny of GA Res 1514 suggests otherwise. Paragraph 6 makes no reference to colonial situations or to States. It reads:

> Any attempt aimed at the partial or total disruption of the national unity and the territorial integrity of a country is incompatible with the purposes and principles of the Charter of the United Nations.

Indeed it is possible to read GA Res 1514 as the reverse of GA Res 2253 seems to contend. First, there is no reference to 'State' in GA Res 1514(6)—the reference is to 'country'. Secondly, GA Res 1514 in its entirety is aimed at the granting of independence to colonial countries. As such the reference in paragraph 6 must be to the territorial integrity of the territory occupied by the colonial people. In other words it is intended to protect the integrity of the colonial country and not the Claimant State. Read as a

[70] Secretary of State for Commonwealth Affairs to Foreign Secretary, 8 February 1968, 149 FCO 60/20 no 16 in Porter, Ashton and Louis (eds), British Documents at the End of Empire Project, Series A, Vol 5, 2004, 64–65.
[71] Louis n 284 above, 707–24.
[72] ibid 707.
[73] ibid 708.
[74] ibid 708, citing Sir Herbert Marchant, British Ambassador to Tunisia.
[75] Cited in Louis n 284 above, 721.
[76] Though it would resume co-operation in the late 1970s: ibid 724.

whole there is nothing in GA Res 1514 that seems aimed at protecting the territorial integrity of States because this resolution is not aimed at States. Thirdly, this assessment would seem to be consistent with two indicators in the wording of GA Res 1514 itself. One of the recitals makes clear that a motivation for the landmark resolution is that 'all peoples have an inalienable right to complete freedom, the exercise of their sovereignty and the integrity of *their* national territory.' (emphasis added). Furthermore, paragraph 7 obliges States to observe the Declaration on the Granting of Independence to Colonial Countries on the basis of 'respect for the sovereign rights of all peoples and *their* territorial integrity.' (emphasis added) The peoples referred to must be those that have the right to self-determination. Read in this way the use to which Spain has traditionally made of paragraph 6 of GA Res 1514 seems to be outside the intention of that paragraph. Nevertheless it is true that in GA Res 2253 of 1967 the Spanish contentions were advanced by the introduction of the above-mentioned paragraph under the guise of a supposed link to GA Res 1514 even though on proper analysis such a linkage must be doubted. However given the non-binding nature of GA Res 2253 the overriding effect of the principle of self-determination[77] could be relied on to negate the effects of any uncertainties caused by the 1967 resolution. In the context of the preceding debate, GA Res 2625 XXV of 1970 states that the principles in it should not be construed to affect the territorial integrity of 'States conducting themselves in compliance with the principle of . . . self-determination of peoples . . . and thus possessed of a government representing the whole people belonging to the territory.' As 'territory' is used in the preceding paragraphs to describe the non-self-governing territory it is submitted that this paragraph should also be interpreted as intended to protect the integrity of the non-self-governing territory as there is no other consistent way of interpreting that the particular government could represent the people of the territory. Interestingly, it also directs 'every State [to] . . . refrain from any action aimed at the . . . disruption of the national unity and territorial integrity of any other state or country'. Here, there is more scope for ambiguity. However, as non-self-governing territories have a status separate from the administering State it follows that decolonising these by achieving independence could not affect the territorial integrity of a State it is not part of. It must also follow that the non-self-governing territory must have a status separate from the Claimant State.

There were further developments in the post 1969 period which were significant in the decolonisation context. In terms of the methods of decolonisation it was declared that:

> The establishment of a sovereign and independent State, the free association or integration with an independent State *or the emergence into any other political*

[77] As either *jus cogens* or at least as a principle of customary international law.

> *status freely determined by a people* constitute modes of implementing the right of self-determination by that people.[78] (emphasis added)

These words are important for two reasons. In the first place they clearly indicate that colonial peoples have the right to elect sovereign and independent Statehood.[79] That stems from their ability to trigger a contingent right. To do so the people of that territory must have that ultimate ability: the basic sovereignty to decide this important question. Aside from that, their right to elect Statehood must under a proper analysis lead to the conclusion that those nations on the list of non-self-governing territories are 'contingent' States.

In a United Nations decolonisation context that is not possible for many of the stateless nations mentioned later in this work: Basques, Catalans and Scots. Any similar move by these would raise issues of secession and the break-up of the State, and would very much require a political negotiation.[80] Gibraltar, on the other hand, can point to a right under international law to elect Statehood.[81] This is an important distinguishing factor in considering the similarities and differences between these sub-State nations.[82] So much is then emphasised by the same Resolution making clear that colonies and self-governing territories have 'a status separate and distinct from the territory of the State administering it', which continues:

> until the people of the colony or non-self-governing territory have exercised their right to self-determination in accordance with the Charter.

Secondly the extract from GA Res 2625 is also important because, while it points to four possible alternatives for decolonisation, the United Nations Committee on Decolonisation and some authors[83] have repeatedly referred to only three. In reality however it could be argued that there are four methods recognised in the 1970 Resolution, namely: independence, integration, free association and ***any*** *other political status freely determined by the people of the territory*. When this point has been made by Gibraltar at attendances before the Special Committee on Decolonisation, the Committee has politely listened but generally re-stated that there are only three recognised forms of decolonisation.

[78] GA Res 2625 (XXV).

[79] As one possible mode of exercise of the right to self-determination.

[80] For the interesting Quebec analogy see *Reference re Secession of Quebec* [1998] 2 SCR 217 and the discussion at S Tierney, *Constitutional Law and National Pluralism* (Oxford, OUP, 2004) 253–71.

[81] Albeit resisted by Spain.

[82] *Realpolitik* may dictate though that Gibraltar's exercise of that right may require negotiations so as to ensure that acquiring Statehood (if that is the preference) is a process that is sustainable, permanent and secure.

[83] eg A Cassese, *Self Determination of Peoples—A Legal Appraisal* (Cambridge, CUP, 1995) 147.

With a slightly revisionist approach it would be possible to read the 1970 Resolution as indicating three forms given that it groups free association and integration together under the same banner of the preservation of a link with an independent State. As such the forms for decolonisation could be recognised as:

1. independence;
2. integration or free association with an independent State; or
3. any other political status freely determined by the people of the territory.[84]

In that way a consistent interpretation is possible which marries the repeated statements of the United Nations that recognise three methods of decolonisation, the perceptions of academics, the actual content of the 1970 Resolution and the arguments put forward by Gibraltar. The latter is important because the proposals for constitutional reform put forward by its Parliament in 2002 were constructed under the so-called 'fourth option'.[85] In fact closer scrutiny of the *Western Sahara* case should encourage the United Nations to more formally recognise that there is such a 'fourth option.' In the context of remarks on the range of options the court stated:

> General Assembly resolution 2625 (XXV) . . . *mentions other possibilities* besides independence, association or integration. But in doing so it reiterates the basic need to take account of the wishes of the people concerned.[86] (emphasis added)

It is implicit in that paragraph that the court is recognising the existence of other options that are plain from a simple reading of the language of the resolution. Crawford[87] recognises the emergence of academic literature on the subject of this 'fourth option' as well as the position taken by the United Kingdom that the United Nations criteria are too rigid to allow a decolonisation of some of the territories left on the United Nations List of non-self-governing territories. Crawford contends that the fault does not lie with the law of decolonisation, as it is sufficient within the various forms of association to accommodate anything from 'virtual independence to virtual integration'[88] and thus allow decolonisation. Additionally he remarks that the 'fourth option' can be a way of ratifying in referenda extant governance arrangements which the people are content with but that fall short of the other forms of decolonisation. Perhaps the issue is not

[84] The 'three' options would then be independence, a form that is linked to an independent state, or any other status freely determined. The alternative is for there to be a formal recognition by the UN of a 'fourth option' that gives more flexibility in a modern legal context.

[85] See ch 3.

[86] Western Sahara Case Advisory Opinion [1975] ICJ Reports 12, [58].

[87] Crawford n 10 above, 635–37.

[88] ibid 636.

the law itself but the fact that there may be a need to revise the guidance of the component elements that should be present when evaluating whether governance and constitutional arrangements are sufficient to achieve a decolonised categorisation.[89] Finally Resolution 2625 is significant for Gibraltar for its statement that, in cases where obligations under international agreements conflict with obligations Member States have under the Charter, 'the obligations under the Charter shall prevail.'[90]

As Fassbender has noted because of the general agreement on which Resolution 2625 of 1970 was based and because of its overriding nature and intent it is said to have become text ' (almost) enjoying binding force.'[91] In the *Nicaragua Case* the International Court of Justice declared that the Resolution sets out provisions that the General Assembly considered to be 'basic principles of international law'.[92] Indeed the Resolution itself in its preambular paragraphs had noted that it was intended to 'constitute a landmark in the development of international law.'

There was little substantive movement at the United Nations on the Gibraltar issue after the late 1960s. The UN General Assembly merely continued the practice of passing annual resolutions calling on Britain and Spain to resolve their differences over Gibraltar. This lay emphasis to the fact that the UN stage acquired less importance as a focal point as the European Community acquired more.[93] It also coincided with Britain's withdrawal from co-operation at the Committee of 24.

Even when conducting this exercise of supervising the decolonisation process the State-centricity of the United Nations came through. In a 1973 Resolution[94] the General Assembly declared itself 'deeply concerned with the potentially damaging effects of the persistence of this problem *on the relations between two Member States*, and keenly aware of the necessity of terminating the source of disagreement between them urges both States' to find a solution. (emphasis added) There seemed to be little consideration of the population even though it was this that faced restrictions from Spain and had faced 'a vicious and misleading campaign . . . in the Spanish press which included sneers at the racial origins of the inhabitants.'[95] As

[89] Currently the guidance is contained in GA Res 742 (VIII) of 27 November 1953 and GA Res 1541 (XV) of 15 December 1960.

[90] Of significance vis-à-vis the Treaty of Utrecht and a reflection of the provisions of the UN Charter: see Art 103.

[91] Fassbender in N Walker (ed), *Sovereignty in Transition* (Oxford, Hart Publishing, 2003), 126.

[92] ICJ Reports 1986 14, 107.

[93] However, the nature and content of the resolutions and the general decolonisation dimension were impacted upon by the Anglo–Spanish rapprochement and the Brussels Agreement of 1984: see ch 4 ff.

[94] 14 December 1973, Official Records of the General Assembly, 28th Session, Supplement No 30 (A/9030) 111, item 23.

[95] This was the position of the British Government as recorded in *Gibraltar: Recent Differences*, 1966, 8. It seems that at a time when Spain was a dictatorship and not a member of the Community Britain felt less of a need to use more diplomatic language.

McCorquodale has noted in another context the behaviour was characteristic of 'an Organisation of States and for States'.[96] Politics rather than law or principle took a dominant role in the application of these standards to Gibraltar through this period. Spain exercised particularly strong influence over Latin American members of the United Nations[97] and those former colonies who found it difficult to understand why the colonial people in this case did not wish to seek a change to the status quo. The simple fact was that, at the time and facing a hostile neighbour, Gibraltar neither had the political nor economic resources to sustain anything other than continuing British sovereignty with some devolution of self-government.[98]

Constitution and Governance

Further Constitutional Reform and Escalating Political Tension

Constitutional attention after 1964 had been distracted by UN events, but there would be renewed impetus in the late 1960s. Before that there were riots during April 1968 as a result of a perception in Gibraltar that some members of the community had been meeting members of the Spanish establishment and Government with a view to finding a negotiated settlement with Spain.[99] An initial letter in a local daily had challenged the Gibraltar Government to seek a settlement with Britain and Spain. That letter had stressed that the group considered that being a Gibraltarian 'signifies and represents a character and a way of life which is our own . . . Because it is our own . . . the responsibility for the survival of the Gibraltarian . . . is ours and ours alone.'[100] The controversy arose when the group revealed that they had explored with officials in Madrid whether Spain would entertain discussions on the basis of their proposals. The culmination came when Spanish sources indicated that these proposals were only acceptable after a transfer of sovereignty. Anger spilled over into violence and damage to property that was quelled by the intervention of military patrols in support of the police.[101] At a time of high political tension

[96] McCorquodale in C Warbrick and S Tierney (eds), *Towards an International Legal Community: The Sovereignty of States and the Sovereignty of International Law* (London, British Institute of International and Comparative Law, 2006) 242.

[97] In 1966, 15 of the 26 members of the Fourth Committee that sponsored GA Res 2231 (XXI) on Gibraltar were Spanish speaking Latin American countries.

[98] In speeches before the C24 Gibraltarian representatives put their ambitions squarely under the free association banner: see ch 1.

[99] The so-called 'Dove' riots because the group signed themselves off as 'the Doves'.

[100] *Gibraltar Chronicle* (Gibraltar, 1 April 1968).

[101] F Cantos, *From Fortress to Democracy—The Political Biography of Sir Joshua Hassan* (Grendon, Gibraltar Books, 1995) 143–48, and J Garcia, *Gibraltar, The Making of a People—The Modern Political History of Gibraltar and its People* (Gibraltar, Medsun Publications, 1994) 151–53. A Commission of Inquiry was convened to examine and report on the incidents: see A Forbes and RC Catling, *Report of the Commissioners Appointed by a Warrant of Appointment dated 1 August 1968*, FCO 42/120, 262258, 20 September 1968.

and restrictions it was clearly impossible to signal a softer approach more willing to engage Spain in direct talks on issues touching on sovereignty.[102]

A constitutional conference was held in 1968 against this background of extreme political tension. The Constitution of 1969[103] was the product of that conference. It set out a human rights chapter and provisions on judicature and finance for the first time. It also expanded the self-governance devolved to elected Ministers. The 1969 Constitution was unique among constitutions of the other British overseas territories in various respects. First, the provisions in the Constitution that specified the demarcation of responsibilities between the Governor and the elected Government were drafted in a very different way to the other territories.[104] Secondly, it was not amended in the period 1969–2006, although, as a result of constitutional conventions arising during that period, some practices changed and sections fell into disuse. Thirdly and most importantly, it carried a Preamble to the body of the Constitution that was inserted as a result of the continuing Spanish claim to sovereignty and the desire of local politicians that a safeguard on this issue be provided to the people of the territory.

The Preamble to the 1969 Constitution was an important step along the road of recognising the people of Gibraltar's right to determine their own future. It stated:

> Gibraltar will remain part of Her Majesty's dominions unless and until an Act of Parliament otherwise provides, and furthermore that Her Majesty's Government will never enter into arrangements under which the people of Gibraltar would pass under the sovereignty of another State against their freely and democratically expressed wishes.[105]

In 1969, in response to the new Constitution which it felt was a breach of the Treaty of Utrecht, Spain closed the land frontier with Gibraltar and did not reopen it for pedestrian crossings until 1982. It would take another three years before the border was opened fully in 1985. In the years since then the border has been the source of much friction because of lengthy delays experienced from time to time to trans-frontier crossings. The criticism laid is that these have generally been politically motivated. The economy during the frontier closure days heavily relied on the ministry of

[102] In fact the letters containing proposals were nationalistic and anti-imperial in tone. They argued that sovereignty was in effect vested in the Gibraltarian people. The combustible aspects, in particular, were the inappropriate timing of proposals and the advances to the Spanish Government. In the context of restrictions and a referendum on sovereignty barely six months earlier the climate of tension could not sustain this approach.

[103] Gibraltar Constitution Order 1969 SI 1969 II p3602. The 1969 Constitution is dealt with in greater detail in ch 3.

[104] For an analysis of the effect of this and the linkage with the issue of constitutional conventions see ch 5.

[105] The Preamble is better described as a right of consent rather than one of full self-determination.

defence as the main employer and on the British government's declared policy of supporting and sustaining it economically during a time of Spanish restrictions.[106] In the first elections after the 1969 Constitution the IWBP, which had been formed around the sole issue of seeking political integration with the United Kingdom), was able to form a coalition with a group of independents to oust Sir Joshua Hassan's AACR. The latter stood for free association.[107]

1969 would mark the constitutional peak for the next 35 years as the process of formal constitutional reform would falter and then lie frozen for years, with the only pressure-valve being the constitutional gains obtained by convention in the 1980s and 1990s. The turning of the tide was slow but was related to the anticipated democratisation of Spain and thereafter the desire to welcome democratic Spain into the European Community. The spectre of sovereignty would once again rear its head as a bargaining chip following the emergence of Spain onto the European stage. The grant of the 1969 Constitution was a surge forward in the constitutional development of Gibraltar. The ministerial system that had been introduced in 1964 was strengthened, a chapter on human rights was included for the first time, legislative powers were enhanced and financial and judicial provisions were widened.

At that time the other British overseas territories were lagging behind in constitutional terms. Anguilla was in the midst of its political troubles with St Kitts[108] and only had an Island Council. The Cayman Islands[109] simply had a Legislative Council. Neither it, Montserrat,[110] the Falkland Islands, St Helena nor the Turks and Caicos[111] had anything resembling an advanced or devolved system of powers or ministerial government. For over two centuries there had effectively been direct rule in Gibraltar through the Office of the Governor. Only a limited franchise had been introduced in 1921. But in the post-war period the people, as in many

[106] *Memorandum by Her Majesty's Government on the Report of the Constitution Committee*, London, 26 June 1976.

[107] The AACR regained power in a hotly contested election in 1972 made necessary as a result of the break-up of the coalition government of which the IWBP was the senior partner.

[108] See *Summary of the Revised Proposals for a new Constitution for Anguilla* (Anguilla, Office of HM Commissioner, November 1975); *Anguilla—Report of the Constitution Review Committee* (Anguilla, Anguilla Printers, April 1988).

[109] *Cayman Islands Proposals for Constitutional Advance: Report by the Constitutional Commissioner, the Rt Hon the Earl of Oxford and Asquith, KCMG* (London, HMSO, 1971); Sir Frederick Smith and Walter Wallace, 'Cayman Islands, Report of the Constitutional Commissioners 1991' (Cm 1547, 1991).

[110] International Development Committee, 'The First Report—Montserrat—Report together with the Proceedings of the Committee, Minutes of Evidence and Appendices' (London, TSO, 1997).

[111] Earl of Oxford and Asquith, *Proposals for Constitutional Advance—Turks and Caicos Islands* (London, HMSO, 1974); Louis Blom-Cooper QC, *Turks and Caicos Islands Commission of Inquiry 1986—Report of the Commissioner Mr Louis Blom-Cooper QC into allegations of Arson of a Public Building, Corruption and Related Matters with Appendices* (Cm 21, 1986).

other colonies, sought greater self-government as reward for their loyalty and made the most of developments across the Commonwealth.[112] Within 40 years Ministerial Government had been achieved with significant powers of self-government. That did not fully meet the expectations of all Gibraltarians, some of whom still called for decolonisation and further reform in subsequent years. However in the context of judging their constitutional gains the people of Gibraltar could reflect that they had come a long way in a relatively short period.

The position of the written Constitution within Gibraltar's legal architecture is of importance to the broader view of the *locus* of sovereignty and extent of the division and distribution of power in Gibraltar. This appreciation assists in understanding the democratic and governance deficit that developed subsequently. Constitutionalism emphasises the place of civil society as the focus of legitimacy and the *locus* of sovereignty.[113] Allied to that is the more modern view that it is the people in whom sovereignty ultimately vests. This combines with the view on the contingent sovereignty of a colonial people in a decolonisation context. These factors need to be put side by side with the factual background of the concerted push for reform by Gibraltar's people and representatives that led to the 1969 Constitution (and preceding and subsequent reforms). The consequence was that the people as a repository of sovereignty triggered a devolution of power, constitutional and legislative sovereignty to its executive and parliamentary institutions.

As a non-independent territory any devolved power or authority has always been subject to limitations in Gibraltar. The doctrine of pure parliamentary sovereignty[114] does not have analogous application in Gibraltar because of the existence of a written Constitution that on its proper application is domestically 'supreme' in Gibraltar. Though even this proposition requires qualification.[115] The 1969 Constitution[116] was granted by Her Majesty by use of the Royal Prerogative and was, for the

[112] For a review of developments see S De Smith, *The New Commonwealth and its Constitutions* (London, Stevens, 1964), R Hyam, *Britain's Declining Empire, The Road to Decolonisation 1918–68* (Cambridge, CUP, 2006), Wm R Louis, *Ends of British Imperialism, The Scramble for Empire, Suez and Decolonisation*, 2nd edn (London, Taurus, 2006), or M Thomas, B Moore and LJ Butler, *Crises of Empire—Decolonisation and Europe's Imperial States 1918–75* (London, Hodder Education, 2008).

[113] See Walker in JHH Weiler and M Wind (eds), *European Constitutionalism Beyond the State* (Cambridge, CUP, 2003) 27–54.

[114] Much has been written on this. See eg AW Bradley, 'The Sovereignty of Parliament' in J Jowell and D Oliver (eds), *The Changing Constitution*, 5th edn (Oxford, OUP, 2004) 26–61; P Craig, 'Public Law, Political Theory and Legal Theory' [2000] PL 211.

[115] In two senses. Pure Parliamentary sovereignty in the UK is no longer so pure: see KA Armstrong, 'UK—Divided on Sovereignty' in N Walker (ed), *Sovereignty in Transition* (Oxford, Hart Publishing, 2003) 327–50. Secondly the Constitution in Gibraltar is not externally superior in terms of certain other UK legislative acts.

[116] As well as the 2006 Constitution. The comments made in these paras apply equally to the 2006 Constitution.

purposes of Gibraltar law, a 'colonial law' within the meaning of the Colonial Laws Validity Act 1865[117] unlike the British North America Act 1867[118] or the constitutions of the other inhabited overseas territories.[119] The effect of this was that as a colonial law it was void to the extent that it was 'repugnant' to an Act of the Imperial Parliament or a Regulation or Order made thereunder which applied in the territory.[120] In fact of the nine main overseas territories the situation of Gibraltar is unique in this. The constitutions of all other inhabited territories are made by statutory Orders in Council under Acts of the United Kingdom Parliament.[121] As such the constitutions of the other territories are not colonial laws within the meaning of the Colonial Laws Validity Act. They are supreme over legislation passed by their legislatures because they are imperial statutes and do not rely for their supremacy on statutory construction—as is the case in Gibraltar. One of the other main distinguishing features is that in the case of at least Bermuda the Constitution is, in case of conflict, superior over preceding Acts of Parliament.[122] By virtue of Annex II to the 1969 Gibraltar Constitution[123] and other provisions made thereunder the Constitution became Gibraltar's supreme domestic law in the sense that it took precedence over all other laws of Gibraltar except Acts of Parliament[124] or Orders in Council made under Acts of Parliament themselves.[125]

By section 32 of the Constitution, the legislature was entitled to pass laws for the peace, order and good government of Gibraltar. This is a power that should be construed widely.[126] However the opening

[117] See ss 1, 28 and 29 Victoria Cap 63 565.

[118] A main source of Canadian constitutional law.

[119] However if there was an application to review the exercise of these prerogative powers in the UK courts the view could be different. See eg Lord Hoffman in *R(Bancoult) v Secretary of State for Foreign and Commonwealth Affairs* [2008] UKHL 61, [41].

[120] Colonial Laws Validity Act 1865 ('the CLVA') s 2.

[121] St Helena under the Government of India Act 1833 and British Settlement Acts of 1887 and 1945; the Falkland Islands under the British Settlement Acts 1887 and 1945; Anguilla under the Anguilla Act 1980 and West Indies Act 1967; Bermuda under the Bermuda Constitution Act 1967 and the British Virgin Islands, Cayman Islands, Montserrat and the Turks and Caicos, all under the West Indies Act 1962.

[122] The definition of 'existing laws' in the 1968 Bermuda Constitution (which on the coming into force of the Constitution must be read in conformity with it) is 'any laws . . . made by any legislature' and thus must include Acts of Parliament. Indeed had they not been specifically excluded from the definition of 'existing laws' in all other Overseas Territories with constitutions made by Order under an Act of Parliament there would have been a case to invoke the normal rules of parliamentary practice and statutory interpretation. Parliament is deemed to know when it legislates about the existence of potentially conflicting legislation and therefore to have intended the result of its actions. The later Acts establishing the Constitution would—if the statutory instrument had been silent—have taken precedence.

[123] And Annex II of the 2006 Constitution.

[124] Of the UK Parliament.

[125] Those take precedence under the Colonial Laws Validity Act 1865.

[126] Halsbury's *Laws of England*, 4th edn (London, Butterworths, 1974) vol 6, para 1074—although it has also been said to be a limitation, as the legislature needs to keep to this remit: see the Court of Appeal of *New South Wales in Building Construction Employees and Builders*

words of the section made it perfectly clear that the power of the House to legislate was subject to the Constitution and this limitation could in turn be subdivided into several areas,[127] for example, the Colonial Laws Validity Act 1865,[128] the Crown,[129] the Governor's powers and obligations,[130] disallowance,[131] human rights,[132] other constitutional provisions which need to be complied with in the law-making process,[133] the doctrine of colonial legislative extra-territorial incompetence,[134] international obligations,[135] emergency powers provisions and constitutional conventions.[136]

Federation of New South Wales v Minister for Industrial Relations [1986] 7 NSWLR 372. This principle was not accepted by the High Court of Australia: see *Union Steamship of Australia v King* [1988] 82 Aust Law Reports 43. See also S Farran, 'Prerogative Rights, Human Rights and the Island People: the Pitcairn and Chagos Islands Cases' [2007] PL 414–24 and Lord Rodger in *R (Bancoult) v Secretary of State for Foreign and Commonwealth Affairs* [2008] 3 WLR 955, [109]: 'it is not open to the Courts to hold that legislation enacted under a power described in those terms does not, in fact, conduce to the peace, order and good government of the territory'.

[127] The Courts have a wide power of review of these matters. For an interesting analysis of the courts and sovereignty from a UK constitutional perspective see P Craig, 'Constitutional Foundations, the Rule of Law and Supremacy' [2003] PL 92–111.

[128] The Colonial Laws Validity Act was passed by Parliament in 1865, to 'remove Doubts as to the validity of Colonial laws' (see the long title of the Act). It was in many senses as Roberts-Wray has described, a 'charter of freedom for colonial legislatures': K Roberts-Wray, *Commonwealth and Colonial Law* (London, Stevens, 1966) 396.

[129] s 86 of the 1969 Constitution (and Annex II, s 8 of the 2006 Constitution) reserves to Her Majesty power to make laws for the peace, order and good government of Gibraltar, thus overcoming the rule in *Campbell v Hall* [1774] 1 Cowp 204. It is also expressed in manner to overcome any possible argument about whether the reservation to make laws for the peace, order and good government would allow the Crown to alter the Constitution. By expressly reserving this power also the problem is neutralised. See *Chennard v Arissol* [1949] AC 127.

[130] In three main areas: the assent and reservation of Bills for Her Majesty's Pleasure, the special powers of legislation and Royal Instructions. The 2006 Constitution restricts the Governor's legislative powers significantly.

[131] But see *Re Disallowance and Reservation of Provincial Legislation* [1938] SCR 71.

[132] See *R v Mejias Reina and Others* [1997–98] Gib LR 1. The Chief Justice in *Mejias Reina* favourably referred to the Supreme Court of Canada in *R v Oakes* [1987] LRC (Const) 492, which recognised that 'In Canada we have tempered Parliamentary Supremacy by entrenching important rights and freedoms in the Constitution.' This analogy also holds true for Gibraltar.

[133] Such as finance Bills.

[134] Though the earlier more restrictive approach has been doubted: see *Croft v Dunphy* [1933] AC 156 and is especially so in a European context.

[135] The ability to legislate may be affected by international treaty obligations (though to be enforceable these must be given domestic legal effect). There has been some provision in Overseas Territory constitutions to that effect—though not Gibraltar.

[136] Though the classic view is that constitutional conventions cannot be enforced unless crystallised by 'statutory adoption'—*Reference re Amendment of the Constitution of Canada 1981* [1982] 125 DLR 1 and see ch 5, 328–37. It is arguable that the House should not legislate in manner that breaches a constitutional convention because the Constitution in Gibraltar has 'adopted' these: see s 78 of the 2006 Constitution (which is in this respect in the same terms as s 79 of the 1969 Constitution). It defines law as 'any rule of law whether written or unwritten'. While this can encompass the common law it is also wide enough to arguably apply to conventions as an example of an unwritten rule of law. Bermuda has a similar definition: see s 102 1968 Bermuda Constitution Order. The constitutions of the other territories would seem to exclude this possibility by requiring the 'law' to be in the form of an 'instrument': see Anguilla s 73; St Helena s 56; Cayman Islands s 50.

The transition from complete dependence to responsible government is characterised by a number of steps. Central among the necessary features are the adoption of constitutional provisions or practices setting out:

(1) an Executive Council (which eventually gives way to Cabinet-style government);
(2) a completely or almost completely elected Legislative Body;
(3) the introduction of a ministerial system with an identifiable head of the elected administration;
(4) the assignment of responsibilities to Ministers who are collectively responsible to the legislature;
(5) the reduction of special responsibilities of the Governor to a minimum;[137]
(6) the possibility of delegation to elected Ministers of even those areas for which the Governor is specially responsible;
(7) the adoption of a modern and liberal relationship between the British Government, the Governor and the elected Government by which procedural practices are followed of minimum interference with the legislative process in the territory;
(8) the insertion of provisions on the judicature, finance and the protection of fundamental rights;[138]
(9) the establishment of executory commissions in relation to the appointment, removal and discipline of public officers and;
(10) the establishment of certain offices in the Constitution of the territory such as Auditor-General, Attorney-General, Complaints Commissioner (Ombudsman) and the provision of a Register of Interests for members of the legislative body.[139]

In that context by 1969 Gibraltar had achieved an advanced form of self-government. While certain constitutional changes arose in response to unique local issues comparison with the other overseas territories is useful as it illustrates the particular official British attitude to reform in each case, highlights individual national issues for each territory and the substantive progress that was made since the late 1960s. The following principles come through in a comparison of the constitutions of the other overseas territories (much of which was in place by 1986). In the first place the United Kingdom had actively participated in the review[140] of the

[137] Even the constitutions of the freely associated territories in the West Indies provided that external affairs and defence should continue to be handled by Britain until independence.

[138] For an interesting study into this area see C Parkinson, *Bills of Rights and Decolonisation—The Emergence of Domestic Human Rights Instruments in Britain's Overseas Territories* (Oxford, OUP, 2007.

[139] O Hood Phillips, *Constitutional and Administrative Law*, 8th edn (Sweet & Maxwell, London, 2001) 785–86 and Roberts-Wray n 128 above, 247–95.

[140] There have been several formal reviews of the Constitution in the respective overseas territories. They provide some useful background: See eg those cited earlier in this chapter

Constitutions of all overseas territories and in all cases there has been formal amendment since 1969.[141] In 1969 there was a Ministerial system in place in only three of the overseas territories.[142] Significant powers of self-government were given to all territories.[143] In the period 1969–2006 the other overseas territories caught up with and in some respects overtook Gibraltar while in formal terms at least many of the local Gibraltar aspirations were not satisfied by written amendment until 2006.[144] There are some differences between the territories[145] but in general in all territories external affairs, defence, internal security and the police are declared to be Governor's responsibilities.[146] Powers to delegate responsibility to Ministers even in these reserved areas have been incorporated into the Constitutions of six territories. This only happened in Gibraltar's case in the 2006 Constitution. The Parliaments of all territories have been enlarged thereby responding to the calls for representation of the populace and accountability of the Executive. Other measures have been introduced to enhance domestic accountability and make provisions for Ombudsmen, human rights and Constitutional Commissions for specific purposes. Self-determination clauses were introduced in two constitutions: those of the Falkland Islands and Montserrat.[147]

Though all territories have the same constitutional template the unique ingredients drive the detail, timing and parameters of constitutional development. For example, Anguilla is only an overseas territory because

and also *Bermuda Constitutional Conference 1966—Conference Report*, BER (66) 29; *Bermuda Civil Disorders 1968, Report of Commission and Statement by the Government of Bermuda* (Hamilton, Bermuda, Government of Bermuda, 1969); *Report of the Royal Commission into the 1977 Disturbances—Bermuda* (Hamilton, Bermuda, Bermuda Government, 1978); Sir Colville Deverell and Harvey Da Costa, *British Virgin Islands Proposals for Constitutional Advance: Report by the Constitutional Commissioners* (London, HMSO, 1974); Walter Wallace, Chairman, Hon Dr Howard Fergus and Alford Penn, *British Virgin Islands Report of the Constitutional Commissioners 1993* (Cm 2527, 1994). The latest Constitution to see substantial amendment is that of the British Virgin Islands: see SI 2007/1678. The process continues with constitutional talks currently ongoing in several territories.

141 In Gibraltar's case there was no formal amendment between 1969 and 2006, largely because of the sovereignty issue.

142 There is now a Ministerial system in seven of the nine OTs referred to throughout this work. In a referendum in May 2005 the people of St Helena rejected the introduction of ministerial government: see FAC Report 2008, Vol II, Ev 160–61.

143 The usual drafting format is to specify the areas specifically reserved to the Governor. In Gibraltar's Constitution the drafting technique was reversed up to 2006, making the position subject to much more ambiguity and constitutional conflict.

144 When the Spanish Government softened its opposition to internal governance reforms.

145 eg in Monserrat, Turks and Caicos and Anguilla the conduct of international financial services is also a reserved matter. In all Territories except Bermuda the public service is also reserved.

146 The position is silent in the Falklands Constitution, but this is also undoubtedly the case in fact.

147 The 2006 Gibraltar Constitution introduced a clause on self-determination: see ch 3.

of the wish of the islanders to sever their links with St Kitts.[148] If Montserrat had not suffered such economic devastation as a result of environmental disaster its level of dependence would not be what it is today.[149] If Bermuda were not such an economic success it would not have been able to seriously countenance independence in 1995.[150] If St Helena were not so isolated they might feel less of a need to try to pull to the centre and seek integration.[151] If the Spanish claim to sovereignty were not there Gibraltar could be independent. If the Falkland Islands had not

[148] There were significant troubles in 1967–69. Anguillans held two referenda to vote for their separation from St Kitts and various attempts dialogue between the parties. A Royal Commission was convened to make constitutional recommendations: see *Report of the Commission of Inquiry (appointed by the Governments of the UK and St Christopher-Nevis-Anguilla) to examine the Anguilla Problem* Misc No 23 (1970) (Cmnd 4510, 1970). The recommendations of the Royal Commission satisfied neither side. Their view was that on balance—because they could not be economically self-sufficient at the time—the island needed to consider a revised relationship with St Kitts, balanced by wide autonomy and greater representation: 59–9. The British Government introduced interim arrangements in the Anguilla Act 1971 and Anguilla (Administration) Order 1971. This was followed by representations that then led to more formal arrangements contained in the Anguilla (Constitution) Order 1976 SI 1976/50: see also *Summary of the Revised Proposals for a new Constitution for Anguilla* (Anguilla, Office of HM Commissioner, November 1975). By then the Anguillan constitutional structure was similar to other dependent territories though technically the state of St Christopher–Nevis–Anguilla still existed. This changed with the introduction of the Anguilla Act 1980.

[149] The drive to obtain maximum self-government depends to a large extent on economics and so while there was talk of independence in political circles in Montserrat in the 1980s this has become much less viable since the Soufriere volcano eruptions. See International Development Committee, *The First Report—Montserrat—Report together with the Proceedings of the Committee, Minutes of Evidence and Appendices* (London, HMSO, 1997) paras 1–13.

[150] In 1995 the Bermudian Government published a Green Paper on Independence: see *A Green Paper—The Implications of Independence for Bermuda* (Hamilton, Bermuda, Government of Bermuda, 1995). as a precursor to a referendum. This stated that 'Discussions have confirmed that there is no option of any intermediate status, such as associated statehood, or the assumption of further responsibility short of independence . . . The 1977 Green Paper advised that no further substantive advance was possible. The UK Government has recently confirmed this, pointing out that the Constitution already provides a very large degree of self-government, and that even the reserve powers have been the subject of delegation. It takes the view that it is unrealistic to expect Britain to maintain responsibility for Bermuda as a dependent territory on one hand, while shedding even more of its remaining power to discharge that responsibility on the other . . . the choice at this time is clear. Bermuda has the option either to remain a dependent territory of Great Britain, or to become an independent state': (7–10). In 1995, 73% of voters rejected the possibility of independence at a specially convened referendum on the subject. In December 2004, a Bermuda Independence Commission was established. Its remit was primarily informative to lay the ground for a domestic debate on the merits or otherwise of independence. It delivered its report in August 2005.

[151] Its great isolation and the desire of its people to secure British citizenship have played a part in recent calls in the territory for integration with Britain: see *St Helena—the Lost County of England* (St Helena, Government Printer, 1996). Subsequent to that a Citizenship Commission produced updated and expanded ideas for the constitutional development of the Islands: see Nicholas Turner, *St Helena; A British Island—a discussion paper produced for the Bishop of St Helena's Citizenship Commission* (London, The Wanderer, 1997). Its call for a new Constitution to be devised 'for the long-term that draws the Island closer to Britain while establishing its own autonomy as a distinct (indeed unique) overseas territory of the Crown.': 32.

been invaded and then retaken, the strength with which the British Government now resists discussions of sovereignty would be far less.[152]

The issues of non-political social unrest also provide evidence of underlying factors that influence the Constitution (albeit to a lesser degree than the self-determination factors). So again Bermuda was encouraged by the Pitt Commission to build up its sense of nationhood to overcome racial tension.[153] Had there not been allegations of regulatory mismanagement in Montserrat the financial provisions of the Constitution would not have been curtailed.[154] If there had not been evidence of ministerial abuses in the Turks and Caicos such radical action as was taken to address the deficiencies during 1986–90 would not have been necessary.[155]

The form of status or governance reform that each territory can opt for will be governed by these factors. Those unique factors also point to certain underlying British and overseas territory political realities that will affect the process. For example, the Bermuda experience clearly highlights

[152] In documents released by the Public Record Office, for example, it is clear that in 1967–69 Britain was giving serious consideration to plans aimed at ceding the sovereignty of the Falklands to Argentina. See also Hyam above n 115, 360–64.

[153] *Report of the Royal Commission into the 1977 Disturbances—Bermuda* (Hamilton, Bermuda, 1978). The Royal Commission into the 1977 Disturbances was set up to enquire into troubles on the Island during the period 1–3 December 1977. These in turn arose out of the dramatic events of 1972–73 in which the Governor and Commissioner of Police were shot dead. On constitutional issues the Commission identified that there were greater prospects for social integration on the basis of a 'shared concept of Bermudian nationhood' (para 12.12) and that those who were alienated would be more likely to identify with an independent territory. They considered that this should constitute 'a principal argument for accelerated nationhood.' It declared, 'we consider it our duty to declare our conclusion that only with independence can national unity be forged and pride in being Bermudian fully develop. We call upon the people of Bermuda to act boldly in fashioning their future.': para 12.16.

[154] In Montserrat concerns were expressed as to money-laundering and lack of regulation in the finance centre. The Governor set up an investigation that included local law officers and Scotland Yard with FBI support. A report was commissioned into the offshore banking regime from Coopers and Lybrand. It made strong recommendations such as the removal of control of the international finance portfolio from local Ministers. The British Government introduced a new Montserrat Constitution of 1989 SI 1989/2401. The main changes were to absorb the portfolio of international financial services into the direct control of the Governor and to allow the Governor to introduce and put into effect legislation on matters pertaining to his reserve powers (even though that legislation had been rejected by the Legislative Council): see H Fergus, *Montserrat—History of a Caribbean Colony* (Montserrat, Macmillan Caribbean, 1995) 206.

[155] In Turks and Caicos the Constitution was amended and subsequently reformed (with certain powers curtailed) after the Chief Minister and other Ministers were convicted of drug trafficking. A Commission was established by the Governor to examine a series of allegations: Louis Blom-Cooper QC, *Turks and Caicos Islands Commission of Inquiry 1986—Report of the Commissioner Mr Louis Blom-Cooper QC into Allegations of Arson of a Public Building, Corruption and Related Matters with Appendices* (Cm 21, 1986). On 25 July 1986, in a statement to Parliament, Tim Eggar, the Parliamentary Under-Secretary for Foreign Affairs, said, 'We have . . . decided that in the interests of the Islanders themselves the administrative structure of the Islands must be changed to prevent ministerial abuses. This is partly because the present Constitution dating from 1976 was drafted on the assumption which was not borne out that local Ministers should be given wide responsibilities in preparation for eventual independence.'

the limits to which the United Kingdom will go in granting powers of self-government. Its contingent liability concern will prevent it from crossing that line beyond which the result is that the territory acquires the powers that it wants but the UK retains some residual liability. Contingent liability concerns not only set the limits for constitutional development but also set limits which the British Government has acted on (in Montserrat or Turks and Caicos) so as to secure good government.[156]

While there was much constitutional activity in other overseas territories between 1969–86 aspirations towards greater self-government in Gibraltar met much resistance because of the Spanish and sovereignty dimensions. That was the state of constitutional development as Gibraltar entered the European Community with Britain in 1973.[157]

THE IMPACT OF EUROPEAN ACCESSION

In 1973 Gibraltar entered the European Community with the United Kingdom. Its membership derives from Article 299(4)[158] of the EC Treaty (formerly Article 227(4)), which applies the provisions of the EC Treaty to 'European Territories for whose external relations a member state is responsible.' Only Gibraltar is currently within the European Union by virtue of this sub-Article. By virtue of the Treaty of Accession[159] Gibraltar was excluded from the Common Agricultural Policy and the harmonisation of turnover taxes (VAT).[160] As a result of secondary legislation Gibraltar has also been excluded from the Common Customs Territory.[161] Gibraltarians are considered United Kingdom nationals for European Union purposes by virtue of the declaration made by the United Kingdom as part of the Treaty of Accession. Membership gave rise to several issues for Gibraltar.[162] The effect on constitutional and legislative sovereignty was shared with all other sub-State authorities but its understanding is essential as it laid the first encroachments on domestic constitutional power. This was then exacerbated when combined with the unique consequences of bilateralism in the post 1986 period.

[156] In July 2008 a Commission of Inquiry was established into allegations of corruption. In March 2009 significant parts of the constitution of the Turks and Caicos Islands were suspended as a result—Turks and Caicos Islands Constitution (Interim Amendment) Order 2009 SI 2009 no 71.

[157] See the European Communities Act 1972 of Gibraltar and the Treaty of Accession of the UK, cited above.

[158] Reference to Article numbers adopt the numbering post the Amsterdam Treaty.

[159] *Treaty concerning the Accession of the United Kingdom of Great Britain and Northern Ireland to the European Economic Community*, Brussels, 22 January 1972 (Cmnd 4862-I, 1972).

[160] Art 28.

[161] See Art 1 EC Council Regulation 2151/84 of 13 July 1984 [1984] OJ L127/1, as confirmed in Art 3 of Council Regulation 2913/92 establishing the Customs Code [1992] OJ L302/1.

[162] The governance issues post-1986 are covered in chs 4 and 5.

Constitutional Sovereignty

Accession to the European Community introduced new principles of law and most importantly fundamentally altered the hierarchy and structure of the constitutional legal order.[163] The doctrines of supremacy, direct effect and implied powers that emerged from cases such as *Van Gend en Loos*[164] and *Costa v ENEL*[165] led to the creation of this supra-national entity which 'constitutes a new legal order of international law for the benefit of which the States have limited their sovereign rights.'[166] These limitations occurred within the strictly defined and limited areas of conferred powers and competences. As has been stated:

> Direct effect can be provisionally defined as the capacity of a norm of Community law to be applied in domestic court proceedings; whereas supremacy denotes the capacity of that norm of Community law to overrule inconsistent norms of national law in domestic court proceedings.[167]

Apart from its effects within the judicial process the principles of direct effect and supremacy inevitably also affect the State's freedom to act and influence its negotiating ability. The doctrine of implied powers by which the Court of Justice accepted that when it was necessary to achieve legitimate ends powers would be implied was also of great significance in expanding the remit of the Community.[168] The dramatic and profound effects caused by accession have both been described as a revolution[169] and as evolutionary[170] in the sense that there has been much discussion whether the UK courts accepted this principle basing themselves on a traditional but refined understanding of Parliamentary sovereignty or in recognition that a new principle had been injected as a result of membership of the Community. Accession transformed the concept of sovereignty

[163] JHH Weiler, 'The Transformation of Europe' in *The Constitution of Europe* (Cambridge, CUP, 1999) 10–101, and see Case 294/83 *Parti Ecologiste, Les Verts v European Parliament* [1986] ECR 1339, in which the court referred to the EC Treaty as the constitutional charter of the Community.

[164] Case 26/62 *NV Algemene Transporten Expeditie Ovderneming van Gend en Loos v Nederlandse Administratie der Belastingen* [1963] ECR 1.

[165] Case 6/64 *Flaminio Costa v ENEL* [1964] ECR 585.

[166] *Van Gend en Loos* 12. In subsequent cases the court extended the application of the direct effect principle laid down in *Van Gend en Loos*. See Case 11/70 *Handelsgesellschaft* [1970] ECR 1125 and for discussion of direct effect in the context of integrationist trends see PP Craig, 'Once Upon a Time in the West: Direct Effect and the Federalisation of EEC Law' (1992) *OJLS* 453.

[167] B de Witte, 'Direct Effect, Supremacy and the Nature of the Legal Order' in P Craig and G de Burca, *The Evolution of EU Law* (Oxford, OUP, 1999) 177–213, 177.

[168] Case 22/70 *Commission of the European Communities v Council of the European Communities* [1971] ECR 263.

[169] W Wade, 'Sovereignty—Revolution or Evolution?' LQR 112 (1996) 568–75, and see also the *Factortame* litigation [1991] AC 603.

[170] TRS Allan, 'Parliamentary Sovereignty: Law, Politics and Revolution' LQR 113 (1997) 443–52.

by redefining it, by diffusing it,[171] by subjecting it to encroachments, by merging, centralising and decentralising it.[172] This has been assisted by the European judiciary and their constitutionalisation of the Treaties.[173] The theory behind this constitutionalisation is that, even though the Community was born out of intergovernmental agreement between States, it evolved in nature to the point that the originating Treaties are treated not as documents of international law but constitutional documents governed by a special constitutional doctrine.[174]

Some countries have struggled with the supremacy question and their courts have initially rejected this, sought to limit it or based the doctrine of supremacy on national constitutional law rather than on recognition of a supra-national, 'special' body of law. The supremacy judgments of the ECJ received a mixed reaction among the Member States of the Community in particular on questions touching on the national Constitution. In part this has been compounded by the fact that there is no reference to direct effect or supremacy principles in the Treaty of Rome. Issues of *Kompetenz-Kompetenz*[175] have invariably arisen and in some cases been exacerbated by the terms of individual national constitutions if these have not specifically provided for cession of sovereignty to supra-national entities.[176] Of the original members, the French, German and Italian experiences were

[171] N MacCormick, *Questioning Sovereignty: Law, State and Practical Reason* (Oxford, OUP, 1999) 70–71.

[172] JHH Weiler, 'European Democracy and its Critics: Polity and System' in Weiler n 162 above, 264–76.

[173] JHH Weiler, 'The Least Dangerous Branch: a Retrospective and Prospective of the European Court of Justice in the Arena of Political Integration' and 'The Reformation of European Constitutionalism' ibid 189–217, 221–37 respectively.

[174] ibid 221.

[175] The competence to decide competences and whether the issue properly falls within the sphere of competence of the Community. The whole matter of allocation of relative competences between Community and Member States has proved a hotbed of contention.

[176] For an extensive overview see B de Witte, 'Direct Effect, Supremacy and the Nature of the Legal Order' in P Craig and G De Burca n 166 above, 177–210.

[177] See the French Court's judgment in *Raoul Georges Nicolo* [1990] 1 CMLR 173. In Germany and Italy, notwithstanding express provisions in the Constitution allowing a transfer of powers, there was resistance to accept supremacy at least when it came to issues of fundamental rights. See the Solange I and II cases: *Internationale Handelsgesellschaft mbH* [1974] 2 CMLR 540 and *Wunsche Handelsgesellschaft* [1987] 3 CMLR 225. In Solange I there was a concern that overriding national human rights provisions at a time when the EC itself had not made certain advances into that field was untenable. By Solange II important developments had occurred, namely an elected European Parliament, development by the European Court of Justice of a doctrine on fundamental rights and the subscription by Member States to the European Convention of Human Rights. See also *Brunner v European Union Treaty* [1994] 1 CMLR 57. A similar approach was followed by the Italian Courts in *Frontini v Ministero delle Finanze* [1974] 2 CMLR 372 and *Fragd v Amministrazione delle Finanze* 232/1989 [1989] RDI 72, in which the Constitutional Court showed it was 'willing to test the consistency of individual rules of the Community law with the fundamental principles for the protection of human rights that are contained in the Italian Constitution.' See also G Gaja, 'New Developments in

substantially different.[177] Additionally, the Constitutions of some countries have either generic[178] or specific[179] provisions conceding the transfer of powers to an international entity such as the Community.[180]

Gibraltar's Constitution did not make specific provision on the transference of powers to the Community. Instead, this was left to domestic legislation, which by its very nature was in a peculiar position, because of the conflict between the supremacy provisions of the Constitution[181] and the principles of supremacy and direct effect developed by the ECJ. But even though there was something of an attempt to exclude the Constitution from the impact of direct effect and supremacy (or at least to lessen its impact), it is clear on a proper analysis that attempt to fine-tune or restrict the principle of supremacy and the encroachment on sovereignty by qualifying its legislative application in cases that could touch upon the 1969 Constitution was inconsistent with the principles applied by the ECJ.

The European Communities Bill was the legislative instrument considered by the House of Assembly in Gibraltar in 1972 to allow accession to the Community.[182] It was amended during the debate to allay Opposition anxieties over the effect of accession on the Constitution. By section 4(1) the Government was given power to introduce regulations to implement Community obligations. Section 4(2) (which is the equivalent of section 2(1) of the UK Act) was then intended to confirm the supremacy of such enactments over other domestic law. However, as a result of issues raised in debate in the House of Assembly, the words 'other than the Constitution' were inserted to make the relevant part of the section (after

a Continuing Story: The Relationship between EEC Law and Italian Law' (1990) 27 *CML Rev* 83, 94, and C Lebeck, 'National Constitutional Control and the Limits of European Integration—the European Arrest Warrant in the German Federal Constitutional Court' [2007] PL 23–32.

178 As in Spain: see Art 93 of the Spanish Constitution.

179 As in Art 29(4) of the Irish Constitution.

180 Thus neatly overcoming the point that has troubled other States, ie whether there is a principle of top-down supremacy, as envisaged by the ECJ, or whether the supremacy has first to be 'authorised' by the domestic law of the States. The position relative countries have taken on this question reveals a fundamentally different ideological approach and view as to what the Community is. Either Community law is a special law because of the special legal order that creates it—in which case supremacy stems from the very special nature of the Community—or it depends on the constitutional law of its respective members. Some of the States without an express constitutional provision have preferred to take the view that the supremacy is conceded as a matter of domestic constitutional law anyway. The Gibraltar Constitution does not have any provisions setting out the consequences of international treaty obligations. This is different in other overseas territories the Constitutions of some of which provide that legislation inconsistent with international obligations may be reserved for the signification of Her Majesty's pleasure.

181 See below—later in this chapter. In fact, on a literal reading, as the Constitution would be supreme over other local Acts, it would result in its superseding even the Act giving effect both to accession and to the principles of direct effect (the European Communities Act 1972). This conclusion would be contrary to EC law and incorrect notwithstanding the apparently clear intention.

182 The provisions of which are generally similar to the UK's Act of the same name.

amendment) read:

> any enactment (which expression shall be deemed to include an Act of Parliament[183] or any instrument made thereunder *other than the Constitution of Gibraltar,*[184] extending to Gibraltar and stated to be passed or made in implementation of the Treaties and of the obligations of the United Kingdom thereunder) passed or to be passed, other than one contained in this Act,[185] shall be construed and have effect subject to the foregoing provisions of this section and section 3.[186] (emphasis added)

The clear intention behind the insertion of these words by Gibraltar's Parliament was to insulate the Constitution from the effects of the supremacy doctrine and the prospect that subsidiary legislation would indirectly amend or qualify the Constitution without debate. While no legal issue or challenge has sprung from the wording of this section since 1972, proper analysis reveals it is unlikely to insulate the Constitution from changes. The UK equivalent of section 4(2) of the Gibraltar Act is in exact terms, except for the insertion referring to the Constitution, and its effect has been held by the UK courts to deliver supremacy.[187] The concerns expressed by members of Gibraltar's Parliament were understandable given the recent constitutional context. Gibraltar had obtained ministerial Government in 1964 and had three years before accession been granted much wider powers of self-government. Spain had closed the border and imposed economic restrictions because of steps that had been taken towards self-government and self-determination. Gibraltar and its political class jealously guarded their devolved powers and were wary of any encroachment on sovereignty. When the Opposition voiced its con-

[183] Of the UK Parliament.

[184] Of course this also implies that there was a misconception as to the source of law of the Constitution given that it is not a statutory Order in Council but one made under the Royal Prerogative.

[185] After the enactment of the 2006 Constitution the nomenclature for principal legislation passed by the Gibraltar Parliament was changed from 'Ordinance' to 'Act.'

[186] s 3(1) incorporated the principle of direct effect. By s 3(2) it was provided that a 'colonial' law (within the meaning of the Colonial Laws Validity Act 1865) that was made in the implementation of the Treaties would not be void for repugnancy with a UK Act of Parliament or because it had some extra-territorial effect.

[187] The UK courts have held that the part of the section that starts 'any enactment passed or to be passed' creates real obligations to ensure the supremacy of EC law. Again—as in other countries—for some time the courts took the view that the doctrine of supremacy was inserted into English law not by the ECJ or by accession to the community but as a matter of domestic law because the sovereign Parliament had intended to achieve that in the 1972 Act. See *Shields v E Coomes (Holdings) Ltd* [1979] 1 All ER 456; *Macarthy v Smith* [1979] 3 All ER 325; *Garland v British Rail Engineering Ltd* [1983] 2 AC 751. But see also the different approach in *Duke v GEC Reliance Ltd* [1988] AC 618. A more generalised acceptance of the need to ensure supremacy came in *Factortame v Secretary of State for Transport* [1991] 1 AC 603 (albeit still as a result of voluntary subjection by Parliament).

cerns it did so from the point of view of safeguarding the domestic governance gains and because of the fear that what had been gained from Britain would be lost in some other way.[188]

The Chief Minister agreed the amendment as a compromise position and said:

> We have excluded the Constitution of Gibraltar because I do not think that anything affecting the Constitution of Gibraltar can be done either by regulations or by Ordinance[189]

Whether this insertion—which has never been tested by the courts—actually achieved its aim is, however, a matter of some doubt. The purported encroachment on the principle of supremacy would run counter to Community law as it has been determined by the European Court of Justice. In the *Simmenthal*[190] case the court emphasised the duty of a national court to give effect to Community law:

> if necessary refusing of its own motion to apply any conflicting provision of national legislation, even if adopted subsequently, and it is not necessary for the Court to request or await the prior setting aside of such provision by legislative or other constitutional means.[191]

In the *Handelsgesellschaft*[192] case the court confirmed that

> the validity of a Community measure or its effect within a Member State cannot be affected by allegations that it runs counter to either fundamental rights as formulated by the Constitution of that state or the principles of a national constitutional structure.[193]

These are statements of the proposition of supremacy at its recognised highest. As has been seen the acceptance of the principle has been far more reluctant. Ultimately if there were a challenge Gibraltar would be faced with deciding how compatible it is for a territory to be within the Union but then attempt to carve its Constitution out of the supremacy of

[188] Their chief spokesman on the Bill, Maurice Xibberas remarked: 'the Gibraltar Constitution Order 1969 including the Preamble thereof and any matter touching on the said Constitution . . . are of obvious significance to the people of Gibraltar and . . . the House should have a good opportunity to discuss and to express its point of view should *any law* or Regulations by the Governor in accordance with other provisions of the Communities Bill have a bearing or come to affect these important matters.' (emphasis added) House of Assembly Hansard, 29 November 1972, 176.

[189] ibid 183.

[190] Case 106/77 *Amministrazione delle Finanze dello Stato v Simmenthal* [1978] ECR 629.

[191] At [24]. And see also Case C-213/89 *R v Secretary of State for Transport, ex p Factortame Ltd* [1990] ECR I-2433 and *R v Secretary of State for Employment, ex p Equal Opportunities Commission* [1995] 1 AC 1, where the court granted a declaration that a statutory provision was contrary to Community law. In a ground- breaking judgment the court has also held that the same duty to disapply is also on administrative authorities: see Case 103/88 *Fratelli Costanzo SpA v Comune di Milano* [1989] ECR 1839.

[192] *Internationale Handelsgesellschaft mbH* [1974] 2 CMLR 540.

[193] At 1134. See also Case C-473/93 *Commission v Luxembourg* [1996] ECR I-3207.

European Community law. The *Factortame* litigation has been said to lead to the conclusion that barring either withdrawal from the Community or Parliament saying it wishes to disregard EC law:[194]

> the courts will continue to accord priority to Community law . . . (and that) . . . 'partial compliance' with community law is not possible; that while the United Kingdom remains in the EEC it cannot pick and choose which norms of EEC law to comply with.[195]

This description seems to fit Gibraltar neatly and must be the proper view of how the court would deal with the nuance inserted in the Gibraltar Act by its Parliament. As such and notwithstanding the efforts of Gibraltar's Parliament the encroachment into Gibraltar's constitutional sovereignty was unaffected. This was to contribute to the general legal panorama with which Gibraltar greeted the start of the period of Spanish accession.

Legislative Sovereignty

Accession has also profoundly affected the legislative sovereignty of the territory. It has both limited these powers and represented a burden on domestic governance because of the Parliamentary time taken for European matters. It has directly affected the processes of day-to-day government and the making of laws in several ways. In the first place, the breadth of issues touched upon by the European Community is significant. These have steadily grown through the years and affect areas as diverse as the environment, education or financial services. The volume and implications of European Community legislation is now extensive. Secondly, this has a dramatic effect on the state of domestic legislation, existing laws[196] and the introduction of new principles as a result of the principle of direct effect. Thirdly, as a result of this it also limits the power of the Parliament to make laws for Gibraltar as these should not conflict

[194] Neither course being realistically available to Gibraltar without the support of the UK.

[195] P Craig, 'Sovereignty of the UK Parliament after Factortame' (1991) 11 YBEL 221, 252, and see also P Craig, 'Britain in the European Union' in Jowell and Oliver (eds) n 114 above, 88–116.

[196] There have been several examples of challenges in the domestic courts of Gibraltar across a variety of fields. See *BiGib Ltd* [1987] (unreported) or *Moroccan Workers Association v A-G* [1995–96] Gib LR 67. There is also a potential overreaching into domestic law. In 2001 the European Commission launched investigations against Gibraltar in respect of legislation providing for tax-exempt and qualifying companies on the grounds that these breached State Aid Rules even in a situation where the main statute predated accession (referred to in ch 4).

[197] In the manner that has already been described. Additionally, s 3(2) of the Gibraltar European Communities Act 1972 is also an important provision in four separate ways. In the first place, the rule (contained in the Colonial Laws Validity Act 1865 that colonial laws) which conflict with English Acts of Parliament applying to the territory are void to the extent of such inconsistency is set aside for EU purposes. Secondly, the section clearly has future

with European obligations.[197] Fourthly, European Community legislation by its sheer volume places special burdens on a small territory like Gibraltar and demand specific human or technical expertise,[198] financial resources or legislative time.

As a result European Community obligations have taken up an increasingly large proportion of the Gibraltar Parliament's legislative time: see the following table.[199]

Table B—Analysis of Legislative Time Originating from European Obligations 1996–2001

Year	Bills of Domestic Origin	Bills Transposing European Obligations	'European' Bills as percentage of total
1996	9	8	47
1997	24	19	44
1998	19	15	44
1999	28	10	26
2000	14	4	22
2001	23	6	21
Totals	117	62	35
Average	19	10	35

application as well as setting out a rule for statutes already applying to Gibraltar. Thirdly, and for the avoidance of doubt, it overturns the normal order of supremacy by making colonial laws (that transpose European obligations) supreme over statutes of the Imperial Parliament. The fact that it is a 'colonial law' itself (the Gibraltar European Communities Act) that does so is significant. Finally it confirms that such laws may have extra-territorial effect. This section, in fact, is very similar in effect to the Statute of Westminster 1931 which removed prohibitions on the legislatures of certain major Commonwealth countries to legislate with extra-territorial effect and removed the supremacy of Acts of the UK Parliament over laws of the territory except that in Gibraltar's case it is limited to the performance of European obligations.

[198] In so far as technical expertise is concerned the Government's Legislation Support Unit generally handles the Government's domestic and European drafting requirements. It initially conducts an assessment of European legislation to examine whether any applicability, legislative or other compliance issues arise as a result of Gibraltar's terms of membership of the Community. If there is a need to transpose any obligation it will liaise with the relevant department. It is also in contact with the UK Government as to information that may need to be forwarded to the Commission or to discuss any issues that may arise in relation with transposition. From time to time specialist drafting expertise will be commissioned in highly complex transposition exercises. The time, personnel and financial consequences of this exercise is therefore very significant.

[199] Even though the table does not cover the pre-1996 period, it is valid to illustrate the main point. Lower numbers in the years 1996 and 2000 are, in part, because these were election years and there was less legislative time available. As can be seen in Table B, approximately 35% of the House of Assembly's average yearly legislative calendar (in the period 1996–2001) was taken up with Bills transposing European obligations. Those figures do not reveal the entire extent of compliance which can only be fully gauged in the context of an evaluation of subsidiary legislation enacted to complete transposition in many cases but they provide a useful assessment which is generally representative of the apportionment of legislative time. Table B is compiled from research of Parliamentary records. For useful com

The effects of accession on constitutional and legislative sovereignty for Gibraltar bring to the fore the need to obtain representation, influence and participation in alternate ways and to review existing constitutional structures to try to obtain more effective democracy. Once again, seen on its own, the effect on legislative sovereignty as a result of accession is neither particular nor special. It is the normal effect on a territory post-accession. The relevance is that it is a further factor that results first in an encroachment of powers and thereafter—after Spanish accession and because of bilateralism—leads to the governance and democratic deficits described in chapter four. It is the accumulated effect of all factors and the bilateral, territorial sovereignty context that is unique to Gibraltar among sub-State governance within the Union.

As Weiler observes, the pooling of sovereignty at a European supranational level has diminished the powers of national parliaments, but in fact this may, in some senses, have been quite convenient for State Executives, in that—subject to unanimity or majority voting—it has enhanced their freedom and power of action but substantially reduced their domestic accountability.[200] The position of the Council of Ministers as the uncontested legislative forum in the pre-1996 period before the enhancement of the European Parliament's powers was achieved by a deliberate policy of the Member States. What Member States thus lost in terms of constitutional and legislative sovereignty or supremacy they sought to recover by obtaining a greater role, participation and influence in the decision-making process and governance of the Community and Union. Many of the developments towards this occurred post 1986.[201] These compensations are missing from sub-State Executives. In Gibraltar's case the deficit is accentuated by its special features and the difficulties in obtaining adequate power, representation and influence elsewhere.

DEMOCRATISATION AND THE REGENERATION OF BILATERALISM

The Anglo–Spanish Approximation

By the early 1970s there was some expectation in Spain, following the appointment of Lopez Bravo as foreign minister, that Britain would at

mentary on the practical effects on the legislative process in Scotland, see A Trench (ed), The State of the Nations 2001: The Second Year of Devolution in the UK (Exeter, The Constitution Unit, Imprint Academic, 2001) and for Europe J Hopkins, Devolution in Context: Regional, Federal and Devolved Government in the European Union (London, Cavendish, 2002).

200 Weiler, 'The Transformation of Europe' in Weiler n 162 above, 10–101.

201 This will be expanded in chs 4 and 5. It has also been said that the European Commission (and by necessary implication possibly the Member States) have been happy to go along with some low-intensity legitimacy aspects of the White Paper on European Governance, because it prevents wider reform which would undermine their hegemony. See C Scott, 'The Governance of the European Union: the Potential for Multi-Level Control' (2002) 8 *European Law Journal* 59–79.

some point contemplate talks on sovereignty. But while Spain was not democratic and the border was closed, this proved an unrealistic aspiration by Spain.[202] Its foreign interests influenced the policy stance of Britain. This was unsurprising. But the merger of the Commonwealth and Foreign Offices in 1968 also affected its attitude to Gibraltar. The former had, traditionally, shown more consideration to the wishes of the inhabitants of territories. The latter's 'main interest being in diplomatic accomodations without the responsibility of actually running any territories . . . the Colonial Office often felt it got no help from the Foreign Office permanent officials and frequently a good deal of hindrance.'[203] Indeed the 'Foreign Office . . . rather resented the fact that British Honduras bedevilled "normal" relations with Guatemala or the Falkland Islands with Argentina.'[204] Differences in approach were clear. In April 1968 in the advent of departmental reorganisation senior officials noted:

> [T]here are aspects of our administration of dependent territories which involve important external considerations—Hong Kong, Gibraltar, the Falklands and British Honduras in particular. Often in these cases our foreign policy interests and our responsibilities to the Dependent Territories concerned pull in opposite directions.[205]

Britain kept its strategic and economic priorities in review to decide how these should influence its policy-making. Such assessments highlighted the importance of the United States relationship and the Soviet dimension.[206] They also set out Commonwealth priorities and the possible importance of Europe. In a 1968 classification of States by relative importance to Britain using the criteria of economic considerations, strategic security priorities and potential to affect British interests Spain was classified in Group C.[207] The assessment was a forecast of British priorities to the mid 1970s but it was then affected by the political shifts represented by British entry into the EEC, Spanish democratisation and subsequent accession to the Community. The approximation was slow but inevitable. The reclassification of priorities together with the absence of the policy counterbalance that would, prior to its abolition as a department of State, been traditionally provided by the Colonial or Commonwealth Office only accentuated the effect on policy towards Gibraltar after the mid-1970s.

[202] P Gold, *Gibraltar: British or Spanish?* (London, Routledge, 2004) 21.

[203] R Hyam, 'Bureaucracy and Trusteeship in Colonial Empire' in J Brown and WM Roger Louis, *The Oxford History of the British Empire—the Twentieth Century* (Oxford, OUP, 2001) 260.

[204] ibid—or the fact that Gibraltar obstructed normal relations with Spain.

[205] 'Combined FCO/CO Organisation: Alternative Scheme for Handling the Dependent Territories—Joint Note by Sir M James and Sir A Galsworthy' 179 FCO 49/137 no 19, 5 April 1968, in Porter, Ashton and Louis, British Documents at the End of Empire Project, Series A, vol 5, 2004, 155.

[206] Hyam above n 115, 256–58.

[207] With the USA and USSR being in Group A and all EEC countries as well as a number of other countries of strategic or economic importance in Group B. 'Letter from EN Larmour

In 1974 from Opposition the IWBP called for further reform and asked that a constitutional conference be convened. The governing AACR agreed to enter into discussions with the Opposition to see if a measure of consensus could be obtained. 1975 marked the start of a distinct phase, for it was in that year that Franco died and Spain commenced its democratic transition, culminating in the signature of its Accession Treaty. That occurred in 1985, which was also the same year that the border was reopened fully with Gibraltar, that the first talks on sovereignty[208] were held and that the EC pushed forward its Single Market reforms. Some of these developments were connected. Even those that were not directly linked were transforming the political, economic and governance backdrop and would influence the pace and direction of Gibraltar's constitutional aspirations.

1975 was also the year that the United Kingdom held its referendum on Community membership.[209] The positive result of the British referendum and the wish to embrace the new democratic Spain had a direct effect on the Gibraltar issue. In the following year the Select Committee of the House of Assembly on constitutional reform submitted its report.[210] The proposals included the transfer of Gibraltar matters to the Home Office, the abolition of the government/opposition system, its replacement with a committee system[211] and an increase in the domestic matters for which Ministers were responsible. In its reply the British Government rejected that there was any need for fundamental constitutional advancement of the type advocated and sent the clear message that in view of Spain's move towards democracy the Spanish factor would play a greater role in shaping British attitudes towards Gibraltar generally and calls for constitutional reform in particular. The Memorandum of the Foreign Office ruled out integration and independence as viable options and added 'it would be wise to avoid innovations which might make the development of a more favourable Spanish attitude less likely.'[212] The feeling on the Rock was that Britain was systematically closing the door to all options leading to decolonisation and locking the territory firmly into either the status quo or contemplation of the Spanish option which was unacceptable to the vast majority of the people.[213]

(FCO) to RL Wade-Grey (Cabinet Office)—Priorities by country for British Interests throughout the world until the mid 1970s' 157 FCO 49/21 no 29, 30 October 1968, in Porter, Ashton and Louis, British Documents at the End of Empire Project, Series A, vol 5, 2004, 96–100.

[208] In the post-accession era.

[209] Gibraltarians were not offered a vote in that referendum.

[210] *Report of the Constitution Committee*, Gibraltar, May 1976.

[211] Similar to the form of governance in place in the Channel Islands at the time.

[212] *Memorandum by Her Majesty's Government on the Report of the Constitution Committee*, 1976, 26 June 1976, referred to commonly as the 'Hattersley Memorandum' after the Minister of State at the Foreign Office at the same time.

[213] Garcia n 101 above, 167–71.

The rejection of integration as a possible constitutional option that the British Government would countenance sent shock waves through the Opposition camp. Instead with the death of General Franco and the end of dictatorship in Spain in 1975 Britain tried to focus on what it needed to do to welcome Spain as a democratic European partner. Against that background the IWBP that had been formed around the idea of pursuing a constitutional option that had now so firmly been ruled out buckled. The party disbanded and the AACR won the 1976 elections easily.[214] The AACR also dominated in 1980 and 1984.

In 1977, shortly after the Hattersley Memorandum, talks between Britain and Spain over Gibraltar were launched in Strasbourg. Gibraltar did not participate as a separate party though its elected leaders attended the talks. Even at that stage links with other stateless nations were evident, in that it became clear that the new democratic administration of Adolfo Suarez sought to solve the Gibraltar issue in the context of domestic accommodations for Catalunya and the Basque Country.[215] Internal constitutional and democratic change was gathering pace with much emphasis on the historic communities within Spain.[216] The Anglo–Spanish process itself was to be progressed in 1980, when Britain and Spain signed the Lisbon Agreement by which they agreed to start a process to negotiate all differences over Gibraltar. The language of the 1980 declaration was eminently bilateral with Gibraltar not guaranteed any separate representation. It stated that:

> The British and Spanish Governments, desiring to strengthen their bilateral relations . . . intend in accordance with the relevant UN resolutions to resolve in a spirit of friendship, the Gibraltar problem . . . Both Governments have therefore agreed to start negotiations aimed at overcoming all the differences between them on Gibraltar . . . To this end both Governments will be pleased to consider any proposals which the other may wish to make . . . the Spanish Government in reaffirming its position on the re-establishment of the territorial integrity of Spain, restated its intention that in the outcome of the negotiations the interests of the Gibraltarians should be fully safeguarded. For its part the British Government will fully maintain its commitment to honour the freely and democratically expressed wishes of the people of Gibraltar as set out in the Preamble to the Gibraltar Constitution.

[214] Some of the integrationists went on to form the Democratic Party of British Gibraltar in 1978 (it was subsequently disbanded in 1984). One of the former members of the IWBP, Joe Bossano, formed the Gibraltar Democratic Movement and contested the 1976 elections. The Party lasted until 1977, when its members went their separate ways and Mr Bossano formed the Socialist Labour Party.

[215] Cantos n 104 above, 207: in effect, Spain wanted first integration of Gibraltar and thereafter to grant it autonomy within Spain.

[216] S Tierney, *Constitutional Law and National Pluralism* (Oxford, OUP, 2004) 117–21; Heywood 1995, 11–82 ; J Navarro, *Nosotros La Transicion* (Madrid, Temas de Hoy, 1995); C Abella, *Adolfo Suarez* (Madrid, Espasa, 1997); P Heywood (ed), *Politics and Policy in Democratic Spain* (London, Frank Cass, 1999), esp therein P Aguilar, 'The Memory of the Civil War in the Transition to Democracy: The Peculiarity of the Basque Case' 5–25, and J Colomer, 'The Spanish 'State of Autonomies' Non-Institutional Federalism' 40–53.

While the prospect of talks decreased during and in the immediate aftermath of the Falklands conflict, a couple of years later, in November 1984 both countries agreed a Joint Declaration at Brussels that established a process of dialogue over Gibraltar in which the 'issues of sovereignty' would be discussed and the border with Gibraltar re-opened.[217] It agreed the

> establishment of a negotiating process aimed at overcoming all the differences between them over Gibraltar . . . Both sides accept that the issues of sovereignty will be discussed in that process. The British Government will fully maintain its commitment to honour the wishes of the people of Gibraltar as set out in the preamble of the 1969 Constitution.[218]

While British Ministers had previously made clear in Parliament that after the 1980 Lisbon Agreement Spain was free to raise the subject of sovereignty[219] the reference in the Brussels Agreement was the first explicit statement in a political declaration by the British Government that it was willing to contemplate such discussions. It caused uproar in Gibraltar. The tide was turning.[220] The 1984 Brussels Agreement was an intergovernmental act between Britain and Spain of significant ramifications. The agreement to discuss sovereignty was not only politically momentous for the two States but for Gibraltar too:

1. It was a further example of bilateralism which was criticised by many in Gibraltar for having insufficient regard to democratic legitimacy and the modern trends towards self-government.[221]
2. It was arguably already a breach of the Preamble to the Gibraltar Constitution,[222] of the right to self-determination or at the very least of the principle of democratic consent.

[217] Spain had already been scheduled to accede to the EC so opening of the border was inevitable if there was not to be a breach of the principle of freedom of movement from inception.

[218] Joint Declaration of 27 November 1984 between the Foreign Secretary, Rt Hon Sir Geoffrey Howe and the Spanish Foreign Minister Sr Don Fernando Moran Lopez ('the Brussels Agreement').

[219] Gold n 201 above, 29.

[220] Shortly after the Lisbon Agreement the British House of Commons Select Committee on Foreign Affairs had considered that regional autonomy within Spain could possibly resolve the dispute and questioned British title over the isthmus and Gibraltar: see FAC Report 1980–81, lv-lvii.

[221] Because it agreed to discuss the sovereignty of Gibraltar when the population had made plain such negotiations were unacceptable to it and a breach of its right to self-determination. There had been no prior public support for such a process.

[222] By the Preamble the UK undertook not to enter into 'arrangements' under which sovereignty would pass to another State without consent of the people. The Brussels process was intended to discuss sovereignty and the possibility of sovereignty change was clearly to be canvassed within it. In some ways these might not be 'arrangements' themselves but arrangements to discuss the arrangements and as such it could be argued that it was one step removed from a breach (unlike the subsequent joint sovereignty proposals of 2001–02 discussed in ch 6).

3. It was an example of the low intensity democracy described by Marks[223] in that the effect was to negotiate sovereignty of the territory without public support or involvement.
4. It was an intergovernmental act that undermined Gibraltar's domestic aspirations and ultimately its participation in the supra-national entity.[224]
5. It advanced EC rights to Spanish nationals in Gibraltar as if Gibraltar and Spain were already participants in the supra-national body. This had legal, political, economic and practical consequences and while not objectionable in itself it showed the extent to which intergovernmental moves could affect the supra-national sphere.
6. It set an unfortunate tone for Spain's participation in the EC and for their ability to exert influence on Britain and consequently on Gibraltar's domestic and European aspirations.
7. It was confirmation of the gradual process by which Britain had grown slowly lukewarm towards the reforms that Gibraltar sought and much more concerned about its wider interests within the Community and its relationship with Spain.

Nothing would be the same after this. It marked the strong revival of a reinvigorated bilateralism which, this time, would be carried over onto the European stage, dominate matters for Gibraltar and obstruct its access to EC measures. The greater closeness between Britain and Spain would also impact on Gibraltar's desire to obtain international recognition for the right to self-determination and to secure an international status in accordance with this principle. After the Brussels Agreement the United Nations' annual consensus resolutions were altered so that they would routinely note the existence of the negotiating process started with that Agreement and urge that negotiations should continue in accordance with that process. In this context it was not the Brussels Agreement that opened up new 'vistas' for a settlement within the European Community[225] precisely because the closed nature of the discussions did not involve the principal party affected—the people of the territory. The Brussels Agreement not only represented bilateralism at work but also demonstrated the slow and gradual convergence of all Gibraltar issues within the European Community. The international status debate was becoming linked to the bilateral negotiations and in turn to the mutual membership of both States within the Community.[226]

[223] S Marks, *The Riddle of all Constitutions* (Oxford, OUP, 2000) 50–160.

[224] In the sense that it clearly set the stage for the policy Spain would then follow towards Gibraltar related issues within the EC: see chs 4 and 5. Both States had devised a bilateral backdrop to negotiating all differences over Gibraltar and this would colour the way Gibraltar-related matters would be handled in the wider Community by themselves, by Community institutions and by other States.

[225] As suggested by Cassese n 5 above, 213.

[226] For a collection of essays from the Spanish perspective on the index period see J Salgado (ed), *Estudios Sobre Gibraltar, Instituto de Cuestiones Internacionales y Politica Exterior* (Madrid, INCIPE, 1996).

In 1985 Spain fully re-opened the border with Gibraltar and in advance of accession to the European Community equivalent rights were advanced to Spanish nationals in Gibraltar. In the same year Spain made sovereignty proposals through its foreign minister, Fernando Moran at one of the initial sessions under the Brussels Agreement. Those proposals envisaged a short period of joint sovereignty or a lease-back solution followed by full Spanish sovereignty with Gibraltarians retaining self-government and their nationality.[227] The arrival of Spain onto the European stage added a new dimension to Anglo–Spanish relations. This would start affecting wider policies concerning all Member States as Spain embarked on a strategy of blocking proposed agreements or legislation at European level because of Gibraltar.[228] This policy gathered pace over the extension of proposed air liberalisation measures to Gibraltar airport.

The bilateral emphasis of Anglo–Spanish relations provided a marked contrast to the evolution of governance trends within the European Community that increasingly had a plurinational, multi-level flavour. In parallel to the introduction of legitimacy and democracy developments that have increased the closer working of the Union there was a programme of economic,[229] institutional[230] and structural[231] reforms to pursue the integrationist agenda.

[227] Gold n 201 above, 65–66.

[228] ibid 87—first doing so over justice agreements and measures concerning commercial transactions in 1987.

[229] Between 1969–74 important agreements were reached establishing the principle of economic union, the self-standing nature of the Community's budget and on the governance of the Community (through the establishment of the European Council). In 1979 the European Monetary System was set up with an Exchange Rate Mechanism as part of it. In 1986 the Single European Act (SEA) established the goal of completing the internal market by 1992. This had been preceded by recommendations set out in the Single Market White Paper of 1985. The Treaty on European Union (TEU) signed in Maastricht in 1992 established a timetable for European Monetary Union and the introduction of a single currency.

[230] The SEA added new policy competences (for example the environment, research and economic and social cohesion), reviewed and strengthened legislative procedures and the powers of the European Parliament (by the introduction of the co-operation procedure and the assent procedure), established a Court of First Instance to assist the work of the ECJ and formalised a degree of foreign policy co-operation. Maastricht then introduced a 'co-decision' procedure, extended Qualified Majority Voting and gave greater powers to the Parliament. The Amsterdam Treaty that followed in 1997 extended the co-decision procedure, making it the most utilised legislative avenue, and gave wider jurisdiction to the European Court of Justice. In the field of legislative process the co-operation procedure was heavily restricted and the co-decision procedure significantly extended and reviewed, thus allowing the emergence of the Parliament as a greatly strengthened player on the European stage.

[231] Concerns that achieving the goals set in 1986 were taking too long led in part to a new impetus that culminated in the TEU. This established the three-pillared structure of the Union—with the European Community forming the first Pillar. The Amsterdam Treaty strengthened the decision-making process in the Justice and Home Affairs Pillar. A number of Justice and Home Affairs issues were transferred to the first Pillar; the Schengen Acquis (on freedom of movement) was integrated into the EU framework by the addition of Protocols to that effect; the JHA Pillar was renamed Police and Judicial Cooperation; the Social Chapter (formerly a Protocol) was integrated into the First Pillar.

The ideological context and roots of the governance debate in Europe that can be traced to the origins of the Community itself have set the scene for the driving influences to the European debate. It is clear that from the start Member States have had different views of what the closer union meant and how it could be achieved. The history of the last 45 years has demonstrated the struggle between the different philosophies and different views as to the purpose of the Community and the form it should take.[232] Tensions between advocates who preferred either a neo-functional or intergovernmental approach to the integration process have been very evident. Neo-functionalists would argue that to achieve specific purposes contracting States would be willing to give up control of certain areas and transfer these competences to a supra-national entity. It is in a sense supra-nationalism driven by political or economic convenience. Integration is not a finite moment in the neo-functional view but rather each stage of transfer of competences leads on to the next phase of integration and positively fosters this subsequent phase—a gradual slice-by-slice method of integration.[233] The intergovernmental[234] view is that the Member States created the Community and that as such it should restrict itself to the standard methodology of action of other bodies that are set up by international treaty. States should therefore continue to act and co-operate on an intergovernmental basis rather than encourage independent action or independent policy-making by the supra-national entity.[235] Specific ends may also be desirable and driven by political factors. But intergovernmentalists would reject the use of supra-nationalism as the preferred way of achieving those ends.

The essential debate centres around the differing standpoints that hold that either the Community is a separate entity created by States that exists above them in a supra-national form and that should have freedom of action and the ability to formulate policy or whether it is the delegate of contracting states and endowed only with delegated power (and should be subordinate to those States). In this debate it would be inter-governmentalists who would more jealously guard the preservation of State sovereignty not because they would be against co-operative integration but because they would see the intergovernmental approach as a way of securing international objectives that were beyond the reach of a State acting alone and because acting in conjunction with other States (while preserving the vestiges of sovereignty) would strengthen State

[232] P Craig, 'The Nature of the Community: Integration, Democracy and Legitimacy' in P Craig and G De Burca (eds) n 166 above, 1–54.

[233] Weiler n 199 above, 10–96.

[234] A Moravcsik, 'Preference and Power in the European Community: A Liberal Intergovernmentalist Approach' in S Bulmer and A Scott (eds), *Economic and Political Integration in Europe: Internal Dynamics and Global Context* (Oxford, Blackwell, 1994).

[235] For further discussion see J Shaw *Law of the European Union*, 3rd edn (Basingstoke, Palgrave, 2000) 20–26, and Craig and De Burca (eds), n 166 above, 1–22.

sovereignty in real terms.[236] This view of course is dependent on the respective standpoint held on the issue of sovereignty. It is not one that assists the perspective or predicament of the sub-State nation.

These approaches to integration are also discernible and replicated as approaches to European governance. Additionally, Weiler has analysed a third approach—the infra-national one that exists side by side with the intergovernmental and supra-national.[237] He describes this as being driven by sectoral interests or technical issues rather than national interest. Each theoretical approach gives a larger role to different participants. Supra-nationalism emphasises the role of the Community institutions. Intergovernmentalism promotes the State governments and infranationalism downplays both in favour of lower levels of governance. The interaction of these with the aspirations of regions for more self-governance is of most interest to this work. More recently multi-level governance has also had an impact on integration theory.[238] In turn this has an impact on the position of regions within the European Union.[239] The emphasis on recognising the European Community as an entity within which there are spheres of competence and a multi-layered polity with diffused sovereignty lies at the heart of the debate of relevance to Gibraltar. It illustrates the deep correlation between sovereignty *qua* power, competence, governance, democracy and legitimacy.

THE NEW ENVIRONMENT

In 1970 the Chief Minister of Gibraltar, excited at the prospect of joining the Community with Britain, sent a telegram to the Foreign Secretary. He replied saying 'this was a major step towards the creation of a more united Europe, in which both Britain and Gibraltar have an important part to play. I am glad we have been able to look after your interests. We shall continue to do so.'[240] But the closer Anglo–Spanish relations grew, the more it drove a wedge between the people of Gibraltar and Britain and the more the hopes for full self-government in Gibraltar were dampened. With Spain as a full partner in the Community from 1986 it was in Britain's interests to seek common ground and to foster alliances of convenience

[236] See P Craig, 'Constitutions, Constitutionalism, and the European Union' (2001) 7 *European Law Journal* No 2, 125–150.

[237] Weiler n 199 above, 272–73.

[238] G Marks, L Hooghe and K Blank, 'European Integration from the 1980s: State-Centric v Multiple Level Governance' (1996) 34 *Journal of Common Market Studies* 341; see also A Stone Sweet and W Sandholtz, 'European Integration and Supranational Governance' (1997) 4 *Journal of European Public Policy* 297.

[239] See chs 4 and 5.

[240] 'Statement by the Chief Minister—The Common Market', House of Assembly Hansard, Gibraltar, December 1970.

that she could deploy at European Council level. It became clear that the interests of Britain and Gibraltar were not the same. In the period that followed Spain would use her position within the Community to contribute to the governance deficit. The accession of Spain and approximation between Britain and Spain transformed the legal context and political panorama for Gibraltar. The European stage would acquire pre-eminence as the main arena in which political scuffles would trickle down and impact on Gibraltar's governance and Constitution. Increasingly Gibraltar's interests became subjugated to the wider interests of both States.

On the 13 June 1985, and barely a day after signature of her Accession Treaty, Spain submitted a Note[241] to the European Community and British Government in a clear signal of her intentions. In it Spain stated that accession did not alter Spain's position over Gibraltar nor the bilateral negotiating process established under the Brussels Agreement.[242] The UK wrote back confirming its understanding that the relative positions of both parties were unaffected by Spanish accession to the Communities. Bilateralism was not only recognised—it was entrenched. To those in Gibraltar who had thought that accession to the Community was an opportunity to resolve historic issues this was a diplomatic side-step to ensure that accession did not encroach on the State-centric bilateralism. The situation would worsen over the following decades.

[241] Exchange of Notes between Spain and the UK dated 13 June 1985, published by the *Boletin Oficial del Estado*, 28 November 1985, Madrid—'*Canje de Notas entre Espana y el Reino Unido de Gran Bretana e Irlanda del Norte Sobre Gibraltar, en relacion con la firma y posterior ratificacion del Tratado relativo a la adhesion de Espana y las Comunidades Europeas, Hecho en Madrid el 13 de Junio de 1985*' Madrid, *Boletin Oficial del Estado, No 291 de 5 Diciembre 1985*, 38508 Iberlex 1985/25452.

[242] Olivie remarks that the purpose of the Note was to make clear that negotiations over Gibraltar would develop at 'arms-length' of Spanish membership of the EC (153) and that the EC could not become the 'guarantor' of the Gibraltar situation (161). At that point he states the EC had two choices—to contribute to a solution in accordance with the United Nations Resolutions, or to disregard the problem and allow Britain and Spain to find a bilateral solution but that in any event Spain had no obligation to Gibraltar because of the territory's EC status until the issue was resolved to her satisfaction (161). F Olivie, '*Gibraltar y La Politica Exterior de Espana de 1975 a Nuestros Dias*' in Salgado (ed) n above, 123–74. The history of subsequent developments illustrate the evident tension between the Commission's relationship towards the European citizens of Gibraltar and its State-centric tendencies that have caused it to shy away from involvement in Gibraltar related disputes. In its *Informe Sobre Gibraltar* in 2007 the Spanish Government set out its view that among other things the purpose of the exchange of notes was to preserve its position that the land known as the isthmus not ceded under the Treaty of Utrecht joined the European Community with Spain in 1986 rather than with Britain in 1973. Spain accepts that the territory of Gibraltar excluding the isthmus joined the Community in 1973: see *Informe Sobre Gibraltar*, 2007, 14.

3

Sovereignty, State and Stateless Nation

INTRODUCTION

SOVEREIGNTY HANGS OVER all facets of constitutional activity in Gibraltar and over the legal and political dimensions of the status and governance questions as a 'disconcerting ghost'.[1] Any examination of the status and governance issues requires analysis of the sovereignty issue as this provides the thematic source of the legal context of this work. The sovereignty issue has been all-engulfing and has hampered progress on the status and governance fronts. It has also deeply influenced the dispute resolution methodologies that the parties have sought to employ.

The States (principally Spain) have guarded against direct involvement of the people of the territory in discussions over the sovereignty of the territory. This in turn bears examination because of the stark contrast between the methodologies of the Gibraltar dispute and the modern trends of multi-level governance fuelled by legitimacy concerns, democracy and constitutional pluralism. Sovereignty as a principle has seen some evolution, but the fixed desire to hang onto the traditional meaning of sovereignty and a strict intergovernmentalist attitude has permeated the issues faced by Gibraltar. There is no real consensus on the ultimate form of decolonised status that should be achieved because the emphasis for Gibraltar has been to achieve recognition of the right to self-determination first and then decide on a method thereafter.[2] Indeed one of the main points in this work is that given the evolution of the concepts of sovereignty and nationalism reliance on the traditional methods of decolonisation[3] can itself be out of step with modern reality.[4]

The criteria and options for decolonisation need to change to take account of developments in the socio-political and legal context. Indeed as

[1] N Walker, 'Late Sovereignty in the European Union' in N Walker (ed), *Sovereignty in Transition* (Oxford, Hart Publishing, 2003) 13.

[2] See below and ch 7.

[3] Independence, free association or integration—though by far the classic method of decolonisation is independence.

[4] Ch 7 will examine a status that could emerge from a proper application of the current legal context.

has been pointed out by Wind 'not all legal problems can be solved legally, especially in a polycentric polity with unity in diversity.'[5] The Gibraltar dispute is not only legal but also intensely political. It is a perfect example for the application of that principle and of the need to consider the linkage between law, society and politics. In that sense too this work is also about sub-state constitutionalism. It is about how the 'constitutive goods'[6] of political dialogue and solidarity combine to create a societal culture fuelled by 'national identity as the battery.'[7] That there are several identities in conflict and even multiple identities will be discussed below.[8] It is about how these principles inform the institutional and normative framework and its relationship with peoples and statehood. It is about the application of constitutionalist principles beyond and below the State in a form of stateless constitutionalism.[9] It is about the threat to these principles and the deficit that has resulted because of bilateralism and intergovernmentalism.

The methodology of State-centric bilateralism between Britain and Spain makes up the first and principal deficit. That then, in turn, fosters and exacerbates further specific elements that make up the overall democratic deficit. This has been facilitated by developments conspiring to set the stage for that deficit to emerge. This chapter looks at the overriding issue of sovereignty that acts as a thematic umbrella for the overall work. It also examines the conflicts of nationalism and the different aspirations of the principal parties. The chapter outlines how the theoretical legal context is evolving and how it provides a marked contrast to the traditional dispute-methodology of the parties. These then affect the status and governance issues highlighted below.

This chapter has four parts. The first touches upon the themes of sovereignty, nationalism, self-determination and the applicable modern evolution of those concepts namely late sovereignty, stateless nationalism, sub-State constitutionalism and multi-level governance. Subsequent chapters will discuss the inter-relationship with multi-level governance as an accommodation of the tensions inherent in the sovereignty dispute. The second part tackles the issue of Gibraltar's claim to be a nation and its political, social and economic sustainability. The third part describes the conflicts between the parties and the tendency to pursue a bilateral policy between Britain and Spain to the exclusion of Gibraltar's representatives. The desire to transform this by injecting trilateralism is a constant theme

[5] M Wind, 'The European Union as a polycentric polity: returning to a neo-medieval Europe?' in JHH Weiler and M Wind (eds), *European Constitutionalism Beyond the State* (Cambridge, CUP, 2003) 126.

[6] N Walker, 'Postnational Constitutionalism and the Problem of Translation', in JHH Weiler and M Wind (eds), *European Constitutionalism Beyond the State* (Cambridge, CUP, 2003) 46.

[7] ibid 47.

[8] See also in ch 6.

[9] This is the natural consequence of the stateless nationalism and polycentric, multi-level trends fuelled by legitimacy.

of this work. The pervasive bilateralism is the main democratic deficit itself. It has also hindered constitutional reform, progress on the international recognition of Gibraltar's right to self-determination, decolonisation and the search for a permanent status. Finally the fourth part outlines the status and governance issues that arise in this dispute and remain to be tackled. It also sets out the paradox of constitutionalism of this case-study.

SOVEREIGNTY AND THE STATELESS NATION— NATIONALISM AND SELF-DETERMINATION

The Tussle Over Sovereignty and Constitutional Gains

Tension over sovereignty in the years after Spanish accession to the European Community continued. In 1987 in a bilateral Joint Declaration between the United Kingdom and Spain under the Brussels Agreement those States agreed a framework aimed at the joint use of Gibraltar airport.[10] This was criticised by broad Gibraltar political opinion because of the view that it made sovereignty concessions to Spain and was not implemented for those reasons. Nevertheless it was a sign of the growing diplomatic co-operation between Britain and Spain within the European Community. The departure of Sir Joshua Hassan from the political scene, the effect of the 1987 airport agreement and the normal erosion of political support after so many years of office all combined to produce the defeat of the AACR and the victory of the socialist labour party (GSLP) in general elections of 1988. The change of administration led to a markedly different approach. The AACR had vigorously campaigned for civil rights in the post-war period and had been instrumental in the achievement of constitutional gains during the 1950s and 1960s. It had also played a significant part in the promotion of a separate Gibraltarian identity. But by the 1980s the movement had been tempered and exhausted by Government. The GSLP unhindered by any previous spell in Government brought a fresh, more nationalistic ethos that placed primacy on economic self-sufficiency. This resulted in much concentration on the growth of the Gibraltar economy as economic development was seen to be inextricably linked to the achievement of constitutional development and political self-sufficiency. The GSLP refused to attend bilateral talks under the Brussels Agreement and the process of discussions between the States failed to progress for a number of years.

The Spanish foreign minister at the time of the full opening of the frontier, Fernando Moran, had espoused a policy of 'osmosis' for the Gibraltar

[10] See chs 5 and 6.

problem which was code for a slow economically-led absorption into the Spanish hinterland combined with a degree of co-operation measures. But there was still friction especially on sovereignty that spilled over into obstruction of Gibraltar access to EC measures and frontier delays. The situation would worsen after the defeat of the Spanish Socialist administration in 1996. During the period 1997–2001 vehicles regularly had to wait two to three hours to cross over into Spain. This led the European Commission to take an interest in the situation and warn Spain that it would have to act if these delays persisted.[11] Tensions between the parties manifested themselves on different fronts. The refusal of the Gibraltar Government to attend talks under the Brussels Agreement led to a policy by the Spanish government of frustration of diverse activities from sporting to military activities.[12] It also spilt over into Gibraltar becoming an obstacle to agreements at EC level.[13]

In 1993 Spain re-tabled proposals, of temporary joint sovereignty followed by full Spanish sovereignty, which had been put to Britain in 1985. For years these proposals lay on the table with Britain refusing to formally respond, Spain expectant for a reply and Gibraltar calling for a rejection. That necessarily resulted in none of the parties being satisfied. Official Spanish government frustration boiled over from time to time. As Javier Solana put it when he was Spanish foreign minister in 1993 Gibraltar obstructed 'the development of bilateral relations between Spain and the United Kingdom and does so increasingly in the development of . . . a new Europe.'[14]

In 1992 the Chief Minister of Gibraltar, Joe Bossano, decided to commence bi-annual interventions before the UN Special Committee on Decolonisation and Fourth Committee. To unblock the impasse in 1994 the then British Foreign Secretary, Douglas Hurd, floated the possibility of talks proceeding on a so-called 'two flags—three voices' formula. This would allow the Gibraltar side to take part in talks on a more even basis. The new formula was used for customs and police co-operation talks during 1995 but was not extended beyond that.

Between 1996 to May 1997 three changes of Government took place. In Gibraltar a social democrat administration led (GSD) by Peter Caruana took the helm. In Spain the socialists were defeated by the conservative *Partido Popular* (PP), led by José Maria Aznar, and Tony Blair led the Labour Party to victory in May 1997. The GSD administration sought to

[11] Border queues were so bad during 1999 that internet cameras were installed at the frontier to transmit the queues over the web.

[12] See chs 2, 4 and 5.

[13] Significant among these was the collapse of the proposed external frontiers convention because Spain insisted its border with Gibraltar needed to be identified as the EC's external border: see P Gold, *Gibraltar: British or Spanish?* (London, Routledge, 2004) 135–45.

[14] *El País* (Madrid 24 March 1993).

participate in talks between Britain and Spain but wished to secure its separate voice and to do so on condition that Britain would not agree to any proposals without the Gibraltar Government's own agreement. Attempts to secure the conditions for attendance at talks all failed.

The Spanish Government position hardened substantially with the centre-right PP in power. This translated into a number of difficulties relating to recognition of Gibraltar issued ID cards and passports. Non-recognition regularly spilt over into the legal arena, with a lack of co-operation by Spanish officials in respect of Gibraltar courts.[15] The lack of recognition of Gibraltar competent authorities was not unblocked until an agreement on competent authorities was entered into in April 2000, by which the UK foreign office acted as a 'post-box' for the transmission of communications to and from Gibraltar, thus side-stepping the unwillingness of Spain to directly engage with Gibraltar authorities, as it considered that this amounted to recognition of the external competence of these.

The new Spanish Foreign Minister Abel Matutes declared at the UN that Spain 'was directly and painfully affected by the question of Gibraltar.'[16] He confirmed that Spain would not lift air or military concessions without sovereignty concessions from Britain. He warned that unless dialogue progressed it was going to 'turn the screw and make life difficult for Gibraltar.'[17] At the next round of talks Matutes presented his own temporary joint sovereignty proposals to the British government with Gibraltar being able to retain autonomy like Catalunya and the Basque country. Again Britain allowed these proposals to remain on the table without express rejection that became a further source of conflict and friction with Gibraltar.

There can be little doubt that, once the European stage acquired greater significance,[18] the sovereignty dispute became interwoven with the bilateralisation of the dispute by Britain and Spain, and its effect was to hamper progress on constitutional reform, decolonisation and produce a democratic and governance deficit at European and domestic levels. The attempt at initiating a process of constitutional reform in the late 1990s was a good example of this. It showed how the more archaic view of sovereignty was promoted in preference to the more diffused modern view. It

[15] This was reflected in both criminal proceedings and civil actions. See also *Gibraltar Homes v Banesto* [1997–98] Gib LR 217, in which the court had to decide whether service had properly been conducted in accordance with the Hague Convention in light of the fact that the Spanish Government had issued a *note verbale* stating inter alia that 'Spain does not recognise the Supreme Court of Gibraltar as an authority and consequently any documents submitted by that body will be considered null and non-existent.' The Spanish Government had issued the *note verbale* on 26 August 1997.

[16] 29 September 1997: Gold n 13 above, 190.

[17] ibid 191.

[18] Post-Spanish accession in 1986.

also shows how the pure intergovernmentalism[19] of bilateralism was a main influencing factor to the detriment of multi-level governance and the achievement of reform and decolonisation.

Exploratory talks to establish the British Government's attitude to the issue of further constitutional reform were conducted in London between September and December 1998. Britain stated that their attitude to reform proposals was guided by four principles.[20] In the first place reform should broadly mirror that which had been or could be introduced in the other overseas territories.[21] This statement ignored the unique and distinguishing factors of Gibraltar, and indeed contradicted the propositions that precisely sought to take these into account. While that statement was not new, had also been stated to other OT Governments and was the tenor of a policy White Paper issued by the British Government earlier that same year[22] it certainly did not take into account the real differences among these micro-territories. The second guiding principle was that the United Kingdom wanted to retain such mechanisms of last resort that were necessary to ensure good government and financial probity. In this context the United Kingdom had exercised interventionist powers in Turks and Caicos and Montserrat.[23] In both cases the incidents that gave rise to British Government interest also led to constitutional changes.[24] These changes proved that constitutional reform is not always a one-way process—it can also entail a resumption of control by the United Kingdom.

Thirdly, the British Government confirmed its concern that arrangements should not affect its ability to comply with its European and international obligations. Indeed several international obligations have influenced British policy towards the overseas territories and Gibraltar in recent years.[25]

[19] For a view of intergovernmentalism at EC level see A Moravcsik, 'Preferences and Power in the European Community: A Liberal Intergovernmental Approach' (1993) 31 *Journal of Common Market Studies* 473: see also ch 4, 270–77.

[20] The British Government's position was also contained in a Response to the Gibraltar Government Non-Paper on Constitutional Change, Foreign and Commonwealth Office, 30 April 1998.

[21] However, in a 'Constitutional Modernisation Check-List' submitted to Overseas Territories' Chief Ministers in October 1999 and issued by the Overseas Territories Department of the Foreign and Commonwealth Office in August 1999 it was stated that the checklist was intended to apply to all territories except Gibraltar, evidencing the special position of Gibraltar in the British Government's eyes (because—but not exclusively—of the Spanish dimension).

[22] *Partnership for Progress and Prosperity* (Cm 4264, 1998).

[23] In Turks and Caicos the Constitution was suspended in 1986 following the arrest of several Parliamentarians on criminal charges. The subsequent Royal Commission recommended certain electoral and constitutional amendments. In Montserrat the volcanic disaster had a serious impact on the ability of that community to govern itself.

[24] There was some significant claw-back of powers in the Turks and Caicos as a result: see ch 2, pp 87–88.

[25] The international regulation of financial services, the common application of human rights principles throughout all its territories, international co-operation in the fight against crime, money-laundering and terrorism are some.

Gibraltar's status within the European Union brings particular challenges and obligations on Gibraltar. It is on these obligations that Britain was focusing when it set out its policy position. Finally, and most importantly for this work, the United Kingdom sounded a cautionary note on the impact that constitutional proposals could have on economic stability in view of the sovereignty claim and urged that the 'Spanish dimension' should be taken into account in any process of reform. This last requirement was a clear indicator that the prospect for reform would encounter serious trouble given the resistance in Gibraltar to factoring in the Spanish view. This emphasised the effect the sovereignty dispute was having on aspirations to progress issues of status and governance. The British position quite candidly was that the Spanish dimension 'adds to the case for proceeding cautiously on constitutional reform in current circumstances.'[26]

All of this demonstrated the British attitude to demands for reform and highlighted some of the reasons that contributed to the delay in making progress. While the other three pillars of British policy were a matter for negotiation the fourth —the Spanish dimension—brought into sharp focus an area of deep conflict between the parties because of the markedly different underlying aspirations. Though Spain's position softened slightly after 2004, when a Socialist administration was elected,[27] it had hitherto repeatedly asserted that it considered any constitutional reform as potentially a breach of the Treaty of Utrecht or (at the very least) as fanning the flame of self-determination in Gibraltar. It is clear from previous statements and conduct—hence the stated British position—that Spain could react negatively to the grant of constitutional reform and would firmly oppose any attempt at decolonisation through an act of self-determination. Spain's most recently expressed position is that reform is not opposed if it is purely internal and does not affect issues of status or decolonisation.[28]

The United Kingdom statement in 1998 highlighted how far it had come in its acceptance of the significant influence that the long-standing Spanish position had acquired on issues of Gibraltar's status and governance. The 1998 episode was a good example of the underlying themes of this work and the point that had been reached at the end of the 1990s. This was a dispute with sovereignty at its heart where the three players tussled for

[26] Response to GOG Non-Paper on Constitutional Change, above, last para.

[27] Previous Governments in Spain had largely insisted that any co-operation from Spain come in parallel to gains on sovereignty. The administration elected in 2004 was willing to aim at sequential measures with co-operation being proffered first and sovereignty lying as the residual goal. While this was a softer line it was still based on an old and rigid view of sovereignty.

[28] Prior to 2004 Spain resisted engaging the Gibraltar Government directly in any form of talks and preferred to engage the UK only (even though they accepted that the UK would involve Gibraltar within the British delegation). This policy of bilateralisation is also reflected in Spain's resistance at recognising the competence of Gibraltar bodies in any field.

power and control and the stateless nation of Gibraltar sought greater power, influence and representation both domestically and at European level. The impasse at that stage was clear.[29]

In July 1999 a cross-party Select Committee of the House of Assembly was formed to examine all aspects of the Constitution and report back to the House. In February 2000 the Spanish foreign minister made clear that Spain viewed any attempts to amend Gibraltar's Constitution with suspicion and dismay and reiterated that his Government would only improve issues of border queues or telephone access if there was co-operation on sovereignty. The Foreign Affairs Select Committee of the British House of Commons recommended the possible commencement of legal action in relation to both border delays and telephone restrictions.[30]

In July 2001 after a gap of three years the Spanish and British Foreign Secretaries, Josep Piqué and Jack Straw, agreed to revive the Brussels process with a new determination to achieve a speedy outcome. The Gibraltar Government did not attend talks under this reinvigorated phase because its previously stated conditions for attendance at talks had not been met. The Minister of State at the Foreign Office, Peter Hain, warned Gibraltarians that they should not get 'stuck in the past'.[31] The talks proceeded in secret on a bilateral basis between Britain and Spain although a number of press leaks revealed that this was an attempt to reach an agreement based on the concept of joint sovereignty. There were a number of so-called 'red line' issues. For Britain these were that the agreement should be permanent, that it should be approved by Gibraltar in referendum and that its military interests should be protected. For Spain the agreement needed to deliver eventual full sovereignty and it did not accept that Gibraltarians should have a right of veto on issues discussed between sovereign states. Talks were expedited and it became obvious that Britain and Spain wished to agree a set of so-called 'agreed principles' and then hoped to invite Gibraltar to participate in the design of the detail. It was made clear, however, that the 'agreed principles' could not be changed. If this included an issue that was objectionable to the people of Gibraltar nothing could be done. Against this backdrop the Gibraltar Government refused to participate in those talks and instead planned a campaign of political and media lobbying, mostly in Britain. At one point there was a demonstration of 25,000 people in March 2002 against the joint sovereignty discussions.

[29] Though the Constitution was not formally amended from 1969–2006 it is still worth noting that there were, on the other hand, significant advancements (achieved by convention) in the area of the powers and competences of the local Government in the years after 1969. The extent of the advances (described in ch 5) should not be under-estimated. These were, in some cases, radical and redrew the competences and de facto relationship between the Crown and the Ministers of Gibraltar.

[30] House of Commons Foreign Affairs Select Committee, Sixth Report, 2000–01, *Gibraltar: Follow-up* (London, HMSO, 2001).

[31] *Gibraltar Chronicle* (Gibraltar, 17 September 2001).

The objective within the British Foreign Office was to agree a joint declaration of principles but talks encountered difficulties on the 'red-line' issues.[32] By the time this became clear the Gibraltar Government ruled out participation in talks, arguing that participation under a set of non-negotiable principles that were bilaterally agreed between Britain and Spain was fundamentally flawed.

In January 2002 the Select Committee on Constitutional Reform finalised its work[33] and the House of Assembly unanimously adopted its Report on 27 February 2002. The objectives stated in the Report were to 'propose amendments to the current Constitution such as would maximise the self-government of Gibraltar by the people of Gibraltar whilst retaining British sovereignty and close links with Great Britain.'[34] In a wide-ranging Report that attached a draft Constitution setting out the proposed changes to the wording of specific clauses the Select Committee made 45 recommendations. Among these were that:

1. the wording of the sovereignty preamble should remain as originally drafted in 1969;[35]
2. a further preamble be added to the draft Order in Council to make clear that acceptance of the Constitution was in accordance with the right to self-determination of the people of Gibraltar;[36]
3. language be added to the Constitution to set out a right to self-determination based on the text of the International Covenant on Civil and Political Rights;[37]
4. a number of amendments be made to the chapter on fundamental rights to reflect consistency with the European Convention of Human Rights and where necessary supplement existing rights;[38]
5. the House of Assembly should be re-styled 'the Gibraltar Parliament', be enlarged, unelected members removed and that the Parliament should have the ability to legislate to achieve further enlargement;[39]
6. the Governor's special legislative powers be curtailed and that powers of disallowance should be deleted;[40]
7. the term 'Government of Gibraltar' be defined, the Gibraltar Council be abolished and cabinet style powers be solely held by the Council of Ministers;[41]

32 *Gibraltar Chronicle* (Gibraltar, 22 February 2002).

33 House of Assembly Select Committee on Constitutional Reform, *Report*, House of Assembly, Gibraltar, 23 January 2002.

34 Report of Select Committee on Constitutional Reform, para (10), 2.

35 ibid para (15), 3.

36 ibid para 1, 3.

37 ibid para 3, 4.

38 ibid paras 4 and 5(1)–(17), 4–6.

39 ibid paras 12–14, 6–7.

40 ibid paras 17–18, 7.

41 ibid paras 21–2, 7–8.

8. the Governor's responsibilities should be strictly demarcated with all matters except defence, external affairs and public/judicial appointments being the responsibility of the Gibraltar Government;[42]
9. the Governor should consult with and wherever practicable act in accordance with the advice of the Chief Minister;[43]
10. there should be a consultative council for EU matters constituted jointly between the British and Gibraltar Governments to consider issues stemming from Gibraltar's membership of the EU;[44]
11. a judicial and senior appointments commission should be constituted for the appointment of a number of judicial and public offices;[45]
12. constitutional responsibility for public finance should vest in a Minister for Finance with the post of Financial Secretary ceasing to be a constitutional office;[46]
13. the land provisions should be amended to make clear that crown land vests in Her Majesty in right of the Government of Gibraltar;[47]
14. the power reserved to Her Majesty to make laws for the peace, order and good government of Gibraltar should be removed;[48]
15. provisions be included to establish a Police Authority maintaining the operational independence of the police but giving the Government competence on policy and resources.[49]

Even though there had been a change of Foreign Minister in Spain and the July 2002 round of Anglo–Spanish joint sovereignty talks had been postponed the Foreign Secretary, Jack Straw, made a statement in Parliament in mid July 2002 that confirmed that Britain and Spain had agreed the principle of joint sovereignty. In reaction the Gibraltar Government organised a referendum in November 2002 to deal head-on with that agreement. The question put to the people of Gibraltar in a referendum asked whether they approved 'of the principle that Britain and Spain should share sovereignty over Gibraltar.'[50] In a massive turnout of 88 per cent of the electorate almost 99 per cent of those who voted rejected the principle of joint sovereignty. While Gibraltarian aspirations had been successfully defended the dispute entered an impasse once again. This would only be lifted by the election of a new socialist administration in Spain in March 2004. The *PSOE*[51] administration of José Luis Rodriguez Zapatero agreed to structure talks on a tripartite basis. These were

[42] ibid paras 24–5, 8.
[43] ibid para 26, 8.
[44] ibid para 28, 8.
[45] ibid paras 30–3, 8–9.
[46] ibid para 40, 9.
[47] ibid para 42, 9.
[48] ibid para 44, 10.
[49] ibid para 45, 10.
[50] Drawn from the text of the question submitted to the electorate on 7 November 2002.
[51] *Partido Socialista Obrero Espanol.*

launched in the autumn of 2004 and led to a number of agreements in the field of telecommunications, pensions, freedom of movement and the use of the Gibraltar air terminal.[52]

The report of the Select Committee on Constitutional Reform was presented to the United Kingdom and formed the basis of several rounds of discussions between United Kingdom and Gibraltar delegations during the period 2004–06. Constitutional negotiations did not commence earlier because of the distraction provided by the joint sovereignty discussions between the United Kingdom and Spain.

Progress on the constitutional talks moved in a parallel though disconnected process to the forum for tripartite co-operation until 2006. In that year the constitutional talks came to an end with the fruit of those discussions being put to a referendum. The acceptance of the new Constitution in referendum led to the commencement of the 2006 Constitution.[53] The new Constitution was the product of those lengthy discussions and resulted in deep-ranging changes and significant advances being made to the 1969 Constitution. A clause on self-determination was added, the human rights chapter was updated, it was made clear that elected Ministers were responsible for all areas except external affairs and defence, powers vested in the Governor or a Secretary of State to disallow, withhold assent or to pass legislation were curtailed and commissions were established for the appointment of senior public officers and judicial officers. A mechanism to allow the amendment of the human rights chapter of the Constitution after parliamentary sanction and approval in a referendum was also agreed. In terms of self-governance major steps forward had been taken even if a residue of proposals had fallen by the wayside and other areas had not been adequately tackled.[54] The detail in respect of the changes is outlined in the comparative table set out in the annex to this chapter. By 2007 the degree of devolution of self-governance and decentralisation of responsibilities to Gibraltar was very significant. It had emerged as an entirely economically self-sufficient territory having managed a successful diversification from a defence economy to one primarily based on shipping, tourism and financial services. The relationship with the military establishment, the British Government and the office of the Governor had been radically transformed. The functions of the Governor had become a shadow of the very central administrative role the office held in the 1950s. Even so a number of issues remained that touched

[52] See ch 6.

[53] The new Constitution was approved by a 60% majority of those choosing to vote. The turnout was about 60%. As such the 'Yes' vote represented about 37% of the total eligible electorate. This was because of domestic party political differences and also because of large-scale confusion on the consequences for Gibraltar's international status of the draft Constitution.

[54] Her Majesty significantly retained the reserve power of legislation and ability to amend or revoke the Constitution.

on aspects of Gibraltar's status and governance. Above all the sovereignty dispute continued making sporadic reappearances to exacerbate old wounds, suspicions and anxieties.

The Córdoba Agreement and Developments of 2006—*plus ça change . . .?*

The hectic autumn of 2006 witnessed a number of legal and political developments affecting Gibraltar that lay emphasis to the fact that the classic and traditional view of sovereignty still hung over the dispute and the status and governance issues in an ominous way. At first sight it was possible to perceive the new developments as representing a progressive trend. For the first time in decades negotiations leading to constitutional reform had concluded successfully with the possibility that this could dramatically address the long-standing calls for reform (and in turn the governance deficit). Additionally a political breakthrough with Spain had been reached that could mark a turning of the tide in the sovereignty dispute. On closer examination it was clear that, while some long-standing obstacles had been removed, the ground rules had not altered in any dramatic fashion.

Long and arduous negotiations had led to the commencement of a new Constitution on 2 January 2007.[55] While this was the fruit of discussions between a Gibraltar cross-party delegation and the British Government it, in substance, concentrated on internal governance.[56] It left the area of external (European) governance largely untouched and was effectively silent on the status of Gibraltar, transferring any evaluation of whether this could lead to formal decolonisation to the United Nations arena. The finalisation of constitutional negotiations was accompanied by protestations from the Spanish Government that the reason they did not object to this new Constitution was because it did not change the international status of Gibraltar, and by side correspondence[57] between the respective Foreign Secretaries, in which Jack Straw[58] gave his Spanish counterpart assurances on status and that the British interpretation on the Treaty of Utrecht had not been breached by the new Constitution.[59] For Spain the Constitution only provided changes to internal governance and

[55] The Gibraltar Constitution Order 2006 was adopted by Her Majesty in Council on 14 December 2006 and commenced on 2 January.

[56] In the sense of increasing powers of self-government. But it did not conclusively enhance democratic checks and political accountability: see earlier.

[57] During the period 28–31 March 2006: see further ch 6.

[58] Mr Straw was Foreign Secretary at the time. By the date of commencement of the new Constitution and the Córdoba Agreements he had been succeeded by Margaret Beckett.

[59] The British Government contend that the Treaty of Utrecht constrains Gibraltar's right to independence because Spain has a right to first refusal under Art X.

not alterations to Gibraltar's international status. For Gibraltar the Constitution not only introduced these governance reforms but provided an opportunity to lobby the United Nations to achieve decolonisation on the basis that by opting to accept the Constitution its people had exercised their right to self-determination. No mention was made in the constitutional text or the Preamble of its effect on the status of Gibraltar leaving the question for decision by the United Nations.[60] In a covering Despatch to the Constitution the United Kingdom stated that:

> it [the Constitution] does not in any way diminish British sovereignty of Gibraltar and the United Kingdom will retain its full international responsibility for Gibraltar including its external relations and defence, and as the Member State responsible for Gibraltar in the European Union. Gibraltar will remain listed as a British Overseas Territory in the British Nationality Act 1981 as amended by the British Overseas Territories Act 2002.

As decolonisation could be achieved without opting for independence this was a deliberately ambivalent declaration designed to meet both Spain's concerns and Gibraltar's anxiety that it should not close the door on its own attempts to lobby the United Nations for decolonisation based on the contents of this Constitution.[61]

On 12 September 2006 the European Court of Justice ruled on Spain's challenge to the manner of enfranchisement by Britain of the people of Gibraltar in European elections.[62] The eagerness to hold onto traditional thinking on Gibraltar and the different approaches of the parties was evident in the positions that Britain and Spain took in that case. Legislation had been introduced by the United Kingdom so as to comply with the ruling of the European Court of Human Rights in *Matthews v UK*.[63] The legislation was expressed to apply to the United Kingdom and Gibraltar and created an electoral region of the South-West and Gibraltar. It also made some mechanical provision as to the registration of voters, compilation of

[60] That in itself was because of the delicate balance between the parties. For Britain silence was the better part of valour. However it should also be recorded that the UK has previously stated that it is not for the General Assembly 'to decide when a non-self-governing territory has reached a level of self-government sufficient to relieve the administering power of the obligation to submit information under Art 73e of the Charter. Such decisions must be left to the Government of the territory concerned and to the Administering Power': Statement of Explanation of Vote by UK Alternative Representative, Paul Arkwright, at UN General Assembly, 48th Session, 4th Committee, Item 116, 29 October 1993. The UN takes a different view: see J Crawford, *The Creation of States in International Law*, 2nd edn (Oxford, OUP, 2006) 622.

[61] The UN has not—so far—heeded any attempt by Gibraltar to obtain decolonisation on this basis.

[62] Case C-145/04 *Spain v UK* (Judgment of Grand Chamber, 12 September 2006). Gibraltarians were unable to vote in European elections until 2004. Their enfranchisement had followed a legal challenge filed at the European Court of Human Rights. The issue is covered in detail in chs 5 and 7.

[63] See *Matthews v UK* (App No 24833/94) ECHR 18 February 1999.

a register of voters and manner of voting within the region. Spain saw the move as a threat to its traditional sovereignty position on Gibraltar and in a rare legal manoeuvre filed a challenge.[64]

Both the European Commission and the court were alive to the delicate nature of the political issue that underlay the legal points taken. The Commission avoided a reasoned opinion when Spain challenged the manner of enfranchisement of Gibraltar because of the 'sensitivity of the underlying bilateral issue.'[65] The European Court of Justice convened its Grand Chamber to deliver its ruling and in a signal of the constitutional importance of the case the Attorney-General, Lord Goldsmith QC, represented the United Kingdom at the hearing. Spain's arguments were quasi-political and the sensitivity of the sovereignty question to it was palpable. The court recorded that part of Spain's central submissions was that

> Gibraltar's situation is colonial and the recognition of a separate electoral district is a step towards independence which runs counter to the international rules which govern that colony.[66]

For Spain the manner of enfranchisement was a breach of an undertaking given in a Declaration by the United Kingdom which had created an obligation under international law.[67] Conversely the United Kingdom in a more phlegmatic focus mostly concentrated on the mechanical convenience of the voting arrangements and denied the alleged breach. The court found the arrangements were within the State's margin of appreciation. The Spanish Government issued a press communiqué after the ruling stating it would respect the decision taken. Nonetheless it had made its position clear and it was little different to its traditional and historic line.[68]

In another development during mid-September 2006 the Governments of Britain, Spain and Gibraltar (that had been involved in tripartite talks since December 2004)[69] announced a series of agreements on communications,

[64] See chs 5 and 7 for detailed discussion of this ruling and of the *Matthews* case.

[65] It issued a press release to that effect on 29 October 2003 stating that it felt that the UK had organised the enfranchisement within its margin of discretion but that 'given the sensitivity of the underlying bilateral issue, the Commission at this stage refrains from adopting a reasoned opinion within the meaning of Art 227 [EC] and invites the parties to find an amicable solution.'

[66] Para 83 of the ruling of 12 September 2006.

[67] That made by it on the 18 February 2002, by which it undertook 'to ensure that the necessary changes are made to enable the Gibraltar electorate to vote in elections to the European Parliament as part of and on the same terms as the electorate of an existing UK constituency.'

[68] It is a fact that the case had been brought by the more nationalistic *Partido Popular* administration in Spain, but the Socialist Government elected in March 2004 made no moves to soften the line in the litigation. It is possible that it may have felt bound to continue the litigation but the maintenance of the more quasi-political legal arguments was an interesting feature.

[69] Described in ch 6, 313–9.

freedom of movement, pensions and aviation measures.[70] These were heralded to demonstrate a new climate in relations by the political participants and by some observers.[71] They certainly promised to achieve the removal of irritants that had been present for some time and to that extent those practical steps forward should not be underestimated.[72] But in terms of the underlying central issue of sovereignty close scrutiny revealed little fundamental movement in positions. The arrangements were said—in the joint communiqué issued by the three Governments—to have 'no implications whatsoever regarding sovereignty or jurisdiction . . . (and to be) without prejudice to the respective positions .' However, the statement was also made that Gibraltar's Government 'understands and accepts that references to sovereignty are bilateral to the UK and Spain'[73]—a reference which highlighted the force of State-centric bilateralism.

It took the Spanish Government only 16 days to assert that the Córdoba Agreements safeguarded its position and enshrined bilateralism on the sovereignty question. The tone of Spain's reassertion to its sovereignty claim provided a striking contrast to the speculation that there had been a change of attitude and a new climate of goodwill. In a speech to the United Nations Fourth Committee on 4 October 2006, the Spanish Ambassador to the United Nations made clear that nothing in the Córdoba Agreements or the new Constitution that Gibraltar was about to be granted 'alter either the fundamental Spanish position on this dispute or the colonial nature of Gibraltar . . . the claim of sovereignty is irrenounceable for Spain.' The hope for Spain was that the Córdoba Agreements would create a 'new atmosphere favourable to advances towards a definitive solution to the dispute between Spain and Britain over Gibraltar.' But it made clear that such a solution had to be premised on a negotiation of decolonisation with Spain adding that 'it would be a big mistake on the part of the UK to believe that using the existence of this Forum[74] as a pretext, it could elude its responsibility . . . to negotiate with Spain the decolonisation of Gibraltar.'

A new dawn or more of the same? This was the unanswered question that remained after these contrasting developments. At the very least it

[70] The so-called 'Córdoba Agreements' named after the Spanish city in which the meeting was held. See ch 6.

[71] *Gibraltar Chronicle* (Gibraltar, 19 September 2006).

[72] eg Spain introduced a green channel at the frontier for the first time with the aim of easing the passage of vehicular traffic and cutting down crossing times. In February 2007 Spain removed the long-standing block on Gibraltar's international dialling code which allowed unhindered telecommunications access in Spain for mobile phones issued by Gibraltar telecommunications carriers.

[73] Communiqué of the Ministerial Meeting of the Forum of Dialogue on Gibraltar and the Ministerial Statement on Gibraltar Airport both issued on 18 September 2006 by the Governments of the UK, Spain and Gibraltar.

[74] The Trilateral Forum for Dialogue created in December 2004 that led to the Córdoba Agreements.

seemed to demonstrate that Spain had as yet not settled in her own mind what her approach to Gibraltar would be in years to come. At worst it indicated that beyond any superficial euphoria it would prove very difficult to alter the underlying status quo.

The Thematic Legal and Political Context: Sovereignty and the Stateless Nation

The claim to the territorial sovereignty of Gibraltar was first prosecuted by Spain militarily and then using diplomatic means. Its resolution has eluded generations of politicians. While this has always been focused as being about a claim to the ultimate territorial sovereignty of Gibraltar it should also be seen as a struggle for power, control and influence over the territory and its domestic constitutional and governance developments. In that sense there is a real link between the territorial claim, the conceptual backdrop and the ability to make progress on status and governance issues. The issues of sovereignty, nationalism and self-determination provoke profound stalling effects on the desire to seek constitutional reform and decolonisation. The thematic umbrella under which the status and governance issues subsist is the sovereignty question.

The roots of the system of sovereign states can be traced most obviously to the Peace of Westphalia in 1648.[75] The elements of state sovereignty required this to be absolute and indivisible and endowed with an external and internal aspect of the same.[76] That traditional view of sovereignty assumed a hierarchical structure with a supreme authority 'be that a person or the people'. Three aspects were central to the power of sovereignty:

> [I]t must be absolute (because independence cannot be qualified or limited), unitary (because it must apply to all matters and cannot be shared or divided) and supreme (because it must be final).[77]

As Fassbender has highlighted the concept of sovereignty acquired a 'mythical quality'[78] and was put to much political use as a tool to wage

[75] See eg S Besson, 'Sovereignty in Conflict' in C Warbrick and S Tierney (eds), *Towards an International Legal Community: The Sovereignty of States and the Sovereignty of International Law* (London, British Institute of International and Comparative Law, 2006) 131–92. Though this has been doubted: see D Grieg, 'International Community, Interdependence and all that Rhetorical Correctness' in G Kreijen (ed), *State, Sovereignty and International Governance* (Oxford, OUP, 2004) 523–24, who contends the developments are much more recent and that the importance of realising that is that it is easier to accept the evolution 'of a new world order . . . from the now outdated system of sovereign States.'

[76] D Held, *Democracy and the Global Order* (Cambridge, Polity, 1995) 78.

[77] R Bellamy, 'Post-Sovereignty and Pre-Sovereignty: Three Models of the State, Democracy and Rights within the EU', in N Walker (ed), *Sovereignty in Transition* (Oxford, Hart Publishing, 2003) 175.

[78] B Fassbender, 'Sovereignty and Constitutionalism in International Law', in N Walker (ed), *Sovereignty in Transition* (Oxford, Hart Publishing, 2003) 115.

war or pursue distinct claims. As such it is a legal notion that 'integrates a political dimension which paradoxically often defies legal control.'[79] And the natural corollary of that is that it is 'not only a political concept but a highly politicised concept.'[80] It remains—notwithstanding its transformation 'the privileged *locus* for reflecting on the problem of the contingent unity of political communities.'[81] It was as Loughlin suggests 'devised for the purposes of giving expression to the distinctively political bond between a group of people and its mode of governance.'[82] It emerged slowly and primarily through the manifestation of royal authority and it has been emphasised that before the development of an 'elaborate institutional framework of the State ... sovereignty did not exist'[83]

Sovereignty has in the most traditional sense been exercised by and 'as a consequence of the formation of the modern state.'[84] This can be described as 'an independent political society occupying a defined territory, the members of which are united together for the purpose of resisting external force and the preservation of order.'[85] But while the Montevideo Convention on Rights and Duties of States[86] sets out the criteria to ascertain the legal personality of a State,[87] Brownlie has warned that it is merely 'a basis for further investigation', because there is much to be discussed around the concepts of Statehood, sovereignty, independence and international legal personality.[88]

The linkage between societies, political communities, rulers, institutional hierarchies and other sources of power is clear. There is a practical interplay with society and power, the law and politics. As indicated above, it is impossible in seeking a resolution to the legal dimensions of the Gibraltar dispute to sever this from the political context. Assertions of sovereignty are expressions of ownership, power or control. As the interplay between organs of governance, civil society and plurinational[89] communities evolve so do the forms through which sovereignty is expressed. In

[79] ibid.

[80] H Lindahl, 'Sovereignty and Representation in the European Union', in N Walker (ed), *Sovereignty in Transition* (Oxford, Hart Publishing, 2003) 87.

[81] ibid 89.

[82] M Loughlin, 'Ten Tenets of Sovereignty', in N Walker (ed), *Sovereignty in Transition* (Oxford, Hart Publishing, 2003) 56.

[83] ibid 65.

[84] ibid.

[85] O Hood Phillips, *Constitutional and Administrative Law*, 8th edn (Sweet and Maxwell, London, 2001) 4.

[86] 1953, Art I.

[87] Namely, a permanent population, a defined territory, government and a capacity to enter into relations with the other States.

[88] I Brownlie, *Principles of Public International Law*, 4th edn (Oxford, OUP, 1990) 80, and see 58–179.

[89] The recognition that more than one nation can co-exist within a particular State. See eg in the case of Spain, M Herrero de Miñón, '*Nacionalismos y Estado Plurinacional en España*', *Politica Exterior* (1996) 51, May–June, 7–20. See also N Walker, 'The Idea of Constitutional Pluralism' (2002) 65 *MLR* 317.

modern forms of governance, sovereignty is re-defined as a more fluid concept of a sharing and overlap of powers. These arrangements are often put in place as a reaction by the State to calls for reform driven by civil society or by the aspirations of a nation within the State. Understanding sovereignty requires a discussion of 'both the normative extent of legal authority and its *locus*'[90] and that the latter does not reside in a specific *locus* and is 'relational not static.'[91]

THE EVOLVING CONTEXT—SOVEREIGNTY, NATIONALISM AND SELF-DETERMINATION

By 1986 the understanding of the concept of sovereignty was evolving to a greater acceptance that it was neither truly unlimited nor did it belong to the exclusive purview of the independent state. The modern analysis in a world of globalisation, interdependence and supra-national entities revolves around the nature and extent of limitations on sovereignty and about understanding the spheres of competence that can be horizontal and vertical, hierarchical and anarchical.[92] The limitations to sovereignty can also be multi-faceted and, for example, encompass legal, governmental, constitutional, legislative or judicial[93] constraints. The dimensions of the sovereignty debate in Gibraltar are various. On the one hand there are territorial aspects—the long-standing claim by Spain. There are also arguments about popular sovereignty represented by the aspirations of the people, the doctrine of self-determination and the Preamble to the Constitution.[94] And even though in a different more general context Brownlie has described sovereignty as 'powers and privileges resting on customary law and independent of the particular consent of another State',[95] it is clear that, in the non-independent territory context, sover-

[90] Tierney in C Warbrick and S Tierney (eds), *Towards an International Legal Community: The Sovereignty of States and the Sovereignty of International Law* (London, British Institute of International and Comparative Law, 2006) 1.

[91] R McCorquodale, 'International Community and State Sovereignty: An Uneasy Symbiotic Relationship' in C Warbrick and S Tierney (eds), *Towards an International Legal Community: The Sovereignty of States and the Sovereignty of International Law* (London, British Institute of International and Comparative Law, 2006) 247.

[92] See further chs 4 and 5, and for a helpful collection of articles see N Walker (ed), *Relocating Sovereignty*, International Library of Essays in Law and Legal Theory (Dartmouth, Ashgate, 2006).

[93] See P Craig, 'Constitutional Foundations, the Rule of Law and Supremacy' [2003] PL 92, and R Bellamy, 'The Constitution of Europe: Rights or Democracy?' in R Bellamy, V Bufacchi and D Castiglione (eds), *Democracy and Constitutional Culture in the Union of Europe* (London, Lothian Foundation Press, 1995).

[94] For an overview of fundamental principles in the Territorial Sovereignty or Popular sovereignty fields see Brownlie n 88 above, 107–71, 553–601.

[95] ibid 290.

eignty—in the sense of devolved authority or power—is exercised very much dependent on consent of the sovereign State.[96]

Practical Sovereignty is in essence about power, the struggle for it, its exercise and its divisions in the modern non-absolutist context. If at the heart of sovereignty is the concept of power and who exercises it in practice, this is both a wider and less definable question than the simple theoretical statements as to unlimited pure sovereignty. The modern reality is that there are few examples of this pure form of sovereignty, with most examples being subjected to limitations or demarcations of competences. In attempting to understand the modern meaning of sovereignty it is important to recognise the variety of different elements and their socio-political and legal context. This modern context is not one of autocracy but of democracy. Its backdrop is interdependence and globalisation—not independence and isolation.

Grappling with the new context is a struggle in itself. As Fassbender highlights, the UN Charter in 1945 was an attempt to move away from 'capriciousness . . . [But] the contradictions have not disappeared . . . [I]mages of sovereignty constructed in past centuries remain.'[97] The extent to which even larger, ostensibly independent, States have struggled with issues of sovereignty is recounted by Oliver, when he describes how Canada, Australia and New Zealand all—during the 1980s—had to confront taking a variety of different steps to assert or 'repatriate' their sovereignty.[98] The fact that these did so is an illustration of the difficulties faced by smaller non-independent territories and also provides an interesting parallel for Gibraltar.

In terms of stateless nations the struggle is to achieve the level of practical sovereignty that secures 'internal sovereignty'[99] and some element of 'external sovereignty.'[100] These by the mid 1980s were making claims 'to sovereign authority not necessarily in the old exclusive manner of the nation-state, but to a sufficient degree to constitute themselves as subjects

[96] It might be argued that there are two limbs to what Brownlie was pointing out—consent on the one hand and 'another State' on the other. It could be said that the consent for the exercise of limited devolved government in a non-independent territory rests on the consent of the sovereign State, which is not 'another' State for the simple reason that the non-independent territory is not a State in the first place. But having said that it is argued throughout this work that in fact given the peculiarities of the Gibraltar situation 'another' State (Spain) is in effect influencing the prospects of constitutional and governance change.

[97] Fassbender in N Walker (ed), *Sovereignty in Transition* (Oxford, Hart Publishing, 2003) 142–43.

[98] P Oliver, *The Constitution of Independence—The Development of Constitutional Theory in Australia, Canada and New Zealand* (Oxford, OUP, 2005).

[99] M Keating, *Plurinational Democracy, Stateless Nations in a Post-Sovereignty Era* (Oxford, OUP, 2001) 194 meaning 'complete control over its territory and ultimate authority within it'.

[100] Meaning the ability to conduct, direct or influence its affairs externally and have recognition and representation internationally.

and not objects of the constitutional debate.'[101] The modern reality is that, after decades of resistance, 'the participants in the international community are not limited to States' and non-State entities are being embraced as actors at that level.[102] These placed their demands on two grounds: original rights and democracy.[103]

That strand of non-separatist nationalism places emphasis on the ability to secure governance reform and constitutional gains without separatism and by a division of competences and powers. This constitutional pluralism[104] recognises the link between society, law and politics that Loughlin has also noted.[105] It does though 'challenge the particular constitutional manifestations of the unitary concept of legal sovereignty.'[106] This proved the motivations for several nations and provides useful analogies for Gibraltar.[107] The expansion and application of these themes of pluralism will form the main thrust of subsequent parts of this work. The shifting sovereignty sands emphasise the competences and pluralism debate and stress the more flexible, less hierarchical, multi-layered nature of this question. It is a concept of practical sovereignty operated against a backdrop of shared, concurrent and exclusive powers.[108] As Tierney has noted, this aspiration to obtain 'constitutional accommodation' is 'a relatively new phenomenon, and one which gained real political currency only since the 1960s.'[109] All of this is tied up with views and expression of national identity by the people of a territory.

Taken together the legitimacy and spheres of competence debates have, at their core, two features essential to the understanding of sovereignty in modern day Europe—consent and power.[110] The importance of considering the people as being at the heart of evolving sovereignty is also relevant to questions of the source, vesting of and exercise of power.[111] The multi-

[101] M Keating, *Plurinational Democracy, Stateless Nations in a Post-Sovereignty Era* (Oxford, OUP, 2001) 202 and see also McCorquodale in C Warbrick and S Tierney (eds), *Towards an International Legal Community: The Sovereignty of States and the Sovereignty of International Law* (London, British Institute of International and Comparative Law, 2006) 2006.

[102] McCorquodale ibid 263.

[103] ibid 203.

[104] S Tierney, *Constitutional Law and National Pluralism* (Oxford, OUP, 2004) 3–45.

[105] M Loughlin, *The Idea of Public Law* (Oxford, OUP, 2003) 83.

[106] S Tierney, *Constitutional Law and National Pluralism* (Oxford, OUP, 2004) 15.

[107] Basques, Catalans and Scots. See chs 4–7.

[108] See G Marks, L Hooghe and K Blank, 'European Integration from the 1980s: State-Centric v Multiple Level Governance' (1996) 34 *Journal of Common Market Studies* 341; B Rosamond, *Theories of European Integration*, 2nd edn (Basingstoke, Palgrave, 2000) and W Wallace, 'The Sharing of Sovereignty: The European Paradox', 47 *Political Studies* No 3, 503–21.

[109] S Tierney, *Constitutional Law and National Pluralism* (Oxford, OUP, 2004) 21.

[110] These features are expanded in ch 6 as part of the keys to resolution of the paradox of governance in Gibraltar.

[111] M Maduro, 'Contrapunctal Law: Europe's Constitutional Pluralism in Action' in N Walker (ed), *Sovereignty in Transition* (Oxford, Hart Publishing, 2003) 501–38; N MacCormick, *Questioning Sovereignty: Law, State and Practical Reason* (Oxford, OUP, 1999), and JHH Weiler, *The Constitution of Europe* (Cambridge, CUP, 1999) 266–355.

layered forms of governance and the devolution of power to sub-State Executives go some way to tempering and managing the aspirations of nations within States. It recognises, fosters, gives vent to but equally lessens the prospect of radicalisation of internal nationalism and self-determination.[112] It has also led to concerns about the divisions of competences,[113] methods of governance[114] within a process that some writers like Olsen or Anderson have described as Europeanisation.[115]

It is worth recalling when contemplating the Gibraltar dispute, as Bellamy has stressed when grappling with the gradual transformation of the concept of sovereignty (especially since 1945), that insufficient attention is paid to 'how recent the doctrine of sovereignty is, originating only in the 16th and 17th centuries to buttress the novel claims of absolute monarchs.'[116] In that process there was a struggle between absolutism advocated by the monarchy and the alternative pre-sovereignty and more republican view that

> power was best distributed and shared rather than concentrated. So republicans advocated a mixed Constitution, involving a balance of powers between different political institutions and sections of the community.[117]

Bellamy puts forward the pre-sovereign mixed constitutional model as a useful model for the world of a multi-layered sovereign polity within Europe, and this provides fertile conceptual ground that could assist the Gibraltar question. The evolution of the concepts of sovereignty and nationalism have spurred on changes to the governance structure which effectively are similar to the republican, pre-sovereignty mixed constitutions

[112] Reference to this will be made in ch 6. See M Keating *Nations Against the State: The New Politics of Nationalism in Quebec, Catalunya and Scotland,* 2nd edn (Hampshire, Palgrave, 2001) (referred to as Keating 2001B) and also J Hopkins, *Devolution in Context: Regional, Federal and Devolved Government in the European Union* (London, Cavendish, 2002). For a study of the British process see the five-volume set entitled *State of the Nations* which examines the state of Scotland, Wales and Northern Ireland post devolution, namely, R Hazell (ed), *The State of the Nations: The First Year of Devolution in the UK* (Exeter, The Constitution Unit, Imprint Academic, 2000), and by the same publishers, A Trench (ed), *The State of the Nations 2001: The Second Year of Devolution in the UK* (2001); R Hazell (ed), *The State of the Nations 2003: The Third Year of Devolution in the UK* (2003); A Trench (ed), *Has Devolution made a Difference?: The State of the Nations 2004* (2004); A Trench (ed), *The Dynamics of Devolution: The State of the Nations 2005* (2005).

[113] eg among a wealth of writings on the subject is W Swenden, 'Is the European Union in Need of a Competence Catalogue? Insights from Comparative Federalism' (2004) 42 *Journal of Common Market Studies* Issue 2 371.

[114] Which are touched on below and expanded in the post-1986 context in ch 4.

[115] J Olsen, 'The Many Faces of Europeanisation' (2002) 40 *Journal of Common Market Studies* 923–25 and JJ Anderson, 'Europeanisation and the Transformation of the Democratic Polity 1945–2000' (2002) 40 *Journal of Common Market Studies* 793.

[116] Bellamy, in N Walker (ed), *Sovereignty in Transition* (Oxford, Hart Publishing, 2003) 169.

[117] ibid 170 and see also J Franklin, 'Sovereignty and the Mixed Constitution: Bodin and His Critics', in JH Burns and M Goldie (eds), *The Cambridge History of Political Thought 1450–1700* (Cambridge, CUP, 1991).

with a system of balance of powers. Certain aspects of the context have changed and the drivers of legitimacy, democracy and peoples have acquired greater pre-eminence but this emergence of layered, balanced, representative governance has as its roots the pre-sovereign philosophy explained by Bellamy.

The concept of sovereignty was seen in some quarters to have played too direct a role in the world wars of the 20th century and to a certain extent 'the idea entered a state of crisis' with predominantly only the recently decolonised States making allusion to it.[118] In the wider sense of international law, as Fassbender has indicated, since the United Nations was founded in 1945 'the traditional notion of sovereignty has experienced a profound modification and limitation.' That year in his view represents a 'deep dividing line in the history of sovereignty.'[119]

These trends were a response to political events and stress the relationship between societal and macro-political developments and how predominant the use of sovereignty as a tool for the promotion of ideals and objectives has been. They also illustrate the deep interrelationship between the concept of sovereignty and the development of more modern ideals of self-determination, democracy, legitimacy and sub-State nationalism. As Aalberts[120] has pointed out it can be argued that 'sovereign statehood [is] . . . a process-dependent institutional fact' and that it is a social reality depending on the interrelationship of subjective processes rather than existing independent of these as a 'brute fact.'[121]

As such it is dependent on and reactive to the people, institutions and entities who exercise it. Sovereignty as a concept is constantly adapting to accommodate socio-political changes. It responds to political pressures and demands for accountability, participation, transparency, ownership, democracy and efficiency among others. All of these different aspects reveal an intricate interplay of elements and themes. They also lay emphasis to the need to be aware and understand these developments so as to appreciate the changing backdrop within which sovereignty is exercised and the shifts that transfer power from one actor to another. In this sense too the interaction between law, society and politics once again comes through.

It is some time since Louis XIV is supposed to have remarked '*L'État c'est moi*.'[122] Nowadays endorsement and acquiescence by the populace is essential in securing participation and co-operation which forms the key

[118] Fassbender in N Walker (ed), *Sovereignty in Transition* (Oxford, Hart Publishing, 2003) 120.

[119] ibid 125.

[120] T Aalberts, 'The Future of Sovereignty in Multilevel Governance Europe—A Constructivist Reading' 2004 *Journal of Common Market Studies* vol 42 no 1 23–46, 23.

[121] JR Searle, *The Construction of Social Reality* (New York, Free Press, 1995).

[122] JM Cohen, *The Penguin Dictionary of Quotations* (Aylesbury, Penguin Books, 1980) 238.

part of the established social order. The people's demands for more participation were so as to have, as Marks has described, equality, influence, representation in the mode of governance and to consent to it.[123] Related to the above elements and a crucial driver in the sovereignty, governance or self-determination debate in Gibraltar as well as elsewhere has been the struggle for legitimacy caused by the awakening of a deeper European consciousness at grass roots level,[124] a greater political awareness, a desire to participate and to demand higher accountability and transparency.[125] Marks urges a balanced, holistic assessment of the value of theoretical principles as an engine for necessary change and of the ethical dimensions of democracy to enhance 'self-rule and political equality against a background of changing historical circumstances.'[126] This is undoubtedly the burning contemporary question for sub-State territories in which there is a search to find balance, workability and a more prominent role for both the sub-State Executive, the individual and populace as a collective.

There are a number of significant developments in the process of European integration that arise in the post-1985 period that will be covered in chapter four and stem from a search for legitimacy and democracy. The rise in democratisation, popular consciousness and evolution of the civilian population in Gibraltar is at the heart of much of the domestic governance debate in Gibraltar. It is a factor in the territorial sovereignty/decolonisation debate as well as in the aspirations at the level of European governance. In Gibraltar the legitimacy and democracy debate has three dimensions—the international status/self-determination level, the domestic level and the European level. The first focuses on the struggle to obtain decolonisation and a revised international status. The second is the attempt to achieve domestic self-government[127] from the administering power in

[123] S Marks, 'International Law and the Project for Cosmopolitan Democracy', in S Marks, *The Riddle of all Constitutions* (Oxford, OUP, 2000) 101–19.

[124] See ch 4 and also Catherine Richmond, 'Preserving the Identity Crisis: Autonomy, System and Sovereignty in European Law' (1997) Law and Philosophy 377–420 and also P Craig and G De Burca (eds), *The Evolution of EU Law* (Oxford, OUP, 1999) and MT Greven, 'Can the European Union Finally Become A Democracy?' In MT Greven and LW Pauly (eds), *Democracy Beyond the State—The European Dilemma and the Emerging Global Order* (New York, Rowman and Littlefield, 2000); WM Reisman, 'Sovereignty and Human Rights in Contemporary International Law' in GH Fox and BR Roth (eds), *Democratic Governance and International Law* (Cambridge, CUP, 2000).

[125] It led Weiler to home in on 1992 as a key 'transformation' moment in the European context when as a result of the concerns expressed in a number of nations the Maastricht Treaty was almost fatally undermined. In *Brunner* the court in Germany stated that a thesis that had previously not been taken into account was that a democratic European Union depended on the evolution of a European Demos (*Das Volk*) which took free decisions and without which it would no longer be legitimate or possible to pursue further radical measures of integration and transfer of sovereignty. JHH Weiler, 'European Neo-Constitutionalism: In Search of Foundations for the European Constitutional Order' 44 (1996) *Political Studies* 517–33.

[126] S Marks, *The Riddle of all Constitutions* (Oxford, OUP, 2000) 74.

[127] Internal self-determination.

the context of the assertion of a separate national identity.[128] The third concerns the search for a role and greater influence in Europe in the context of a still embryonic sense of European identity and a Europe-wide struggle for legitimacy.[129] It is in those three senses part of a search for identity and then an assertion of it. It is a search for decolonisation in accordance with self-determination, domestic self-governance, influence and real participation at European level. It is a search and assertion process that is fully compatible and consistent with the diffusionism and decentralisation described by MacCormick in the context of the re-evaluation of the concept of sovereignty. It is what Schlesinger has called the paradox of 'centralisation and fragmentation' which passes through States, raising questions of identity.[130]

As Marks has observed it is no longer possible for the State to be 'democracy's container . . . [because it] cannot flourish in nation-states unless efforts are made to democratise the processes of transnational and global decision-making as well.' To that should be added the rider that the same applies to the internal sub-State level and (in the case of Gibraltar and other non-independent territories) the colonial level. Without dealing with the 'low intensity democracy' of colonial and immediately neocolonial situations that assertion will not be complete. Of relevance to Gibraltar MacCormick notes the compatibility between nationalism and democracy, because

> democracy locates the ultimate source of legitimacy in a people as in principle a pre-political entity. National self-determination similarly alludes to the people as a pre-political body, and asserts each people's right to determine its own destiny through its own processes of decision-making.[131]

But even as sovereignty developed into a plural polycentric concept and greater emphasis was being placed on the people as the relevant constituent form Gibraltar was about to encounter a revitalised more absolutist interpretation represented by resurgent bilateralism.

There are useful parallels for Gibraltar in the internal sovereignty, political and legal dynamics of modern plurinational states. The unique feature

[128] External self-determination. Thus there is a link between the first and second dimensions. See T Musgrave, *Self-Determination and National Minorities* (Oxford, OUP, 2000) for a summary of these differences.

[129] Weiler n 111 above, 324–57 and also J Shaw *Law of the European Union*, 3rd edn (Basingstoke, Palgrave, 2000).

[130] P Schlesinger, 'Europeannesss—a New Cultural Battlefield?' in J Hutchinson and A Smith (eds), *Nationalism* (Oxford, Oxford Readers, 1994) 316–26 See also E Christodoulidis, 'Constitutional Irresolution: Law and the Framing of Civil Society' (2003) *European Law Journal* 401–32 and H Lindahl, 'Acquiring a Community: The Acquis and the Institution of European Legal Order' (2003) *European Law Journal* 433–50 and on the principles of democracy as drivers and the linkage between law and politics M Wilkinson, 'Civil Society and the Re-Imagination of European Constitutionalism' (2003) *European Law Journal* 451–72.

[131] MacCormick n 111 above, 125.

for Gibraltar is the nuance that a third-party State claims its territorial sovereignty.[132] That inevitably produces conflicts between the current holder of ultimate territorial sovereignty (Britain), those claiming ultimate and exercising practical sovereignty (Gibraltar and its people) and the third party sovereignty claimant (Spain). All lay claim to sovereignty. The dispute is a conflict of aspirations and national interests. In that sense too it is a conflict of nationalisms—the Spanish ambition to recover sovereignty it last held in the 18th century is a reflection of national ambition. The aspiration of Gibraltar and its people to achieve full self-government and a 'right to our land' is driven by ambitions towards national self-determination. This drive led to the constitutional reforms of the 1950–69 period and those of 2006. It also led to the greater use of referenda on sovereignty issues[133] and to the Preamble to Gibraltar's 1969 and 2006 constitutions.

As stated in the previous chapter that qualified and negatively expressed right to self-determination in the Preamble to both Constitutions states that:

> Gibraltar will remain part of Her Majesty's dominions unless and until an Act of Parliament otherwise provides, and furthermore that Her Majesty's Government will never enter into arrangements under which the people of Gibraltar would pass under the sovereignty of another State against their freely and democratically expressed wishes.[134]

It was inserted as a result of the continuing Spanish claim to sovereignty and the demands by the people of the territory that a clear safeguard be provided. While there may be concerns as to the legal enforceability of the Preamble,[135] its moral and political weight is considerable. That Preamble is testimony to the tussle of sovereignty that has formed the key dispute between the parties. The question over Gibraltar has very much become one of 'whose sovereignty?', with Britain holding it, Spain claiming it and the people of the territory counter-claiming, in accordance with a more modernist understanding of late sovereignty and sub-state constitutionalism

[132] Additionally it is not part of the same State either constitutionally or geographically.

[133] In 1967 and 2002.

[134] The Preamble is better described as a right of consent rather than one of full self-determination. The Preamble has two distinct parts. First, there is a qualification of the prerogative right of cession by subjecting any proposed breakage from Her Majesty's Dominions to a requirement that statute be passed for that purpose. Second it restricts the British Government's ability to negotiate over Gibraltar.

[135] Because of the formalistic views of the status of a Preamble to legislation: see later. It will be argued that it amounts to an effective transfer of the Crown's Prerogative and a legitimate expectation as well as an act of sovereignty. The Preamble would be consistent with the legal rights of a people vested with the right to self-determination—as the people of Gibraltar claim to be. There is thus a difference between legal enforceability of the *wording* of the Preamble, which is a matter of statutory construction under Gibraltar/English law, and *expectations* that are derived from it that may have greater flexibility of enforcement. Such legal rights as may be bestowed on the Gibraltar people under international law would also fall to be considered separately. See ch 6.

(which places emphasis on people as a source of power and legitimacy), that the civil society of Gibraltar is vested with such sovereignty. The Preamble is not only evidence of the dispute but also arguably provides a strong qualification on the Crown's prerogative and one to which the people of Gibraltar would claim to have an enforceable legitimate expectation.[136] It was also a positive move towards vesting the people with basic rights that endowed the Constitution with greater legitimacy even if the right was framed negatively. Additionally as has been pointed by Hooghe and Marks it can be said that the right to a veto is the ultimate instrument of sovereignty.[137] This argument was significantly bolstered by the addition in the 2006 Constitution of an express right of self-determination.[138]

Self-determination is an expression of political decision-making that has as its core a recognised principle of international law. It has an external and internal form. In a United Nations decolonising context having it is the condition precedent to the ability of a people to decide its future and is also the mechanics through which the decision is exercised. It has been taken to equate to independent statehood but this is inaccurate. The assumption that self determination or nationalism was necessarily equated with a desire for statehood or sovereignty was a view that has dominated constitutionalism but is not

> valid in a longer historical perspective and as the global political order changes the State is increasingly demystified and deconstructed opening up new avenues for national accommodation.[139]

While there is 'no logical reason why self-determination should be linked to statehood' Keating cautions that there is a 'sovereignty trap' and that the greatest 'obstacle to accommodating nations and nationalities . . . is the doctrine of sovereignty itself.'[140] But as he indicates it is possible to:

> de-link sovereignty from the State in an altogether more radical manner by formulating it as a right to self-determination. Here an entity whether it be a people or territorial unit may be sovereign where it has the right to determine its own future.[141]

This theme which recognises and puts the sub-State nation at the centre of solution-building will be expanded later in this work as it represents an

[136] See ch 6, pp 301–9. A similar principle, described as Executive Estoppel, has been outlined by Francis Bennion: [2007] PL, Spring, 1–12.

[137] G Marks, L Hooghe and K Blank, 'European Integration from the 1980s: State-Centric v Multiple Level Governance' (1996) 34 *Journal of Common Market Studies* 341.

[138] See ch 6, 306–8. Albeit that the language of the right was qualified in some respects and the UK stated that its view was that Gibraltar's right to self-determination was restricted in that it did not consider that Gibraltar could apply for independence.

[139] M Keating, *Plurinational Democracy, Stateless Nations in a Post-Sovereignty Era* (Oxford, OUP, 2001) 6.

[140] ibid 12.

[141] ibid 15.

element that forms an integral part of any reassessment which aims at breaking the traditional view of the sovereignty dispute of Gibraltar. An additional theme will be that independent statehood is not necessarily the option for decolonisation, which can accommodate the Gibraltar conundrum. In a context that applies the modern legal context of constitutionalism to the sub-State nation, an option that falls short of independence provides much greater flexibility and security.[142] This would be more attuned to modern forms of governance and the re-definition of sovereignty and nationalism. It also illustrates the linkage with self-determination and sub-State constitutionalism. Self-determination is about the ability to decide. This may be exercised in favour of independence but need not be. Equally nationalism is about emphasising national identity and separateness. In a modern sense both can be accommodated. Indeed it must be of the essence of constitutionalism that the civil society vested with that right of self-determination should have the freedom to opt for a non-separatist accommodation of its aspirations.

If the right to self-determination and its application is an 'elusive concept'[143] so too is its philosophical backdrop—the concept of sovereignty. The theme of sovereignty was heavily impacted upon by the principle of self-determination during the decolonisation era. Colonialism, which had been promoted during the 19th century, became completely unacceptable. The task moved from enlightening colonial people to freeing them by endowing them with independence irrespective of whether they had the capacity to govern at that stage or not. The respective Belgian, French, Dutch and Portuguese experience of decolonisation is illustrative of similar themes and a useful comparator to the decolonisation of British territories.[144] It led to new understandings of Statehood 'where State-building did not precede but followed recognition of Statehood . . . independence may precede ability for self-government.'[145] In essence decolonisation was a 'legal revolution instigated by moral considerations . . . [and] a typical instance of using the law as a vehicle for change.'[146]

Sovereignty is currently in evolution as much as other component elements such as nationalism, democracy or governance. How the meaning

[142] This would accommodate the United Nations, European and domestic contexts in that: (1) it is already envisaged by the United Nations Resolutions as the so-called 'fourth option' or can be structured as a form of free association; (2) it would not lead to a Treaty change and could be accommodated within Art 299(4) EC and; (3) it would accept Gibraltar's aspirations while insulating it from a hostile Spanish reaction.

[143] H Quane, 'The United Nations and the Evolving Right to Self-Determination' (1998) 47 ICLQ 537–72.

[144] M Shipway, *Decolonisation and its Impact—A Comparative Approach to the End of the Colonial Empires* (Oxford, Blackwell, 2008) and M Thomas, B Moore and LJ Butler, *Crises of Empire—Decolonisation and Europe's Imperial States 1918–75* (London, Hodder Education, 2008).

[145] Kreijen in Kreijen (ed) n 75 above, 100–01.

[146] ibid 102.

of each of these is changing has influenced the political and legal environment of the European Union. Sovereignty is now increasingly pooled as a voluntary act of Member States within the Union, but is still capable of raising a ferocious debate especially among those who more zealously wish to safeguard national sovereignty. Governance is no longer dominated solely by intergovernmental acts but now more sensitively recognises the necessary existence and inclusion of different levels of players in the governance structure. This multi-level governance goes hand in hand with the desire for greater legitimacy and a wish to embrace participatory democracy. As a consequence, the methodology and objective of nationalist movements has also been transformed. No longer the sole terrain of separatist nationalists (in particular within European Member States)[147] these have increasingly adopted a discourse which relies on plurinationalism and whose objective is no longer independence but accommodation within a larger entity—what has been described as stateless nationalism. All of these themes and concerns are present in the case of Gibraltar.

But while the concepts around them were changing the parties in the Gibraltar dispute still doggedly spoke the language of the 1960s and consistently failed to take into account these evolving concepts. The emphasis was still on the view, seen through a 1960s prism, of a territorial sovereignty claim versus traditional decolonisation. There was insufficient realisation that the methods of achieving greater self-government, democracy and changes in constitutional architecture were changing against the evolving conceptual backdrop of governance and sovereignty.[148] Nationalism was now less of a one-off event by which a nation-State was created and more of a process of pragmatic negotiation.[149] The ground rules were changing and the parties needed to find a way through the conundrum. The process of seeking Statehood[150] could be pursued in a different way or be abandoned altogether in recognition that in a practical sense aspirations could be achieved without the formal acquisition of Statehood.[151] As the meaning of sovereignty evolved, so too did the meaning of nationalism. Traditional separatist nationalism gave way to plurinationalism and an acceptance of federalism. Plurinationalism entails recognition of several nations within one State and of several actors within the same constitutional framework. This then within the governance sphere manifested itself as multi-level governance theory. Federalist and

[147] Britain and Spain are two good examples.

[148] For a useful set of articles reviewing this see N Walker (ed), *Sovereignty in Transition* (Oxford, Hart Publishing, 2003).

[149] W Norman, *Negotiating Nationalism; Nation-Building, Federalism, and Secession in the Multi-national State* (Oxford, OUP, 2006). Catalunya is a good example of this: see later.

[150] For an extensive examination of this question, see Crawford n 60 above.

[151] Hence the description that this is stateless nationalism: see also M Keating, 'Territorial Politics and the New Regionalism' in P Heywood, E Jones and M Rhodes, *Developments in West European Politics* (Hampshire, Palgrave, 2002) 201–15.

quasi-federalist models can provide viable options for resolving the self-government demands of stateless nations. The democratic- and governance deficit that Gibraltar faces was created because of the disconnection between old concepts and the new governance environment. That new environment which has driven a better accommodation of sub-State nations has, according to Kymlicka been driven by demographics,[152] rights consciousness,[153] democracy, desecuritisation[154] and liberal-democratic-consensus.[155] These should also be factors for application in Gibraltar's case even though it does not sit neatly within the categories identified by Kymlicka as most commonly arising examples of forms of multi-culturalism.[156]

At the heart of the evolving definitions in sovereignty and nationalism are two key points. The first is that inherent in the rise of multi-level governance there is an acknowledgement of voluntary power transference to the key players in the governance structure. The second is that stateless nationalism represents a realisation of the architecture of modern political interdependence. The first is about governance, the second about status. They both illustrate the thematic connection between status and governance as the normal consequences of the evolution of the concepts of sovereignty and nationalism. Both multi-level governance and stateless nationalism recognise the need to secure representation and influence and rate this above secession and independence. Both raise issues of how legitimacy and participatory democracy are best achieved and place the relevant people or sector of civil society at the centre of its consideration. Gibraltar provides an interesting case-study for the application of the evolved meaning of those concepts even though for years traditional views have had primacy. The evolving sovereignty and nationalism definitions and the trends towards multi-level participation in governance all create a backdrop that could more easily accommodate it within the modern European legal context.

GIBRALTAR—A NATION

As Smith has pointed out, there are four main approaches to the analysis of questions of nationalism, namely primordialism, perennialism, modernism

[152] The fact that minority groups have endured and not disappeared.

[153] The rise of human rights issues and greater awareness of the same.

[154] Issues that relate to global or regional geo-political security.

[155] Meaning that it is assisted if there is broad approval for any proposed form of constitutional accommodation. See W Kymlicka, 'The Global Diffusion of Multiculturalism' in S Tierney (ed), *Accommodating Cultural Diversity* (Aldershot, Ashgate, 2007) 25–29, and see also W Kymlicka, *Multicultural Odysseys—Navigating the New International Politics of Diversity* (Oxford, OUP, 2007).

[156] Kymlicka in Tierney (ed) n 155 above, 19–21.

and ethno-symbolism.[157] In summary, primordialists see 'kinship, ethnicity and the genetic bases of human kinship' as the keys to explaining nations and nationalism.[158] Perennialists contend that nations, although not part of a natural order, have always existed and have been regular actors in the global order.[159] Modernists argue that nations are in essence novel political constructs fuelled by the idea that sovereignty was vested in peoples and driven by social, cultural and political elites who took advantage of economic and industrial shifts. But by seeing nationalism as only a modern phenomenon the modernist analysis has been criticised for failing 'to come to grips with cultural identity (and) . . . ideology.'[160] Leading advocates of modernism such as Gellner, Hobsbawm and Benedict Anderson have dominated the recent analytical approach to nationalism. For Anderson 'the imagined political community, imagined as sovereign, finite and horizontal'[161] was spurred on by technological progress and advances in communications that allowed people to 'imagine the nation.'[162] The modernist agenda does not allow a proper 'understanding of the popular roots and widespread appeal of nationalism' or give weight to pre-existing cultural or ethnic features.

As such Smith puts forward his own preferred ethno-symbolic approach. This maintains that

> what gives nationalism its power are the myths, memories, traditions and symbols of ethnic heritages and the ways in which a popular living past has been and can be rediscovered and reinterpreted by modern nationalist intelligentsias. It is from these elements of myth, memory, symbols and tradition that modern national identities are reconstituted in each generation, as the nation becomes more inclusive and as its members cope with new challenges.[163]

This allows proper weight to be given to historical and conflictive territorial claims. Ethno-symbolism assesses the historical memories and traditions of the people forming part of the nation and applies these. It also emphasises the connection between an 'ethnie', meaning a collective grouping with 'myths of common ancestry, shared historical and one or more common elements of culture including an association with a homeland and some degree of solidarity'[164] and modern nations. Even in the

[157] A Smith, *Myth and the Memories of Nation* (Oxford, OUP, 1999) 3.

[158] ibid 4. Smith talks of three main types of primordialism: popular (which sees nations as elements of nature); socio-biological (which argues that nations are extensions of kinship units) and cultural (which lends primacy to key features of human linkage such as custom, religion and territory).

[159] In turn Smith sets out distinctions between two types of perennialism that he terms continuous and recurrent, 5–6.

[160] ibid 7.

[161] ibid 8.

[162] ibid.

[163] ibid 9.

[164] ibid 13.

case of former colonies with a short record as new nation-states it is necessary to 'forge a cultural unity and identity of myth, symbol, value and memory that can match those of nations built on pre-existing ethnic ties if they are to survive and flourish as nations.'[165] In a colonial situation it is possible for colonist and immigrant elements to merge to 'create a plural or polyethnic immigration nation and culture.'[166]

Generally, the more flexible accommodation of a civic rather than an ethnic model of nation could result in a combination of 'linguistic-cultural with territorial aspects of the nation and generate an inclusive, assimilative cultural nationalism' which could facilitate the construction of 'more polyethnic nations held together by cultural, territorial, economic and legal bonds . . . with adequate safeguards for ethnic minorities.'[167]

As Hobsbawm[168] has indicated, a dense fog surrounds questions of national consciousness, especially before modern nationalism became a political force. That was not assisted by the casual interchange of phraseology. As such in the same way that claims based on self-determination have been regularly but wrongly equated with a search for independence for many years the words State and nation were used as if they were synonymous even though plainly they represented quite different concepts. What Hobsbawm has described as the 'quadilateral' State–People–Nation–Government[169] really only converged in select few cases. This notwithstanding, the classic view that nationalism that fuelled the state-building process in many localities is 'a political principle which holds that the political and the national unit should be congruent.'[170] However, as Kymlicka has observed 'there is nothing "natural" about such nation-states.'[171] Indeed, Connor has pointed out that, in a 1971 survey of 132 countries generally considered to be States, only 12 could 'justifiably' be described as nation-states. In the majority of countries the predominant nation accounted for anything between 50–90 per cent of the population. In nearly 30 per cent of those 132 countries the largest nation accounted for less than 50 per cent of the population.[172] Those statistics reveal the lack of real convergence between nation and state and the reality that in few States this converges with singular purity. The greater socio-political reality is that most States have within them significant minorities and in some several nations all cohabiting within the same space. Indeed as has been

[165] ibid.

[166] ibid 18.

[167] ibid 201.

[168] E Hobsbawm, *Nations and Nationalism Since 1780—Programme, Myth, Reality*, 2nd edn (Cambridge, CUP, 1992) 79.

[169] ibid 188–89.

[170] E Gellner, *Nations and Nationalism* (New York, Cornell University Press, 1983) 1.

[171] Kymlicka n 155 above, 18.

[172] W Connor, 'A Nation is a Nation, is a State, is an Ethnic Group . . .' in J Hutchinson and A Smith (eds), *Nationalism* (Oxford, OUP, 1994) 39.

noted the only element that provided 'internal cohesion' to some African States formed in the age of decolonisation was the 'decades of colonial administration.'[173]

The predominance of the concepts of nation and nationalism is a relatively recent development having particularly surged forward since the late 19th century.[174] It acquired some prominence during the 18th century, linked to the concept of democracy and the idea that people were the *locus* of sovereignty. This then gathered momentum after the revolutions throughout Europe during the 19th century. Linked to political mobilisation and enfranchisement it became identified as 'the body of citizens whose collective sovereignty constituted them a State which was their political expression.'[175] Until the late 19th century the more common definitions of nation relied on ethnic or geographical characteristics rather than on any linkage with political status or notions of independence.[176] In the era of decolonisation emerging States adopted colonial boundaries that were not based on ethnic divides. They were simply an acceptance of imperially imposed ring-fencing.

Nationalism during the 19th century was essentially a unifying and nation-building force.[177] In many ways this ideologically sat well with imperial and conservative national unifying policies. In contrast nationalism during the late-20th century in the post-war period of decolonisation was anti-imperial and not about unification but about deconstruction of colonial dynastic regimes into smaller political units. In many ways such thinking sat well with centre-left ideologies that promoted democracy, emancipation, universal enfranchisement and egalitarianism as central political goals.

In either case, as has been stated in the modernist analysis, it is 'nationalism which engenders nations and not the other way round.'[178] Hence the statement by D'Azeglio during the first meeting of the Italian Parliament that 'we have made Italy, now we must make Italians.'[179] In essence the driving force for nation-building processes in the late 19th and 20th centuries have been nationalisms of two distinct kinds—first, a unifying force, and second, an anti-imperial decolonising one. These generalisations do not of course cover the whole range of situations encapsulating nation-building motivations. In particular they do not accurately describe the emergence of various nation-States in Eastern Europe during the late 20th century or the aspirations of nations within established States—such as

[173] Hobsbawm n 168 above, 67.
[174] Hobsbawm n 168 above, 14–18.
[175] ibid 19.
[176] ibid 18.
[177] ibid 33.
[178] Gellner n 170 above, 55.
[179] Cited in Hobsbawm n 168 above, 44.

may relate to Basque or Scottish nationalism. In any event the concept of nation has been promoted by political forces of different kinds, and generally by educated elites that have sought to identify and collect a series of features and then transmit these to the populace with a message that this constitutes the canvas of their existence as a cohesive territorial ethnic or political unit. In transmitting these ideas of 'imagined communities'[180] or of 'invented traditions'[181] the central realisation to draw from that is the ability of these political forces to construct a sense of nationhood on specific features and the role of education, symbolism and communication in that process. Indeed the acceptance that 'nation-formation is a process not an occurrence'[182] is important. The point at which it can be said that a nation is formed is uncertain as it depends on the absorption and acceptance of the emotional, psychological and emotional mutuality of a common and distinct identity by a populace which in itself is a less than tangible event. But it is that uncertain exercise which is what must be sought, because too often it is the views of intellectual elites that are used as an analytical basis for discerning the feeling of nationhood of a populace. Clearly using this as a barometer can heavily influence the results and the proper collation of indicators of mass awareness and collective feeling are more reliant if these can be obtained.

Nevertheless an examination of the process itself in each case should identify distinct results. Smith has highlighted that this would include: a transition from a relatively passive to an active political community; a movement to assert a clearly demarcated 'homeland'; economic control over resources; the mobilisation of citizens; the endowment of these with common rights; and the education, celebration and placement of people as the central *locus* of political and moralistic concern.[183] Sometimes in that process it is easier for people to understand things in the negative—to appreciate 'what they are not before they know what they are'.[184] Indeed, as has been stated 'like many another liberated people, Germany was more easily defined by what it was against than in any other way.'[185]

The environment of nationalism is one that focuses on individual features of the community to produce 'politically induced cultural change'.[186] What underpins nations or nationalism must also respond to a rapidly moving evaluation of the threshold for political or legal principles.

[180] B Anderson, *Imagined Communities: Reflections on the Origins and Spread of Nationalism* (London, Verso, 1983).

[181] E Hobsbawm, 'The Nation as Invented Tradition' in Hutchinson and Smith (eds) n 172 above, 76–78.

[182] Connor in Hutchinson and Smith (eds) n 172 above, 59.

[183] A Smith, 'The Origins of Nations' in Hutchinson and Smith (eds) n 172 above, 154.

[184] Connor in Hutchinson and Smith (eds) n 172 above, 45.

[185] Hobsbawm in Hutchinson and Smith (eds) n 172 above, 82.

[186] P Brass, 'Elite Competition and Nation Formation' in Hutchinson and Smith (eds) n 172 above, 87.

Indeed, self-determination was very much linked to economic viability when initially linked to the aspiration of nations to seek their separate status or governance and it is only in the post-war period 'and even more since decolonisation that we have made way in the community of nations for entities like Dominica or the Maldives or Andorra.'[187] In fact, the United Nations' declaration on colonial peoples expressly states that economic inadequacy or lack of preparedness cannot 'serve as a pretext for delaying independence'.[188]

There have been a number of attempts to find a definition of nation. In his often quoted definition Stalin[189] once remarked that a nation is 'a historically constituted, stable community of people, formed on the basis of a common language, territory, economic life and psychological make-up in the form of a common culture.' The presence of all six elements was, according to Stalin, crucial in the determination. However, Hobsbawm has pointed to the failure of objective definitions, because exceptions always appear and because in their application the criteria have lead to diverse and ambiguous results.[190] Renan,[191] who already in 1882 was forecasting a European confederation, in his attempt at defining the important elements, identified two distinct and important features. The first was the continuing consent of the populace to live and exist together—the most basic and raw aspect of what now would be called legitimacy. The second is a history of shared suffering, because Renan recognised the binding effect of national sorrow. For him, the spirituality inherent in the concept of nation was crucial. The combination he highlighted was the possession of 'a rich legacy of remembrances' and the 'actual consent, the desire to live together, the will to continue to value the heritage which all hold in common.'[192] The common suffering was to produce a body of 'grand solidarity constituted by the sentiment of sacrifices which one has made and those that one is disposed to make again.'[193]

In a rather more functional definition, Gellner has stated that 'nationalism invents nations where they do not exist.'[194] This last statement, which places emphasis on the evolution of nations as a consequence of economic and industrial diversification acknowledges the role of economic prosperity in helping to develop a stable, consolidated population. To this last extent, this point of the importance of economics to political self-

[187] Hobsbawm n 168 above, 32.

[188] GA Res 1514 (XV) of 14 December 1960, para 2.

[189] J Stalin, 'The Nation' in 'Marxism and the Natural Question' in B Franklin (ed), *The Essential Stalin: Major Theoretical Writings 1905–52* (London, Croom Helm, 1973) 57–61.

[190] Hobsbawm n 168 above, 5–6.

[191] E Renan, '*Qu'est-ce qu'une nation?*' in Hutchinson and Smith (eds) n 172 above, 17–18.

[192] ibid 17.

[193] ibid.

[194] For an exposition of his views see Gellner n 170 above.

sufficiency is relevant to Gibraltar.[195] Industrialisation and advances in science and technology, improved communications, higher standards of living, education, access to external markets and generated wealth were all important factors. These also acted as a driver for nationalism and colonialism. Equally, as Gellner observes, there is a link between nationalism and decolonisation, in that empires were established by 'nations increasingly oriented towards industry and trade not by a militaristic machine.'[196] Similarly, the 'diffusion of this technological and economic might'[197] led to the loss of empire.

But if there are many more nations than States, what makes nationalism in a particular place lead to the construction of a nation? And what then makes an aspirational nation a viable one? These questions rely on the emergence and combination of sufficient raw materials of communication, education, symbolism, desire, conflict and culture. Customarily moulded by political actors, some nations will succeed in establishing themselves as a separate State as a result, and others will wither, disappear or find a peaceful accommodation within an existing or new State. In that sense 'nationalism . . . sometimes takes pre-existing cultures and turns them into nations, sometimes invents them.'[198] Understanding that this is the way many nation-building processes are facilitated does not invalidate the claim it merely is a recognition of the factors that combine to foster it. A critical analysis is still required to identify any underlying features that strengthen the claim to be a nation.

At its heart the emotional and psychological dimension to the process of nation-building cannot be under-estimated as 'a nation is a community of sentiment.'[199] As a psychological linkage it is necessarily 'shadowy and elusive'.[200] But what is commonly the case is that 'nationalist elites [are] only able to mobilise support from peasants, merchants, artisans or factory-workers because many persons in these various classes were disenchanted with political and social conditions.'[201] For modernists the evolution of nations is usually an *ex post facto* exercise.[202] Even so there is recognition of the need for patriotism as a 'civic religion'[203] and that if the 'State did not succeed in converting its citizens to the new religion before

[195] See below: the economy grew and stabilised first in the 19th century and thereafter in the 20th century, especially in the post-1945 period.
[196] Gellner n 170 above, 42.
[197] ibid 43.
[198] ibid 49.
[199] M Weber, 'The Nation' in Hutchinson and Smith (eds) n 172 above, 25.
[200] Connor in Hutchinson and Smith (eds) n 172 above, 36.
[201] H Seton-Watson, 'Old and New Nations' in Hutchinson and Smith (eds) n 172 above, 136.
[202] E Hobsbawm, *Nations and Nationalism Since 1780—Programme, Myth, Reality*, 2nd edn (Cambridge, CUP, 1992) 71.
[203] ibid 85.

they listened to rival evangelists it might well be lost'.[204] The ease with which there could be mass mobilisation was not only important to secure legitimacy of the new nations but also, in practice, to forge an identification with a new system, nation or State. By becoming a 'people' it created a sense of community and collectivity whether it was an 'imagined' one or not.

Smith's definition of a nation is a 'named human population sharing an historic territory, common myths and historical memories, a mass, public culture, a common economy and common legal rights and duties for all members.'[205] Nationalism itself is for him an 'ideological movement for attaining and maintaining autonomy, unity and identity for a human population deemed by some of its members to constitute an actual or potential nation.'[206] The political reality is that the contextual drivers spurning movements advocating nationalist objectives are 'always with us'[207] because the presence of a combination of socio-economic, political, geographic, ethnic and cultural factors will lead to the emergence of such movements.

In Gibraltar's case the elements that have combined to produce that civic nationalism and the claim that Gibraltar is a nation fall under four broad headings—socio-economic issues; conflict; physical location-based features; and historical-cultural matters. Of these, the first two headings encompass the main drivers for nationalism with the latter two covering an array of components that add ingredients to the fertile ground produced by the socio-economic and political canvas developed as a result of the main features. Under each of those there are a number of sub-elements and manifestations which seen holistically have produced the overall canvas for the consideration of whether the people of Gibraltar are indeed a nation.

Socio-economic Issues

There are four principal drivers under this heading—the growth of the population, educational progress, economic success and language and communication issues. The production of a larger highly educated population fuelled by economic success provided fertile ground for political agitation for civil rights.

[204] ibid.
[205] A Smith, *Myth and the Memories of Nation* (Oxford, OUP, 1999) 11.
[206] ibid 256.
[207] ibid 259.

Population

In the context of self-determination Jennings has remarked 'the people cannot decide until someone decides who are the people.'[208] There has been considerable discussion about the applicability of that definition. There is no doubt though that calls reliant on popular sovereignty have come thick and fast in both the Commonwealth context[209] and in the sub-State arena.[210] The difficulty in defining 'people', especially when there is a territorial dispute, is compounded in the colonial context, because on occasion there has been some dispute as to the application of the principle of self-determination in cases where there is an allegation that the principle of territorial integrity is at risk.[211] As pointed out this is precisely Spain's contention. Britain, on the other hand, has maintained the long-standing position that Gibraltar's people evolved with a separate and distinct identity and 'for longer than many immigrant communities in the New World.'[212]

In the foreword to Howes' book in 1951 the Governor of Gibraltar, Sir Kenneth Anderson described the Gibraltarian as being a people with 'mixed stock who represent a fusion of very many races' having 'naturally developed characteristics of (their) own derived from his forebears and it is not too much to say that the Gibraltarian race is unique.'[213] In its 1964 paper on the future of Gibraltar the Legislative Council had observed:

> [T]he people of Gibraltar are British but this does not mean they are English: they live very near Spain, but this does not mean they are Spanish. They are a unique community which has a character of its own and which seeks to continue to live as such.[214]

In 1965 Franco set out his position in trenchant terms, saying that Gibraltarians were 'Spanish almost in their entirety, even though they benefit from English citizenship, and the rest [of the population are] Jews and foreigners who can live under one flag or another.'[215] In the democratic

[208] I Jennings, *The Approach to Self-Government* (Cambridge, CUP, 1956) 55–56.

[209] For Australia, Canada and New Zealand see P Oliver n 98 above.

[210] eg, S Tierney, '"We the Peoples": Constituent Power and Constitutionalism in Plurinational States' in M Loughlin and N Walker (eds), *The Paradox of Constitutionalism, Constituent Power and Constitutional Form* (Oxford, OUP, 2007) 229–46.

[211] See GA Res 1514 (XV).

[212] *Gibraltar, Recent Differences with Spain*, Misc No 12 (Cmnd 2632, 1965) 11, and also British Information Service, Central Office of Information, *Gibraltar—The Facts* (London, Fox Printing Press, 1966) (a pamphlet issued by the UK Government).

[213] K Anderson, 'Foreword to the 1950 edition', reprinted in Howes, *The Gibraltarian—The Origin and Evolution of the People of Gibraltar*, 3rd edn (Gibraltar, Medsun, 1991) iii.

[214] *The Future of Gibraltar*, Legislative Council, Gibraltar, May 1964.

[215] *'Los llanitos son espanoles en su casi totalidad, aunque se aprovechen de la ciudadania inglesa, y el resto, judios y extranjeros, que lo mismo pueden vivir bajo una bandera que bajo otra'*, *Documentos sobre Gibraltar presentados a las Cortes Espanolas por el Ministerio de Asuntos Exteriores* (Madrid, 1965), cited in EG Archer, *Gibraltar, Identity and Empire* (London, Routledge, 2006) 1.

Spain more enlightened views have also been expressed. In March 1978 the Spanish foreign minister, Marcelino Oreja Aguirre, in an interview with a Gibraltar newspaper recognised that the Gibraltarian community was 'a reality that cannot be ignored. We have great respect and affection for the Gibraltarian population and it is with this respect for the *Gibraltarian identity* that it will be possible to achieve common progress towards certain objectives.'[216] (emphasis added) Other similar statements have also been made more recently. These have been balanced against rather more equivocal statements and a policy of seeking to persuade Britain to negotiate over the territory without adhering to the wishes of the population. The statements emanating from Spanish officials or politicians that have shown respect for the existence of Gibraltarians have fallen short of recognising that Gibraltarians constitute a nation or that their wishes should be adhered to. It is that disconnection between people and territory that lies at the heart of the conundrum. Around the same time Manuel Fraga, leader of the conservative *Alianza Popular*[217] informed the House of Commons, Foreign Affairs Committee that Gibraltarians 'cannot dispose of a territory which is not theirs.'[218] Sir Joshua Hassan observed in a submission to the Commons Foreign Affairs Committee in 1981 that among the basic political realities evident to any visitor to Gibraltar were 'the separate identity of the people of Gibraltar, small in number but clearly neither English nor Spanish [and] . . . the passionate attachment which the Gibraltarians feel for Gibraltar.'[219]

The growth of the population has already been traced in chapter one. Gibraltar is a Southern European British territory with a predominantly Latin Mediterranean population.[220] Cassese has stated that the Gibraltar and the Falklands issues have been treated similarly by the United Nations because both populations are essentially of 'colonial stock'.[221] That assertion is simply sociologically incorrect, as the majority of Gibraltar's population is not derived from British stock—quite the contrary is the case.[222] As far back as 1777 the register of inhabitants revealed that no more than one-sixth of the civilian population was of British extraction.[223] The large amount of immigration from Genoa, Malta and North Africa subsequently would dilute that significantly to the extent that Howes notes that 'never

216 *Panorama*, 6 March 1978, cited in Foreign Affairs Committee Report 1981, 85.

217 Predecessor of the *Partido Popular*. Mr Fraga had been Spanish Ambassador in London.

218 FAC Report 1980–81, 119.

219 ibid 87. He added that the intensification of those feelings were due to Spain.

220 At the last census the population was about 32,000, of which about 24,000 are Gibraltarians as defined by statute: see below and *Census 2001* (Gibraltar, Gibraltar Government Publications Office, 2002).

221 A Cassese, *Self Determination of Peoples—A Legal Appraisal* (Cambridge, CUP, 1995) 87.

222 Howes n 213 above, and also L Sawchuk and S Burke, 'Through the Looking Glass: An Anthropological Reflection on the Roots of the Gibraltarian People', vol 1 (Gibraltar, *Memoirs Gibcemed*, 1997).

223 Howes n 213 above, 12–13.

again did the British reach such a proportion.'[224] By the 1844 census persons from 'British Isles stock' formed less than 10 per cent of the civilian population[225] and had fallen to less than five per cent by 1891.[226] The 1947 Colonial Annual Report on Gibraltar shows that the British born element of the civilian population had grown to about 10 per cent again. In a more recent assessment based on the ethnic origins of family names of Gibraltarians Archer concludes that the British element was understated by Howes and that in his view around 27 per cent of family names reflect British ancestry with other major ancestral ethnic groups being Spanish (24 per cent), Italian (19 per cent), Portuguese (11 per cent) and Maltese (8 per cent).[227] Whatever the fine proportions the roots of the Gibraltarian people are diverse, cosmopolitan and a result of a few centuries of migration. Predominantly southern Mediterranean there are also traces of Anglo-Saxon or even North African lineage. While the population is largely Catholic[228] there are also small but prominent Anglican, Jewish, Hindu and Moslem communities.

The 'Gibraltarian' is a product of this mix of cultures and nationalities over the last three centuries. The residue of the inhabitants that remained after the British conquest combined with those elements of the Garrison or British civilians that made Gibraltar their home, the flood of immigrants from Genoa, Malta, North Africa or Portugal and the injection of some residents from adjoining Spanish towns as a result of marriage between the communities. According to the British Government in 1965 'this community has now existed in Gibraltar for over 250 years and since 1830 when a Charter of Justice was proclaimed has had legal recognition.'[229] The Gibraltarian is a culturally and ethnically diverse mediterranean people.[230] Its characteristics as a micro-community in some senses help rather than hinder the development of nationhood. As Frendo has said about Malta 'the smaller a nation is, the more its territory has the characteristics of a natal soil. Smallness retains integrity, facilitates human contact and is more likely to have natural boundaries.'[231]

In terms of the accepted evolution of a separate identity this was recognised in law in an implicit way by the first references to 'natives' of

[224] ibid 13.

[225] ibid 121.

[226] From a total of 'other British' inhabitants of in excess of 10% made up of British subjects from other parts of the Dominions, ibid 136.

[227] Archer n 215 above, 3.

[228] 80%, *Abstract of Statistics*, Gibraltar, Government of Gibraltar, 2006.

[229] *Gibraltar—Recent Differences with Spain*, Misc No 12 (Cmnd 2632, 1965) 3.

[230] L Sawchuk and S Burke, 'Through the Looking Glass: An Anthropological Reflection on the Roots of the Gibraltarian People', vol 1 (Gibraltar, *Memoirs Gibcemed*, 1997); Howes n 213 above.

[231] H Frendo, 'National Identity' in H Frendo and O Friggeri (ed), *Malta—Culture and Identity* (Malta, Grima Printing, 1994) 1.

Gibraltar in the Census of 1777.[232] By the end of the 19th century the Strangers Ordinance 1889 prescribed that only native residents and persons exempted under the Aliens Order Extension (Gibraltar) Order 1900 could enter Gibraltar without a permit and reside in the colony.[233] The legislation was principally aimed at non-British persons but it also provided that most British subjects who were not 'native' to Gibraltar apply for permits of residence. It has been said that this amounted to one of the first official recognitions in legislation that the identity of the Gibraltarian population was distinct from British subjects not born in Gibraltar.[234] One of the first references to 'Gibraltarians' as a specific named classification appears to have been made in a 1955 amendment to the 1948 Aliens Order in Council. In 1962 the Legislative Council passed the Gibraltarian Status Ordinance 'to define and regulate Gibraltarian status'. The Act prescribed the establishment of a Register of Gibraltarians[235] and provided for criteria that, if satisfied, entitled a person to be registered as a Gibraltarian.[236] In essence British nationals born in Gibraltar on or before 1925, descendants and spouses of these persons and other persons who fulfil certain criteria and are, on application, granted such application are entitled to be so registered.[237] Gibraltarians have the right to reside in Gibraltar without a permit.[238] This law was important in providing legal definition to the concept of a separate people and is especially relevant in the context of the United Nations impetus on decolonisation as this requires a palpable exercise of self-determination by the people of a territory. It was the yardstick of voting entitlement to the 1967 referendum on sovereignty.[239] Two other instances relating to the categorisation of the people of Gibraltar are relevant. The first is that after being excluded from the initial definition of British citizens under the British Nationality Act 1981 a campaign with large support in the House of Lords secured an amendment that allowed registration of Gibraltarians as British citizens.[240] The second is that by the Treaty of Accession to the EC Gibraltarians were considered UK nationals for EC purposes.[241]

[232] L Sawchuk, *Deadly Visitations in Dark Time—A Social History of Gibraltar* (Gibraltar, Gibraltar Government Heritage Division, 2001); Howes n 213 above.

[233] See also the Aliens Order 1885.

[234] J Garcia, *Gibraltar, The Making of a People—The Modern Political History of Gibraltar and its People* (Gibraltar, Medsun Publications, 1994) 9.

[235] Though this had actually been created in 1955. See also Immigrants and Aliens (Amendment) Ordinance 1955.

[236] By s 4 a 'Gibraltarian' is a person who is registered on the Register of Gibraltarians.

[237] Gibraltarian Status Act 1962 s 5.

[238] s 20 ibid.

[239] See below.

[240] Now overtaken by events because of the effect of the Overseas Territories Act 2002. There was a major political campaign in the early 1980s to achieve that because of the emotional attachment of people to Britain.

[241] See ch 2.

The evacuation of the population at the start of the Second World War threatened the survival of a cohesive people, with families divided to Britain, Northern Ireland, Morocco, Madeira or Jamaica. The subsequent efforts to repatriate the civil population has been well documented elsewhere.[242] The successful repatriation allowed for the consolidation and further development of the population. It also injected human resources for the economic rebuilding of post-war Gibraltar and re-energised the political aspirations of the civil population. These were then further fuelled by economic development and the growth of the civilian population itself.

Language

The position of language as a cultural driver and a political tool has been recognised in other countries.[243] Gibraltarians are almost all bilingual.[244] Ironically there has been a rise in the social and domestic use of English in the last 20 years notwithstanding the opening of the frontier.[245]

During the eighteenth century Spanish, Genoese, Italian and Hebrew were largely the languages of the civilian population. Maltese immigration in the 19th century added that semitic language. The military and small group of British officials and settlers spoke English and this had pride of place as the official language and that of the courts. As happened in Malta there was a process of Anglicisation and a real impetus to impose English as the dominant language.[246] This put 'pressures on the native Gibraltarians to demonstrate their loyalty and to learn English when engaged in commerce or in any dealings with officialdom . . . essential for aspiring members of the community.'[247] The introduction of English through the educational system also fostered the greater assimilation of the language.

The local patois '*yanito*',[248] which is a fusion of English and Spanish with a range of words from other linguistic sources such as Hebrew or Genoese is a linguistic amalgam which reflects the cosmopolitan cultural influences.[249]

[242] TJ Finlayson, *The Fortress Came First—The Story of the Civilian Population of Gibraltar During the Second World War* (Grendon, Gibraltar Books, 1991).

[243] H Frendo, *Party Politics in a Fortress Colony: The Maltese Experience* (Malta, Midsea Publications, 1991) and S Tierney (ed), *Accommodating Cultural Diversity* (Dartmouth, Ashgate, 2007).

[244] English and Spanish.

[245] Probably because of the advent of satellite television and telecommunications. For some comparison in Catalunya of the role and significance of language see E Roller, 'The 1997 *Llei del Catala*: A Pandora's Box in Catalunya' (2001) 11 *Regional and Federal Studies* 39.

[246] Frendo n 243 above.

[247] Archer n 215 above, 108.

[248] Also spelt '*llanito*'.

[249] M Cavilla, *Diccionario Yanito* (Gibraltar, Medsun Publications, 1990).

The most familiar element of *yanito* is the use of both English and Spanish-sourced words in the construction of individual sentences. This 'code-switching' has been said to be 'related to social class, to linguistic competence and to national identity.'[250] It has offered a linguistic refuge when trying to grapple rather ambivalently in seeking to assert a separate identity that was neither English nor Spanish. Simultaneous code-switching made a very clear symbolic manifestation of difference. As Archer highlights:

> [W]ithout doubt, language is important to Gibraltarians and to the debate about identity. It takes them back to their beginnings in the early eighteenth centuries . . . many in Gibraltar make the more plausible assertion that the founding layer of the population was Genoese. Evidence of ligurian Italian has long gone and in line with the language of commerce and social life in the Strait, a form of Spanish held sway in its place. English gained ground over time encouraged, expected or imposed by the British. A bilingual community has resulted with its own accent in both languages and with Yanito astride the two, for some Gibraltarians at least. In significant ways English now dominates . . . overall the place of language in society . . . reinforces the Gibraltarians' perception of themselves as separate and distinct.[251]

Economic Viability—The Particular Challenge of Small Territories

Economic self-sufficiency facilitates political aspirations by giving a people the freedom, latitude of action and knowledge that consequences from political actions will have some economic insulation. Before turning to the micro Gibraltar picture it is important to consider the economic context and challenges for small States.

There are several socio-economic issues that are common to all overseas territories. They are all small territories with small populations. Their combined population does not exceed 250,000 people. They are the remnants of an empire that stretched across continents and has now dwindled significantly. The English language and aspects of a shared Commonwealth history bind these together and are some of the features that are also common to most of the other 54 independent countries of the Commonwealth. Their economies tend to be service-led, with strong finance sectors and tourism being common to the majority of Caribbean territories, Bermuda and Gibraltar.[252]

In 1998 a joint task force was established between the Commonwealth and the World Bank to assess the particular challenges faced by small

[250] Archer n 215 above, 111 citing M Moyer, 'Analysis of Code-Switching in Gibraltar', PhD thesis (University of Barcelona, 1992).

[251] Archer n 215 above, 114.

[252] Each territory will have other unique sectors individual to it and suited to its physical characteristics.

States and to make recommendations on how the predominantly economic, social, infrastructural and geographic issues could be addressed. This led to Commonwealth Heads of Government commissioning a report on small States. The report that emerged was aimed at highlighting the strains small States suffer to maintain economic self-sufficiency.[253] In its conclusions the Report uses a benchmark of populations of under one and a half million as its criteria of definition of a small State.[254] The range of countries caught by this is so diverse and numerous that special consideration should be given to using the additional category of population of under one hundred thousand and describing these as 'micro states'.

If population is used as a benchmark then it is clear that 30 out of the 54 member States of the Commonwealth can be classified as small States. But the concerns of the Bahamas are different to those of Malta, even though they have similar populations. By the same token the needs of a country near a population mark of one million is vastly different to Tuvalu or Niue in the Pacific with a few thousand islanders making up its population.[255] It is always difficult to define small States. Usually an attempt to do so is based on the premise that the problems of small States are shared. This is sometimes so. But it is equally inadvisable to generalise. Not all small States are poor, or lack human or technical resources. Not all of them share the same priorities and goals. Even though general sweeping yardsticks are not helpful in discerning the true subdivisions it is possible to categorise states by similar geographic, social, economic, political characteristics or shared needs and priorities. The report makes the point that

> [e]ach small state is unique, and needs to address its development prospects in the context of its own cultural, historical and social realities. There are also differences between regions. But most states share a number of common characteristics.[256]

[253] *Small States: Meeting Challenges in the Global Economy—Report of the Commonwealth Secretariat/ World Bank Joint Task Force on Small States* (London, Commonwealth Secretariat, April 2000) ('the Small States Report').

[254] But accepts that the population figure is arbitrary and cites the example that a previous study had classified small nations using an upper limit of ten million people which would mean that 134 countries would be termed as small today (or more than 70% of the countries of the world). See S Kuznets, 'Economic Growth of Small Nations' in EAG Robinson (ed), *Economic Consequences of the Size of Nations: Proceedings of a Conference Held by the International Economic Association* (London, Macmillan, 1960). On the other hand other Commonwealth organisations use lower benchmarks. So for example the Commonwealth Parliamentary Association uses a yardstick of populations of under 400,000 to classify territories as 'small countries' for the purposes of its annual Small Countries Conference.

[255] Equally countries of similar populations may have vastly differing GNP *per capita* figures (cf Cape Verde $1200 and Malta $10100). Additionally some micro-states may have better GNP figures than larger territories (compare Antigua $8500 with Trinidad and Tobago $4520). All figures are World Bank sources as per 1998. See 4 of the Small States Report.

[256] Page i of the Small States Report.

The Report only considers sovereign States but the same principles apply to largely self-governing non-sovereign territories such as the nine main British overseas territories. It considers that the eight special challenges to the development of small States, which are often present in many of these, are their remoteness and isolation,[257] economic exposure,[258] susceptibility to natural disasters and environmental change,[259] limited opportunities for diversification,[260] poverty,[261] limited institutional capacity,[262] income volatility[263] and restricted access to external capital. Seven of the eight factors are present to a greater or lesser extent in the case of Gibraltar.[264] So, for example, while Gibraltar is not an island its economy is largely run as if it were one because of the uncertainty that political restrictions introduced by Spain from time to time have caused. This brings about a sense of remoteness, isolation and economic exposure. The economy is also almost entirely services based and has limited diver-

[257] Three out of four small States are islands. Large distances bring high transport costs and are an additional hurdle to innovation and efficiency. With the exception of Gibraltar the overseas territories are all islands and even in the case of Gibraltar the political and economic restrictions sometimes cloud the reality that it is a peninsular. Some of the islands (in particular St Helena and its dependencies) are located in far-flung locations and this geographical fact provides its own intricacies.

[258] Given their relative inability due to their size to influence global markets. The size of the respective economies is such that the overseas territories have marginal clout at international level and this makes them vulnerable to changes.

[259] The overseas territories are all small with finite resources and are inherently vulnerable to natural disasters and the environment. In particular the islands in the Caribbean are located in a region that frequently faces hurricanes or severe storms. The small islands are also extremely vulnerable to climate change issues and tidal increases. eg Montserrat faced a volcanic disaster that was a direct cause for the reduction of its population by 60% from 1995 levels (11000) and has partially devastated the island.

[260] This is an issue that faces all the territories. Some of these turned their focus on growing their expertise in financial services or to tourism because the more traditional agricultural or fishing industries suffered a downturn. The latter being the case of the Cayman Islands, for example. Dependence on few industries means that even if successful they remain extremely susceptible to suffer great impact on their small economies if one particular sector is exposed.

[261] While the territories suffer physical and resource constraints some of them have been remarkably successful in carving out a niche for themselves in a particular industry which has made them prosperous—for example Bermuda, the British Virgin Islands, Cayman Islands and Gibraltar in financial services and the Falkland Islands in fishing. However there are others that still require financial assistance to meet their liabilities, eg St Helena and Montserrat. All (whether prosperous or not) remain vulnerable because of limited diversification which reveals the fragility of small economies.

[262] Small populations lead to the territories encountering problems in possessing the necessary human, technical or financial resources. They often have to resort to recruiting expertise from overseas. This problem is larger for the smaller, poorer and more isolated territories.

[263] All overseas territories are reliant on imports and exports to a higher or lower degree and therefore vulnerable to fluctuations in world markets. The economy of Gibraltar has no agriculture, fisheries or food production industries and is particularly reliant on imports of goods.

[264] Gibraltar is not afflicted by poverty issues.

sification opportunities. This emphasises the importance of accessing EU economic rights unhindered.[265] The formal acceptance that these issues also affect non-sovereign small territories with socio-economic constitutional competences would be entirely consistent with the situation on the ground. The greater realisation that non-sovereign territories have to be included in discussion about decisions that affect them led to the inclusion of some of these territories in the OECD's 'Global Forum' established in consequence to the harmful tax initiative.[266]

The modern financial panorama of Gibraltar has allowed a political agenda to be pursued more radically. Built on a solid and diverse economic base of financial services, shipping and tourism the Gibraltar economy has grown significantly. GDP for 2008–09 is currently estimated to hover around GIP800 million.[267] Government revenue in 2006–07 was about GIP230 million from a figure of less than GIP50 million in 1982–03 (the financial year of the re-opening by Spain of its border with Gibraltar for pedestrians).[268] Economic growth has been fairly robust with recent figures of nine per cent in 2006 and 12 per cent in 2007. Inflation is low at between two to three per cent. Government borrowing stood at GIP93 million in 2006–07, which represented about 12 per cent of GDP.[269] Net public debt during the same year was around 5.5 per cent of GDP at 43 Million. The economic picture has strengthened since the major infrastructural overhaul of the late 1980s and early 1990s, when in 1995 net public debt stood at 24.5 per cent of GDP.[270] The 2007 estimate by Government experts of the Ministry of Defence contribution to GDP was three per cent[271] with total jobs in the economy growing to just under 20,000.[272] Bank deposits grew from GIP500 million in 1988 to about GIP3.5 billion in 2006.[273] Equally the growth in companies under management, licensees in a number of financial services fields, cruise or merchant shipping calls and tourist arrivals are key indicators of the large shift from a defence based economy to one that is now a private sector-led services economy.[274] While Gibraltar is now clearly economically self-sufficient and viable in terms of financial resources, personnel and governance

265 See eg the long-standing telecommunications issues referred to in chs 4 and 5.

266 Concern was also expressed at the Commonwealth Parliamentary Association's Small Countries Conference held in Namibia in September 2002 that non-independent small countries were not given a right to attend the Commonwealth Ministerial Group of Small States with the Meeting agreeing to pass these concerns on to the Commonwealth Secretariat.

267 Chief Minister's budget speech 3 June 2008: www.gibraltar.gov.gi.

268 For 1982–03 figures see Abstract of Statistics, 2005, 67. 2006–07 figures are taken from speech by Chief Minister to Parliament on 3 June 2008.

269 Relatively low in comparison to UK averages: see ibid 13.

270 ibid.

271 ibid 15.

272 ibid 16.

273 Abstract of Statistics 2006, 71.

274 ibid 72–83.

experience it is worth recalling that effectiveness was never the test for non-self-governing territories aspiring to independence.

The underlying strength of an economy allows political aspirations to be fostered and emerge confidently without fearing that these might be financially unsustainable. Conversely if a community is not self-sufficient it runs the risk of its aspirations being curtailed by extraneous factors that subjugate political wishes to economic realities. During the 19th and most of the 20th centuries the economy relied heavily on the Ministry of Defence as the major employer and contributor to GDP. As recently as 1980 the Government estimated that MOD activity generated about 60–65 per cent of GDP.[275] As has been seen estimates of MOD contribution have now fallen to about 3 per cent. With the military exercising major economic force this also led to direct and indirect political influence. It was direct in the sense that the MOD was actively consulted on constitutional reform during the post-war period and often retained a role or influence in the constitutional architecture and governance mechanisms established under law in Gibraltar.[276] It was indirect in the sense that elected Governments of Gibraltar had to be conscious of the economic power of MOD in its own economic planning. For example, right up to the late 1980s the MOD held vast areas of land in Gibraltar with the majority of the population living on a small part of the land. As the economy changed, diversified and strengthened and as the MOD role diminished politicians acquired more freedom to voice and pursue reform. The challenge of the 1980s and 1990s was to manage the transition from the heavy defence influence to the economy to a greater private sector emphasis.

Conflict

Conflict, restrictions and suffering sustained from the internal and external political issues faced by the civil population fostered a sense of togetherness, common aims, aspirations and bonds that in turn assisted those driving the Gibraltarian political agenda.

Internal Conflict—Governance

With a larger and more economically successful civil population the focus changed to political aspirations. Chapter 1 has described the slow pace of

[275] FAC Report 1980–81, xli, fn3.

[276] eg the Commander British Forces was a member of the Gibraltar Council under the 1969 Constitution and MOD representatives have sat on the principal Planning Commission since 1973.

domestic reform. This was largely due to the size of the civil population and the control exercised by the military. As the civil population grew and then heavily outnumbered the military population aspirations to secure first influence and then limited responsibility over internal governance were inevitable aspirations.

Nonetheless as long as the military remained a large economic contributor and employer and had a direct role in the constitutional architecture it necessarily acted as a check on any aspirations. The military's influence in that regard would only diminish heavily in the 1980s. In 1989 the British Government announced that the resident military garrison would be reduced by 50 per cent. This was then finally removed in 1991 with the Gibraltar Regiment becoming the resident battalion. This had a consequent effect on the economy. The civilian population is now over 30,000 with the population of Gibraltarians having grown 10 per cent in the 10 years since the last census. Conversely the military population is now down to about 300 United Kingdom based individuals[277] from the thousands stationed regularly in Gibraltar in the past. There is no longer a permanent RAF base and the naval base was severely contracted in the 1980s. The military role is now less physical and more strategic. All those measures caused a significant shift in the economy of Gibraltar that accounts for the sharp descent in contribution to GDP.

Necessarily this also caused an effect on any domestic political influence that local politicians might have been willing to accept. In the 1950s the military was not only consulted as a matter of course on any constitutional proposals but these were not granted absent their consent. In taking fledgling steps towards self-government under the shadow of such a dominant economic force local politicians had to defer to reality. Pragmatic politics required that. The current climate is very different with the military role confined to a small presence. The struggle of the political classes against the colonial administration and the British Government who were resistant to reform on the grounds that the fortress should be protected and that it was inappropriate for civilian self-government to co-exist with the military because of the potential for interference in military activities was a unifying force for the civilian population.

In general terms aspirations to obtain participation, influence and control of internal governance were shared by the spectrum of social groups represented by labour organisations and merchant bodies. The emergence of the first political parties in the 1940s and 1950s also acted as a catalyst for political organisation, lobbying and were focal points for efforts

[277] In a press interview the Commander British Forces (the most senior British officer stationed in Gibraltar) made clear that the current levels of personnel were only 'Royal Navy 162; RAF 97 and total Army 280 of which the majority are the Gibraltar Regiment with about 50 regular army from the UK. A total of about 300 UK-based people.' See *Gibraltar Chronicle* (Gibraltar, 18 August 2008).

towards constitutional reform. Apart from capitalising on the growth of the population and on economic development both of which facilitated the requests for self-government these politicians were influenced by the international drive towards self-determination and decolonisation. In that way the civic nationalism that had its origins in the collectivity fostered by the socio-economic evolution of the populace within this living fortress entered a distinct phase in the post-war period. There was then a regeneration based on the language of civil liberties and the rewarding with self-government of Commonwealth populations that had manifested their loyalty to Britain during the war years.

Civic nationalism throughout the Commonwealth was in that sense anti-imperial, as described by Hobsbawm.[278] While in some countries it manifested itself in volatility, internal turmoil and aggression, the moves in Gibraltar requesting self-government were, by comparison, relatively docile. In making these claims for civil rights, nationalism in Gibraltar never manifested itself as promoting an ethnically-based case, even though the distinctions between a population that was largely Catholic[279] and had Latin Mediterranean social ancestry and an imperial Anglo-Saxon Anglican establishment were obvious. Even so, the mix of religions, the lack of a clearly dominant immigrant grouping, the need to close ranks in relation to external conflict and to promote internal civil aspirations tended to ensure that religious or immigrant differences as between various sectors of the civil population were down-played in the interests of greater social lobbying cohesion. Over time and as the civil population faced a number of internally and externally sourced conflicts it produced a solidarity and feeling of collectivity which laid the ground for the identification of the separateness of the people of Gibraltar. A feeling of identity is as much an emotional, psychological state of being as a historical or political fact. By the post-war period this was there in both senses.

While social groups shared self-government aspirations the main political organisation of the post-war years and throughout the intense constitutional activity up to the late 1960s was the AACR. Linked as it was for many years to one of the main unions, and with a broad base of support, it was ideologically a centre-left party. This was in keeping with many developments throughout newly decolonised countries and the Commonwealth where nationalism had 'acquired a strong association with the left during the anti-fascist period . . . which was subsequently reinforced by the experience of anti-imperial struggle in colonial countries.'[280]

The domination in Gibraltar political and social groupings by 'local elites imitating European national self-determination'[281] also falls neatly

[278] Hobsbawm n 168 above, 137.
[279] 80%: see *Abstract of Statistics 2006*.
[280] Hobsbawm n 168 above, 148.
[281] ibid 151.

within the modernist classification of nationalist movements worldwide. As Hobsbawm identifies, in the colonised dependent world, these movements were 'the main agents for the political emancipation of most of the globe, that is to say for an elimination of imperial administration and more significantly, direct military domination.'[282] In Gibraltar it was no different with the post-war struggle concentrating on loosening the military grip on the day-to-day affairs of the territory. It is important to acknowledge that the impetus to achieve civil rights was not based on any ethnic unison but rather on the emergence of an ethnically diverse State unified by a struggle based on political emancipation.[283]

External Conflict—Status

Even though Gibraltarian political aspirations have been aimed at achieving internal self-government there has never been any attempt to pursue any latent separatist ambitions. Indeed, political parties have been traditionally cautious about going any further than free association. The dominant tendencies that emerged during the 1960s in Gibraltar were based on aspirations for free association[284] or constitutional integration with Britain.[285] It can be argued that the latter was a purely defensive reaction that had no firm social or anthropological roots. In later years a more vigorous strand of nationalism became noticeable during the years of the socialist administration after 1988. Again that was consistent with the Commonwealth trend of anti-colonial, nationalist centre-left politics.[286] The social democrat party that has served in Government since 1996 has adopted a moderate nationalist stance combined with a desire to engage Spain in a process of dialogue. One political party during the late 1970s and early 1980s promoted a softer line of appeasement and negotiation with Spain. It had a brief existence and scarce political support.[287]

The people of Gibraltar have evolved in an imperial container under assault from an external re-colonising force. Struggling to obtain devolution and civil rights from the British colonial power Gibraltarians faced the prospect that the Spanish claim would simply replace a colonial situation

[282] ibid 169.

[283] ibid.

[284] The AACR.

[285] The IWBP.

[286] The growing nationalism was also evidenced in the launch of a National Party in 1991, which then changed its name to the Liberal Party but retained its moderate nationalist objectives.

[287] The Party for the Autonomy of Gibraltar (PAG). Its objectives are encapsulated in a memorandum contained within the FAC Report 1980–81 on Gibraltar, at 93. Principally the ideological content was also nationalist in its promotion of 'Gibraltarians as a democratically sovereign people', but this was lost in the language that promoted an Anglo–Spanish treaty of reconciliation.

not with decolonisation but with recolonisation by another claimant. This reality both concentrated nationalist forces and produced the defensive reaction of a movement seeking constitutionally closer links with Britain through integration.

As Hobsbawm has stated 'there is no more effective way of bonding together the disparate sections of restless peoples than to unite them against outsiders.'[288] In that sense the Spanish sovereignty claim, and the political fall-out from the clash of aspirations was the principal unifying force of Gibraltar nationalism. While Spain made plain its territorial sovereignty claim during the military sieges of the 18th century it is the 20th century post-war period dominated by the political pursuit of the sovereignty claim that would give an impetus to Gibraltarian nationalism. Several instances during that post-war period coincided with Gibraltarian attempts at securing domestic self-governance. As the Spanish claim, in effect, denied the existence of a separate people and rendered nugatory the claims towards status and governance reform based on self-determination it was seen as a distinct threat to Gibraltar's aspirations and thus helped to solidify and unify the populace.

There are a number of instances that contributed to these developments, most of which have been mentioned in the previous chapters. So for example the culture of conflict and antagonism produced by economic,[289] social[290] or political restrictions on the population inevitably led to a counter-reaction of resistance and recoil. The climate of friction got substantially worse during the 1950s and the subsequent decade of UN attention. United Nations interest in Gibraltar came during a time of decolonisation, but rather than resolving the Gibraltar issue, it tended, as a result of the General Assembly resolutions, to enshrine the bilateral, UK–Spain, treatment of the Gibraltar problem. Pronouncements by Spain and responses by Gibraltar during the period all led to an accentuation of tension that peaked with the 1967 referendum, the decision to grant the 1969 Constitution and Spain's closure of its land frontier with Gibraltar in the same year. That had been preceded by a gradual escalation of restrictive measures.

The border closure created a generational disconnect with mainland Spain. The border would only be fully re-opened 16 years later, by which time almost an entire generation had grown up with little or no contact with Spain. The number of Gibraltarians that formed part of the civil population in 1970 was 18,873.[291] By 2006 the number of Gibraltarians had grown by over 20 per cent to 23,447 from a total population of about

[288] Hobsbawm n 168 above, 91.

[289] eg aviation restrictions.

[290] Such as on freedom of movement across the frontier or obstacles faced by sporting bodies.

[291] *2006 Abstract of Statistics*, 2.

29,000.[292] In that time the military population had been reduced by two-thirds, to just 745.[293] The average number of births during the frontier closure years was in excess of 500, with the number of annual deaths at less than 300. With the vast majority of births and deaths during the period being Gibraltarians the figures reveal that, by the time the frontier re-opened, about 25 per cent of the population were 'new' Gibraltarians, meaning that they had not been born when the frontier closed. If to that figure the number of Gibraltarians below the age of eight in 1969 (who would have had little memory of contact with Spain but who spent their formative years in a closed-frontier Gibraltar) is added the figure grows to more than 40 per cent of the Gibraltarian population. The result of all this was the emergence of a large proportion of the population by 1985 that had never known anything other than conflict with Spain and had had very little or no contact with Spain. This bred an insular suspicion and apprehension that was inevitable because of the imposed isolation. That state of mind and psychology was then easily transmitted to successive generations. For those generations that were of adult age at the time of the frontier closure, the isolation brought people together but also engendered a negative climate towards Spain. While restrictions had also been there prior to the 1960s the fact that the border had been open had led to much greater social interchange. The regular transit of goods across the land fuelled economic trade between Gibraltar and the hinterland. Intermarriage between communities was commonplace, Spanish was the language of the masses in Gibraltar, with English the official language and that of the establishment.

The irony of Spain's closure of the border was that it fostered togetherness, a desire for survival of the civil population and excluded Spanish influences except those that arrived via television and radio. By the time the socialist administration of Felipe González had decided to re-open the frontier in the post-Franco democratic Spain, the forced isolation had proved to be the single most unifying feature for the people of Gibraltar. For a generation the people were contained within a small land mass. Surviving economically dependent on a defence-based economy Gibraltar became a social development laboratory. When the door to the laboratory was re-opened the Gibraltarians that stepped through the door were very different to those that had been placed in it in 1969.

The re-opening of the border would also fuel an unparalleled economic expansion and diversification into other areas such as financial services. Reliant on a defence economy in which the big player was the MOD and accustomed to using Britain as a shield the Gibraltarian became more self-reliant because of economic success. The political approximation between

[292] ibid.
[293] ibid 3.

Britain and Spain also led to Gibraltarians becoming more vociferous about aspirations and more conscious that the wishes and interests of the people of Gibraltar were different to those of Britain. By the early 1990s Gibraltar was seeking constitutional reform and had pro-actively recommenced attendances at the United Nations after an almost 30-year absence, so as to claim its right to self-determination. Assertions of the distinctiveness of the people of Gibraltar in social or legal terms can be traced back to the 19th century. It became more prominent in the political speeches of Gibraltar representatives at the United Nations during the 1960s in response to the Spanish claim. Use of the description of 'country' for Gibraltar became more common-place from the late 1980s with the election of the Socialist Labour Party in Gibraltar and its more nationalist programme of hard-line political resistance, economic self-sufficiency, constitutional reform and assertion of self-determination. All these were gradual political manifestations of the claim to nationhood of the people of Gibraltar.

Physical Location Issues

The size, physical location, geographical nature and boundaries of Gibraltar make the territory clearly finite, and facilitate socio-political and economic activities within it. During the years of closure of the land frontier access to the territory was only possible by air links to London or Morocco and sea links to the latter.

Three formative benefits stem from the physical features of Gibraltar. First, the territorial boundaries are easily identifiable. Second, the small size of the territory contributes to the ease with which communication of issues of mutual concern could be conveyed or shared feeling engendered. Third, the period of forced inaccessibility through the land frontier created a human sociological experiment that brought people together much more strongly. The idea behind the economic and physical restrictions on Gibraltar placed by Francoist Ministers was to coerce the population so that Gibraltar would fall like a 'ripe fruit'.[294] The need to overcome these gave Gibraltarians a much stronger feeling of community.

A sense of belonging and attachment to an easily identifiable common territory is an important aspect of nationhood. That attachment was made easier by the frontier closure but it had already been there in previous generations. The war-time song of evacuees that longed for repatriation, '*llevame donde naci*'[295] spoke of the return to Gibraltar in romantic and

[294] P Preston, *Franco* (London, Fontana Press, 1995) 731–32. Though he goes on to say that Franco refused to sanction one of Castiella's more extravagant plans to fly barrage balloons around Gibraltar to prevent air access to the territory.

[295] Take me to where I was born.

mystical terms. It remains widely sung especially on National Day in remembrance and evocation of the sense of togetherness and suffering of the population. It both has a past value of re-creation, a present value in engendering togetherness and a future forward-looking value as the common traditions and evidence on which the sense of nationhood is based.

The efforts to achieve the repatriation of the population when it could have been so easy to simply live elsewhere rather than return to a heavily bombed territory where housing was scarce and many people had to live in war-time nissen huts for some time was in itself testimony to the desire and attachment to the territory of the population.

Historical–Cultural Issues

The use of symbols—flags, ceremonies, monuments—as the backdrop to assertions of nationhood or the emphasis on cultural distinctions have also proceeded in parallel. Politicians and community leaders have drawn on bonds of cultural origin to maintain distinctiveness and unity. This is common elsewhere in emergent modern nations, as Smith points out:

> Though these nationalisms were modern and the nations they helped to create relatively new, their cultural and social bases, the ethno-symbolic elements that made each nation, and nationalism individual and distinctive and gave to each its persistent characters derived from specific repertoires and resources of ethno-history, religious, myth and ancestral history. This is true of nationalisms in every continent and all economic backgrounds.[296]

Hence, Smith notes the 'relatively recent nationalist upsurge among the Quebecois which started in the 1950s' and derives support from its history, territorial attachment and religious beliefs 'which now undergird its modern secular expressions.'[297] So it is in Gibraltar that territorial attachment is strong and that politicians invoke the shared history and suffering of the evacuation and repatriation of the population, the development of the origins of the immigrant populace and the emergence from military domination. Above all, the centuries of resistance to a Spanish claim to sovereignty is the strongest historical bond.

These bonds are then manifested in modern times by the greater use of flags, ceremonies and monuments. The erection of an evacuation/repatriation monument and the establishment of an annual 'national day' in 1992, at which the vast majority of the population don red and white and celebrate the distinct identity of the people of Gibraltar and their right to self-determination, and assert a claim to nationhood, are clear invocations of that. National Day combines political events and cultural and leisure

[296] A Smith, *Myth and the Memories of Nation* (Oxford, OUP, 1999) 275.
[297] ibid 276.

celebrations in a clear attempt to merge and highlight the culinary, cultural, historical and political elements in an annual celebration. As Brass has stated, whether the culture of a group

> is ancient or is newly fashioned the study of ethnicity is in large part the study of politically induced cultural change . . . by which elites and counter-elites select aspects of the groups' culture, attach new value and meaning to them and use them as symbols to mobilise the group.[298]

This is in part what has occurred in Gibraltar though there is some irony in that the national flag of Gibraltar is not the defaced blue ensign given to Gibraltar by Britain but rather the red and white flag with a castle and key emblem given to their 'most loyal' city by the Spanish monarch in 1502. Equally the coat of arms was granted to the city by the Spanish Crown at the beginning of the 16th century and in modern British times was formally adopted as Gibraltar's coat of arms in 1926.

The fact, though, is that these symbols and flags have been fully adopted as home-grown indicators of nationhood, whatever their original source. This experience is shared with many other Commonwealth territories that have morphed elements of their social roots, their 'invented traditions' and acquired symbols. So for example there was a deliberate policy in the early to late 20th century of naming housing estates or roads after colonial Governors providing a subliminal message of contribution and control to the society. The recent trend has seen the naming of public housing after prominent Gibraltarians. This again is indicative of changing times.

Gibraltar—The Stateless Nation

The level of involvement and mobilisation of the civil population has been high, especially at times of conflict. First demonstrations and public meetings of an organised or of a more spontaneous nature have occurred at different points, especially over the last 40 years. So, for example, mass demonstrations of support greeted the Gibraltar representatives returning from the United Nations in the 1960s. Large demonstrations mobilising in excess of 50 per cent of the total electorate have been held at times of conflict on specific issues of a sovereignty or nationalist flavour, such as in respect of the 1987 Anglo–Spanish airport agreement, the non-recognition of Gibraltar passports and ID cards by Spain in 1998, and significantly of about 20,000 people against the joint sovereignty plans in 2002, among other instances. The populace has also been effectively and overwhelmingly mobilised in two sovereignty referenda in 1967 and 2002.[299] While

[298] Brass in Hutchinson and Smith (eds) n 172 above, 87.

[299] Described in chapter 1 and this chapter. And by the annual National Day events: see above.

objectively there can be some caution in taking political mobilisation of people as an indicator of any particular thought process of the collective populace, two points must be made. The first is that the size of mobilisation is so large in the examples given that it must demonstrate a collective feeling by the people. Secondly, when given options in a free ballot the numbers supporting Spanish sovereignty (44 in 1967) or joint Anglo–Spanish sovereignty (187 in 2002) were negligible and indicated the strength of collective feeling on the nationhood issue. Granted, both were negative exercises in the sense that, on both occasions, the people were asked to reject sole or joint Spanish sovereignty with no alternative offer other than the *status quo* in mind. But even so, the mass turnout and mass support for the option that rejected a Spanish dimension was clear. It is also true that in neither referendum was there a credible camp putting an opposite case, so those advocates of rejection of the Spanish sovereignty proposals had a fairly unhindered attempt at persuading the population. Equally, the leader of the more dove-ish Party for the Autonomy of Gibraltar at elections in 1976 and 1980 did obtain a personal vote of 10–15 per cent, although this may be accounted for by personal following and a much softer message of negotiation. In either case it cannot deflect in any significant way from the fact that the vast amount of the population in different generations have expressed their clear view on sovereignty proposals linked to Spain. Indeed, rather than the population getting more amenable to a solution with Spanish sovereignty at its core it is contended that the indications are the reverse. A more confident and highly educated younger generation cut-off from Spain for many years has developed that unlike previous generations now see a much larger distinction between the concepts of being British and Gibraltarian. For some promoting the British connection was done out of conviction. For others it was more of a defensive reaction. When the IWBP was launched in the 1960s it was the height of UN tension. The pro-British referendum of 1967 followed, and the IWBP became the senior partner in the coalition Government of 1969. While it collapsed as a Party when Britain rejected the idea of integration in 1976, the markedly different fate of those who sought to revive it is interesting. A few years ago some of the old faces in the IWBP tried to relaunch a political movement with very similar constitutional objectives. It drew a small membership exposing a generational divide with few younger people openly backing the idea.

Fuelled by growth in population and economic self-sufficiency political aspirations grew. Strengthened and made more cohesive by conflict the collectivity of the people of Gibraltar was forged. Drawing on the historical, cultural, physical and symbolic features most politicians used these to highlight the nationhood of the people of Gibraltar. This focus brings together sectors with differing cultural roots and cuts across these. It is not an ethnically based nationalism but rather a civic nationalism that has the advantage of appealing widely across the community and fostering inclusion rather than disintegration. In the case of Gibraltar there are different historic strands though a couple are predominant—a quasi-unionism that places much importance on constitutional integration with Britain and a moderate non-separatist nationalism that seeks to maximise self-government. In recent decades the latter has predominated.

The mix of all these factors makes for a unique concoction: British education[300] and Latin temperament; predominant Catholicism with a smattering of other religious groups; and a bilingual population. It has through the centuries demonstrated a survival instinct (in the face of a sovereignty claim) with an entrepreneurial flair that ensures that its economy is vibrant, constantly changing and robust. Economic self-sufficiency in turn fuels the political aspirations of the population. It is a community under siege that has faced political and military assault throughout the ages. Restrictions placed by Spain, such as the inability to fly over Spanish aerospace, have only served to bind the community further together. The irony thus is that the siege mentality, the national aspirations and the feelings of nationhood were, in part, accentuated by the restrictions imposed by the Spanish Government. That combination of positive nation-building factors—common language, shared values, shared adversity, economic self-sufficiency, largely common political values, geographically demarcated entity among others—all contribute to encouraging the identity and sense of nationhood that in turn fosters political nationalism.[301]

The people of Gibraltar have multiple identities in terms of religion, national origin and culture. They are European, British and Gibraltarian.[302] While the idea of European citizenship is nascent and has not been embraced widely by the diverse populations of Member State countries the prevalent identities will be nationality- and locality-based. In Gibraltar cultural, educational or sporting affinities with both Anglo-Saxon and Latin roots are present in parallel and can easily be misconstrued. These need to be factored in properly and not misunderstood.[303] They highlight the distinctiveness of identity rather than the absence of distinction from Spanish identity. The presence of multiple identities is common to many societies and nations. Generally speaking, these aspects co-exist, though there is

[300] The role of education in the development of identity of the people should also not be under-estimated. It helped to anglicise the community and also as a result of Government policies led to many more young people having the opportunity of an English university education (especially after 1988). For a detailed survey of the education system see Archer n 215 above, 115–152, and also EG Archer and AA Traverso, *Education in Gibraltar, 1704–2000* (Grendon, Gibraltar Books, 2004).

[301] See also M Creveld, *The Rise and Decline of the State* (Cambridge, CUP, 1999).

[302] Approximately 85% of the population hold Gibraltarian Status under domestic law: see Abstract of Statistics, 2006.

[303] Indeed Smith has cautioned about making assumptions concerning collective-identity-based individual behaviour: see Smith n 296 above, 230.

potential for identity conflict. The multiple identity facets combine to create a single and distinct identity base for the people of Gibraltar. This identity then merges into the politically charged environment to lay a fertile ground for pluralistic and multi-dimensional approaches to governance that respect the complex arrangement of elements and the culturally cosmopolitan identity mix.[304] Once a collective identity has been forged,

> they are less subject to rapid changes and tend to be more intense and durable, even when quite large numbers of individuals no longer feel their power ... [I]t is particularly true of national identities today when the power of mass political fervour reinforces the technological instruments of mass political organisation so that national identities can outlast the defection or apathy of quite large numbers of individual members.[305]

The combination of all the features outlined above are best recognised as forming the ethno-symbolic layer of elements that together make the Gibraltar identity.

The placement of Gibraltar onto the UN list of non-self-governing territories in 1946 indicated its status separate from the administering power and that the colonial people had a right of self-determination. All colonial peoples are nations[306] though not all nations are colonial peoples. In that sense too Gibraltar has a stake to a claim for recognition of its nationhood. The contingent claim to statehood of the nation of Gibraltar is based on that right to self-determination.[307] But as Smith has pointed out it is important for these purposes to retain the awareness of the distinction between nation and State, as the

> latter is a legal and institutional concept ... [T]he idea of the nation, by contrast, is fundamentally cultural and social. It refers to a cultural and political band which unites in a community of prestige all those who share the same myths, memories, symbols and traditions.[308]

Towards the Future

There has been a surge in the feeling of nationhood of the people of Gibraltar, especially in the post-war period. This has seen a merger of elements some indigenous, some imported and some born out of cultural, religious and ethnic fusion. That is common with other countries that have

[304] As is the case with Switzerland: see W Linder, *Swiss Democracy—Possible Solutions to Conflict in Multi-Cultural Societies* (Hampshire, MacMillan, 1998).

[305] Smith n 296 above, 230.

[306] Or groups of nations.

[307] Though Hobsbawm would urge caution: 'we need hardly remind ourselves that the mere setting up of a State is not sufficient in itself to create a nation.' Hobsbawm n 168 above, 78.

[308] Smith n 296 above, 232.

emerged in the decolonisation era and aspirations that have been promoted in 'nominally national but actually plurinational States.'[309] Of course, the difference with Gibraltar is that its people do not co-exist within a State but rather live in a territory with a status that is distinct from Britain under international law. In any event there are many parallels in the drive for accommodation of sub-State nations identified by Kymlicka.[310] What Gibraltar is best described as is a 'polyethnic nation',[311] forged over the last few centuries by all the elements described in this and the preceding chapter. But the concept will not remain static. It will continue to evolve because nationalism as a doctrine is 'chameleon-like, capable of almost infinite adaptation and reformulation while preserving its underlying purposes.'[312] Nationalism may evolve but it is unreal to contend that there is no place for the concept or that we are in a post-national world when self-evidently the importance of the concept remains. Being 'beyond a world of nations . . . may remain a dream for some time'[313] as much as it is unrealistic only to explain self-determination as purely a symptom of the crisis of the concept of the nation-State.[314] True that nations or States are no longer the simplistic answers to demands for emotional or political accommodation but that is due to an evolution and not an elimination of the concepts of sovereignty and nationalism.

The accommodation of the various nations within Member States of the European Union provides fertile analogous ground for comparison with Gibraltar.[315] In that sense the pluralism of nations and—as a consequence—the participants within them accentuate the need for a modern governance solution consonant with the legal and political realities. It is even more important for sub-State nations to be accommodated because of the historic rights claimed by those civil societies. This is made possible within the various States if there is an adjustment of the State's internal constitutional architecture and changes are reflected as benefits at the supra-national level.

As such plurinationalism within the European stage manifests itself as the marriage between non-secessionist sub-State nationalism and the drive for multi-level governance. It relies on the same principles of democracy, legitimacy and participatory governance that will be encountered later in this work. This stateless nationalism seeks cohabitation within federalist, quasi-federalist or supra-national solutions rather than secession. This makes quasi-federalist models more interesting when examining the

309 Hobsbawm n 168 above, 139.
310 Kymlicka in Tierney (ed) n 243 above.
311 Smith n 296 above, 201.
312 ibid.
313 ibid.
314 Hobsbawm n 168 above, 186.
315 S Tierney, *Constitutional Law and National Pluralism* (Oxford, OUP, 2004) 131–244.

concept of status-change. It also makes the adjustment of the constitutional framework of the State a practical key to enable the amelioration of national tensions. Substantive reforms only work if the twin objectives of domestic constitutional progress and representation, power and influence at supra-national or State level are achieved. These issues are faced by Britain and Spain in Catalunya, the Basque Country and Scotland. They are similarly encountered in respect of Gibraltar. The approach to ensure the resolution of these issues is the pragmatic one of 'negotiating nationalism'.[316] Looking at the British and Spanish comparators is important in two respects—the first because Gibraltar does not operate in a legal vacuum and the second because the fact that there may be consequences for Britain or Spain in relation to its own internal constitutional arrangements will influence their attitudes towards Gibraltar.[317]

Among these the sharpest, most relevant contrasts for Gibraltar within the European Union are therefore Scotland, Catalunya[318] and the Basque Country[319] (and to a lesser extent Northern Ireland). These are relevant in a couple of ways, namely because they are all within the EU and are within the two countries that bilaterally dominate the Gibraltar panorama. Additionally, there is (in both States) a degree of asymmetrical devolution or regional government, with Scotland, Catalunya and the Basque Country as the leading and most advanced exponents of sub-State self-government. The parallels reveal why it makes sense to monitor developments affecting these within Spain[320] and the United Kingdom[321] as constitutional movement within those national structures can affect the Gibraltar issue.[322] There are also differences, namely that the relevant territories are all constitutionally integral parts of Spain or the United Kingdom—Gibraltar is

[316] Norman n 149 above, 95–169.

[317] At other stages of this work analogies have been drawn from the Belgian and German experiences, not because these are the strongest comparators to the Gibraltar situation, but because in an aspirational sense they represent useful illustrations of how sub-State governmental demands have been accommodated especially in a federal context.

[318] A Balcells, *Catalan Nationalism: Past and Present* (London, McMillan, 1995).

[319] JL De La Granja Sainz, *El Nacionalismo Vasco: Un Siglo de Historia* (Madrid, Tecnos, 1995).

[320] J Colomer, *Catalunya como cuestion de Estado: la idea de nacion en el pensamiento politico catalan (1939–79)* (Madrid, Tecnos, 1986); A de Blas Guerrero, *Nacionalismos y naciones en Europa* (Madrid, Alianza, 1994); F Requejo, '*Diferencias Nacionales y Federalismo Asimetrico*', *Claves de la Razon Practica* (1996), Jan–Feb, 24, 1996; JP Fusi, *España: La Evolución de la Identidad Nacional* (Madrid, Temas de Hoy, 2000); F Moral, '*Identidad Regional y Nacionalismo en el Estado de las Autonomias, Opiniones y Actitudes*' (Madrid, Centro de Investigaciones Sociologicas, 1998).

[321] W Ferguson, *The Identity of the Scottish Nation: An Historic Quest* (Edinburgh, Edinburgh UP, 1998); R Weight, *Patriots—National Identity in Britain 1940–2000* (London, Pan MacMillan, 2002).

[322] Gibraltar's claims to self-determination or to the external manifestations of sovereignty (in its representation at EU level) make Britain keep one eye on comparable Scottish claims and Spain keep one eye on comparable Basque claims. Conversely, developments that entrench constitutional recognition of Scottish or Basque claims through a stronger federalisation facilitate concessions to Gibraltar.

not. Gibraltar is unique in that it sustains a territorial sovereignty claim from a third party and it has more constitutional responsibilities but in some respects less influence than these comparators.[323]

As has been explained, there is a causal link between the sovereignty dispute, the conflicts of nationalism and aspirations of the different parties. The next Part of this chapter outlines these.

Conflicts of Nationalism, Parties, Aspirations and Methodologies

(i) Objectives of the Parties

In many ways the sovereignty dispute represents the clash of nationalism and national interests of the three parties involved in the dispute. These have markedly different objectives which, at first sight, appear difficult to bridge.

Gibraltar

As indicated at the beginning of this work, Gibraltar is faced with concerns that affect its status and governance. It is clear that on the internal self-determination and governance sphere there has been a significant development of the population, a marked democratisation of Gibraltar and a rise in national consciousness. All these aspects are important to appreciate the current aspirations of the people and their role within the paradox of governance.

The people of Gibraltar have developed a sense of nationhood that has acquired greater prominence and expression during the last 20 years.[324] While the calls for self-determination were principally masked behind parallel expressions of loyalty to the British Crown, there has been a distinct rise of moderate nationalism.[325] All political parties are united on calls for the international recognition of the people's right to self-determination and the people have demonstrated their very clear majority view on the subject of sovereignty in two referenda convened on the subject. Such clarity of feeling gives the call for decolonisation based on the principle of self-determination greater weight even though there may be differences on the form of decolonised status that Gibraltar should enjoy. The calls for decolonisation do not take a separatist form and there is no mainstream political party in Gibraltar that advocates independence.

[323] The paradox is described below.

[324] See F Cantos, *From Fortress to Democracy—The Political Biography of Sir Joshua Hassan* (Grendon, Gibraltar Books, 1995) 150–200.

[325] In part because of a reaction to the perceived Foreign Office policy on Gibraltar.

There is thus to a large extent a merger between the calls for constitutional reform and those for decolonisation based on a non-independent status freely chosen by the people in a referendum (even though the questions of reform and decolonisation are distinct). In this sense the main political parties adopt a position similar to that adopted by other Stateless nationalists in Catalunya.[326] Stateless nationalism is one of the better ways to describe modern political movements in Gibraltar and the collective aspirations of its people.

Britain

There has always been a clash of interests between the British garrison and the civilian inhabitants. The former viewed Gibraltar as a garrison town with the interests of the fortress being paramount. To them, the civilian population was there to service the needs of the military. As the civilian population grew so did their aspirations to obtain more control over their lives and break away from this stereotype.[327] The British outlook was that the strategic imperative needed to be protected and that any element of self-government was undesirable and should be resisted. This had a real effect on the attitude of the colonial establishment to the aspirations for self-government of the local populace.[328]

Britain retains certain priorities some of which are held in common in relation to other overseas territories,[329] and some of which are particular to Gibraltar, which influence the decolonisation, reform and governance agenda. But the two aspects that have principally influenced Britain's stance on Gibraltar through the ages have been its strategic interests and Spain. In many respects the degree of responsiveness of Britain has been largely proportional to the degree of acceptability of measures in Spain. So for example during the Conservative PP administration of José Maria Aznar (1996–2004) the most austere reactions and difficulties were experienced.[330] The wider interests of Britain within the EU require a system of alliances and bargaining with other States. Britain is keenly aware of the need to promote its interests. Spain has proved a useful ally—especially

[326] The position of the Scottish National Party is more radical in its openly advocated more separatist policy. See eg 'Choosing Scotland's Future, A National Conversation: Independence and Responsibility in the Modern World' (Edinburgh, Scottish Executive, August 2007).

[327] TJ Finlayson, *Stories from the Rock* (Gibraltar, Aquila, 1996) 110–27.

[328] See ch 1.

[329] Such as compliance with its international financial obligations, good governance and environmental issues.

[330] This was because the PP is traditionally more hard-line on Gibraltar and because the Blair–Aznar relationship was close. For a perspective on the Spanish view of EU membership, see C Closa and P Heywood, *Spain and the European Union* (London, Palgrave International, 2004).

over the last decade—in countering the Franco-German axis and this necessarily impacts on Gibraltar's aspirations by colouring Britain's attitude. The objectives of Britain are primarily driven by the desire to retain its strategic interests while ensuring that any proposals for constitutional changes or decolonisation strike a fine balance and are not unduly confrontational to Spain.

Spain

Franco used Gibraltar as a distraction from Spanish internal troubles as 'a cheap and effective way of whipping up nationalist support by stressing the sinister intentions of imperialist Britain.'[331] Even though he was discouraged because of lack of United States support Franco 'always kept public agitation on the matter as a useful residual device to divert attention from other issues.'[332] That attitude has continued and has also affected other stateless nations. Balfour and Quiroga[333] have highlighted how the 'invention of Castile as the dominant region in the formation of Spain was a direct response to the birth of Catalan and Basque nationalisms at the end of the 19th century.'[334] They go on to outline the role of the media[335] or of the central Government in pursuing policies to promote Spanish nationalism over the 'historic nationalities' of Catalunya, the Basque country and Galicia. These lost their newly acquired devolution statutes as a result of the civil war.[336] For many years Spanish politicians anguished about the concept of Spain as a nation and whether it faces the prospect of disintegration. Franco made national unity a key principle and it was often used to distract the population from domestic troubles.[337] But in fact Spanish national identity has been far from 'monolithic' and 'illustrates the kaleidoscopic nature of nationalism.'[338] In the construction of the Spanish Constitution post Franco, 'compromise, concession and the reconciliation of different concepts of nation were the guidelines of the constitutional debate.'[339] However, the Spanish angst over nation and identity remains, and it signposts the fact that for many in Spain the Gibraltar issue is not merely about asserting an extra-territorial claim but is also about managing the internal cohesion of Spain so as to balance

[331] P Preston, *Franco* (London, Fontana Press, 1995) 621.
[332] ibid.
[333] S Balfour and A Quiroga, *The Reinvention of Spain: Nation and Identity Since Democracy* (Oxford, OUP, 2007).
[334] ibid 23.
[335] ibid 33.
[336] The Catalan statute was approved in 1932; the Basque and Galician ones in 1936.
[337] Balfour and Quiroga n 333 above, 29.
[338] ibid 43.
[339] ibid 44.

the constitutional architecture in the face of Basque and Catalan pressures.[340]

That angst over nation has resulted in some conceptual ambiguity over Gibraltar. In 1980 the House of Commons Foreign Affairs Committee while noting that 'Spain will not compromise on sovereignty' also noted that Spanish academics had given evidence of

> fresh concepts of sovereignty opening new possibilities. They were alluding to the current preoccupation of Spanish political philosophers with the meaning to be given to 'sovereignty', 'nation', 'nationality' in the light of modern thinking on human rights.[341]

That tension and lack of complete philosophical comfort with those concepts continues today and is evident from time to time in the handling of Spanish stateless nations as well as Gibraltar.

The principal objective of the Spanish State in respect of Gibraltar is to achieve Gibraltar's sovereignty. If full sovereignty cannot be achieved because of the objections of the population, the Spanish Government has been willing to contemplate other structures, such as joint sovereignty, as an interim mechanism. In the meantime, Spain has sought to achieve a measure of influence, jurisdiction or control by indirect or gradual means or by opposing measures designed to enhance Gibraltar's self-governance.[342] Spain has demonstrated that it is not prepared to sit still on the matter and has traditionally chosen the more abrasive of two obvious policy options open to it.[343] Recently, Spain has pursued a more open co-operative stance,[344] but even this is described by Spain as a means to the same end.[345] The sovereignty claim is the predominant overriding influence and reveals the dramatically converse aspirations of one of the main players. This has contributed to the external governance deficit described later in this work.

Methodologies: Bilateralism v Trilateralism—The Different Approaches

The initial absence of a significant civilian population enhanced the bilateral nature of the sovereignty dispute. As the population grew dramatically during the 19th and 20th centuries, it led to two developments. On the status front the interposition of a resident civilian population

340 ibid 16.

341 FAC Report 1980–1, liii, para 189.

342 See ch 4.

343 The other option—wooing the people of Gibraltar with a concessionary policy, which successive British Governments have urged them to do, has not been consistently attempted.

344 See ch 6 and the period post 2004.

345 See the Speech of Spanish Ambassador José Luis Yague before the Fourth Committee on 4 October 2006.

would challenge the traditional bilateralism. On the governance front it would eventually give rise to demands for devolution of powers and participation in Government. For many years Britain and—most notably—Spain strived to reserve any discussion of the sovereignty issue to themselves to the exclusion of the people of Gibraltar. This bilateral and State-centric approach, which inevitably affected progress on issues of status or governance, is evident from developments in three fields.

The United Nations

The United Nations affirms annual consensus resolutions that call for Britain and Spain to resolve the Gibraltar issue, taking into account the interests of the population.[346] The focus of those resolutions is clearly bilateral and does not create sufficient space for the people of Gibraltar as a direct participant in those discussions. They also make clear that it is only the 'interests' of the people and not their 'wishes' that need to be taken into account. This distinction is important. Respecting the wishes of the population would have the support of the principle of self-determination and the endorsement of legitimacy of the people. Taking into account a people's interests is not an exercise that is guaranteed to reflect the people's views or gain their consent. Mechanically it also does not guarantee their participation in any process.[347] The annual resolutions by the United Nations do not call for negotiations between all parties concerned, as it excludes from that call for negotiations the representatives of the people of the territory. It would be more consistent with the principles of self-determination and legitimacy if the annual call included a recommendation that the people of the territory participate in any discussions as a 'party concerned' through their elected Government. Cassese has noted that 'by reaffirming the principle of self-determination as the basic standard of conduct while at the same time calling for direct negotiations between all parties concerned the UN has assumed an active and important role in the field of self-determination.'[348] This is far from the case because in fact the United Nations has adopted a passive and State-centric

[346] See eg GA Res 3286 (XXIX) of 13 December 1974. Successive annual resolutions followed a similar pattern and were only influenced by the launch of direct Anglo–Spanish talks over Gibraltar (see later) and GA Decision 41/407 of 31 October 1986, 43/411 of 22 November 1988 or 48/422 of 10 December 1993, all of which were in substantively identical terms.

[347] Unless interests are equated with wishes. On the one hand this would be the only way to read the concept so as to make it consistent with pluralism and constitutionalism. On the other hand the long-standing Gibraltar–Spain struggle over the distinction demonstrates it would not be unproblematic to persuade all parties of this.

[348] Cassese n 221 above, 88.

stance in relation to Gibraltar that has placed the interests of the States above those of the population of the territory.[349]

In October 2005 the wording of the annual resolution was slightly altered to welcome the commencement of Trilateral Dialogue between Britain, Spain and Gibraltar in December 2004.[350] However the General Assembly Resolutions[351] still continue to be framed in the language of bilateralism that the Government of Gibraltar, in its annual attendances before the UN, has described as 'ineffectual' and incompatible with the right to self-determination.[352] The latest format of annual decisions on Gibraltar urge the United Kingdom and Spain

> while listening to the interests and aspirations of Gibraltar, to reach, in the spirit of the statement of 27 November 1984,[353] a definitive solution to the question of Gibraltar, in the light of the relevant resolutions of the General Assembly and applicable principles, and in the spirit of the Charter of the United Nations.[354]

The clash of positions is evident in that the Spanish representatives at the UN regularly emphasise that for its part the decolonisation of Gibraltar can only be decided as a result of a bilateral negotiation with the United Kingdom that cannot involve an application of the right to self-determination.[355] The United Kingdom position is that the people of Gibraltar have the right to self-determination but not the right to independence without Spanish consent.

Intergovernmental Arrangements

The direct agreements between Britain and Spain in the post-war period have also taken a markedly bilateral approach. As has been outlined, there were several bilateral political agreements over Gibraltar between the States in the period following 1975 and during the period of Spanish democratisation that immediately preceded Spain's accession to the

[349] The Special Committee on Decolonisation has eg shrugged off a number of invitations to visit Gibraltar. In some respects the UN has adopted a passive role akin to the stance taken by the European Commission: see chs 4 and 5.

[350] See ch 6.

[351] See eg Decision 59/519 of 10 December 2004 adopted by the General Assembly on the Question of Gibraltar and that put forward by the Fourth Committee to the UN General Assembly on 13 October 2005.

[352] See the Speeches delivered by the Government of Gibraltar at the UN Fourth Committee, October 2003–05, Government Press Office, Gibraltar. Perhaps insufficient attention has been given to the possibility of involving the Human Rights Committee at an appropriate juncture through the mechanisms at the disposal of that Committee: see D McGoldrick, *The Human Rights Committee: Its Role in the Development of the International Covenant on Civil and Political Rights* (Oxford, Clarendon Press, 1994).

[353] The Brussels Agreement entered into by the UK and Spain.

[354] See General Assembly decision 61/522 of 14 December 2006 and that of December 2007, United Nations, General Assembly, 62nd session, Agenda Item 40, A/62/412, 33.

[355] Speech of Spanish Ambassador, October 2006, cited above.

community.[356] Britain was keen to facilitate the democratisation process and to remove any friction between the States. This, combined with its overall strategy of pursuing alliances within the European Community and with prospective entrants. Notwithstanding its public pronouncements these factors coloured its immediate stance and long-term strategy in respect of Gibraltar.

European Union

State-centric bilateralism has hampered the enjoyment of Gibraltar's European Union rights and impeded access to certain measures. These are described in detail in chapters 4 and 5. All in all, the bilateralism of the Gibraltar dispute has hampered constitutional reform, access to EU benefits and rights and obstructed the path to decolonisation. The European Commission has deferred to the State-centric bilateralism at European level and at United Nations level.[357] At the latter, it is worth highlighting that the European Commission used to make a statement supportive of self-determination in the context of decolonisation until, as a result of the Gibraltar dispute and Spanish objections, it ceased to do so in the mid 1990s.[358] In that statement, support for the right was confirmed by the EU 'irrespective of the geographic location and population size of the remaining non-self-governing territories.'[359] This was the standard phrase in previous statements and clearly encompassed Gibraltar. However no express reference to it was made. When raising 'two regional issues' of special importance to the EU it referred to East Timor and Western Sahara and not to the only European territory on the List: Gibraltar.[360]

The bilateralism of the Gibraltar dispute is in stark contrast to the trends within the European Community that have caused a fundamental reassessment of the methods of governance. This has been driven by a wider struggle for legitimacy in Europe which has manifested itself in several ways.[361] Pressures have come from different quarters—from

[356] These were described in the previous chapter. The bilateral dealings in subsequent years post Spanish accession to the EC are described in chs 4 and 5.

[357] For a general review see A Clapham, 'Where is the EU's Human Rights Common Foreign Policy and How is it Manifested in Multilateral Fora?' in P Alston (ed), *The EU and Human Rights* (Oxford, OUP, 1999) 627–83. For a review of the EU in the field of external affairs see P Koutrakos, *EU International Relations Law* (Oxford, Hart Publishing, 2006); A Dashwood and C Hillion, *The General Law of EC External Relations* (London, Sweet and Maxwell, 2000) and I Macleod, I Hendry and S Hyett, *The External Relations of the European Communities* (Oxford, OUP, 1996.

[358] See eg the Statement on behalf of the European Union by Hans-Pieter Kaul, Representative of Germany, 49th Session of the General Assembly, Agenda Items 12, 18, 81, 82, 83 and 84 on Decolonisation, New York, 12 October 1994.

[359] ibid 1.

[360] ibid 2–3.

[361] See ch 4.

supra-national and sub-State levels and from the citizen. The basic aspirations have been characterised by claims for greater transparency and accountability of the Community institutions and for more power, influence and participation at various levels of the governance spectrum. The calls for legitimacy and the primacy of 'peoples' were such that there were statements in the Amsterdam and Maastricht Treaties and the Treaty establishing a Constitution for Europe (referred to hereafter as the 'CE')[362] on respect for peoples. The European integration and reform agenda has sought to deal with these demands by introducing key measures designed to endow the citizen, sub-State and supra-national institutions with a greater role in the governance of the Union in moves that can best be described as decentralisation of a horizontal and vertical manner. The pressures have also seen internal national constitutional changes to address governance deficits. In Gibraltar's case there has been a double democratic deficit because it has neither had the benefit of changes at European level nor has it has seen the establishment of sufficient national mechanisms to alleviate these concerns.[363]

The redefinition of sovereignty and nationalism and the rise of pluralism come against a background of a greater stimulus to principles of participatory governance by which different societal groupings, individuals or institutional entities may each derive a more defined and larger role in the governance process. The principle of participatory democracy itself was introduced into the CE in Article I-47 that was directed to three different spheres. First to require the institutions to allow citizens and representative groups to express their views on areas of Union action. Secondly, to require institutions to 'maintain an open, transparent and regular dialogue' with representative groups and 'civil society.' Finally, it was intended to require the Commission to 'carry out broad consultations with parties concerned.' The European and Social Committee have made the point that the concept of participatory democracy is already incorporated in the theory of civil dialogue.[364] As Obradovic[365] has pointed out the

[362] CIG/87/2/04 of 29 October 2004. Ratification of the CE collapsed when this was rejected in referenda in France and Netherlands. A new Treaty was subsequently signed at Lisbon: see *Treaty of Lisbon amending the Treaty on European Union and the Treaty establishing the European Community*, Conference of the Representatives of the Governments of the Member States, Brussels, CIG 14/07, 3 December 2007 ('the Lisbon Treaty'). Ratification of that was also affected by the rejection of the Lisbon Treaty in referendum by the people of Ireland in June 2008. There is current speculation that further amendments will be made and a new document will emerge in due course. Which provision of the old CE or the Lisbon Treaty will survive this process and reappear in an eventual amending Treaty is unknown at this stage. References to provisions in the CE throughout this work should therefore be read in that light.

[363] The EU trends are described in ch 4.

[364] European Social and Economic Committee, Opinion addressed to the 2003 Intergovernmental Conference (2003) CESE 1171/2003, Brussels, September 2003.

[365] D Obradovic, 'Participatory Democracy and the Open Access Policy for Interest Groups in the European Union', Paper presented at EUSA Ninth Biennial International Conference, April 2005, Austin, Texas (cited with permission of the author). See also D Obradovic and

essence of participatory democracy is that parties affected by legal provisions 'should be given the opportunity to bring their wishes to bear in this (opinion-forming) process and to put forward their proposals.'

This last point is central in Gibraltar's case and indeed reveals the crux of the democratic deficit underlying the historic bilateralisation of the Gibraltar issue. For years the view was held by Britain and Spain that they were the only valid interlocutors in respect of the sovereignty of Gibraltar and that while the interests of the population should be taken into account the States should be at liberty to decide what those interests required.

In an interesting study on Switzerland, Linder,[366] describes the wide-ranging methods that can be used to enhance democracy, participation and power-sharing in culturally diverse, plural or quasi-federalist societies. While informal consultation has happened within the European Union for some years, there is now a much more conscious and active encouragement of dialogue with various interest groups and other representatives of civil society. Indeed, as Obradovic has noted, the European Commission considers itself 'legally bound' to pursue such consultation and its 'duty to wide consultation flows from Protocol No 7 on the application of the principles of subsidiarity and proportionality.'[367] To that end access to information, transparency, accountability and consultation have become the bywords of this impetus to achieving more formalised structures for civil dialogue with the Commission. A call for more structured dialogue was made in the White Paper on Governance in 2001.[368] Minimum standards for such consultation have been introduced[369] and a range of measures have stemmed from that to secure those principles of dialogue. The aim of that dialogue is to obtain input from representative groups and civil society, to secure their understanding and as a consequence their support,[370] to allow these groups adequate influence into the law-making process and allow the progression of European Union development.[371]

JM Alonso Vizcaino, 'Good Governance Requirements Concerning the Participation of Interest Groups in EU Consultations' (2006) 43 *CML Rev* 1049–1085.

[366] Above.

[367] D Obradovic, 'Participatory Democracy and the Open Access Policy for Interest Groups in the European Union', Paper presented at EUSA Ninth Biennial International Conference, April 2005, Austin, Texas, at 4 (cited with permission of the author).

[368] Commission of European Communities, European Governance: White Paper COM (2001) 428, Brussels, 25 July 2001.

[369] Commission of European Communities, Communication from the Commission 'Towards a reinforced culture of consultation and dialogue—General principles and minimum standards for consultation of interested parties by the Commission' COM (2002) 704, 11 December 2002.

[370] The effective legitimisation of the Commission's work.

[371] See eg the extensive review by D Oliver in *Constitutional Reform in the UK* (Oxford, OUP, 2003) esp chs 2, 3, 19.

The governance debate is relevant to the sovereignty dispute and the conflict of nationalisms because it can help soften and accommodate the all or nothing absolutist tendencies of the traditional sovereignty dispute into an acceptance of a more plural and polycentric environment without provocative assertions of ownership.

In the remainder of this chapter the status and governance issues that arise for Gibraltar and are considered in the following chapters of this work are traced.

THE STATUS AND GOVERNANCE ISSUES FOR GIBRALTAR AND THE PARADOX OF CONSTITUTIONALISM

The Status Issue

There are three dimensions to Gibraltar's status that require examination:

Domestic Dimension—Colony Under Domestic Law?

In the 300 years since the Anglo-Dutch force landed on Gibraltar shores the territory has gone from being described as 'the garrison of Gibraltar in the Kingdom of Spain' to being the fortress 'colony' and to simultaneously being described as the 'garrison and city of Gibraltar'. Subsequently it became simply the city of Gibraltar and from being a dependent territory became an overseas territory. But all that was nomenclature only. The basic status change that had arrived in 1830 when Gibraltar became a colony would require much more to be altered. It required substantive change—in domestic and international law. That could be achieved by convention or by actual amendment. In either case it depended, at some point, on some international and domestic recognition.

The word 'colony' is defined in British domestic law within the 1978 Interpretation Act.[372] Jersey and Guernsey fall within the definition of 'British Island' in the same Act and not in that of 'colony'.[373] Overseas territories acquired their new nomenclature in 2002 after some soul-searching to alight on a name that did not imply dependence and colonialism.[374] That however did not stop overseas territories from falling

[372] Interpretation Act 1978 Sch 1. Essentially these are any territories part of Her Majesty's Dominions outside the British Islands except countries having fully responsible status within the Commonwealth, territories for whose external relations a country other than the UK is responsible, and associated states. Dominions were taken out of the definition of colony pursuant to s 11 of the Statute of Westminster 1931: see Hood Phillips n 85 above, 787–95.

[373] Though this is not always the case as other statutes make some anomalous provisions in respect of both islands.

[374] The former name was dependent territories.

within the definition of colony in the Interpretation Acts, at least for the purposes of English law or domestic law in the territories. While of late[375] Gibraltar's constitutional relationship with the United Kingdom has been described as non-colonial in nature,[376] the inevitable conclusion of the interplay between the different provisions seems to be that for Gibraltar to formally cease to be a colony there would not only have to be a qualitative change in its relationship with the United Kingdom but also (preferably) formal amendment to the Interpretation Act[377] and formal de-listing at the United Nations. Decolonisation requires recognition that Gibraltar is not a colony under domestic law or international law. Until this happens it is possible to argue that the territory is constitutionally advanced but technically still a colony under domestic or international law. The battle lines are not so black and white of course, as the history of Canada and New Zealand demonstrates. As Crawford has stated the 'fact that until the Statute of Westminster 1931, Canada was still in British law a "colony" was not decisive as to its international status.'[378] Those countries were regarded as independent as a result of a cumulative process of constitutional steps and not as a result of a one-off event. In some respects it was the acquisition of independence by stealth. The Statute of Westminster, for example, came five years after the Balfour Declaration of 1926, which was the first political recognition of the change in effective status of the so-called Dominions.[379] Oliver described how the Balfour Declaration and Statute of Westminster

> avoided the legal nettle of calls for constitutional independence, and wrapped it up instead in the flexible material of constitutional convention. While constitutional convention could achieve a perfectly satisfactory level of independence in practice it was never likely to be an acceptable peg on which to hang full and permanent constitutional independence.[380]

As Crawford cites 'international law does not require complete independence before regarding governmental units as States.'[381] In essence

[375] Post the 2006 Constitution.

[376] See the Written Ministerial Statement by the Foreign Secretary, Hansard HC vol 444 pt 132 cols 44–46W (27 March 2006) and the Statement by Minister of State Geoff Hoon at Handard HC vol 448 pt 177 col 932W (4 July 2006).

[377] Or some other explicit statutory provision which would deal with the formal issue of status in domestic law and disapply the definition 'colony' to Gibraltar. Otherwise, the only argument that remains is that, by constitutional convention and as a result of legitimate expectations created by statements made by British Ministers, Gibraltar's domestic status has been transformed into a non-colonial one. This is an unsatisfactory position devoid of certainty, and certainly at peril of being unenforceable in fact. When political statements were made in the Balfour Declaration of 1926 in respect of the Dominions this had to be followed up by statutory change in the Statute of Westminster of 1931.

[378] Crawford n 60 above, 363.

[379] Hood Phillips n 85 above, 787.

[380] P Oliver n 98 above, 8.

[381] Crawford n 60 above, 358.

this requires an evaluation of the stage the devolving unit has reached and can be

> considered independent when it possesses virtually complete autonomy and some substantial competence in international relations which the metropolitan State is bound by law, convention or Treaty to respect and when the remaining restrictions vis-à-vis the metropolitan State in internal and external affairs are not such that if they were consented to by an existing State the restrictions so created would be inconsistent with its independence. After the critical date remaining fetters on local autonomy are to be explained on grounds of agency, representation or consent.[382]

Gibraltar's process has also been evolutionary (because of the political sensitivities with Spain) and leads to the potential for further gradual changes at both status and governance level. That will also be an argument of this work. The substantive point though is that, unlike the Dominions, Gibraltar is not at the constitutional stage these had reached in 1926 or at the stage Crawford outlines above, hence the need for clarity and certainty by legislative change and political recognition or further evolution by convention.

European Dimension

As stated in the previous chapter, Gibraltar joined the European Community with Britain in 1973. Membership of the Community raised several issues for Gibraltar. First it led to an impact on constitutional and legislative sovereignty. Secondly, it gave rise to a number of deep legitimacy and governance issues. Thirdly, there was a need to re-define the constitutional relationship with the United Kingdom, and fourthly, the effect that the continuing Spanish claim to the sovereignty of Gibraltar had on access to rights and implementation of obligations of the European Union required examination[383] especially after Spanish accession to the Community in 1986. Recently, a couple of issues have arisen that have had the potential to affect Gibraltar's EU status either directly[384] or

[382] ibid.

[383] See chs 3–5.

[384] In 2001 the European Commission challenged the non-implementation by Gibraltar of directives to do with the freedom of movement of goods under Arts 94 and 95 of the EC. The implications of such a challenge—if lost—would have meant that Gibraltar's Treaty exemption to the 'goods freedom' would have been undermined, with potentially adverse economic effects. It would also have meant a great deal of administrative and legal burden in meeting the backlog of transposition of directives that had historically not been implemented, because of the assumption that Gibraltar was exempt from doing so. However in 2003 the European Court of Justice (following the Opinion of Advocate-General Tizzano) ruled that Gibraltar did not have to transpose such directives and retained the exemptions intact: see Case C-30/01 *Commission v UK*, Judgment of 23 September 2003 [2003] ECR I-09481.

indirectly.[385] These cases however are generally outwith the sovereignty dispute that has led to or exacerbated the central governance deficit and are not dealt with in great detail in this work.

International Dimension—the United Nations, Decolonisation, Self-Determination and International Status

The inability to achieve formal decolonisation as defined by the United Nations is largely because of the sovereignty dispute and the prevailing bilateralism. Spain's attitude conveyed at the United Nations is clear—the UN cannot accede to any demands by the population that the territory be decolonised in accordance with the principle of self-determination. It maintains that this can only be achieved by a bilateral negotiation with the United Kingdom. That position was forcefully re-stated in speeches by the Spanish Ambassador to the Fourth Committee of the United Nations during the sessions held in 2006–08. It remains one of the central obstacles to overcome.

The Governance Issue

Internal Governance

Gibraltar's 1969 Constitution was granted at a time of significant escalation in tension between Britain and Spain over the territory. It did not satisfy the aspirations of its people for long, though these were temporarily dampened by the lack of economic self-sufficiency during the years of economic blockade and frontier closure with Spain. Even so, by the 1970s there were attempts to reform the 1969 package to achieve several

[385] The European Commission and the Gibraltar Government were engaged in litigation over proposed reforms to Gibraltar's fiscal system during the period 2001–08. In the latest phase to that litigation one of the key issues between the parties was an argument over so-called 'regional selectivity' in which the Commission argued that Gibraltar could not have a different tax system to the UK because it considered it to be a 'region' of that Member State for State Aid purposes. That argument did not recognise the constitutional relationship between the UK and Gibraltar or the fact that Gibraltar has always had a different tax system to the UK. The ruling in the *Azores* case (Case C-88/03 *Portugal v European Commission*, Judgment of the Grand Chamber of 6 September 2006) is indicative of the criteria that should be met. An adverse ruling would have had repercussions way beyond the fiscal because any inability to have a separate tax system would have raised issues of economic sustainability which would have brought Gibraltar's current relationship with the EU sharply into focus. On 18 December 2008 the European Court of First Instance dismissed the Commission's contentions that Gibraltar's tax system was regionally selective: see chs 6–7 for the constitutional significance of this case.

objectives.[386] Attempts at seeking constitutional reform foundered after clear statements by Britain that Spain had to be taken into account.[387]

As stated the 2006 Constitution was introduced as the culmination of a process of negotiations between the Gibraltar and United Kingdom Governments that took place during the period 1998–2006. It introduced a number of significant advances in the field of demarcating domestic competences, devolving further powers of self-government, reforming the Parliamentary and other institutions of governance and modernising the chapter on human rights. It took that long for Gibraltar, even though other overseas territories had seen quicker reform processes in the preceding 30 years, because of the impact of the sovereignty claim. But even on the eve of negotiations, the issue of the drafting of the Second Preamble,[388] the language of the Despatch[389] and the reference to self-determination[390] in the 2006 Constitution all led to complicated and protracted wrangling over wording. The reason for that stemmed clearly from the sovereignty

[386] To achieve greater self-government, to enshrine constitutional conventions and to assist in obtaining formal decolonisation.

[387] The best example being the response to constitutional proposals by the Labour Government in 1976: see ch 2 and Cantos n 324 above, 1995.

[388] The Preamble to the 1969 Constitution—set out in ch 2—was repeated in the 2006 Constitution. A so-called Second Preamble was inserted to set out the mechanical context and consequence of the acceptance of the Constitution by the people of Gibraltar in referendum. The intention behind this—for Gibraltar—was that it would assist in lobbying the United Nations for decolonisation. It stated, 'And whereas the people of Gibraltar have in a referendum held on 30 November 2006 freely approved and accepted the Constitution annexed to this Order which gives the people of Gibraltar that degree of self-government which is compatible with British sovereignty of Gibraltar and with the fact that the UK remains fully responsible for Gibraltar's external relations.'

[389] The 1969 Constitution had carried a Despatch (an explanatory covering letter) from the Foreign Secretary to the Governor. The purpose of it was to explain certain provisions or set out British Government policy more appropriately described outwith the Constitution proper. The 1969 Despatch was quite lengthy because of the nature of the inverted domestic competences demarcated by that instrument. The 2006 Despatch is relatively short, but equally was the opportunity to set out relevant British policy on sovereignty and the Treaty of Utrecht. The Gibraltar delegation insisted on setting out Gibraltar's position too, so that there was no doubt that there was disagreement on this issue. Accordingly among other things the Despatch states 'this Constitution does not in any way diminish British sovereignty of Gibraltar . . . Gibraltar will remain listed as a British Overseas Territory . . . Her Majesty's Government supports the right of self-determination of the people of Gibraltar . . . except that independence would only be an option for Gibraltar with Spain's consent. Her Majesty's Government takes note that Gibraltar does not share the view that this constraint exists and that their acceptance of this Constitution is on that basis.'

[390] The 2006 Constitution inserts a preambular paragraph just before the chapter on human rights, which declares 'Whereas all peoples have the right to self-determination . . . And whereas the realisation of that right must be promoted and respected in accordance with the provisions of the Charter of the United Nations and any other applicable international treaties . . .' Substantial debate flowed from the inclusion of the words 'and any other applicable international treaties'. This phrase was ambiguous enough to allow different interpretations as to whether it included the Treaty of Utrecht or not. The use of the plural and the word 'any' was inserted at the request of the Gibraltar delegation to the constitutional talks to allow flexibility for Gibraltar's interpretation that there may not be any Treaty that fulfils the requirement of being applicable to Gibraltar's case and that Utrecht was inapplicable.

dispute and the prospect of Spanish objections. It also resulted in a parallel exchange of correspondence between Foreign Secretaries aimed at conveying British assurances that the reforms did not affect the Treaty of Utrecht and in turn allowed Spain to make statements that these had no effect on Gibraltar's international status or amount to a sufficient degree of reform for decolonisation.[391] Two points arise: first, that the obstacles represented by Spain and the traditional view of the sovereignty claim remain; secondly, that the 2006 reforms have in any event not substantively (still less conclusively) tackled the external governance or status issues for Gibraltar.

The External Governance Dimension—Representation, Power and Influence within the Union

When Gibraltar chose to accede to the Community, politicians expressed the hope that this would contribute towards finding a solution to the Gibraltar issue. Instead there has been a growing erosion of legislative and constitutional sovereignty, a deepening democratic and governance deficit and a marked disenchantment of the local populace. The hope that Europe is or would ever be willing and able to respond to Gibraltar's needs has greatly diminished.

It is beyond dispute that EC membership fundamentally altered the constitutional balance established by the 1969 Constitution through the doctrines of supremacy, direct and indirect effect and State Liability. If the process of constitutional development can be described as two scales—one representing the colonial power, which is the source of any transfer of powers to the colony, and the other scale representing the competences that have been transferred to the territory, the 1969 Constitution very firmly tipped the scales in the direction of significant self-government. Political pressure post-1969 was directed at securing a greater distribution of power. EU accession added a third scale with pressure being brought to bear to tip the scales the way of the EU with a consequent shift of powers to Brussels. If accession brings difficulties to a Member State it brings particular challenges to a stateless nation for the simple reason that the acquisition of greater power, representation and influence requires a negotiation with the State responsible.[392] In parallel, there has also been some pressure from the United Kingdom for some powers to be revisited or clawed back in response to internal situations or international trends (an experience which has been shared with other overseas territories). These attempts have been immeasurably complicated by the sovereignty dispute with another Member State.

391 The exchange of letters are referred to in greater detail in ch 6.
392 See chs 4–5.

The European context has brought to the fore the need to redefine the UK-Gibraltar relationship and how governance arrangements are handled and structured in areas that touch on and are affected by European issues. Gibraltar has suffered real problems in accessing EU measures that have been introduced to address sub-State calls for greater power, the European Parliament's concern for a greater role or the ordinary citizen's desire for greater participation in or greater transparency and accountability of Community Institutions. This has been hindered by the absence of national constitutional mechanisms that would allow smooth access to those measures and the flow of those benefits to Gibraltar. The territory also lacks the ability to effectively influence the policy or decision-making process at EU level as this would first require the securing of real influence over the way the United Kingdom represents or defends Gibraltar's interests at EU level. The subsidiarity[393] debate has in many ways passed Gibraltar by. In the meantime the United Kingdom remains accountable for the implementation in Gibraltar of EU obligations by virtue of the provisions of Article 299(4) EC[394] against a backdrop of growing frustration within Gibraltar that it is suffering a distinct deprival of EU benefits.

The struggle to obtain advancement on the external governance agenda has become increasingly important because of the day-to-day effect that the European Union has on domestic governance. In that sense it also takes primacy over the status debate because it is in the governance arena that Gibraltar has sustained the deepest and most regressive encroachment into its powers.[395] It is also this area that could be addressed first and more effectively without necessarily encountering the perennial territorial sovereignty claim.

The Paradox of Governance/Constitutionalism and the Growing Democratic Deficit

The cumulative effect of the domestic push for constitutional reform and decolonisation, the effect of the sovereignty dispute and the context of European governance reveal the paradox of self-governance and constitutionalism[396] in Gibraltar. The paradox is that:

[393] The issue of subsidiarity is developed in chs 4–5.

[394] Pre-infraction letters or proceedings brought to enforce EU obligations are brought by the Commission against the UK. The principles of State Liability, the implementation of EU obligations and the relationship with the UK are mentioned in chs 4–5.

[395] Outlined below and in chs 4–5.

[396] For an interesting analysis on the subject across a variety of fields see M Loughlin and N Walker (eds), *The Paradox of Constitutionalism, Constituent Power and Constitutional Form* (Oxford, OUP, 2007).

1. through a domestic process, Gibraltar has acquired greater powers of self-government than most other European sub-State Executives or stateless nations;[397]
2. but in turn, through an external process, those powers are being eroded without compensation[398] and progress on achievement of decolonisation and a permanent status is being resisted;
3. therefore leading to the conclusion that sub-State Governments with fewer powers of self-government have actually secured greater influence within their own State context and at European level and that the constituent power of Gibraltar (its people) are presently unable to achieve that advancement on external governance and status.

Even after the introduction of internal governance reforms in the shape of the 2006 Constitution and a more trilateral process of dialogue with Spain, Gibraltar continues to suffer a clear democratic and governance deficit. It needs reform and agreement from the United Kingdom if it is to address these issues. At the heart of this problem lies the unresolved question of its sovereignty and international status that exacerbates and is an obstacle to the resolution of the governance deficit.

The principal deficit is the State-centric bilateral stranglehold. This then manifests itself in a series of sub-deficits. On the domestic front it arises because of the failure of the reform process to introduce mechanisms that could adequately guarantee better accountability, representation and workability of its institutions and system of government. The slow process of reforms is a manifestation of how difficult it is to lift the spectre of sovereignty. In the context of its EU membership the deficit has arisen as a result of the failure to put such governance structures into place that could provide an appropriate response to the trends within the European Union and the need to secure better influence, participation and representation in it. Gibraltar is suffering a slow but constant erosion of powers without adequate compensation. To unblock these issues there is a need for further reform to agree how the British Government will interact with the Union on behalf of Gibraltar. At European level, Gibraltar would need to secure enjoyment of and access to its European Union rights, for which it needs the co-operation of the United Kingdom as the relevant Member State, the acquiescence of other States and the Community institutions.

The main obstacle to progress on those fronts is Spain's continuing claim to the sovereignty of Gibraltar. This has various effects. It hinders domestic constitutional reform because of the British Government's concern that it should avoid upsetting its European ally. It hinders progress on the European stage because of the preponderance by Spain to use any tool at that level to obfuscate the achievement, performance or enjoyment

[397] Comparisons will be made in chs 4–5.

[398] In the form of power, influence or representation elsewhere.

of European rights by Gibraltar and its people. On the international stage—at the United Nations—there has been an impasse for decades because of the seemingly unbridgeable gap between the aspirations of the different parties. While the United Kingdom has for many years adopted a policy of avoiding any course of action that would increase friction with Spain over Gibraltar, it was easier to avoid this happening when the only constitutional stage was the domestic one. Accession to the European Community changed all that, and the gradual and inexorable acquisition of more importance by the European stage combined with the reality that Spain could exercise more direct influence froze some necessary progress within Europe.

The result has been the creation of the mentioned paradox. On the one hand, domestic developments led to constitutional progress over the last 30 years. On the other hand, such progression has been neutralised or curtailed because of the encroachment into the domestic arena that accession to the European Union represents. For other sub-State Governments such encroachments were compensated by the acquisition of power and influence at different levels throughout the Union. This has not adequately occurred in Gibraltar. It thus acquired more theoretical powers of self-government than many of its counterparts among both the overseas territories and the more powerful self-governing regions or sub-State nations of Europe. Conversely it has also seen these being eroded as a result of its European status and the dispute on sovereignty.

The paradox arises because of the combination of the unique features that distinguish Gibraltar from other overseas territories and the methodology of bilateralism. To address this paradox requires a complete re-evaluation of the context within which the Gibraltar dispute operates. This requires an understanding and application of the changing definitions of the underlying component principles of sovereignty, nationalism and governance. The environment of changing concepts—once understood—needs to be applied by all parties in a more consensual, multi-level, plural or polycentric approach that could break the deficit and achieve progress on the vexed issues of status and governance. As the story in the next chapters unfolds it will be seen how Gibraltar encountered a very different environment in the European Union after 1986.

Annex to Chapter 3

Table C—Comparison of the Constitutions 1964–2006

Provision	1964 Constitution	1969 Constitution	2006 Constitution
Definition of Gibraltar	The city and garrison of Gibraltar[1]	The city of Gibraltar[2]	A part of Her Majesty's dominions known as the city of Gibraltar[3]
Preamble on Sovereignty	No	Yes[4]	Yes[5]
Second Preamble[6]	No	No	Yes[7]
Self-determination clause	No	No	Yes
Human Rights Chapter	No	Yes[8]	Yes—amended and updated in manner consistent with ECHR
Mechanism to amend Human Rights Chapter	No	No	Yes[9]

[1] 1964 Constitution s 1(1).

[2] Dropping the 'garrison' from the nomenclature for the first time: Gibraltar Constitution Order 1969 SI 1969 II p3602 s 2.

[3] Gibraltar Constitution Order 2006, s 2.

[4] Preamble to the Gibraltar Constitution Order 1969.

[5] In the same terms as in 1969 Constitution.

[6] That makes clear that constitution has been freely accepted by the people in referendum.

[7] 'And whereas the people of Gibraltar have in a referendum held on 30 November 2006 freely approved and accepted the constitution annexed to this order which gives the people of Gibraltar that degree of self-government which is compatible with British sovereignty of Gibraltar and with the fact that the United Kingdom remains fully responsible for Gibraltar's external relations.'

[8] 1969 Constitution Order ss 1–15, which set out a wide range of rights including rights to life, personal liberty and protections from forced labour, inhuman treatment, deprivation of property, of privacy of home, to secure protection of law, freedoms of conscience, expression, assembly and association, movement, to establish schools and protection from discrimination.

[9] 2006 Constitution s 18(9)—if there is a motion supported by 75% of the members and that proposal is then supported by majority in referendum.

Provision	1964 Constitution	1969 Constitution	2006 Constitution
Governor	There shall be a Governor and Commander-in chief[10] Need not consult Gibraltar Council if in public interest or too urgent or too unimportant[11] May act against the advice of the Gibraltar Council[12]	There shall be a Governor and Commander-in-chief . . . who shall be Her Majesty's representative in Gibraltar[13] Power to act against advice of Gibraltar Council and Council of Ministers in wider range of cases than under 2006 Constitution	There shall be a Governor and Commander-in-chief . . . who shall be Her Majesty's representative in Gibraltar[14] Governor's powers limited in scope following abolition of Gibraltar Council, clear demarcation of competences and redefinition of powers of Council of Ministers[15]
Executive Authority		Vested in the Governor on behalf of Her Majesty[16]	Vested in Her Majesty and exercised by the Government of Gibraltar[17]
Definition of Government of Gibraltar	No[18]	No, but as across	Council of Ministers and Her Majesty represented through the Governor shall constitute the Government of Gibraltar[19]
Executive (Gibraltar) Council	Presided by Governor[20] and made up of four *ex officio*– and five elected members[21] Elected members appointed by Governor after consultation with Chief Minister[22]	Presided by Governor[23] and made up of four *ex officio*– and Chief Minister and four Ministers The last appointed after consultation with Chief Minister[24]	Abolished

[10] 1964 Constitution s 4.
[11] 1964 Constitution s 21.
[12] 1964 Constitution, s 22.
[13] 1969 Constitution, s 18.
[14] 2006 Constitution, s 19.
[15] 2006 Constitution ss 45–50.
[16] 1969 Constitution, s 45.
[17] 2006 Constitution, s 44.
[18] Though in practice it was the Governor in Council.
[19] 2006 Constitution s 45(1).
[20] 1964 Constitution s 20.
[21] 1964 Constitution s 12.
[22] 1964 Constitution s 13(3).
[23] 1969 Constitution s 51.
[24] 1969 Constitution s 46.

Provision	1964 Constitution	1969 Constitution	2006 Constitution
Chief Minister and Ministers	Governor charges elected member with responsibilities after consultation with Chief Minister[25]	Ministers appointed by the Governor after consultation with the Chief Minister[26] and charged with responsibility for defined domestic matters[27]	Ministers appointed by the Governor acting in accordance with the advice of the Chief Minister[28] and charged with responsibility of any business of Government of Gibraltar[29]
Council of Ministers	'May make recommendations to the Gibraltar Council' concerning matters for which ministers were responsible[30]	Composed of Chief Minister and between four and eight other Ministers[31] Governor shall act in accordance with the advice of Council of Ministers in respect of defined domestic matters but retained some discretion in specific circumstances to depart from that[32]	Composed of Chief Minister and not less than four other Ministers[33] Subject to enlargement of the Parliament it is possible to increase the number of Ministers to 15[34] Governor shall act in accordance with advice of Council of Ministers on all matters not set out in s 47(1) Very few examples of when can depart from that[35]
Agenda and Minutes of Council of Ministers	To be sent to Permanent Secretary, Attorney-General and Financial Secretary[36]	To be sent to Governor[37]	Simple duty on Chief Minister to provide regular briefings to Governor on policies of Government and public affairs[38]

[25] 1964 Constitution s 23.
[26] 1969 Constitution s 47.
[27] 1969 Constitution s 48.
[28] 2006 Constitution s 45(4).
[29] 2006 Constitution s 46(1).
[30] 1964 Constitution s 14(3). The 1964 Despatch stated that 'its recommendations on matters of purely domestic concern will as a general rule be endorsed by the Governor in Council.'
[31] 1969 Constitution s 47 .
[32] 1969 Constitution s 50.
[33] 2006 Constitution s 45.
[34] Presently there are nine Ministers and a Chief Minister: see 2006 Constitution s 45.
[35] 2006 Constitution s 50.
[36] 1964 Despatch para 4.
[37] 1969 Constitution s 53.
[38] 2006 Constitution s 52. Equal duty on Governor to brief the Chief Minister on his responsibilities under s 47: see 2006 Constitution s 49.

Provision	1964 Constitution	1969 Constitution	2006 Constitution
Areas of Responsibility/ Competence	Not defined but cross reference needed to Royal Instructions 1964	Ministers responsible for defined domestic matters[39]	Governor responsible for external affairs, defence, internal security and functions in relation to public offices conferred on him by the Constitution—other functions are the responsibility of Ministers[40]
Police Authority	No	No: area not devolved	Established by s 48 and then prescribed in the Police Act 2006
Legislature	Legislative Council	House of Assembly: Legislature defined as the Governor and the Assembly[41]	Gibraltar Parliament: Legislature defined as Her Majesty and the Gibraltar Parliament[42]
Composition	Speaker, plus 11 elected members: two *ex-officio* members[43]	Speaker, plus 15 elected members: two *ex-officio* members[44]	Speaker, plus at least 17 elected members[45]
Governor's special legislative powers	Wide powers of law-making in default of Council passing a measure at Governor's discretion[46]	Wide powers of law-making vested in Governor in default of Gibraltar Council supporting or Assembly passing a measure but to be exercised only after prior approval of	Law-making power vested in Governor in relation to matters within the Governor's responsibilities[47] if the Government is unwilling to support the introduction of a Bill or the Parliament is

39 1969 Constitution s 55 and para 3 of the 1969 Despatch, which made clear that the arrangements were to devolve matters in a more formal way and that what was intended to be devolved were matters 'hitherto within the competence of the City Council and the existing Council of Ministers.' While directions were not formally made, a list of those areas was annexed to the Secretary of State's Despatch. These areas ranged from municipal services, public utilities, social services, education, housing, welfare, employment and industrial issues, medical and public health issues, economic development, tourism, trade, commerce, public services (air terminal, fire services, public works), personal status (amongst which were issues of Gibraltarian Status). The Despatch also stated that 'everything which is not a defined domestic matter automatically remains within the Governor's direct responsibility.'

40 2006 Constitution s 47.

41 1969 Constitution s 24.

42 2006 Constitution s 24.

43 1964 Constitution s 24.

44 1969 Constitution s 25.

45 2006 Constitution s 25(2). The enlargement of Parliament may be prescribed by law if a motion has first been passed in Parliament with a two-thirds majority.

46 1964 Constitution s 45.

47 External affairs, defence, internal security (including the police) and functions in relation to public offices: see 2006 Constitution s 47(1).

Provision	1964 Constitution	1969 Constitution	2006 Constitution
Governor's special legislative powers (*cont.*)		Secretary of State[48]	unlikely to pass a Bill so introduced Such power to be exercised with Secretary of State approval only[49]
Finance Bills	Cannot be proceeded with unless have Governor's consent[50]	Cannot be proceeded with unless have Governor's consent signified by the Financial Secretary or a Minister[51]	Cannot be proceeded with unless have consent of Minister for Finance[52]
Disallowance	Any law may be disallowed by Secretary of State[53]	Any law may be disallowed by Secretary of State[54]	Removed Power retained to withhold assent to bills repugnant to good government or incompatible with any international legal obligation or to reserve for signification of Her Majesty's consent any bill inconsistent with the constitution[55]
Dissolution of Legislature	By Governor 'at any time'[56]	By Governor 'at any time' after consultation with the Chief Minister[57]	By Governor 'at any time' acting in accordance with the advice of the Chief Minister[58]
Public service appointments	Governor may constitute offices, make appointments, discipline officers and terminate the appointments[59]	Governor may constitute offices, make, confirm and terminate appointments and execute disciplinary control over public officers[60]	Government may constitute offices for Gibraltar Governor, acting on advice of the Public Service Commission, may make, confirm,

48 In defined domestic matters, only after having previously introduced a bill for debate into the Assembly and this having failed to pass. In matters other than defined domestic matters there was no requirement to introduce a Bill into the House: 1969 Constitution s 34.

49 2006 Constitution s 34.

50 1964 Constitution s 46(2).

51 1969 Constitution s 35.

52 2006 Constitution s 35.

53 1964 Constitution s 48(1).

54 1969 Constitution s 37.

55 2006 Constitution s 33. Wide powers to withhold assent or to reserve bills for the signification of Her Majesty's pleasure were also present in the 1964 and 1969 constitutions.

56 1964 Constitution s 50(1).

57 1969 Constitution s 39.

58 2006 Constitution s 38.

59 1964 Constitution s 9. This was subject to the mechanics set out in the Public Service Commission Ordinance 1956: now repealed by the Public Appointments Act 2007.

60 1969 Constitution s 71.

Provision	1964 Constitution	1969 Constitution	2006 Constitution
Public service appointments (*cont.*)		Governor acting in his discretion may refer questions of the appointment, transfer, promotion, termination, dismissal or disciplinary control of public officers to the Public Service Commission but the Governor may not act in accordance with their advice[61]	terminate appointments and exercise disciplinary control over officers Discretion to depart from that advice only if it will 'prejudice Her Majesty's service'[62] Specified Appointments Commission established for a certain number of senior appointments[63]
Judicature	No provisions in constitution	New Part added specifying provisions on Supreme Court, appointment of judges and appeals to Privy Council Court of Appeal established[64]	Judicial Services Commission established for judicial appointments and discipline
Judicial Appointments	No provisions in constitution	See above	By Governor in accordance with advice of Judicial Services Commission
Finance		New Part added setting out the manner of expenditure from consolidated Fund and the presentation of estimates of expenditure[65]	Finance provisions updated and linked to Minister for Finance and not Financial Secretary
Crown Lands	Power vested in Governor to dispose and make grants of crown lands[66]	Power vested in Governor to dispose and make grants of crown lands acting after consultation with the Gibraltar Council[67]	Power vested in Governor to dispose and make grants of crown lands in accordance with the advice of the Chief Minister[68]

[61] 1969 Constitution s 73.
[62] 2006 Constitution s 54.
[63] 2006 Constitution s 56.
[64] 1969 Constitution ss 56–62.
[65] 1969 Constitution ss 63–70.
[66] 1964 Constitution s 8.
[67] 1969 Constitution s 75.
[68] 2006 Constitution s 75(1). In respect of lands under the possession, occupation, use or control of the Ministry of Defence or any other such authority of the UK Government the

Provision	1964 Constitution	1969 Constitution	2006 Constitution
Power to make laws	Vested in the Governor with the advice and consent of the Legislative Council[69]	Vested in the Legislature[70]	Vested in the Legislature[71]
Supremacy of constitution	Existing laws shall be construed in compliance with constitution[72]	Existing laws shall be construed in compliance with constitution[73]	Existing laws shall be construed in compliance with constitution[74]
Existing Laws Definition	All ordinances, laws etc 'having effect as part of the law of Gibraltar before the appointed day'[75]	All ordinances, laws etc 'made or having effect as if they had been made in pursuance of the existing Order and having effect as part of the law of Gibraltar'[76]	All ordinances, laws etc 'made or having effect as if they had been made in pursuance of the existing Order and having effect as part of the law of Gibraltar'[77]
Reserved Power to Her Majesty[78]	Yes[79]	Yes[80]	Yes[81]

Governor can also make such grants or dispositions but only on the instructions of a Secretary of State and 'with the consent of the Chief Minister.' For reasons set out in ch 6 this is considered to be a major reform.

[69] 1964 Constitution s 36.

[70] 1969 Constitution s 32.

[71] 2006 Constitution s 32.

[72] Gibraltar (Constitution) Order 1964 s 5(1).

[73] 1969 Constitution, Annex 2, paragraph 2(1) and for an interpretation of the scope of that provision see *Rojas v Berllaque* [2004] 1 WLR 201.

[74] 2006 Constitution Annex 2, para 2(1).

[75] Gibraltar (Constitution) Order 1964 s 5(4).

[76] 1969 Constitution Annex 2, para 1.

[77] 2006 Constitution Annex 2, para 1.

[78] The standard provision is 'to make laws from time to time for the peace, order and good government of Gibraltar (including without prejudice to the generality of the foregoing laws amending or revoking this Order)'.

[79] Gibraltar (Constitution) Order 1964 s 9.

[80] 1969 Constitution s 86.

[81] 2006 Constitution Annex 2, para 8.

4

'The Sensitivity of the Underlying Bilateral Issue':[1] Bilateralism and the Governance Deficit 1986–2004

INTRODUCTION

IN 2003 THE European Commission became caught up in a controversy between Spain and the United Kingdom on the manner of enfranchisement of Gibraltar's citizens in European elections. It sought to sidestep the controversy by adopting a non-interventionist stance, anxiously conscious of the 'sensitivity of the underlying bilateral issue'.[2] That perception from the Commission that the dispute was bilateral instead of trilateral coloured their attitude and made it take a back seat in relation to it.[3]

Bilateralism as an applied methodology does not sit well with the modern legal context. It stems from the territorial sovereignty dispute and has had a marked impact on the status and governance ambitions of Gibraltar, as highlighted in earlier chapters. After 1986 bilateralism emerged regenerated with the European Community becoming the principal theatre of developments. Status issues and the decolonisation level at the United Nations would continue to take a back seat.[4] Formal attempts at constitutional reform were also frozen during the same period. But in a Community post Spanish accession the internal and external governance issues took centre-stage. The 1986–2004 period was dominated by the external governance deficit and the inability to pursue formal constitutional reform or status change.

[1] From the European Commission press release on Gibraltar, 29 October 2003.

[2] See n 1 above.

[3] Though it is accepted that the commission has a broad discretion as to whether to pursue enforcement action in the general course of things.

[4] The prospect of formal decolonisation remained frozen during the period 1969–86 as explained in ch 2.

The principal deficit was the lack of legitimacy epitomised by the insistence on bilateralism to the exclusion of Gibraltar and its representatives. That in turn spurns further examples that make up the overall democratic deficit. This chapter traces the causes of the democratic and governance deficit suffered by Gibraltar by examining the causal and theoretical context that pits the intergovernmentalism inherent in bilateralism against more modern trends of multi-level governance.

The causal roots of the deficit are assessed. Albeit after some struggle, there has been a fairly generalised acceptance upon the European stage that governance involves a variety of parallel levels. In Gibraltar pure intergovernmentalism has been the order of the day during the same period. As this and the next chapter progress, it will become clear that the different component elements of the democratic and governance deficit are due to one or a combination of factors. They are either:

a. directly caused by bilateralism or;
b. exacerbated by it because of the effect of bilateralism as an additional complication; or
c. (when neither) they are caused by the failure to address specific circumstances within the United Kingdom-Gibraltar constitutional relationship (which when it requires constitutional reform has seen such aspirations being frozen during the period 1986–2006 in part because of the Spanish angle); or
d. caused by purely internal and domestic Gibraltar reasons.

Examples within the last two points exist in a self-standing category unrelated to bilateralism and form a small part of the causal roots of the Gibraltar democratic deficit, the products of which are then analysed in the next chapter. Bilateralism as a pure form of intergovernmentalism also causes the paradox of governance for Gibraltar. At European supranational level the acceptance of multi-level governance dynamics was brought about as a way of trying to secure greater legitimacy.[5] Sub-State territories then depended on these mechanisms being facilitated at national level by those same Member States.[6] In that sense, the ultimate irony is that intergovernmentalism is always central. The State level is at the heart of bilateralism and is also at the heart of facilitating sub-State self-governance. To end the bilateralism Gibraltar relies on the principal participants in that bilateralism to replace it with structures more reflective of participatory governance and the evolved meaning of sovereignty.

[5] See the introduction of the principle of subsidiarity in Art 5 of the EC Treaty, below. Certain Regions also fostered change by applying pressure before each Treaty was concluded, particularly German Länder.

[6] Albeit often very reluctantly.

The Sub-State Context of Governance

The chapter assesses the nature of sub-State power and the levels at which this is exercised. It emphasises that the best and most direct way of achieving effective democracy and participation in the institutions of power is by endowing the sub-State Executive level with adequate power and influence. It compares the relative importance of the State and European levels in securing greater sub-State power and concludes that to secure access to the mechanisms of multi-level governance[7] it is the Member State that is in the principal position of securing real and effective access for the sub-State territory. In analysing the deficit this part of the chapter studies the two principal dimensions at which the deficit is sustained—the sub-State Executive Power level and the non-Executive level at which greater influence and representation is sought. For the reasons explained in this chapter it is contended that the sub-State Executive is of most practical significance.

THE CAUSAL CONTEXT—BILATERALISM: THE PRINCIPAL DEFICIT

The Conflicting Trends—Intergovernmentalism (Bilateralism) and Multi-Level Governance

In Gibraltar's case the last two decades have seen a clash between the forces of bilateralism and the influences behind the process of European integration. Contrary to European trends, the pure intergovernmentalism represented by bilateralism has triumphed over attempts at introducing adequate power, representation and influence for Gibraltar at European level. The period 1986–2004 has been one of significant change in the composition, constitutional framework and institutional balance of the European Union.[8] It has also led to a reassessment of the layers of governance[9] and the position of the individual European citizen within the ambit of the process of European integration.[10] In parallel to these changes, the

[7] Referred to herein for ease of reference as 'MLG'.

[8] Craig, in Craig and De Burca, *The Evolution of EU Law* (Oxford, OUP, 1999) 1–20.

[9] The White Paper on European Governance, 'Report by Working Group 3b, Decentralisation—Better Involvement of National, Regional and Local Actors', June 2001, conceded that 'The EU integration process originated with a centralised top-down approach . . . it is however clear that better involvement of all levels of government as well as civil society and the general public in EU policy-shaping and implementation are prerequisites for the necessary credibility, legitimacy and acceptance of EU policy and law.'

[10] J Shaw, 'The Interpretation of European Union Citizenship' (1998) 61 *MLR* 293; C Closa, 'Citizenship of the Union and Nationality of the Member States' (1995) 32 *CML Rev* 487; C Closa, 'The Concept of Citizenship in the Treaty on European Union' (1992) 29 *CML Rev* 1137 and S O'Leary, 'The Relationship between Community Citizenship and the Protection of Fundamental Rights in Community Law' (1995) 32 *CML Rev* 519.

incremental bilateralisation by Britain and Spain of the Gibraltar issue at European level has led to turbulent clashes with governance trends that sought to include all relevant levels—whether at executive (State or sub-State), parliamentary or individual level—as participants within their respective spheres of influence in the new governance framework.[11]

Both forces have aroused and responded to the same themes: legitimacy, democracy and sovereignty.[12] Both have necessitated a reassessment of the participants to the process of governance, an evaluation of the structures of government, an assessment of compliance with principles of effective democracy and a redefinition of the concept of sovereignty especially within a larger, more integrated Europe. Both have witnessed the strains between structural cohesion, effective government, democracy and legitimacy of the integration process and the institutions of governance. Within this was a struggle between a colder, more technocratic and utilitarian view that placed efficiency at the top of the list of objectives and a trend that argued that success of the supra-national model depended on its adaptation to allow greater participation of the individual governmental, State, regional and individual components of the European entity.[13] This last philosophical approach placed greater importance on identity and a more individualised, reflexive and interactive participation in governance.

While there were thematic similarities in the processes of bilateralism and European integration the clash between them—in the case of Gibraltar—came as a result of the very different end-results that both processes envisaged. In Europe, after a conflict between different proponents of governance theory, the advocates of multi-level governance started to slowly get the upper hand and this was increasingly reflected in measures that sought to define competences, rebalance and increase the accountability of institutions, give opportunities for sub-State executives to influence the European governance process,[14] and recognised the importance of the support of the ordinary European citizen to secure legitimacy in an enlarged Union.[15]

The by-word for European governance trends was the recognition of inclusion as a key to legitimacy.[16] In contrast for many years the effect of the process of bilateralisation of the Gibraltar issue was exclusion. The

[11] For the European struggle: H Wallace, 'European Governance in Turbulent Times' (1993) 31 *Journal of Common Market Studies* 293.

[12] JHH Weiler, *The Constitution of Europe* (Cambridge, CUP, 1999) 10–96, 264–76.

[13] W Wallace and J Smith, 'Democracy or Technocracy? European Integration and the Problems of Popular Consent' in J Hayward (ed), *The Crisis of Representation in Europe* (London, Frank Cass, 1995).

[14] By introducing the principle of subsidiarity or the ability for sub-State Executives to be represented on Ministerial delegations at Council level, eg, below.

[15] S Garcia (ed), *European Identity and the Search for Legitimacy* (London, Pinter, 1993).

[16] Even though within a large supra-national entity made up of such different national or regional components this was always going to be very difficult to achieve.

natural consequence of the emphasis by the UK and Spain on bilateralism was to greatly exclude the people of Gibraltar and its Government from access to power, representation or influence within key areas. This clash led to the democratic and governance deficit described in this chapter and was compounded by the paradox that during the same period Gibraltar had acquired significant constitutional competences vis-à-vis the UK but had in fact lost more power.

The Importance of 1986 And Beyond

It is in that context that 1986 was a watershed for Europe and for Gibraltar.

For Europe

For the Community the launch of the Single Market White Paper marked the start of a drive to complete the internal market and boosted the integration process.[17] This in turn led to several developments in subsequent years. These were not confined to the economic arena—they cut across all the institutions of the Community and had significant ramifications for the political, social and constitutional framework of Europe.[18] In relatively quick succession this led to three Treaties at Maastricht, Amsterdam[19] and Nice.[20] The developments overhauled the governance of the Union and created a more cohesive economic and politically integrated unit. The pace of change has been such that the present extent and structure of the Union would have been difficult to foresee for anyone contemplating the Europe of 1985.

By 1 May 2004 a European Union had been established consisting of 25 Member States.[21] The enlargement process—first southwards and most recently eastwards—altered the economic balance and required a profound readjustment of the way the EU was governed.[22] Apart from problems fostered by conflicting cultural, social or political priorities

[17] See Craig n 8 above, 5–25, and C Barnard and J Scott (eds), *The Law of the Single European Market—Unpacking the Premises* (Oxford, Hart Publishing, 2002) 10–150.

[18] See eg the greater use of Qualified Majority voting.

[19] The Amsterdam Treaty, among other matters, incorporated a heavily qualified last resort mechanism into the first and third pillars that allowed 'closer co-operation' between a majority of Member States (short of unanimity) thus institutionalising the trend of flexibility in the integration process in recognition to the reality that not all States would agree on the pace of integrationist measures.

[20] See also the Laeken Declaration which was a significant development in the integration process.

[21] By the time of the Lisbon Treaty in October 2007 the EU had 27 members.

[22] In terms of the re-weighting of votes for example and the allocation of structural regional funding for example.

the smaller States in the Union have found that their size leads to a distribution of power that puts them at a relative disadvantage vis-à-vis the block of larger States.

A single currency has been adopted for a majority of Member States with the European Central Bank having a wide impact on the internal economies of those States. There is a common flag, a common citizenship[23] and passport. Citizens have the right to vote in elections to a European Parliament with enhanced influence and strengthened powers. Sub-State representation has also been improved by the creation and strengthening of a Committee of the Regions.[24] The Community Institutions have slowly assumed more powers but also subjected themselves to greater accountability.[25] With a wider range of competences has come a wider raft of legislation. In turn, the influence that European measures have on daily life in Member States has grown substantially.[26] The natural consequence of this has been that Member States and sub-State self-governing regions have ceded powers and national vetoes on increasing areas of policy. While the ratification processes of the CE[27] and the Lisbon Treaty were thrown into turmoil because of adverse referenda their content does illustrate the significant steps taken over the last couple of decades.

The pace of integration since 1985 now seems remarkable in retrospect. But the path has understandably not been easy. The tensions between the theories of federalism and intergovernmentalism have run deep sparking off national and European rows over loss of sovereignty[28] and legitimacy. The power struggle on different levels—supra-national, State and sub-State—has led to the greater acceptance of multi-level governance and in parallel to it to a fundamental reassessment of the meaning of sovereignty within the Union.[29]

[23] Albeit one with limited rights ascribed directly to it: see Art 18 TEC.

[24] In 1992 although doubts have been cast on its effectiveness: see ch 7, pp 346—7. Gibraltar does not have representation on this Committee and this will be covered in greater detail later.

[25] P Magnette, 'Appointing and Censuring the European Commission: The Adaptation of Parliamentary Institutions to the Community Context' (2001) 7 *European Law Journal* 292–310; E Vos, 'Reforming the European Commission: What Role to Play For EU Agencies?' (2000) 37 *CML Rev* 1113–34.

[26] See the Table set out in ch 5 below on the volume of legislation within areas of competence of Gibraltar's Executive.

[27] Among other measures the Constitution sought to clarify the competences of the Union, remove the three pillar structure and create the EU into a single legal personality, extend the competences of the Union in a number of areas, further enlarge the Parliament, increase the role of national parliaments in the approval of European legislation and the powers of the Committee of the Regions.

[28] Witness eg how difficult it was to achieve an agreement on the weighting and assignment of votes at Council level in the run up to and following the Nice Treaty.

[29] This reassessment has however somewhat concentrated on practical power and not on the more complex question of trying to resolve the dimension of emotional sovereignty in the sense of its link with identity, ownership, individual and societal inclusion and participation.

The advent of greater political, social and economic cohesion has also brought a number of challenges and pressures that have required resolution. For a period, the priority was driving economic integration and accumulating power around Community institutions and State Executives even if this was to the detriment of other players. State Parliaments, sub-State government and the average European voter all felt a mixture of threat or simple disenchantment. While measures to encourage decentralisation—such as the insertion of the principle of subsidiarity and proportionality—or to temper the competences of the institutions were introduced, many concerns remained and it was widely thought that these reforms did not go far enough to address the governance deficit.[30] There were pressures for further developments in the period leading to and during the Convention on the Future of Europe[31] (that led to the CE). It was agreed that there would be a meeting in 2001, as a precursor to the convening of a conference, that would make recommendations on the Future of Europe. Before that the Commission issued a White Paper on 'European Governance' in response to the loss of confidence and dissatisfaction with the Union and its perceived remoteness. It recognised the need for a broader debate about the future of the Union, for more coherence, for the policy-making processes to be opened up and for greater openness, accountability and responsibility. It made certain proposals amongst which were the recognition of a greater need to interact with regional and local Government and to 'bring greater flexibility into how community legislation can be implemented in a way which takes into account regional and local conditions.' The Anglo–Spanish bilateralism over Gibraltar during the period tended to obstruct the delivery of these objectives for Gibraltar.

At the pre-Convention meeting in Laeken in December 2001 it was acknowledged that several areas needed to be tackled, including many of those mentioned in the Treaty of Nice. The trends and pressures all consistently demand a review of powers, simplification of the Treaties, a clear demarcation of powers and greater involvement and participation at all levels of the governance spectrum by civil society and sub-State governments.[32]

[30] See S Weatherill and U Bernitz (eds), *The Role of Regions and Sub National Actors in Europe* (Oxford, Hart Publishing, 2005).

[31] Annex IV to the Treaty of Nice set out a Declaration on the Future of the Union which called for a 'deeper and wider debate about the future development of the Union'. That process was called to address several questions: a 'more precise delimitation of competences between the European Union and the Member States reflecting the principle of subsidiarity'; the status of the Charter of Fundamental Rights; the role of national Parliaments; a simplification of the Treaties; and an improvement and monitoring of the 'democratic legitimacy and transparency of the Union and its institutions to bring them closer to the citizens of the Member States'.

[32] The process of European integration has as a consequence promoted at its mildest a national redistribution of competences and at its most dramatic could foster any latent tendencies there might be for national disintegration.

For example, the Commission has supported simplification measures, the greater use of framework directives and other policy tools, the wider availability of information, the greater use of consultation methods and a review of objectives and methods to ensure coherence. It highlighted five principles of good governance—openness, participation, accountability, effectiveness and coherence—and suggested ways in which the institutions could abide by those principles and address the alienation that the citizen felt. Within that context it stressed the importance of compliance with the principles of subsidiarity and proportionality. It acknowledged the growing importance of regional and local government in many Member States and recommended that the Committee of the Regions should play a more proactive role in matters. The whole ethos of the White Paper was the realisation of the need to improve dialogue, consultation and participation so as to contribute to its relationship and interaction with civil society.

Self-governing regions within Member States felt their hard won constitutional powers of self-government were being eroded.[33] State Parliaments felt their very existence as forums to debate the initiation of legislation and hold their State executives to account was being undermined by transfers of power elsewhere.[34] Conversely the European Parliament also felt it had insufficient powers to influence or initiate legislation. Worse still for many Europeans, the Union was alien to their aspirations or daily lives.[35] They did not feel they could identify with European ideals or that they owned the integration process. The levels of participation in European Parliamentary elections were a clear illustration of the crisis of legitimacy and democracy suffered by the Union which was compounded by corruption scandals at the level of the Commission, the perceived remoteness of European legislators, scant accountability, inability to access core information or to influence the process through any Parliamentary, political or legal route.

These concerns emerged over a period of years. In parallel to the integration process, a realisation grew that this so-called crisis of legitimacy and the concerns at different governmental, political and administrative level had to be addressed.[36] Attempts were made to address these through a variety of measures combining a redistribution of power, provisions to

[33] Submissions in the consultation exercise run by the Convention on the Future of Europe are indicative of that. In particular see those made by German Länder, Belgian Regions and NGOs all posted on the relevant website: http://european-convention.eu.int/.

[34] Note the proposed Protocol on National Parliaments in the Lisbon Treaty that would enhance national parliament power (though in a manner—which in practice could make its exercise cumbersome, impractical and ineffective).

[35] This was clear in a number of 'eurobarometer' surveys run by the European Commission during the period.

[36] See White Paper on European Governance COM (2001), cited above. Whether the White Paper went far enough to deal with these concerns is another matter—eg J Scott and D Trubek, 'Mind the Gap: Law and New Approaches to Governance in the European Union' (2002) 8 *European Law Journal* 1.

ensure greater accountability, transparency and access to information and mechanisms to promote more representation and influence at European level to compensate for any loss elsewhere.[37] Central to these reforms was the growing awareness—as evidenced by multi-level governance theory—of two key realities. The first was that there were a number of players in the political, governmental, legal and administrative architecture of the modern European Union. The second was that all those players needed to be involved in the governance of the Union. There was a realisation too that the various players co-existed both at horizontal and vertical levels and that ultimately securing the endorsement and support of the individual citizens of the Union was paramount.[38]

The extent of success of these measures in addressing the conflicts and pressures created by the integration process has been the subject of much debate but there have been clear moves at both State and European level to introduce reforms and create more constitutional space for the various players.[39] The recognition of this decentralised federalism or multi-level polity has been a key facilitator in the integration process[40] and has (at least in part) helped to accommodate the conflicting pressures from the different levels.[41]

For Gibraltar

1986 was also an important year for Gibraltar but for a very different reason. It marked the accession of Spain to the Community and the transposition of the growing bilateralisation of the Gibraltar issue onto the European stage. Given the historical legal and political context described in previous chapters the arrival of Spain onto the mainstream European stage would progressively impact on Gibraltar's participation within the Union and its governance and status aspirations. Indeed, at a time when the theory of intergovernmentalism was giving way to a growing acceptance of multi-level governance at European level the clear supremacy of bilateralism in the Gibraltar case stands out as a micro-trend that runs against the macro-European trends. The exclusion of Gibraltar's elected Government from effective modes of representation and the relatively

[37] G de Burca, 'The Quest for Legitimacy in the European Union' (1996) 59 *MLR* 349; A Cygan, 'White Paper on European Governance—Have Glasnost and Perestroika Finally Arrived to the European Union?' (2002) 65 *MLR* 2.

[38] As demonstrated by the problems over the ratification of the CE and Lisbon Treaty.

[39] There have been significant reforms to State governmental arrangements in Germany, Belgium, Scotland and Spain for example: see below.

[40] Report by Working Group 3b, Decentralisation, June 2001, above.

[41] The assimilation process has been complicated by the significant enlargement of the Union which raises debate on how to maximise cohesion, collective action, subsidiarity, decentralisation and legitimacy.

little influence that its people exerted was its principal crisis of democratic legitimacy from which the rest of the deficits stemmed.

The Consolidation of Bilateralism as a Factor in the Governance of Gibraltar

As described in chapter 2 there is no doubt that there was a bilateral approximation between Britain and Spain during the years 1975–86. Britain was eager to welcome the newly democratic Spain into the European fold. It also viewed a democratic European partner in a very different light in respect of the Gibraltar issue. Initially, discussions over Gibraltar were designed at breaking the physical blockade the territory had endured since Spain closed the frontier with Gibraltar in 1969. But Spain made clear it wanted to trade the lifting of restrictions and economic co-operation for some advancement on sovereignty discussions.

The 1987 round of Brussels talks[42] led to the signing of a bilateral Airport Agreement, the effect of which was simply to exclude Gibraltar's airport from the European air liberalisation package unless Gibraltar accepted joint control of its airport.[43] The Gibraltar Parliament rejected the agreement because of its implications over the sovereignty of the airport. Successive Gibraltar Governments committed themselves not to implement it. For a period during 1988–97 the Brussels talks ground to a halt as a result of a combination of factors: a Government in Gibraltar that refused to participate in these; a pre-occupied and weak Government in Britain;[44] and an exhausted socialist administration in Spain.[45] While sovereignty discussions stuttered the growing bilateralism was slowly having an effect on the governance of Gibraltar.

In 1997 Spain tabled proposals[46] seeking eventual Spanish sovereignty preceded by a period of joint sovereignty. It combined these proposals with a wave of obstructionism and restrictions.[47] Achieving recognition of

[42] Under the 1984 Brussels Agreement: see ch 2.

[43] Joint Declaration between the Governments of the UK and Spain of December 1987. It led to litigation when the Government of Gibraltar challenged the subsequent exclusion of Gibraltar from the benefit of the air liberalisation directive because of the bilateral agreement. See Case C-298/89 *Government of Gibraltar v Council of the Communities*, [1993] ECR I-03605. The Gibraltar Government lost that litigation because the court held it was not directly and individually concerned with the decision, narrowly construing the test, as Wade has observed: W Wade and C Forsyth, *Administrative Law*, 8th edn (Oxford, OUP, 2000) 212.

[44] Especially in the mid-1990s.

[45] Especially after the early 1990s.

[46] The so-called 'Matutes Proposals' known after the Spanish Foreign Secretary at the time, Abel Matutes.

[47] See House of Commons Foreign Affairs Committee, 1999–2000, Ninth Report *Gibraltar: Follow-Up*, HC 863 (London, TSO, 25 July 2000) and by the same Committee, 2000–01, Sixth Report, *Gibraltar*, HC 319 (London, TSO, 3 April 2001). In both, the Committee recommended that Britain take Art 227 proceedings against Spain over its behaviour at the frontier, as well

its claim by Britain and the tabling of a process of dialogue that involved the issue of sovereignty proved insufficient for Spain, which sought to move along its claim by using its position of influence within the EU and—where necessary—threatening to or actually vetoing European measures so as to gain concessions over Gibraltar. The reality in the post-Franco period is that there was an inexorable bilateral approximation and a successive watering down of the British position over Gibraltar. From a refusal to entertain talks and assertions of support for the right to self-determination of the people of Gibraltar at the United Nations in the 1960s, Britain first accepted a tabling of discussions in 1980, then formally agreed that sovereignty would be discussed in 1984 and, in 2002, that Britain would support a joint sovereignty deal over Gibraltar.[48] This last development was the culmination of a slow process that led to an emergence into the public glare of a view that had been held in some senior Foreign Office circles for some time. It was one of the most dramatic sovereignty developments in 300 years. For the first time in Gibraltar's history a British Government openly declared it was willing to sanction a sovereignty deal which clearly was objectionable to the people of the territory.[49]

This inexorable approximation had a profound effect on the domestic constitutional aspirations of the people, the participation and enjoyment of European benefits and trends of governance during the period from Spanish accession to 2004.[50]

The Forms of Bilateralism

Bilateralism in the case of Gibraltar does not merely result from Britain and Spain agreeing to pursue a policy of simple co-operation or joint subordination of issues. It comes in different forms. Sometimes there is dual and joint action between Britain and Spain. Sometimes action is consecutive,

as making other recommendations on lifting of other restrictions. See also *Memorandum of Evidence from the Chief Minister of Gibraltar to the House of Commons Foreign Affairs Committee*, Gibraltar, 23 March 1999.

48 There was also a macro-European reason for the emergence of heightened bilateralism, namely the wish of Britain to get Spanish co-operation at European level in the face of a strong Franco–German axis.

49 As evidenced by the referendum result of that year: see previous chapter. Whether the UK Government could in practice have entered into these arrangements or agreed the principle of ceding territory without the consent of the UK Parliament is another matter: see O Hood Phillips, *Constitutional and Administrative Law*, 8th edn (Sweet & Maxwell, London, 2001) 329, ch 6. Whether a majority would have been obtained in the House of Commons was moot (as there was a strong pro-Gibraltar lobby). It was even doubted by the Foreign Secretary, who admitted as much to Parliament on 5 February 2002.

50 The absence of legitimacy was condemned by the House of Commons, Foreign Affairs Committee, Eleventh Report, Session 2001–02, HC 973 (London, TSO, 7 November 2002) ('FAC Report 2002').

consequential and reactive. In this way it can be seen to be an underlying influence behind the stance taken by the UK on matters such as constitutional reform which, at first sight do not appear to be linked to the Spanish dimension. The reality is that it is clear after proper investigation that the United Kingdom driver in Gibraltar's affairs is, almost always, influenced by the Spanish dimension.

The examples of bilateralism that emerge in this chapter can in turn be categorised into four types:

Passive v Active Bilateralism (Direct Obstructionism)

This resulted from Spain's direct policy to obstruct the application of general European Union measures, undermine the constitutional aspirations of Gibraltar and question its status. The situation was so prevalent that the Cabinet Office produced a checklist of 'Gibraltar pitfalls against which to guard in such negotiations' because of 'instances of Spain seeking to exclude Gibraltar from draft legislation under discussion.'[51]

What marks these examples is passivity on the part of the United Kingdom and activity on the part of Spain. Within this field would fall examples of hindered access to European measures that stem from a policy of Spanish obstructionism exerted at different levels within the Union (sometimes combined with a concessionary United Kingdom attitude). There are a number of examples of Spanish obstructionism to the extension of European legislation or measures to Gibraltar. In the field of telecommunications, Spain for many years prevented the recognition of Gibraltar's international direct dialling code. It was the subject of a complaint before the Commission filed by the main Gibraltar telecommunications providers.[52] In the course of that complaint, *Telefonica*—the former

[51] See App 8 to Memorandum of Evidence, FAC Report 2002, setting out the 'Checklist of Gibraltar Pitfalls in EU Business', Cabinet Office, March 1997.

[52] eg in 1996 the main Gibraltar mobile telecommunications carrier (Gibtel) filed a complaint with the Commission (complaint no C1/36.036). In 2003, after some lengthy delays and investigation, the Commission found that *Telefonica* did not infringe Art 82 because it had received binding instructions from the Spanish State that were matters of foreign policy not to enter into mobile roaming agreements with Gibtel or to recognise Gibraltar's international dialing code and that the Spanish State's position was that roaming agreements were dependent on a resolution of the sovereignty dispute over Gibraltar. The Commission also considered that there was no breach of Art 86 by *Telefonica* because at the time of the determination of the complaint it was no longer the dominant operator. Finally, in considering a possible infringement of Art 10 as read with Art 82, the Commission relied on its discretion to decide not to start infringement proceedings against Spain. In doing so it noted inter alia that Britain and Spain had pledged to find a solution to the telecommunications issues as well as sovereignty issues within the process under the Brussels Agreement. The Commission noted it had sent a letter to both Governments encouraging the importance of telecommunications services between Gibraltar and Spain in 2000, but decided that it would not, in 2003, take enforcement action: see House of Assembly Hansard, 2003–04.

Spanish national monopoly—admitted it was under instructions from the Spanish State not to recognise the code, thereby blocking telecommunications access to Gibraltar from Spain via that route.[53] In the field of freedom of movement complaints about frontier flows have also been commonplace with vehicular and pedestrian queues of several hours materialising and then disappearing in an apparently arbitrary way. Difficulties over the Spanish Government's refusal to recognise the competence of Gibraltar authorities led to an Agreement in April 2000 on the methodology of communication from and to Gibraltar authorities. The obstructionism has produced peculiar examples of failure to recognise a Gibraltar entity or organisation in any sphere. This programme of measures has affected activities and access to rights at international[54] and European[55] levels, inclusion in measures,[56] the membership or participation of representative groups in wider international bodies[57] or the competence of authorities.[58]

CONFLICTIVE BILATERALISM

Conflict is the prevailing theme of this type of bilateralism that manifests itself because of the different demands and interests of the United Kingdom and Spain on a particular matter of Gibraltar interest. Examples in this category are the right to vote or State Aid cases[59] or the free

[53] House of Assembly Hansard, Gibraltar, June 2001. In February 2007, as part of the 2006 Córdoba Agreement, Spain finally recognised Gibraltar's international dialing code.

[54] The most significant being their denial of the right to self-determination of the people of Gibraltar.

[55] eg the failure, over decades, to recognise Gibraltar's international dialing code was an anti-competitive measure and a breach of provisions of the EC Treaty: see above.

[56] Gibraltar has been excluded from a variety of EU measures as a result of Spanish pressure. eg, the exclusion of Gibraltar from the air liberalisation package in 1993 was challenged by the Government of Gibraltar before the European courts: see ch 5 for this and other instances. Another poignant example of how seriously Spain views these issues was its insistence that Gibraltar should be excluded from the External Frontiers Convention in 1992. The draft Convention sought to demarcate Europe's external borders. Spain wanted these demarcated at La Linea (the frontier town most proximate to Gibraltar on the Spanish side). On that occasion the British Government resisted Gibraltar's exclusion and the draft Convention collapsed.

[57] In the field of sport Spain has intervened to oppose Gibraltar's application for membership of the International Olympic Committee or UEFA (the latter as recently as 27 January 2007). It is not only in sporting matters where this policy is evidenced. In the more sensitive field of international co-operation on serious crime the Spanish Financial Intelligence Unit (SEPBLAC—a quasi-police body) in 1998 blocked the application of the Gibraltar financial intelligence unit (GFIU) for admission to an international organisation of financial intelligence units (the Egmont Group).

[58] Which at European level led to an agreement of 19 April 2000 to unblock the recognition of Gibraltar bodies by Spain by using the British Foreign Office as a conduit for communications—the so-called system of post-boxing. This has been of main benefit in financial services.

[59] Both covered in greater detail in the next chapter.

movement of goods case.[60] In the latter the Commission—supported by Spain—challenged Gibraltar's status within the Union and its Treaty exclusion from the Common Customs Tariff unsuccessfully. It is an example though of Spain being prepared to litigate in assistance of the EU in a way that could potentially affect the status of Gibraltar. It had no other obvious interest to do so. There are also a number of instances of Spain intervening in Gibraltar specific litigation to make submissions on the competence of the Government of Gibraltar[61] or its authorities.

CO-OPERATIVE BILATERALISM[62]

These examples are dominated by a more deliberate policy that combines elements of consent, consultation, acquiescence or the simple conscious factoring in of the views of Spain by the United Kingdom.[63]

The trend of bilateralism and its influence over European and international measures of application to Gibraltar has clearly been incremental. During the first few years of Spanish accession to the Community, Britain had resisted the pressure from Spain with more vigour, to the point that no agreement was possible over the proposed External Frontiers Convention in 1992. For a while Spain concentrated its efforts on simple bilateralisation and in obtaining reservations that the extension of any measure to Gibraltar was without prejudice to its sovereignty claim over Gibraltar.[64] After a while, Spain graduated from that to full-blown exclusion of Gibraltar from the measure. A without prejudice reservation of itself was no longer enough to satisfy Spanish aspirations. So for example in the Common Position on the 'Single Sky' proposal it was made clear that the aviation measures in that package are not extended 'until the bilateral arrangements on Gibraltar airport of 1987 enter into operation.'[65] This

[60] Case C-30/01 *Commission of the European Communities v UK* [2003] ECR I-09481.

[61] The Air Liberalisation Case 1987 or litigation launched in 2001 challenging a Commission State Aid decision in respect of Gibraltar companies legislation (See Cases T-195/01 and T-207/01 *Government of Gibraltar v Commission* [2002] ECR II-02309)—later in the next chapter.

[62] As Spain and the UK are EU partners a certain amount of bilateral co-operation is, to a certain extent, inevitable. However the instances concentrated on in this work are those that either run contrary to the clearly expressed wishes of the people of the territory or that by their methodology have excluded its representatives from participation or consultation.

[63] Exclusion from air liberalisation and the 1987 Airport Agreement.

[64] See eg the Spain (Extradition) (Dependent Territories) Order 1991.

[65] Additionally the UK and Spain agreed a bilateral mechanism to exclude the application of EC aviation measures to Gibraltar. The reason for this was the Spanish Government's position that the airport was built on disputed land and the general sovereignty dispute. As stated in the Gibraltar Government's press release of 22 March 2002, 'In essence the UK has agreed that when a new aviation measure is brought forward in the EC, the UK and Spain will ask the EU Commission whether or not the measure places any obligations on airports. The Commission will consider its response specifically in the context of Gibraltar Airport. If the Commission's answer is yes, then Spain will request the Gibraltar suspension clauses

was notwithstanding the clear rejection of the Airport Agreement of 1987. Issues of legitimacy were engaged by the absence of popular support from the people of Gibraltar or its elected representatives. This was only possible because of the acquiescence of the United Kingdom.

TACIT BILATERALISM (INDIRECT OBSTRUCTIONISM)

In this group of examples bilateralism takes the form of a tacit acceptance that the other Member State (Spain) is a presence in the background to be considered in the discussion over specific measures.[66] This category is in some ways related to the first. The main difference is that Spain adopts a less pro-active and vociferous public stance (though this does surface from time to time). Rather, this sphere of activity is more discreet and less immediately obvious.

While the net governance deficits described herein are present as a result of the combination of all instances of bilateralism,[67] the deepest effects producing inadequate power, lack of influence or unrepresentative structures are felt as a consequence of (i) and (iv). Some instances have features of different categories. The European Union—through the Commission—and the United Nations both deferred to this bilateralism and preferred to maintain a role as an encouraging supervisory entity rather than as active participant in the resolution of the dispute.[68] A number of instances have drawn criticism by Gibraltar political parties as to perceived inaction, insufficient action or a reluctance to act by Community institutions:

> At the height of 2–3 hour border queues and after submission of extensive dossiers the Commission reported back that it did not see that it could act in the matter;[69]

when the proposal reaches the Council, and the UK will agree. If the answer is no, then Spain will agree that Gibraltar should not be excluded. Both the UK and Spain will accept the Commission's judgment on this question as final.' As a result, Gibraltar airport was excluded from a variety of aviation measures: see Government of Gibraltar Press Office, Press Release 105/2002 of 31 May 2002, and 51/2002 of 22 March 2002.

[66] The prime example is the discussion on prospects for constitutional reform. Governance structures established as a direct or indirect result of reforms could enhance Gibraltar's power and influence. The Spanish dimension casts a shadow over constitutional reform, in that the UK tacitly accepts Spain as an unspoken factor in the consideration of reform. As Spain has made evident her historic opposition to moves perceived to imply self-determination this has hampered the process of reform.

[67] And the few examples of factors unrelated to bilateralism alluded to (above).

[68] As described in ch 3 245 the European Union confirmed annual support for the principle of self-determination at the United Nations until Spanish objection was made—as a result of Gibraltar.

[69] In October 2000 the Commission sent Spain a Letter of Formal Notice raising that the border checks might be incompatible with EC law. After an 18 months investigation the Commission announced it was to close its investigation because it had found no evidence of

The Commission refused to act on complaints by Gibraltar's telephone carriers against *Telefonica* and the Spanish State's anti-competitive action.[70] This led to action by the carriers against the Commission for failure to act;

As mentioned at the outset of this chapter the Commission baulked at intervening in the dispute over the enfranchisement of Gibraltarians in European elections because of the sensitivity of the bilateral issue;

The reference to Gibraltar as a bilateral dispute has now become standard at Community level and there is an expectation that the matter is best left to the two States concerned.

While the Commission has a wide discretion in deciding if to act in any given situation, all this has created deep dissatisfaction in Gibraltar. Concerns have been expressed about the role of the Community institutions and the lack of pro-active intervention to tackle the causes of the governance and democratic deficit. The Commission has been described as the guardian of the legal framework of the Community.[71] On the one hand, it has a wide discretion in deciding whether to institute enforcement action but equally the Commission has general duties to act, among other matters, in cases of restrictive practices. It has been accepted by Nugent, however, that 'political considerations can inhibit the Commission from acting as vigorously as it might ... [and that] ... the Commission does not normally wish to upset or politically embarrass the governments of Member States if it is at all avoidable.'[72] This is the issue that haunts Gibraltar and affects the achievement of progress in other spheres. It is the sphere of bilateralism rearing its head once more but without abatement. Indeed it carries the acquiescence of the Community at institutional level.[73] This attitude is perhaps consistent with other developments for as Petersmann has noted in an analogous context there is a distinction and a 'tension between citizen-oriented interpretation of internal EU rules and state-centred interpretations of the EU's foreign policy powers.'[74]

incompatibility—this despite queues of several hours for vehicular crossings over the border. Two days later Spain announced that it would open a second channel for vehicles thereby raising the spectre that there had been an agreement behind the scenes to ensure the closure of the investigation on terms: see European Parliament, Reply E-2283/2002 to Parliamentary Question of 12 August 2002.

[70] In 1977 direct telephonic links to Gibraltar were restored by Spain on a limited basis, and as if Gibraltar were part of its own national numbering plan. The consequential effect of this policy was that Gibraltar had a maximum set of numbers available as part of its own numbering plan if it wished to retain telephonic links with Spain. Gibraltar carriers were heavily critical of non-recognition of the international dialing code, the limitation on the Gibraltar numbering plan and the failure to allow mobile roaming. They contended that such action prevented commercial expansion and was anti-competitive.

[71] N Nugent, *The Government and Politics of the European Union* (Hampshire, Palgrave, 1999) 133.

[72] ibid.

[73] It can lead to complaints that could be laid against the Institutions affected.

[74] E Petersmann, 'From State Sovereignty to the "Sovereignty of Citizens" in the International Relations of the EU?' in N Walker (ed), *Sovereignty in Transition* (Oxford, Hart Publishing, 2003) 145–166, 153.

It is this—the prevailing, all-engulfing State-centric bilateralism—that is the principal deficit suffered by Gibraltar. It is the single and most prominent example of lack of legitimacy. This was not only markedly different to the European governance trends but also then provoked further governance issues across a range of fields.[75]

The Trend of European Governance: Conferred Powers, Subsidiarity and Proportionality

In contrast to the pure intergovernmental influence sustained by Gibraltar, the European trend has been to increasingly embrace multi-level governance as a way to maximise the legitimacy and stability of the Union, because States

> no longer provide the sole interface between supra-national and subnational arenas, and they share rather than monopolise, control over many activities that take place in their respective territories.[76]

State-centricity is what marks the bilateralising impetus of the UK and Spain over Gibraltar. Conversely the rise of multi-level governance is based on a pluralistic rather than a hierarchical view of the Union–national law divide.[77] Neither the State nor the supra-national level has full control over the pace of integration. This is also influenced by different players across all fields of governance and society by a multilateral interchange at State and sub-State level rather than simply a unilateral flow from the supra-national body. This explains the tensions between the players and the intense level of interactivity that necessarily has spurred on the State and sub-State debates on sovereignty and loss of competences.

There is also a conflict between the technocratic and democratic views of how the Union should be run as Scott has noted.[78] The impetus for the new methodologies of governance have been identified by Scott and Trubek,[79] as the increasing complexity of issues, the irreducible diversity of these, the developments in public and administrative law, the competence 'creep'[80] and the struggle for legitimacy and subsidiarity. The

75 These are described below after reviewing these governance trends.

76 G Marks, L Hooghe and K Blank, 'European Integration from the 1980s: State-Centric v Multiple Level Governance' (1996) 34 *Journal of Common Market Studies* 346–47.

77 N MacCormick, *Questioning Sovereignty: Law, State and Practical Reason* (Oxford, OUP, 1999) 118–19.

78 C Scott, 'The Governance of the European Union: The Potential for Multi-Level Control' (2002) 8 *European Law Journal* 59, 62: what he terms the 'quality of outputs and inputs' debate.

79 Scott and Trubek n 36 above, 6–8.

80 For a very useful table that illustrates how competences have shifted in the period see P C Schmitter 'Imagining the Future of the Euro-polity with the help of new concepts' in G Marks, P Schmitter, W Streeck and F Scharpf, *Governance in the European Union* (London, Sage, 1996) 125–26.

trends and characteristics of the new methodologies are 'participation and power-sharing, multi-level integration, diversity and decentralisation, deliberation, flexibility and revisability and experimentation and knowledge creation'[81] This is evident in the use of so-called soft law mechanisms or in the introduction of the Open Method of Co-ordination as a legislative technique.

The key question for EU governance 'lies in bridging the gap between transnational governance and its democratic legitimation.'[82] The legitimisation of power and its intercourse with civil society is a key battleground, with a number of views on how this can be achieved.[83] The White Paper on European Governance has come in for some criticism as not going far enough, fostering technocratic control and not embracing innovation.[84] At a more radical level, Moravcsik has mounted an interesting defence of the legitimacy of the European Union, analysing its processes and modes of governance and concluding that 'as long as political procedures are consistent with existing national democratic practice and have a prima facie normative justification ... we cannot draw negative conclusions about the legitimacy of the EU from casual observation of the non-participatory nature of its institutions—a dictum that could usefully be applied in many contexts outside the EU.'[85]

The essential underlying thread of subsidiarity[86] is that decisions should be taken at the most appropriate level, which is usually the lowest one possible. The theory puts at its centre the interests of the individual and insists that these can be secured by action taken by the social unit most proximate to the individual. It encourages decentralisation as a fundamental philosophy—accepting centralisation only where absolutely necessary.[87] Article 5 of the Treaty that establishes the principle of subsidiarity contains three

[81] Scott and Trubek n 36 above, 5–6.

[82] K Armstrong, 'Rediscovering Civil Society: The European Union and the White Paper on Governance' (2002) 8 *European Law Journal* 102, 104.

[83] See the Convention on the Charter of Fundamental Rights and the CE. Both involved national politicians and representatives of civil society—though none from Gibraltar.

[84] J Scott and D Trubek, 'Mind the Gap: Law and New Approaches to Governance in the European Union' (2002) 8 *European Law Journal* 1–18, and K Armstrong, 'Rediscovering Civil Society: The European Union and the White Paper on Governance' (2002) 8 *European Law Journal* 102–32.

[85] A Moravcsik, 'In Defence of the "Democratic Deficit": Reassessing Legitimacy in the European Union' (2002) 40 *Journal of Common Market Studies* 603, 622. Christopher Lord has advocated that performance indicators be devised to assess this: see 'Assessing Democracy in a Contested Polity' (2001) 39 *Journal of Common Market Studies* 641.

[86] P Birkinshaw, *European Public Law* (London, Butterworths, 2003) 219–54.

[87] For reasons of effectiveness: see De Burca, 1996 and also P Marquardt, 'Subsidiarity and Sovereignty in the European Union' (1994) 18 *Fordham Int L J* 616.

separate (but interrelated) concepts:[88] those of conferred powers,[89] subsidiarity[90] and proportionality.[91]

Subsidiarity and proportionality concern the scope and extent within which conferred powers can be exercised. The definition of such competences or the lines of demarcation between Union and Member States has been the subject of much debate,[92] with some focus placed also on whether the fact that the Union has not legislated in a field of, prima facie, exclusive competence affects the exclusivity of it. The issue was analysed in a document prepared by the Secretariat for the Convention on the Future of Europe,[93] which described five basic problems and made a number of recommendations.[94] The system of competences it is said[95] needs to balance the need for more precise delimitation and the need for flexibility. The proposed amendments to Articles 2B and 2C of the TEU put forward in the Lisbon Treaty set out a catalogue of exclusive and shared competences. Concerns have been expressed as to issues that

[88] There is also reference to the principle of subsidiarity in Art 2 TEU, which states that the Union's objectives will be achieved 'respecting the principle of subsidiarity'.

[89] That the Union should only act within its attributed powers and objectives. Given the Court of Justice's liberal construction of the doctrine of implied powers and the use of Art 308, the reality is that its powers have expanded through the years.

[90] Which is only triggered if the area is not one within the exclusive competence. It is concerned with the exercise of shared powers. The concept has been described as a 'hotly contested aphorism': Birkinshaw n 86 above, 221.

[91] That the measure should be appropriate, proportionate and not excessive. The three concepts are inter-related, in that there is a fluid domino effect in the analysis of the key questions and the points at which each element is invoked. The underlying emphasis running through the three elements is a wish to demarcate competences to ensure balance and certainty. The principle of conferred powers was in many ways useful for advocates of very different positions. On the one hand, it suited those who wanted to attribute specific powers to the Community that could then be built on. On the other hand, it suited decentralisers or sovereigntists as it created parameters for the exercise of that power which together with subsidiarity could enhance the multi-level governance balance. The article places emphasis on a definition of the areas of exclusive competence. Finally, the subsidiarity principle and proportionality clause act as a double safety net to ensure that the Community does not stray beyond what is strictly necessary.

[92] The starting point is to examine where an issue lies. If it is an issue of exclusive competence of the EC (or the Member States), then the principle does not apply. The principle contained in Art 5 is only of application in cases of overlapping competences—a majority of areas. The range of exclusive competences is summarised in a document produced for the Convention on Europe's Future. See CONV 47/02, 29.

[93] Entitled 'Delimitation of Competence between the European Union and Member States—Existing System, Problems and Avenues to be Explored' CONV 47/02, Brussels, 15 May 2002.

[94] (1) The 'system's lack of clarity', in that there are no specific provisions governing the allocation of competences; (2) the 'lack of precision of certain provisions of the Treaty', making particular reference to Arts 94, 95 and 308; (3) the 'failure to comply with the principles of subsidiarity and proportionality'; (4) the fact that 'powers of the Union do not match citizens' expectations'; and (5) the insufficiency of 'checks to ensure compliance with the delimitation of competence', especially at national level.

[95] CONV 47/02, 10.

require more attention.[96] It is clear, though, that (together with other measures) the injection of the principle of subsidiarity into the Treaty was intended to respond to State and sub-State concerns about the need to put a brake on an unrestricted extension of supra-national power and more closely demarcate the principles which should govern the law-making powers of the Union.[97] The subsidiarity amendment made to the EC Treaty in 1992 did not adopt the ambitious agenda of the regions. The Article currently only refers to the Union and Member States as if they were the only relevant actors, and focuses on a functional mechanism/divide rather than on the conceptual objective of subsidiarity. The amendment put forward in the Lisbon Treaty was aimed at recognising that in the application of subsidiarity the measure could be introduced at central, regional or local level.[98]

The adoption of the subsidiarity principle reflected these concerns and the wider debate of the level at which initiatives should be driven. Subsidiarity was a key demand of the powerful regions and was used at Maastricht in response to their calls for a greater role. In the protocol attached to the Maastricht Treaty, only Belgium, Germany and Austria asserted that the principle had application at sub-State level, but it is clearly applicable by sub-State governments in all Member States to press their claims at least within their State constitutional structures.[99] The larger regions continued to press for an amendment to the subsidiarity article so that it explicitly referred to organs of Government other than Member states.[100] Indeed this was reflected in the insertion of 'either at central level or at regional and local level' in the proposal in the Lisbon Treaty to introduce a new Article 3b TEU. Those developments resulted from an impetus to multi-level governance as the real engine of the Union machinery. Its essence was to regulate the actions of the different players to ensure that law-making was at the correct level.

[96] N MacCormick, 'Problems of Democracy and Subsidiarity' (2000) *European* PL vol 6, Issue 4, 531. Concerns have been expressed that the EU has legislated in areas in which it was not competent or in which it was inappropriate to do so. The lack of clarity also led to confusion in the mind of the EU citizen and disenchantment with how the EU works. These concerns were recognised in the Nice and Laeken Councils.

[97] J Scott, 'Member States and Regions in Community Law: Convergence and Divergence' in P Beaumont, C Lyons and N Walker (eds), *Convergence and Divergence in European Public Law* (Hart Publishing, Oxford, 2002) 19–38.

[98] See proposal to insert a new Art 3b to the TEU (Art 1 para 6 Lisbon Treaty).

[99] As has been noted, Spain did not sign up to the Declaration annexed to the Amsterdam Treaty, which extended the principle of subsidiarity to regions with legislative competence (unlike Germany and Austria, who did support this) on the grounds that 'subsidiarity runs counter to the Spanish distribution of competencies between central and regional authorities': see C Closa and P Heywood, *Spain and the European Union* (London, Palgrave International, 2004) 103.

[100] The internal national application of this principle to sub-State Government would seem to follow from Art 1 TEU, which requires decisions to be taken 'as closely as possible' to the citizen.

There were recommendations in the Protocol annexed to the Amsterdam Treaty that there should be an annual report on subsidiarity. In the 2000 Report,[101] the Commission remarked that both the Charter of Fundamental Rights and the process of enlargement would put pressure on the need to strictly apply the principle of subsidiarity, and conceded that the 'balanced application of this principle' was a demand of several bodies.[102] It called for 'active subsidiarity' to achieve the objectives of the Union, and recognised the need for greater co-operation with Member States, local and regional authorities and civil society. The CE and Lisbon Treaty proposed a number of changes to the functional base of the Treaties and the provisions on subsidiarity. While these changes have sought to address sub-State concerns these have been criticised as being ineffective. Weatherill has noted the 'competence creep' and that 'the textual limits . . . have had little impact in confining the exercise of legislative power.'[103] The 'legislative bottom-line offers little indication that subsidiarity has quelled expansionism.'[104]

Decisions of the European Court of Justice seem to have confirmed the court's reluctance to upset legislation based on a plea of non-compliance with the subsidiarity principle.[105] The main decisions—the *Working Time Directive Case*,[106] *the Tobacco Advertising Directive Case*,[107] *Germany v Parliament and Council*[108] and *R v Secretary of State ex parte BAT and Imperial*

[101] Commission Report to the European Council, 'Better Lawmaking 2000' (2000) COM, 772.

[102] See the Opinion of the Committee of the Regions on the Principle of Subsidiarity, 'Developing a Genuine Culture of Subsidiarity. An appeal by the Committee of the Regions' [1999] OJ C198/73.

[103] S Weatherill, 'Finding a Role for the Regions in Checking the EU's Competence' in Weatherill and Bernitz (eds) n 30 above, 134.

[104] ibid 137.

[105] Starting with Case C-415/93 *Union Royal Belges des Societes de Football Association v Bosman* [1995] ECR I-4921.

[106] Case C-84/94 *UK v Council* [1996] ECR I-5755. The UK challenged the introduction of the legislation as a health and safety measure under old Art 118A (now Art 137 EC) on various grounds. First, it argued that it should have been introduced under Arts 94 or 308 (which required unanimity). The UK's contention was that this type of legislation should be left to Member States, but the court rejected this, using the argument of effectiveness. It placed emphasis on its competence to harmonise and stated that the Council had a duty to impose minimum requirements to safeguard health and safety of workers (squarely placing the judgment within its conferred powers). The court also failed to address the issue of proportionality ([55]).

[107] Case C-376/98 *Germany v Parliament and Council* [2000] ECR I-8419 and Case C-74/99 *R v Secretary of State for Health and Others, ex p Imperial Tobacco and Others* [2000] ECR I-8599. The court held that the Treaty basis that had been used for the Directive was inappropriate as it was contrary to its express wording and also 'incompatible with the principle embodied in (Art 5) that the powers of the Union are limited to those specifically conferred upon it.' It therefore based its judgment on the principle of conferred powers and not of subsidiarity.

[108] Case-233/94 [1997] ECR I-2405. The court did not consider that a directive on deposit guarantee schemes had been adopted without regard to the principle of subsidiarity because an objective assessment had been carried out before legislating. The inappropriate legal basis plea was one of seven pleas put forward in *Germany v Parliament* and while in [83] of the

Tobacco[109]—demonstrate how interrelated the three principles of Article 5 have become in arguments before the court. Even against the backdrop of a clear reluctance of the court to intervene on the grounds of a breach of the principle of subsidiarity the Commission has taken a proactive position to propose less intrusive measures; directives, decisions or recommendations[110] rather than Regulations. As Weatherill observes, the Commission's aim is 'to do less but to do it better'.[111]

The European Convention secretariat acknowledged that subsidiarity as a means of regulating the Community's non-exclusive powers 'has not produced the expected results', because political factors have intervened and the result has been that action has been taken by the Community when action by Member States 'could have been sufficiently attained', and that the principle of proportionality has similarly been breached, with occasions of action beyond what was necessary. The secretariat has raised the question of the sufficiency of the current Protocol and the need for a more specific demarcation of powers. This emphasises the fact that any advance at European level can only necessarily be a partial progression. It illustrates why a firm commitment at Member State level is essential, and confirms the analysis that puts the State level at the centre of the sub-State conundrum.

The pressure of the regions and the concerns expressed in the 1992–2002 period as to the lack of definition of the principle of subsidiarity in the Treaties and its general ineffectiveness led to amendments being incorporated in the CE and subsequently in the Lisbon Treaty. A number of diverse fields were covered. The Lisbon Treaty attached declarations on the principles of primacy over Member State law[112] and on the delimitation of competences.[113] The Treaty outlined the categories of competence,[114] exclusive competence[115] and shared competence.[116] National Parliaments were to be given a role as an extra layer of monitoring and control on the exercise and categorisation of these competences. The Protocol on the Application of the Principles of Subsidiarity and Proportionality was

judgment it specifically referred to the attribution of powers and impliedly to the doctrine of subsidiarity, the court emphasised in [118] that its judgment was based on the inappropriateness of legal basis and that 'it is unnecessary to consider the other pleas' which included the argument that there had been a breach of the principle of subsidiarity and proportionality.

[109] Case C-491/01 [2002] ECR I-11543. The case recognised that the principle of subsidiarity applied, but adopted a pragmatic approach in assessing whether the particular objectives could be carried out without action at Union level. It decided that it could not.

[110] So-called soft law.

[111] S Weatherill and U Bernitz (eds), *The Role of Regions and Sub National Actors in Europe* (Oxford, Hart Publishing, 2005) 137.

[112] Declaration 17 to the Lisbon Treaty.

[113] Declaration 18 to the Lisbon Treaty by which competences not conferred upon the Union by the Treaties remain with the Member States.

[114] Art 2(12) Lisbon Treaty introduced new Art 2A to TEC (to be re-named the Treaty on the Functioning of the European Union, 'TFEU').

[115] Art 2(12) Lisbon Treaty setting out new Art 2B to TEC/TFEU.

[116] Art 2(12) Lisbon Treaty setting out new Art 2C to TEC/TFEU.

intended to introduce changes to give greater influence to the parliamentary and sub-State level, but has been criticised by Weatherill for falling short of expectations and of what is necessary to achieve real influence for the sub-State level.[117] He has noted that subsidiarity 'sharpened by the Amsterdam Protocol may have prompted wider consultation and more specific reasoning in the legislative process but that it is far from plain that any genuine change in institutional culture and assumption has been achieved.'[118]

It is clear—whether or not the Lisbon Treaty is finally ratified[119]—that the clear trend is to better define and demarcate competences. The concerns at different levels by Regions[120] as to the encroachment into devolved areas and the wider legitimacy debate has led to the introduction of a number of Treaty amendments to promote a clearer demarcation of competences, effective subsidiarity and influence at the pre-legislative stage at European level.

Additionally, as will be expanded on below, any measures taken at European level, be it the demarcation of competences, access to Article 203 (that provides for representation of the State at ministerial level at Council meetings)[121] or real influence within the national stage, require support at Member State level. The adoption of measures at European level does not—by itself—address that. They usually provide a means through which better access could be obtained as long as the State concedes real access to influence and power within its national constitutional architecture

SUB-STATE EXECUTIVES: POWER, GOVERNANCE AND SUB-STATE ASPIRATIONS

For sub-State territories aspiring to more self-government the debate does not end at European level. While multi-level governance may be fostered at supra-national or infra-national level it cannot be *delivered* through those means as this is dependent on intergovernmental or State action to succeed. The enhancement of sub-State power is in some respects in contradiction to intergovernmentalism, as it would undermine the latter's very mode of action. However it is the Member State level which is both a key participant at intergovernmental level and holds the key to sub-State

[117] See the collection of articles in Weatherill and Bernitz (eds) n 30 above.

[118] ibid 138.

[119] On 11 December 2008 an agreement was reached with Ireland the effect of which was that on the basis of certain concessions the Irish Government declared its intention to hold another referendum by October 2009.

[120] Assembly of Regions Declaration and Papers submitted by Bavaria, Scotland or North Rhine-Westphalia to the Convention on the Future of Europe.

[121] Some Member States have allowed sub-State representation via this mechanism: see below.

power. The State is a necessary party because the hope that MLG can be delivered indirectly to the regions without invoking State governments is a forlorn hope. The best that can be hoped for is that a supra-national decision will lead to agreement of a template of access provisions for sub-State power. How and when these are invoked will be up to the Member State concerned. While the sovereignty debate within the Community may have evolved to recognition of multi-level spheres of power and governance, the inevitable reality is that the ability to determine internal State constitutional and governance structures lies with the Member State. It is this, the State, that is the ultimate arbiter. Pressure can be exercised from different levels, but the final decision must come from the State's centre. As Weatherill has noted, it is up to 'the Member States to choose whether to activate the power . . . and then to cope with the potential awkwardness of a schism between the promotion of State interests and sub-State interests. This breeds inevitable diversity in practice.'[122]

MLG that involves stateless nations is thus only truly possible if power is extended by the Member State.[123] This must decide to voluntarily decentralise and limit its power. The EU cannot actually deliver on this. It can only foster the debate and introduce framework provisions that then rely on States deciding to fully invoke these. While MLG provides an opportunity for 'governance beyond the state'[124] it depends on the State to get to that 'beyond', and this causes predictable national tensions in all States. Bourne[125] has identified seven sources of regional power; legal-constitutional, legal-administrative, co-operation, legitimacy, financial resources, institutional resources and internal regional characteristics. She highlights the lack of clarity, and ambiguity in perception as to whether the integration process empowers or disempowers regions.[126] In reviewing the different arguments, she notes how it is said that European integration can be said to empower regions by improving the supra-national/sub-State axis. Alternatively she records how it is also said that it has no effect because State governments block improvements.[127]

In some ways it is neither. The focus on the influence of European integration as a grantor of power is mistaken. It is more of a catalyst than a grantor. Even when it introduces new participatory structures or prin-

[122] S Weatherill and U Bernitz (eds), *The Role of Regions and Sub National Actors in Europe* (Oxford, Hart Publishing, 2005) 14.

[123] eg as in the case of Scottish devolution arrangements.

[124] T Aalberts, 'The Future of Sovereignty in Multilevel Governance Europe—A Constructivist Reading' 2004 *Journal of Common Market Studies* Vol 42 No 1, 28, citing M Jachtenfuchs, 'Conceptualising European Integration' in KE Jorgensen, *Reflective Approaches to European Governance* (Basingstoke, Macmillan, 1997).

[125] A Bourne, 'The Impact of European Integration on Regional Power' (2003) 41 *Journal of Common Market Studies* 597–620, 599.

[126] Applying her analysis to the case study of the Basque country, she decides that it disempowers the Basque country.

[127] Bourne n 126 above, 601–02.

ciples (such as subsidiarity) this can only happen because of Member State agreement. Of course, the European Commission can still adopt certain 'softer' techniques to deliver newer forms of governance, but in general terms the influence of Member States as the ultimate arbiters is still quite concentrated. Failing a new and radical era of judicial intervention[128] the role of EU institutions[129] as a catalyst is of immense value but depends on the States to deliver on these new measures of a more substantial nature.

It is certainly true that accession diminishes sub-State executive power because of the impact of the doctrine of supremacy, direct effect and the restrictions on the legislative process.[130] But the effect of the integration process on sub-State territories is more indirect. Member States are relatively comfortable that they can still exert enormous influence over the law-making process through their State executive governments. They tend to get compensation for the loss of national sovereignty by obtaining direct influence and participation elsewhere. Many times it reappears elsewhere in a different form. This relationship between Member States and sovereignty *qua* governance is like a squashed balloon. When sovereignty is squeezed from one end it reappears at the other end. It is a diffusionist transfer and balance. For sub-State nations, however—and especially for Gibraltar—this is not the case, because these nations are not in control of the integrationist agenda, nor can they exert the same influence on European events as Member States. Sub-State territories, by their very nature, are never, for example, going to be in the position that they can cause a Luxembourg Accords situation[131] or veto proposed legislation as Ireland or Luxembourg[132] when necessary or as Malta or Cyprus are now in a position to do (even when all those countries are smaller than some stateless nations).[133]

For sub-State territories, power transfer depends on two drivers. The primary driver is the acquiescence of the Member State to the particular national arrangements. The secondary driver is the EU level and its trends and measures. Primary and secondary here are used in terms of importance, not in a chronological sense of when the pressures are exerted. Indeed, often the origination of reforming measures may emanate from the EU level. Put another way, the Member State level is usually the grantor and the European level is often (but not always) the catalyst.

128 See Case T-135/96 *UEAPME v Council* [1998] ECR II-2335.

129 Discounting the Council.

130 It can be said though that direct effect empowers the citizen against the Member State.

131 As France did in the 1960s when it disagreed with qualified majority voting in the Community of six. It was resolved after an impasse by an agreement referred to as the Luxembourg Accords which effectively restored the need to obtain unanimous consensus. See J Shaw, *Law of the European Union*, 3rd edn (Basingstoke, Palgrave, 2000) 50–52.

132 eg on the Savings Directive which then led to concessions being made to it in 2002–03.

133 cf the populations of Luxembourg, Malta and Cyprus (all under a million) with Scotland's 7m, Catalunya's 5m, eg.

The pre-eminence of the State in the acquisition of power by the sub-State level is clear. It is the Spanish State that has sought to block the attempt by the Basque Country and Catalunya for greater fiscal or external powers.[134] It is the German federal—as Cygan[135] points out—or the Belgian national arrangements—as Kerremans[136] highlights—that permit the Länder or Regions greater power and influence. It is the heavy centralisation of France[137] and Italy[138] that produce little for those Regions. It is the United Kingdom State that decided to grant and in what form to offer the devolution arrangements to Scotland, Wales and Northern Ireland.

In a Europe of such constitutional diversity—national federalism of Germany or Austria, high regional autonomy in Spain, high centralisation in France and asymmetrical devolution in the United Kingdom—it cannot be expected that there will be either harmonisation of sub-State power or that European trends will be finally determinative of the level of power in the regions. Certainly, European integration trends will be catalysts for change, but it is still very often up to the Member State to exert the final and decisive aperture of power.[139] Indeed because of this reality of being '*united in diversity*',[140] it is natural that, while the EU can suggest a yardstick of measures, it is the Member State that is best placed to gauge how best to organise the constitutional arrangements of the State and accommodate the sub-State diversity.

Gibraltar sustains the same issues, but these are exacerbated because of its special circumstances. For Gibraltar it is clear that the interrelationship between people and the Primary Driver led to the national constitutional reforms in the period up to 1969. It is equally clear that the Primary Driver (with the aid of Spain as third party) has stood in the way of resolution of the governance and democratic deficit.[141] As regards Gibraltar this is the

[134] Though now Catalunya has achieved more fiscal powers by negotiation. See also M Perez, F Marino and F Aldecoa, '*La Acción Exterior y Comunitaria de los Länder, Regiones, Cantones y Comunidades Autonomas*' (Onati, Basque Country, *Instituto Vasco de Administracion Publica*, 1994).

[135] A Cygan, *National Parliaments in an Integrated Europe—an Anglo-German Perspective* (The Hague, Kluwer Law International, 2001).

[136] B Kerremans, 'The Belgian Sub-national Entities in the European Union: Second or Third Level Players?' in C Jeffrey (ed), *The Regional Dimension of the European Union—Towards a Third Level in Europe?* (London, Frank Cass, 1997) 41–55.

[137] A Smith, 'The French Case—the Exception or the Rule?' in Jeffrey (ed) n 137 above, 117–30.

[138] C Desideri and V Santantonio, 'Building a Third Level in Europe: Prospects and Difficulties in Italy' in Jeffrey (ed) n 137 above. Though there have been some interesting recent reforms: see P Leyland, J Frosini and C Bologna, 'Regional Government Reform in Italy: assessing the prospects for devolution' [2002] PL 242–51.

[139] eg, as will be seen, the arrival of principles of subsidiarity or a reshaped Art 203a still requires the co-operation of the Member State to deliver real power to the Regions.

[140] As pointed out in the Preamble to the CE.

[141] Notwithstanding that at the level of the Secondary Driver, there is evidence of a push for governance reform.

double democratic deficit in action. In that context Spain is in some respects best described as a Tertiary Barrier and this is evident in the manifestations of bilateralism and its effects.

THE PRIMACY OF SUB-STATE EXECUTIVES

Given the size of the Union, the ever increasing complexities of governing a larger entity, the different international, State and sub-State pressures, and the ease with which sub-State concerns could be lost or subjugated within the broader whole, the key for the peoples of the non-independent but largely self-governing regions is for their sub-State Executives to acquire a sufficient degree of power, representation or influence at appropriate levels. Without this those self-governing peoples (which because of their special circumstances have a particularly deep sense of identity) will not realistically acquire that effective and influential political democracy. It is the sub-State executives of those territories that must be empowered and facilitated at supra-national level and within their national constitutional set-up.

For stateless nations, a strong sense of identity or nationhood often motivates the aspirations for self-government or self-determination. Additionally, as will be seen below, the third level authorities can be liable in damages for failure to implement European obligations correctly. The natural riposte from the third level is not unexpectedly that, if it has obligations it should also have rights, powers and influences. The conflicts that occur with State executives (and which are, in the case of Gibraltar, uniquely exacerbated by bilateralism) have led to a blockage of these aspirations and that in turn produces a sense of lack of democracy or legitimacy. This feeling is additional to the ordinary disenchantment felt widely by citizens throughout Europe.[142]

In that sense this different dimension of democratic legitimacy must not only be recognised as separately existing, but tackled as such so as to dissolve this democratic deficit and achieve the wider legitimisation of the Union by all its peoples. This would have to be addressed not only at European level but also within the State's constitutional framework, by putting arrangements in place safeguarding those objectives.[143] The

[142] See also Report by Working Group 4c, 'Multi-Level Governance: Linking and Networking the Various Regional and Local Levels', May 2001, prepared in advance of the White Paper. The actual implementation of the measures to foster MLG is sometimes slow. eg the reaching of tripartite agreements between the Commission, Member State and Regional Government is an issue which is encouraged. However the first tripartite agreement was signed on 15 October 2004 (between the Commission, Italian Government and the Lombardy Region).

[143] Art 6 TEU is also relevant in its recognition of fundamental rights arising from particular national constitutional tradition and the respect for national identities.

benefit for sub-State territories of a system of MLG is the opportunity to acquire power at the appropriate levels. The benefit for the EU is the greater participation of all governance players and the opportunity to secure more legitimacy that will enhance cohesion. The benefit for the Member States is that they retain much control over the pace and manner of State and supra-national arrangements. They also achieve stability within a clearer demarcation of competences. It is potentially a system of co-operative cohabitation not conflict.[144]

THE NATURE AND EXTENT OF SUB-STATE SELF-GOVERNANCE

As Hopkins has pointed out,[145] there are certain discernible features and key elements to regional self-governance. The presence or absence of these is a useful yardstick to the extent of self-government. The various elements include the power to legislate,[146] financial self-sufficiency, the extent of and areas of competence, the extent of constitutional entrenchment, the independence of policy-making, and the ability to have some form of international capacity, administrative autonomy and separate judiciary. These should in turn all be underwritten by the necessary degree of democratic legitimacy. Seen holistically, the wider-ranging nature of these features in Gibraltar makes it a highly advanced self-governing territory. This can be seen by comparison at different levels.[147]

In the finance area Gibraltar's powers, administrative and policy autonomy are akin to an independent micro-state. It is entirely self-financing.[148] It derives no financial contribution from the United Kingdom and all its tax and other revenues are retained in Gibraltar. The importance of this cannot be underestimated in that the ability to carry out infrastructure projects or to implement social or economic programmes very much depends on financial capability and freedom.

In that sense, Gibraltar is very different to certain European self-governing regions that hold less power and are much more dependent on central finance. The consequence of this is also that it is more difficult to move away from central policy if the sub-State level is dependent on central State monies. In his review of financing powers, Hopkins[149] recognises

[144] See Case T-135/96 *UEAPME v Council* [1998] ECR II-2335. The principle of representative democracy is also recognised in Art 1 (draft Art 8A) of the Lisbon Treaty, and it is this which is at the heart of the philosophical approach behind the desire to involve all levels of players in the decision-making process.

[145] J Hopkins, *Devolution in Context: Regional, Federal and Devolved Government in the European Union* (London, Cavendish, 2002) 211–64.

[146] Of a primary or secondary nature.

[147] Illustrated below and in the next chapter.

[148] It does also receive EU structural funds.

[149] Hopkins n 146 above, 211–44.

four different ways of financing regional government: independent finance (raised by the region); block funding; borrowing;[150] and specific grants and mandated expenditure. He notes that only in France and Denmark is there any significant element of self-financing.[151]

Of course the consequence of a lack of self-financing is that the regions are less able to pursue independent policies and are also less 'accountable to the regional electorate'.[152] It also makes them more reliant on the Member State level for either financing or constitutional reform of a financing nature.[153] Conversely, in Gibraltar the manifestos of political parties will provide alternative social and economic programmes entirely focussed on local needs and in the knowledge of the funds that are available. That ability to carry out an electoral programme and to respond to local needs does much to marry accountability and legitimacy at Gibraltar sub-State level.

In the case of Scottish or Welsh devolution, Trench has noted that one of the paradoxes of devolution has been that it has failed to produce a fundamental financial change, and that these countries continue heavily dependent on the central allocation of financial resources.[154] This acts 'as a brake on the spending increases' of the devolved administrations.[155] The ability or failure to obtain the allocation of central funding can have a dramatic effect on the landscape of regional politics.[156] It also means that they are less fiscally accountable to their Parliaments and electorates. The observation has been made that the financing arrangements of devolution could provide a source for controversy and friction.[157] Gibraltar is largely free from those financial pre-occupations. However, as a result of a combination of the consequences of accession and the impact of bilateralism, it suffered an encroachment into the powers of its executive without receiving a commensurate ability to shape law or policy-making, institutional representation, or governance compensation elsewhere.[158] This has

[150] Which would usually be subject to some limits as in Spain or Belgium: see Hopkins n 146 above, 231–36. Gibraltar is subject to borrowing limits under its domestic law: the Public Finance, Control and Audit Act.

[151] Hopkins n 146 above, 213–20.

[152] ibid 214.

[153] See eg the Catalan Government's proposals of 2005–06.

[154] Based on the Barnett formula. See A Trench (ed), *The State of the Nations 2004* (Exeter, The Constitution Unit, Imprint Academic, 2004) 172.

[155] ibid 173.

[156] J Osmond, 'A Constitutional Convention by Other Means: the First Year of the National Assembly in Wales' in R Hazell (ed), *The State of the Nations: The First Year of Devolution in the UK* (Exeter, The Constitution Unit, Imprint Academic, 2000) 37–76.

[157] D Bell and A Christie, 'The Barnett Formula: Nobody's Child?' in A Trench (ed), *The State of the Nations 2001: The Second Year of Devolution in the UK* (Exeter, The Constitution Unit, Imprint Academic, 2001) 135–52.

[158] See next chapter.

happened at different stages of the European decision-making process and continues to occur.[159]

Having reviewed the theoretical context the next chapter traces the consequences of the climate of bilateralism that has dominated the Gibraltar dispute, its affairs and its participation in the European Union.

[159] It can be identified as occurring at four different points, namely: pre-decision; pre-legislation and the decision stages; and then at the post-decision phase.

5

Sub-state Power, Representation and Influence, and the Zenith of Bilateralism

INTRODUCTION

THE PREVIOUS CHAPTER described the trends of European governance, the quite different intergovernmental State centricity sustained by Gibraltar and the resulting governance deficit. This chapter is about the consequences of that democratic deficit. It concentrates on the direct or indirect effects of bilateralism that cast a long shadow over Gibraltar's constitutional development and prevail as both the main democratic deficit and the principal issue behind the remaining sub-deficits. This chapter also covers the principal mechanisms by which greater power, influence and representation within Europe could be obtained.

There are a number of themes to the democratic deficit. In the first place, the emergence of an absence of legitimacy as a by-product is worthy of note. The second is the pre-occupation with the territorial sovereignty claim that remains as a constant reminder of the application of an ill-fitting constitutional context to this long-standing dispute.[1] The third theme is the emergence of the paradox of governance and constitutionalism, resulting in Gibraltar having more responsibility but less power or influence on the European stage. A comparison with self-governing regions within the European Union confirms the existence of the paradox. Gibraltar has more theoretical constitutional responsibilities than those regions, but is hampered to a greater extent than some of those regions from accessing effective influence to deal with the European dimension. It is important to address this, because the more time passes the more this encroachment into the domestic sphere is exacerbated.

Bilateralism between Britain and Spain, and the exclusion of Gibraltar as an active participant and interlocutor at all levels of Gibraltar-related

[1] Expanded in next chapter.

matters, contributed to the creation of an environment which fostered several elements in the governance and democratic deficit. These were manifested in examples of lack of power, representation or influence. While important for their own effects, these were net deficits that caused constitutional discomfort through their accumulation. By far the main deficit was the climate of bilateralism itself. This chapter analyses these net deficits and builds on the explanation of the causes and categories of bilateralism given in the previous chapter. It surveys the main manifestations of bilateralism during the 1986–2004 period, which were threefold:

1. a failure to define and demarcate both the duty of the United Kingdom in respect of external affairs and the powers and competences of Gibraltar;
2. the freeze in constitutional reform;
3. the lack of representation and influence at several levels.

Each of these is dealt with in turn. The first was a deficit shared with several other sub-State nations as a result of EC membership. It was worsened by bilateralism. The second was largely due to bilateralism, and the third was indirectly accentuated by bilateralism. The latter two are, in great part, unique to Gibraltar. Analysis of the deficits highlight a point made in the previous chapter that the best way of obtaining the resolution of the external European governance deficit is for the executive of the stateless nation to be comprehensively empowered.

THE EXTERNAL AFFAIRS V DOMESTIC POLICY AGENDA

The Encroachment and the Meaning of External Affairs: A Deficit Shared with Others

The extent to which Community legislation is now being introduced in areas within the traditional competences of the Gibraltar Government can be seen in Table D.[2] The Table spans a period of 15 years, and assesses the legislation transposed into Gibraltar law from a Community source. While the subsidiarity principle and the legislative approach now recommended by the Commission have tempered that practice,[3] this is still a real issue for sub-State Executives. This has spurred on a search for mechanisms at both State and supra-national level to address the loss of

[2] Below: compiled from my research of legislative records, Hansard and the *Gibraltar Gazette*.

[3] The use of 'soft law': P Birkinshaw, *European Public Law* (London, Butterworths, 2003) 10–11. The European Commission has recognised in its work before and since the White Paper that the use of more general and softer legislative approaches would encourage legitimacy, participation and decentralisation.

power/influence of the third level of government. The Table illustrates the extent to which legislation originating from a European source impacts on the domestic scene and the width of such impact, across diverse areas. Taken over the 15-year period there are an average of about 15 transposition instruments per year. It has already been seen[4] that about 35 per cent of the Gibraltar legislature's time is dedicated to European-sourced matters. In a small territory with a small legislature and finite resources, those numbers are significant, and demonstrate the need to secure better influence lest all its hard-won constitutional gains are eroded without adequate compensation.

Concerns as to the real loss of powers and encroachments into the domestic constitutional framework has been replicated in many Member States,[5] especially those with highly regionalised or federal structures. In Germany the Länder argued that while external affairs was a matter for the Federal Government, transfer of powers to the European Union should not be achieved via the constitutional provision which authorised transfer of competences to international bodies, because such an action encroached on domestic affairs.[6] Areas in which the Community sought to legislate were, properly analysed, areas of domestic policy, and did not become matters of external affairs just because it was the Community at supra-national European level that was seeking to legislate. As such they argued that in fact these were domestic matters being discussed at European level. At the heart of the encroachment is the definition of external affairs and how it should be conducted.

THE NATURE OF THE DUTY (EUROPEAN DOMESTIC POLICY DEBATE—THE CONDUCT OF EXTERNAL AFFAIRS)

Gibraltar's membership of the Community stems from Article 299(4) of the TEC and is based on the fact that a Member State is responsible for its external affairs. The Commission looks to the United Kingdom when it seeks information about Gibraltar's compliance with EU legislation. Similarly it is the accepted position that the United Kingdom is responsible for the fulfillment by Gibraltar of international obligations entered into by the United Kingdom on Gibraltar's behalf and extended at Gibraltar's request.

4 Ch 2.

5 For Scotland and Wales see *The State of the Nations* (Exeter, The Constitution Unit, Imprint Academic, 2000–05).

6 C Jeffrey, 'Farewell the Third Level? The German Länder and the European Policy Process' in C Jeffrey (ed), The Regional Dimension of the European Union—Towards a Third Level in Europe? (London, Frank Cass, 1997), 56–75.

Table D—Overview of Transposition by General Subject Areas 1987–2001[7]

Subject Area	Number of Transposition Instruments
Employment	
General	7
Equal Pay and Treatment	4
Residence etc of Workers	1
Health and Safety	17
Education and Training	
General	9
Professions and Recognition of Qualifications	11
Environment	
General	13
Water[8]	9
Waste[9]	11
Wildlife (including domestic animals, fish and sites designation)	6
Noise	4
Air Quality, Emissions and Pollution	15
Radiation and Radioactivity	5
Petroleum	6
Consumer Measures	
General Protection and Contracts	6
Food	5
Product Safety	1
Medicines and Pharmaceutical Products	3
Financial Services	
General	7
Insurance	11
Banking	8
Other Industry	
General	1
Communications, Media and Technology	7
Companies and Business	13
Tourism	3
Transport	
(Including Land and Sea and General Shipping)	22
Miscellaneous	
General	10
International Co-operation and Crime	2
Public Procurement	5
Total	222

[7] Table setting out legislation introduced by Gibraltar transposing Community obligations, compiled from my research of primary and subsidiary legislation during the index period.
[8] Including drinking, bathing water and the aquatic environment.
[9] Including disposal.

There is little specific reference to Gibraltar in directives, for example,[10] and these are always addressed to the Member States.[11] Due to the self-government bestowed on Gibraltar, it is an obligation of the Gibraltar Government to legislate and implement these, but the party that remains accountable at European level is the United Kingdom Government. The party that is accountable on a domestic level (within the constitutional framework of Gibraltar) is the Gibraltar Government—at least at first instance.

Whenever the Commission decides to open any informal or formal procedure of investigation on an EU-related matter, it will address the correspondence or notification to the United Kingdom.[12] Indeed whenever the Commission feel that proceedings are required, these will be issued against the United Kingdom.[13] This makes the United Kingdom take a keen interest in the implementation of European obligations in Gibraltar. It also means that, as European Union legislation may be made within many areas devolved to the Gibraltar Government and the United Kingdom is ultimately accountable for the enforcement of these, it (the UK) has in fact re-entered this side of the constitutional arena, not by virtue of formal constitutional amendment but because of the impact that European Union membership has on a stateless nation.[14] Their re-entry is in an interested observer role rather than an active legislative one.[15] In another sense it has re-entered in a far more proactive way—in the sphere of the conduct and definition of the remit of responsibility for external affairs.[16]

[10] What little there is in Community legislation tends to concern either territorial applicability or competent authorities.

[11] Pursuant to Art 249. And as has been pointed out the reference to 'United Kingdom' does not refer to the territory of Gibraltar. Rather the proper view is that the Treaty applies to the territory of Gibraltar by Art 299(4): it then applies to the people by virtue of the Declaration of the UK on accession. The fact that the directive is addressed to the UK merely reflects the fact that the UK is responsible at Community level for Gibraltar's compliance. It does not mean that Gibraltar can evade transposition of obligations because these are not specifically 'addressed' to it. This argument (ie that the UK = Gibraltar for EU purposes) would be a retrograde step in attempting to keep the respective constitutional spheres of influence of the UK and Gibraltar intact and would be an invitation to the UK to take a more interventionist attitude in Gibraltar's affairs.

[12] eg when a pre-Art 226 letter warning of infraction proceedings is issued.

[13] See eg Case C-30/01 *Commission v UK* [2003] ECR I-09481.

[14] This principle that a Member State is responsible for regional government default is recognised in cases such as Case C-298/97 *Commission v Spain* [1998] ECR I-3301.

[15] Though of course, as has already been pointed out, certain powers of legislation are retained by the UK, and if Gibraltar were to resist implementation of European obligations the UK could have recourse to these powers.

[16] See below.

IMPLEMENTATION OF OBLIGATIONS AND RESPONSIBILITY

However whatever it agrees at European level the United Kingdom then relies on Gibraltar for domestic implementation of the particular agreement. An interesting analogy can be had with the Canadian experience. When considering the federal system of Government in Canada before repatriation[17] and the separation of functions between the federal and provincial levels, the Privy Council in the Ontario industrial relations case[18] held that:

> the obligations imposed by Treaty may have to be performed, if at all, by several legislatures; and the executive have the task of obtaining the legislative assent not of the one Parliament to whom they may be responsible, but possibly of several parliaments to whom they stand in no relation. The question is not how is the obligation to be formed, that is the function of the executive,[19] but how is the obligation to be performed, and that depends upon the competent Legislature or Legislatures.

This comparison holds true for Gibraltar and other sub-State European nations. It is the sub-State parliament and executive that determines the performance of an obligation, once it is formed and entered into.[20] The added feature is that, within the Union, and in accordance with principles of multi-level governance, sub-State territories (and Gibraltar) also seek influence in the manner and content of the 'formation' of the policy measure.[21] The German courts[22] followed a similar line when considering the implementation of an international obligation arising between Germany and the Vatican. This view was also shared by the Spanish constitutional court in 1982. Indeed, as Aurrecoechea notes, the possibility of the central government implementing an international obligation under the Spanish Constitution arises only if the particular autonomous community refuses.[23]

[17] So-called 'patriation' of the Constitution took place in 1982 (though to all intents and purposes the principle in the Ontario case cited below is of effect in respect of Federal–Province relations).

[18] *A-G for Canada v A-G for Ontario* [1937] AC 326, 348.

[19] To construe this in a polycentric manner 'executive' would need to be interpreted to either mean both the State and sub-State level or be given the most favourable construction in the singular to the sub-State level.

[20] Though in some respects if the Executive in Gibraltar had real and consistent influence it would also have a hand in the 'formation' of such an obligation.

[21] For some discussion of arrangements in Australia, Switzerland and the US, see also JHH Weiler, 'The External Legal Relations of non-unitary Actors: Mixity and the Federal Principle' in Weiler, *The Constitution of Europe* (Cambridge, CUP, 1999) 130–187.

[22] 8 BVerfGE 309. See J Hopkins, *Devolution in Context: Regional, Federal and Devolved Government in the European Union* (London, Cavendish, 2002) 187. It led to the Lindau Agreement: see later.

[23] I Aurrecoechea, 'The Role of the Autonomous Communities in the Implementation of European Community Law in Spain' (1989) 38 ICLQ 74.

However, if there is a failure to fulfill an obligation and the Commission acts under Article 226 TEC to require compliance (either by the reasoned opinion procedure or in default by referring the matter to the Court of Justice), the United Kingdom will pressure the Gibraltar Government to secure implementation. Discussions between the two Governments will invariably then lead to compliance.[24] There is no reported instance of the United Kingdom having to use its residual power of legislation in the Gibraltar Constitution to achieve this.[25] There has been a number of Article 226 letters sent in respect of non-or incomplete transposition of Community legislation by Gibraltar.[26]

The practice that has evolved in relation to international conventions and treaty obligations is that the United Kingdom will not extend these to Gibraltar without its Government's consent. Some would then require ratification or implementation via domestic law.[27] In that case, the Gibraltar executive would have the option of introducing measures via the Gibraltar legislature or to consent to the United Kingdom parliament legislating.[28] The latter is a rare course, with the Gibraltar Government preferring to legislate or otherwise introduce the measure directly.[29] To give domestic effect to the Maastricht and Amsterdam Treaties the Gibraltar legislature introduced amendments to the Gibraltar European Communities Act. This practice is akin to the convention that has been recognised in respect of other territories in the Commonwealth before independence[30] or in Wales and Scotland. The latter—described as the Sewel Convention[31]—has not however ended the role of Westminster in Scotland. Quite the contrary. In the first three years of devolution the Convention was used in respect of 39 Westminster Bills by which the London parliament legislated for Scotland (with its consent).[32]

[24] Unless, as in the Mutual Tax Directive case, the issue was that both UK and Gibraltar decided to (unsuccessfully) maintain the position before the ECJ that it need not be transposed: Case-349/03 *Commission v UK*, Judgment 21 July 2005.

[25] Though this last resort mechanism is available.

[26] There are examples in the fields of the environment, tax and financial services.

[27] See eg the Merchant Shipping (Safety etc) Act 1993, which implements the SOLAS and Load Lines Convention into Gibraltar law.

[28] Or allowing the matter to be introduced by Order in Council.

[29] See the comments of the Chief Minister to that effect—House of Assembly Hansard, June 1999 and May 2000—when introducing a measure in respect of UN sanctions on the Former Yugoslavia.

[30] Though the convention has been recognised, it has also been held not to limit the powers of the UK Parliament: see *Madzimbamuto v Lardner-Burke* [1969] 1 AC 645; K Roberts-Wray, *Commonwealth and Colonial Law* (London, Stevens, 1966) 991–93.

[31] *Memorandum of Understanding and Supplementary Agreements between the UK Government, Scottish Ministers, the Cabinet of the National Assembly for Wales and the Northern Ireland Executive Committee* (Cm 5240, 2002) 13.

[32] A Trench (ed), *The State of the Nations 2004* (Exeter, The Constitution Unit, Imprint Academic, 2004) 168.

These duties to give effect to Community law[33] give rise to responsibilities and liabilities on executive and public authorities alike in what is often described as State liability or responsibility.[34] This dimension is the natural extension of duties of implementation and accountability for that failure.[35] Apart from the need to account to the Commission under Article 226 the principle of State liability ensures that, if a failure to implement such an obligation causes damage, the State may be liable to pay compensation.[36] There are two main pillars for this reasoning: the supremacy of Community law and the direct interrelationship with Article 10 TEC, which outlines the necessity for Member States to guarantee compliance with Community law.[37] The principles have been construed to apply to governments and public authorities of all types.[38] In *Konle v Austria,*[39] in a case on compensation in a federal state, it was held that it was up to Member States to secure compensation rights for individuals, irrespective of which public authority was responsible. EU law has no regard to nor interferes with division of State powers but merely seeks to ensure that remedies are provided to allow individuals to protect and enforce their rights.[40]

In the Memorandum of Understanding that underpins the British devolution arrangements, an obligation to indemnify the United Kingdom in respect of 'financial penalties . . . damages and costs' is accepted by the devolved administrations.[41] If the reality is that there are possible financial consequences to the self-governing regions for non-implementation or

[33] Reports are published annually by the Commission on the application of Community law: see 'Eighteenth Annual Report on Monitoring the Application of Community Law' (2000), COM (2001) 309.

[34] Liability only arising if there is a breach of that responsibility.

[35] See eg Case 205–15/82 *Deutsche Milchkontor* case [1983] ECR 2633 and Case C-8/88 *Germany v Commission* [1990] ECR-I 2321, which ruled that sub-State authorities were bound to ensure compliance with laws within the sphere of their competence but that the court could not rule on the division of competences within the national constitutional framework.

[36] Case 60/75 *Russo v AIMA* [1976] ECR 45; Cases C-6 to C-9/90 *Francovich* Cases.

[37] This requires Member States to take appropriate measures to ensure fulfillment of Treaty obligations and facilitate the achievement of the Community's tasks.

[38] It includes: the Legislature—Case 167/73 *Commission v France* [1974] ECR 359; Regional/local authorities—Case 1/86 *Commission v Belgium* [1987] ECR 2797; States within a Federation—Case 9/74 *Casagrande* [1974] ECR 773; a private party controlled by the State—Case 249/81 *Commission v Ireland* [1982] ECR 4005.

[39] Case C-302/97 [1999] ECR I-3099.

[40] Proceedings have been brought in a number of cases alleging a breach of Treaty obligation by the State in Gibraltar. See eg *Moroccan Workers Association v A-G* [1995–96] Gib LR 67 (alleged breach of Art 48 TEC and EC-Morocco Cooperation Agreement 1978); *R v Governor and Collector of Customs ex p A.S.Marrache and Sons Ltd* [1997–98] Gib LR 348 (alleged breach of Arts 85 and 221 TEC). The cases have all been resolved by the Gibraltar courts and to date there has not been a reference determined by the ECJ from a Gibraltar court.

[41] *Memorandum of Understanding* etc (Cm 4444, 1999), para 20. See also R Hazell, 'Intergovernmental Relations: Whitehall Rules OK' in R Hazell (ed), *The State of the Nations: The First Year of Devolution in the UK* (Exeter, The Constitution Unit, Imprint Academic, 2000) 149–81.

wrong implementation of Community obligations, the desire of the sub-State level to exercise real influence before legislative decisions are taken is easy to understand. This emphasises the practical dimension of the need to break the negative influence of bilateralism that holds back reform.

The power dimension is related to bilateralism because this largely requires constitutional reform for its unblockage. In turn any suggestion of reforms allowing 'external action' tends to arouse Spain's objections because of the perceived connotations of quasi-Statehood. Indeed, as has been seen in previous chapters, Spain has historically also sought to contain primarily internal reforms.

THE NATURE AND EXTENT OF ARTICLE 299(4)

The nature and extent of the United Kingdom's powers and duties as a result of its constitutional relationship with Gibraltar, and the reference to external affairs in Article 299(4), are at the centre of the sub-State Executive power conundrum. This sub-Article states that the Treaty applies to Gibraltar because it is 'a territory for whose external *relations* a Member State is *responsible*.' (emphasis added). This, of course encapsulates the constitutional difference between Gibraltar and the regions with which comparisons are being made. Gibraltar is in a unique situation. It is not constitutionally integrated into the United Kingdom, has all the institutional, parliamentary and governmental trappings of a self-governing territory, but the workings of Article 299(4) potentially drive a coach and horses through its self-government[42] and the principle of democratic legitimacy.

There are two main questions requiring examination: the nature of the duty, and the way the duty should be conducted in practice. As to the first dimension, what is important is whether the word 'responsible' includes connotations that the United Kingdom has acquired not only the representation of the issues but also the substantive carriage of them. This is particularly relevant when matters arise within the constitutional competence of the Gibraltar Government. Does the United Kingdom have responsibility at European level for matters of an external nature only, or does its responsibility include domestic affairs discussed at European level? If the latter, is the case is their duty to *represent* Gibraltar only, or is the actual carriage of the domestic issues transferred to them for the purposes of that European discussion?

[42] The general nature of the external affairs powers of the Crown are set out in Halsbury's *Laws of England*, 4th edn (London, Butterworths, 1974) vol 6, para 1022, and O Hood Phillips, *Constitutional and Administrative Law*, 8th edn (Sweet & Maxwell, London, 2001) paras 15–021 to 15–033. And see also the recent cases that have touched on the issue of the Prerogative in Foreign Affairs—*Quark Fishing* and *Bancoult* (the Diego Garcia case) referred to in ch 6, pp 289—305.

If, for example, an employment measure is being discussed at EU level, does the United Kingdom merely represent Gibraltar, or does it actually acquire responsibility for employment when it is dealing at European level on behalf of Gibraltar? By way of example, the method of pollution control within a nation's borders does not become an external affair, because the decision about which method to follow is taken in Brussels in the interests of greater harmonisation of preventative environmental measures. The latter interpretation would be a heavy encroachment into domestic matters that would undermine the substantive devolution of power. The former interpretation—while still an encroachment—could be addressed more easily by rectifying the mechanics of representation.[43] Does the duty entail that the United Kingdom must act on Gibraltar's wishes, in a role akin to that of principal and agent?[44] The analogy with the evidence given by the former Secretary of State for Wales, Paul Murphy, before a Parliamentary Committee is interesting, for he asserted that he presented the views of the Welsh administration within Cabinet but did not represent it.[45]

Britain's authority to bind Gibraltar with measures that its Government has openly opposed, or to exclude Gibraltar from the application of measures, has been a matter of controversy for some years. In 2001–02 Gibraltar was excluded from a raft of aviation measures, most notably the so-called 'Single Skies' measures.[46] The exclusion prompted its Government to consider taking legal action over Britain's power to exclude and bind Gibraltar. There are two options that at some point could be taken further. Either the Government of Gibraltar could seek to litigate such questions before the domestic courts in an attempt to clarify the position,[47] or the Gibraltar Courts—in an appropriate case—could refer a question to the ECJ for clarification of Article 299(4).[48] Without clarity in the demarcation of

[43] As eg in the case of Germany and Belgium: see below. For a review of similar issues see J Kottman 'Europe and the Regions: sub-national entity representation at Community level' EL Rev 26 (2001) 159–176.

[44] As in the Cook Islands–New Zealand arrangements: see J Crawford, *The Creation of States in International Law*, 2nd edn (Oxford, OUP, 2006) 630.

[45] House of Lords Select Committee on the Constitution, Evidence of Paul Murphy, 10 April 2002.

[46] Designed to harmonise air traffic control, air safety and other air passage issues across a common and defined European airspace. See eg the *Proposal for a Regulation of the European Parliament and of the Council on the Organisation and Use of the Airspace in the Single European Sky*, COM (2001) 564 final, OJ C103E, 30 April 2002.

[47] If a useful intergovernmental accommodation cannot be reached by negotiation.

[48] The danger of the latter may be that so far—in all unrelated cases coming before the ECJ—the court has sought the guidance of the UK to understand the constitutional arrangements of Gibraltar in deciding questions of *locus standi* for example. Gibraltar would have to be careful that in deciding those unrelated matters the ECJ has not already assumed a position contrary to Gibraltar's desired outcome on the nature of the external affairs responsibility question. Given the present dynamics, Spain is likely to intervene in such litigation and argue that the Article should be construed in the most restricted fashion for Gibraltar. Admittedly, previous cases have construed the 1969 Constitution. The enactment of the 2006 Constitution has improved Gibraltar's position by introducing further clarity.

competences and definition of the nature of the duty in the field of external affairs, there is a very significant risk of erosion of constitutional sovereignty, not to Europe and arising as a normal consequence of accession, but rather to the United Kingdom and arising out of the UK's interpretation of its powers post accession. This is in fact the German European domestic policy debate,[49] taken to its natural conclusion. For the constitutionally devolved areas to be preserved as much as possible, the UK's responsibility needs to be construed in accordance with the nature of Gibraltar's self-government in mind. This does not ignore the fact that the Treaty applies, nor is it a contradiction of that position. This is because, as previously indicated, the extent of self-government is very dependent on the Primary State Driver. If necessary, constitutional arrangements could be established to ensure that the boundaries and manner of representation of Gibraltar are more usefully demarcated and enforced.

The Crown Prerogative in a particular area is limited or suspended if legislation has been introduced in that area. Accordingly, the fact that Her Majesty granted wide powers of self-government to Gibraltar in the written Constitution means that her prerogative powers on external affairs should not be conducted in an unlimited fashion but in light of the Constitution.[50] In areas like public health, education or the environment, this duty should require that the United Kingdom transmit the Gibraltar view on any matter that would specifically impact on Gibraltar—so there would be no exclusions from EU measures, as in the case of aviation, without the express agreement of the Gibraltar Government. In areas not devolved to the Gibraltar Government, such as defence or internal security, the United Kingdom could exercise her responsibility in a more liberal manner and consult the Gibraltar Government as appropriate.[51]

The position after 1986 provided a source of friction. It was important to provide for a clear mechanism that both created a consultative framework and clearly demarcated the constitutional responsibilities of the Gibraltar and United Kingdom Governments.[52] The same issue troubled self-governing regions within the Union. Litigation by Bavaria to force the federal German Government to vote in a particular way at the Council of Ministers was unsuccessful, but there was recognition by the German Courts that Community law could be reviewed to ensure compliance with the German Basic Law.[53]

[49] Mentioned in greater detail below. The German experience on how Länder have struggled with similar questions is illuminating.

[50] *A-G v De Keyser's Royal Hotel Ltd* [1920] AC 508.

[51] eg if there is a proposal to introduce a measure under Art 11–28 of the Treaty on European Union. In practice this happens often though not always at an early stage.

[52] See House of Assembly Select Committee on Constitutional Reform, Report, 23 January 2002 (Gibraltar, 2002).

[53] This is an interesting judgment, which may be unique to the careful balance of the German federal system. See M Herdegen, 'After the TV Judgment of the German Constitutional

The essential elements to any arrangements introduced to address these issues are co-operation, a degree of formality (preferably of a binding nature), definition of the nature and extent of the duty and a clear demarcation of powers. Indeed, given that the interrelationship between duties, respective competences, power to create and implement obligations, and liabilities for non-implementation, affect both the State and sub-State level, it is essential for there to be a partnership at the different levels of governance. It is said that the German system is one of co-operative federalism, where co-operation between the Länder and the Federal Government is the key.[54] But this works because Governments know that the definitions and demarcations are constitutionally entrenched and are not subject to the whims of any incoming administration. The system is also carefully weighted so the Federal Government is not in a position of overwhelming strength in relation to the Länder. It must also try to make the governance arrangements with the sub-State executives work. The British devolution arrangements are somewhat different. The Concordats made under the Memorandum of Understanding are expressed to be without binding legal effect and are heavily weighted towards the central government in London. They do—as Rawlings notes[55]—stress co-operation, communication, confidentiality and consultation, but they have been observed to develop in a fragmented and less than open and transparent way.[56] In a way, the embryonic and asymmetrical system of devolution in the United Kingdom could hinder any progress in respect of Gibraltar, as any gains made by it—at European level—could upset the arrangements in place for Scotland and Wales. These compare unfavourably with the highly resourced and intricate intergovernmental arrangements in Canada and Australia.[57]

In 2002 the Select Committee on Constitutional Reform recommended:

—that the United Kingdom retain responsibility for external affairs but that the Governor should 'as far as practicable act on the advice of the Chief Minister.'[58]

Court: decision-making within the EU Council and the German Länder' (1995) 32 CMLR and N Foster, *German Law and Legal System* (London, Blackstone, 1996).

54 Hopkins n 24 above, 264.

55 R Rawlings, 'Concordats of the Constitution', *LQR* 116 (2000) 257–86.

56 Hopkins n 24 above, 268.

57 R Cornes, 'Intergovernmental Relations in a Devolved UK: Making Devolution Work' in R Hazell (ed), *Constitutional Futures: A History of the Next Ten Years* (Oxford, OUP, 1999). See G Carney, *The Constitutional Systems of the Australian States and Territories* (Cambridge, CUP, 2006).

58 Proposed s 48(1). This was accepted in part in the 2006 reforms: see s 47(1) of the 2006 Constitution, which requires the Governor in respect of external affairs to 'as far as practicable act in consultation with the Chief Minister'—watered down from the original proposals. However, this can be substantially circumvented by s 47(4), which states that the exercise by the Governor of his responsibility for external affairs is 'without prejudice to the overall responsibility of Her Majesty's Government in the UK for those matters.'

—that the obligation should be tighter in the handling of European Union matters because the United Kingdom should be 'bound to act in accordance with the advice of the Gibraltar Government . . . within the European Union in matters in respect of which the Gibraltar Government has responsibility under this Constitution or any other law.'[59]

The Committee also recommended that there should be a declaratory section making clear that domestic matters remain domestic, notwithstanding any European dimension.[60] The intention behind this was not to reverse the fact that the Community would take action[61] that would affect Gibraltar, but rather to ensure that the competences of Gibraltar were protected against UK unilateral encroachment.[62]

The entire issue of how the United Kingdom Government should fulfill its role in its 'responsibility' for external affairs is a contentious and deeply political one. The Select Committee's proposals also made clear[63] that what politicians in Gibraltar aspired to is a relationship akin to political agency.[64] Thus, for example, international obligations should not be entered into without the consent of the Government. While it has been the long-standing practice not to extend Conventions or International Treaties to Gibraltar without the consent of the Gibraltar Government, the United Kingdom Government can take the view that, in the EU sphere, it cannot or will not argue for special or different treatment for Gibraltar. Even where there is a case for doing so,[65] it may balance acting against its own national interests and decide that its wider interests mean that the Gibraltar point must be sacrificed.[66] The Select Committee also recommended that, while external affairs should remain a United Kingdom responsibility, powers could be delegated to local Ministers. This constitutional power is common in the Overseas Territories constitutions[67] so this was not a radical recommendation. Indeed, while this did not appear in the final 2006 Constitution, it could be argued that the practice has already developed by constitutional convention.[68]

[59] This provision did not find its way into the final draft of the 2006 Constitution.

[60] To address the so-called European Domestic Policy debate, described above.

[61] Or to introduce a provision which was in any way incompatible with EC law.

[62] Accepted in modified form: see s 47(3) of the 2006 Constitution: see ch 7.

[63] See proposed ss 46 and 48 and below.

[64] Crawford n 44 above, 630.

[65] eg because of the size of Gibraltar: see Minimum Guarantee Scheme Directive in relation to insurance companies.

[66] See the case of the Savings Directive—referred to below. The predominance of UK national interests over those of the territory have most recently been recognised in the October 2008 judgment of the House of Lords in the *Bancoult* case.

[67] The power is eg present in the constitutions of Bermuda, British Virgin Islands or Anguilla.

[68] See below.

INTERNAL AND EXTERNAL POWER

Without the formal power to delegate functions in external affairs[69] the ability to enter into international agreements or to acquire representational rights at European level[70] depends on a voluntary cession of such powers or the argument that these have been acquired by convention.[71] The Belgian sub-State governments have, since 1993, been able to enter into international agreements in areas of their exclusive competence. The regional legislatures must also approve any international agreements entered into by the Belgian Government in areas of their competence.[72] In Germany, Länder have the constitutional right to be consulted before a Treaty which affects them is entered into,[73] and may (with the consent of the Federal Government) enter into international agreements with foreign States in areas of their legislative competence.[74] Additionally the Länder's consent is necessary if the Federal Government proposes to enter into international agreements in areas of the Länder's exclusive competence. In Spain there are similar rights to be informed and consulted but there is no obligation on the central government to seek the consent of the regions to enter into agreements.[75]

While there may be a convention under which international agreements are not entered into without the agreement of Gibraltar its ability to enter into external agreements itself or to operate with external competence is a much more contentious issue. In the first place, the spectre of bilateralism raises its head, with Spain mounting a systematic campaign to refuse to recognise the competence of Gibraltar authorities and Gibraltar-issued documentation.[76] It also lobbied other Member States to refuse recognition. Spanish pressure led to the signing of a so-called 'Competent Authority' Agreement in April 2000,[77] under which a system of 'post-boxing' was introduced as a result of which Spain lifted its objections to the recognition of Gibraltar authorities within a defined context. Under that system, official notifications or communications to and from Gibraltar statutory authorities[78] were to be channeled through the Foreign Office in

[69] But the requirement on the Governor to act in consultation with the Chief Minister: see 2006 Constitution s 47(1).

[70] Either by simple participation within the UK delegation or, if there are no other UK issues at stake, by fully representing the UK.

[71] The latter is a complex argument to field.

[72] Hopkins n 24 above, 191.

[73] Art 32, Basic Law.

[74] A Cygan, *National Parliaments in an Integrated Europe—an Anglo-German Perspective* (The Hague, Kluwer Law International, 2001) 178; and the Lindau Agreement, which dates back to the 1950s and allows Länder to enter into these agreements.

[75] Aurrecoechea n 25 above, 99. However the powers of Catalunya were enhanced in 2006.

[76] eg passports and ID cards.

[77] House of Assembly Hansard, 19 April 2000.

[78] In any field—be it Financial Services or Customs for example.

London as the conduit for the passage of information. In practice, this is often not observed with foreign authorities seeking to make direct contact with Gibraltar Governmental authorities.

By the same token the Gibraltar Government zealously guards its competences and constantly tries to push forward the bounds of what is possible. During the OECD's harmful tax initiative[79] the international body sought commitments from a variety of non-independent finance centres, amongst which was Gibraltar. Once again the bilateralism theme sprang to life. While Gibraltar had been negotiating with the OECD in the spring of 2001 so as to give the OECD certain financial commitments, Spain tried to resist Gibraltar's international capacity by objecting to the fact that Gibraltar was engaged in direct talks with the OECD and—more fundamentally—tried to attack the standing of any commitment that Gibraltar was contemplating giving, by requesting separate letters from the United Kingdom endorsing the action.[80]

This capacity to enter into international commitments is a controversial area, though there have been some interesting developments in recent years. When the United States and Bermuda entered into a tax information exchange agreement, the actual agreement was entered into between the Governments of the United States and the United Kingdom.[81] The interesting feature was that the then Premier of Bermuda, John Swan, actually signed on behalf of the United Kingdom under delegated power. More recently, however, Jersey, Guernsey and the Isle of Man have entered into direct agreements with the United States.[82]

In its memorandum of evidence before the Foreign Affairs Committee in 2008 the Foreign Office has confirmed that there are standing instructions to enable consultation with the overseas territories in relation to the proposed ratification or extension of any treaty.[83] While the British Government position is that, unless specifically authorised, the territories

[79] OECD Report on Harmful Tax, OECD, 1998.

[80] Ostensibly so that it could take the position that any commitment with the OECD was in reality a British commitment. In practice, neither Gibraltar nor the UK could be comfortable with that pretence: Gibraltar because it would resist the encroachment into its powers; the UK because it did not wish to become embroiled in a Gibraltar commitment to an international organisation, for accountability reasons. In the end, the tussle over the language Spain wanted delayed the publication of the 2001 OECD Report, substantially threatening the blockage of the entire initiative.

[81] In 1999.

[82] See the exchange of information agreements entered into between those territories and the US of 2002, though the entrance into these agreements was far from unproblematic. It appears, for example, that Jersey's capacity to enter into such an agreement was a live issue between the Jersey and UK Governments before its signature.

[83] FAC Report 2008, Ev 153–54. Though there is a difference in practice between considering a possible extension and devising a negotiating position of the UK before a treaty is entered into. In the former scenario there is a clearer line of consultation; in the latter case the views of a territory are only sought 'where applicable'.

do not have capacity to enter into treaties there is a recognised practice of providing an 'entrustment' to an overseas territory Government to allow it to negotiate agreements in specific areas:

It is possible for an entrustment to be general, covering all treaties within certain categories. But it is more usual for an entrustment to relate to a particular treaty. An entrustment should be sought by an overseas territory prior to commencing the negotiation of an international agreement. Bermuda and BVI have a 'standing entrustment' in specified areas. Bermuda, Gibraltar and the Caribbean Overseas Territories have standing entrustments to negotiate tax information exchange agreements. The principles behind standing entrustments are the same as those for the much more common treaty-specific entrustments. Where a standing entrustment exists the territories must keep the UK Government informed of negotiations in individual agreements and the UK has the right to refuse to allow an overseas territory to sign an agreement to which the UK objects.[84] In 2009 Gibraltar entered into exchange of information agreements with the United States and Ireland and was negotiating the signature of a series of other similar agreements.

THE FREEZE IN CONSTITUTIONAL REFORM

The Demarcation of Domestic Competences: Their Extent, Extension, Demarcation and Change by Convention

Spanish accession to the Community created a specific governance deficit for Gibraltar, because Spain could exert influence over EC measures applicable in Gibraltar. The failure to address the impact of accession by establishing constitutional structures to preserve alternative influence, representation and power was another main result of the governance deficit that developed in the two decades since 1986. During the same period the legitimacy debate spurred on similar discussions around Europe and fostered the development of national and European arrangements to secure power, representation and influence for State and sub-State executives, Parliaments and individuals.

One of the principal effects of bilateralism was that the constitutional aspirations in Gibraltar were frustrated for a long time. While Britain was keen to repeat assurances that it would listen carefully to any proposals put forward, it also, privately, expressed concerns that it would not wish to offend Spain or fail to take into account 'the Spanish dimension'. This policy went back some time and was emphasised after Spanish accession to the Community. It affected the constitutional aspirations of Gibraltar in two respects. The first related to the status of Gibraltar. Britain accepted

[84] ibid.

that the decolonisation of Gibraltar was a live bilateral issue for Britain and Spain as soon as it agreed to discuss sovereignty. Secondly, it affected any moves towards gaining greater self-governance, even when it was short of full-blown decolonisation. This position softened slightly with the election of a new administration in Spain in 2004,[85] and facilitated a package of constitutional reforms by 2006. Even then Spain's position was heavily qualified.[86] Bilateralism was in full force and the limits to the domestic competences of Gibraltar were dictated by such changes that had been gained by constitutional convention against the background of what was the legal formality of the 1969 Constitution.

While formal constitutional reform proved impossible between the years 1986–2004, it is also true that the Constitution had not stood still. In this way, the bilateralising influence was partially but inadequately ameliorated. There were many examples of evolution by convention formed with British Government acquiescence. In the same way as the United Kingdom was reluctant to formalise further constitutional reform it also, to a large extent, did not seek to resist the pushing forward of constitutional boundaries by convention.[87] Broadly speaking, these fell into two categories: in the first place the assumption of greater responsibility by the elected Government and secondly general changes in practice that reflected that greater acquisition of power.[88]

[85] Covered in the next chapter.

[86] See chs 3 and 6.

[87] For general discussion on the principles of constitutional conventions see G Marshall, *Constitutional Conventions—The Rules and Forms of Political Accountability* (Oxford, Clarendon Press, 1986); and P Oliver and A Tomkins, 'Constitutional Change in the UK', in M Andenas (ed), *The Creation and Amendment of Constitutional Norms* (London, British Institute of International and Comparative Law, 2000) 319–57. A convention, being an unwritten custom or rule of practice, is unenforceable. See the Supreme Court of Canada in *Re Resolution to Amend the Constitution* [1981] SCR 753, where this seems to be accepted on the basis that they are unenforceable unless 'crystallised' by statutory adoption. And also 'it is perfectly appropriate to say that to violate a convention is to do something which is unconstitutional although it entails no direct legal consequence' (at 883–4). They can though be used as an aid to statutory construction. See also *Osborne v Canada (Treasury Board)* [1991] 2 SCR 69. They can also be incorporated into statute, and therefore endowed with certainty and enforceability. What a convention so transformed gains in enforcement it also loses in flexibility. Part of the attractions and the reason for the survival of conventions is that they can adapt themselves to the requirements of the moment. Most conventions therefore arise in one of three situations: because there is no written Constitution; or (if there is one) because it is either silent on the specific issue; or it has remained unamended and has fallen out of step with actual practice. A rule of practice may subsequently be incorporated into (or, as some would argue, be superseded by) a statutory provision resulting, not in the natural death of the convention, but in its replacement by statute motivated by the need to ensure survival of the principle or practice on which it is based.

[88] For an interesting comparative review of the amendment process of different national Constitutions, including the issue of conventions, see Andenas (ed) n 89 above.

DOMESTIC DEMARCATION OF COMPETENCES OF 1969

The 1969 Constitution envisaged that a list of defined domestic matters would be designated under it. These were to be delegated to local Ministers. The Governor's responsibilities were not defined in the Constitution. In most of the other British overseas territories the Governor's special responsibilities were expressly defined with everything else being local.[89] The intention behind the different drafting technique was set out in the explanatory despatch from the Foreign Secretary, to the Governor which was annexed to the Constitution.[90] The purpose of the despatch was said to be to 'supplement' the Constitution on certain points.[91] The despatch, which had to be deemed to be an aid to construction of the Constitution, stated that

> Since everything which is not a defined domestic matter automatically remains within the Governor's direct responsibility it is unnecessary and undesirable to attempt an exhaustive definition of all matters retained by the Governor.[92]

The Foreign Secretary annexed a list of suggested matters[93] which 'should be specified as defined domestic matters'. He went on to confirm that '[it] must be recognised that this list may need adjustment from time to time' and that the devolution of authority to Ministers should be read together with the statements made in the despatch.

As acknowledged in the Despatch itself, the list was valid as a starting point for guidance and it was subject to change. There were some changes, some of which are described in the following paragraphs, that should be seen in the context of the wider evolution of the constitutional practices set out in the Order and Despatch respectively. Indeed, the most fundamental statement that fell away is that which asserted that anything not defined as a domestic matter was the Governor's responsibility. In practice, the reverse became constitutional practice by 2004.

[89] All territories except the Falkland Islands.

[90] *Despatch from the Secretary of State to His Excellency the Governor Admiral of the Fleet Sir Varyl Begg*, 23 May 1969.

[91] ibid para 1.

[92] It did go on though to state examples of possible areas where 'wider considerations require responsibility to be retained by the Governor', such as honours, the implementation of international agreements, appointments to public bodies (other than when the powers had been specifically devolved) and administrative responsibility of the public service. The despatch also noted that 'responsibility for the financial business of the Government of Gibraltar should continue to be entrusted to the Financial and Development Secretary.'

[93] Including health, municipal matters, education and a wide range of domestic matters.

EXTENSIONS OF COMPETENCES AND POWERS SINCE 1986—REFORM BY STEALTH

By 2004 the areas generally accepted[94] as responsibilities of the Governor were only external affairs, defence, internal security and the police,[95] and it would not have accorded with the practice developed over the last three decades for the Governor to have sought to direct matters within other areas. Indeed, even in respect of the accepted reserved areas there had developed much discussion between the Governor and the Chief Minister, either as a general process of consultation or because of any grey areas of overlap of responsibility that arose.[96] This should not be seen in isolation. Several other instances pointed to this trend of greater devolution by convention. First, some of the matters highlighted in the despatch as being areas for which the Financial and Development Secretary should be responsible passed to Ministers.[97] Secondly, notwithstanding the hope expressed in the despatch that the Financial Secretary should be invited to Council of Ministers whenever financial matters were to be discussed, this did not happen after the late 1980s. The modern practice developed that only elected Ministers attended Council of Ministers, and neither the Attorney-General nor the Financial Secretary was accorded Ministerial standing.[98] Thirdly, while the Financial and Development Secretary and the Attorney-General were *ex officio* members of the House, they did not answer for the Government in the House of Assembly on financial matters, issues of law and order or on matters reserved to the Governor. Practice evolved that the Chief Minister would usually take questions on the police, law and order or financial matters within the Assembly. In Bermuda, use of the express powers to allow delegation of business within an area specifically reserved to the Governor has been necessary to allow Ministers to answer questions in the House on the Bermuda Regiment or

[94] But there is scope for disagreement as to whether Britain formally conceded this position: see the submissions filed by the UK at the European Court of Justice in the airport liberalisation or tax litigation—below; and Spain also contested this. Both instances are further examples of the wide bilateralisation of this dispute.

[95] The Public Service was a half-way house. Theoretical responsibility and discretion of making appointments lay with the Governor, but in practice there was a great deal of consultation with the elected Government on public appointments, and the recommendations of the statutory commission entrusted with the administration of appointment and discipline of public officers (the Public Service Commission) were followed in practice. Finance had been devolved in all but name.

[96] eg between the operational and administrative responsibilities for the Police. The budget for the Police is decided by Ministers and voted on by the House. The Police are operationally independent. Since the 2006 Constitution, a Police Authority has been established under a new Police Act.

[97] And more specifically to the Finance Centre Director—a senior official.

[98] By the 2006 Constitution both ceased to be members of the Parliament, and separate elected Ministerial portfolios for Finance and Justice were created.

on certain administrative issues concerning the police.[99] In Gibraltar, elected Ministers have both presented legislation in the House on the Gibraltar Regiment or have fulfilled similar functions in relation to the Police without express delegation. Fourthly, the presentation of legislation also followed the convention outlined in the above paragraph. So, for example, the Chief Minister presented the Budget for nearly 20 years[100] before a formal ministerial responsibility for finance was created in 2007, and regularly presents legislation that could be construed as affecting a reserved matter of the Governor.[101] Fifthly, while the Constitution did not provide for consultation with the Government, it was consulted in practice before senior public service and judicial appointments were made. The usual channel of consultation was between the Deputy Governor (an appointment of the British Government usually seconded from the Foreign Office) and the Chief Secretary.[102] Notwithstanding constitutional silence on this issue, a clear practice developed since at least 1979, by which the Chief Minister was consulted before certain appointments, such as Justices of the Peace, Magistrate, Judges of the Supreme Court, Attorney-General and other senior public service appointments, were made.[103]

Finally, another substantial issue where there was change by convention concerned the Gibraltar Council,[104] which was in effect defunct by the end of the period. This had been established under section 46 of the 1969 Constitution, and was made up of the Governor, the Chief Minister, four other Ministers, the Commander British Forces, the Deputy Governor, the Attorney-General and the Financial Secretary. It was empowered to advise the Governor on many of his functions. In other territories, a Governor-presided Executive Council still fulfils a crucial day-to-day role in the affairs of administration of the territory.[105] However, in Gibraltar it had not met since 1990.[106] Normal Government

[99] E Davies, *The Legal Status of the British Dependent Territories* (Cambridge, CUP, 1999) 184–85.

[100] In fact adopting and fulfilling a role akin to a Minister of Finance.

[101] eg the Gibraltar Regiment Ordinance 1999, legislation under the Imports and Exports Act on police powers, or legislation relating to weapons of mass destruction.

[102] The renamed title of the most senior civil servant in the employ of the Government of Gibraltar—the effective Head of the Civil Service.

[103] See the Statement of November 1999 issued by the Government. Formal involvement in the appointment and consultation process was built into the 2006 constitutional structures through the establishment of a Judicial Services Commission.

[104] The descendant of the Executive Council.

[105] eg in territories such as St Helena, Cayman Islands and the Falkland Islands. See also FAC Report 2008, where, in its Memorandum, the Foreign Office makes the point that 'Bermuda has almost full internal self-government . . . [T]he situation is similar in Gibraltar' (Ev 146, para 8).

[106] The position had evolved since the hope expressed in para 7 of the despatch 'that the fullest use would be made under the new Constitution of the Gibraltar Council . . . The Council is so constituted as to bring together the senior elected representatives of the people of Gibraltar with the Governor's senior official advisers in a body small enough and flexible

business was organised through the Council of Ministers that includes all Ministers and is chaired by the Chief Minister. The rationale of the practice that had evolved in Gibraltar by 2004 was that, as more powers had in practice been assumed by the elected Government, its business should be driven through a cabinet-style body made up of the elected arm of the Executive. In this way the modern form of executive governance had become akin to the Bermudian Cabinet structure and was some distance away from those territories in which the Executive Council still had an ordinary and daily function. As Roberts-Wray points out, this is a normal way of acquiring greater powers of self-government in the standard transition between dependence to self-government.[107] The practical disappearance of the Gibraltar Council was clearly a step in the direction of full self-government.[108]

These conventions are notable for three main reasons of importance to Gibraltar:

—The development of conventions is absolutely necessary for the good government of a territory. It cannot be supposed, just because a Constitution has been confined to writing, that the practices that were originally envisaged by its draftsmen at the time of conception will not require evolution. While it is right that such parts of the Constitution that lay down rights or principles should be entrenched, those practices that on the other hand govern the definition and relationship between the Crown (or its representative in a territory) and the elected government are by necessity capable of change depending on the mutually agreed or evolved political circumstances;

—In extreme examples constitutional development leading to independence can be secured by convention. This fact is of importance to Gibraltar because its Constitution was the only one—among the current overseas territories of the United Kingdom that had not been formally amended before 2006. But the lack of amendment did not mean there

enough in its procedures to permit frank intimate and confidential discussion of problems of mutual concern. The great importance of such a forum needs no emphasis in the special circumstances of Gibraltar today.' As circumstances changed so did the need for the existence of the Gibraltar Council.

The Gibraltar Council did retain a small administrative role in signing off long leasing arrangements reached by Government and which were required to be signed by the Governor. However, no meetings were held. Circulars were distributed to members on a round-robin basis and on terms that 'unless objection is received' by a certain date 'the necessary action will proceed.' By 2003 not more than a dozen or so Papers were circulated to members every year.

[107] Roberts-Wray n 30 above, 247–89, and S De Smith, *The New Commonwealth and its Constitutions* (London, Stevens, 1964) 38–76.

[108] The effectiveness of this practice and its capability of being challenged is an interesting question. Examples drawn from Canadian experience provide useful analogies. See P Hogg, *Constitutional Law of Canada* (Toronto, Carswell, 1993), *Re Resolution to Amend the Constitution* [1981] SCR 753, and *The Queen v Beauregard* [1986] 2 SCR 56.

had been no constitutional progress. This could and had been achieved by convention.[109]

—The acquisition of power by convention circumvented—at least in part—any reluctance or inability to progress matters because of the spectre of bilateralism.

As Zines points out, there was often difficulty defining the demarcation of responsibility between imperial and local government, but this lack of clarity also produced the advantage that 'more and more executive power [could] . . . be transferred to the Dominions without any alteration to constitutional law by simply changing the rule or understanding as to who advises the Crown.'[110] Judges also assisted by confirming that the Constitution should be given the interpretation 'which changing circumstances require.'[111]

Though the lack of express constitutional rigidity allowed for flexible development, which could advance local aspirations, it also led to some confusion.[112] But however clear the practices, the situation was unsatisfactory. As conventions are recognisable but not enforceable,[113] if there were ever an attempt to turn back the constitutional clock, the small territory would be placed in an invidious position. The supreme reality is that the pressure that could not be exerted on a country with the political muscle of Canada (if practices were either disliked or were moving too fast for some in the British Government) could certainly be brought to bear on a small territory. The achievement not so much of certainty then (as it is clear that these conventions had developed) but of a degree of enforce-

[109] In an interesting comparative analysis of the position in Canada, New Zealand and Australia, Zines remarks on the evolutionary manner in which independence was achieved by these countries noting that the 'growth in status . . . [was] achieved mainly not by changes in law or alterations to the constitutions of those countries but by the development of constitutional conventions and understandings.' L Zines, *Constitutional Change in the Commonwealth* (Cambridge, CUP, 1991). See also P Oliver, *The Constitution of Independence—The Development of Constitutional Theory in Australia, Canada and New Zealand* (Oxford, OUP, 2005).

[110] Zines n 111 above, 4.

[111] *A-G for Canada v A-G for Ontario* [1947] AC 127.

[112] In that the Australian States were still described as 'self-governing dependencies of the British Crown' by the British Government as recently as 1981: see Zines n 111 above, 11. The UK Parliament enacted the Canada Act in 1982 to allow the 'patriation' of the Constitution to Canada. (It provided that no UK Act of Parliament would apply to Canada from that date: in *Re Amendment of the Constitution of Canada* (1982) 125 Dominion Law Reports 1 the Supreme Court of Canada had remarked on the omnipotence of the UK Parliament in respect of Canada in 1981, the year prior to the Act). Acts were also passed in Australia and New Zealand in 1986 to deal with similar issues of constitutional supremacy. That these Acts were felt necessary to clean up a residue of issues which compromised the image of independence of these countries seems remarkable. On the other hand, *realpolitik* also ensured that the UK Government was relatively sensitive in handling this issue and did not provoke a constitutional issue with these countries before these Acts. It would be somewhat different with a small territory such as Gibraltar because of the relative political weight of these.

[113] See Marshall n 89 above, 210–217.

ability was at the heart of the desire to enshrine the conventions that had largely developed since the 1980s into the new Constitution. This was one of the aims of the constitutional process that was commenced in 1998.

COMPARING AND REDRAWING STATE AND SUB-STATE COMPETENCES

Even though there was a struggle to ensure constitutional entrenchment of these advances by convention, it seemed clear that by 2004 Gibraltar was, in practice, almost entirely self-governing and economically self-sufficient. It administered its public services with complete responsibility for policy and administration. It set its own taxes, collected its revenues and managed public finances without any degree of involvement from the British Government. It is interesting to examine how this compared with self-governing sub-State polities elsewhere in Europe.

The internal structures of Member States are very diverse. There are States that are organised on a unitary,[114] devolved,[115] regionalised[116] or federal[117] basis, with each category representing an incremental level of decentralisation and transfer of powers. The highest levels of constitutional delegation of powers are found in the federal or highly regionalised countries.[118] In the latter there is wide autonomy, legislative power and constitutional provisions that provide for directly elected regional Government, and at the highest federal level a sharing of power set out in the Constitution with the central Government either having no power or a restricted ability to change the nature of federally demarcated powers. In many Member States the powers of different regions or devolved entities is asymmetrical, which highlights the disparity of internal national structures of liaison with the central Government. However, as Hopkins has suggested, 'mere lists of regional responsibilities give us a very misleading picture . . . [because] . . . the extent to which regions exercise authority within these areas is very different.'[119] He highlights that not

[114] With high centralisation and very little devolution other than at local level. Denmark is a good example.

[115] Following Scottish and Welsh devolution, the UK properly falls into this category.

[116] Spain.

[117] Austria, Belgium or Germany.

[118] A Project Report published by the Scottish Office, entitled 'Summary of Devolved Parliaments in the European Union' (Edinburgh, University of Edinburgh, August 1998), describes the situation in eight Member States; and see also 'The Constitutional Status of Local Government in Other Countries' (Birmingham, School of Public Policy, University of Birmingham, Central Research Unit, Scottish Office, 1998).

[119] Hopkins n 24 above, 245–47. There is a useful table of comparative competences on 246. The areas within which most competences commonly exist are matters such as planning, health, culture, education transport, economic development and, interestingly, the police.

only constitutional issues, but financial and practical ones, will have an impact on how and to what extent these powers are exercised.

In Germany, Belgium and Austria there are definitions of exclusive, mixed and shared competences. In Belgium exclusive sub-State competences are mainly restricted to the economic, cultural, educational or urban planning fields.[120] In Germany it has been noted that 'the Länder possess only a very limited range of exclusive legislative responsibilities.'[121] The same is the case for sub-State entities in Austria,[122] Italy[123] or France.[124] In Spain, the more advanced Regions, like Catalunya or the Basque Country, have a wider range of exclusive competences (and then also a number of shared competences with the central Government in other fields).[125] Bengoetxea has argued that apart from fiscal issues the levels of autonomy of the Basque Country are lower than Scotland or German Länder in many respects.[126] In Scotland the revenue raising powers of the Parliament are severely restricted in accordance with the choice given to voters in the devolution referendum.[127] In Wales the Assembly's legislative power is generally confined to secondary legislation only.

The form of regional devolution can be either vertical or horizontal but, because it is difficult to ring-fence some areas of Government from others, it

> leads most federal and regional systems to utilise horizontal forms of functional definition. A horizontal system of federalism does not grant specific policy areas

[120] B Kerremans and J Beyers, 'The Belgian sub-national entities in the European Union: Second or Third Level Players?' in C Jeffrey (ed), *The Regional Dimension of the European Union—Towards a Third Level in Europe?* (London, Frank Cass, 1997) 41–55, 46.

[121] C Jeffrey, 'Farewell the Third Level? The German Länder and the European Policy Process' in C Jeffrey (ed), *The Regional Dimension of the European Union—Towards a Third Level in Europe?* (London, Frank Cass, 1997), 56–75, 58.

[122] M Morass, 'Austria: the case of a Federal Newcomer in European Union Politics', in C Jeffrey (ed), *The Regional Dimension of the European Union—Towards a Third Level in Europe?* (London, Frank Cass, 1997) 76–95 and I Seidl-Hohenveldern, 'Constitutional Problems Involved in Austria's accession to the EU' (1995) 32(3) *CML Rev* 1.

[123] C Desideri and V Santantonio in C Jeffrey (ed), *The Regional Dimension of the European Union—Towards a Third Level in Europe?* (London, Frank Cass, 1997) and P Leyland, J Frosini and C Bologna, 'Regional Government Reform in Italy: assessing the prospects for devolution' [2002] PL 242.

[124] A Smith, 'The French Case: The Exception or the Rule', in C Jeffrey (ed), *The Regional Dimension of the European Union—Towards a Third Level in Europe?* (London, Frank Cass, 1997) 117–30, 118.

[125] See the *Estatuto de Autonomia* of Catalunya or the Basque Country, the official website of the Catalan Government, www.gencat.cat and also Art 148 of the Spanish Constitution, which lays down the exclusive competences of the State.

[126] J Bengoetxea, 'Participation of Infra-State Entities in European Union Affairs in Spain' in S Weatherill and U Bernitz (eds), *The Role of Regions and Sub National Actors in Europe* (Oxford, Hart Publishing, 2005) 61.

[127] In many ways the ability to both raise revenue and keep the revenue collected in the territory is an important indicator of the extent of self-government. In Gibraltar all revenue raised is deployed by the Government to run public services, public administration and for capital projects. There are no financial contributions from the UK Government.

to specific levels of government. Instead particular aspects of policy will be given to the most appropriate levels.[128]

Effective interdependence and co-operation is essential for sub-State government to operate. Practical State mechanisms need to be in place to avoid friction between the areas of responsibility. If a region is responsible for the provision of healthcare or transport services there will be clear overlaps—in prescription charges[129] or the maintenance of a shared railway network. Should the region be able to decide what to do with green areas or should the remit of activity have to comply with national environmental policy? This all demonstrates the high level of devolution of competences and financial autonomy that Gibraltar had achieved. This developed side by side with the erosion it was suffering by the inadequate structures that deprived the Gibraltar executive of representation, power and influence at supra-national level. It is to this to which we must now turn.

REPRESENTATION, POWER AND INFLUENCE IN THE EUROPEAN UNION

The overall truism is that:

> regional government . . . is not born free. It is a limited institution of governance integrated into a system alongside other forms of governance. It comes with intergovernmental relations as standard and there is no pretence that it can operate independently of other levels of government particularly its parent state.[130]

Here lies the crux of the issue for Gibraltar. Instead of its devolution stemming from this culture, its pattern of self-government is that shared with other Commonwealth territories. The horizontal functional divide described as the common feature within many EU Member States is the reverse of the way that the constitutions of British Overseas Territories are structured. These are based on a vertical functional divide. The unique challenge for Gibraltar is that it is the only Overseas Territory to which the TEC applies, and as such it is trying to find a constitutional accommodation, while it has a scheme of governance that is organised in a different functional way to that of most other stateless nations within the Community. This is not impossible but it is always important to bear in mind these structural differences and the impact they have on governance. For devolution to work in an integrated state the devolution of powers to

[128] Hopkins n 24 above, 253.

[129] eg should the region have power to alter these and collect the revenue or should these be done at State level?

[130] Hopkins n 24 above, 267.

nations within the State must go hand in hand with the establishment of intergovernmental mechanisms so as to address issues of overlap and friction. This ensures co-operation and administrative efficiency. In devolving power to the former Commonwealth colonies usual practice saw a gradual withdrawal of the UK from all areas of responsibility gradually leaving the administration to the government of the territory. Self-government was a preparation for independence, not for interdependence within a supra-national entity.[131]

As such, while Gibraltar does not achieve independence and remains within the EU, the more traditional method of meeting local aspirations of self-government and self-determination is deficient and causes substantial functional difficulty. In combination with the overarching bilateralism that is so present in Gibraltar's case, the absence of formal intergovernmental structures more akin to a federal system undermines Gibraltar's actual level of self-government. For the time that it remains within the European Union and in a non-independent state, Gibraltar and the United Kingdom must depart from the colonial method of assumption of self-government and instead accept that membership of the Union—in practice—has transformed the relationship from a colonial one to a quasi-federal one. The realisation of this would be essential to address the governance deficit that emerges from bilateralism and is exacerbated by the fact that Gibraltar is treated—still—as a colony and not as a sovereign stateless nation with a quasi-federal relationship with the United Kingdom and the Union.[132]

This is why, although Gibraltar has more exclusive competences than the more powerful regions, it has less power in some respects. The 'exclusivity' it acquired has been systematically eroded without being compensated by the award of influence elsewhere which would maintain that power. In other countries, the regions or states may have fewer exclusive competences but, in some, they have acquired better governance structures and access to mechanisms of influence to allow them a better chance of maintaining their power. In a small group of cases they have acquired a national voice to co-determine policy in matters which interests or will affect them. The acquisition of a clearer demarcation of competences by Gibraltar in the 2006 Constitution has not changed the fundamental point that the structures to secure and preserve representation and influence at supra-national level are deficient.

[131] Whether it follows that constitutional integration—as in the case of the French Overseas departments combined with direct Parliamentary representation—is therefore a viable or desirable option is touched upon in ch 7. It will be submitted that it is not for a variety of social, economic, cultural and political reasons.

[132] This theme will be expanded later. There is a need for a clear reassessment of the nature, context and quality of the key relationships with Gibraltar (ie with Europe; with Britain and with Spain).

The German Constitution sets out areas of exclusive, mixed and concurrent competences that demarcate the relationship between the Federal Government and the 16 Länder.[133] The German system has sometimes been described as one of co-operative federalism. Indeed, it seems to have been the inspiration behind the competence provisions of the CE and the Lisbon Treaty. During the debate that led to the Maastricht Treaty and in the years that followed, the Länder have consistently held two broad aspirations. The first has been to address the European domestic policy debate (an inward-looking objective) and the second to obtain a greater role at European level (the outward-looking objective). Securing representation, consultation and participation in national mechanisms in the fields of parliamentary scrutiny, decision-making, administration, legislation and governance furthered the first.[134] For example, in so far as proposed transfers of powers to Europe relate to exclusive competences of the Länder, then the Bundesrat[135] must be consulted and agree to this by a two-thirds majority. Transfer of competences will not be agreed if it would affect the Federal structure of Germany or the involvement in legislation of the Länder.[136]

Scotland, Wales and Northern Ireland do not have the constitutional mechanisms which secure the position as steadfastly as in Germany. Instead, their legislative and (in the case of Scotland or Northern Ireland) executive power is set out in the respective Acts of Parliament,[137] but is always subordinate to the overriding power of the UK Parliament to legislate for the particular devolved nation.[138] Cooperative arrangements to improve participation in European matters are set out in Intergovernmental Concordats.[139] The Belgian and Austrian situations also constitutionally protect the competences of sub-State authorities.[140]

[133] Germany is a democratic and social federal state—Art 20 Basic Law.

[134] See below.

[135] The Bundesrat is composed of Cabinet Ministers from the 16 Länder.

[136] Cygan n 76 above, 181–83.

[137] Scotland Act 1998 and Government of Wales 1998 Act—though, as stated earlier, this is subject to the Sewel Convention.

[138] Scotland Act 1998 s 35, for example.

[139] Hood Phillips n 44 above, 83–109; Cygan n 76 above, 189–217 and V Bogdanor, *Devolution in the United Kingdom* (Oxford, OUP, 2001) 276–86.

[140] Kerremans in C Jeffrey (ed), *The Regional Dimension of the European Union—Towards a Third Level in Europe?* (London, Frank Cass, 1997) 42, and Morass ibid 76.

EXECUTIVE AND NON-EXECUTIVE PRE-LEGISLATIVE REPRESENTATION, INFLUENCE AND ROLE IN POLICY FORMULATION AND DECISION-MAKING

At EU Level

The introduction of Article 203 into the TEC provided that[141]

> [t]he Council shall consist of a representative of each Member State at Ministerial level, authorised to commit the government of that Member State.

This has two distinct elements. The first—the simple representation element—widened the previous position, which had only permitted representatives from Governments of the Member States. For the first time sub-State Ministers would be able to represent the Member State at meetings of the Council. The second element was that the representative must have authority to bind the Member State Government. Thus this provision invited and led to a carve-up of roles and responsibilities within Member States to reflect constitutional competences and to make this Article work in practice.

Belgium, for example, on the basis of a demarcation of competences and a co-operation agreement between the State and sub-State governments, has operated a system of mixed delegations and rotation,[142] unless the matters on the agenda concern exclusive federal competences. In Germany, the Bundesrat nominates the German representative at Council of Ministers level if the matters to be discussed relate to exclusive Länder competences.[143] Wider powers of representation (when they affect federal competences) are only given on the clear understanding that the Member State's national policy is advocated and defended. So much is clear in the Inter-Governmental Concordat between the United Kingdom Government and the Scottish Executive, and provides the logistical umbrella for attendance by Scottish Ministers at the EU Council of Ministers.[144] A Gibraltar Minister has never represented the United Kingdom in Council meetings under

[141] See J Kottman, 'Europe and the Regions; Sub-national Entity Representation at Community Level' 26(2) (2001) EL Rev 159–176.

[142] Kerremans in Jeffrey (ed) n 142 above, 46–47.

[143] Art 23(6) Basic Law and Jeffrey (ed) n 142 above, 61.

[144] See V Bogdanor, *Devolution in the United Kingdom* (Oxford, OUP, 2001) 280–81, and Cygan n 76 above, 164–65, 210–17, and also Memorandum of Understanding and Supplementary Agreement (Cm 4444, 1999 and Cm 5240, 2002). Also of interest is J Poirer, 'The Functions of Intergovernmental Agreements: Post-Devolution Concordats in a Comparative Perspective' [2001] PL 134; A Cygan, 'Scotland's Parliament and European Affairs: Some Lessons from Germany' (1999) 24(5) EL Rev 483–98, and G Pearce, 'British Sub-National Government Engagement in Europe' (2000) 6(4) *European Public Law* 595.

Article 203[145] or even been a member of the Member State's delegation in that respect.[146]

At parliamentary level, the CE and Lisbon Treaty proposed the introduction of a new mechanism to enhance the powers of national parliaments and their role in the legislative scheme of the Union. National parliaments would be given the right to review draft legislative acts on subsidiarity grounds. If the national parliaments of one-third of the Member States were to submit a reasoned opinion within the time-limit the Commission would be obliged to review its proposal.

At State Level

But however good the framework to allow sub-State representatives to attend Council meetings under Article 203 or the new mechanisms to give National Parliaments more power, these are but one side of the coin. Internal national structures are also needed if the coin is to have any value.

Domestic Parliamentary Scrutiny and Representation

The proposed mechanism enhancing the role of State parliaments sets out that these will—where appropriate—consult sub-State parliaments with legislative powers.[147] It was unclear whether there was an intention to apply this to Gibraltar because of its unique constitutional position. The British Government's White Paper on the CE did make the point that 'the Government welcomes the progress already made by Parliament's Scrutiny Committees in giving thought to how this mechanism can be made to work effectively, and how the devolved Parliaments and assemblies can be consulted on its use.'[148] It is premature to know how this could work,[149] and nor is it clear whether the treatment given to devolved home administrations would be extended to Gibraltar.[150] The different approach taken by Belgium is worthy of note. In a declaration annexed to the Lisbon Treaty, it stated that:

[145] This might be unrealistic unless it occurs within narrowly defined situations.

[146] Ministerial representation with the UK delegation on key issues should be feasible.

[147] Protocol on Subsidiarity to Lisbon Treaty.

[148] White Paper on the Treaty Establishing a Constitution for Europe (Cm 6309, 2004) para 23.

[149] If the Lisbon Treaty is ratified by all States or, absent that, if piecemeal introduction of certain reforms is undertaken.

[150] Gibraltar might not wish to describe or categorise its Parliament as regional to avoid confusion about its own constitutional status. Any application of these arrangements would have to be on an analogous basis only.

> in accordance with its constitutional law not only the Chamber of Representatives and Senate of the Federal Government *but also the parliamentary assemblies of the Communities and the Regions act,* in terms of the competences exercised by the Union, as components of the national parliamentary system or chambers of the national parliament.[151] (emphasis added)

There is an additional parliamentary area within which Gibraltar's influence falls short of other sub-State territories. Given their constitutional status as integral parts of a Member State, these are always represented within the State parliaments. In some countries with bicameral systems there is a strong regional element to these.[152] Gibraltar has no representation in the United Kingdom parliament and if the proposed new scrutiny mechanism were not extended to it then its ability to scrutinise intended legislation would be further curtailed.

Executive Influence

This is achieved via a variety of methods in certain Member States:

Influence in the Drafting and Formulation of Legislation

Currently, Gibraltar has insufficient power to influence proposed Community measures. This is especially relevant when the proposed legislation allows the Member State to make certain choices as to its form before it is transposed into national legislation. The Gibraltar Government is widely consulted by the United Kingdom on proposed measures,[153] and it has a free hand when drafting and putting forward legislation for enactment by the Gibraltar Parliament once European legislation is in place. But sometimes issues come to the fore (especially in the formative period of Community legislation) that illustrate the strains that can be caused by different interpretations, the fact that real influence needs to be exercised at the pre-legislative stage and that this is missing.[154]

The debate surrounding the terms of the so-called Savings Directive provides an interesting example. The proposal at its inception put forward a system by which Member States could opt to either introduce a withholding tax on savings or agree to exchange information with the tax authorities of other member states. Eventually, circumstances changed—principally because the United Kingdom was against the dual system—and an agreement was reached in Portugal in June 2000 by which all

[151] Declaration 51 to the Lisbon Treaty (formerly Declaration 49 to the CE).
[152] Austria, Belgium and Germany. See Hopkins n 24 above, 270–77.
[153] Indeed there is a special unit within the Foreign Office which provides this liaison.
[154] Absent are the formal arrangements in place for Scotland, Belgium or Germany.

countries agreed to exchange information as an ultimate goal but allowed themselves the right to choose to impose a withholding tax for a transitional period of seven years. The agreement was conditional on the implementation of equivalent measures in key third countries and the Caribbean overseas territories, the Channel Islands and the Isle of Man.[155] This measure was of great importance to jurisdictions operating finance centres and emphasis was put on the need to ensure that any new regulatory environment had to be applied to all competitor jurisdictions. If it did not then clearly some jurisdictions would benefit at the expense of others. Countries such as Austria and Luxembourg elected to introduce a withholding tax for a transitional period of seven years. Other jurisdictions outside the Union also opted for a withholding tax. As such the uneven fiscal environment, with only some countries applying the more stringent exchange of information requirements, inevitably affected the attraction of banking deposits and private client finance centre work.

In that context the Gibraltar Government wished to retain the option of electing to introduce a withholding tax on the same terms as Luxembourg and other non-EU competitors. The United Kingdom replied that as a matter of policy it was not willing to attempt to obtain any reservation for Gibraltar in the draft directive as the United Kingdom herself did not want to introduce the tax.[156] This was an example of the United Kingdom exercising her responsibility in manner that protected her national interest and not those determined by the Gibraltar Government.[157] The situation was only finally resolved and ameliorated after long negotiations between the Gibraltar and UK Governments that led to the publication of an Agreement between the Governments in December 2005.[158]

Input into policy at pre-decision stage

On the pre-legislative or policy formulation level, Gibraltar does not have access to any formal constitutional structures of discussion or co-operation with the United Kingdom Government. It is only on an ad hoc basis

[155] Among others.

[156] Even though it subsequently emerged that the Isle of Man and Channel Islands would in practice have that choice.

[157] Further examples are found in the Investor Compensation Directive, where the UK wished the Gibraltar Government to introduce a scheme containing the same financial limits as set out in English legislation, whereas Gibraltar wanted to transpose on the financial basis set out in the directive itself (see House of Assembly Hansard, November 2002), and in the exclusion, in 2001, of Gibraltar from several aviation measures to which the UK agreed, to unblock an impasse with Spain. The aviation measures concerned the so-called 'Single Skies' regime and a package of safety, compensation and noise control measures: House of Assembly Hansard, December 2001.

[158] The Agreement also resolved the outstanding issues on investor compensation and allowed access to the UK market.

that views are sought from Gibraltar on proposals or other communications. It is rarer still for there to be any Gibraltar participant (even at non-ministerial level) in a United Kingdom delegation at any EU level.[159] Though of course, given the size and resources of Gibraltar, it is assumed that any new arrangements for this would be premised on participation whenever it is assessed that a proposed measure would have a significant or disproportionate effect on Gibraltar.[160]

In the absence of this it is usually left to Gibraltar to monitor most issues and to raise matters of concern with the United Kingdom from time to time. The fact that issues arise post Directive is proof that the consultative processes between the United Kingdom and Gibraltar are not working to the satisfaction of Gibraltar.

Consultative Structures

This all makes the lack of formal consultative mechanisms with the United Kingdom and representation within United Kingdom delegations seem more stark and in need of change. There is some contrast elsewhere. In Belgium, a co-operation agreement was signed between Federal and sub-State Government to set up mechanisms by which the sub-State entities are involved in the State decision-making process.[161] Regular meetings are held, at which the instructions for Belgium's Council delegation are fixed. If no agreement is possible the Belgian delegate will abstain (the so-called sub-State right of veto). This is what Kerremans has described as granting sub-State government 'the status of a second level player within the Belgian legal order.'[162]

As has been seen in Germany, the Bundesrat (the Länder constituted body) has to agree transfers of competences to Europe. The Länder's views are required and participation in the formulation of national policy is guaranteed not only on exclusive Länder competences but also in relation to Federal competences.[163] The Bundesrat opinion is binding when it affects

[159] There are rare examples of Gibraltar Government officials forming part of UK delegations to discuss issues at EU level (such as in relation to the review of certain health provisions stemming from Council Regulation 1408/71, or in respect of a particular State Aid investigation on Gibraltar legislation; these, though, are very infrequent and when arise do so as part of an attempt to respond to unplanned issues). Interestingly, the position is reversed in the case of the Western Mediterranean or South-West Mediterranean Interreg structural funds programmes, within which Gibraltar has effectively represented the UK, as there is no other British territory within the scope of the programmes. It is the only example of this happening.

[160] Within those parameters the decision of whether Gibraltar, the UK or both make that assessment would be a crucial factor.

[161] Kerremans in Jeffrey (ed) n 142 above, 45–46.

[162] ibid 54. This is effectively Gibraltar's aspiration, given its unique constitutional status.

[163] Cygan n 76 above, 171–86.

Länder exclusive powers and is consultative (non-binding) in relation to other matters. This is significant, and markedly different to the position in Scotland,[164] Gibraltar or most small non-independent territories.

In 2002 the Gibraltar Parliament's Select Committee on Constitutional Reform proposed that a special Inter-Governmental Council be set up to deal with EU affairs. That Council was to be supported by an Agreement between the Governments that would demarcate roles and responsibilities akin to an Intergovernmental Concordat. It was suggested that the Council be composed of three persons nominated by the Chief Minister and three persons nominated by a Secretary of State,[165] and that its remit would be to 'consider matters relating to Gibraltar's membership within the European Union'[166] and to consider all proposals, whether legally binding or not, on matters which the Gibraltar Government wished pursued by the United Kingdom Government on her behalf.[167] In the bartering that was inevitable in formal negotiations with the United Kingdom that spanned so many years this mechanism was dropped from the final package that became the 2006 Constitution.

Clearly a constitutional mechanism is always preferable from the point of view of certainty and longevity but this can be achieved by less formal means—like a concordat. The disadvantages of the non-legally binding form of British concordats have been described as very firmly weighting the power in favour of the State.[168] The establishment of clear structures fosters certainty, clarity, legitimacy, democracy and co-operation. The disadvantage may be that there is less flexibility for changing circumstances but to a large extent that can be addressed through language that allows such leeway and a multi-lateral desire to keep the reform process under review.[169]

Ministerial Meetings

Länder have created European policy departments and organise meetings of Länder European ministers. Interdependence marks the relationship

[164] R Hazell, 'Intergovernmental Relations—Whitehall Rules OK?' in Hazel (ed) n 43 above, 149–81.

[165] s 48(1).

[166] Proposed s 48(2).

[167] Proposed s 48(2)(i), (iii).

[168] Hazel (ed) n 43 above, 157–62 and see also C Jeffrey, 'Devolution and the European Union: Trajectories and Futures' in A Trench (ed), *The Dynamics of Devolution: The State of the Nations 2005* (Exeter, The Constitution Unit, Imprint Academic, 2005) 179–96.

[169] In other Commonwealth examples the importance of these structures has been highlighted, as it goes to the heart of giving effect to the national constitutional settlement. eg the Canadian model has been described as one of 'executive federalism' because of the volume and nature of intergovernmental structures (see DV Smiley, *The Federal Condition in Canada* (Toronto, McGraw-Hill, 1987) 83).

between Länder and State government[170] In Germany the Conference of Minister–Presidents provides a regular interface with central State government. There are also analogies in Spain[171] and Italy. Similar ministerial meetings are held in Canada between the Provinces and Federal Governments.[172] In the British devolution arrangements the lack of frequency and ad hoc nature of the Joint Ministerial Committees has been criticised. They have been described as more ceremonial than effective and not transparent or open.[173] Comparison of the powers and mechanisms made available to the devolved regions within several Member States reveal progressive differentials between them. From the constitutionally entrenched, binding, justiciable, interdependent and co-operative federalism of Germany[174] there are also the non-justiciable, co-operative agreements of Scotland or Wales to the very informal, almost non-existent arrangements of Gibraltar.[175] What emerges from all this is that Gibraltar has more competences and more to protect from supra-national encroachments but less means to do so.

Representation

The Right to Vote in European Parliament Elections

The fact that during 1979–2004 Gibraltar was the only part of the Union not enfranchised for the purposes of European elections is a clear and further example of a democratic deficit suffered by Gibraltar. Its partial eradication must be put into perspective and be seen in the overall context of the wider governance deficit being sustained and the fact that while significant its resolution was not the most important governance advance for Gibraltar to make.[176] The story of how the deficit came about and an analysis of how it has been addressed reveals four points under the general theme of this chapter:

[170] C Jeffrey (ed), *The Regional Dimension of the European Union—Towards a Third Level in Europe?* (London, Frank Cass, 1997) 61–63 and Cygan n 76 above, 160–61 and 175. This is particularly important because approximately 55% of Federal legislation needs Länder approval.

[171] Conference of Presidents of autonomous regions.

[172] P Hogg, *Constitutional Law of Canada* (Toronto, Carswell, 1998) 138.

[173] R Hazell (ed), *The State of the Nations 2000: The First Year of Devolution in the UK* n 43 above, 150–64, R Hazell (ed), *The State of the Nations 2003: The Third Year of Devolution in the UK* (2003) 145–48, and Trench (ed), *The Dynamics of Devolution: The State of the Nations 2005* n 170 above, 187–88.

[174] And to a lesser extent Belgium and Austria.

[175] Governance arrangements are also a live issue in Spain in relation to the more advanced autonomous communities.

[176] See this chapter and ch 7. In both it is argued that obtaining representation and influence for the sub-State Executive level provides the most significant governance advance.

That the ECHR Judgment Was Significant

The exclusion from the vote was a result of the interpretation of an Annex to the 1976 Act on Direct Elections that gave rise to the first European Parliament elections in 1979.[177] A long political campaign was waged in Gibraltar to acquire the vote. The matter was ultimately resolved as a result of litigation in the European Court of Human Rights in a test case brought in the name of a young Gibraltarian student, Denise Matthews. She alleged that there had been violations of Article 3 of Protocol 1[178] and Article 14 of the European Convention of Human Rights.[179] The European Commission on Human Rights declared the application admissible in April 1996.[180] In its report of 29 October 1997 it expressed the view that there had been no violation of Article 3 of Protocol No 1[181] or of Article 14.[182] As required, the Commission then referred the case to the court in January 1998.[183]

The court was asked to determine several other main questions[184] but the principal one became whether the European Parliament at the relevant time had the characteristics of a 'legislature' for Gibraltar? The court held that it needed to consider not only 'the strictly legislative powers which a body has, but also that body's role in the overall legislative process.' Since the Maastricht Treaty, the European Parliament's powers were no longer expressed to be 'advisory and supervisory.' The removal of these words were to be taken as an indication that the European Parliament had moved

[177] Act concerning the Election of the Representatives of the European Parliament by Direct Universal Suffrage 1976, OJ 1976 1/278/5. The Act applied to the UK and the British Government maintained that as a matter of interpretation the Act did not extend to the territory of Gibraltar.

[178] Which reads, 'The High Contracting Parties undertake to hold free elections at reasonable intervals by secret ballot under conditions which will ensure the free expression of the opinion of the people in the choice of the legislature.' She alleged that the European Parliament was now a legislature within the meaning of the Article and she should thus be entitled to vote.

[179] That while being a British national because of her status as a Gibraltarian she was deprived of the right to vote in European elections. She also alleged a violation of this Article because pursuant to Directive 93/109 she was entitled to vote in European Parliamentary elections in any territory in the European Union in which she resided except Gibraltar and alleged discrimination against citizens of Gibraltar in this respect.

[180] European Commission of Human Rights Decision as to the Admissibility of App No 24833/94 *Matthews v UK* 16 April 1996.

[181] By 11 votes to six.

[182] By 12 votes to five.

[183] Both majority and minority decisions of the Commission concentrated on the same main issues—the significance of the introduction of the co-decision procedure for the powers of the European Parliament and its standing within the European legislative architecture; the impact of European legislation on Gibraltar; whether the European Parliament could be construed as forming part of the legislature of Gibraltar; whether the principle of state responsibility could be invoked against the UK.

[184] Similar to those that concerned the Commission.

away from being a purely consultative body and towards being a body with a decisive role to play in the legislative process of the European Community:[185]

> *The European Parliament represents* the principal form of democratic political accountability in the Community system . . . *whatever its limitations the European Parliament which derives democratic legitimation from the direct elections by universal suffrage must be seen as that part of the European Community structure which best reflects concerns as to 'effective political democracy.* (emphasis added)

The court further held:

> that the European Parliament is sufficiently involved in the specific legislative processes leading to the passage of legislation under Articles 189b and Article 189c of the EC Treaty and is sufficiently involved in the general democratic supervision of the activities of the European Community to constitute part of the 'legislature' of Gibraltar for the purposes of Article 3 of Protocol 1.[186]

Once this point was overcome the court went on to hold that though the choice of electoral system was a matter for the State issues of a practical nature (such as disproportionality or difficulty of involving Gibraltar in elections) could not be allowed to become insurmountable obstacles. As the applicant had been completely deprived of expressing any electoral choice there had been a breach of Article 3 Protocol 1.[187] Apart from Gibraltar's perspective, the case is significant because it is recognition of the effect of Treaty amendments on the role of the Parliament within the institutional architecture of the Union and because the court describes the Parliament as the '*principal form of democratic political accountability.*' Access and representation to the Parliament was therefore, in that context, of major importance. From Gibraltar's standpoint the case represented an important victory in securing rights in this sphere of governance. More detail on this case will be discussed in chapter 7.

That bilateralism in different forms is present throughout this issue

The democratic deficit had arisen—not strictly because of bilateralism—but because of an initial decision by the United Kingdom not to extend the Act on Direct Elections to Gibraltar, and thereafter by omitting to rectify it.

185 *Matthews v UK* at 16: see Arts 137, 138b, 144, 158, 189b, 189c, 203 and 206 of the Treaty.

186 Ignoring the arguments of the Respondent (reflected in the dissenting opinion) that, as the European Parliament could not have been considered a legislature in 1976, the exclusion of Gibraltar from the Act in 1976 was perfectly legal then, and that to rule otherwise was to construe the matter retrospectively. The majority of the court disagreed with this view. See above.

187 *Matthews v UK* at 19–20—by 15 votes to two. Given this conclusion the court felt it unnecessary to determine whether there had also been a breach of Art 14 of the Convention (enjoyment of rights without discrimination).

There was extensive political lobbying during the 1980s and 1990s to try to remedy this and achieve the vote in Europe. It became clear that the United Kingdom Government would not voluntarily act to address this point so litigation was launched at the European Court of Human Rights.

The intervention of the United Kingdom in the creation, omission to rectify and then partial rectification of the democratic deficit is clear. Subsequent to the court's decision the United Kingdom Government first considered rectifying this by proposing an amendment to the 1976 Act. It made clear that it would seek Spanish consent to this.[188] When this was firmly refused by Spain[189] the United Kingdom confirmed it would introduce legislation to extend the franchise to Gibraltar by redrawing one of the British electoral regions and include Gibraltar in time for the 2004 European elections.[190] In 2003 Spain filed a request with the Commission under Article 227 TEC[191] alleging that the United Kingdom's enfranchisement of the people of Gibraltar through the above-mentioned Act of Parliament breached a Treaty obligation.[192] The Commission had three months—which expired on 29 October 2003—to issue a reasoned opinion on the matter.[193] Instead of doing so when the period expired the Commission issued a political statement that it considered:

> following an in depth analysis . . . that the UK has organised the extension of voting rights to residents in Gibraltar within the margin of discretion presently given to Member States by the EU law. However given **the sensitivity of the underlying bilateral issue**, the Commission at this stage refrains from adopting a reasoned opinion within the meaning of Article 227 of the Treaty and invites the parties to find an amicable solution.[194] (emphasis added)

Several things are significant from that statement. First, it emphasised the priority and acute scrutiny that Spain gives to Gibraltar related issues. Secondly, it shows that though the requirement to issue a reasoned opinion is mandatory the Commission side-stepped this requirement because of the sovereignty claim. It emphasises the caution with which Community institutions tread in encountering the Gibraltar issue and the breadth of the impact of the sovereignty dispute on the material performance of practical rights. This is a prime example of the prevailing bilateralism of the Gibraltar issue affecting the achievement of fundamental rights sought by the people of Gibraltar. The Commission was not only

[188] An example of Tacit Bilateralism.

[189] An example of Active v Passive Bilateralism.

[190] Initially, the UK had sought to consider other options, but when it became clear that Spain would object to enfranchisement even after the judgment, the UK Government decided to proceed by way of domestic legislation.

[191] Unusually because the more usual mechanism is Art 226.

[192] An example of Confrontational Bilateralism.

[193] A hearing was held on 1 October.

[194] Commission Declaration of 29 October 2003.

recognising bilateralism as the key panorama in Gibraltar's case, but it was entrenching it by trying hard to take a back seat on the issue.[195] Once more the primacy of the State (or bilateral) driver over the EU driver in the Gibraltar situation comes to the fore.

Spain subsequently referred the matter to the European Court of Justice under Article 227 for clarification of the extent of the franchise. Direct action between Member States under this Article is very unusual and is a further example of bilateralism.[196] The court's judgment in the case came in September 2006, and has been outlined in chapter 3.

That the deficit has only been partially addressed

It is certainly true that the powers of the European Parliament as an effective political organ, its role as a forum for democratic debate and mouthpiece for the European electorate have been enhanced significantly.[197] But it is also clear that achieving the right to vote is, of itself, little more than a symbolic victory that does not deliver any significant political influence or power. The effect of the UK legislation that enfranchised the people and territory of Gibraltar was to submerge the tiny electorate of Gibraltar into a predominantly English electorate. After a consultation exercise conducted by the Electoral Commission, Gibraltar was joined to the South-West Region for the 2004 elections.[198] However there are good reasons[199] on the grounds of the current interpretation of Article 189, effective political democracy, self-determination, size, affinity with an English region, other practicalities and legitimacy, why the simple enfranchisement of Gibraltar is insufficient and why Gibraltar should be given separate representation of its own.[200]

[195] The Commission has the benefit of a wide discretion on many issues. While this is so, it is also clear that it is extremely conscious of the politically controversial nature of the Gibraltar issue and has factored this in when considering whether to exercise any discretion it has had on particular matters.

[196] In this case an example of Combative Bilateralism.

[197] By the introduction of a variety of measures in successive Treaties enhancing its legislative powers (such the co-decision procedure) and its overall role in ensuring accountability in the Community architecture.

[198] Both the Gibraltar Government and the public at large were consulted on this issue.

[199] Expanded in ch 7, pp 347–56.

[200] The case for separate representation on political, constitutional, social and cultural grounds will be set out in the next chapter in the context of practical arrangements that could be introduced to secure governance improvements. The next chapter will also touch upon the issue of whether the current arrangements could be legally challenged.

That even if the deficit was entirely addressed it might still not deliver effective influence to Gibraltar

In *Brunner* the German Constitutional Court, observed that it is citizens:

> who must legitimise action through the democratic process. This democratic legitimacy is achieved by referring the activities of European bodies to the Parliaments of the Member States . . . as the nations of Europe grow closer together, democratic legitimacy will increasingly be supplied . . . by the European Parliament which is elected by the citizens of the Member States.[201]

This also raises the philosophical question of the means by which to best achieve legitimacy and power. Is the Union more legitimised by a Parliament with larger powers or by ensuring that the principle of subsidiarity is effective and decisions are truly close to the citizen? For these purposes it is sub-State executives that are more proximate to the citizen and it is these that should be suitably empowered. Even if Gibraltar did receive an MEP by either political concession or through litigation this Member would be one among a body of 785.[202] In terms therefore of practical effect the acquisition of a Member of Parliament is far less significant than securing influence at European Council of Ministers level or at State level with the United Kingdom Government. Similar issues that are described in relation to the European Parliament arise from the fact that Gibraltar does not have representation on the Committee of the Regions.[203] This is especially relevant in the context of the growing role of the Committee within the Union.[204]

Post-Decision: The Courts—Access and Influence

In the absence of effective national governance structures the question arises whether resorting to the courts can exert sufficient influence.

[201] *Brunner v European Union Treaty* [1994] 1 CMLR 57, 155.

[202] 750 under the Lisbon Treaty.

[203] The body constituted in 1992 which is supposed to provide a forum for the expression of sub-State opinion. See J Jones, 'The Committee of the Regions, Subsidiarity and a Warning' (1997) 22(4) EL Rev 312–26. This compounds the representational and governance deficit suffered by Gibraltar. The UK's allocation of members was (pre-devolution) assigned to local authority and county council level. Post-devolution provision has been made for Scottish and Welsh members to be drawn from the Regional assemblies. No provision has ever been made for Gibraltar. In other Member States there is either a balance between regional and local authority representation (Italy), or there is a marked preponderance of either regional (Germany), or local (UK) government representation. Representation on the Committee of the Regions is important because it already has been granted some influence in the European legislative process, and it is clear that Regional Governments see its future enhancement as a way of securing further direct influence at European level.

[204] Both the CE and Lisbon Treaty proposed an increase to its role in the introduction of legislation and its ability to challenge legislation.

Gibraltar's infrequent interaction with the European Court of Justice in the post-1986 period has led to two clear conclusions. First, Gibraltar—like other sub-State governments—does not have the status of privileged applicant for the purposes of Article 230. It must therefore meet the much more stringent direct and individual concern test.[205] Additionally, when trying to establish its direct and individual interest it has faced the intervention of the United Kingdom or Spain in opposition.

Recourse to litigation to secure clarification or enforcement of rights is an important element in giving legitimacy to the Union and providing proper accountability and transparency of the institutions. Both the European courts and national courts can be asked to determine these rights. National courts are required to apply the principles of supremacy, direct and indirect effect and State liability. The Commission monitors their performance annually. The European courts may receive actions directly under Article 230 TEC or indirectly via a reference from one of the national courts under Article 234 TEC. The Gibraltar experience with Article 230 actions is dealt with below. As for Article 234 references, no case from the Gibraltar courts has been determined by the ECJ. Any party or the Government could raise the possibility of this in pleadings if it wished to have a determination of any particular Article of the Treaty. It could, for example, be a vehicle to clarify the terms of the external affairs duty under Article 299(4), although this strategy has the inherent risk that an adverse ruling would be politically counter-productive. In the context of intergovernmental relationships it is sometimes easier not to seek a conclusive determination by the court and allow a more fluid political process of constitutional gains by negotiation or convention. The possibilities are still there for private parties in litigation. While the infrequent use by individuals of this mechanism could be due to a lack of awareness of their private law rights it is more likely to be down to the simple size of the jurisdiction. So, for example, in the years 1990–2000 the smallest Member States, Luxembourg and Ireland only produced an average of two references per year.[206]

[205] It failed to achieve this in the air liberalisation case and succeeded in the State Aid Case—both cited above. An interesting difference between one and the other is that in the 1993 case the UK opposed the application for locus standi of the Gibraltar Government. In the State Aid case it did not intervene in the proceedings and merely supplied some information on competence to the court, which assisted in their determination. Only the institutions and the Member States can challenge a measure of general application under Art 230(2) and (3) before the Court of Justice. The European Parliament formally acquired the status of privileged applicant at Nice. The ECJ had recognised that the Parliament should have that status in certain circumstances.

[206] In Ireland's case in five out of those 11 years there were no references at all. The population of Gibraltar is roughly 1% that of Ireland and about 8% that of Luxembourg. The proportions in respect of the other Member States are also directly related to their size, with the most active being the largest: Germany, Italy, the UK and France in that order. If that mathematical data were simply extrapolated it would be expected that there would only be one or two references from Gibraltar courts every 10 years. Such calculations while based on

Article 230 TEC presents a second important tool of democracy for both the Executive and individuals. The ability of national courts to give effect to EU principles or refer cases to the European Court of Justice and the ability of individuals to have recourse to the national courts or the ECJ is of real relevance in the legitimacy debate. It is a key element in the legal enfranchisement of the individual and the psychological adoption of the ideals and principles of the Community for there to be effective and speedy access to the courts. It is part of the same legitimacy debate that has given greater prominence to the quality and nature of citizen's rights, the need to empower supra-national and sub-State institutions to balance the power of national executives and the principles of openness, accountability and transparency. As was stated in *Union de Pequenos Agricultores*,[207] the European Community:

> is based on the rule of law in which its institutions are subject to judicial review of the compatibility of their acts with the Treaty and with the general principles of law which include fundamental rights. Individuals are therefore entitled to effective judicial protection of the rights they derive from the Community legal Order and the right to such protection is one of the general principles of law stemming from the constitutional traditions common to the Member States. That right has also been enshrined in Articles 6 and 13.[208]

The point of Article 230[209] (and in relation to individuals paragraph 230(4)) is 'to provide appropriate judicial protection for all persons, natural or legal, who are directly and individually concerned by acts of the Community institutions.'[210] National law must be construed to make this or the ability to challenge measures of general application an effective right by which there is access to national courts.[211] This is consonant with the view of the ECJ of Article 234 that has been said to entail a 'special field of judicial co-operation'[212] which 'is essential for the preservation of the Community character of the law'[213] and is intended to produce legal consistency and cohesion.

In *Government of Gibraltar v Council*,[214] a case challenging a Directive on air liberalisation failed because the applicants had not discharged the presumption that this was a measure of general application and not a decision

average predictions would be displaced by the individual facts of particular cases justifying reference to the ECJ. See 'Eighteenth Annual Report on Monitoring the Application of Community Law (2000)' Annex VI 24 COM (2001) 309.

[207] Case C-50/00, Judgment 25 July 2002.

[208] ibid paras 38–39.

[209] The main provision that gives the ECJ jurisdiction to review matters.

[210] Case T-288/97 *Regione Autonoma Friuli Venezia Giulia v Commission* [1999] ECR II-1871.

[211] Case C-50/00 P *Union de Pequenos Agricultores* [42]: see http://eur-lex.europa.eu/LexUriServ/LexUriServ.do?uri=CELEX:62000J0050:EN:HTML.

[212] *Firma Schwarze* case [1965] ECR 877, 886.

[213] *Rheinmuhlen-Dusseldorf* case [1974] ECR 33, 43.

[214] Case C-298/89 [1993] ECR I-3605.

that directly and individually concerned them.[215] There are a number of significant aspects to this case. First, that—as is a constant theme in this work—it stemmed from the sovereignty dispute over Gibraltar. Secondly, the measure under challenge in the case came about because of Anglo–Spanish bilateralism. In December 1987 Spain and the United Kingdom entered into an agreement over the joint use of Gibraltar airport.[216] Implementation of the agreement was suspended until the Gibraltar House of Assembly[217] passed the necessary legislation to give effect to the arrangements. Instead the agreement was heavily criticised in Gibraltar for making sovereignty, jurisdiction and control concessions in respect of the airport and because of the fact that, by a bilateral agreement, both States should enter into arrangements in respect of Gibraltar airport without the express agreement of the Gibraltar Government. In the event Gibraltar political parties pledged not to implement it. In 1989 a directive was introduced to amend a former directive on the authorisation of inter-regional air services.[218] The original directive[219] had already been amended in 1986[220] to temporarily exempt certain airports in the Azores or Oporto from the measure. The 1989 Directive introduced further amendments to the regime on inter-regional air transport by extending the arrangements to flights with more than 70 seats. Article 2(2) of the 1989 Directive also contained exclusionary wording, as follows:

> Application of the provisions of this Directive to Gibraltar airport shall be suspended until the arrangements in the Joint Declaration made by the Foreign Ministers of the Kingdom of Spain and the United Kingdom on 2 December 1987 have come into operation. The Governments of the Kingdom of Spain and the United Kingdom will so inform the Council on that date.

The Gibraltar Government launched proceedings seeking an annulment of Article 2(2) of the 1989 Directive. The Council, supported by the United Kingdom and Spain, argued that the Gibraltar Government did not have capacity to bring the action under the 1969 Gibraltar Constitution and that Article 2(2) of the 1989 Directive did not constitute a decision that was susceptible to challenge. Additionally, the Commission also intervened to argue (supported by Spain and the Council) that the 1989 Directive was

[215] Though since that judgment the court has more liberally construed the circumstances when a Regional authority vested with autonomy can be considered to be individually concerned even if a Decision is addressed to the Member State: see Case T-288/97 *Regione Autonoma Friuli Venezia Giulia v Commission* [1999] ECR II-1871.

[216] Joint Declaration made by the Foreign Ministers of the UK and Spain of 2 December 1987.

[217] The name of the Gibraltar Parliament at the time.

[218] Council Directive 89/463/EEC of 18 July 1989 amending Directive 83/416/EEC concerning the authorisation of scheduled inter-regional air services for the transport of passengers, mail and cargo between Member States, OJ 1989 L226, 14.

[219] Council Directive 83/416 EEC of 25 July 1983, OJ 1983 L237 19.

[220] Council Directive 86/216/EEC of 26 May 1986, OJ 1986 L152, 47.

not a measure that individually or directly concerned Gibraltar. The court found that the suspension clause (Article 2(2)) applied to all air carriers and that the Gibraltar airport was not the only airport suspended from the measure.[221] It added that the 1989 Directive justified the exclusion of Gibraltar airport, because

> there is an obstacle of an objective nature to implementation of the directive, having regard to its aims. In view of the differences between the Kingdom of Spain and the United Kingdom, discussed at length by the applicant itself, concerning *sovereignty* over the territory on which Gibraltar airport is situated and the operational problems resulting from those differences, the development of air services between that airport and the other airports within the Community is conditional on the implementation of the co-operation arrangements agreed between those two States. In those circumstances, Article 2(2) of Directive 89/463 cannot be regarded as constituting a decision within the meaning of the second paragraph of Article 173,[222] but on the contrary is of the same general nature as that Directive.[223] (emphasis added)

The case is indicative of the prevailing effect of bilateralism and the sovereignty dispute and how these converged to lay obstacles to the enjoyment by Gibraltar of Community wide measures.

More recently however in *Government of Gibraltar v Commission*[224] (the State Aid case) the court held that the applicants challenge was admissible under Article 230(4). These cases concerned decisions notified by the Commission in July 2001[225] by which it considered that certain corporate legislation in Gibraltar contravened State Aid rules.[226] The Gibraltar Government sought annulment of both decisions. Initially it made an interim application for the suspension of the decisions and to restrain their publication. In considering those applications the European Court of First Instance heard objections from the Commission as to the legal standing of the Gibraltar Government to bring the proceedings. An important contrast between these cases and the 1993 air liberalisation case, cited above, is the attitude of the British Government. While it opposed the Gibraltar Government's *locus standi* in the challenge to Article 2(2) of Directive 89/463 the United Kingdom Government did not file any objections of that nature in the State Aid challenge. Indeed it confirmed certain constitutional provisions and the view of the UK that the Gibraltar Government did have power to bring such actions. This allowed the Court of First Instance to hold that in view of that response the actions could not be

[221] The examples of the Azores and Oporto have already been mentioned.

[222] Now Art 230.

[223] The Court went on that it did not need to deal with other arguments—such as the capacity of the Gibraltar Government—and dismissed the application as inadmissible.

[224] Cases T-195/01 and T-207/01 [2002] ECR II-02309.

[225] Decisions SG(2001) D/289755 and SG(2001) D/289757 of 11 July 2001.

[226] The Companies (Taxation and Concessions) Ordinance 1967 and the Income Tax (Amendment) Ordinance 1983.

declared manifestly inadmissible.[227] The UK response did though reveal a constitutional tension which had been described by Advocate-General Lenz in the air liberalisation case as the 'overlapping spheres of competence in matters affecting external affairs.'[228] In distinguishing its position from that it had adopted in the air liberalisation case it stated:

> It is for Her Majesty's Government, and not for the Council of Ministers[229] to determine by exercise of prerogative powers whether an international agreement shall be concluded in respect of Gibraltar, or whether an international agreement concluded by the UK shall be applied in respect of that territory.
>
> Nevertheless a matter does not cease to be a defined domestic matter,[230] or to be treated as such by reason only of the fact that it has a nexus with international obligations, including European Community law. Indeed if that were the case the Assembly and executive would be deprived of a substantial part of the competences expressly conferred . . . by the Constitution . . . the EC Treaty constitutes both an international agreement and the constitutional charter of a Community based on law.[231]

When the case came up for substantive consideration, Spain intervened to oppose the application on a number of grounds, including the *locus* of the Gibraltar Government. Relying on the UK response in 2001, the court held that:

> under the relevant British law the applicant has competence in the specific field with which the present cases are concerned, namely company taxation, as a defined domestic matter. There is nothing to invalidate that response. In those circumstances the reference by the Commission and by the Kingdom of Spain to *Gibraltar v Council* in which the United Kingdom disputed the *locus standi* of the Government of Gibraltar, is irrelevant, since that case concerned air transport within the Community and was therefore fundamentally different from the present case.[232]

The United Kingdom's variable position on the recognition of Gibraltar's constitutional competence (especially in those areas where power had been acquired by convention) lent weight to the argument of those who felt exposed by the lack of enforceability of changes by convention and called

[227] Cases T-195/01 R and T-207/01 R, *Government of Gibraltar v Commission* [2001] ECR II-03915.

[228] Opinion of Advocate-General Lenz 4 May 1993 in Case C-298/89 *Government of Gibraltar v Council of the Communities* [1993] ECR I-03605 at para 43.

[229] The name of the Gibraltar Cabinet under the Gibraltar Constitution.

[230] The terminology under s 55 of the 1969 Gibraltar Constitution.

[231] Letter of 11 October 2001, Response of the UK Government to the Questions posed by the President of the Court of First Instance pursuant to Art 21 of the Statute of the Court of Justice of the EC at paras 12–14.

[232] Cases T-195/01 R and T-207/01 R *Government of Gibraltar v Commission* [2002] ECR II-03915, [53]–[54]; though it is difficult to discern from the position taken by the UK in 1993 that this was, in fact, the basis of its distinction; rather, it seemed to be based on a policy decision that it should insulate its bilateral agreement on the airport of 1987 from challenge and that the 2001 decisions of the Commission did not give rise to the same issues.

for formal amendments to the Constitution.[233] It is pertinent within the context of the theme of bilateralism, to also note that Spain has intervened in most major litigation involving Gibraltar at the ECJ[234] to (inter alia) file arguments intended to dilute the status of Gibraltar or constitutional competences of the Gibraltar Government. It is of course perfectly entitled to do this under Community law, but the zeal with which interest in Gibraltar is shown in Spain goes well beyond the norm of customary intervention and just reveals how Spain considers that it is an intrinsic part of its national interest to set out its position over Gibraltar, to seek to preserve the State-centric bias of the dispute, and to contain any expansion of self-government.

There has been some attempt at widening the scope of Article 230(2) to enable sub-State Government to challenge measures of general application on the same basis as Member States but so far these attempts have failed. In *Regione Toscana v Commission*[235] the court held that Article 230(2)

> refers only to government authorities of the Member States . . . and cannot include the governments of regions or of autonomous communities irrespective of the powers they may have. If the contrary were true, it would undermine the institutional balance provided for by the Treaties, which determine inter alia the conditions under which the Member States . . . participate in the functioning of the Community institutions. It is not possible for the European Communities to comprise a greater number of Member States than the number of States between which they were established.

The court in the *Toscana* case seemed very concerned about applying the Treaty strictly and maintaining the institutional balance. It had been far less worried about both issues when it had held, albeit in a different context, in *Parliament v Council (Chernobyl)*[236] that, while there was no specific provision to that effect, the Parliament should be able to take action in order to protect its prerogatives. The court's view was then subsequently integrated into the Maastricht Treaty amendments.

There was a renewed attempt to expand the definition of Article 230(2) in the first *Nederlandse Antillen* case.[237] In that case the applicants argued that they had extensive self-government and that, if there was something within their constitutional prerogatives, then by analogy with the European Parliament *locus standi* should be recognised without having to meet the test of individual and direct concern. The court rejected the application of Article 230(2) to sub-State Government on the basis of cases such

[233] See earlier.

[234] The Air Liberalisation case (1993); Art 94/95 Case (Freedom of Movement of Goods case (2003)); State Aid/Tax Case (2002); The Right to Vote case (2006); and the State Aid II case (2007–08): the references to all these cases are cited earlier in this chapter.

[235] Case C-180/97 ECR [1997] I-5245.

[236] Case C-70/88 [1990] ECR I-2041, overturning its previous decision in Case 302/87 *Parliament v Council (Comitology)* [1988] ECR 5615.

[237] Case C-452/98 *Nederlandse Antillen v Council of the European Union* [2001] ECR I-8973.

as *Regione Toscana*[238] and rejected that Article 230(3) could be extended by analogy with the precedent of the European Parliament. The court did though hold at first instance that the Netherlands Antilles were individually and directly concerned, but even this aspect of the ruling was reversed on appeal.[239]

The specific elevation of sub-State Government to the status of privileged applicant[240] rather than non-privileged applicant[241] has been a regular call of the more powerful regions in successive intergovernmental conferences since 1992. They have sought this in areas within their competence under their respective national constitutional law. This has not only been resisted by the court. Member States have been very reticent to allow an amendment to the Treaty to this effect.[242]

Contrast the position of the court under Article 10 of the Treaty.[243] The Article specifically refers to the Member States having the duty to 'take all appropriate measures'. Nowhere in the Article is there an express or implied reference to sub-State government. However in *Casagrande*[244] the court held that, if there was a breach of a measure of general application, it was

> irrelevant that the conditions of their implementation are laid down by rules issued by the central power, by the authorities of a country forming part of a federal state or of other territorial entities or even by authorities which the national law equates with them.[245]

And in *Salomone Haim*[246] in deciding who should be liable for the reparation of loss and damage suffered by an individual the court held that this

> need not necessarily be provided by the Member State . . . [when] certain legislative or administrative tasks are devolved to territorial bodies with a certain degree of autonomy or to any other public law body legally distinct from the State . . . reparation for loss and damage caused by national measures . . . by a public law body may therefore be made by that body.[247]

The court has clearly held that the principle of State responsibility and the duty to compensate for breaches of that principle extends to entities beyond the central Government. If it is necessary for there to be a trickle-

[238] And Case C-95/97 *Region Wallone v Commission* [1997] ECR I-1787.

[239] Case C-142/00 P *Commission v Nederlandse Antillen, Judgment* [2003] ECR I-03483.

[240] Art 230(2), (3).

[241] Art 230(4), which needs to satisfy the direct and individual concern test.

[242] For a variety of different reasons particular to their own situation. For many, retention of control of these mechanisms was important to move legislation ahead with the maximum cohesion. This of course did not deal with sub-State aspirations.

[243] Which sets out the doctrine of State Responsibility.

[244] Case 9/74 *Casagrande v Landeshaupstadt Munchen* ECR [1974] 773—a case about the interpretation of Art 12 of EC Regulation 1612/68 in State law.

[245] Case 9/74 *Casagrande v Landeshaupstadt Munchen* ECR [1974] 773, [15].

[246] Case C-424/97 [2000] ECR I-5123.

[247] [29]–[31].

down of the principles of responsibility and liability in respect of damages (with the consequential stretching of the definition of the 'State') to secure proper implementation of EC law and to make the rights of individuals properly effective, then conversely it should also be the case when considering a liberalisation of Articles 230(2) or (3).

If there is a concern about the individual having properly effective rights, then a key right on the European stage is the ability to present legal challenges. To allow individuals or sub-State governments to have a more direct avenue of recourse to the European courts would be an important move forward. The focus so far has been on functional effectiveness without too much linkage by the courts or Member States with the legitimacy debate. The Union would acquire greater legitimacy in the eyes of individuals and sub-State government if they did not feel that the Member States and Institutions had reserved for themselves the simple procedures for the challenge of measures of general application that they themselves play a part in devising, in particular when these will then in many cases have to be applied by sub-State government and will affect individual rights. The legal framework will continue to be alien unless individuals and sub-State government acquire a sense of ownership at two different ends. In the first place, securing a degree of participation at different levels of governance so as to influence the design of legal architecture is important. Secondly, at the production end it is also necessary to acquire wider ability to challenge measures. This is central to the legitimacy issue.

In *Union de Pequenos Agricultores* the court conceded that, while

> it is admittedly possible to envisage a system for judicial review of the legality of Community measure of general application different from that established by the founding Treaty . . . it is for the Member States, if necessary, in accordance with Article 48 EU to reform the system currently in force.[248]

The court could have taken a more liberal view, as it did in the Parliament's case, when it allowed challenges under Article 230 that were then followed by Treaty amendment, or as it did in construing the word 'State' for the purposes of Article 10. However, if this happens it may also require an examination of how proceedings are brought by the Commission to enforce Community obligations. At present, these are directed against the Member States notwithstanding the internal national constitutional arrangements. For it to be possible for sub-State Government to bring actions challenging measures of general application in areas within their constitutional competence the *quid pro quo* could be that a mechanism is also devised to enable sub-State government to be joined in such cases. While the clear case law is that internal constitutional structures are not relevant 'to justify a failure to comply with obligations

[248] [45].

and time-limits resulting from Community directives',[249] the inclusion of sub-State government as a party would (rather than a challenge to this stream of authority) be a recognition akin to that already acknowledged under Article 10 that there are sub-State government responsibilities that can both give rise to judicial proceedings.[250]

Even though it is primarily responsible for the domestic implementation of Community obligations and could face litigation or claims for compensation if it fails in its duties Gibraltar has been unable to have unproblematic recourse to the European courts.[251] It is therefore left with a scenario within which it has obligations under the Treaty to transpose obligations or be liable in default. It does not have automatic access to the courts, and must make out its case as a non-privileged applicant when contemplating litigation. To compound that, it faces an uphill struggle to establish direct interest as it will almost certainly face the intervention of Spain (and perhaps the United Kingdom) in the proceedings. Finally, it cannot rely on adequate governance structures or national arrangements to minimise the need to seek recourse from the courts.[252] If better governance structures were in place by which greater influence could be secured at the pre-legislative stage then contemplating litigation would be less necessary. It is in any event an avenue with a difficult initial threshold to overcome should the decision be taken to commence an action.

THE ZENITH OF BILATERALISM AND THE CRISIS OF LEGITIMACY

On 12 July 2002, in the House of Commons, the British Foreign Secretary rose to make a Parliamentary statement. It was near lunchtime on a Friday, close to the summer recess, and the benches were almost empty. Within 60 minutes Gibraltar's Council of Ministers was in special session. In a long and calculated statement that was the culmination of a process that had started with vigour in mid-2001,[253] the Foreign Secretary said that the two Governments had agreed the principles around which a Joint Declaration could be made, on the basis:

> that Britain and Spain should share sovereignty over Gibraltar . . . including the disputed territory of the isthmus; that Gibraltar should have more internal self-

[249] Case 386/85 *Commission v Italy* [1987] ECR 1061 and *Commission v Belgium* [1987] ECR 2797.

[250] A Cygan, 'Protecting the Interests of Civil Society in Community decision-making—The Limits of Art 230' (2003) 52 ICLQ 995–1012 and Case C-321/95 *Stichting Greenpeace Council (Greenpeace Council) v Commission* [1998] ECR I-1651. The CE and Lisbon Treaty would expand the equivalent article to enable the Committee of the Regions to be a privileged applicant.

[251] It could also as an additional option move to intervene in litigation concerning decisions against another party in relation to its specific interests under Art 230.

[252] To make it a measure of last resort.

[253] And had been opposed by Gibraltar with equal vehemence.

> government; that Gibraltar should retain its British traditions, customs and way of life; that Gibraltarians should retain the right to British nationality, and should gain the right to Spanish nationality as well[254] . . . that Gibraltar should retain its institutions—its Government, House of Assembly, Courts and police service; and that Gibraltar could if it chose, participate fully in the European single market and other EU arrangements[255]

In one fell swoop it dramatically changed the emphasis of 300 years of history. While Britain had been increasingly lukewarm towards Gibraltar since the death of Franco, it had never previously taken a public official position that suggested that it was prepared to enter into such arrangements. Now and for the first time, it declared that it was ready to share the sovereignty of Gibraltar with Spain. The decision was dramatic and immediately pitted the people of Gibraltar against the British Government. The Straw declaration of July 2002—as it became known—was a watershed in Gibraltar's modern constitutional history and highlighted two quite contrasting features that are prevalent throughout this chapter.

In the first place it was—once again—an instance of bilateralism; of pure intergovernmentalism that ran counter to the trends of multi-level governance and inclusive participation in decision-making in Europe. Britain and Spain had decided that a joint sovereignty arrangement was in their respective national interests, and had determined to announce their decision notwithstanding the well-known opposition of the people of Gibraltar. This marked change of emphasis was the result of the process of transformation that had started with the end of the Franco dictatorship in the mid 1970s. The approximation of Britain and Spain in the three decades since then had eventually led the parties to that moment. Spain, no longer a dictatorship, now a fellow Member of the European Union and a powerful ally of Britain was keen to forge alliances at European level.[256] Britain that had first agreed to negotiate the resolution of all differences,[257] and then agreed to discuss sovereignty,[258] had finally in 2002 accepted the principle of joint sovereignty.

This last development was fostered by the election of a more pro-European Labour administration in Britain in 1997. Labour Ministers and senior Labour Parliamentarians close to Government had been indicating since 1998[259] that in their view Gibraltar had to take account of the 'Spanish

254 While the ability to acquire Spanish nationality was described as a non-coercive 'right' rather than an obligatory imposition, it was seen in Gibraltar as illustrative of the continued misunderstanding of the sovereignty context. By placing emphasis on the presentation of the Spanish dimension as the only alternative to the British dimension it maintained the less modernist understanding of territorial sovereignty.

255 HC Deb, 12 July 2002, col 1166.

256 Especially in the face of a powerful Franco-German axis on certain issues.

257 Lisbon Agreement 1980.

258 Brussels Agreement 1984.

259 Ken Purchase MP did so in a visit to Gibraltar in 1998.

dimension'.[260] Then in a more vigorous change of tack the then Minister of State in the Foreign Office, Peter Hain, said in 2001 that Gibraltar's status was unsustainable and that Gibraltar had to accept the new trends or be left behind.[261] Quite what was precisely meant by this is unclear, but this was not only a signal of the determination and belief of the British Government that it could conclude a deal which it perceived to be in its interests, but it illustrated the willingness to ignore the clear opposition by the people of Gibraltar (and public opinion in Britain) to this strategy.[262]

The theme of bilateralism was self-evident, in that this was an example of Britain and Spain agreeing to share sovereignty over a territory without first getting the participation, still less the agreement, of the population. What was presented as the package of benefits of internal self-government, retention of British nationality, way of life, institutions and access to European measures, was conditional on acceptance of the principle of joint sovereignty in referendum. Additionally, the artificiality of the historical obstacles Spain had placed in the path of Gibraltar's access to European measures came through in a poignant fashion. As part of the package, Spain was prepared to lift any difficulties in front of Gibraltar to allow full participation in EU arrangements. The fact that historic, and previously considered insurmountable, obstacles could be promptly removed seemed to lead to only one conclusion.

Quite what were the operating factors in the motivations of Britain and Spain is a cause for speculation. Different issues seemed to operate in parallel. On the one hand at macro-level there was a clear strategy by Britain to foster Anglo–Spanish alliances at EU level to counter the Franco–German axis.[263] On the other hand, the desire to conclusively

[260] In some ways this aspect was not earth-shattering as Roy Hattersley had come close to saying the same thing in 1976 when he issued the so-called 'Hattersley Memorandum'.

[261] In the balancing of interests between Gibraltar and wider British interests, it became clear—because it was mentioned on several occasions—that some Labour politicians were conscious of the number of Britons that lived in Spain, and that this was more significant than the population of Gibraltar. This was mentioned by Peter Hain in speeches on a couple of occasions and reference to this was even included in the text of a House of Commons Motion in January 2002 which stated that, 'since 1969 Spain has become a successful open democracy where 17 times more Britons live than do in Gibraltar; welcomes the Government's determination to take advantage of the present excellent relations between Spain and the UK to push ahead . . . [with the bilateral talks].' The House of Commons was during 2001–02 the scene of lobbying by Members of Parliament on both sides of the divide.

[262] All Gibraltar political parties were vociferously opposed. Public opinion in Gibraltar had been tested by polls and by massive demonstrations against the joint sovereignty negotiations. In Britain the Gibraltar Government office in London received 400,000 letters of support after a media campaign. There was significant media interest throughout the period. The Conservative Party publicly opposed the joint sovereignty negotiations and pledged to abandon that policy. The Chief Minister was invited to address the Conservative Party conference on the issue.

[263] On 10 February 2002 the *Sunday Telegraph* reported on the basis of a leaked confidential Foreign Office Report that this was a specific strategy agreed at very senior level and that this had involved a discussion of the stance Britain would need to take in relation to the Gibraltar issue.

resolve the Gibraltar problem through the device of joint sovereignty must be doubted because of the impact that the acceptance of such an arrangement would have on Spanish internal constitutional arrangements. Any implementation of arrangements of that type would see mirror calls in the Basque Country or in Catalunya[264] and more worryingly for Spain would make the Moroccan Government intensify their lobbying over their claims to the Spanish North African enclaves of Ceuta and Melilla.[265] Factored into that theory is the reality that opposition to the principle of joint sovereignty in Gibraltar was both overwhelming and entirely predictable.[266] If all that holds true, the joint sovereignty plan was really more about neutralising self-determination and the quasi-separatist aspirations of nationalists in Gibraltar,[267] and less about actually resolving the Gibraltar issue through the vehicle of joint sovereignty. The closeness of the relationship between the relevant Prime Ministers at the time also contributed to this. Additionally, and in terms of the particular Spanish national party political strategy, Closa and Heywood[268] have commented that, while the biggest mainstream parties in Spain, the PP (conservatives) and the PSOE (socialists) both favour the process of European accession and integration, the PP is more nationalist in outlook, hence why the PP Government of Aznar proactively tried to capitalise on its close relations with the British Government in an attempt to make sovereignty inroads over Gibraltar.

The construction of a package based around a fundamental principle—joint sovereignty—which the vast majority of people in Gibraltar were against, and which sought to deliver benefits that Gibraltar already considered it had as of right, was doomed to fail. The absence of Gibraltar representatives during the Anglo–Spanish talks also made the task to sell the announced package in Gibraltar much more difficult.

The second thematic element that emerges from the Straw Declaration is precisely this disregard of Gibraltar, British and Spanish opinion. For a good 12 months before the Declaration, Gibraltar, through its elected representatives and in public acts of solidarity[269] had made its opposition to any deal on Gibraltar well known. During an advertising campaign in the British media over 400,000 letters of support were received from UK

[264] Already this was the case through the Anglo–Spanish process.

[265] How could Spain then resist the parallel that it should share sovereignty of Ceuta and Melilla with Morocco.

[266] And subsequently consummated in the 2002 referendum.

[267] Or, for Britain, about demonstrating to Spain how willing Britain was to resolve the dispute on terms potentially acceptable to Spain but which were blocked not by British but by Gibraltarian objection.

[268] C Closa and P Heywood, *Spain and the European Union* (London, Palgrave International, 2004) 40–53.

[269] A demonstration was held on 18 March 2002 under the banner 'NO In Principle Concessions Against Our Wishes—YES to Reasonable Dialogue', at which more than 70% of the population demonstrated against the bilateral talks on joint sovereignty.

nationals. At the same time a poll in *La Vanguardia*,[270] a prominent Spanish newspaper, put the support in Spain for a deal on the basis of joint sovereignty at two per cent and went on to conclude that about 49 per cent wanted a Spanish Gibraltar and—more surprisingly—that 41 per cent of respondents favoured independence for Gibraltar.[271] In a subsequent report published by the *Instituto de Cuestiones Internacionales y Politica Exterior*[272] the concept of joint sovereignty received only 31 per cent support, with 20 per cent expressing that the decision on Gibraltar's future should be left to the people of Gibraltar.[273] It seemed that a hybrid solution was not even the preferred option in Spain.

The Straw Declaration led the Gibraltar Government to hold a referendum in November 2002 on whether the principle of joint sovereignty was acceptable.[274] This was rejected by Britain as eccentric and by Spain as illegal and undemocratic.[275] The result of the referendum was conclusive in its opposition to the Anglo–Spanish strategy. In an electoral turn-out of 89 per cent only 187 people (or just over one per cent) voted in favour of the principle of joint sovereignty.[276] It had been the clear intention of the British Government to finalise discussions with the Spanish Government and then put the final and complete package to a referendum of the people of Gibraltar whether or not the Government of Gibraltar had attended the talks that devised that package or approved it.[277] The criticism of the Gibraltar organised referendum and the intention behind the organisation of a plebiscite on conclusion of the bilateral talks could be seen as exercises in the type of low-intensity democracy exposed by Marks.[278]

NEVER THE TWAIN SHALL MEET?

It was clear that the Anglo–Spanish process of 2001–02 completely either misread the aspirations and mood of the people of Gibraltar or proceeded in disregard of these. Any attempt at examining a resolution to this inter-

[270] The main Catalan daily.

[271] The poll was conducted during April 2002 and had over 25,000 respondents.

[272] INCIPE—the Spanish Institute of International Questions and External Affairs—in July 2003.

[273] Also of interest was the observation that only 10% of Spaniards now saw Gibraltar as an obstacle to Anglo–Spanish relations as opposed to 22% in 1991 and that 37% of Catalans and 46% of Basques felt that the ultimate decision should be left to the people of Gibraltar.

[274] The referendum was supervised by a panel of Election observers chaired by Gerald Kaufmann MP and which included several MPs, Parliamentarians from other Commonwealth countries and the Electoral Commission.

[275] It was the second time that Spain rejected a referendum—the first time was in 1967: see ch 2.

[276] Opposition to the Anglo–Spanish strategy was also voiced in the FAC Report 2002 published just after the referendum was held—cited above.

[277] A tactic that seemed drawn from the Northern Ireland experience.

[278] S Marks, *The Riddle of all Constitutions* (Oxford, OUP, 2000) 50–75.

national dispute had to consider the questions of culture, identity and citizenship that influence the Gibraltar issue. The period of negotiations leading up to the Straw Declaration fostered ill-feeling and acrimony and the opposite of any constructive popular legitimacy. To a large extent this was because the attempted resolution ignored the representations, views and aspirations of the people of Gibraltar and was based entirely on what the two States deemed to be in their national interest.

The fundamental problem with the proposed conceptual method of resolving the long-standing view was that it—once again—was based on traditional sovereignty and nationalism models.[279] This was, in large part, influenced by both Spanish and United Kingdom State drivers (more passive in the United Kingdom, more active, radical and forceful in Spain). For Spain the acquisition of Gibraltar has always been more of a priority than its defence has been for Britain. It has been a matter of pride and a symbol of frustration for Spain.

The morning after the referendum result so conclusively defeated the principle of joint sovereignty, a daily newspaper in Gibraltar, *Panorama*, led with the headline 'What Next?'[280] In the aftermath of the referendum result—for a while—the entire issue seemed to be placed in flux because it was plainly impossible to proceed with the discussions along a basis that had been so overwhelmingly rejected. The conflicting aspirations of the parties seemed quite dramatically different and irreconcilable. Bilateralism seemed entrenched.[281] The task to bridge those differences needed time and a new approach.

[279] It also emphasised how at odds with democratic legitimacy, governance and sovereignty trends this process was.

[280] *Panorama* (Gibraltar, 8 November 2002).

[281] This is a further example of Active v Passive Bilateralism that demonstrates that the official British Government policy tended to acquiesce to the bilateralism that was the principal deficit for Gibraltar. A bilateral Declaration between the UK and Spain on Gibraltar was annexed to the CE and Lisbon Treaty which confirmed the extension of it to Gibraltar and then added the following line that: 'This shall not imply changes in the respective positions of the Member States concerned' (Declaration 46 to the CE and Declaration 55 to Lisbon Treaty). This was entirely consistent with the fact that Spain had submitted a Note to Britain the day after signing the Treaty of Accession in 1985 to hurriedly emphasise that the dispute over Gibraltar remained bilateral. Its use of 'changes' seemed broader and could encompass a sanction of the obstructionism and bilateralism that was at the heart of the democratic deficit. It implied a continuation of the status quo with all it represented. But it was precisely this bilateral status quo that needed to be changed to address the deficit. While innocuous at first sight, the Declaration seemed to both enshrine into writing the unproductive status quo and an acceptance of Spanish action. An interesting insight into the respective attitudes of Britain and Spain is the admission in the White Paper issued in response to the CE (cited above). When referring to its negotiating position on individual clauses a Table is published setting out matters proposed by Britain and others that were amended by it in the national interest. It also publishes a list of clauses proposed by others to which Britain adopted a neutral stance. The Declaration on Gibraltar is on that list.

6

Negotiating a Way Through the Mist—Old Concepts, New Meanings

INTRODUCTION

HAVING ENCOUNTERED DIFFICULTIES in accessing governance measures that flowed from the Treaties of Maastricht, Amsterdam or Nice, and facing a continued wall of obstructionism, the arrival of a new and invigorated round of Anglo–Spanish talks in 2001 had been greeted with trepidation. The Gibraltar Government was concerned about how it could take forward its own agenda of constitutional reform and how it could unblock the obstacles it faced within the Union. Gibraltar also faced the paradox of governance described in earlier chapters. Instead, the Anglo–Spanish talks brought Gibraltar to the peak of the bilateralising impetus and put the three parties in direct conflict in a clear challenge to democracy and legitimacy. Once the spectre of immediate joint sovereignty was overcome, the aftermath of the bilateral talks left the parties more distant than ever in their aspirations. Spain still wanted to recover sovereignty over the Rock. Britain still wanted to protect its own strategic interests, and Gibraltar still wanted to pursue a solution in accordance with its right to self-determination (which invariably meant a solution without Spain). This chapter is about the necessary reassessment of negotiating possibilities that remained post the collapse of the joint sovereignty initiative.

A radical revision of the approach and methodologies of the parties was needed. This had to be designed in the context of moves to guarantee greater participatory democracy and legitimacy within the Union as well as against the background of the evolving concepts of sovereignty and nationalism. The most important and discernible aims that needed to be secured were: an end to the bilateralism that had so impinged on the ability to be flexible and inclusive in the dialogue process; an achievement of measures of greater practical self-governance; and the diffusion or elimination of the sovereignty dispute of Gibraltar. While new structures of dialogue, created in 2004, led to some co-operative agreements between the three parties by 2006, and while a package of internal constitutional reform was introduced in early 2007, this chapter and the chapter that follows will demonstrate that those developments left a range of issues untouched. They were an important but contextually misguided and ambivalent step towards resolution of the overall conflict.

This chapter considers the keys to the resolution of the governance deficits suffered by Gibraltar. It emphasises that it is first important to consider the modern constitutional context and the principles that stem from that. In applying those principles, it highlights that it is important to fully adopt a trilateral method, diffuse the sharper dimensions of sovereignty that can hamper progress and allow Gibraltar to achieve greater power, influence and representation.

In many ways the traditional focus when considering the Gibraltar dispute has been to home in on a status-first approach by which immediate attention goes to the end-product rather than the mechanics, methodologies or philosophy underlying the approach itself. By doing so, the dispute has become intractable and almost irreconcilable. Spain bases its case on territorial integrity and on achieving the integration of Gibraltar into Spain. Gibraltar bases its case on self-determination and on achieving a decolonised status which it has chosen. Gibraltarians fear absorption into Spain as much as the Spanish Government worries about what it perceives as separatist tendencies in Gibraltar. The status-first approach can only lead to a sharpening of the conflict and the resulting impasse. This perpetuates the governance issues faced by Gibraltar. Adopting a context-first approach that focuses on the constitutional context, mechanics and underlying philosophy and postponing the status issue could bring the unblockage of this seemingly intractable situation brought forward. This approach would then seek to apply the context and principles to the methodologies of the parties and would address the governance issues. The status issue would deliberately be left till last as it would accord with sequential sense to do so, because it would be influenced by what precedes it and because the status issue itself would evolve with time. Finally, it is not possible to definitively resolve the status issue unless the parties accept the extant legal context.

The recognition of Gibraltar as a stateless nation in a period of late sovereignty would allow a radical reappraisal of the governance and status issues that have frustrated generations. It would both dissipate the democratic and governance deficit and unblock the decolonisation and status debate. Above all that, it would create a better practical climate for the enjoyment of cohabitive and co-operative structures within a Europe 'united in diversity'. Following a recognition of its ultimate ability to sanction and legitimise events as an act of sovereignty the people, elected representatives and parliamentary institutions of Gibraltar, in exercise of their sovereignty, could very well elect to encourage a diffusion of these powers.

1. THE KEYS TO THE RESOLUTION OF THE PARADOX

To resolve the paradox of self-governance that Gibraltar faces, the overarching methodology, context and outputs of any approach must be assessed. There are three keys to the unblockage of the governance and status[1] issues faced by Gibraltar. Two are dealt with in this chapter. The third[2] is covered in the next chapter:

Placing the Dispute in its Modern Legal Context

Any attempt at resolving the conflict must first evaluate its placement in the modern constitutional context. An analysis of this has as its heart the concepts of sovereignty, nationalism and governance and, more specifically, what is now defined as late sovereignty,[3] stateless nationalism and participatory governance. Those three concepts and their constituent elements (namely pluralism, practical self-government, influence, power, representation, democracy, legitimacy and participation) form the main background of influences which would give the Gibraltar issue not only its proper perspective but the opportunities for its own resolution. All of these issues intertwine and are reflected within the European Union in the contemporary debate on multi-level governance and subsidiarity.[4]

The contexts and principles described above increasingly converge. It is in their convergence and application that the conflict can be resolved. The conscious invocation of these principles should occur within the four arenas in which Gibraltar needs to break down the governance, democratic and status deficit:

1. the UK–Spain–Gibraltar territorial dispute (the macro-dispute Level) by consistently pursuing methodologies of solution-building which will facilitate a thawing of the obstacles to reform;
2. the European Union (the EU Level) by access to the benefits of reforms, governance trends, legislation and increasing participation in governance;
3. the UK–Gibraltar constitutional relationship (the State Level) by allowing sufficient constitutional reform that delivers access to greater internal self-government, greater power, representation and influence

[1] It does not necessarily follow that this will immediately lead to a new status but rather that in achieving an unblockage of the power-responsibility paradox and an acceptance of the correct legal context it may facilitate the emergence of a new status through time.

[2] Securing greater sub-State governance first.

[3] N Walker (ed), *Sovereignty in Transition* (Oxford, Hart Publishing, 2003) 3.

[4] C Jeffrey, 'Sub-National Mobilisation and European Integration' (2000) 38 *Journal of Common Market Studies* 1.

at EU level and adequate national constitutional structures to safeguard these;
4. at pure domestic sub-State level (the domestic Level) by a programme of internal domestic reform to secure greater efficiency, accountability of the Executive and participation of civil society in the process of governance.[5]

While limited improvements can be achieved at EU, State and domestic levels the most holistic changes could be gained by tackling the macro-dispute level, because of the inevitable trickle-down of progress or obstruction from that to all other levels. It is at that level, therefore, that attempts should be made to apply the principles identified within the modern constitutional context.[6] This is in keeping with what has been stated in the previous chapters that the inter-State level is crucial in ending the bilateralism that has obstructed resolution to the dispute and then liberating the primary[7] and secondary[8] progress drivers.[9]

After recognition[10] of the true legal context, there must be an effort to neutralise the language, emotions and sensitive connotations of sovereignty so as to break down barriers. The evolution of the meaning of sovereignty with all that it means for the redistribution of powers and adoption of new forms of governance should also act as a driver for that process. The debate should centre on why the traditional concepts of sovereignty, nationalism and governance are now out of place and the promotion of pluralism, subsidiarity, sub-State constitutionalism and co-operative multi-national structures. Hand in hand with that is the parallel analogy that, in a supra-national environment, traditional status change may be as defunct as a solution-model as the traditional view of sovereignty is inappropriate as the theoretical basis for application to the dispute.

[5] The detail of which is outside the scope of this work.

[6] The importance of unblocking at this level has been seen in the previous two chapters. The shadow of bilateralism stifles much of Gibraltar's constitutional and European progress. There has been somewhat of a tendency to try to address matters only at the internal or State level and this clearly has not worked to tackle the main deficit.

[8] State.

[8] EU.

[9] See ch 4, pp 214–7.

[10] Recognition would itself entail an analysis and implied acceptance of where sovereignty lies in the modern legal context. But the parties can then voluntarily move on to a softer environment where this need not be constantly emphasised. As such, recognition could be followed by more pragmatic neutralisation and diffusion.

TACKLING THE METHODOLOGY OF SOLUTION-BUILDING AT MACRO LEVEL

By applying the modern context to the macro dispute, the most marked improvement would be a permanent end to the pure bilateralism that has haunted any prospect of resolution to this issue. Adopting a lasting commitment to trilateralism will go a long way to laying the foundations of an enduring new era. The mechanics of dialogue between the parties play a crucial part in this. A coherent trilateral process on all fronts should achieve improvements in the political climate by fostering trust, legitimacy, goodwill, confidence and ending any spectre of harassment. This methodology would also have to be consistent with the cohabitive federalisation that is fostered by the governance trends of the European Union. This chapter follows the central theme of this work that much progress could be achieved by applying the modern legal context and principles to the Gibraltar dispute, concentrating on practical self-government (through participatory democracy), practical nationalism (nation-building and pluralism but not separatism) and practical sovereignty (through a diffusion and de-fusion of sovereignty). This effort would be consistent with the trends of economic globalisation, political interdependence and international initiatives at co-operation on a wide range of policy. The next chapter sets out some detail on the achievement of practical self-governance improvements that could be gained if the dispute was placed in its proper theoretical context.

THE MODERN LEGAL AND THEORETICAL CONTEXT

Preliminary Issues, Parallels and the European Dimension

The first preliminary observation to make when analysing Gibraltar's governance dilemma is that the traditional common disregard by all parties of the larger political and constitutional environment within which Gibraltar co-exists has made little sense. There are useful parallels within both British and Spanish States that illustrate the diversity and complexity of the problems faced by nations within States and can provide influences for application to Gibraltar. To that extent, it is pertinent to consider developments touching on these stateless nations within Europe.[11]

[11] eg in Scotland, the Basque Country or Catalunya: see S Tierney, *Constitutional Law and National Pluralism* (Oxford, OUP, 2004) for a review of developments in connection with these and M Keating, *Plurinational Democracy, Stateless Nations in a Post-Sovereignty Era* (Oxford, OUP, 2001).

It is unrealistic that the Gibraltar issue should trail-blaze solutions for all these nations or that the Gibraltar situation should be tackled without reference to these other territories. They are both examples and constraints for Gibraltar. They are examples in the sense that they can provide useful precedents for Gibraltar, and constraints because it is unrealistic for constitutional models to be applied to Gibraltar if this would upset the internal constitutional arrangements of Britain and Spain. To expect the Gibraltar issue to be addressed without consideration of the debates that affect 7,000,000 Catalans[12] or 5,000,000 Scots[13] is unrealistic and swims against all tides that inextricably globalise the trends of governance. The European Union debates especially with regard to subsidiarity,[14] or the nature of multi-level governance[15] that so affect Gibraltar also profoundly affect Basque, Catalan, Scottish, Welsh and Northern Irish self-governance and there will be developments in all these that can usefully provide templates and indicators for Gibraltar. The unique features of the Gibraltar dispute—sovereignty claim within the EU—need to be considered side by side with these other stateless nations in case there are developments to draw upon.

The fact that Gibraltar does not operate in a constitutional vacuum and that developments concerning the other nations in Britain and Spain have the potential of influencing matters in Gibraltar is evident from a number of examples. The first Conference of Presidents of Autonomous Communities was held in Spain during the autumn of 2004.[16] A couple of months later the Basque Parliament approved the Free Association Plan of its Premier by a slim margin. It demanded recognition of the right to self-determination, greater powers within Europe, and a revised association with the Spanish State.[17] In a more moderate fashion, the Catalan Government was at the same time pressing for revision of its autonomy.[18] All these developments were occurring at a time of heightened constitutional activity in Gibraltar. While radical movement within the Gibraltar issue may be complicated because of Spain's fear that this would prejudice its position with regard to its own constitutional regions, it is also true that as the internal situation evolves in Spain it is possible for Spain to relax her stance with regard to Gibraltar's non-separatist aspirations. Equally the

[12] www.gencat.cat.

[13] www.scotland.org.

[14] S Smismans, *Law, Legitimacy and European Governance—Functional Participation in Social Regulation*, Oxford Studies in European Law (Oxford, OUP, 2004).

[15] I Bache and M Flinders (ed), *Multi-Level Governance* (Oxford, OUP, 2004).

[16] Bengoetxea in S Weatherill and U Bernitz (eds), *The Role of Regions and Sub National Actors in Europe* (Oxford, Hart Publishing, 2005) 54.

[17] Published on the Basque Government website at www.euskadi.net/r33-2219/es.

[18] Achieved in its *Estatuto de Autonomia* 2006 approved in referendum on 18 June 2006: see www.gencat.cat.

well-publicised plans of the current Scottish Government[19] may drive constitutional changes that can transform the panorama to such an extent that facilitates a more radical 'reconfiguration' of Gibraltar's constitutional architecture, in the sense that it would liberate British Government officials from any fears they may have that changes achieved by Gibraltar might provide an uncomfortable precedent for it when addressing Scottish demands.[20] If advances in Scottish arrangements are made, then it is much easier for Gibraltar to seek similar treatment than to be seen to be asking for trail-blazing mechanisms. This applies more to the external governance arrangements and the issue of status rather than to the internal constitutional powers because in this last sense Gibraltar has more devolved powers than Spanish or British stateless comparators.[21]

As matters evolve it is difficult to foresee how the internal constitutional panorama of Britain and Spain could look in a few years' time.[22] To that extent it is important when considering possible permanent solutions to the Gibraltar issue to factor in parallel developments within the European Union that can influence local developments.[23] This can best be described as the European dimension that affects the affairs of these nations. Indeed not only is it a more accurate description of the constitutional backdrop for Gibraltar, but it would also be a much more palatable driver for a co-operative process with Spain. There has been much resistance to the introduction of the so-called Spanish dimension,[24] and the 2002 referendum is recent proof of that. Gibraltarians saw the 2001 Anglo–Spanish process as a vehicle to ensure that Spain obtained influence and sovereignty over Gibraltar and to that extent it was, for an overwhelming majority of the population, objectionable from the start. The European dimension on the other hand does not have those connotations and simply is a description

[19] 'Choosing Scotland's Future, A National Conversation: Independence and Responsibility in the Modern World' (Edinburgh, Scottish Executive, August 2007), and 'Raising the Standard', Scottish National Party, 2005. While recognising that there are other options available the current Scottish SNP administration 'believes that an independent, sovereign Scotland is the best option for the country's future and that the people should be invited to support that option through a referendum.' It is committed to introduce a referendum bill by 2010, leading to a referendum on 'enhanced devolution or independence': see www.scotland.gov.uk/Home. There have been less radical developments in Wales: Government of Wales Act 2006 (c 32). For the general UK Government position on constitutional reform see *The Governance of Britain* (Cm 7170, 3 July 2007).

[20] S Tierney, 'Reframing Sovereignty? Sub-State National Societies and Contemporary Challenges to the Nation-State' (2005) 54 ICLQ 161–83.

[21] Ch 5.

[22] N Walker, 'Beyond the Unitary Conception of the UK Constitution' [2000] PL 384.

[23] Though the principles and parameters that could govern a solution framework can be mapped out, this should be amended to take into account developments at EU and State level. That is the basis on which the status ideas towards the end of the next chapter should be considered.

[24] A euphemism usually used by advocates within British Government circles to obliquely describe that Spain is a factor in Gibraltar's constitutional or governance panorama.

that encapsulates the legal reality of Gibraltar's participation within the European Union.

If the European dimension is not addressed both the slow uncompensated loss of sovereignty to Europe and the indirect acquisition by Spain of a slice of practical sovereignty (through its weight as a Member State and its ability through the governance, parliamentary and policy-making structures of the Union to influence Gibraltar's affairs) will continue unabated. A consistent and enduring process of dialogue with Spain, within a reassessed sovereignty climate and adequate constitutional reform with the United Kingdom, would be important to redress the balance. This chapter will examine the trilateral process initiated in 2004 and the constitutional reform package of 2006. The former has, so far, not proved entirely consistent and still smacks of bilateralism; the latter is insufficient in a number of important respects.

The Modern Application of Sovereignty

Sovereignty has been described 'as a mystic and dangerous word',[25] and the resolution of this dispute that has sovereignty at its heart has proved very vexing. In some ways the Anglo–Spanish process of 2001–02 attempted to sever the concept of legal sovereignty (in its sense of ultimate theoretical source of authority in a particular polity) from a more political understanding of sovereignty as power. That would explain the British Foreign Secretary's statement in November 2001 that negotiations were looking to tackle the issue of 'legal sovereignty'.[26] In trying this the miscalculation that was made was to think that even though sovereignty has several dimensions[27] the legal dimension could in any way be dislocated from the emotional dimension of sovereignty that is inextricably linked to the existential meaning that the concept has to the relevant demos. As Maduro has pointed out, while ' the question of ultimate authority is mainly presented as a question about legal sovereignty . . . it also impacts on these aspects of political sovereignty'[28] and to that should be added the inevitable impact on emotional sovereignty and legitimacy. Until a time arrives—unlikely in practice—when the word sovereignty can operate in an emotional vacuum then any view that in Gibraltar's case 'legal'

[25] HF van Panhuys, 'The Netherlands Constitution and International Law' (1953) 47 *American Journal of International Law* 537, 552.

[26] It was denied subsequently that any distinction was meant but this seems improbable given the declared intentions of the States.

[27] As described in ch 3 sovereignty represented by exercises of power merged with society and governance principle can operate on different dimensions.

[28] M Maduro, 'Contrapunctual Law: Europe's Constitutional Pluralism in Action' in N Walker (ed), *Sovereignty in Transition* (Oxford, Hart Publishing, 2003) 502.

sovereignty could be sliced away was a forlorn hope.[29] Indeed the purported dislocation of legal sovereignty was proposed while the *demos* that had a strong claim to sovereignty itself had not expressed an opinion on it and this was doomed to failure.

While the concept of sovereignty has been critically examined in recent years to the point that there have been suggestions that we are now in a post-sovereign world[30] this description does not fit neatly with the Gibraltar situation. As highlighted in previous chapters the traditional view of sovereignty has been transformed not only within the EU but also throughout the world. Equally greater political, social and economic co-operation and interdependence over the last few decades has had a global impact. Financial initiatives promoted by the OECD or the FATF,[31] for example, have recently emphasised how all countries irrespective of geography, size, resources or membership of a relevant supra-national entity can be affected by international measures. The process of European integration and governance trends has acted as drivers to the redefinition of sovereignty by a process of division, demarcation, pooling, participation and diffusion.[32] In the realms of international law 'the reality today is that the participants in the international community are not limited to States'[33] and that non-State actors are now in fact effective participants. This to a large extent swims against traditional 'legal doctrine (which) reinforces colonialist imperial gendered power structures of exclusion.'[34]

In terms of the European Union 'absolute or unitary sovereignty is entirely absent from the legal and political setting' of the Union, in that no Member State is:

> in possession of ultimate legal power over its own internal affairs ... [T]he sovereignty ... of the Member States has not been lost but subjected to a process of division and combination internally and hence in a way enhanced externally. But the process of division and combination has taken us beyond the sovereign state.[35]

[29] For a summary of the relationship between political and legal sovereignty see S Besson, 'Sovereignty in Conflict' in C Warbrick and S Tierney (eds), *Towards an International Legal Community: The Sovereignty of States and the Sovereignty of International Law* (London, British Institute of International and Comparative Law, 2006) 148–51, who takes the view that they are 'not logically separable in the long run' (at 150).

[30] N MacCormick, *Questioning Sovereignty: Law, State and Practical Reason* (Oxford, OUP, 1999) 156.

[31] Financial Action Task Force created by G7 nations.

[32] MacCormick n 30 above, 133.

[33] McCorquodale in C Warbrick and S Tierney (eds), *Towards an International Legal Community: The Sovereignty of States and the Sovereignty of International Law* (London, British Institute of International and Comparative Law, 2006) 263.

[34] ibid 249.

[35] MacCormick, 1999, 132–33 and see also by the same author 'Beyond the Sovereign State' (1993) 56 *MLR* 1–18. Some authors make the point that there has not strictly been division but delegation: see Besson in C Warbrick and S Tierney (eds), *Towards an International Legal Community: The Sovereignty of States and the Sovereignty of International Law* (London, British Institute of International and Comparative Law, 2006) 154–55.

In that sense a 'non-sovereign confederal Commonwealth' emerged, within which the 'sovereign territorial state' has ceased to be the 'only legitimate form of European polity.'[36] The dominance of state-centric models of sovereignty has dissipated[37] to be replaced with a push for wider participation, legitimacy and decentralisation. There has been a diffusion of power upwards to the supra-national entity and downwards to sub-State government.[38] Given that State governments dominate as central players at supra-national level it is also true that even within this 'new communicative universe'[39] there is an irony that the fragmentation of levels of governance actually facilitates the centralisation of power in State governments.[40] This issue is compounded for Gibraltar by the strong bilateralism that has obstructed access to European measures facilitating greater participatory democracy and frozen moves towards domestic constitutional reform.[41]

Within the EU the interplay of many actors in the governance system has produced 'a shift away from territorial sovereignty to functional sovereignty.'[42] However as Brus reminds us 'one should not lose sight of the important fact that non-territorial governance should be based on political authority that is rooted in the people's consent and loyalty.'[43] Change also marked the international sphere. The era of decolonisation and doctrine of self-determination with a regeneration of concepts of popular sovereignty has 'radically reshaped the economic and political tenor of international law.'[44] This also provides a relevant backdrop for the non-self-governing territory of Gibraltar and emphasises how human rights provide an increasing ideological role in theories of governance and status. Fundamentally it should be recalled, as Jennings has observed, that the 'doctrines of sovereignty down the ages have differed from time to time for the very reason that they reflected the needs and problems of their own particular times and were designed to do so.'[45]

[36] MacCormick n 30 above, 37.

[37] See J Scott and D Trubek, 'Mind the Gap: Law and New Approaches to Governance in the European Union' (2002) 8 *European Law Journal* 1–19; K Armstrong, 'Rediscovering Civil Society: The European Union and the White Paper on Governance' (2002) 8 *European Law Journal* 102–33.

[38] Evidenced by the push towards subsidiarity.

[39] A von Bogdandy, 'Links between National and Supra-National Institutions: A Legal View of a New Communicative Universe' in B Kohler Koch (ed), *Linking EU and National Governance* (Oxford, OUP, 2005) 24–52.

[40] By weakening the prospect of consistent accountability of the State or indeed the supranational entity. See A Moravcsik, *'Warum die Europaische Union die Exekutive starkt?'* in KD Wolf (ed), *Project Europa im Ubergang?* (Baden-Baden, Nomos, 1997) 211–69.

[41] Ch 5, 326–340.

[42] A van Staden and H Vollaard, 'The Erosion of State Sovereignty: Towards a Post-territorial World?' in G Kreijen (ed), *State, Sovereignty and International Governance* (Oxford, OUP, 2004) 180.

[43] M Brus, 'Bridging the Gap between State Sovereignty and International Governance: The Authority of Law' in Kreijen n 43 above, 22.

[44] M Craven, *The Decolonisation of International Law—State Succession and the Law of Treaties* (Oxford, OUP, 2007) 86.

[45] R Jennings, 'Sovereignty and International Law' in Kreijen n 43 above, 29.

Meaningful or Meaningless?

As stated above there are aspects of the Gibraltar conundrum that bring to the fore whether the word 'post-sovereignty' is in any way an apt description for the Gibraltar-sovereignty dilemma. The post-sovereignty theory is premised on an evolution of the concept to such an extent that not only is it divided and shared in practice but that it has lost its original meaning and emotional repercussions. It is this last aspect that does not sit well with the realities on the ground.

The Anglo–Spanish process of 2001–02 had several flaws, one of which was to miscalculate the significance of the sovereignty question to the electorate that would be called upon to reject or endorse any agreement.[46] Throughout the failed process British Ministers kept insisting that there would be major gains that would flow from a joint sovereignty agreement,[47] and that this made sense in a Europe where sovereignty was now being pooled among States. However, neither Britain nor Spain behaved in a way that convinced Gibraltarians that these States themselves believed sovereignty was unimportant. In a dramatic turn of irony, the very night that Peter Hain[48] gave an interview on Gibraltar television saying that symbols of sovereignty were meaningless in the modern Europe (and that if a Spanish flag had to fly anywhere in Gibraltar it should—rationally and coldly—be seen as unimportant in the overall modern context) Spanish helicopters and elite troops were landing on *Isla Perejil*[49] (off the Moroccan coast) because of an alleged infringement of Spain's sovereignty. It appeared sovereignty and symbols were not meaningless to Spain and the diplomatic impasse between Morocco and Spain required the intervention of US Secretary of State Colin Powell before the conflict was defused.[50]

In a political environment within which Spain and Gibraltar are hypersensitive about anything with the remotest sovereignty implications, it was unrealistic to try to sell a process on this premise. Indeed, instances like this convinced the people of Gibraltar that sovereignty was far from

[46] Its legitimacy was also criticised by the Gibraltar Government as it contended that it was invited to participate in the talks on the basis that it had no right to reject the sole constitutional model being designed by the States.

[47] Foreign Secretary Jack Straw in Parliament on 5 February 2002.

[48] Minister of State for Foreign Affairs at the time.

[49] A rocky outcrop the size of two football fields and home only to a few animals. The islet is a few hundred metres from the Moroccan coast (with the nearest point of the Spanish mainland almost 14km away). Spain considers it to be sovereign Spanish territory: 'A Row Over Rocks; If you want Gibraltar, says Morocco to Spain, why can't we have some Rocks?' *The Economist* (London, 20 July 2002).

[50] Secretary Powell reputedly referred to *Isla Perejil* as 'that stupid little Island': see S Balfour and A Quiroga, *The Reinvention of Spain: Nation and Identity Since Democracy* (Oxford, OUP, 2007) 187.

'meaningless' and that the actions of the two States was inconsistent with the marketing line they were promoting. As MacCormick has noted, if:

> the sovereign state is taken as the self-evident and only available framework for democracy, it becomes vital to struggle over boundaries and membership, vital to define the nation as possessor and master of the sovereign state, the nation-state.[51]

It seemed clear from their actions that Spain considered the boundaries and symbols of territorial assertion vital. With such a tiny homeland, and facing a large neighbour, the symbols were no less important to Gibraltarians. Additionally, there had been no serious attempt at any time to persuade all sides that they were operating within a new and redefined climate of sovereignty, where the concept of the sovereign state as the only possible vehicle for pluralistic self-government and democracy had been eroded.[52] The inconsistency was too difficult to reconcile. If, as Peter Hain pronounced, sovereignty was less important because it was being shared in the modern European Union, why first require an actual partial transfer of sovereignty as part of a settlement of this long-standing dispute.[53] This methodology did not sit well with the evolved sovereignty philosophy. Rather the attitude seemed to have clear echoes of traditional sovereignty.

In fact, and while it may have been re-defined, the concept of sovereignty still retains its importance. In its redefinition it is more closely equated with de facto power and associated with the determinative source of that power. In that sense there is a recognition that true sovereignty vests in the legitimate exercise of the voluntary will of the people of the particular territory and that their role in the decision-making process is crucial.[54] Elected executives may have decided in the context of a more politically interdependent and economically globalised world to pool certain powers in the supra-national entity. To that extent there is a conscious and deliberate loss of sovereignty. But it is that ability to decide to pool or give up these powers that is the act of sovereignty that reveals who actually holds this power. As such, the holding and giving up of sovereignty is in itself an important practical and symbolic act. Against that background to have asked the people of a disputed territory—who have for years campaigned to assert their right to self-determination—to accept

[51] MacCormick 1999, 134–35.

[52] The situation was no different in the State-centric United Nations: see earlier.

[53] As has been stated the 2002 Anglo–Spanish plan was based on joint sovereignty between Britain and Spain.

[54] M Maduro, 'Europe and the Constitution: What if this is as good as it gets?' in JHH Weiler and M Wind (eds), *European Constitutionalism Beyond the State* (Cambridge, CUP, 2003) 81. Though it has also been stated that the locus of sovereignty is not static: see McCorquodale in C Warbrick and S Tierney (eds), *Towards an International Legal Community: The Sovereignty of States and the Sovereignty of International Law* (London, British Institute of International and Comparative Law, 2006) above.

joint sovereignty (in other words a transfer of the very sovereignty that they perceive is rightly theirs to the claimant territory) and all in the name of the post-sovereignty era was a contradiction in terms. It was the old, unadulterated doctrine of the assertion of sovereignty[55] masquerading as post-sovereignty philosophy.

The symbols and trappings of sovereignty—especially in a dispute such as Gibraltar—have not ceased to be important. As Lord Mance has stated in another context, 'symbols can themselves be important, more so in some cultures than others. Recognition of a wrong can be as valuable as, sometimes valued more than, concrete compensation.'[56] Rather to deal with these symbols sensitively, they need to be neutralised, diffused or dissolved. While there has been much debate over the trends of European governance and multilevel constitutionalism[57] within the European Union, 'sovereignty hovers as a somewhat disconcerting ghost at this particular conceptual feast.'[58] Walker records that, for advocates of disaggregated sovereignty the word now does not maintain the meaning it once did, but notes that 'they dismiss too easily the persistence of sovereignty in official constitutional discourse.'[59] He accepts that sovereignty may be a case of 'organised hypocrisy[60] in that it can be invoked selectively and self-servingly but that does not stop it being taken seriously by significant political actors.'[61] As such, any explanation needs to take into account the social reality that sovereignty is still a used and recognised concept to transmit authority and power as an institutional and governmental fact. To that extent constitutional pluralism which accepts that 'states are no longer the sole *locus* of constitutional authority (and) . . . are now joined by other sites or putative sites of constitutional authority'[62] does recognise that:

> just as we cannot dismiss the constitutive power of those claims which continue to be registered in the language of sovereignty, we cannot either ignore the objective reality of globalisation and multi-dimensionality which has caused many at the meta level to forsake the claims of sovereignty.[63]

In that context, Walker prefers to describe this view as 'late sovereignty' rather than post-sovereignty, which suggests a period after sovereignty.

[55] R Bellamy, 'Sovereignty, Post-Sovereignty and Pre-Sovereignty' in N Walker (ed), *Sovereignty in Transition* (Oxford, Hart Publishing, 2003) 167–90.

[56] *R (Bancoult) v Secretary of State for Foreign and Commonwealth Affairs* [2008] 3 WLR 955, [172].

[57] See eg I Pernice, 'Multilevel Constitutionalism in the European Union' (2002) 27 EL Rev 511–29.

[58] N Walker (ed), *Sovereignty in Transition* (Oxford, Hart Publishing, 2003), 13.

[59] ibid 16.

[60] Quoting SD Krasner, *Organised Hypocrisy* (Princeton, Princeton University Press, 1999).

[61] N Walker (ed), *Sovereignty in Transition* (Oxford, Hart Publishing, 2003) 17.

[62] ibid 4.

[63] ibid 18.

By describing this phase as late-sovereignty he seeks to transmit the elements of continuity, distinctiveness, irreversibility and transformation potential of the concept of contemporary sovereignty, and in doing so recognises that sovereignty still has an extant, though albeit modified, meaning.[64] This insight, coming at a time when sovereignty is not merely territorial but also exists in multi-dimensional functional terms, leads to his conclusion that:

> the advent of functionally limited polities co-existent within the same territorial space means that the assertion of authority around a disputed boundary does not necessarily impugn the integrity of the other polity qua polity.[65]

This allows the conception of autonomy 'without territorial exclusivity—to imagine ultimate authority or sovereignty in non-exclusive terms.'[66] This is an important observation for Gibraltar and the prospects of co-operative cohabitation with Spain without entailing symbolic or territorial concessions. This is similar to the 'co-operative sovereignty' of Besson, which she describes as a

> reflexive and dynamic concept . . . stimulating constant challenging of the allocation of power thus putting into question others' sovereignty as well as one's own . . . none of them is ultimately and entirely submitted to another.[67]

And this because in a Europe of 'many overlapping *demoi*' the 'convergences should be made the most of but . . . should also be respected in a constant dialogue.'[68] This co-operative sovereignty can reconcile 'conflicting claims of sovereignty . . . with constitutional pluralism and the co-existence of many different legal orders.'[69] Tension between old, more territorial, spaces and these new governance spaces are inevitable and to a certain extent this is 'not the end of territory but its reinvention as the relationship among space, function, identity and representation changes.'[70]

Rather than being in a period that has seen the demise of sovereignty, the proper view is to recognise its evolution and its continued existence in a modified form. In this multi-dimensional world there are more subtle and a greater number of boundaries. This fits in well with the Gibraltar situation—a complex international dispute with sovereignty at its crux. If the parties can be persuaded to operate within the modern subtleties of

[64] ibid 19.
[65] ibid 23.
[66] ibid 23.
[67] Besson in C Warbrick and S Tierney (eds), *Towards an International Legal Community: The Sovereignty of States and the Sovereignty of International Law* (London, British Institute of International and Comparative Law, 2006) 159.
[68] ibid 173.
[69] ibid 176–77.
[70] M Keating, 'Europe's Changing Political Landscape: Territorial Restructuring and New Forms of Government' in P Beaumont, C Lyons and N Walker (eds), *Convergence and Divergence in European Public Law* (Hart Publishing, Oxford, 2002) 3–18, 4.

constitutional pluralism without seeking to impose a territorial formula then there can be a neutralisation or diffusion of the sovereignty debate and in turn a de-fusion in the sense of ' a plethora of organisational fragments which do not fit comfortably within the representational perspective of an existing sovereign but which do not themselves, yet, or perhaps ever, make independently effective sovereignty claims.'[71] Indeed, if 'sovereignty does . . . give expression to the distinctively political bond between a group of people and its mode of governance . . . to do justice to the value of these multiple bonds, a pluralisation of the very concept of sovereignty seems logically and normatively to be required.'[72]

Gibraltar is in a European Union where the traditional view of sovereignty and its connection with ultimate authority is under assault.[73] In Gibraltar itself the sources and dimensions of sovereignty are multi-dimensional. Gibraltar is a Crown territory, and while Her Majesty holds territorial sovereignty over Gibraltar the Crown has devolved wide powers of self-government to her elected Government of Gibraltar. Many of those wide-ranging powers are exclusive in nature. Any focus on purely institutional governance risks disregarding the role of the *demos* in ensuring legitimacy for the constitutional system and (at its highest) staking a claim as the ultimate repository of sovereignty itself or as the organ that bestows legitimacy on it.[74] There are at the very least a range of competing sovereignty players and claimants within the Gibraltar domestic and external context and all claim and tussle for a slice of sovereignty in an environment of pluralism. The modern understanding of the concept of the Crown in the overseas territories also provides a backdrop which influences the analysis of governance and status issues for Gibraltar.

The Crown in the Overseas Territories and Gibraltar

The definition of the Crown in the overseas territories is not an unproblematic question, and it inevitably has some impact on issues of status and governance and how constitutional arrangements can be viewed. The concept that there is 'one undivided realm', which contains Her Majesty and her territories, exists in parallel with the recognition that, once there is representative or responsible Government, that distinct Executive for the territory is described as 'the Crown in right of' the Government of the territory.

[71] N Walker (ed), *Sovereignty in Transition* (Oxford, Hart Publishing, 2003) 27.

[72] S Tierney, *Constitutional Law and National Pluralism* (Oxford, OUP, 2004) 17.

[73] Or, to fine-tune this position slightly, the entity that is vested with ultimate authority is (voluntarily) accepting the transfer of powers to another locus.

[74] Both in terms of sovereignty *qua* international law concept (through the right to self-determination) and of sovereignty *qua* power and competence in the governance sense.

In the seminal *Alberta Indians* case[75] it was made clear that the 'divisibility' of the Crown in that sense—connoting a recognition of a separate Executive—did not depend on independence. Indeed divisibility for these purposes takes place much earlier than that. So to that extent it has been held that there was a Crown in right of Mauritius[76] or for South Georgia[77] among many others. But tensions and problems still arise even in territories that are at a stage of what any layperson would recognise as independence. So in Canada in 1981 an evident tension arose between the views expressed by the United Kingdom House of Commons Foreign Affairs Committee and that of the Federal Government of Canada as to the respective duties or otherwise of the United Kingdom Parliament to legislate in the manner requested by the Canadian Government.[78] The position in Australia during the same period revealed the difficulties between Crown in right of the Australian Commonwealth and that of the United Kingdom given the status of Australian states as theoretical colonial dependencies of the UK, co-existing within what the international community regarded as a sovereign, independent country.[79] These constitutional issues led to the moves to ensure the 'patriation' of the Canadian Constitution in 1982 and the Australia Act in 1986.[80]

Those issues arose for Canada and Australia most particularly because the transition of those countries to political independence was achieved by constitutional evolution that never hinged on an independence Act. The combination of the 1926 Balfour Declaration, 1931 Statute of Westminster and a series of conventions and practice led those countries through that transition. The Acts of the 1980s revealed the need to clear up constitutional residue because of the gradual process those countries had been involved in.

If those countries faced those dilemmas because constitutional lawyers struggled with the impact of a lack of a categorical Act of political independence and sought to bridge the theoretical gap similar dilemmas are understandable in territories that fall short of that constitutional stage. The recent decisions in *Quark Fishing*[81] and *Bancoult*[82] have not definitively

[75] *R v Secretary of State for Foreign and Commonwealth Affairs ex p Indian Association of Alberta and Others* [1982] 2 WLR 641.

[76] Before independence—*R v Secretary of State for the Home Department, ex p Bhurosah* [1967] 3 WLR 1259.

[77] *R (Quark Fishing Ltd) v Secretary of State for Foreign and Commonwealth Affairs* [2005] 3 WLR 837.

[78] For an account see G Marshall, *Constitutional Conventions—The Rules and Forms of Political Accountability* (Oxford, Clarendon Press, 1986) 180–200, and also P Oliver, *The Constitution of Independence—The Development of Constitutional Theory in Australia, Canada and New Zealand* (Oxford, OUP, 2005).

[79] L Zines, *Constitutional Change in the Commonwealth* (Cambridge, CUP, 1991).

[80] It also led to similar moves in New Zealand.

[81] [2006] AC 529.

[82] [2008] 3 WLR 955.

clarified these issues.[83] On the one hand, the House of Lords considered that the Order in Council made under the British Settlements Act 1887, that was the Constitution for South Georgia, was not part of the law of the United Kingdom.[84] On the other hand, it was common ground between Counsel that the prerogative Order in Council under challenge in *Bancoult* had been made by Her Majesty in right of the United Kingdom,[85] and the same judge referred to the 'amphibious nature of the Order in Council as both British and colonial legislation.'[86] Thus, he held that:

> from the point of view of the jurisdiction of the courts of the United Kingdom to review the exercise of prerogative powers by Her Majesty in Council the Constitution order is not a colonial law, although it may well have been from the point of view of a British Indian Ocean Territory court applying BIOT law.[87]

Lord Hoffman added 'Her Majesty exercises her powers of prerogative legislation for a non-self-governing colony on the advice of her Ministers in the United Kingdom.'[88]

In what seemed to be at least a partial abandonment of his speech in *Quark Fishing*, Lord Hoffman said that, having considered a recent analysis on the powers of colonial legislatures 'I am inclined to think that the reason which I gave for dismissing the cross-appeal in [*Quark*] was rather better than the reason I gave for allowing the Crown's appeal and that on this latter point Lord Nicholls was right.'[89] In that context it is unclear

[83] See the critique written before the 2008 *Bancoult* ruling by A Twomey, 'Responsible Government and the Divisibility of the Crown' [2008] PL 742.

[84] [2006] AC 529, [64] (Lord Hoffman).

[85] [2008] 3 WLR 955, [76].

[86] ibid para 40. However, Lord Rodger in the same case remarked that 'such an interpretation would leave the status of the law in limbo—valid in the courts of the colony, but open to challenge in the English courts': [97].

[87] ibid [40].

[88] ibid para 47, citing the passage at Halsbury's *Laws of England*, 4th edn (London, Butterworths, 2003 reissue) vol 6, para 716: 'The UK and its dependent territories within Her Majesty's dominions form one realm having one undivided Crown . . . To the extent that a dependency has responsible government, the Crown's representative in the dependency acts on the advice of local ministers responsible to the local legislature, but in respect of any dependency of the UK (that is, of any British overseas territory) acts of Her Majesty herself are performed only on the advice of the UK government.' But see later—advice tendered will be to Her Majesty in right of the territory and acts done subsequently will be on her behalf in that guise.

[89] In *Quark* the issue raised by the Crown's appeal was 'whether the Court of Appeal was correct to conclude that the instruction . . . issued by Her Majesty through her Secretary of State was issued by Her Majesty in right of the UK.' The cross-appeal related to the decision by the Court of Appeal that, because the UK had not extended the First Protocol of the ECHR to the territory, a claim for damages for breach of s 7 of the Human Rights Act 1998 could not proceed. Lord Nicholls had stated that the case should not have been decided on the issue of the capacity in which the Secretary of State had acted when giving his instruction to the Commissioner of South Georgia: 'In my view this line of argument is misdirected in the present context . . . this is a non-issue. Quark's claim fails . . . because the Secretary of State's instruction was not incompatible with a Convention right within the meaning of the Human Rights Act. Had the instruction been incompatible, the capacity in which the Secretary of

whether Lord Hoffman was suggesting that he had reflected on the rationale in *Quark* or on the conclusions. To that extent, it was indicative that perhaps on a further occasion their Lordships would consider related issues afresh. However, it is submitted that South Georgia and the British Indian Ocean Territory are both in a special category, given that they are presently territories with very limited government (no legislature or elected executive) and no indigenous population. If the Privy Council or House of Lords were to consider a case concerning one of the nine other overseas territories which have active civilian populations and their own devolved institutions of Government, the *Quark* position should be upheld.

The decisions in *Quark Fishing* and *Bancoult* could only be reconciled in one of several ways:

1. In the first place, the court was making a distinction between the source of legislation and holding that in relation to constitutions made under statutory orders in council those were made *qua* the territory and that prerogative orders in council were made *qua* the UK. The distinction would be based on the fact that as no representative Parliament was involved in the particular prerogative orders in issue in those cases this justified a finding of substantive difference.[90] The problem with that is that the reality is that UK Ministers advise Her Majesty in the making of prerogative as well as statutory orders in council that contain a Constitution for a territory[91] and so do the elected Ministers of the territory. The issue in territories like South Georgia and BIOT was who was the representative advising Her Majesty? Was it the UK Government or the executive of the territory? As vice-regal entities cannot advise Her Majesty (only Ministers can)[92] the absence of an executive in the territory meant that the only body advising Her Majesty was that comprising UK Ministers. As there was no representative Government in the territory the distinction seems less about the nature of the Orders in Council and more about the advisory entities to Her Majesty.

State gave his instruction would not have afforded him a defence.' He considered that whether the instruction was issued in right of the UK or South Georgia was irrelevant. He did accept that in other contexts 'the capacity in which a minister of the Crown was acting may be all-important': see 548–49, [45].

[90] So eg Lord Hoffman said, 'the principle of the sovereignty of Parliament, as it has been developed by the courts over the past 350 years, is founded upon the unique authority Parliament derives from its representative character. An exercise of the prerogative lacks this quality; although it may be legislative in character, it is still an exercise of power by the executive alone' (*Bancoult* [35]).

[91] See eg the minutes of 14 December 2006 of the meeting of the Privy Council in its executive capacity that advised Her Majesty to make the Order in Council annexing the 2006 Constitution.

[92] R Brazier, *Constitutional Practice—The Foundations of British Government*, 3rd edn (Oxford, OUP, 1999).

2. Alternatively, the court was making a distinction not as to the nature of the Order (and whether it was statutory in nature or made under the prerogative) but as to whether the act was *de facto* one of the UK Government. This involved an analysis and recognition of the political reality that in the absence of an actual representative Government of the territory the act of legislation was one of UK Ministers. Some of the speeches in *Bancoult* seem to indicate this was a real issue of concern for the court.[93] But that cannot have been the basis of the distinction in *Bancoult* (for the BIOT) and *Quark Fishing* (for South Georgia). The obvious point is that in both territories there was no representative government to speak of and yet the decisions arrived at in respect of the territories was different.[94]
3. Perhaps the better distinction is between the stages of commencement and then subsequent enjoyment of self-government. So in this way the constitutions for the territories whether made by prerogative or statutory Orders in Council are all made by Her Majesty *qua* UK Government. These establish self-governing structures for the first time or repeal and replace existing structures with alternative measures of self-government. There is no contradiction to say these are colonial laws made for the territory that are both part of the law of the territory and that of the United Kingdom. It would be a consistent reading with the undivided realm of Her Majesty and her territories within which the Crown is divisible because it creates a concept of sub-divisibility and not parallel divisibility (which would only happen in an independence situation.[95]

This view may not seem consistent with Lord Bingham's opinion in *Quark*, but is it not consistent with the classic principle recognised in the *Alberta Indians* case that on the grant of a representative legislature and the establishment of other institutions of government Her Majesty's government of the territory is to be considered to be distinct to that of the United Kingdom? It follows that, until that happens, the government of a territory cannot be considered distinct. As such, Kerr LJ observed in *Alberta Indians* that this was the case in Canada by 1867. In Gibraltar the process was somewhat slower. So, for example, there was a colonial government in

[93] At [109] of *Bancoult* Lord Rodger remarked, 'the difference—and it is, of course, very important—is that orders in council are made without the concurrence of Parliament or of any other representative legislature and so the political control is less direct.', though he made this remark in a different context.

[94] An abject surrender of substance to form as the Court of Appeal criticised in *Quark*. In a dissenting judgment in the House of Lords, Baroness Hale, concurred with that approach by the Court of Appeal (at 562, [95]). The distinction she drew from Kerr LJ's approach in *Alberta Indians* was 'in the case of territories which are in reality governed by and from the UK.' *Quaere* whether Baroness Hale would have reached the same conclusion in the case of the more advanced overseas territories like Gibraltar or Bermuda.

[95] Twomey n 83 above.

place under the Governor but little civilian involvement. The first moves towards some democratic mechanisms of participation through elections to a city council and the appointment of some civilian representatives to the Executive Council did not substantially alter the balance of power. It is arguable that, by 1957, with the grant of an elected majority in the Legislative Council, or by 1962, when elected members became 'associated' with departments, firm moves had been taken that could be perceived as having laid the foundation for that divisibility. By 1964 the introduction of ministerial government, supported by other governance reforms, established responsible government and the distinct and divisible Crown in right of Gibraltar beyond any doubt. Subsequent constitutional reforms in 1969 and 2006 were achieved seamlessly without disturbing or re-calling the divisibility that had already been established. It continues without interruption—so there is always a Crown in right of Gibraltar in place since 1964 and it is that that arguably has been issuing subsequent Orders in Council to replace the original one which was granted by the Crown in right of the United Kingdom because at *that* point there was no responsible devolved executive for the territory and no divisibility. Once the original Constitution providing for responsible government was granted any powers stated therein to belong to Her Majesty, including those of amending, revoking or replacing the Constitution are retained by her in her capacity as Queen of Gibraltar. Her Majesty grants subsequent amending instruments in that capacity albeit on advice of both her Ministers in Gibraltar and, because of sub-divisibility, from UK Ministers.

An added issue when examining particular situations is to understand the nature of the representative government in the territory and the extent to which in practice acts of Her Majesty to trigger those constitutions or actions taken under them are of the UK or of Her Majesty on advice of local Ministers. So for example is the prerogative Order in Council establishing the 2006 Constitution an act of Her Majesty *qua* the United Kingdom or not? On one reading of *Bancoult* it must be. On the other hand if the conclusion[96] was only based on the fact that it was either common ground in *that* territory[97] or because there was a lack of representative government in *that* territory then the conclusion could and should be different in the case of the highly developed overseas territories like Bermuda and Gibraltar.[98]

The 2006 Gibraltar Constitution was the result of protracted negotiations between Gibraltar and the United Kingdom that spanned an eight-year

[96] At [76].

[97] Without extending the principle to other territories.

[98] The issue is of some importance because the majority in the House of Lords in *Bancoult* held that, in legislating via the Order in Council that had been made *qua* the UK, the interests of the UK could take primacy over those of the people of the territory.

period. At the conclusion of those negotiations a final package of agreed reforms was reached which the Gibraltar Government was politically committed to put to a referendum of the people of Gibraltar. Equally the Gibraltar Government's commitment was not to advise Her Majesty to introduce the Constitution unless a majority accepted it.[99] When it was, to all intents and purposes, Gibraltar Ministers advised Her Majesty through the Governor to make the prerogative Order in Council containing the 2006 Constitution. At a meeting of the Privy Council of the 14 December 2006, Her Majesty issued the Order in Council. Present at that meeting were a number of United Kingdom Ministers. To that extent, Her Majesty received advice both from her Gibraltar Ministers in her guise as Crown in right of Gibraltar to repeal and replace the existing Constitution with a new one and from UK Ministers to do likewise.

The fact that Her Majesty can receive advice from both the territory Government and UK Ministers reflects political reality.[100] It also finds a way through the complex interrelationships that arise when there are sub-divisible royal components under an undivided realm. Advice received by Her Majesty is non-exclusive in the context of advanced territories with responsible government. Expressed in a different way advice is provided from different organs of governance and received in different capacities. In that way the constitutional dynamic accommodates the actual political substance.

In that sense the 2006 Constitution was the result of an act of sovereignty by the people of Gibraltar and subsequent advice to Her Majesty by both Gibraltar and UK Ministers. Her Majesty *qua* Crown in right of Gibraltar was advised by her Government of Gibraltar that its people had approved the Constitution negotiated at intergovernmental level and put to them in referendum and that it was time to introduce it. Her Majesty also received advice from UK Ministers in Council that the 2006 Order should be made. In what capacity she received that advice is a matter of some debate. There are two possibilities: the first, that she received that advice as Crown in right of the UK on the basis that it was in that capacity that she introduced the 2006 Constitution; the second, that she received such advice from UK Ministers also in her capacity as Queen of Gibraltar but in recognition of the sub-divisibility that co-exists in the non-independent overseas territories. Central to that debate would be to identify who holds the reserved power of revoking, altering and replacing the Constitution and to consider how the Order was made and the Constitution enacted.

[99] If it had been rejected presumably it would not have been introduced. In that way both the UK and Gibraltar Governments had agreed to subordinate the introduction of the 2006 Constitution to the acceptance by its people. This was an act of sovereignty in the constitutional sense.

[100] See Twomey n 83 above for discussion on the tension surrounding the receipt of advice by Her Majesty from the Commonwealth Government of Australia and from the Australian States.

In that sense, different features point in different directions, revealing the presence of hybrid and complex constitutional relationships. The 2006 Constitution, like its predecessor, was expressed as having been made by Her Majesty 'by virtue and in exercise of all the powers enabling Her to do so . . . by and with the advice of Her Privy Council.' The practice then is to set out the Constitution being granted to the territory in an annex to the Order. Under section 86 of the 1969 Constitution

> There is reserved to Her Majesty full power to make laws from time to time for the peace, order and good government of Gibraltar (including, without prejudice to the generality of the foregoing, laws amending or revoking this Constitution).[101]

In other overseas territories the practice has been to insert such a provision in the body of the Order and not in the Annex to it. Indeed, that was the case in Gibraltar's 1964 Constitution.[102] Whether that is material is an issue of some relevance in this search for the identification of the fountain of constitutional powers. In that constitutional maze the conclusion may simply be that after a somewhat lengthy journey dissecting the strolls in both directions the discovery would be made that both avenues return to the same source.

When Her Majesty granted the 1964 Constitution the exercise was somewhat simpler. At that point there was no responsible government and as such no Gibraltar ministers from which to take advice. It can be argued that divisibility, in the sense explained in *Alberta Indians*, occurred at that point and no earlier. If so, then the making of the 1964 Constitution was an exclusive act of Her Majesty in right of the UK. The difficulty arises after that when considering the Orders of 1969 and 2006 that were phrased in similar mechanical terms to that of 1964, even though the substantive content of each Constitution was markedly different. Had the nature and capacity in which the 1969 and 2006 Orders were made changed because it was after the moment of constitutional divisibility?

Given that section 9 of the 1964 Order reserved to Her Majesty the power to amend, revoke or replace the Constitution, and that before that moment there could be no firm basis to argue that divisibility had taken place, the reservation must be for Her Majesty *qua* the UK. If so then the 1969 Order can be explained as having been made by Her Majesty in right of the United Kingdom too. But is that too easy a way out of the conundrum? And can a distinction really be drawn because the reserved powers are not in the body of the Order but in the 1964 Constitution being granted to the territory? The argument would run that that Constitution is one that is enacted in a post-divisibility environment and the reservation is for Her Majesty as Queen of Gibraltar. Is a distinction based simply on the location

[101] There is a similar provision in s 8 to Annex 2 to the 2006 Constitution.
[102] s 9 of the 1964 Order.

of the reserved power (which might be subject to other unrelated considerations) too tenuous a basis to place a major constitutional argument? The answer is that it would be best to find a more solid footing for an argument that the reserved powers are those of Her Majesty *qua* Crown in right of Gibraltar.

The successive constitutions of 1964, 1969 and 2006 created and re-enacted a system of almost full internal self-government.[103] The executive responsibility for Gibraltar is expressed to vest in Her Majesty.[104] The Government of Gibraltar is defined as being made up of the Council of Ministers and Her Majesty.[105] Certain responsibilities are held by the Governor as Her Majesty's representative *qua* Queen of Gibraltar.[106] If the reserved powers to alter or revoke the Constitution are powers vested in Her Majesty in right of Gibraltar, what would happen if Gibraltarian Ministers refused to advise that the Constitution be amended but this was desired by the UK Government? As the Crown constitutionally acts either in accordance with the advice of Ministers, after consultation with them, or in its discretion, it would be possible to conclude that the reserved powers of Her Majesty under Annex 2 of the 2006 Constitution are retained for her to exercise in her discretion. In those circumstances, in the very extreme case of Gibraltarian Ministerial objection, Her Majesty would seem to have that residual ability to act in terms of those powers reserved given the plain meaning of the section. But does Her Majesty retain those powers in right of Gibraltar or in right of the United Kingdom?

In *Quark* Lord Bingham stated:

> What is in issue is the constitutional standing of the instruction. The factual matrix might, I accept, be relevant if there were in a given territory no government, or no government worthy of the name, other than the United Kingdom Government. There would then be no government other than that of the United Kingdom Government on whose behalf an exercise of executive power could be made, no other government in right of which the Queen could act. But that is not this case. Here, there is nothing to displace the initial inference that the instruction was given by Her Majesty, through the Secretary of State, in right of the government of SGSSI.[107]

If this was the case for South Georgia with its almost non-existent form of representative Government it would certainly be the case in an analogous situation in one of the advanced overseas territories. But this does not settle the issue as this paragraph refers to an instruction made under the

[103] This is accepted by the British Government: see FAC Report 2008.

[104] s 44 of the 2006 Constitution.

[105] ibid s 45.

[106] See the reference is s 45(1) to the fact that 'Her Majesty . . . is represented in Gibraltar by the Governor.' The Governor's special responsibilities are set out in s 47. They are principally external affairs, defence and internal security. In relation to external affairs there is a requirement as far as practicable to act after consultation with the Chief Minister.

[107] [2006] 1 AC 529, 542, [19].

particular order in council but not to the Order itself.[108] Lord Hope, more conclusively, deals with that question when he stated:

> If one approaches the 1985 Order,[109] as one should, as an instrument which sets out the Constitution of SGSSI, the references that it makes to *Her Majesty fall to be read as references to Her Majesty in the exercise of her rights as Head of State and Queen of the territory unless that there is a clear indication to the contrary.*[110] As I have already said, that is the meaning that one would give to the first reference that is made to Her Majesty in section 5(1).[111] I can see no good reason for altering the meaning of the phrase when she is referred to again in the same subsection or elsewhere in the 1985 Order just because the references on these occasions are to her giving instructions through a Secretary of State. These references reflect the constitutional reality that the government of SGSSI is subordinate to that of the United Kingdom. It is subject to instruction from time to time as to what it can and cannot do. But the constitutional reality is that, although the government of SGSSI is a subordinate government, it is nevertheless the government of the territory. The Secretary of State is not acting, when Her Majesty gives instructions under section 5(1), on behalf of Her Majesty as Head of State of the United Kingdom. What he is doing is providing the vehicle by which, according to the Constitution of SGSSI, instructions are given and other acts done by Her Majesty as its Head of State.[112] (emphasis added)

Lord Hope reached this view reliant on that part of Kerr LJ's judgment in *Alberta Indians*, where the latter had stated that:

> Indeed, independence, or the degree of independence, is wholly irrelevant to the issue, because it is clear that rights and obligations of the Crown will arise exclusively in right or respect of any government outside the bounds of the United Kingdom as soon as soon as it can be seen that there is an established government of the Crown in the overseas territory in question.[113]

The conclusion in *Alberta Indians*, based as it was on other paragraphs that recognised the importance of representative Government in Canada after 1867 could have been construed as requiring at least a modicum of

[108] It would therefore be the case if Her Majesty issued an instruction in accordance with any power retained in the Constitution itself but would not definitively explain whether Her Majesty qua Gibraltar itself made the Order that gave authority to the instruction made under it.

[109] The Order setting out a Constitution for South Georgia.

[110] In a recent decision of the Gibraltar Court of Appeal, Otton JA, delivering the judgment of the court held that references to Her Majesty in the Gibraltar Constitution were to Her Majesty in right of Gibraltar: see *Cripps v OEM Rosia Developments Ltd*, 17 September 2008, unreported. Equally the European Court of First Instance surveying the 1969 Constitution and the relationship between the office of the Governor and the Crown held that his appointment was made by the 'Queen of Gibraltar' and that the 'Governor of Gibraltar could [not] be equated with the central government of the UK': see Cases T-211/04 and T-215/04 *Government of Gibraltar v Commission of the European Communities*, Judgment of the Court of First Instance, 18 December 2008, [97].

[111] s 5 of the relevant Order for South Georgia set out the powers of the Commissioner for South Georgia who was the officer appointed to administer the territory.

[112] At 556, [76].

[113] [1982] QB 892, 927.

representative institutions. If that was the case it would have justified a court holding that references to Her Majesty in a territory without representative institutions or responsible Government were to Her Majesty in right of the UK. References in a territory with responsible Government would be to Her Majesty in right of the territory. That would have been a result that would accord with realities linked to representation, democracy and governance in a much closer way. It would marry political reality with constitutional theory.

Instead the speeches of the majority in *Quark* point to a bolder decision which construes references to Her Majesty as being that relating to her role as Queen of the territory whether or not there were representative institutions or responsible government. If this is applied to Gibraltar then a strong case could be made for the divisibility going back to the 18th or 19th centuries. It is possible given the potential for inconsistency between the *Bancoult* and *Quark* cases that this question may be reassessed. This work prefers the more conservative approach that takes the acquisition of representative institutions and responsible government as the point of divisibility.[114] In either case it has taken place in the case of Gibraltar.

If Lord Hope's statement is used as a yardstick references in the Gibraltar Constitution to Her Majesty's reserved powers would be to powers she retains as Queen of Gibraltar 'unless . . . there is a clear indication to the contrary.' Subject therefore to it not being argued that the context requires that it be understood as necessarily meaning the Crown in right of the UK, the application of this statement to Gibraltar would mean that it is Her Majesty in right of Gibraltar that made the 2006 Constitution order and retains certain powers. Even if it is argued that Her Majesty in right of the UK made the Constitution[115] this does not affect the view of what subsequently transpired in the case of Gibraltar.

The trigger of commencement of the 2006 Constitution and the revocation of the 1969 Constitution was an act of the Crown in right of Gibraltar. The Constitution was commenced not by Order in Council but by the gazetting by the Governor in Gibraltar of a notice specifying that the Constitution would be commenced as from 2 January 2007. This was an act of the Crown in right of Gibraltar pursuant to the power prescribed in the principal Order itself.[116] This was also evident from the terms of the despatch accompanying the Constitution itself.[117]

[114] The point though is that if this had been the test *Quark* could have been decided differently because of South Georgia's special situation.

[115] As was common ground in *Bancoult*. It could be argued though that this was, again, because the BIOT had no representative institutions or responsible government.

[116] Under s 1 of the Order the Constitution came into force when published in the Gazette, but the Governor was to set the 'appointed day' from which it was to have effect and from which the 1969 Constitution would be considered revoked.

[117] In the despatch to the 2006 Constitution, the Foreign Secretary stated, 'as was the case in 1969, Her Majesty's Government in the UK in this despatch confirm the position in

Aspects of the 2006 Constitution reflect the complex interrelationships that still co-exist. For example, section 47(1) provides that the Governor is responsible for external affairs and defence (*qua* representative of the Crown in right of Gibraltar), and then section 47(4) says that this is without prejudice to the overall responsibility of the UK Government for these issues. The juxtaposition of these sections neatly encapsulates the fact that other references to the Governor and Her Majesty must indeed be references in right of the Government of Gibraltar.

While Twomey considers the impact of *Quark Fishing* on the United Kingdom and whether Her Majesty should now be described as Crown in right of Scotland, Wales or Northern Ireland,[118] there is a clear distinction between the status of the overseas territories and those nations that are part of a United Kingdom. The latter constitute a constitutionally integral unitary State,[119] within which there is asymmetrical devolution to responsible executives in respect of each nation. As the group of overseas territories with responsible governments have never had constitutional integration, it is easier to conceive that on acquisition of responsible government Her Majesty acts on the advice of Gibraltar Ministers without suffering a distortion to the constitutional structures. As Twomey states 'to identify the capacity in which the Queen acts, one must identify the source of her advice. The capacity in which the Queen acts is determined by the identity of her advisers and the source of their responsibility.'[120]

The sub-divisibility would be transformed into parallel divisibility on independence. But even then, identifying when there has been an 'alienation' for the purposes of sovereignty is a vexed question, which becomes obvious when the Canadian and Australian examples are considered. If there has not been an act of independence, it may be particularly complex to home in on a precise constitutional moment. Indeed, that is not in the nature of a gradual transformation. The alienation issue is important from the point of view of the proviso to Article X of the Treaty of Utrecht. As in cases of pure constitutional evolution, the timing of the moment of alienation or independence is a creeping concept that is noticed once it has

relation to certain matters in the Constitution. I would therefore be obliged if you could arrange for this despatch to be published in the Gibraltar Gazette at the same time as the Gibraltar Constitution order itself.' The request was to publish the despatch with the Constitution—it was not a direction to publish the Constitution. In any event and following *Quark* even if this was construed to be an instruction to publish the Constitution from a Secretary of State to the Governor it would be considered that the Secretary of State was for these purposes Her Majesty's 'mouthpiece or medium . . . passing on her instructions as Queen [of Gibraltar] not acting as Secretary of State for Foreign and Commonwealth Affairs of the UK': see *R (Quark Fishing Ltd) v Secretary of State for Foreign and Commonwealth Affairs* [2005] 3 WLR 837, [10] (Lord Bingham).

118 A Twomey, 'Responsible Government and the Divisibility of the Crown' [2008] PL 742, 764.

119 Twomey ibid, citing R Brazier, *Constitutional Practice—The Foundations of British Government*, 3rd edn (Oxford, OUP, 1999).

120 ibid 766.

occurred. For the reasons explained earlier in this work, it is outwith this book to consider that issue in detail. What is the case is that both the identification of the source of constitutional power and the exercise of it are questions that raise the continuing importance of the currency of sovereignty in all its dimensions.

Whose Sovereignty?

Sovereignty has thus evolved but not disappeared. In that context the question asked often is whose sovereignty is it to exercise? With Britain holding territorial sovereignty, Spain claiming it and Gibraltar arguing that its people are the true source of sovereignty and legitimacy—all stake a rival claim. Even though the *locus* of sovereignty may shift through time given the raw importance of this issue to civil society the question is best tackled rather than ignored.

The tension between competing claimants came to the surface most prominently during the joint sovereignty discussions. These had occurred notwithstanding a commitment in the Preamble to the Gibraltar Constitution that Britain 'would *never* enter into arrangements' (emphasis added) by which the people of Gibraltar would pass under the sovereignty of another State against their freely and democratically expressed wishes.[121] Seen restrictively, it could be argued that while Britain had agreed the arrangements of joint sovereignty there had been no breach of the Preamble because actual implementation of the 'in principle agreement' was subject to a referendum of the people of the territory. However if the commitment was read more generously the fact that Britain had proclaimed that it had agreed certain principles with Spain by which sovereignty could be shared was already an *entrance* into arrangements which affected the sovereignty under which the people of Gibraltar would live in the knowledge that this was profoundly rejected by these.

The Preamble is useful in clarifying the context and purpose of the Constitution, but it may be arguable whether it is enforceable in the absence of any other legal right arising.[122] Rather, it may be that it is necessary to identify a substantive constitutional or quasi-public law right. Any argument as to a potential breach would then be tagged onto a particular right so as to trigger the enforceability of the commitment

[121] See ch 2.

[122] The Preamble is an aid to construing the enacting provisions but 'it is only when it conveys a clear and definite meaning in comparison with relatively obscure or indefinite enacting words that the preamble may legitimately prevail.' If the enacting words are only capable of one construction then they will prevail over the Preamble. The Preamble is part of the context of the statute and must be read in its widest sense: *A-G v Prince Ernest Augustus of Hanover* [1957] AC 436, 461, 467–68, 474 (Simonds VC). However this must now be subject to the point made below as to legitimate expectation or human rights.

inherent in the Preamble. Having said that, in the human rights context there have been examples of a wide teleological construction of rights. So, for example, when trying to establish the object and purpose of a right it has been held that this can only be seen in the wider context of values, democracy and pluralism. As has been pointed out in *Golder v United Kingdom*[123] the court construed a right of access to the courts when there was no specific language to that effect in the Article. It did so 'mainly by reference to guidance as to the object and purpose of the Convention to be found in the Preamble.'[124] It must also be construed liberally and widely to ensure that the objects of the Convention are achieved.

There was no clear and express language in the fundamental rights chapter of the 1969 Constitution (or any other part of it other than the Preamble) that was offended by the joint sovereignty arrangements,[125] unless it had been argued that in a very indirect fashion there was a breach of section 32[126] and that the joint sovereignty arrangements directly/indirectly affected these. Subject to fielding arguments on the construction of a Preamble or an ambitious teleological construction of the Constitution[127] the principal domestic legal argument appeared to rest on legitimate expectation.

In previous decisions in both the *Quark Fishing* and *Bancoult* sagas the courts have made clear that decisions of the Foreign Secretary to direct a specific administrative decision in an overseas territory[128] or introduce legislation for a territory[129] are judicially reviewable on the usual grounds of legality, rationality and procedural impropriety.[130] While in the *Quark*

[123] [1975] 1 EHRR 524; and see DJ Harris, M O'Boyle and C Warbrick, *Law of the European Convention of Human Rights* (London, Butterworths, 1995) 5–7.

[124] ibid 6.

[125] Both the Falkland Islands and Montserrat constitutions include a right to self-determination in the body of the text. If similar provisions had been in place in Gibraltar at the time, it would have been easier to argue a direct breach without seeking recourse to more ambitious or strained construction. However, attempts at domestic enforcement of a jus cogens norm of international law might encounter State immunity issues in some circumstances: see *Jones v Saudi Arabia* [2007] 1 AC 270. While the majority in the 2008 decision in *Bancoult* did not consider that international law provided a route to challenge an Order in Council Lord Mance left the possibility open: see [145]. See also S Fatima, *Using International Law in Domestic Courts* (Oxford, Hart Publishing, 2005).

[126] The power to make laws for the peace, order and good government of the territory. And also S Farran, 'Prerogative Rights, Human Rights and the Island People: the Pitcairn and Chagos Islands Cases' [2007] PL 414.

[127] And the powers devolved to Gibraltar.

[128] *R v Secretary of State for Foreign and Commonwealth Affairs, ex p Quark Fishing Ltd* [2002] EWCA Civ 1409.

[129] *R (Bancoult) v Secretary of State for Foreign and Commonwealth Affairs and another* [2001] 2 WLR 1219 ('*Bancoult 2001*'). That is so even when the legislative power is based on an exercise of the prerogative power to legislate because it is 'an executive act alone': see *Council of Civil Service Unions v Minister for the Civil Service* [1985] AC 374, and *R (Bancoult) v Secretary of State for Foreign and Commonwealth Affairs* [2008] 3 WLR 955, [35] ('*Bancoult 2008*') (Lord Hoffman).

[130] *Bancoult 2008*, [105].

Fishing or *Bancoult* cases both acts complained of were directed at the Foreign Secretary, these were not cases concerning anything other than domestic acts within the territories concerned. The decisions complained of were not acts of foreign affairs. The *Bancoult 2001* decision came closest in that the complaint was targeted at local legislation that had been introduced to expel the Chagossians from islands in the Indian Ocean as a result of an agreement between the United States and British Governments. But the agreement between the Governments themselves was not directly impeached. Such a target would have been much more complex as the courts might have taken the view that an act of foreign affairs was not justiciable as in *Rees-Mogg*.[131] Though in that case it was keen to point out that the 'principle of non-justiciability is not universal and absolute'[132] pointing out that in *Molyneaux*[133] the court had considered whether the intergovernmental conference established by Britain and Ireland 'contravened any statute or rule of law or constitutional convention.'[134] It was also said not to be in dispute that 'the Government could not lawfully transfer any part of the Crown's prerogative powers in relation to foreign affairs without statutory enactment.'[135] In *Christian v Queen*[136] Woolf LJ pointed out that:

> today it can no longer be taken for granted that the courts will accept that there is any action on the part of the Crown that is not open to any form of review by the courts if a proper foundation for the review is established.[137]

In the most recent consideration of the *Bancoult* case[138] by the High Court in England it was suggested that 'where fundamental or constitutional rights are at issue, judicial review may be more intrusive and the margin of discretion to the legislator narrower.'[139] On appeal the Court of Appeal squarely placed its judgment in favour of the Chagos islanders on the basis of legitimate expectation and of the ability to judicially review the

131 *R v Secretary of State for Foreign and Commonwealth Affairs, ex p Rees-Mogg* [1994] QB 552.

132 ibid 570 (Lloyd LJ).

133 *Ex p Molyneaux and Others* [1986] 1 WLR 331.

134 *Rees-Mogg*, 570. See also *R v Prime Minister of the UK and Others, ex p Campaign for Nuclear Disarmament* [2002] EWHC 2777 (QB), in which the grant of advisory declarations sought in relation to UN Security Council 1441 was rejected inter alia because it was unnecessary to interpret these to determine a person's rights under domestic law and because it would be damaging to the public interest in the field of international relations, security or defence. The complexity of obtaining declarations on the basis of constitutional conventions or political promises to hold referenda can be seen in *R (Southall and Anor) v Secretary of State for Foreign and Commonwealth Affairs* [2003] EWCA Civ 1002 and *R (Wheeler) v Office of the Prime Minister and Others* [2008] EWHC 1409 (Admin).

135 *Rees-Mogg*, 570.

136 The Pitcairn Islands case—*Christian v The Queen* [2007] 2 WLR 120.

137 ibid para 33.

138 *R (Bancoult) v Secretary of State for Foreign and Commonwealth Affairs and Another* [2006] EWHC 1038.

139 Farran n 126 above, 421. Lord Hoffman in *Bancoult 2008* approved that concept in principle: see para 53.

acts of the executive.[140] On further appeal the House of Lords by 3:2 majority reversed this decision.[141] It held inter alia that the Chagossians did not have a claim to a legitimate expectation. As highlighted it was common ground between the parties that the prerogative Order in Council under challenge had been made by the Crown in right of the UK. In judging what interests should drive the making of the Order the court accepted that, while the interests of the territory should be considered if any conflict arose, United Kingdom interests could legitimately be preferred.[142] However, the European Court of First Instance in a recent ruling implied that, when considering how to exercise the United Kingdom's residual powers of legislation or other powers bestowed in the Governor, these must be used to implement the United Kingdom's obligations under international law to promote self-governance.[143] If so it could be argued that these powers must be discharged with the 'sacred trust' of promoting the rights of colonial peoples under Article 73 of the UN Charter in mind as the primary obligation. In those circumstances if choices needed to be made they would err on the side of favouring the people of the territory and not otherwise. The difference of approach is clear.

The fact that the 2006 Constitution was put to a referendum for approval or rejection was significant. The United Kingdom Government had agreed to introduce the new Constitution only if the people of Gibraltar approved it in referendum.[144] To that extent it had agreed to qualify its constituent sovereignty and transfer that to the people of Gibraltar for decision. That is both a distinguishing feature to the *Bancoult 2008* decision and endowed the Constitution with representative character and the ingredient of popular sovereignty.[145] The third distinguishing feature between the BIOT case and that of Gibraltar is that the United Kingdom is subject to obligations under Article 73 of the UN Charter in respect of Gibraltar. By this the UK is obligated to progress the 'sacred trust' of taking colonial people to self-determination, self-government and decolonisation. The fourth distinction is that the sovereignty preamble to Gibraltar's Constitution gave specific assurances capable of a clear legitimate expectation.

The collective result of all those propositions, when applied to the Anglo–Spanish process that Gibraltar faced in 2002, seems to be that an

[140] *R (Bancoult) v Secretary of State for Foreign and Commonwealth Affairs and another* [2007] EWCA Civ 498.

[141] *Bancoult 2008*.

[142] ibid [47]–[49].

[143] Cases T211/04 and T215/04 *Government of Gibraltar v Commission of the European Communities*, Judgment of the Court of First Instance, 18 December 2008, [99].

[144] Not too dissimilar in effect (albeit without a referendum) to a mechanism set out in the Statute of Westminster: see the discussion in the case of Canada in *Manuel v A-G* [1982] 3 WLR 821, 846.

[145] Contrast *Bancoult 2008* [35] (Lord Hoffman).

agreement between Britain and Spain may not have been a Treaty,[146] but as it was akin to one it would, as in *Molyneaux,* have been capable of review by the courts. The complication would have been that an agreement on sovereignty was an act within the prerogative on foreign affairs, and as such it would have been difficult to persuade the courts to prevent this from proceeding in any form. However, for a joint sovereignty agreement to have been consummated, there would have had to have been United Kingdom legislation to transfer (at least) part of the Crown's prerogative in foreign affairs to Spain (or to transfer part of the territory or a share in the overall sovereignty). Legislation would also have had to be introduced in Gibraltar to give practical meaning to the mechanics of such arrangements. The opportunity for challenge in the United Kingdom or Gibraltar courts would in such eventuality be greatly enhanced, as constitutional and fundamental rights questions, as in *Bancoult,* would potentially be thrown open for adjudication.[147] However, this would be made difficult in light of the fact that the House of Lords has recently stated that, while the United Kingdom should take account of the interests of a colony when legislating, it can, in the case of conflict, prefer its national interests.[148] It is submitted that this view pays insufficient regard to the 'sacred trust' under which the United Kingdom operates and is distinguishable in the case of Gibraltar.[149] For territories on the UN list of non-self-governing territories, the people of which are vested with the right of self-determination, this work contends that the view of Lord Mance in *Bancoult 2008* should be preferred.

In terms of legitimate expectations the courts accept that these arise by statements or conduct and can give rise to procedural[150] and substantive[151] expectations which, if breached or at risk of being breached can be enforced. The statement in the Preamble clearly gives rise to a legitimate expectation by the people of Gibraltar or, as has in more recent times been

[146] Though it was the declared intention to proceed to have a Treaty signed should the people of Gibraltar accept the joint sovereignty model.

[147] A nexus with a substantive right or other provision of the Constitution would be necessary. It might also be possible to mount a challenge on breach of the ECHR or the UK Human Rights Act in respect of extra-territorial activity of the UK in Gibraltar: see *R (Al-Skeini) v Secretary of State for Defence* [2007] UKHL 26. The English High Court has jurisdiction to entertain judicial review proceedings in respect of all Her Majesty's territories: see *Bancoult 2001,* 'but that does not mean that the acts in question are acts of UK public authorities. On the contrary, the jurisdiction exists whether the act is one of a UK public authority or not': *Bancoult 2008* [65] (Lord Hoffman). In the case of breaches based on Convention rights, Lord Nicholls in *Quark* stated that, when the ECHR is extended to overseas territories it does not lead to claims under the Human Rights Act as 'the rights brought home by the Act do not include Convention rights arising from the extended obligations assumed by the UK in respect of its overseas territories' (546, [36]).

[148] *Bancoult 2008* [114].

[149] See below.

[150] *A-G of Hong Kong v NG Yuen Shin* [1983] 2 AC 629.

[151] *R v North and East Health Authority, ex p Coughlan* [2001] QB 213.

described, an executive estoppel[152] of the British Government that arrangements would not be entered into that, in effect, would transfer sovereignty to another State against the wishes of the people. Equally it could be argued that it has qualified the freedom of action of Her Majesty *qua* UK to be able to legislate for Gibraltar in manner that prefers UK national interests. In the absence of a specific right to self-determination in the Constitution, the people of Gibraltar would have been left with arguing such expectations in the context that that principle of international law, while not incorporated domestically, gave rise to the contingent sovereignty of its people. The British Government has recently argued that the concept of the distinct and divisible Crown in the overseas territories is based on the 'distinct sovereignty' of the Government of the territory.[153] That must also assist in reading the sovereignty as displaced and localised.[154] Taken together with the *Alberta Indians* case, the Preamble on sovereignty and now the self-determination reference in the 2006 Constitution, it leads to an analysis that in effect the Treaty obligations of the Crown under the Treaty of Utrecht are held or shared by the Crown in right of Gibraltar. In that scenario the Crown in right of Gibraltar has stepped into the shoes of the original British Crown. The effect of that would be that the British Government view that the Treaty of Utrecht is a bar to independence, because of the alienation clause, would be difficult to sustain. Quite apart from the fact that the UN Charter takes precedence over the Treaty of Utrecht in case of conflict, the point would be that, in the situation described above, the achievement of independence would be an evolution of the Crown that holds current sovereignty under the Treaty of Utrecht—that is, the Crown in right of Gibraltar. There would therefore not be an 'alienation' to another Crown and the first option clause would not be triggered.[155] The corollary of that is that the right of first option of Spain is intact but vested in the Crown in right of Gibraltar *qua* the people of Gibraltar.[156] Section 75(1) of the 2006 Constitution is also relevant in that light, in that, in effect, it is declared that Crown lands in Gibraltar are lands of the Crown in right of Gibraltar.

[152] Bennion [2007] PL, Spring, 1–12.

[153] In the 2001 *Bancoult* decision the UK Government argued that 'the government of the (British Indian Ocean Territory) . . . must be taken to possess a separate and distinct sovereignty of its own' (at 1240), although the court then went on to look beyond the 'form' and analyse which Government had in fact made the Order.

[154] Although see the discussion in *Madzimbamuto v Lardner-Burke* [1969] 1 AC 645, 722–23.

[155] In some ways this is similar to the Scottish argument that, on independence, 'Her Majesty the Queen would remain the Head of State in Scotland.' See 'Choosing Scotland's Future, A National Conversation: Independence and Responsibility in the Modern World' (Edinburgh, Scottish Executive, August 2007) para 3.25.

[156] This argument is bolder, but whether issues of State Succession would eventually arise or the doctrine of reversion could be applied to this last obligation are moot points. Additionally self-determination could in a case of State succession 'create a presumption in favour of the successor State': see I Brownlie, *Principles of Public International Law*, 4th edn (Oxford, OUP, 1990) 654–675.

A reference to a right to self-determination has now been inserted into Gibraltar's Constitution by virtue of the 2006 amendments. The approval of the Constitution in referendum has, according to Britain, been, in itself, an act of self-determination.[157] The inclusion of that right to self-determination can only strengthen the view that the people of Gibraltar have a legitimate expectation in respect of the sovereignty of the territory to decide what happens over it.[158] This would be perfectly justiciable and in fact amounts to an argument that the people of Gibraltar are now the actual repositories of sovereignty[159] and that the Crown's prerogative in respect of Gibraltar has been voluntarily qualified by these rights and statements.[160] Additionally, there is a more fundamental argument that on proper analysis the sequence of constitutional developments has in effect displaced[161] sovereignty to its people acting through its Executive to such an extent that the British Government can no longer enter into such arrangements without the consent of the people.[162] To an extent the British Government have voluntarily provided a similar recent commitment, observing on a number of occasions since 2006 that it would 'never enter

[157] Letter dated 22 January 2007 from the Permanent Representative of the United Kingdom of Great Britain and Northern Ireland to the United Nations addressed to the Secretary General, United Nations General Assembly, 23 January 2007, A/61/710.

[158] The clause is phrased in declaratory terms, and even though this may give rise to issues of construction and direct enforcement when it is placed side by side with the sovereignty Preamble and Despatch, the arguments for reliance on it seem strong. The clear statements amount to a right of the people of Gibraltar to self-determination barring only independence and providing that no arrangements on sovereignty will be entered into without consent. Arguments of legitimate expectation arise throughout these elements.

[159] On three grounds: because of the modern assessment of where sovereignty lies (see Maduro); because of the domestic rights (Preamble, self-determination reference and legitimate expectation); and the right under international law of the people of Gibraltar to self-determination (which is in itself a right to contingent sovereignty). To the last can be added the language of the 'ever closer Union' in the EC Treaty, the need to maintain identity of the peoples of Europe and the more recent language that acknowledges the EU as being created on the basis of peoples 'united in diversity'.

[160] One would also have to consider any possible recourse to the UN Human Rights Committee: see D McGoldrick, *The Human Rights Committee: Its Role in the Development of the International Covenant on Civil and Political Rights* (Oxford, Clarendon Press, 1994).

[161] Rather than merely qualified.

[162] See also J Crawford, *The Creation of States in International Law*, 2nd edn (Oxford, OUP, 2006) 613–5, where he refers to the *Western Sahara* case, in which it is said that Chapter XI does not affect territorial rights or sovereignty, but this must be because Administering Powers are doing precisely that—administering territories that have contingent sovereignty but have not, as yet, attained full self-government in accordance with the solemn trust created by Art 73 of the Charter. Rights of sovereignty are unaffected because it is up to those in whom it vests—the people—to do what they will in exercise of their right to self-determination. Additionally, Farran notes that in the Diego Garcia case it was argued on behalf of the Chagos Islanders that the power to legislate was limited by the UK's 'obligations to respect human rights and its treaty obligations—including the United Nations Charter and customary international law regarding the right to self-determination of colonies' (Farran n 126 above, 423–4). The Court did not feel the need to rule on those arguments in either the High Court or Court of Appeal (see [2007] EWCA Civ 498) or House of Lords though Lord Mance left the point open for future argument.

into an agreement on sovereignty without the agreement of the Government of Gibraltar and their people. In fact we will never even enter into a process without that agreement.'[163] In the overseas territory of Gibraltar that is on the UN list of territories with contingent sovereignty have we now not come full circle to Bodin's proposition that this is a democracy where there is an elected structure holding sovereignty on trust for its people? The monarch has devolved a Constitution to a people who chose their system of Government freely and who could equally choose independence with or without that monarch as Head of State. What more demonstrative fact of sovereignty?

In contrast Spain has made clear that its objections to internal governance have been lifted because it considers that the international status of Gibraltar remains unchanged. In that context it has made clear that its sovereignty aspirations are still to acquire territorial sovereignty.[164] There is of course a distinction between sovereignty and decolonisation in that one can obtain the latter without necessarily altering the sovereign status of the territory. For example, if integration with the Administering Power is sought, then this does not change the sovereignty of the territory. The issue is whether the people have the right to self-determination and, if so, how they have exercised that contingent right to sovereignty. The debate lies in recognising it and thereafter considering how it will be exercised, manifested and asserted.

It is impossible in the burning cauldron of the Gibraltar dispute to artificially ring-fence sovereignty *qua* status from its governance manifestations. In all those circumstances sovereignty has far from disappeared. Rather, it has evolved into a concept which is now more malleable and flexible and is capable of greater nuances. In that inherent flexibility it is also able to accommodate various dimensions and spheres of competences. The task

> is not to imagine . . . a world in which new political values and virtues flourish in the absence of sovereignty but to imagine and anticipate ways in which such values and virtues may flourish through the operation of sovereignty.[165]

As this and the next chapter develop it will be seen that much of the concerns of Gibraltar are about the exercise of power and influence. That relates to the sovereignty concept because of the linkage with power as the currency of sovereignty in its most basic form. To some extent therefore the concept at this level can best be understood in its political context. The exercise of power after it has been vested in the institutions of Government is an 'explication rather than a division of sovereignty.'[166] And political power itself, as Loughlin notes,

[163] House of Commons, Foreign Affairs Committee, *Overseas Territories*, 2008 at para 392, citing the evidence of Minister of State, Jim Murphy MP.
[164] Spanish Ambassador to UN, October 2006, cited in chs 1 and 3.
[165] N Walker (ed), *Sovereignty in Transition* (Oxford, Hart Publishing, 2003) 31.
[166] Loughlin, in ibid 70.

can be divided without decreasing it and the interplay of powers with their checks and balances is even liable to generate more power, so long, at least, as the interplay is alive and has not resulted in a stalemate.[167]

The challenge thus is that, while sovereignty may remain as a currency of international law, the 'thinking about this sovereignty needs to be developed into new directions' so as to create 'new structures . . . [and a more] effective method of employing sovereignty rather than . . . a surrender of it.'[168] This is the challenge for Gibraltar: to seek to achieve an unblockage of its attempts to obtain a greater slice of power, influence and representation without having to cede ground in its position on territorial sovereignty.

The Irish Parallels

During the abortive Anglo–Spanish process, many British officials and Ministers made comparisons to Northern Ireland when discussing Gibraltar. The Irish link was clearly in their mind and provides some interesting parallels that can be drawn between the way that the Labour administration in the United Kingdom approached the Gibraltar and Northern Ireland issues. It also provides some material for comparative application for Gibraltar. The general approach in tackling the so-called Irish dimension was that it was necessary for Britain and Ireland to solve this because, as Morgan[169] has pointed out, there were bigger international questions on which both countries had to co-operate.[170] This too was the Labour approach when it urged Gibraltar to take into account the 'Spanish dimension'. It wanted to resolve a problem that caused unnecessary difficulties in the close relationship between Tony Blair and José Maria Aznar and soured the gentle fostering of Anglo–Spanish alliances at EU level.

A central issue in the Irish context was the acceptance of the principle of consent by the South and the removal of the territorial claim.[171] In exchange, Britain was prepared to recognise that the people of Northern Ireland could

[167] ibid 71, citing H Arendt, *The Human Condition* (Chicago, University of Chicago Press, 1958) 201.

[168] Jennings in Kreijen n 43 above, 42.

[169] A Morgan, 'Permeating the Irish Border: Practical North–South Co-operation under the Belfast Agreement' IBRU Boundary and Security Bulletin, Autumn 1999, 52. He also observed (at 55) that the term 'Irish dimension' was coined in the British Government document, 'The Future of Northern Ireland: a Paper for Discussion', October 1972, London, HMSO.

[170] This approach is not individual to Labour, though, as the initial efforts to address this dispute can be traced to the Conservative administration of the 1980s.

[171] J Doyle, 'Governance and Citizenship in Contested States: The Northern Ireland Peace Agreement as Internationalised Governance' (1999) 10 *Irish Studies in International Affairs* 201–19.

remain British or choose to be integrated with the Republic. In other words there was no recognition of the principle of full self-determination for the people of Northern Ireland. They could consent to or resist a transfer of sovereignty to Ireland, but could not choose a different course.[172] Any pretence of a right to self-determination was thus heavily qualified and expressed in a negative form.[173] So too with Gibraltar. While the Preamble vests the people with the right of consent and the 2006 Constitution incorporates a right to self-determination the positions of both Britain and Spain resist an acceptance of the full ramifications of this right.

The people of Northern Ireland, like the Gibraltarians, have multiple identities[174] and were offered the acquisition of Irish nationality,[175] as the Gibraltarians were offered the chance to acquire Spanish nationality in the Straw Declaration of 12 July 2002. However, no element of Gibraltar's political make-up incorporates a desired Spanish identity component, so the offer was more a disincentive than an attraction. In terms of the mechanics of the process itself, there were also similarities. The Anglo–Irish discussions since the 1980s had been premised on the basis of bilateral declarations between the two States.[176] These set out a general objective and a multi-party conference was convened as a result. The result was to produce an agreement that would then be put to referendum of the Northern Irish electorate. The process during the Anglo–Spanish talks was similar. The discussions were aimed at first achieving a bilateral declaration of principles between the United Kingdom and Spain (which would include the principle of joint sovereignty). Following this (and only then) the Gibraltar Government would be invited to take a full part in drawing up an agreement on the details of the implementation of those principles at a multi-party conference. That would then lead to the agreement being put to a referendum in Gibraltar.

But there were some important differences too, that were not adequately taken into account in the formulation of policy. Had they been, it would have become clear that, however close the parallels, there were some differences that suggested different treatment of both problematic situations. In the first place, the Irish process was clearly more sovereignty-neutral and conscious of being sensitive in the use of symbols and emotional gestures. The attempt at persuading Gibraltarians to park a settlement under what they considered to be the unacceptable umbrella of

[172] B Hadfield, 'The Belfast Agreement, Sovereignty and the State of the Union' [1998] PL 599.

[173] 'Agreement between the Government of the United Kingdom of Great Britain and Northern Ireland and the Government of Ireland', Belfast, 10 April 1998, Treaty Series No 50 (Cm 4705, 2000) (the 'Good Friday Agreement').

[174] FSL Lyons, *Culture and Anarchy in Ireland, 1890–1939* (Oxford, OUP, 1982).

[175] Art 1(vi) of the Good Friday Agreement.

[176] N Mansergh, *The Unresolved Question: The Anglo-Irish Settlement and its Undoing* (New Haven, Yale UP, 1991).

joint sovereignty was a serious flaw, in that it by-passed the population and sought to pre-determine the key first part of the exercise, rather than attempt to persuade the populace in a way that was less destined to fail. Secondly, Gibraltar—unlike Northern Ireland—is not a divided community.[177] In Northern Ireland there is a significant nationalist community (favouring Irish integration) and a strong Unionist community (favouring retaining the current constitutional links to the British Crown). In Gibraltar, the population is almost unanimous in its rejection of the Spanish dimension having any formalistic role in the sovereignty of the territory. No political party advocates giving Spain a role and nor is there any discernible strand of public opinion advocating it. To fail to take adequate account of this stark reality limited the ability of formulating acceptable options.

Thirdly, in Gibraltar—unlike Northern Ireland—the main differences are between a strand of quasi-unionism that advocates integration with Britain and moderate stateless nationalism that advocates greater self-government short of independence.[178] That realisation should provoke a discussion of a wider range of options that would go beyond the status quo and accommodating the Spanish dimension.[179] Fourthly, the Anglo–Spanish process was aimed at producing a *fait accompli* on the principle of joint sovereignty, following which the detail could be influenced. The principle itself, though, was meant to be immovable. The Anglo–Irish discussions were more inclusive and shunned any attempt at imposing a status model *ab initio* (especially one that did not have the support or endorsement of the people of Northern Ireland).

Fifthly, while in Northern Ireland self-government had been suspended for some time (and to that extent it was normal that the British Government might take the lead in administering the affairs of the territory), Gibraltar has had its own elected Ministerial Government for more than 40 years, and to deny its Government full equality at talks was always going to create the feeling that the people of Gibraltar were being excluded from discussions over their very future. To that extent the Gibraltar process was less inclusive and more deprived of legitimacy. It was difficult for Gibraltar to understand, still less accept that the British Government was prepared to allow Spain to have a greater say over the future of the territory than its own Government. The offer of a referendum on the model of joint sovereignty that was the oft-used riposte by British officials facing that criticism was seen as falling well short of the exercise

[177] For a general review of multiculturalism see W Kymlicka, 'The Global Diffusion of Multiculturalism: Trends, Causes and Consequences' in S Tierney (ed), *Accommodating Cultural Diversity* (Dartmouth, Ashgate, 2007) 17–33.

[178] And not between unionism and acceptance of the Spanish dimension. The model of joint sovereignty therefore appealed to no significant sector.

[179] The analogy of what is on offer in Northern Ireland.

of real influence on the political agenda.[180] Sixthly, the Good Friday Agreement model replaced the Anglo-Irish bilateralism with a multi-party discussion method and thereafter with a more acceptable form of bilateralism (Northern Ireland/Ireland) in the administration of some of the bodies established by all sides.

Similarities and differences apart there are some aspects of the Irish model that provide useful guidance for a properly constituted and administered process. These will be expanded below, but include:

—the neutralisation of the hard edges to the sovereignty debate;
—the voluntary pooling of sovereignty to supra-national constitutionally created bodies;
—the acquisition of direct influence in the decision-making process by the Government of the territory;
—the conscious avoidance of symbolism and the emotional aspects of sovereignty;
—the injection of co-operation to replace conflict;
—the subjection of the European dimension to the 'implementation' bodies created by agreement;
—the adoption of the Agreement by an exercise in popular legitimacy on both sides;
—the offer of constitutional concessions by the claimant party rather than the claimed territory.

To this extent elements of the Irish experience are indeed relevant for analogous consideration in the constitutionally plural approach to the Gibraltar issue.

THE METHODOLOGY OF SOLUTION-BUILDING AT MACRO LEVEL

The Mechanics of Dialogue and Co-operation and the Sovereignty Mist

For nearly two years after the 2002 Referendum, the issue of Gibraltar was largely in abeyance. It was clear that the positions of the three parties were polarised and it was time for cold reflection on the methodology of the Anglo–Spanish process. While the British Foreign Secretary had (before the Referendum had been held) referred to it as eccentric,[181] by the Spring

[180] As it was only a choice to accept or reject a model designed by others. It was not an opportunity to vote on a wide range of options (some of which at least could have been suggested by the electorate or its representatives), nor was it a chance to vote on a model which had been drawn up after agreement and with the input of its Government.

[181] A position which was heavily criticised by the House of Commons Foreign Affairs Committee in their Report of November 2002—above.

of 2003 the Minister for Europe admitted that the referendum result could not be ignored.[182]

In March 2004 the Socialists won a surprise election victory in Spain. This prompted a reassessment of the policy that the Conservative and more sovereigntist *Partido Popular* had been unable to abandon even in the face of overwhelming rejection. While Spanish Socialists and Conservatives share similar objectives within Europe and are not as divided as the mainstream British parties on the question of Europe, the Spanish socialist attitude to sub-State government has traditionally been more welcoming.[183] Accused, for example, of being intransigent on the Basque question, the Conservative Leader of the Opposition, Mariano Rajoy, retorted that the PP 'was not intransigent but there is nothing to talk about on national sovereignty.'[184] By the early autumn of 2004 there were moves to open a new chapter.[185] While the PP Government had said that its policy was that progress on the issue of sovereignty should go hand in hand with any progress made on the twin track of co-operation with Gibraltar, the Socialist Government was prepared to abandon this insistence on dual progress. It did emphasise that it stood by the long-term goal of recovering sovereignty of Gibraltar. But it talked of restarting discussions over Gibraltar with a new perspective and wanting to involve Gibraltar in a co-operative process, so as to 'recover the sentiment, friendship and the involvement of the citizens.'[186] The British Government echoed those sentiments. In a marked shift of position at a Joint Press Conference with the Spanish Foreign Minister, Jack Straw stated that 'unless they [the people of Gibraltar] are there fully able to participate . . . and their active consent is there, there is no point, frankly in having the discussions.' He added that the only way ahead on this difficult issue is 'on the basis of democracy and consent.'[187] At that press conference the Foreign Ministers issued a statement that seemed to indicate a radical departure from the policy that had been followed up to mid 2002. The

[182] Denis MacShane in an interview with *El País* (Madrid 8 June 2003). A position that the Spanish Government seemingly came to share, see *Financial Times* (London 27 October 2004) and Spanish Foreign Minister's interview with *El País* (Madrid 3 August 2004).

[183] For an analysis of the differing motivations and perspectives of the two main parties see C Closa and P Heywood, *Spain and the European Union* (London, Palgrave International, 2004) 40–53.

[184] Remarks made to Spanish television on 4 May 2005.

[185] Even though the tension with old style bilateralism was ever present and came through in different developments. eg, in a Council Regulation on co-operation in relation to the External Borders of the Union, it was recorded that 'a controversy exists between the Kingdom of Spain and the UK on the demarcation of borders of Gibraltar', with the consequence that the applicability of the Regulation to the borders of Gibraltar was suspended—Council Regulation EC 2007/2004 Art 12(3).

[186] Statements made by Spanish Foreign Minister, Miguel Angel Moratinos, at a Joint Press Conference between the British and Spanish Foreign Ministers on 27 October 2004, see—*Gibraltar Chronicle* (Gibraltar 28 October 2004).

[187] ibid.

Joint Statement included a commitment 'to consider and consult further on how to establish a new forum for dialogue in which Gibraltar would have its own voice.' This followed on from indications that Spain wanted to foster a so-called 'Two States, Three Parties' formula for dialogue.[188]

In an interview with *The Times* on 28 October 2004, Miguel Angel Moratinos[189] stressed that 'we are not renouncing or putting aside sovereignty, but we also want to create an atmosphere that will facilitate a better understanding'. He went on to emphasise that in an effort to rebuild its alliance with Britain it wanted to lift 'the siege' of Gibraltar and court Gibraltarians, recognising that

> we have to take into account not only the future of the land itself but also its people, so instead of creating blocking obstacles, making them the objective of reactive policies, we prefer to foster co-operation in order that everybody in the region benefits.

The Opposition PP chastised the new Spanish Government's overtures towards Gibraltar accusing the socialists of abandoning the joint sovereignty gains. This led the Spanish Government to emphasise in its Parliament that the Government had not given up its sovereignty claim, but was merely pursuing it along different means.[190] The conservative PP introduced a Motion into the Senate, which was narrowly defeated 125–123, that had sought to ensure that there should be no acceptance of the principle of self-determination of the people of Gibraltar, that the claim to sovereignty should be maintained and that at no time should any Gibraltarian authority be recognised as having any sovereign powers or competence.

These instances illustrate:

—that beneath the surface there exists an easily provoked latent view among certain political sectors which would resist the application of European trends and a redefinition of sovereignty to Gibraltar;
—that, however unresponsive to the modern context this view is, it demonstrates that there is tremendous resistance in certain Spanish political quarters that resist embracing a softer line over Gibraltar;
—that Spain must tread a difficult balancing act between its hawks and those prepared to consider new ways of dealing with Gibraltar (and that moderates must have one eye on Spanish hardliners and another on regional nationalists as potential destabilising and driving forces throughout the process).

[188] Mentioned by Spanish Secretary of State Bernardino Leon in an interview with the *Gibraltar Chronicle* (Gibraltar 27 October 2004), though this in itself was not new, as it had been talked about by the UK as its position during the failed joint sovereignty talks: see the Statement to the House of Commons on 5 February 2002 by Foreign Secretary, Jack Straw.

[189] Spanish Foreign Minister.

[190] Answers to Questions by Spanish Foreign Minister to Senate on 3 November 2004.

While the traditional political establishment in Spain may have difficulties accepting the right of the people of Gibraltar to independence (or even self-determination) because of its own internal constitutional arrangements, it should be less difficult to accept Gibraltar as a stateless nation and as a historic community if aspirations fall short of separatist intentions. Spain has been described as a 'regionalised unitary state'.[191] Articles 1 and 2 of the Spanish Constitution explicitly recognise three important principles—constitutional pluralism, the vesting of sovereignty and the right to self-government as a historic nation.[192] These form the core of the issues faced by Gibraltar. Spain already recognises the Basque 'country' and the Catalan 'nation' as part of its constitutional architecture as well as other historic nations.[193] For Spain to apply just equivalent philosophy in its approach to the Gibraltar issue would not entail either an acceptance of separatist aspirations or a renunciation of its claim to sovereignty. It would though represent a significant psychological and practical advance in the negotiating body language. If Spain did proceed on a basis that de facto there is a stateless nation in Gibraltar, with a history and cohesion, that require it (at the very least because Britain is constitutionally, politically and morally bound) to have regard to its expressed wishes, then a footing for genuine and enduring discussions leading to progress and resolution of this conflict could be laid. In exchange, Gibraltar could—while maintaining its own belief and assertion of its right to self-determination—not necessarily require Spain to formally accept this as a lever to facilitate a resolution. Participation of Gibraltarian civil society represented through its elected representatives in enduring talks with Britain and Spain in accordance with the correct constitutional and pluralistic context and the consequent debilateralisation of the attempts to discuss Gibraltar's future status would be a significant first step at resolving this issue.

On 17 December 2004, after technical talks between the three Governments, a statement was issued which seemed to herald a new opportunity. In it 'and without prejudice to their respective positions, the Governments of the United Kingdom, the Kingdom of Spain and Gibraltar [confirmed] . . . the establishment of a new three-sided forum for dialogue on Gibraltar, separate from the Brussels process.'[194] The key elements of the forum were agreed to be that:

[191] A Ross and M Salvador Crespo, 'The Effect of Devolution on Implementation of EC Law in Spain and the UK' (2003) 28 EL Rev 210.

[192] S Tierney, *Constitutional Law and National Pluralism* (Oxford, OUP, 2004) 117–21.

[193] M Herrero de Miñón, *Derechos Historicos y Constitucion* (Madrid, Tecnos, 1998).

[194] Joint Declaration of 17 December 2004 between the Governments of the UK, Spain and Gibraltar. Implicit though was that the bilateral Brussels process that included discussions on sovereignty could still be considered alive.

—dialogue will be on an open agenda basis and therefore any of the participants may raise any issue relating to or affecting Gibraltar;

—without prejudice to their constitutional status (including the fact that Gibraltar is not a sovereign independent State) each of the three parties will have its own separate voice and each would participate on the same basis;

—any decisions or agreements reached within the forum must be agreed by all three participants; if the three parties wish to take a decision on an issue in the forum where formal agreement would properly be between the United Kingdom and Spain it is understood that the UK will not agree thereto without the Government of Gibraltar's consent.[195]

The stated purpose was to 'endeavour to create a constructive atmosphere of mutual confidence and co-operation for the benefit and prosperity of Gibraltar and the whole region, in particular the *Campo de Gibraltar*.'[196] There is no doubt that this was a radical breakthrough in putting any talks over Gibraltar on a proper footing. The Conservative Opposition in Spain renounced it and asserted that they would review the legalities of the Agreement to see if this was capable of challenge in the Spanish courts.[197]

2006—The Córdoba Agreements and Constitutional Reforms: Two Steps Forward, One Step Back

In September 2006, after a series of technical meetings, the Governments of Britain, Spain and Gibraltar announced a series of Agreements at the picturesque Spanish town of Córdoba. As highlighted in chapter 3, there were a number of agreements to improve and remove long-term irritants to the relationship between Spain and Gibraltar. These spanned issues such as frontier flows,[198] telecommunications[199] and pensions to trans-

[195] Joint Declaration of 17 December 2004, ibid. This last phrase and the previous para implied that there was at least 'an issue'—code for sovereignty—that was bilateral for the UK and Spain. It therefore demonstrated this was not a complete break with the past.

[196] The Campo de Gibraltar is the common description given to the Spanish region most proximate to Gibraltar. It is made up of several towns and municipalities and has a population of about 200,000.

[197] Statements by Opposition Leader Mariano Rajoy to *El País* (Madrid 17 December 2004).

[198] As has been highlighted through this work border delays and perceived hindrance to freedom of movement has been a constant for years. The Agreements at Córdoba promised to establish a system of two red and green channels 'in both directions' to ease the flow of traffic. A mechanism was also agreed to monitor the functioning of those arrangements and to continue to improve commercial and non-commercial frontier fluidity.

[199] It was agreed that Gibraltar's international dialling code would be recognised. This unblocked the usage in Spain of mobile telephones issued by Gibraltar carriers and released an unlimited supply of numbers into Gibraltar's telephone numbering plan. It also ended a long-standing economic dispute between Gibraltar fixed-line and mobile carriers with Spanish carriers that had been a major political dispute between Gibraltar and Spain.

frontier workers.[200] There was also an agreement on expanded use of the airport.[201] While the various political parties in Gibraltar approved the majority of these agreements there was divergence of opinion as to whether the airport agreement gave rise to concessions at the level of sovereignty, jurisdiction and control.[202]

Neither the effect of these agreements, nor the fact that the parties were engaged in a trilateral process of discussions so soon after the joint sovereignty proposals, should be under-estimated. It was in fact a dramatic step forward of some importance that the three Governments should not only be meeting but that co-operative agreements should emerge. Indeed, the parties were also able to navigate the complex military and strategic issues that arose.[203] However closer scrutiny reveals not only that the aspirations of the parties remained fundamentally unchanged but that the traditional unreformed legal context continued to be applied.

The Córdoba Agreements themselves[204] included a declaration that the 'Government of Gibraltar understands and accepts that references . . . to sovereignty are bilateral to the UK and Spain.'[205] Within the trilateral

[200] For many years Spain and Spanish pensioners groups had sought a resolution to their demands to be paid full pensions for the time spent working in Gibraltar before the frontier was closed in 1969. Those workers had paid nominal social insurance contributions during their time of employment. The UK Government assumed 'indefinite responsibility' for the payment of enhanced pensions to former Spanish workers. Entitled Spanish pensioners were offered to either accept a lump sum payment under the terms of the Agreement (and withdraw from entitlement of regular payments from the Gibraltar Social Insurance Fund) or to continue receipt of regular payments from the Fund. The Spanish pensioners' issues had caused much political pressure and social pressure from interest groups on the three Governments. It had also led to litigation in Gibraltar in 1995 when an attempt was made to judicially review the decision by the Gibraltar Government to wind up the then existing Social Insurance Fund: see *In the Matter of Guzman and Others* [1995–96] Gib LR 217.

[201] Annex 2 to the Córdoba Agreement set out the terms for the 'enhanced' use of Gibraltar airport. The agreement replaced the more controversial 1987 Airport Agreement. It was agreed that as part of the arrangements 'there will also be an end to the current discriminatory restrictions imposed by Spain over use of Spanish airspace by civilian aircraft flying in and out of Gibraltar Airport.' Spain also agreed not to request the exclusion of Gibraltar airport from any more EC measures of general application. One terminal would be built adjacent to the frontier to replace the current terminal. The replacement building would include provision of a level that would overhang the Spanish side in which Spanish officials would be located so that they could conduct advanced clearance and delayed exit checks into and out of the Schengen area. The arrangements would be supervised by a Joint Committee.

[202] For two reasons in particular. First, because of the declaration on sovereignty made in the Agreement: see below. Secondly, the Agreement prescribed relatively complex passenger procedures, the effect of which, critics said, was to allow Spanish officials to exert jurisdictional customs and immigration controls in Gibraltar that touched upon sovereignty.

[203] For a summary of British and Spanish strategic interests see L Romero, '*Lo Estratégico en la Cuestión de Gibraltar*' Madrid, UNISCI Discussion Papers, No 12, October 2006, 135–152.

[204] In both the communiqué and the text of the Airport Agreement that is annexed to it: see below.

[205] Communiqué of the Ministerial Meeting of the Forum of Dialogue on Gibraltar, 18 September 2006, para 3. The Airport Agreement itself drops the words 'in this Communiqué' simply stating that the 'Gibraltar Government understands and accepts that the references to sovereignty are bilateral to the UK and Spain.'

forum it raised the image of bilateralism on the most important issue of all: sovereignty. The Agreements also included a statement that they had 'no implications whatsoever regarding sovereignty and jurisdiction' and that they were 'without prejudice to the respective positions on sovereignty and jurisdiction.' Mere statements that matters were 'without prejudice' were not the end of the matter. Political parties in Gibraltar disagreed as to whether, in practice, there had been concessions on jurisdiction and control in the logistical arrangements of the airport agreement.[206] These were concerned about the powers given to Spanish customs and immigration officials in respect of passengers physically situated in Gibraltar.[207] These arrangements, together with those on supervision[208] and structural ownership of the management of the air terminal[209] raised issues of whether Spanish officials or commercial interests were gaining control or jurisdiction of the airport. There were views on both sides of the issue. The official Spanish Government line was that these agreements were positive for the Spanish State and left untouched its aspirations on sovereignty. The more right-wing PP was heavy in its criticism. In a politico-legal analysis rooted in classic conservative politics, Areilza Carvajal,[210] launched a stinging attack on the Agreements, which represented 'revolutionary concessions'[211] and 'a radical turn in Spanish foreign policy over Gibraltar.'[212] He chastised the Spanish Government for recognising Gibraltarian jurisdiction over the airport and its status at the talks, as well as the loosening of economic restrictions which would allow Gibraltar's economy to expand in a way that would make it not have 'incentives to reconsider its status.'[213] Areilza Carvajal's analysis of the implications of the Agreements would not be borne out by subsequent events.

Whether or not matters were sovereignty-neutral depended on an assessment that looked beyond the label. There was a telling precedent. In 1987 the attempt at a previous Airport Agreement had also carried an almost verbatim statement that it was 'without prejudice' to sovereignty positions. All mainstream Gibraltar political parties had opposed it on the basis that it contained sovereignty concessions in practice. Eventually it

[206] See the press releases of the Progressive Democratic Party of 21 September 2006 and of the Socialist Labour / Liberal Alliance of 25 September 2006.

[207] See cl 7 of the Airport Agreement, 3/4, Annex II to Communiqué cited above.

[208] A Permanent Joint Liaison Committee: cl 5.

[209] A joint venture company owned by Gibraltar and Spanish commercial interests: cl 10.

[210] JM de Areilza Carvajal, '*Los Acuerdos del Foro Trilateral de Diálogo Sobre Gibraltar, Un Análisis Critico*', *Politica Exterior, Papeles FAES*, No 32, 11 October 2006.

[211] ibid 2.

[212] ibid 1.

[213] In effect this urged a return to the policy of the past, when Spain had traditionally relied on restrictions to pressurise Gibraltar to accept a political deal. There has been little evidence that this strategy has produced anything other than the reverse effect. It has been tried unsuccessfully, on and off, for nearly three centuries.

led to the Gibraltar challenge at the European Court of Justice.[214] Indeed statements were made by Spain at the United Nations barely two weeks later, in October 2006, which planted a firm seed of doubt as to whether Spain really considered the matter to be sovereignty-neutral.[215] This fear was bolstered by statements during early November 2006 by the Spanish Foreign Secretary who, in a television interview in Spain, asserted that Spain had made major gains in the Córdoba Agreements and that the airport segment of the agreements was akin to the 1987 Airport Agreement.[216] As this had been rejected in Gibraltar because it had been widely considered to have created sovereignty encroachments, it aroused widespread concern. This almost collapsed the trilateral process and led to a joint statement being issued by the three Governments after a hectic round of patch-up discussions that inter alia stated, 'the Córdoba Airport statement has no implication for sovereignty, jurisdiction or control of Gibraltar Airport. No participant has made a sovereignty advance and no participant has made a sovereignty concession.'[217] This mere re-statement however left unanswered many of the objections raised by Opposition parties in Gibraltar[218] and raised the clear spectre that some Spanish politicians felt the need to transmit a radically different message to their own audience.

Constitutional talks had progressed in parallel to the trilateral talks. The new Constitution was a package that introduced the most significant set of internal governance reforms in 40 years. It clearly demarcated internal competences, devolved more powers to the Gibraltar Government, updated the human rights chapter, reviewed the powers and composition of the Parliament, and generally improved the functions of the institutions of Government. The Constitution also added a reference to self-determination for the first time. All of this was significant, as was the assertion by the United Kingdom to the UN that the acceptance of the

[214] Described in ch 5.

[215] Mentioned in ch 3.

[216] In an interview to the Spanish regional daily, *Area*, in early November 2006, the Foreign Minister remarked that the 2006 Airport Agreement was in almost exact terms to the 1987 Airport Agreement 'word for word and comma for comma.' He observed that the Spanish sovereignty position emerged reinforced from the Córdoba Agreements, that for the first time all three sides had accepted the validity of the Treaty of Utrecht and that sovereignty was bilateral. Mr Moratinos also asserted that Spanish customs and immigration officials would exercise real control over flights into the Schengen area and that the terminal would be jointly managed by Spain. Spanish officials would later say that the Foreign Minister had 'slipped up with a minor imprecision'. For its part, the Gibraltar Government, which had at first rejected the veracity of reports that the Spanish Foreign Minister could have made such remarks, pressed for a correction: *Gibraltar Chronicle* (Gibraltar, 9 November 2006).

[217] Joint Press Release issued by the *Ministerio de Asuntos Exteriores y Cooperación* of Spain, the Foreign and Commonwealth Office of the UK and the Government of Gibraltar, 9 November 2006.

[218] These largely concerned the customs and immigration arrangements and whether Spanish officials would be exercising jurisdiction and control in Gibraltar.

Constitution in referendum was an 'act of self-determination',[219] and that it believed that Gibraltar should not be on the list of non-self-governing territories.[220] The engagement of Gibraltar in trilateral talks by Spain was also a positive innovation. Even though constitutional reform had been on the cards for a long time with the start of exploratory talks as far back as 1998 it is true that the climate—post 2004—that had fostered a process of trilateral talks on co-operation had certainly also facilitated the achievement of constitutional reform. Without that constitutional reform would still have been achievable but it would have developed in a climate of confrontation so, almost certainly, it would have made the package look different.[221] In that way, it was an opportunity seized with both hands, even though for reasons that are set out below it did not deliver a conclusive package of reforms.

The Select Committee had, when making its proposals in 2002, made clear that the twin objectives were achieving internal reform (so-called 'modernisation') and decolonisation in accordance with Article 73 of the United Nations Charter.[222] However, while internal governance reforms had been achieved, the advances on external governance or status were much more limited. A section was inserted into the Constitution[223] that made clear that matters devolved to the Gibraltar Government remained the responsibility of Gibraltar, irrespective of whether they acquired a European dimension. Gibraltar did achieve significant internal progress and some 'sovereignty' gains, the most important change in the latter category being the clause on self-determination inserted into Chapter One of the Constitution. Undoubtedly, seen as an overall package, the 2006 Constitution represented a major advance from the 1969 Constitution along the road to full self-government. However, sufficiency of power, representation and influence at the European and external governance level was what was missing from the 2006 constitutional reforms and remained the issue to be principally tackled.

The Spanish position, made clear at the conclusion of the negotiations between the United Kingdom and Gibraltar, was that Spain acquiesced to and dropped its long-standing objection to constitutional reform, because it considered these were only of an internal governance nature and did not touch upon decolonisation or status.[224] The United Kingdom position was

[219] Letter of 22 January 2007 n 157 above.

[220] Of course, that last statement in itself does not guarantee an enlightened constitutional status, but merely the acquisition of formal decolonisation, if consummated.

[221] The prospect of achieving a reference to self-determination in the Constitution was opposed quite strongly for several years throughout the process, and there is no guarantee as to what would have happened to this in a different climate.

[222] Select Committee Report, 23 January 2002, House of Assembly, Gibraltar, 2.

[223] Referred to in ch 5, 232–3.

[224] See the exchange of letters during 28–31 March 2006 between Foreign Secretary Jack Straw and Spanish Foreign Minister Miguel Ángel Moratinos ('the Straw–Moratinos' letters).

that Gibraltar (as well as other overseas territories) should be taken off the UN list of non-self-governing territories, and that the referendum by which the Constitution had been accepted was an act of self-determination.[225] It confirmed that the United Kingdom retained responsibility for external affairs and that the Constitution in no way diminished British sovereignty over Gibraltar.[226] The United Kingdom added that its view was that by Article X of the Treaty of Utrecht 'independence would only be an option for Gibraltar with Spain's consent.'[227] Importantly—and at the request of the Gibraltar delegation to the constitutional talks, who were concerned about the implications of accepting the Constitution in the face of an assertion that was strongly rejected by them—the Despatch then continued, 'Her Majesty's Government takes note that Gibraltar does not share the view that this constraint exists and that their acceptance of this Constitution is on that basis.'[228] Interestingly and while the Straw-Moratinos letters recorded in almost verbatim terms parts of the Despatch to the 2006 Constitution this last qualification was not part of it.[229]

The attitude expressed by the Spanish Foreign Minister in correspondence was poignant. Internal governance reforms were only acceptable if they did not entail any change in the international status of Gibraltar.[230] In his letter, Mr Moratinos asserted that neither the Constitution nor referendum[231] would affect 'the ongoing process of decolonisation under the United Nations mandate.' Spain went on to make the point that its interpretation of the inclusion of a reference to self-determination in the Constitution was that its language recognised 'the different circumstances that affect Gibraltar' and that the Constitution was without prejudice to Spain's long-standing position on the sovereignty of the isthmus.[232] Finally, Spain called on the United Kingdom to pursue sovereignty discussions with it over Gibraltar.[233] Given the Spanish Government's

[225] Letter of 22 January 2007 from the Permanent Representative of the UK to the United Nations n 157 above.

[226] Despatch to the 2006 Constitution: cited in ch 3.

[227] Para 5 of the Despatch. Though for the reasons expressed earlier in this chapter the solidity of this position is doubted.

[228] ibid para 6.

[229] The Despatch had substantially been agreed at the conclusion of the constitutional talks on 17 March 2006. It was not formally made public until July 2006. The Straw–Moratinos letters occurred between 28–31 March 2006. Whether the Spanish Government had privately been shown a draft of the Despatch that was being canvassed with that qualification is unknown.

[230] Letter from Miguel Ángel Moratinos to Jack Straw dated 28 March 2006.

[231] He described this as 'this poll' that 'is no more than the democratic expression . . . by the inhabitants of Gibraltar of their right to choose an improved system of modern and effective Government.': letter of 28 March 2006, cited above.

[232] As stated previously, the Gibraltar airport is built on a strip of land referred to as 'the isthmus'. Spain claims that the isthmus was not ceded to the UK under the Treaty of Utrecht and that Britain has no title to this land under Utrecht. The British position rejects that and in the alternative claims title under prescriptive rights.

[233] Under the Brussels Talks—thus once again confirming its wish to retain bilateralism and the context of old sovereignty.

assertions of the consequences of the Constitution on status and on sovereignty, the British Government felt compelled to reply on 31 March 2006 that Mr Straw's first letter 'made no reference to a change to Gibraltar's international status, nor to a link between the new Constitution, any referendum by which it may be accepted by the people of Gibraltar and the process of decolonisation.' Mr Straw re-stated the British view that the relationship between the UK and Gibraltar could not be described as colonial. The United Kingdom went on to record the fact that Britain's historical position on the principles applicable to the Gibraltar dispute in the context of the right to self-determination was different to that held by Spain. Mr Straw concluded by saying there was no prospect of sovereignty negotiations 'with which Gibraltar was not content.'[234]

The eagerness to obtain decolonisation was evident in certain political quarters in Gibraltar.[235] The view of Government and Opposition in Gibraltar in 2006 was that the new Constitution should be accepted by the United Nations as sufficient to obtain formal de-listing and decolonisation.[236] However, this emphasises the fact that decolonisation does not necessarily guarantee adequate reform or a final status. Not having adequately dealt with the external governance structures and, given that the self-government achieved fell short of independence, all it would mean, if formal decolonisation was obtained, is that the achievement of further reforms would have to come at another time and that decolonisation was being achieved on the basis of an incomplete governance package. Whether in fact the United Nations would agree to remove Gibraltar from the list of non-self-governing territories on the basis of this 2006 Constitution or not is uncertain, though initial signs since enactment of the Constitution do not seem encouraging. The attitude of the UN on a status that has fallen short of independence has not been untroubled.[237] This is especially complex, given that the package upon which to achieve decolonisation is put forward within the so-called 'fourth option' that the United Nations Committee of 24 has seemed reluctant to accept. Though the effect of the reforms on the UN decolonisation stage is still to be

[234] This last statement was in some respects one of the more important statements in that letter as it was a markedly different position to that adopted in 2001.

[235] See eg Leader of the Opposition's speech to UN Seminar on Decolonisation in Grenada, *Gibraltar Chronicle* (Gibraltar 25 May 2007).

[236] Of late the stance by the GSLP/Liberal opposition has also been to ask the UN to confirm—if de-listing cannot be achieved on the basis of the 2006 Constitution—what else would need to be introduced to achieve decolonisation. The Gibraltar Government by contrast have informed the UN that it considers that Gibraltar has now achieved a decolonised status and in June 2008 decided to stop attending the UN Committee of 24.

[237] See the experience of the West Indies associated status territories and Puerto Rico, Crawford n 162 above, 626–27. For a review of the federation and free association experiments in the West Indies, see SR Ashton and D Killingray (eds), *The West Indies*, British Documents on the End of Empire, Series B, vol 6 (London, TSO, Institute of Commonwealth Studies, 1999).

determined, it is safe to say that the reforms did not significantly alter Gibraltar's domestic status.[238] The package of reforms was a stepping-stone to further internal reforms, external governance reforms and progress on decolonisation (at two levels—the UN level[239] and under domestic law).[240]

An Evaluation of 2006

So while 2006 brought internal governance reforms and trilateral agreements on co-operation, the legitimate questions raised were how much progress had actually been achieved on status and had the principal deficit—the methodology of bilateralism—been definitively and effectively cured? The answers to those questions were disappointing. Undoubtedly, the 2006 developments were a major step forward on internal governance and promoting dialogue and co-operation between the parties, but they neither conclusively addressed the principal deficit of bilateralism nor applied the correct legal context to the sovereignty environment, without which definitive progress on external governance and status would remain hampered.

It is important to resist the temptation to be over-critical, given that the parties had successfully stepped back from the desolate political brink in which they had found themselves by the end of 2002. But the factor that was the virtue of the 2004 tripartite formula was also the reason it was unable to address the core theoretical issues. Rather than deal head-on with the issue of sovereignty the 2004 process sought to park it. While this minimised political sensitivities and was able to deliver some progress on historic grievances, it did not realistically apply any modern legal thinking to the dispute or give sufficient primacy either to the views of peoples or the recognition of key issues. It may be that the 2004 process was structured in the only manner possible to forge a way forward at that time. In that way its value could be to provide a transitional step towards a clearer understanding of the context between the parties.

[238] If at all—the Despatch proclaimed that 'the UK will retain its full international responsibility for Gibraltar . . . Gibraltar will remain listed as a British Overseas Territory': para 4 of the Despatch. A wider range of considerations would need evaluating to assess whether Gibraltar had in effect acquired Statehood under the criteria indicated in ch 3. It is submitted that this has, as yet, not occurred. Even if the political declarations of 2006–07 by the UK were to be akin to a 'Balfour Declaration' for Gibraltar—it would still be necessary to have a Statute of Westminster equivalent.

[239] At which formal de-listing was necessary.

[240] To ensure that the territory is excluded from the definition of 'colony' and to achieve such other reforms that are consonant with that. It could be done, in a free association context, by extending the definition of 'associated State' to Gibraltar or by creating a specific provision.

Several instances highlighted the ambivalent signals sent by the parties following the 2006 Córdoba Agreements, or simply the application of the traditional but now ill-fitting legal context to this dispute. First, the obstructionism, by now a familiar trait to bilateralism, continued. The obstacles associated with classic bilateralism continued to manifest themselves, notwithstanding the impetus to achieve practical co-operation at trilateral talks. Spain blocked an international sanctions agreement on North Korea,[241] deployed political objections to derail Gibraltar's application to UEFA[242] and continued to block the ratification by the European Union of the International Convention on the Protection of the Child because of its reluctance to recognise the external competence of Gibraltar authorities.[243] All this was the situation arrived at in early 2007 in the supposed 'new climate' fostered by the trilateral talks. In fact the better assessment is that, while there had been significant advances, equally, a number of examples demonstrated the limitations of these talks and the need to overhaul the theoretical and legal context being applied.[244] In a Written Reply, the Commission confirmed[245] that, apart from the 1996 Hague Convention, 'the *bilateral* problem' between Spain and the United Kingdom was preventing 'all other Member States from ratifying' four other Conventions. In December 2007 agreement was reached between Spain and the United Kingdom, after consultation with Gibraltar, to extend the mechanical arrangements on the transmission of communications from Gibraltar competent authorities, agreed in 2000 for EU Agreements to mixed competence agreements.[246] While this agreement unblocked the problems on ratification of international conventions it was a compromise based on the assumption that little had substantially changed.[247] A practical mechanical

[241] See Replies to Written Question E-0854/07 and E-0853/07 by the European Commission, available at www.europarl.europa.eu and also Gibraltar Government press release of 12 February 2007.

[242] Referred to in ch 3.

[243] See the Reply to Written Question E1839/44 by the European Commission, at which it expressed a degree of powerlessness: 'the Commission can only but strongly encourage the Member States concerned to continue their *bilateral* efforts to find a solution in the near future.' (emphasis added)

[244] There is also some local political criticism that key issues such as an improvement in frontier flows have not been delivered as promised.

[245] European Parliament, Reply to Written Question E2576/07 of 20 June 2007.

[246] The Agreements reached in 2000 were touched upon in ch 4. In essence a system of so-called 'post-boxing' was introduced, by which communications with Spanish competent authorities to and from Gibraltar competent authorities would be sent via an office in the UK's Foreign Office. Mixed competence agreements were defined as 'an international instrument that contains provisions some elements of which fall within the competence of the Member States and to which the Community—if that is permissible under the instrument in question—and the Member States are parties following a Council Decision.' See the exchange of correspondence between Rt Hon David Miliband MP and HE Miguel Ángel Moratinos of 19 December 2007 and annexes thereto.

[247] The principal letters between respective Foreign Secretaries also included the standard rider that the arrangements did not imply 'any change in [the] respective positions on the question of Gibraltar or on the limits of the territory.'

understanding was easier to understand in the politics of 2000, when there was no pretence of a new climate. The 2007 agreement on competent authorities was not one that established the recognition of the external competence of Gibraltar authorities, but rather enshrined the non-recognition by Spain of the external competence of these. It was evidence of *status quo*, not of a new climate of understanding. To underscore this point, the Spanish Council of Ministers recorded that the reason for its agreement to the arrangements was to 'lay emphasis to the merely local nature of Gibraltar authorities that have their origin . . . on the distribution of competences effected by the United Kingdom which is the sovereign State on which this territory which has no international competence is dependent.'[248] To 'reinforce our position on this matter' Spanish Ministers also agreed the text of a unilateral declaration that would be made whenever such an agreement was ratified. This declaration would among other statements set out Spain's view on the 'merely local nature' and 'internal competence' of Gibraltar authorities and that Gibraltar is a territory subject to a UN process of decolonisation for whose external relations the UK is responsible.[249]

Secondly, as highlighted above, the statements set out in the Córdoba Agreements of 2006 were not all they seemed. Notwithstanding the use of sovereignty-neutral language, a critical analysis revealed an ambiguity that could only foster confusion and scope for misunderstandings. Thirdly, at the level of constitutional reform, Spain made clear that its position had not fundamentally changed and remained positioned in 'old sovereignty'. In 2006 Spain had confirmed that it opposed any change in the international status of Gibraltar or progress on external governance issues, because these would have been suggestive of external competence and implicit steps towards external sovereignty/independence. At its heart, Spain continued to believe in the application of the traditional sovereignty context and not its modern meaning. The aspirations of Spain remained remarkably intact. Indeed, in a document issued in April 2007 the Spanish Government reiterated that the policy of co-operation via the tripartite forum had not resolved the fundamental question and that Spain had not 'abandoned its historic claims'.[250] It made clear that it 'maintained its claim over the sovereignty of Gibraltar—that is irrenounceable.'[251] Equally the objectives of Britain seemed also remarkably similar to those it had followed during the unacceptable phase of the joint sovereignty proposals.[252]

[248] See the text of agreements of Spanish Council of Ministers published on the official Spanish Government site: www.la-moncloa.es/consejodeministros.

[249] Spanish Council of Ministers meeting of 28 February 2008, ibid.

[250] *Informe Sobre Gibraltar*, 2007, 49.

[251] ibid. Also confirming that the way ahead was the bilateral process established under the Brussels Agreement.

[252] Jack Straw had told the Commons on 5 February 2002 that Britain had four objectives: to preserve the unique way of life of Gibraltar; to achieve greater internal self-governance; to

What had changed was the British approach to the methodology of conflict resolution. Britain now seemed to accept that proceeding on sovereignty discussions without Gibraltar was not viable. For Spain, not even its methodology had definitively changed. Its commitment to trilateralism was on issues of co-operation but not on sovereignty. It considered the latter to be firmly ensconced in bilateralism and that the only valid interlocutor for talks on sovereignty remained Britain—hence its insistence on the sovereignty declaration in the Córdoba Communiqué and its statements about sovereignty and status on the constitutional reforms. This nuance was not lost on Spanish academics, and even those with a more liberal approach, such as Del Valle Gálvez,[253] who accepted Gibraltar as a 'sub-State entity that must be taken into account in the search for Anglo–Spanish solutions' rooted such recognition in a policy of bilateralism.[254] Del Valle Gálvez makes clear that the trilateral dialogue was part of a hierarchy of levels of dialogue with the *Comisión Mixta*[255] at its base followed by the Trilateral forum at its intermediate level for trans-boundary co-operation and a 'superior level . . . constituted by the Brussels process for bilateral sovereignty negotiation.'[256] At such a level there are 'two participants, Spain and the UK' and though he accepts that Gibraltar would have its 'own separate and distinct voice' he asserts that this would be with 'no vote.'[257] This analysis falls well short of a realisation of the modern legal context and the realities on the ground.

Difficulties that seem inconsistent with the 2006 Agreements or the climate engendered by them continue to surface from time to time.[258] The fact that these problems continue may not be so difficult to reconcile if the premise of the observation made earlier is accepted—namely, that the 2004 tripartite process has tried to ignore the issue of sovereignty. A climate based on such foundations was bound to be fragile and frequently pierced by reminders of mutual sensitivities. While more cathartic a

achieve practical benefits through co-operation (with Spain); and to put the dispute about sovereignty 'to rest'.

[253] A Del Valle Gálvez, '*Los Acuerdos del Foro de Diálogo Sobre Gibraltar: la Apuesta por la Normalizacion*', Real Instituto Eclano, ARI No 107/2006, 19 October 2006.

[254] ibid 2: NB that the search is for an Anglo–Spanish solution and that Gibraltar must be taken into account, but this does not necessarily mean the wishes of Gibraltar would be adhered to.

[255] The municipal forum—described earlier.

[256] Del Valle Gálvez n 253 above, 5: the only concession he makes to stem bilateralism is that such dialogue could take place under the 'two flags three voices' formula and that Gibraltarian 'consent' is necessary for Anglo–Spanish agreements.

[257] ibid.

[258] In December 2008 Spain blocked a regulation amending four regulations introduced in 2004 establishing the so-called 'Single European Sky' because of issues related to its concerns over the applicability of the regulation to Gibraltar. The Spanish Minister for Transport asked that adoption of the measure be postponed so that it could agree a text that did not affect its sovereignty concerns over the isthmus of Gibraltar. The UK's Transport Secretary in a statement to the House of Commons confirmed that he was hopeful that the matter could be resolved bilaterally: *Gibraltar Chronicle* (Gibraltar 18 December 2008).

process of co-operation that recognised and accepted a new contextual framework based on rights of peoples might engender a climate that, in the long term, could prove more fruitful.

For the agenda of external governance and status issues to be unblocked, the legal context of late sovereignty, stateless nationalism and constitutional pluralism must be fully embraced and acted on. Resolution requires a marriage between the philosophy of the correct legal context and the practicalities of trilateralism. Run properly in application of an acceptance of that plural environment, trilateralism could deliver not only co-operation but a lifting of obstacles that affect further internal self-governance, external governance reforms (achieved at sub-State level and at European Union level), decolonisation and status change. All three parties would engage at all levels and not seek to exclude another from participation in a particular field, as does Spain when it expresses an unwillingness to accept Gibraltar's representatives as participants on the issue of sovereignty. Progress on constitutional reform, external governance and decolonisation could come without a proper atmosphere of trilateralism, but in that event such changes would develop in a spirit of confrontation[259] and there would, no doubt, be problems of enjoyment of such measures. While trilateralism is focussed on co-operation and understanding, the subliminal climate it creates can facilitate a removal of obstacles, further reform and real change. For that to happen, however, the commitment to trilateralism must be combined with an acceptance and application of the proper modern legal context of late sovereignty and stateless nationalism. Understandably the co-operative benefits of the Córdoba agreements and the package of constitutional reforms were seized, but the parties still had some way to go to apply a fundamental reassessment of the conceptual and theoretical legal background to the dispute. In a review of the tripartite process, Oda-Angel observed that it is crucial to recognise the gains made so far if further progress is to be made on the basis that 'co-operation . . . can generate a fluid relationship and normalisation for ever.'[260] However, he also notes:

> It is obvious that the fundamental problem is not solved. The historic claim of Spain over the sovereignty of Gibraltar remains in place and has not changed one iota. Nevertheless given the new climate created by the tripartite forum it could in the medium to long term facilitate the taking of new initiatives like, for example, that of joint sovereignty . . . if that proposal were made it might not obtain the backing of Gibraltarians but at least these could not assert that such a proposal had been made without their participation.[261]

[259] If at all.

[260] F Oda-Angel, *'Gibraltar a un año de la Declaración de Córdoba: la recuperacion de la confianza'*, *Real Instituto Eclano, Documento de Trabajo* 45/2007, www.realinstitutoelcano.org, 20.

[261] ibid 21.

A return to the policies so overwhelmingly rejected in 2002 would demonstrate a failure to understand the reasons for the rejection of the joint sovereignty proposals. This was not based on pure mechanics of representation at the talks designing those proposals but involved a substantive rejection of the principle itself.[262] The fact that fundamentally things did not seem to have changed was not lost on the International Affairs and Defence Section of the House of Commons, who in a Research Paper stated:

> The Tripartite dialogue and the UK-Gibraltar negotiations have to some extent been parallel processes, with issues becoming occasionally intertwined. While the sovereignty question was deliberately put aside by all parties to the dialogue, sovereignty was inevitably at the centre of the constitutional talks. Spain was not a party to the constitutional negotiations, but Spanish contributions to United Nations debates on decolonisation and self-determination—along with those of Gibraltar and UK representatives—punctuated the negotiations and were a reminder that fundamental positions had not wavered in spite of the new spirit of dialogue and co-operation.[263]

There will be no solutions to either the status question or the practical dimension of external governance unless the proper context is applied and there is a true end to bilateralism on everything—including sovereignty. The basis for that solution building lies firstly in recognition that sovereignty is meaningful to all parties. Secondly that Gibraltar is a stateless nation in whose people sovereignty as now defined ultimately vests. Alternatively, at the very least Spain should recognise that rival claims exist and debilateralise sovereignty. In the same way that, for historic reasons, Spain finds it difficult to accept the inclusion of Gibraltar in sovereignty talks, it is equally complex for Gibraltarians to embrace the fact that Spain should participate in talks over the land of Gibraltar. The creation of equal political space and mutual respect is an essential component to take matters forward. Thirdly, it is necessary to recognise that Gibraltar does not, currently, wish to press a separatist agenda and that in exchange for that there should be recognition of it (the stateless nation) and a lifting of any block on decolonisation and external governance reforms. There is no reason why the Spanish Government could not permanently end its more obstructionist stance within the EU and elsewhere given that mainstream Gibraltar political parties seek an interdependent accommodation rather than Statehood.

Bilateralism holds back constitutional reform, decolonisation, status change and governance improvements. The next chapter touches on

[262] This seems clear from the very overwhelming nature of the result. The 2002 referendum rejected the 'principle' of joint sovereignty. In the campaign leading up to the vote it was also clear that the mechanics and structure of the bilateral talks were objected to.

[263] *Gibraltar: Diplomatic and Constitutional Developments*, House of Commons Library, Research Paper 06/48, 11 October 2006, 22.

certain governance changes that could be made to deliver improvements but these must be seen in their proper context. They are suggestions of net improvements to net aspects of the deficit. The biggest obstacle is bilateralism itself and the inability to embrace the new legal context. Once this is overcome it will be much easier to deal with the net deficits.

All-issue Comprehensive Trilateralism

Operated properly a permanent and successful trilateral approach is a key to the solution-building process between the parties, and can provide a variety of initial benefits, namely:

—an end to acrimony and obstructionism and the opportunity to create a new climate of trust;
—the provision of time so as to be able to consider any parallel or analogous developments carefully so these can, if necessary, be factored into their particular context;
—the removal of emotion and symbolism, which hampers the conflict resolution effort;
—securing normality (or as much of it as possible).

Without these benefits accruing it is unrealistic to expect a successful transition to a modified relationship in accordance with the modern theoretical context. A permanent end to bilateralism[264] must as a necessary first step bring a lasting end to acrimony and obstructionism and create a climate of trust. This should be followed by Spain removing the visible issues of obstructionism at different levels. While the 2006 Córdoba agreements brought solutions to long-standing hindrances in a number of fields more than anything else the parties face the hurdle of long-standing scepticism as to whether these are genuine or will endure. There are signs that some of the restrictions[265] remain and this operates as a constitutional, practical and psychological drag. Indeed, there is always the fear that even this partial and imperfect process will be retrenched in the event of the re-election of the more hard-line Spanish Conservative opposition.[266]

264 On everything including sovereignty.

265 In January 2007 Spanish frontier officials again refused to recognise Gibraltar-issued ID cards as valid travel documents, blocking access temporarily. This was resolved after discussions between officials that had been preceded by tit-for-tat non-recognition by Gibraltar.

266 Encouraged by JM de Areilza Carvajal in his article '*Los Acuerdos del Foro Trilateral de Diálogo Sobre Gibraltar, Un Análisis Critico*', *Politica Exterior, Papeles FAES*, No 32, 11 October 2006, 7. There was a contrast between the political manifestos for the 2008 general elections of the PSOE and that of the PP. While stating that the objective of recovering sovereignty was irrenounceable the PSOE maintained that efforts at co-operation through the tripartite should be intensified—*Programa Electoral 2008*, PSOE, 296 www.psoe.es. For the PP the bilateral Brussels talks had to be restarted with the objective of finding a solution to the dispute because the 'existence of the colony fractures Spain's territorial integrity.' The basic

It would be important to break boldly with the obstructionism of the past to increase confidence and the prospects of real and lasting co-operation. This would foster the basis for cohabitive federalism in all areas of policy and administration.[267] As Herrero de Miñón[268] notes, instead of boldly recognising the claims of historic nations, States have tended to grant functional concessions on powers and competences, which both fail to satisfy the nations and weaken the State. The vicious cycle then recommences with further claims and further insufficient concessions whereas recognition of the principles of plurinationalism would stabilise the Constitution. While recognition of *locus standi* in the trilateral talks is possible, it is politically difficult to expect any degree of acceptance amounting to capitulation to historic arguments by any party in the Gibraltar macro-dispute. More politically realistic, as explained above, is the strategy of gradual movement and parking the form of final status until last.

The provision of time is important, first because lasting improvement in a dispute that has endured for nearly three centuries can only be judged over time. Secondly, as previously highlighted, it is crucial so as to be able to take account of any analogous developments within Britain and Spain that may influence and affect the perspective within those States to the Gibraltar issue. There must also be a conscious effort to ensure that the symbolism associated with sovereignty does not rear its head in any provocative guise. As part of the Good Friday Agreement package, the parties in Northern Ireland acknowledged:

> the sensitivity of symbols and emblems for public purposes, and the need in particular in creating the new institutions to ensure that such symbols and emblems are used in a manner which promotes mutual respect rather than division. Arrangements will be made to monitor this issue and consider what action might be required.[269]

The parties need to move from focussing on the methodology of dialogue to the methodology of co-operation, and do so by looking at and establishing adequate intergovernmental, regional and supra-national structures. The function of trilateralism is first to achieve dialogue and then co-operation.[270] Having achieved the initial objectives, a permanent

difference was that the more conservative and nationalist PP placed a policy of regional co-operation more in the background than the PSOE that gave this more importance. The policy on the fundamentals of sovereignty was similar: see *Las Ideas Claras*, PP, para 561, 2008, www.pp.es.

267 See below.

268 Herrero de Miñón n 193 above.

269 Good Friday Agreement, 34.

270 In a communiqué of 2 July 2008 the parties to the Tripartite Forum confirmed that talks were occurring on a wide range of matters such as the environment, maritime communications, judicial, customs and police co-operation, financial services and tax: see *Communiqué of the Ministerial Meeting of the Forum of Dialogue on Gibraltar*, 2 July 2008, Government of Gibraltar, Press Office, 161/2008. This was confirmed in a further communique on 21 July 2009.

climate of trilateralism could also in its second phase adopt cross-border structures that could foster co-operation in the context of full recognition of multi-national pluralism, the diffusion of power and the de-fusion of practical sovereignty.[271] In essence, the crux of this would depend on the voluntary pooling of power as an exercise of the sovereignty of each side, and without threatening the sovereignty of either. This would reflect what is occurring in Europe as a matter of course and is part of the gradual gravitation towards this cohabitive multi-national federalism encouraged by European trends and Gibraltar's special features.

The Northern Irish Good Friday Agreement provides interesting parallels. It created in '*Strand Two*' a North-South Ministerial Council bringing together those with Executive responsibilities in both Northern Ireland and the Republic of Ireland to develop co-operation on matters of interest.[272] '*Implementation Bodies*' were then to be established under this Council on specific areas of co-operation. The Council is specifically endowed with power to 'consider institutional or cross-sectoral matters (including in relation to the EU).'[273] In this way, it combines the need for ordinary co-operation on a cross border basis in this contentious dispute and also for co-operation on the European dimension. In many ways these are also the two levels of co-operation on which Gibraltar and Spain need to find a *modus vivendi* for their cohabitation. The Council sets up a Joint Secretariat and, specifically on Europe, the Agreement provides that it will

> consider the European dimension of relevant matters, including the implementation of EU policies and programmes and proposals under consideration in the EU framework. . . . Arrangements to be made to ensure that the views of the Council are taken into account and represented appropriately at relevant EU meetings.[274]

This last aspect—interactivity before the EU—is an important feature. The Council is a supra-national body established under this agreement designed to foster co-operation and decision-making on matters of mutual interest as well as representing that position at EU level.[275] The context of its operation under the umbrella of the European dimension is an interesting analogy.

While the mere existence of a partial trilateral process for Gibraltar is a good sign it is too informal in structure and frequency. The North–South

[271] For a variety of methods based on the Swiss experience see W Linder, *Swiss Democracy—Possible Solutions to Conflict in Multi-Cultural Societies* (Hampshire, MacMillan, 1998).

[272] Good Friday Agreement, 22–25.

[273] Para 3(iii) at 22.

[274] Para 17, 24.

[275] Though in practice of course the Northern Irish arrangements encountered difficulties as a result of the 'stalling' of devolution see A Trench (ed), *The State of the Nations 2001: The Second Year of Devolution in the UK* (Exeter, The Constitution Unit, Imprint Academic, 2001) 156–57.

Council is funded by both administrations and given permanent technical and human resources. The Gibraltar process falls well short of the Irish model, which demonstrates a capacity for co-operation with safeguards for the sovereignty of each side.[276] Decisions can be taken separately for each jurisdiction or for cross-border policies.[277] An Irish-type model cross-border Council could be established by statutory endorsement[278] and empowered to take decisions by each jurisdiction. It could provide funding for specific projects and a working secretariat of officials. These structures should not represent a threat to the emotional issue of sovereignty as each side would be voluntarily co-operating (with the clear ability to also decide to cease to participate). Co-operation—as in the Irish model—could be established across a clearly demarcated list of subjects such as tourism, economic co-operation, social, cultural and sporting matters or any other issue of mutual interest that could deliberately avoid the more controversial subjects.[279]

The important aspect of the Irish model is also the representation of views at EU level. If followed in any model set up between Gibraltar and Spain this could provide a vehicle which could agree positions of common interest and remove the imagery of litigation between the Commission and Gibraltar in which Spain intervenes to oppose positions taken by Gibraltar.[280] The constitutionalisation of the Irish model had in fact also been preceded by an act of legitimacy through the endorsement in referenda in both Northern Ireland and the Republic. In that analysis the Irish model includes many elements that recognise the modern constitutional context: an act of legitimacy; a structure based on cross-border constitutional pluralism; its constitutionalisation; and the creation of supranational entities to deal with the European dimension.[281]

Clearly steps to establish these bodies need to be cautious, because of the sensitive political climate and the dramatically opposed positions. As Keating notes, when considering cross-border collaboration:

> a critical element in the success of these ventures is precisely that they should not challenge State borders and they only work where border issues are settled. In this way it is possible to work around the border, to penetrate it peacefully;

[276] Though clearly there are also aspects of the Good Friday Agreement that would be unwelcome and perceived as encroachments into sovereignty if paralleled in Gibraltar. The secret would be to draw on the positive aspects of the Northern Irish Model.

[277] Para 5(iv) at 23.

[278] eg the Irish Constitution was amended to recognise the powers of the bodies set up under the Agreement and to sanction this transfer of 'sovereignty' *qua* power to these supranational bodies.

[279] For a review of recent areas of co-operation (as well as EU areas) see R Hazell (ed), *The State of the Nations 2003: The Third Year of Devolution in the UK* (Exeter, The Constitution Unit, Imprint Academic, 2003) 149–50.

[280] See ch 5.

[281] Though clearly there were numerous obstacles that led to the temporary suspension of devolution arrangements. The review of these is outwith this work.

where borders are contested, then almost any proposal for collaboration can be seen by State elites as a threat to the border itself.[282]

This is what commonly happens in Gibraltar when voices of dissent and concern are raised whenever the idea of cross-border co-operation is mooted. It is also important that the cross-border arrangements are seen to be firmly focussed on the objective of inclusive, lasting and fully trilateral co-operation and not so as to promote an undesirable spectre of territorial annexation. In Northern Ireland, as Wilford and Wilson note, this point was made by the Democratic Unionist Party in its counter-proposals to Strand Two.[283] In that sense it is an unfortunately ambivalent position when Spain stresses that 'we want co-operation independent of sovereignty. That does not mean that Spain give up its claim. The co-operation is done in the context of the claim on sovereignty.'[284]

Setting the dispute into a proper and modern legal context that recognises the conceptual evolution of sovereignty, nationalism and the importance of people as the essential element in the achievement of any solution will provide an opportunity to break definitively with the methodologies of the past. But this is proving more difficult than anticipated.

282 M Keating, *Plurinational Democracy, Stateless Nations in a Post-Sovereignty Era* (Oxford, OUP, 2001) 154.

283 R Wilford and R Wilson, Northern Ireland, 'While you take the High Road' in A Trench (ed), *The Dynamics of Devolution: The State of the Nations 2005* (Exeter, The Constitution Unit, Imprint Academic, 2005) 72–73.

284 Interview with Bernardino de León, Spanish Secretary of State for Foreign Affairs, *Gibraltar Chronicle* (Gibraltar 27 October 2004).

7

Making Advances—Power, Influence and Representation Within the European Dimension and the Status Dilemma

INTRODUCTION

AS HIGHLIGHTED IN the previous chapter, the major issues that remained unresolved following the 2006 Constitution were those of external governance and international status.[1] Removing the negative influence of bilateralism and replacing this with productive, enduring, all-issue trilateralism would facilitate improvements at both levels. Given the pre-eminence of the Union as the main theatre of external governance for Gibraltar, obtaining these advances at European level is important. Some of the practical self-governance improvements depend on general reforms being adopted at supra-national level and on progress at the macro-dispute level. Other changes can be achieved with the co-operation of the United Kingdom and within national constitutional arrangements. The role of the United Kingdom Government at all levels in facilitating the climate for these changes has already been touched upon. To the extent that change is dependent on the UK as the Primary Driver the disappearance of Spanish objection will at the very least create a positive psychological constitutional climate for change.

This chapter traces key areas within which Gibraltar could acquire more power, representation and influence in the context of the prevailing themes of participatory governance, democracy, legitimacy and the evolved concepts of nationalism and sovereignty. Practical advances could be secured at all four levels described in the previous chapter.[2] Apart from these practical improvements constitutional developments within the European Union, and especially within Britain and Spain, should be monitored, as

[1] Even though there was also scope for further internal governance reform.
[2] Macro-dispute level, EU level, State and domestic levels.

these might influence the pace and manner of change that can be applied to Gibraltar.[3]

The chapter concludes by suggesting that proceeding in a genuinely trilateral manner could even facilitate the emergence of a new understanding between the parties, leading to decolonisation and a development of a special international status. The underlying ethos behind this endgame should be to proactively seek or gradually drift towards a status which accords with the trends that are transforming Europe into a non-traditional 'federalised system':[4] in essence, to embrace a cohabitive federalism based on multi-national constitutional pluralism. The quest in attempting to resolve this dispute is to find an avenue toward the emergence of a new status by consent and by evolution.[5] The more conventional way of achieving maximum self-government is by an easily identified constitutional event on a declaration of independence.[6] However, as Oliver identifies in the case of Canada, New Zealand and Australia, it is possible to achieve this constitutional change by a series of conventions and evolution.[7] While the clarity of an overall constitutional agreement is attractive it has the potential of arousing acrimony, confrontation, misunderstanding and as a consequence obstructionism. In view of the political sensitivity of the Gibraltar issue it would make sense, as an alternative possibility, for change to be settled by practical evolution rather than bold one-off events. This could emerge as conflict-resolution prospers.

THE EUROPEAN UNION AND SUB-STATE MANAGEMENT

It has been said that the European Union is 'region-blind'[8] in failing to adequately recognise and provide regions with proper influence into the Union's decision-making process. Sub-State executives with law-making powers have the obligations to transpose European directives and imple-

[3] While EU institutions have primarily adopted the stance of witness rather than participant in the Gibraltar issue, this could also change in an environment that leads to an enduring methodological change, real governance improvements and a new status.

[4] J Loughlin, 'The Regional Question, Subsidiarity and the Future of Europe' in S Weatherill and U Bernitz (eds), *The Role of Regions and Sub National Actors in Europe* (Oxford, Hart Publishing, 2005) 170.

[5] As in Canada, there is a place for constitutional change by convention. Spanish consent may not be obtained, and so in that sense consent and evolution are alternatives.

[6] The majority of Commonwealth States.

[7] P Oliver, *The Constitution of Independence—The Development of Constitutional Theory in Australia, Canada and New Zealand* (Oxford, OUP, 2005) 153–95. The point has been made in ch 5 that for a variety of reasons—principally size and political muscle—Gibraltar is at a disadvantage to such large nations and cannot strictly be compared to these or rely on such comparators.

[8] S Weatherill, 'The Challenge of the Regional Dimension in the European Union' in Weatherill and Bernitz (eds) n 4 above, 2–6.

ment European obligations. Unless protected by adequate national arrangements they suffer the 'competence creep' described in the previous chapter. Moreover, the greater use of 'soft law' mechanisms, rather than signifying a positive reduction in the process of encroachment into powers, has represented indirect erosion of these.[9] Subsidiarity—whilst heralded as a major advance—has not really halted the competence creep or the lack of consultation and influence suffered by regions because 'subsidiarity depends on the internal arrangements activating it'[10] and in many cases—such as Gibraltar—these are poor.

It is true that not all Member States have a 'regional issue' to deal with: hence, why obtaining advances within the State constitutional arrangements is so important, as it is unrealistic to expect a template solution to emanate from Europe when those issues may not arise for all Member States or might cause further internal constitutional issues for some others. Nevertheless, the regional issue affects a significant number of Member States and it has been noted that 'in the European Union 56.3 per cent of the population (pre-enlargement) live in a region with legislative power.'[11] Pre-enlargement there were 75 regions with legislative power in the European Union. Post-enlargement 'the Union will comprise about 250 regions and 100,000 local authorities.'[12] The Committee of the Regions made clear in its contribution to the Convention on the Future of Europe that it believed several steps had to be taken to improve the consultative structures, power and influence of the regions. Doing so is not just about 'effective management of the problem of governing. They are associated with identity, representation and democratic legitimacy.'[13] Indeed it is important that supra-national institutions and State executives perceive and accept this correlation to legitimacy, because marginalising sub-State executives stands a greater risk of alienating the citizen too. An absence of adequate safeguards can provoke a 'let us in—leave us alone'[14] reaction by regions that first struggle to have a voice and then, if repelled vociferously, reject the European process. This in turn has an effect on the citizen who is constantly exposed to a barrage of criticism about the European Union and explanations based on the remoteness of European institutions from the average European. In that sense, as Weatherill has remarked, while the Convention was an opportunity to secure these 'durable safeguards for local autonomy' it failed to do so, and also ' missed a chance to bring the

[9] ibid 8.
[10] ibid 14.
[11] Kimmo Kiljunen MP, CONV 321/02, 7 October 2002, 2.
[12] Contribution from the Six Observers of the Committee of the Regions to the Convention 'The Role of the Regional and Local Authorities in European Integration' CONV 520/03, 30 January 2003.
[13] Weatherill in Weatherill and Bernitz (eds) n 4 above, 10.
[14] C Jeffrey, 'Regions and the European Union: Letting them In and Leaving them Alone' in Weatherill and Bernitz (eds) n 4 above, 35.

EU closer to the citizen.'[15] The CE and Lisbon Treaty included provisions to achieve greater consultation of national parliaments or a strengthening of the standing of the Committee of the Regions but have fallen well short of regional demands for involvement in the decision-making process.[16]

THE PRIMACY OF THE SUB-STATE EXECUTIVE LEVEL

There are several spheres within which it is necessary to obtain progress to secure greater power, representation and influence for the benefit of sub-State executive Government, the domestic Parliamentary institution and individual citizens.[17] As highlighted,[18] by far the most important level at which to obtain the most direct and senior influence on policy formulation and law-making is that of executive influence. Other areas are important too, but do not hold the primacy of influence that can be achieved if structures to deliver better influence for sub-State government are in place. It is important in considering the adequacy or mechanics of those structures to understand the process of decision-making within the European sphere and the central importance of influence being obtained within civil service circles and at non-ministerial level.[19]

From a cold perspective of the raw influence that tiers of players in the governmental process can exercise, the influence of executive Government is much higher than that of the legislature, the individual citizen or the NGO participant in the process of governance. For sub-State territories the same is true, except that there are challenges within State constitutional arrangements and the European integration process that also give rise to obstacles in the path towards securing that degree of influence. For Gibraltar the ordinary issues that affect other non-independent Governments are further complicated by the special challenge of the territorial sovereignty dispute.

From the point of view of the acquisition of legitimacy it is important to identify how the greatest sense of 'ownership', participation and civic inclusion will be achieved. As Weatherill points out 'this matters—there is an evident thematic connection to a broader sense of citizen alienation from the complexity inherent in subjection to multiple sites of governance.'[20] It is of course unrealistic to expect the Commission or Member States to consult all citizens or give all regional or local actors the same level of participation. The reasonable citizen understands that there are

[15] Weatherill and Bernitz (eds) n 4 above, 132–33.

[16] It did though set out the principle of local and regional self-government in Art I-5 of the CE.

[17] See ch 5.

[18] In ch 4.

[19] The role of COREPER for example is important. For a review of process see N Nugent, *The Government and Politics of the European Union* (Hampshire, Palgrave, 1999).

[20] Weatherill and Benitiz (eds) n 4 above, 139.

certain rights of access to information, consultation and influence he can aspire to at individual level and appreciates that the rights of either representative associations or groups at non-governmental societal level may be greater than individual rights (and that even those will be limited). Incremental rights of influence, power and representation should be granted to sub-State Parliaments and principally to sub-State Executives for the simple reason that these are the closest to the citizen, who is in danger of feeling alienated. If sub-State Executives are alienated there is little prospect of the citizen feeling included in the process.

It is not realistic to suppose that the Governments in Madrid or London are more representative or attune to the wishes and views of the citizens in Falkirk or Jerez than the sub-State Governments in Edinburgh or Seville. This likelihood is particularly pronounced when particular nations or regions within a State vote consistently in one ideological direction and a party of a different ideological complexion occupies the central Government. For example, Andalusia has, for the last couple of decades, consistently voted in regional socialist administrations. When conservative administrations are in power in Madrid it is often clear that its views on particular issues are different to the Socialist Government of Andalusia, the Basque nationalist Government in the Basque country or the Catalan Government. Is the central Government in Madrid more attuned to Catalans or Andalusians than their peers in the respective regional administrations, or is it likely that, by doggedly marginalising regional executives, the State Government also risks marginalising citizens too? In Gibraltar the party-political and legitimacy divide is permanent, in the sense that the possibility that the party in power in London would at some point at least also be in power in Gibraltar will not arise, as parties in Gibraltar are self-standing and unrelated to mainstream British parties. Secondly, and as Gibraltar is not an integral part of the United Kingdom, it is not seen as a domestic issue by British politicians. Thirdly, the geographical divide and the fact that Gibraltarians do not vote in United Kingdom elections means that there is more of a feeling of alienation of the average citizen. These elect Gibraltar Governments on a platform of defending their interests as against Spain and the United Kingdom. There are always two sides to Gibraltar elections. There are ordinary domestic issues (health, education, tax and other social or economic issues) and also 'international'-type issues (sovereignty, relations with Spain, constitutional reform, relations with the United Kingdom or EU related matters). Elections are often won or lost on 'international' issues. It is not unusual for policy differences to arise, highlighting that the interests of the United Kingdom and Gibraltar on any one matter are not the same.[21] In those scenarios the British Government defends its interests first and only supports

[21] Some have been identified in earlier chapters.

Gibraltar when there is no conflict with its position. Citizens in Gibraltar are fully aware of this fact and elect Gibraltar Governments to defend their particular interests. If the view were put forward that it would be possible to secure legitimacy without adequately involving the elected representatives of citizens this would most likely be rejected by Gibraltar given its sensitivity to the fact that it is not sufficiently protected by the Member State Government. In this sense, the elected representatives are not just the governing administration of the territory but its citizens' chosen interlocutors with the Member State and the European Union. To ignore or marginalise these would, in turn, alienate the ordinary citizen. The following are different points under specific headings that could facilitate more power, better representation and influence at European level.

Power

The reforms achieved in the 2006 Constitution could be further enhanced by a variety of means, amongst which could be:

—joint responsibility / co-ordination in external affairs between the United Kingdom and Gibraltar—the assignment of responsibilities and demarcation of theoretical and practical arrangements for this purpose;

—alternatively the constitutional enshrinement of an agency relationship in external affairs;

—delegation of wide formal power to enter into certain agreements with other territories and States—especially in the case of domestic competences.[22] This would build on the convention that already exists that the British Government should not extend international agreements to a dominion or a territory with representative government without the consent of the government of the territory.[23] In essence that constitutional convention has been in place for Gibraltar for some time. A similar understanding—the Sewel Convention—is in place for the devolved arrangements of Scotland.[24] In some respects this would be a natural extension of those arrangements and would accord with the grant or assumption by a sophisticated, resourced Government of more proactive responsibilities affecting the territory. The basis for such arrangements exist in the 'entrustment' system described in the previous chapter that would need to be applied more widely and reviewed in its terms so as to meet the conditions of particular territories.[25]

[22] F Aldecoa and M Keating (eds), *Paradiplomacy in Action. The Foreign Relations of Subnational Governments* (London, Frank Cass, 1999).

[23] Oliver n 7 above.

[24] See eg R Hazell (ed), *The State of the Nations 2003: The Third Year of Devolution in the UK* (Exeter, The Constitution Unit, Imprint Academic, 2003) 129–30, 160–61.

[25] See FAC Report 2008 vol 2, Ev 146–151.

Influence

Greater influence needs to be secured both before and after the politico-legislative decision-making process. It is, though, in the area of *ex ante* influence where the largest improvements need to be made.

Ex Ante Influence

Several reforms could be contemplated in this area with the overriding aim of enhancing consultation and participation at different levels in the law-making and decision-making process.

Consultative Mechanisms

Greater consultation can be achieved by formal and informal means. In a formal sense a constitutional mechanism establishing a Consultative Council between the UK and Gibraltar on European Union matters would be an important first step. This could be achieved by formal constitutional reform[26] or by less formal intergovernmental agreement. A general constitutional provision would be useful to ensure entrenchment of consultation and increase the prospect of its binding nature and effect. It would be impossible to capture all supporting detail in such a provision so it would also be necessary to agree a Memorandum of Understanding between the Gibraltar and United Kingdom Governments to encapsulate the mechanics of these arrangements.[27] In further support of any MOU human, technical and financial resources would have to be deployed by both Governments to fuel these arrangements. The practice of the United Kingdom Government is to establish Concordats with the devolved administrations in a context of what has been described as co-operative governance.[28]

Informal arrangements already exist between both Governments that allow some consultation at technical level on the impact and suggested form of transposition of proposed legislation. However these arrangements are often inadequate to provide effective discussion before the proposal becomes law and to secure any influence in its drafting. The arrangements are also not comprehensive enough and, while flexible, err

[26] As suggested in the 2002 Select Committee report—but not included in the final 2006 package.

[27] As for the standing of MOUs see A Aust, *Modern Treaty Law and Practice* (Cambridge, CUP, 2002).

[28] C Carter and A McLeod, 'The Scottish Parliament and the European Union' in Weatherill and Bernitz (eds) n 4 above, 72–79.

on the side of excessive informality.[29] These do not properly provide regular opportunities of effective influence. Any structures set up need to take account of the fact that much European decision-making takes place at sub-ministerial level.[30] In the German model, constitutional structures are entrenched and there can be no constitutional amendment which abolishes the participation structures through which Länder participate in federal law-making.[31] Additionally, transfers of power to the European Union are subject to the consent of the Bundesrat (which is controlled by the Länder).[32] Further constitutional reform in Gibraltar, to achieve a similar degree of clearly demarcated, entrenched structures, would guarantee more secure participation. Current deficiencies were acknowledged by the Foreign Affairs Committee in its 2008 report, when it concluded that it was

> disappointing that the UK did not properly engage with the Government of Gibraltar about its concerns regarding the text of the Lisbon Treaty. We recommend that the FCO must ensure it takes overseas territories' interests into account in its relations with the EU.[33]

Participatory Mechanisms

Greater consultation should then facilitate the natural corollary of greater participation at EU level. More comprehensive and precise discussion on policy proposals would clarify the nature of sub-State concerns and could then if necessary find some appropriate support in other fora. There have been some more radical proposals made by self-governing regions, such as splitting a State's votes at Council level when a matter that concerns regional competences is put to the vote, or establishing a Regional Affairs Council made up of regional Ministers.[34] The latter is more relevant for Gibraltar if it ever came about. Representation on United Kingdom ministerial delegations under Article 203 could be made available where a proposal that affects an area of Gibraltar's competence is envisaged as having

[29] See the discussion in the House of Commons FAC Report 2008 on the Overseas Territories, at para 115. This records the fact that there is a technical forum, designated the Whitehall/Gibraltar Tracking Group, made up of officials from both the UK and Gibraltar Governments that meets twice a year.

[30] Nugent, 1999 n 19 above, 100–85.

[31] See chs 4 and 5 for comparisons with Belgium, Germany and Scotland.

[32] PC Muller-Graf, 'The German Länder: Involvement in EC/EU law and policy-making' in Weatherill and Bernitz (eds) n 4 above, 111–12.

[33] FAC Report 2008 paras 11 and 117–18. The lack of consultation noted was in respect of both the Inter-governmental conference that led to the CE, the CE and Lisbon Treaty. The Government of Gibraltar had put forward memoranda on both occasions but it was not felt that its concerns had properly been taken into account. One of the particular issues was the insertion of a reference to 'territorial integrity' in the Lisbon Treaty that gave rise to anxiety in Gibraltar: see FAC Report 2008 vol 2, Ev 47–8, Q230–3.

[34] C Jeffrey, 'Regions and the European Union' in Weatherill and Bernitz (eds) n 4 above, 42.

the potential to have a disproportionate effect on Gibraltar or raises some other substantial concern. It would be unrealistic and unnecessary to expect regular attendance. Indeed this would not generally be required and would unnecessarily engage resources. But there are occasions on issues of policy or proposed legislation where the measures discussed can seriously affect a pillar of Gibraltar's economy such as shipping or financial services in which it would be desirable to have some influence. Secondly—and while it is unrealistic to expect the United Kingdom delegation to vote in the way Gibraltar would wish on any particular measure when the UK national interest requires a decision in the opposite direction it is not unreasonable to expect that an earlier realisation of fundamental Gibraltar concerns could lead to the greater use of Gibraltar-specific derogations in EU legislative instruments. This would cater for such special circumstances affecting Gibraltar.

Intra-Sub-State Arrangements

Participation in extant structures that have been set up to support the introduction of devolution arrangements for Scotland and Wales or the introduction of analogous arrangements could also assist in improving this aspect of Gibraltar's governance.[35] In some respects Gibraltar suffers from political isolation. Meetings with other overseas territory Governments whilst useful do not improve the issues of isolation as regards the European Union dimension, as none of these have the same status as Gibraltar with regard to the Union. The ability to meet with officials and Ministers of the devolved administrations in Scotland, Wales and Northern Ireland more regularly would assist in the finding of common ground, sharing of mutual concerns and experiences in areas of interest. There is potential for the creation of a Council between Gibraltar, Scotland, Wales and (assuming some longevity of the restoration of arrangements there) Northern Ireland in particular, to consider European Union matters. Clearly, there will be issues of great concern to the other countries that will be largely irrelevant to Gibraltar but there is scope for—at least—an annual conference to discuss issues of mutual interest. While the Channel Islands and the Isle of Man are not members of the European Union, the consideration, over the last decade, of international initiatives on financial services has demonstrated that even though a territory is not a member of the European Union it is not guaranteed immunity from the impact of prospective measures. With that in mind there is also scope for greater co-operation between Gibraltar and these territories by either creating a separate forum for regular meetings or extending the proposal for a

[35] For a review of these see ch 5 and *State of the Nations* (Exeter, The Constitution Unit, Imprint Academic, 2000–05).

Council with Scotland and Wales to these territories too.[36] Whether the United Kingdom Government participates in these forums or not would depend on the consensus that emerges within those stateless nations.[37]

Different States have responded in different ways to accommodate the sub-State dimension in the process of EU decision-making. In Spain a Conference of Presidents of the Autonomous Communities has been created, with central Government and regional officials increasingly making use of comitology with the Commission.[38] In the United Kingdom a variety of Joint Ministerial structures have been set up to support the devolved arrangements. In Germany there is a Europaminister Conference of Länder, and other constitutional mechanisms have been established to allow the channelling of views and representations.[39]

Parliamentary Arrangements

The extension of the proposed early warning system to Gibraltar's Parliament[40] would also be an improvement.[41] To that extent, and while there is mention in the United Kingdom's published political position as to the extension of these arrangements to Scotland and Wales, there is a marked silence in respect of Gibraltar.[42] Improved domestic parliamentary scrutiny would also assist in securing an effective opportunity to influence proposals, draft legislation and consider the most suitable method to transpose legislation.[43]

Ex Post *Influence*

The most significant way of ensuring *ex post* influence would be to achieve a greater ability of judicial challenge by the sub-State Executive. As was

[36] Alternatively the British–Irish Council established under the Good Friday Agreement could be extended to include Gibraltar. More radically a sub-State Council could be established between Gibraltar, Scotland, Wales, Catalunya, Andalucia, Northern Ireland and the Basque Country (and other interested Regions).

[37] Any particular body established should first cater for the sub-State agenda.

[38] Bengoetxea, in Weatherill and Bernitz (eds) n 4 above, 55–61.

[39] Muller-Graf, ibid 112–115.

[40] If introduced across Europe at some stage. If not there is nothing to stop analogous internal arrangements being agreed. The draft Protocol was cited in chs 4 and 5.

[41] The CE and Lisbon Treaty also sought to introduce a system of monitoring competences for national parliaments and subsequent challenge that would be dependent on a third of Parliamentary votes being the trigger challenge mechanism. There have been calls for a wider right to challenge: see Weatherill and Bernitz (eds) n 4 above, 147.

[42] See chs 4 and 5. The arrangements could—in principle and subject to any necessary local adaptation—be applied to Gibraltar in the same way.

[43] The European Scrutiny Committee of the House of Commons visited Gibraltar for the first time in mid 2007. Closer liaison with this Committee would assist.

indicated in the previous chapter, on the handful of occasions that Gibraltar has sought to challenge measures, it has had to satisfy the direct and individual concern test as a non-privileged applicant. It has been a regular demand of self-governing regions that the category of privileged applicant be extended to allow sub-State Executives more direct access to the ECJ.[44] It is a common theme for such a call to be made on behalf of sub-State government from Spain to Germany, Belgium to the United Kingdom.[45] The direct and individual test is quite onerous and it would certainly facilitate matters for such access rights to be granted. This would be consistent with the principles of legitimacy that underlie much of the governance reforms that need to be secured. It is an important aspect of legitimacy that the sub-State executive, which is the duly elected representative body of the electorate, should be able to test its concerns in the ECJ. A failure to have such access rights can only contribute to the psychological disconnection between the European citizen and the supranational centre and operates in direct opposition to principles of participatory governance.

Representation Beyond Sub-State Executive Level

Representation within a number of institutions would enhance the quality of participatory governance and democracy for Gibraltar and its citizens. These bodies are the European Parliament (the 'EP'), the Committee of the Regions and REGLEG[46] in that order, because of the relative powers of the first two in the law-making process of the Union.[47] By far the more important institution in which non-Executive representation could be gained is the Parliament. As was seen in the previous chapter, the achievement of the right to vote in European elections only came about at the 2004 European elections after a political and legal struggle that spanned many years. In fact simple enfranchisement has not dissipated the democratic deficit and the grounds for a claim to a separate MEP for Gibraltar still subsist. Many of the principles justifying this claim are also relevant in support of a claim to representation within the Committee of Regions ('CR') and these are set out below. Representation in these bodies (as well as in REGLEG) is important from the perspective of securing an overall package of benefits that addresses the governance deficit in accordance with the principles of multi-level governance, subsidiarity and constitutional plurinationalism.

[44] Weatherill in Weatherill and Bernitz (eds) n 4 above, 30.

[45] ibid.

[46] Regions with Legislative Powers—a body formed by some of the more powerful regions and stateless nations—www.regleg.eu.

[47] Participation by Gibraltar within other, less formally constituted, bodies, such as the Assembly of the Regions, would also be useful.

From the practical governance point of view, it is important in terms of ensuring participation at all levels of influence in the different decision-making processes. Added to that, and in the context of Gibraltar's position as a stateless nation, it is important in ensuring that its people do not feel marginalised or alienated. In that last sense it accords with the widest sense of pluralism of all nations within a State and across all States within the Union.

Seeking participation in these bodies does not detract from the wider point made earlier that it is the achievement of sub-State executive power and influence at all levels within the governance process that is the most important in securing effective influence for Gibraltar and its representatives. The basis of representation is an important distinction in the case of each and is not simply a nuance. The Council of Ministers represents the States. The EP represents the peoples. The CR represents the regions and local authorities and REGLEG represents the so-called 'constitutional regions'. The EP is part of the institutional framework of the Union and the CR is advisory to it. In that sense to obtain the broadest representation possible Gibraltar needs to seek this at all these levels.

The CR and REGLEG

The CR is advisory to the Union's institutions, and if the reforms that were in the CE and the subsequent Lisbon Treaty were introduced, it would see its role and powers enhanced.[48] It was created in response to demands by regions in the run-up to the Maastricht Treaty,[49] but has consistently failed to meet the demands of the larger regions. These consider the CR to be too widely drawn, cumbersome and ineffective (as it has representatives from local authorities sitting together with representatives from the major stateless nations). There has been a consistent call for the powers of the CR to be strengthened.[50] REGLEG was set up partly in response to the view of those larger, more powerful regions that their needs could not be met in the CR.[51] There have been calls by regions represented within REGLEG that mechanisms should be found to allow the larger regions greater access, influence and power within the Union.[52] A variety of suggestions

[48] It would acquire a limited right to challenge decisions for example.

[49] For an overview of its creation see A Warleigh, *The Committee of the Regions, Institutionalising Multi-Level Governance* (Kogan Page, London, 1999).

[50] J Nergelius, 'The Committee of the Regions Today and in the Future—A Critical Overview' in Weatherill and Bernitz (eds) n 4 above, 119–129.

[51] It has also been stated that the Convention on the Future of Europe disappointed the REGLEG group. See C Jeffrey, 'Regions in the European Union' in Weatherill and Bernitz (eds) n 4 above, 42–45 and the article by one of the editors in that same volume: S Weatherill, 'The Challenge of the Regional Dimension in the European Union' ibid 1–29.

[52] Neregelius in Weatherill and Bernitz (eds) n 4 above, 126.

have been made, amongst these that there be a special status for REGLEG regions,[53] that REGLEG be represented as observers at Council meetings,[54] or that there be a Second Chamber for the regions.[55] While REGLEG is a body outside the formal structures of the Union, it does bring together important sub-State executives and could be a forum for useful exchange of ideas and collective lobbying. As is apparent though, its mere existence is down to the fact that the regions do not feel adequately represented or protected within the Union. The achievement by Gibraltar of representation in both CR and REGLEG would be consistent with an attempt to obtain an overall package of measures to enhance its influence and address the democratic deficit it faces. It would accord with the principles of participatory governance described above for such representation to be granted by the United Kingdom in the CR.

European Parliament—Enfranchisement without Separate Representation

Gibraltar and the South-West of England were constituted as an electoral region for the purposes of the 2004 elections to the European Parliament. The Conservatives capitalised on their stance against the failed 2002 joint sovereignty proposals by giving a manifesto commitment that they would formally reject these in Government. In the resulting elections the Conservatives obtained 73 per cent of the vote in Gibraltar with Labour, Liberal Democrats and the Greens obtaining about seven to ten per cent each with the small balance being divided among the minority formations.[56] However enfranchisement has not delivered real parliamentary influence or adequate representation. While Gibraltar has not been given an MEP of its own the case for separate representation on political, constitutional, social and cultural grounds is strong. Some of the following points can also similarly be applied to the case for membership of the CR.

The principle of democracy is a general principle of law on which the EU is based and has been respected as such by the courts.[57] In 1992, the Treaty on European Union made first mention of human rights and endowed the European Court of Justice with jurisdiction to apply this in respect of Community institutions.[58] Even before 1992, the ECJ had been

[53] ibid 125–26.

[54] N Jaaskinen, 'The Case of the Aland Islands', in Weatherill and Bernitz (eds) n 4 above, 98.

[55] P Muller-Graf in Weatherill and Bernitz (eds) n 4 above, 115 (though categorised by him as a 'monstrosity').

[56] Statistics published by Electoral Registration Officer for Gibraltar, 11 June 2004. Turnout was about 58%.

[57] Case T-135/96 *UEAPME v Council* [1998] ECR II-2335—in that case by labour groups in a negotiation with management groups.

[58] Art 46(d) TEU.

developing jurisprudence recognising underlying human rights protections as part of Community philosophy.[59] Most succinctly in *Kremzow*[60] the ECJ recognised the integral role of fundamental rights in Community law and other more recent cases have continued to develop this jurisprudence.[61]

Under Article 189 (TEC) the European Parliament 'shall consist of the *peoples of the States* brought together in the Community.' This use of the double plural clearly allows scope for the argument that States are composed of a number of groups, peoples or even nations.[62] Article 190 then sets out the number of representatives for each Member State and goes on to say 'the number of representatives elected in each Member State *must ensure appropriate representation of the peoples* of the States brought together in the Community.'[63] (emphasis added)

The CE recognised that the Union is based on peoples 'united in diversity' and this is at the heart of the aspiration to ensure this maximum representation at all levels and this peaceful cohabitation of all peoples with their respective national identities. The electoral arrangements established by the United Kingdom for Gibraltar have submerged the electorate of Gibraltar, about 20,000 people, into an electoral region in which they will vote but their votes in themselves or as a collective total will, effectively, be electorally meaningless.[64] This proposed practice can be criticised on several grounds which support instead the case for a separate MEP for Gibraltar.

Appropriate Representation of the Peoples and Stateless Nations

Articles 189 and 190 refer to the appropriate representation of the peoples of the States in the European Parliament. Whether there is appropriate representation of the peoples depends first on defining who the 'peoples' of the State are.[65] Thereafter there needs to be a national allocation of seats

[59] P Birkinshaw, *European Public Law* (London, Butterworths, 2003) 55–61 and P Alston (ed), *The EU and Human Rights* (Oxford, OUP, 1999) 687–88.

[60] Case C-299/95 [1997] ECR I-2629.

[61] For a list of cases see Birkinshaw n 59 above, 57.

[62] But see Advocate-General's opinion in Case C-145/04, *Spain v UK*: see below.

[63] Art I-20 of the CE and Art I-15) of the Lisbon Treaty (which proposed the insertion of new Art 9A(2) of the TEU) would change the reference of 'peoples' to 'Union's Citizens'.

[64] The electorate of the Gibraltar-South-West region is approximately 4,000,000.

[65] If this is at all possible: see below. The CE and Lisbon Treaty stated that the Union is based on the principles of representative democracy and participatory democracy—(See eg Arts 46–47 CE or Lisbon Treaty Art I-12), inserting proposed Art 8A TEU). Additionally Art I-46(2) CE states that 'citizens are directly represented at Union level in the European Parliament.' The acceptance of the principle of pluralism as a key value of the Union (Art I-2 CE and Lisbon Treaty Art I-3), inserting proposed Art 1a TEU) would retain the core relevance of these same arguments that would be intended to ensure participatory democracy.

that ensures that 'representation' of those particular 'peoples'. So, for example, if Wales were joined as an electoral Region with London, because of the size of the population of London it could be said that the people of Wales would have been assured of the vote but not of 'representation' in the Parliament. Scotland, Wales and Northern Ireland each have a specific allocation of seats as do the Basque Country, Catalunya or the different Belgian peoples.

In *Spain v United Kingdom* the Advocate-General doubted that the expression 'peoples' had a 'precise legal meaning.'[66] In response to a submission by Spain that 'peoples' in the relevant Article was linked to the concept of nation in the sense that it meant citizens that shared the same nationality[67] the Advocate-General stated:

> 79. First of all, considerable doubts are raised by the attempt to interpret that expression as embodying a choice of an ideological nature, as it were, identifying the 'peoples' to which those articles refer with the concept of 'nation'. Without going into a long theoretical disquisition here, suffice it to observe that the term 'nation' is normally used to describe the totality of individuals linked by the fact of sharing traditions, culture, ethnicity, religion and so on, regardless of whether they belong to the same organised State (and therefore regardless of their status as citizens thereof). But if that is the case, it then seems clear to me that that cannot be the meaning attributed by those Treaty articles to the term 'people'. If that were the case, first, it would necessarily include people who are not citizens of the Member States, since all individuals who share the above-mentioned values form part of it, even if, as a result of historical and political circumstances, they belong to other State entities. Second, it would be necessary to exclude those individuals (or entire communities) who do not belong to the 'nation' even though they are citizens of the State (consider, for example, ethnic and linguistic minorities). And that clearly, other considerations apart, is not the aim of the Treaty; it is not a result that is found in practice, nor do I believe it to be the result intended by the applicant government.
>
> 80. If therefore it is actually intended that the expression 'peoples of the States brought together in the Community' should have a precise legal meaning (and, in truth, I find that doubtful), it is much more plausible to take the view that it purports to refer to the concept of 'people' as such, that is to say a community of individuals politically organised within a specific territorial area and linked by the legal bond of citizenship. In other words, it can be considered that, in principle, the concepts of 'people' and 'citizens' overlap.

Advocate-General Tizzano concluded that:

> where they provide that the European Parliament is 'to consist of representatives of the peoples of the States brought together in the Community', Articles 189 and 190 EC clearly do not purport to say (for the reasons set out just above)

[66] Case C-145/04, *Spain v UK*, Opinion of Advocate-General Tizzano, 6 April 2006, para 80.
[67] And not the 'population' of a particular territory sectors of which might share different nationalities: ibid [76].

that all the citizens of those Member States are actually entitled to vote and be represented in that assembly, but, on the other hand, they do not necessarily limit that right to citizens.[68]

Finally the question arises whether a separate MEP is 'appropriate' for Gibraltar. Practical issues outlined below are of relevance here. The application of principles of democracy, representation and good governance support the case for such a separate voice.[69] It is also clear that in the enlargement process the Union has accepted the principle of assigning representation in the EP on a 'degressively proportional'[70] basis. This level has been set to protect a minimum level below which it is thought that smaller States would have insufficient representation within the EP. The thinking behind this principle is relevant in determining whether separate representation should be granted. Scotland has been allocated eight seats from the United Kingdom total, with Wales having five. The same is the case in other Member States. In Belgium much care has been taken to ensure that the Dutch-, French- and German-speaking parts are protected and all have separate representation.[71]

Effective Political Democracy

In *Matthews* the European Court of Human Rights specifically reiterated that the principle underlying the right to vote[72] is the principle of effective political democracy.[73] It held that 'the Convention is intended to guarantee rights that are not theoretical or illusory but practical and effective.'[74] The court accepted there is a margin of appreciation in introducing such arrangements but cautioned that the conditions should not 'impair its very essence and deprive it of effectiveness . . . [or] thwart the free expression of the people on the choice of the legislature.'[75] Gibraltar is a highly charged political environment and its people are sensitised due to the long-standing Spanish sovereignty claim. They are accustomed to having to struggle for political rights and to do so through their local representatives at various international forums. It is certain that Gibraltarians would prefer to elect another Gibraltarian to the European Parliament purely because that person would be more attune with their aspirations and more

[68] ibid [88].

[69] D Oliver, *Constitutional Reform in the UK* (Oxford, OUP, 2003) and S Marks, *The Riddle of all Constitutions* (Oxford, OUP, 2000), both cited above.

[70] Art I-20 CE and Lisbon Treaty Art I-15) proposing new Art 9A TEU.

[71] 14 in the Flemish Region, 10 in the French Region and 1 in the German Region.

[72] Art 3 Protocol 1 which secures 'the free expression of the opinion of the people in the choice of the legislature.' The expression must not only be free—there is a direct linkage to the 'choice' issue that relates inevitably to the candidates before an electorate.

[73] *Matthews v UK*, ECHR, 18 February 1999, [42].

[74] ibid [34].

[75] ibid [63].

knowledgeable as to the issues that affect Gibraltar. Most of the mainstream United Kingdom political parties do not have a presence in Gibraltar.[76] The major local political groupings are all purely domestic outfits. In that context even if the electorate of Gibraltar all voted for the same candidate from one of those parties they might still be deprived of their choice of Parliamentarian by virtue of the fact that Gibraltar has been included in a combined region with an electorate of several million. Additionally, the absence of any Gibraltarians from the electoral lists of the mainstream British parties in the 2004 elections meant that a vote for these was not a vote for one of their countrymen.[77] Admittedly, the fact that a region is allocated seats does not guarantee that the people will want to elect regional parties or other countrymen (even from national parties) but it gives electors an unhindered and realistic chance to do so.

In the 1999 European elections five regional parties in Spain—*Convergència i Unió; Coalición Europea; Coalición Nacionalista—Europa de los Pueblos, Bloque Nacionalista Gallego* and *Euskal Herritarrok*[78] (with national voting percentages between 1.4 per cent and 4.4 per cent)—obtained seats to the European Parliament; in Scotland, the Scottish Nationalist Party won two out of eight seats; in Wales *Plaid Cymru* won two out of five seats; and in Italy both the *Lega Nord* (which admittedly has a national profile) and the regionally-based *Südtiroler Volkspartei* also won seats. Among the other seats won in those nations many of these (even though not won by strict regional groupings) went to Scots, Welsh, Catalans or Basques representing national parties.[79] In the 2004 and 2009 elections similar results were recorded. In Spain, for example *Convergència i Unió, Partido Nacionalista Vasco, Iniciativa per Catalunya,* and *Europa de los Pueblos/Esquerra Republicana de Catalunya* either won seats outright or formed part of electoral coalitions that obtained seats.[80]

Those 'peoples' or nations that make up the Spanish State or the British State not only had seats allocated to their region, country or territory but also had an unhindered chance to select representatives drawn from specific territorially constituted groupings and did so. Alternatively, they elected representatives from their own 'national' groups even if they had a broader party political affiliation.[81] Scots could and did elect Scots.

[76] Only the Conservatives opened an office in the run-up to the 2004 European elections.

[77] Only the Greens included the Leader of the local minority Reform Party on its list. However, this was done on such a low position in the list that it was of token value only. At the 2009 elections the Liberal Democrats placed a Gibraltar Liberal party member last on its list. The electoral system meant that this did not provide a genuine opportunity to elect a local candidate.

[78] From the Catalan, Basque, Galician, Andalusian Regions and from the Canaries.

[79] All electoral statistics drawn from *Dod's European Companion 2003* (London, Vacher Dod Publishing, 2002).

[80] See www.elections2004.eu.int. and www.elections2009.eu.

[81] Though this argument must be tempered and qualified by the extracts from Advocate-General Tizzano's Opinion in *Spain v UK*, cited above.

Basques could and did elect Basques. It is unlikely that Gibraltarians will be able to elect a Gibraltarian without being assigned a specific seat.[82] The electoral system introduced denies Gibraltarians effective representation. It denies them a real chance to elect a Gibraltarian or a member of one of Gibraltar's mainstream parties. It would 'routinely exclude from all effective influence a discrete minority'[83] and it would 'thwart the free expression of the opinion of the people.'[84]

The choice for people must not simply be to cast a vote every four years. For the democratic right to be effective it must be valuable in a qualitative and continuous sense.[85] Part of that relates to the immediate electoral arrangements but part must also relate to the nature of the representation. That in itself must involve two dimensions: who represents?; and how it is done? Answering the first question by maximising the possibility that the people of the stateless nation are actually represented must accord with the full expression of this right to effective democracy and indeed, by analogy, the principle of degressive proportionality referred to above. First, there is a need to be extensive in ensuring the allocation of seats across the Union so as to ensure that the 'diversity' is represented within the EP. Secondly, tokenism in the allocation of seats does not guarantee effective influence and as such there may be a need to set a minimum threshold to ensure this. As the court noted in *Matthews*, the Convention is a 'living instrument which must be interpreted in the light of present day conditions.'[86] As constitutional pluralism and participatory democracy are increasingly recognised so too must be the notion that stateless nations should—in the interests of safeguarding representation and constitutional stability—be separately represented in the EP. In a Parliament of 750 it should be possible to secure this for the stateless nation of Gibraltar. The 'creative approach' adopted by the ECHR in developing positive obligations in respect of Convention rights is well-documented.[87] The ground seems fertile for a possible test case on this issue of separate

[82] Art 14 of the ECHR is also relevant in situations of this type. The electoral choice must operate in a non-discriminatory environment and in a way that does not discriminate against Gibraltarians because of their 'national or social origin' or because of their 'association with a national minority': see *Mathieu-Mohin v Belgium* [1987] A 113 (a case about voters in the French speaking region of Belgium and the electoral arrangements put in place as a result).

[83] DJ Harris, M O'Boyle and C Warbrick, *Law of the European Convention of Human Rights* (London, Butterworths, 1995) 555.

[84] Case nos 6745/74 and 6746/74 *W, X, Y and Z v Belgium*, [1975] 2 DR 110.

[85] See S Marks, *The Riddle of all Constitutions* (Oxford, OUP, 2000) 50–75.

[86] *Matthews v UK*, ECHR, 18 February 1999, [39].

[87] A Mowbray, *The Development of Positive Obligations under the European Convention on Human Rights by the European Court of Human Rights* (Oxford, Hart Publishing, 2004) 230.

[88] The increasing sensitivity of the ECJ to human rights principles together with the strong trends towards participatory governance that in some respects the Commission already considers legally binding: see D Obradovic, 'Participatory Democracy and the Open Access Policy for Interest Groups in the European Union', Paper presented at EUSA Ninth Biennial International Conference, April 2005, Austin, Texas (cited with permission of the author)—

representation.[88] While obtaining one seat for a Gibraltar MEP among 750 will not dramatically alter the balance of influence wielded by Gibraltar the symbolism of the move would be important and sufficient in fostering a feeling in Gibraltar of having achieved greater representation and influence.

Self-Determination

The right of colonial peoples in non-self governing territories is to what has been described as external self-determination. There is an internal dimension to the principle of self-determination that endows national minorities or racial groups with the right to participate fully in the decision-making process, but safeguards the territorial integrity of the State by not bestowing on such groups the right of secession.[89] Internal self-determination has been defined as the right to 'authentic self-government . . . the right for a people really and freely to choose its own political and economic regime . . . the right to have a representative and democratic government.'[90] Gibraltarians as a colonial people are entitled to external self-determination. If peoples that do not have that external right can stake a claim to influence and representation in the democratic governance of a country, then these rights should also exist for those peoples that are capable of an external right to self-determination. A people with the right to self-determination should not have their democratic expression neutralised at European elections by virtue of the particular electoral arrangements that are established. What is relevant is that Gibraltar, for historical, cultural, geographic, social and political reasons, is very different to the United Kingdom, and this separateness of its people—the identity question—must be a factor in the determination of the fairness of the electoral arrangements.[91] The separate identity must be specially protected through separate representation or it will lead to the stifling of the expression of the people.[92] Once a separate Parliamentary seat is assigned, the people can then choose whomever they want.

together with the parallel possibility of recourse to the ECHR (as in *Matthews v UK*) makes this a plausible scenario.

[89] A Cassese, *Self Determination of Peoples—A Legal Appraisal* (Cambridge, CUP, 1995) 124. Internal self-determination is 'neither destroyed nor diminished by its having already once been invoked and put into effect, unlike external self-determination' 101.

[90] A Cassese, *Self Determination of Peoples—A Legal Appraisal* (Cambridge, CUP, 1995) 101.

[91] See also the section on practical arrangements below.

[92] For the Quebec analogy on special protection, see P Oliver, 'Quebec and the Amending Formula: Protection, Promotion and Federalism' in S Tierney (ed), *Accommodating Cultural Diversity* (Dartmouth, Ashgate, 2007) 167–97.

Practicalities

Size

In the *Matthews* case the United Kingdom Government argued that it 'would have distorted the electoral process to constitute Gibraltar as a separate constituency, since its population of approximately 30,000 was less than 5 per cent of the average population per European Parliament seat in the United Kingdom.'[93] But that headline figure does not tell the whole story. Turnout in Gibraltar elections is traditionally high, with the average of the last four elections exceeding 80 per cent. In an election with a Gibraltar presence in the form of a candidate with a real chance of being elected or a list of candidates, it would be more likely that the imagination of the electorate could be captured and electoral participation fostered. The turnout at the 2004 European elections in Gibraltar was 58 per cent (a figure which was well below the 90 per cent of the electorate that had signed a cross-party Petition that was presented at the British Houses of Parliament in 1999 requesting the vote at European elections). The lower turnout was contributed to by the fact that no Gibraltar candidate or party was contesting the elections and that these had decided to support different UK mainstream parties.[94] In 2009 the turnout in Gibralter was 35 per cent. Voter-candidate identification is more complex in those circumstances. The issue of the disconnect between the citizen and the European project is also an intangible but real factor.

Given the traditional low turnout at European elections in Britain and because the United Kingdom now uses electoral arrangements based on the *d'Hondt* system to elect its European Parliamentarians, a better comparison for Gibraltar is made by examining the minimum number of votes necessary to obtain a seat in one of the English Regions. In the 1999 European elections, between 87,000 and 120,000 votes were needed to win a seat depending on the region.[95] In the 2004 election, a higher turnout in Britain meant that the figure rose to 138,000.[96] While these figures still make it impossible for the Gibraltar electorate to obtain a seat (unaided by a significant vote from British residents who arguably would have little reason to do so) they make for a more realistic comparison that reveals that the true differences are not between millions of people and a few thousand but between the likely block vote of the Gibraltar electorate[97]—20,000—

[93] *Matthews v UK*, ECHR, 18 February 1999, [60].

[94] Even so the turnout was well above the UK average.

[95] The lowest, 87,545, was the Green Party in the London Region; the highest, 119,376, for the Liberal Democrats in the North West. In four out of the nine regions, votes under 100,000 secured a seat. *Dod's European Companion 2003*, n 79 above.

[96] In the North East Region (the lowest). The highest minimum necessary was registered in the North West for UKIP (257,000). By contrast, in Northern Ireland, the minimum necessary was 91,000 (Ulster Unionist Party).

[97] The majority of which could probably be relied on to support a unity candidate.

and the likely minimum necessary to obtain a seat (about 100,000). In that context, assigning a seat to Gibraltar does not seem so disproportionate. In fact, historically, the smaller countries have been disproportionately represented in the European Parliament. Luxembourg, for example, has six seats, with a population of 400,000 (about 70,000 per seat). Ireland has 15 seats, with a population of 3.5 million. The accession of Malta and Cyprus provide further examples of relatively small populations on a per seat basis.[98] That, of course, again, does not reveal the complete picture. At the 2004 European elections only about 50,000 votes were needed to obtain a seat in Ireland and on a turnout of 90 per cent only 18,000 votes were necessary to secure a seat in Luxembourg.

Affinity with an English Region

In trying to resist the applicant's claim in the *Matthews* case, the United Kingdom Government also stated that 'redrawing constituency boundaries so as to include Gibraltar within a new or existing constituency was no more feasible, as Gibraltar did not form part of the United Kingdom and had no strong historical or other link with any particular United Kingdom constituency.'[99] However, this is precisely what the United Kingdom did subsequently by legislation.[100] It would have been better if, for that absence of specific cultural, historical or social affinity with any of the English regions, Gibraltar had been allocated a specific seat.[101]

Other Practicalities

Gibraltar was attached to the English South-West region for European election purposes. It is clear that the issues that matter to constituents in the south west England part of the region are very different to those of concern in Gibraltar. While there may be some local domestic differences, the European issues that touch upon Devon and Cornwall will at least bear some resemblance. The European issues that concern Gibraltar are very different because of very specific political, economic and geographic factors. Gibraltar has Treaty exemptions that the South-West region does

[98] In accordance with the principle of degressive proportionality any Member State—irrespective of size—would at least have six seats.

[99] *Matthews v UK*, ECHR, 18 February 1999, 60.

[100] At the time of a consultation exercise by the Electoral Commission, there were some representations on the basis that there was an affinity based on naval and historical connections with the South-West but even that was in reality quite tenuous in any modern-day context.

[101] See also *Podkolzina v Lettonie*, ECHR, Judgment of 4 April 2002 as to the State's margin of appreciation.

not. The policy positions of the United Kingdom Government in relation to European questions are different to those held by the Gibraltar Government.[102] There are many political and legally complex issues faced by Gibraltar. The average Gibraltarian—being on mainland Europe—is less Euro-sceptic than his English counterpart. The measure of delegated power of the devolved administrations in Scotland or Wales or local authority government in the South-West is far removed from the level of real self-government of Gibraltar. The seven MEPs that were elected to represent the South-West and Gibraltar in 2004 (three conservatives, two UKIP, one Labour and one Liberal Democrat) faced two very different worlds in trying to adequately represent or balance the interests of their constituents in Gibraltar.[103] They were drawn from national United Kingdom parties and, in case of conflicts of interests, most likely felt the need to adhere to national party policy.[104] By the European Parliament (Number of MEPs and Distribution between Electoral Regions) (United Kingdom and Gibraltar) Order 2008[105] the number of MEPs to form part of the South-West and Gibraltar electoral region was reduced to six. This can only place more pressure on MEPs seeking to cover responsibilities in Gibraltar.

All these factors deny Gibraltarians genuine representation to the European Parliament. These factors may be at the heart of why most of Gibraltar's MEPs were relatively inactive over Gibraltar in the initial 12 months following the June 2004 elections. Out of a total of 447 written questions put by British MEPs in the period June 2004–May 2005, only six were on Gibraltar.[106] However those six questions were put by Graham Watson who—without having been elected for Gibraltar previously—had already in the 1999–2004 Parliament shown an interest in Gibraltar and asked questions on subjects of interest to constituents in Gibraltar.[107] In fact of the other MEPs elected for 'Gibraltar' only Glyn Ford seems to have asked any written questions on Gibraltar in the last two Parliaments.[108]

[102] On matters such as the Euro or the Savings Directive.

[103] To compound this, two UKIP MEPs support a deeply Eurosceptic manifesto that would have little immediate relevance to Gibraltar.

[104] Apart from these issues, it requires a large amount of travel to stay in touch with Gibraltar constituents and the acquisition of this knowledge will be largely irrelevant to mainland constituents. It would be natural that the mainland part should receive primacy of attention as a result of the combination of factors stated.

[105] SI 2008/1954.

[106] And all of those were put by Graham Watson (Liberal Democrat). There were two other written questions on Gibraltar in the same period: one by a Spanish MEP, the other by a Cypriot.

[107] Information from European Parliament website.

[108] The others are Neil Parish, Dr Caroline Jackson and Giles Chichester (Conservative), Roger Knapman and Graham Booth (UKIP). Mr Parish, Mr Ford and Mr Watson are proving the most active on Gibraltar, regularly visiting Gibraltar and attempting to foster certain local links.

The Search for a Status at the End of the Rainbow

The Colonial Context

As the years go by and the decolonisation process reaches its practical culmination, there may be a need to redefine what decolonisation and self-determination means in the United Nations context, especially in so far as the remaining territories on the list of non-self-governing territories are concerned. Some of those do not have the resources to opt for independence or the wish to seek free association or integration. A similar point was made in a letter submitted to the UN on the subject of Gibraltar by the British Ambassador in January 2007, in which he stated Britain's position to be that it was:

> the long-standing view of the United Kingdom that none of its remaining overseas territories, including Gibraltar, should remain on the United Nations list of non-self-governing territories . . . (and that) . . . we regard the criteria used by the United Nations Special Committee on Decolonisation as outdated, and believe that the criteria fail to take account of the way that relationships between the United Kingdom and its overseas territories have been modernised, in a way acceptable to both parties.[109]

Subsequently, and in compliance with its obligation to transmit reports to the UN under Article 73e of the Charter, the United Kingdom delivered the 2007 Report under cover of a letter dated 9 February 2008, which stated:

> I would draw particular attention to the adoption of a new Gibraltar Constitution which came into force on the 2 January 2007, following its earlier approval by the people of Gibraltar in a referendum conducted by the Gibraltar Government. Our view is that this new Constitution provides for a modern relationship between the UK and Gibraltar which is now non colonial in nature. Accordingly, the UK does not believe that Gibraltar should remain on the UN list of non-self-governing territories.[110]

[109] Letter dated 22 January 2007 from the Permanent Representative of the UK to the United Nations, addressed to the Secretary General, United Nations General Assembly, 23 January 2007, A/61/710.

[110] Letter dated 9 February 2008 from J Godwin, UK Mission to the United Nations, New York to Chief, Decolonisation Unit, DPA, United Nations. The letter also re-states the UK view that decolonisation criteria are outdated and implies from its terms that the delivery of the report is made grudgingly because the UK is 'obliged by the terms of the Charter to continue to do so.' In that context the UK probably has in mind its experience in the West Indies. After introducing free association arrangements in the 1960s it had described these as 'something between that of a colony and of a totally independent State.' On that basis it had ceased to report to the UN under Art 73. This was 'regretted' by the UN, which in GA Res 2701 XXV of 14 December 1970 stated that 'in the absence of a decision by the General Assembly itself that the territories . . . have attained a full measure of self-government . . . [the] UK should continue to transmit information under Art 73': see J Crawford, *The Creation of States in International Law*, 2nd edn (Oxford, OUP, 2006) 630–31.

Similar points were re-stated by the UK representative in its reply to the Spanish intervention before the UN Fourth Committee in October 2008.[111] Conversely, the Spanish Permanent Representative made clear that, for Spain:

> [i]t cannot be accepted that the United Kingdom attempt to use the new constitutional decree it has granted to Gibraltar or the vote in a referendum . . . to justify not complying with United Nations resolutions. The colonial situation of Gibraltar continues, and consequently, its consideration by the Special Committee on decolonisation . . . It cannot be accepted either that the United Kingdom pretend that its commitment to the people of Gibraltar, that is, [that] the UK would not reach any agreements or understandings over the issue of sovereignty that go against the wishes of the people of Gibraltar, as provided in the new constitutional decree, serve as a justification to not take up negotiations with Spain again over the issues of sovereignty. In no way can these arguments serve as an excuse to not comply with the UN mandate on Gibraltar which is reiterated each year since 1984. This mandate establishes that the decolonisation of this territory can only come about as a result of a *bilateral* negotiation between Spain and the United Kingdom based on the fact that there is a controversy over sovereignty and the infringement of the territorial integrity of Spain is concerned. Therefore the principle of self-determination cannot be applied to the case of Gibraltar.[112]

The governing guidance that describes the constituent elements necessary to categorise a status as free association or independence are contained in two principal UN Resolutions which date back to 1953 and 1960 respectively.[113] Understandably, there is some concern that, after more than 50 years, the key criteria should be revised in accordance with the general governance trends, the evolution of underlying concepts, the practicality of what the remaining residue of listed territories can aspire to, and the global culture of interdependence.[114] The eradication of colonialism is supposed to happen by 2010 but there are no real signs that all these remaining territories can be decolonised in one of the conventional ways recognised by the UN. In that case there is possibly a need for that redefinition—for a declaration of a period of 'late decolonisation' as much as there has been a review of the meaning of sovereignty. The answer—outwith this work but which would similarly impact on the future of Gibraltar—would be to concentrate on constitutional pluralism as the baseline for such a redefinition of the criteria for decolonisation. It is

[111] Statement of UK at the 63rd Session of the General Assembly, Fourth Committee, 7 October 2008.

[112] Statement by the Permanent Representative of Spain at the 63rd Session of the General Assembly, IV Committee, 7 October 2008.

[113] See chs 1 and 2.

[114] Crawford does make the point that perhaps the criteria need not change as there is enough flexibility in the term free association to accommodate a range of alternatives: see Crawford n 110 above, 636.

because the remaining sixteen territories on the United Nations list do not fit within the classic categories of independence, free association or integration that some politicians in a number of jurisdictions have hung on to the language of UN Resolution 2625 of 1970 as laying the legal basis for a so-called fourth option.[115] There is much scope in the language of that particular resolution for that view.[116] Indeed, as has been highlighted in an earlier chapter, it can be argued that the International Court in the Western Sahara case implicitly recognised the existence of this fourth option.[117] But even if this is not accepted as a formal de-colonising option, it could be seen, as Crawford highlights, as an intermediate and hybrid stage in the process of self-determination, where the people have expressed their preference for a particular status but remain subject to Article 73.[118] In that context it would be a 'partial fulfilment of the right to self-determination . . . [but] would not end their right . . . to elect a change in status.'[119]

As the Foreign Affairs Select Committee Report of 2008 recognises, there is little appetite for moves to independence among the remaining British overseas territories.[120] Equally, these generally value their internal self-governance and are not in favour of integration.[121] Unless significant accommodation can be found by re-drawing the criteria for 'association', or the fourth option is embraced with more enthusiasm, then it may be difficult for formulae to be found for these territories. They could be left in an undesirable constitutional purgatory without international recognition and relying on simple political assurances for an assertion of their status. In the case of Gibraltar, a Minister of State at the Foreign Office has recently stated that the relationship with Gibraltar was not colonial, adding that 'if you do not have a colonial relationship, it [Gibraltar] is not a colony.'[122] But political assurances are not legally enshrined covenants. Nor do they actually deliver a general acceptance of a new international status or categorical domestic settlement of the colonial question.[123] These statements without international recognition deliver a transitional and hybrid status not unlike a gentle constitutional drift towards the shore of Statehood.

[115] Crawford n 110 above, 636–37.
[116] As pointed out in chs 1 and 2.
[117] See ch 2.
[118] Crawford n 110 above, 637.
[119] ibid.
[120] House of Commons Foreign Affairs Committee, *Overseas Territories*, Seventh Report of Session 2007–08, HC 147-I (London, TSO, 6 July 2008) paras 31–34.
[121] With the possible exception of St Helena, where this was mooted some years ago.
[122] Jim Murphy MP in comments to the press on a visit to Gibraltar: see *Gibraltar Chronicle* (Gibraltar 26 April 2008). Echoing comments made by other Ministers of the UK Government since the 2006 Constitution. However, barely a month earlier he had said to the Foreign Affairs Committee 'It [the Constitution] is a modernisation and it has been described by others as an end to the colonial relationship, although I have never described it in those terms.' See FAC Report 2008 vol 2, Ev 52, Q246.
[123] For the reasons explained in ch 3 legislation would be needed.

The 2006 Constitution was accepted by the people of Gibraltar in a referendum held in November 2006. Both Gibraltar and the United Kingdom have argued for de-listing and decolonisation on this basis. Spain's view, as highlighted, is markedly different. For the moment, the United Nations resists the removal of Gibraltar from the list of non-self-governing-territories. There are three difficulties to that aspiration: two substantive, and one political. The first substantive issue is the long-standing difficulty that the UN has had about accepting the plea that the fourth option actually exists.[124] As such, any formula constructed on that basis may suffer from the fact that the UN would wish to categorise it in accordance with traditional models and this may make that task impossible. The second substantive question lies in an actual assessment of the extent of self-government now enjoyed by Gibraltar.[125] In that context the residual powers of the UK to legislate may prove a stumbling block. But that would amount to a misunderstanding of the modern legal context that Gibraltar exists within. As it is part of a supra-national entity and the UK can be held to account at that level, then this mechanism is a justifiable inclusion until a negotiation finds a way to replace it in a manner acceptable to the UK and Gibraltar.[126] The acceptance of such mechanisms in an interdependent governance environment is consistent with modern trends of constitutionalism. The constitutional clean-break or the sharp institutional ring-fencing may be unnecessary and impractical. Residual powers need not threaten the core spirit of self-governance and can be understood as providing the equivalent sovereignty balance that is provided in a State's membership of a supra-national entity such as the EU.

In some ways the European Court of First Instance has in its recent decision on the fiscal regime of Gibraltar edged towards those conclusions. First, it held that the Governor's residual powers to introduce legislation were held *qua* Crown in right of Gibraltar and not on behalf of the United Kingdom.[127] Secondly, it made clear that the 'residual power which the United Kingdom retains to legislate for Gibraltar[128] and the various powers granted to the Governor under the 1969 Constitution that entitle him

[124] Though the 2007 Chair of the UN Committee of 24 made positive comments implying that she was more willing to have an open mind on this issue. This has not changed official UN policy: *Gibraltar Chronicle* (Gibraltar 6 June 2007).

[125] While an empirical assessment is being required of Gibraltar's extent of self-governance this is quite different to the lack of qualitative assessment of ability to govern in cases where independence has been chosen as an option: see G Kreijen in G Kreijen (eds), *State, Sovereignty and International Governance* (Oxford, OUP, 2004) 90–4, ch 2.

[126] There are also other issues the removal, amendment or fine-tuning of which may assist: see Conclusion below.

[127] The court was reviewing the Governor's powers to introduce legislation under ss 33 and 34 of the 1969 Constitution, which was in place at the time: see Cases T-211/04 and T-215/04 *Government of Gibraltar v Commission of the European Communities*, Judgement of the Court of First Instance, 18 December 2008, [97]. The case is currently under appeal with a decision expected in 2010.

[128] Presumably, the court was alluding to old s 86 of the 1969 Constitution.

to participate in the legislative process *must be interpreted in the light of the status of Gibraltar . . . as a non-self-governing territory under Article 73 . . . of the Charter*.'[129] (emphasis added). In doing so the court recognised that the responsibility under the Charter was to promote self-governance and development of the people and the territory:

In the light of the foregoing, the United Kingdom's residual power to legislate for Gibraltar and the various powers granted to the Governor *must be interpreted as means enabling the United Kingdom to assume its responsibilities towards the population of Gibraltar and to perform its obligations under international law, and not as granting an ability to intervene directly* as regards the content of a tax measure adopted by the Gibraltar authorities, in particular since those residual powers have never been exercised in matters of taxation.[130]

As Jennings has noted 'changing times need different approaches.'[131] If the UN were willing to conduct a more qualitative assessment of the constitutional mechanisms in light of the changes in the global environment of governance then its reluctance about the presence of residual powers may be overcome. In doing so it would be important to bear in mind that the central objective is the decolonisation of colonial peoples in accordance with their wishes. The criteria for meeting that objective must accommodate changes in constitutional architecture, as otherwise it is in danger of not delivering that end to colonialism.[132] Perhaps therefore the best way to modernise the analysis of options, short of independence, is to require that the option be put to the empirical test of a referendum. If that happens and the people elect to choose such a status this act would accord with a modern assessment of sovereignty and should be a powerful indicator towards decolonisation.

Indeed, it is ironic that being removed from the UN list has depended not on ability to govern, capacity or resources, but on having the enshrined mechanical right to do so, only as long as the option chosen is independence.[133] As such, Gibraltar could in one scenario acquire independence and be decolonised and de-listed but currently be more politically exposed or have more limited resources to conduct its self-governance than in a status short of independence. In modernising the criteria for decolonisation, principles of effective Government as well as adherence to the wishes of the people must form the driving rationale for

[129] My emphasis. See Cases T-211/04 and T-215/04 *Government of Gibraltar v Commission of the European Communities* n 127 above, [98].

[130] ibid [99].

[131] Jennings in Kreijen (ed) n 125 above, 27.

[132] Indeed the European Court of First Instance's judgment of 18 December 2008 could also assist in the obtention by Gibraltar of better structures of governance given that it reminds the parties of the overall duty the UK retains.

[133] RH Jackson, *Quasi-States, Sovereignty, International Relations and the Third World* (Cambridge, CUP, 1990).

change. It seems pointless to retain criteria that may have suited countries of several million but do not suit Tokelau[134] or Pitcairn.[135] To consummate the UN Secretary General's desire for an eradication of colonialism, the criteria now need to be redrawn with the special situations thrown up by the territories on the current UN list in mind. Perhaps a task-force towards that end could be established by the Secretary General, which would include representatives of States and from the territories. This possibility of further reviewing the criteria to take account of present-day circumstances was expressly reserved in the pertinent UN resolutions.[136]

The political issue that remains is the continued resistance by Spain that Gibraltar should be decolonised in a manner other than by Spain acquiring sovereignty.[137] Even though the process of decolonisation is not about determining third party claims to sovereignty[138] obtaining it is not a political magic wand. Even if Gibraltar finds itself off the list of non-self-governing territories it will not necessarily signify the end of the Spanish claim to sovereignty.[139] The only prospect that this should disappear lies in the acceptance by all parties of the modern legal context of late sovereignty and stateless nationalism and a consequent review of status options in that light. Obtaining decolonisation without an end to bilateralism and the Spanish sovereignty claim is not impossible, but would be to do so while retaining a negative climate of confrontation.[140] Again, the Belize example given earlier provides a useful analogy. The decolonisation and independence of Belize was achieved notwithstanding the sovereignty claim from Guatemala that for years had seemed to prevent this from materialising. Negotiations were needed subsequent to decolonisation to seek an end to the Guatemalan claim.[141] Indeed, in Belize's case, first bilateral and then tripartite discussions occurred, both before and after decolonisation, given the complexity of addressing historic sovereignty issues. The analogy with Gibraltar is clear.

Even though third party sovereignty claims should be kept quite separate from the decolonisation process, this view is not universally shared.

[134] Rejected independence twice in referenda organised in 2007.

[135] With a very small population of under 50.

[136] See ch 2.

[137] A change in status will also require a suitable amendment to domestic law as highlighted in ch 3.

[138] As the case of Belize illustrates.

[139] Nor does it necessarily deliver constitutional finality—witness for example the case of New Caledonia which was de-listed in 1947, but which has seen a number of constitutional developments since then: D Custos, 'New Caledonia, A Case of Shared Sovereignty within the French Republic: Appearance or Reality?' (2007) 13(1) *European Public Law*, 97–132.

[140] *Quaere* whether it is even politically possible given the State-centricity of the UN and the current desire of the UN that any agreement over Gibraltar should have the bilateral endorsement of Britain and Spain.

[141] Sylvestre, 2002; SR Ashton and D Killingray (eds), *The West Indies*, British Documents on the End of Empire, Series B, vol 6 (London, TSO, Institute of Commonwealth Studies, 1999).

Indeed Spain's traditional position has been markedly different.[142] For it decolonisation is only possible 'once a definite solution is reached regarding the issues of sovereignty.'[143] And this, for Spain, can only be achieved in a bilateral process of discussions with the United Kingdom. The issue of sovereignty has reared its head within recent debates both before the Committee of 24 and the Fourth Committee of the United Nations, laying emphasis to the controversy that continues to rage and the enduring importance of sovereignty as the currency of symbolism and power. For Spain the 2007 regional seminar on decolonisation organised by the Committee of 24 'highlighted the singularity of those territories in which a sovereignty dispute exists.'[144] Indeed the Committee of 24 submitted a report to the Fourth Committee that self-determination should be applied as the governing principle in the decolonisation process to all territories 'where there is no dispute over sovereignty.'[145] This lead to an 'intense debate', with a number of countries voicing concerns that this would raise new hurdles for colonial peoples and would affect fundamental principles of decolonisation.[146] The proposal was made that the phrase 'and where there is no dispute over sovereignty' be deleted from the omnibus draft resolution.[147] The amendment was carried by a vote of 61 in favour, 40 against and 47 abstentions. Even though the threat to qualify the application of the principle of decolonisation where there were third party sovereignty claims had failed, the relative narrowness of the victory reflects the division on such questions at the United Nations. The States backing each position was also revealing. Of the 40 States opposing the amendment and favouring the sovereignty claim qualification were Spain, Argentina and 15 other Latin American countries.[148] Equally there was a relatively high figure of abstention and absenteeism from Commonwealth States.[149] The omnibus resolution was aimed at addressing the questions of eleven non-self-governing territories.[150] Even though this was not

[142] A position shared by Argentina in light of its claim to the Falkland Islands.

[143] Statement by the Permanent Representative of Spain at the 63rd Session of the General Assembly, IV Committee, 7 October 2008.

[144] ibid.

[145] Communiqué entitled 'Following Intense Debate, Fourth Committee Approves Amended Omnibus Text on Non-Self-Governing Territories', report on 63rd Session, Fourth Committee, General Assembly GA/SPD/406, Department of Public Information, News and Media Division, United Nations, New York, 20 October 2008.

[146] ibid.

[147] Omnibus Draft Resolution VI (A/63/23 64).

[148] This in some ways reflected the position of the 1960s, when several Latin American countries backed the Spanish position. No Latin American State other than Belize voted among the 61 States opposing the sovereignty qualification.

[149] Over 20 States.

[150] It was not aimed at dealing with the questions of Gibraltar, Western Sahara or Falkland Islands—the territories where there were controversial third party sovereignty claims. The specific question of Gibraltar was dealt with by a decision that was adopted on 13 October 2008, which stated that the 'General Assembly, recalling its decision 62/523 of 17 December 2007 and the statements agreed to by the Governments of Spain and the United Kingdom of

strictly aimed at the other territories by implication it would have affected the decolonisation process of each, given that there were sovereignty claims in relation to some of the others.

In the same way as the decolonisation criteria should change, so too should the United Nations' understanding of sovereignty. Not unidimensional, this is not simply a question of territorial sovereignty. The principle of self-determination vests a colonial people with contingent sovereignty, and they may choose to exercise this to elect a status short of independence. This decision would not be a denial of sovereignty but an exercise of it. In doing so, if it is undertaken in acknowledgment of a new era of governance within which traditional concepts have evolved, and the decision is taken in full exercise of free will, such an act should be unimpeachable. To introduce a modern contextual understanding of sovereignty the UN must accept that 'the doctrines of sovereignty down the ages have differed from time to time for the very reason that they reflected the needs and problems of their own particular times and were designed to do so.'[151] The continuing process of change fuelled by geo-political factors must inform the criteria of decolonisation and the use of sovereignty concepts by the United Nations. That would cause a departure from the language of the 1960s and the acceptance that the ground-rules for decolonisation must be more responsive to the modern sovereignty and nationalism context and not conflict with those. This would be achieved by devising formulae for decolonisation short of independence that acknowledge the underlying force of stateless nationalism and multi-level governance within the re-defined sovereignty environment. The colonial people would then take choices within new decolonisation criteria freely and democratically, in accordance with the principle of self-determination. If a basis for that transformation in understanding were needed it would be that the era of human rights provides the philosophical driver to the special protection of colonial peoples.

Great Britain and Northern Ireland in Brussels on 27 November 1984 and in Madrid on 27 October 2004 and noting the establishment pursuant to the latter of the tripartite forum for dialogue on Gibraltar, separate from the Brussels process, under the statements made jointly by the Governments of Spain, the UK and Gibraltar on 16 December 2004: URGES both Governments, while listening to the interests and aspirations of Gibraltar to reach in the spirit of the statement of 27 November 1984, a definitive solution to the question of Gibraltar, in the light of relevant resolutions of the General Assembly and applicable principles and in the spirit of the Charter of the United Nations [and] welcomes the ongoing implementation of the first package of measures concluded at the tripartite forum for dialogue on Gibraltar and the shared will to reach new agreements by July 2009.'

[151] Jennings in Kreijen (ed), n 125 above, 29.

The Conceptual Approach and Trilateralism

After a sustained and enduring period of productive trilateralism that fosters new understandings within the proper theoretical context, it may at some point be possible to turn attention to the vexed issue of the status of Gibraltar.[152] Indeed it may even be possible, by agreement, to involve the EU more directly in the attempt to seek a resolution to the conflict or in the model for that resolution. Given the cautious attitude adopted by the Commission, the EU is unlikely to get involved in this without the specific invitation of the States, though this might be a constructive and useful way forward.[153] The driver of positive neutrality would be the feature that proves decisive as to whether such participation would be welcomed by all.[154]

The possibility for a new status need not be immediate, and can emerge by evolution or negotiation. In terms of evolutionary processes, this can develop through time, in part responsive to how constitutional trends have modified the relationship of other stateless nations within Member States of the European Union. Alternatively, it can edge forward in a gradual way, as was the case with the former Dominions.[155] The third evolutionary possibility is for a status to emerge following a re-evaluation of the criteria towards decolonisation and a re-categorisation of the forms of decolonisation. If novel re-classifications were devised, they could more easily accommodate the remnant territories on the list of non-self-governing territories. In attempting to try to find a solution to the Gibraltar issue, it is important to take a fresh look at possible scenarios. As Keating[156] has pointed out, 'in order to understand the complexities of nationality and political order in the modern world we need to get beyond the old models of statehood based on a uniform order whether federal or unitary.' To aspire to find a solution to the Gibraltar conundrum and produce a status that all parties can endorse (or at the very least acquiesce to) requires an immersion in the politics of this new constitutionalism that recognises the core values of pluralism, participation and respect. A

[152] In 2008 the Chief Minister of Gibraltar indicated that he would be prepared to discuss proposals with Spain at the current tripartite forum. Two immediate points arise. The first, that the current construct of the tripartite process would not seem to allow that: see ch 6. As such, there would need to be a departure from the original structure for that to occur. Secondly, without an acceptance of the modern context of sovereignty and a sustained end to bilateralism this would be fraught with difficulty.

[153] Its pronouncements on the 'sensitivity' of the political issue (see ch 4) suggest that the Commission has shied away from involvement on Gibraltar because of political reasons and a lack of desire to upset Member States.

[154] Gibraltar may view the EU with some caution because of the fear that it will proceed with a State-centric bias and as such any involvement would have to be clearly demarcated.

[155] L Zines, *Constitutional Change in the Commonwealth* (Cambridge, CUP, 1991) 1–33.

[156] M Keating, *Plurinational Democracy, Stateless Nations in a Post-Sovereignty Era* (Oxford, OUP, 2001) 160.

constitutionalism that recognises that the nation-state is not democracy's sole 'container'[157] and that there are issues that occur in a dialogue with supra-national interlocutors as much as sub-State ones. It is recognition of this constitutionalism[158] beyond the state that would provide the first and important precursor to facilitating the emergence of a settled status that is in consonance with the modern pluralistic context.

This constitutionalism within, above and below the State recognises, as Maduro has pointed out, that the ' borders of national democracy no longer correspond to the actions of the modern citizen' and that to acquire control of decision-making and true participation requires the adoption of thinking that dispenses with 'abstract models and artificial boundaries.'[159] This is where the traditional models often mooted as solutions for Gibraltar would fall well short, as they would neither satisfactorily address all dimensions of the Gibraltar conundrum nor marry the deeply conflictive aspirations of the various parties. Most fundamentally, none of those would take adequate account of the modern context. To that extent, it is constitutionalism and mechanics of power, pluralism and participation that are the key partners to the aspirations of and legitimacy conferred by the demos.

The current discussion on abstract models operates on several false and artificial premises. First, there is a sense that it is very much an entirely abstract debate, given that models and permutations are bandied about which are clearly neither on offer nor able to resolve the democratic deficit suffered by Gibraltar—a deficit not unlike the 'two-fold' deficit observed by Maduro in respect of national polities that:

> do not control many decision-making processes that impact on those national polities but occur outside their borders . . . [and instead] exclude from participation and representation many interests which are affected by their decisions.[160]

Secondly, the presentation of those old models as being instantly capable of resolving Gibraltar's constitutional or governance difficulties and the historic impasse with Spain is somewhat artificial.[161] Neither obtaining decolonisation nor a particular status are solutions in themselves that can in some way eradicate the Spanish sovereignty claim. The only way to seek to do that is either to deal with it pro-actively or with a conscious policy of the reverse—namely, to pursue a policy of slow constitutional progress and political containment until such time as Gibraltar has been

[157] S Marks, *The Riddle of all Constitutions* (Oxford, OUP, 2000) 100.

[158] N Walker, 'European Constitutionalism and European Integration' [1996] PL 266.

[159] Maduro, in JHH Weiler and M Wind (eds), *European Constitutionalism Beyond the State* (Cambridge, CUP, 2003) 75, 83.

[160] ibid 83.

[161] eg, it has long been the argument of those favouring integration with Britain that achieving this status would resolve the Spanish claim. This is an unrealistic aspiration.

able to drift to a satisfactory constitutional moment.[162] If an attempt is made to tackle Spain's claim head-on it should be in a de-bilateralised environment, in comprehensive all-issue trilateral talks without the current attempt to exclude Gibraltar from the sovereignty dimension. Placing antiquated or previously rejected constitutional models at the preconceived start of a solution-building exercise almost guarantees derailment. It would be an approach that would not have drawn sufficient lessons from the Anglo–Spanish joint sovereignty negotiations of 2001–02. This model-first approach starts at the wrong end. The correct approach would be to put principles, methodologies and context first, and then aim for a particular status that comfortably meets aspirations or allow a status to emerge through time that respects the canvas of pluralism, democracy, participation, legitimacy, late sovereignty, late decolonisation and stateless nationalism.

The Review of Status Models

Not surprisingly the patent inability of traditional models to present a cogent base for resolution of the historic dispute has bred confusion and disenchantment among Gibraltarians. This lack of enthusiasm for any particular option has been reflected in the few opinion polls conducted in Gibraltar on the subject.[163] Rather, the consistent tendency has been for people to react defensively, manifesting greatest support for the options of constitutional integration with Britain or *status quo*, even though plainly neither would address the deficit of bilateralism and the other net deficits identified in this work, conclusively deal with the Spanish question or meet aspirations of self-governance. Constitutional choices need to be more imaginative and properly factor in the overall constitutional context.

As has been previously noted there are different strands of nationalism that can be discerned among sectors of the Gibraltar population. There is the quasi-unionism of those who favour integration with Britain that generally tends to adopt a defensive stance to the Gibraltar issue. At the other extreme, there is a more radicalised nationalism that seeks a solution without taking any account of the Spanish dimension. Both do not properly factor in the modern constitutional context of contemporary Europe. The European dimension is the aspect that must be tackled to resolve governance issues. The macro-dispute level is also a part of that attempt at

[162] That would also pre-suppose that Spain's internal constitutional architecture would evolve to a point at which stable political cohabitation with Gibraltar will be more possible.

[163] eg, in polls conducted by the daily *Gibraltar Chronicle* in 2001 and 2002, no option (ranging from integration with Britain, free association, independence or Spanish sovereignty among others) received clear majority backing, with most opinion substantially divided among integration with Britain and free association.

solution-building. The largest failing of this strand of opinion is to mistake a willingness to recognise the mere existence of the Spanish issue as an acceptance of it. More practical nationalism would wish to factor in the presence of the Spanish dimension, so as to be able to circumvent it and to achieve a lasting constitutional status. In any event, what unites all strands of opinion—save for a very small minority—is a desire to find a solution that does not entail political absorption into the Spanish State.

The tendency of parties to the dispute towards maintaining traditional thinking and focussing on old prejudices and aspirations has hindered resolution of the conflict. Embracing modern pluralistic and democratic constitutionalism that gives primacy to peoples and both diffuses and de-fuses sovereignty will provide a serious prospect of resolution. Traditional models of status-change are out of step with this modern context. They are in any event premised on a conclusive sovereignty-win by one of the three parties that invariably makes this unacceptable to the other parties and fails to provide the necessary finality to the issue. The most commonly talked-about options for Gibraltar are integration with Spain; joint or partial Spanish sovereignty; *status quo*; integration with Britain; free association and independence. A brief examination of these demonstrates the patent deficiencies.

In the first place, those with a sole or partial Spanish sovereign element would not overcome the first hurdle of acceptance by the people of Gibraltar. Any attempt based on these would suffer from the same democratic deficit as the 2001–02 process as well as having firmly turned its back on the de-fusion of sovereignty that is so necessary in the solution-building process. The *status quo*—if by that is meant the pure retention of the current constitutional status (with by necessity the periodically reoccurring governance deficit too)—is undesirable and unrealistic. The current situation where the sovereignty dispute spills over onto the European stage and hampers Gibraltar's enjoyment of Union membership is less than productive. To that extent the *status quo* is unsustainable, because Gibraltar is being held back in a political time warp. To exacerbate matters, lack of access to governance reforms fostered by European integration trends, combined with encroachments on legislative sovereignty and insufficient participation in European decision-making, mean that there is a slow erosion of the powers of the Gibraltar executive and legislature in a way that continues to gradually undermine the self-government of Gibraltar. In this last sense this is not *status quo* at all, but rather a slow exacerbation of the current paradox of constitutionalism. The 2006 constitutional reform package has ameliorated the situation, but cannot, by itself, provide such lasting solutions.

Integration with Britain was a popular aspiration 40 years ago, and recently made a comeback, albeit with only qualified success. The current Integration with Britain Movement has its roots in the 1960s, when it started life as a political lobby group that slowly increased its prominence until it became a political party just before the 1969 general elections. It briefly formed Government in coalition with other members of the House until 1972. When the then Minister of State at the Foreign Office, Roy Hattersley, rejected the possibility of offering integration to Gibraltar,[164] the party disbanded.[165] The movement was revived in the late 1990s as a political pressure group. This continues to campaign on a relatively low-key basis for integration with Britain but has somewhat refined its demands since its predecessor movement by seeking a form of what they describe as 'devolved integration'.[166] The British Government has equivocated over integration by regularly saying that it is not on offer,[167] but also sometimes implying that (if the majority of people wanted it) it should be examined.[168] The devolved integration model propounded by its recent advocates is predicated on retention of wide powers of self-government, the achievement of representation in the House of Commons and the extension of an Act of Union to Gibraltar.[169] It does not, though, respond to the governance or constitutional trends that have been described in this chapter, and in this sense is socially, culturally, economically and politically defective.[170] It is also misconceived in its representation as the constitutional model that would cure the Spanish issue. It plainly would not.

There has never—hitherto—been any strong desire for independence in Gibraltar. Support for such an option in opinion polls has been low.[171] This would fit with the stateless nationalism of the majority of the population and its political representatives. The Gibraltar community has historically mainly divided into support for either constitutional integration with Britain or some form of free association. Indeed, the 2002 constitutional proposals were in practice a form of hybrid free association even though it has also been described as falling under the parameters referred to as the UN 'fourth option'.

More controversially some commentators have referred to an Andorra-style model for Gibraltar. This has proved controversial, only because the current constitutional status of Andorra is often misrepresented in the

164 Britain had offered it to Malta in the late 1950s.

165 Described in ch 2.

166 At the 2003 elections this was also supported by a couple of minority political parties (both of which together accounted for about 9% of the voting turnout).

167 Ministers from Roy Hattersley to Robin Cook or Jack Straw have stated that it is not available.

168 Interview with Denis MacShane, *Gibraltar Chronicle* (Gibraltar 5 July 2003).

169 Article by former IWBP member of the House of Assembly, Maurice Xibberas, *Gibraltar Chronicle* (Gibraltar 22 April 2003).

170 It would—significantly—swim in a directly opposite direction to full self-government, and this is probably why it does not achieve majority support. A more detailed exposition of these reasons is beyond the scope of this work.

171 Less than 10% in *Gibraltar Chronicle* polls conducted in 2001–02.

Gibraltar media as a form of joint sovereignty. A solution based on the Andorra model[172] would be a hybrid formula that would not fall under this heading. During the 2002 Anglo–Spanish process, Foreign Secretary Jack Straw made some equivocal reference that States were trying to construct a process based on the concept of legal sovereignty, without explaining what he specifically meant by this reference. He would later say that he did not seek to create any distinctions between 'legal sovereignty' and territorial sovereignty, but this seemed to be a clear allusion to how some misconstrue the Andorra model. Andorra was not a suitable precedent for the joint sovereignty model put forward in 2002 because, as a result of its 1993 Constitution, Andorra had become an independent State[173] and not a territory whose sovereignty was held jointly by two other States.

However, the Andorran model does provide an interesting example of an imaginative way of addressing the sovereignty issue albeit against a historical background that facilitated this. The preamble to the Andorra Constitution states that it is approved by 'the Andorran People, with full liberty and independence and in the exercise of their own sovereignty.' It goes on to declare in Article 1(3) that 'sovereignty is vested in the Andorran people, who exercise it through the different means of participation and by way of the institutions established in this Constitution.' The political system in Andorra is termed a parliamentary co-principat,[174] and Andorra is recognised to be a democratic and social independent State.[175] The Andorran Constitution recognises 'in accordance with the institutional tradition of Andorra'[176] that the Co-Princes are 'jointly and indivisibly' the Head of State of Andorra. The Co-Princes are a historical institution and 'are in their *personal* and exclusive right, the Bishop of Urgell and the President of the French Republic'[177] (emphasis added). The Co-Princes perform normal constitutional functions as Head of State within the Andorran system.[178] They also have functions in relation to certain categories of Treaties[179] or may initiate a process of constitutional revision and appoint some members of the judiciary.[180] It seems clear that the Andorran model is not one of joint sovereignty, but rather a model based on sovereign independence of Andorra where the people of Andorra, who are sovereign, have consented to the Co-Princes performing

[172] See the 1993 Constitution of Andorra: www.consell.ad/micg/webconsell.nsf.
[173] And a member of the United Nations.
[174] Art 1(4).
[175] Art 1(1).
[176] Art 43(1).
[177] Art 43(2). Note the use of the concept of a 'personal right'.
[178] See Arts 45 and 46. eg, the calling of general elections, the appointment of the Prime Minister, the accreditation of diplomatic representatives.
[179] Art 66 (in relation to internal security or defence).
[180] Art 96.

governmental functions and representing Andorra as their joint and indivisible Head of State. The Co-Princes are not sovereign in Andorra but representative of those who are sovereign—namely the people of Andorra.[181] To that extent, and while it is possible to speak of the Co-Princes having the titular sovereignty in Andorra, even that is a slight misnomer which does not accurately reflect the constitutional position, in that it insufficiently describes the sovereign legitimacy of the people of Andorra.[182] It is a moot point whether Spain would accept an Andorra-style solution, as it is tantamount to an acceptance by it of Gibraltarian independence.[183]

An analysis of these options can distil some key elements for inclusion in an evolved status that can be reached in application of the modern legal context. Some of the following constituent points could help demarcate the institutional and governmental framework of a constitutional status, and would need to be sensitively handled because of the potential for controversy. In general, the distinction between the entity in whose name titular sovereignty is placed, as opposed to the body vested with sovereignty (as in Andorra) is interesting. Recognition of the Crown as the holder of sovereignty on behalf of the people of Gibraltar would accord with that principle. Maduro notes that the people are the lifeblood from which the democratic process gains its legitimacy.[184] If sovereignty were vested in an entity on behalf of the people, then it would be possible to consider other permutations, even though it is clear that there is an affinity and desire of the people to retain a strong association with the British Crown.[185] It would be important to bear in mind that the sharpness of the current sovereignty dispute would need to be removed and that the symbols and trappings of unreconstructed nationalism are unhelpful to the resolution of the debate. As such, any possible de-fusion and diffusion of the sovereignty aspects should be encouraged through the neutralisation of some of these features.[186]

In terms of power structures, the aspiration of full internal self-government should be combined with the establishment of appropriate constitutional mechanisms that guarantee influence to the sub-State executive at European level. Inter-governmental structures could also be

[181] Art 43(1): the Co-Princes 'assume its [Andorra's] highest representation.'

[182] The Co-Princes are, eg—under Art 44—'the symbol and guarantee of [Andorra's] independence.'

[183] Though this option has never been formally mooted by any side and could have its face-saving attractions to Spain.

[184] Maduro in JHH Weiler and M Wind (eds), *European Constitutionalism Beyond the State* (Cambridge, CUP, 2003) 81.

[185] An aspiration not unlike current proposals of the Scottish SNP administration who favour retaining a link with the Crown as an independent nation on the basis that Her Majesty would remain 'Queen of Scotland'.

[186] The introduction of the EURO as the official currency of Gibraltar (as long as there were no good economic reasons to refuse to introduce this) is an example of this.

fostered outwith the Constitution, but in keeping with the division of competences set out in it to deal with the spill-over of decision-making that occurs outside a national polity's borders, as observed by Maduro. In broad terms, the formal vesting of sovereignty in the people of Gibraltar should be conferred in a form which secures constitutional entrenchment and which also places the judgment of the nature of the association with the European Union and the testing of the quality of membership of the Union in the hands of the Gibraltar demos. This would guarantee the overall fabric and social, political and economic integrity of the constitutional system. It would also secure its legitimacy.

Conscious of the dangerous fixation with constitutional labels and models it is with a great degree of caution that the loose term of 'European Free Association' is put forward as encapsulating all those elements of full internal self-government, Crown association, European Union membership, vesting of sovereignty in the people of the territory, supra-national intergovernmental bodies for economic, social and political co-operation and adequate constitutional mechanisms to secure representation, influence and power for civil society and the sub-State executive. It represents a marriage between free association, the so-called 'fourth option', stateless nationalism, late sovereignty and constitutional life within a supranational entity. It provides an accommodation of the modern legal context through an acceptance of statelessness. This could be the *quid pro quo* for Spain accepting that it cannot acquire sovereignty and that the people of Gibraltar are the key repository of sovereignty.[187] Pluralism and pragmatism are the threads underlying late sovereignty and stateless nationalism. An imaginative analysis of the elements of such a constitutional settlement could entail, for example, the President of the European Commission being given a nominal and personal constitutional role—jointly or subordinate to the Crown—to be exercised on solemn trust for the people of Gibraltar.[188] Indeed the parties may wish to enter into a tripartite Agreement or Treaty to replace the Treaty of Utrecht, to which the EU may become a fourth party if it is to have some involvement in the resolution of the conflict.[189] Such a Treaty could provide for the vesting of sover-

[187] Though it may be possible to retain a contingent aspiration to independence.

[188] With sufficient political will of the parties a specific amendment to the Treaties could be considered to give sufficient support for the involvement of the Commission in the conflict resolution or any constitutional model that emerges. Presumably this could alter Gibraltar's relationship with the Union. New Art 313(6) in the Lisbon Treaty provides an interesting analogy, by which the status of a Danish, Dutch or French territory could be changed by unanimous decision of the Council after consulting the Commission. To ensure legitimacy and safety any mechanism which allows a similar alteration would have to provide for the prior agreement of the sub-State executive of Gibraltar.

[189] The possibility of such an Agreement or the details of which would be canvassed at talks between the parties, and further consideration of this is outside the scope of this work. As for the EU's general competence to enter into Agreements on external affairs see P Koutrakos, *EU International Relations Law* (Oxford, Hart Publishing, 2006).

eignty in or for the people of Gibraltar on trust. Other aspects would have to be critically looked at to deliver sufficient self-governance that meets aspirations and resolves the current deficit. Such a solution would develop in parallel to the production of other organs of co-operative governance devised to assist the different nations co-habiting in this southern European governance space.[190]

The first task, as has been stated, is for all parties to fully accept that they are operating within an environment of late sovereignty, constitutional pluralism, stateless nationalism and participatory governance, in which the key elements are democracy, participation, legitimacy and a diffusion and de-fusion of sovereignty. Equally, there would have to be a realisation that it is the people[191] that are central to the solution-building process. In that modern context, and having then adopted solution-building mechanisms for dialogue and unblocked the governance deficit, the parties would either then turn to the issue of status or merely allow one to emerge in accordance with the parameters of pluralism. Indeed it is consistent with stateless nationalism for the focus and objective to be on practical power and not on theoretical status. To that extent, and as these concepts of sovereignty, nationalism and governance continue to evolve within the European arena, the solution to the sovereignty question of Gibraltar might even, paradoxically, lie in simply allowing the focus, objectives, principles and parameters governing the dispute to change and the principal governance deficits to be unblocked. Though it would deliver clarity and certainty to settle a new status for Gibraltar, participants should not zealously pursue status change as if it were the sole, elusive and coveted constitutional elixir. Indeed, in some ways, the pursuit of a mystical new status is a complete distraction from the real debate that must first be had in relation to the current legal context. By getting to the heart of the governance and democratic deficit and first placing the sovereignty issue into its proper perspective, it may eventually be possible to find a solution to the status debate which to many now would seem akin to finding an Eskimo in the desert.

[190] A new status could then lead to the inclusion of Gibraltar within the definition of 'associated State' under British domestic law, thereby removing Gibraltar from the definition of 'colony.'

[191] In Gibraltar, Spain and the UK.

Conclusion: Sovereign within Spheres of Influence

Sovereignty is no longer the recognition of a power over a people but the collective right of a people to participate in, and benefit from, an independent political community participating as an equal in the community of nations. To put it another way, sovereignty becomes a human right.[1]

INTRODUCTION

ANYONE WONDERING HOW 2009 greeted the long-standing Gibraltar dispute would be forgiven for getting lost in the contradictions and ambiguities of the most recent developments. Weeks before HRH Princess Anne was due to open a medical centre in Gibraltar, the Spanish Government called in the British Ambassador to Madrid to file a diplomatic protest at the visit, calling it 'inopportune' and insensitive, because the ceremony was to take place on the 'disputed isthmus'.[2] In July 2009, for the purpose of a Ministerial round of the Tripartite talks, the Spanish Foreign Minister made the historic first official visit of a serving Spanish Minister. This was a significant political gesture along the road to formal recognition of Gibraltar. Mr Moratinos was heavily criticised by elements of the Spanish press.[3] In terms of sovereignty he made clear, however, that Spain's claim was 'irrenounceable' and that it viewed the tripartite process as a means to regaining Gibraltar.[4] In 2007 and 2008 Spain had, once again, put across its traditional line on sovereignty before the UN Special Committee on Decolonisation—that this could only be discussed bilaterally with the United Kingdom and that self-determination was not to be applied to Gibraltar's decolonisation.[5] When a United States

[1] TM Franck, 'Fairness in International Law and Institutions' (1995) cited in J Nijman, 'Sovereignty and Personality: A Process of Inclusion' in Kreijen (ed), *State, Sovereignty and International Governance* (Oxford, OUP, 2004) 144.

[2] The Opposition *Partido Popular* described the visit as 'an affront to Spain'—see *Gibraltar Chronicle* (Gibraltar 24 February 2009). The diplomatic protest followed on from comments days earlier by the Foreign Affairs spokesman of the ruling Spanish Socialist Party in the Senate, who had called for bilateral talks on sovereignty and also remarked that the intended visit by Princess Anne to Gibraltar was a 'provocation' and could derail the tripartite process—see *Gibraltar Chronicle* (Gibraltar 16 February 2009 and 21 February 2009).

[3] The headline in *El Mundo* was 'Photograph of Shame', 22 July 2009.

[4] *Gibraltar Chronicle* 22 July 2009, *El Pais* 22 July 2009, *ABC* 22 July 2009.

[5] See eg the intervention of Ambassador Sr Iñigo de Palacio España to the UN Special Committee on Decolonisation, 4 June 2007.

company found a haul of gold off Gibraltar, a Spanish police vessel arrested the company's boat and Spain issued a statement that the arrest had taken place within Spanish territorial waters and that Gibraltar had, in effect, none.[6] While agreement had been reached on a formula to unblock the applicability of conventions that had lain frozen because of the dispute over Gibraltar problems of a similar type continued to arise. All this made the House of Commons Foreign Affairs Committee recommend to the UK Government that it should make

> strong representations to Spain and within NATO at the highest level about the unacceptability of Spain's continuing restrictions on direct naval, army and air-force movements or military communications between Spain and Gibraltar . . . [and Spain's] failure to recognise Gibraltar's territorial waters and its objections to international conventions being extended to Gibraltar.[7]

Notwithstanding this the classic manifestations of the dispute resurfaced with Spanish claims to Gibraltar territorial waters reappearing in 2009.[8] The sovereignty dispute seemed as intractable as ever. The Gibraltar issue was a source of discord at the UN and continued to be the subject of difficulties at European level. While there had been some improvements Gibraltar continued to suffer from the governance and democratic deficit that stemmed from the stifling bilateralism and hampered access to adequate power, representation and influence. The State-centricity that was the hallmark of bilateralism between UK and Spain remained a strong feature. Both the United Nations and the European Union continued to defer to the bilateralism.[9] Spain felt little if any pressure from these levels. There was some justification for the feeling that this was symptomatic of a trend observed by McCorquodale in another context by which, taken to an extreme, 'States live happily ever after as the creators of all international law for their own international community.'[10]

But this was scarcely three years after the constitutional and trilateral developments of the autumn of 2006 had promised a complete overhaul in relations. The Córdoba arrangements had unblocked long-standing irri-

[6] The saga of the *MV Odyssey*: *Gibraltar Chronicle* (Gibraltar 13 July 2007). A position reiterated by the Spanish Ambassador to the House of Commons Foreign Affairs Committee in 2008: see the FAC Report 2008 at paras 408–13.

[7] ibid para 414.

[8] In mid-December 2008, a second list of sites of Community importance for the Mediterranean bio-geographical region was adopted under Council Directive 92/43 EEC (the Habitats Directive). In it Spain purported to designate an area of Gibraltar waters as its national site of Community interest. It raised a political storm with the British Government saying it would investigate the circumstances of that designation—see *Gibraltar Chronicle* (Gibraltar 28 February 2009) and Commission Decision of 12 December 2008, 2009/95/EC, OJ L43/393, 13 February 2009. The Gibraltar Government launched legal proceedings to challenge the designation on 6 May 2009 Case T-176/09 *Government of Gibraltar v Commission*.

[9] chs 3 and 6.

[10] McCorquodale in C Warbrick and S Tierney (eds), *Towards an International Legal Community: The Sovereignty of States and the Sovereignty of International Law* (London, British Institute of International and Comparative Law, 2006) 242.

tants and been heralded as a new climate in trilateral relations between the parties. The new 2006 Constitution was the most significant package of reforms Gibraltar had ever been offered. Undoubtedly 2006 had delivered improvements to the often fraught relationship between the parties which would have seemed difficult to foresee at the height of the joint-sovereignty talks barely a few years earlier.[11] But the steps forward were guarded and the Spanish Government was keen to emphasise whenever it got the opportunity that it was not agreeing to de-bilateralise the issue of sovereignty. Equally, the new constitution provided much by way of internal self-government and achieved the long-standing desire for a clause on self-determination, but it did not deliver sufficient external governance mechanisms or adequately deal with the European governance dimension. Gibraltar still lacked proper power, representation and influence at the all-important European level. The paradox of governance and constitutionalism remained.

In terms of the possibility of formal decolonisation on the basis of the new Constitution this was placed for determination before a UN that seemed paralysed by State-centricity. The subsequent 'intense debate' in late 2008 that saw fundamental disagreement between States as to whether territorial sovereignty claims should qualify the application of the principle of self-determination demonstrated how the interests of some States clearly conflicted with those of colonial peoples. Additionally a lukewarm attitude by the British Government—that resisted actively lobbying for de-listing or ceasing to report on Gibraltar under Article 73[12]—and a very pro-active and diplomatically hostile Spain made the prospect of progress at the UN seem distinctly improbable for Gibraltar. It seemed unlikely that the UN would agree to de-list Gibraltar. The cause of that did not seem to be based on a detailed analysis of the content of the 2006 Constitution against specific criteria but rather seemed more to do with the culture of bilateralism.[13] It may be that, critically seen, the package of reforms was deficient in some aspect. Unfortunately the perception had been created that the UN might even resist a set of reforms that met the necessary criteria, on the grounds that the dispute has not been

[11] Further agreements are envisaged by 2010 on a number of matters. It is expected that financial services, environment and culture issues will feature in the next round of possible specific areas of discussion.

[12] On the basis that it was now decolonised. Although the letter sent by the UK in January 2007 (see ch 7) was positive in that it made clear that it did not think any of its 'remaining territories, including Gibraltar, should remain on the United Nations List', it went on that as the UK believed the criteria were outdated it did not 'engage formally with the Committee in seeking the de-listing of any of its territories.'

[13] There seems to have been no concerted attempt by the C24 to conduct an extensive critical analysis of the reforms against existing criteria. If it does not meet these it would, at least, fall within the staging-post category suggested by Crawford: see ch 3. In any event a clear qualitative assessment of any deficiencies would at least provide clarity for the territory which would allow it to take constitutional stock of the situation.

resolved to the satisfaction of both States concerned and thus did not meet the spirit of the bilaterally-rooted annual decisions on Gibraltar.[14]

Even so, given the depth and width of the reforms the acceptance of the 2006 constitutional package provided a stepping-stone to further reforms and kept alive the possibility of decolonisation. It moved the constitutional debate forward substantially. Equally, seizing the opportunity to pursue trilateral talks with Spain was also positive imperfect though this process was. It did achieve large strides in the amelioration of irritants over frontier flows, transport and telecommunications, that in overall terms improved the lives of citizens on both sides of the border.[15] Even though Gibraltar had achieved certain constitutional and practical advances towards the end of 2006, it became clear that any talk of a dramatically new era had been a false dawn. The fundamental backdrop to the sovereignty dispute was still the classic bilateral one and insufficiently paid regard to a more modern legal context. The combination of all this held back any effective long-term resolution of the dispute. Prospect of real change at the level of status and governance on the issues that needed to be unblocked—a permanent decolonised status and an enhancement of external / European governance—seemed a distant prospect.

CONTINUED BILATERALISM, OLD SOVEREIGNTY AND THE GOVERNANCE AND DEMOCRATIC DEFICIT

At its conceptual core, the language that Spain deployed at the UN in 2007–08 seemed a carbon copy of the 1960s. There were distinct parallels in the fact that recognition of Gibraltar ID cards or international conventions were blocked in 2007 in a similar way to the manner they were objected to 30 years earlier.[16] Spain's proposals for decolonisation still promoted perceptions of old sovereignty cloaked in absolutism and territorial ownership. The 1997 Matutes proposals on sovereignty were little different to those fielded by Castiella in the 1960s and in turn these were not fundamentally different to the joint-sovereignty proposals of 2002.[17] The aspirations voiced at the UN by Spain in 2006–08 were firmly rooted in that legal and historical approach and had seen scarce ideological movement.[18]

What had changed since the 1960s were the British attitude and the ability of Spain to exert more direct governance influence on Gibraltar.

[14] It should also be noted that the UK position has previously been that de-listing is a matter for the Administering power and the territory: see ch 3, p 119.

[15] Though even here old grievances like long delays in crossing the border resurface periodically.

[16] ch 2.

[17] ch 2, pp 70–71 and ch 3, p 111.

[18] For example the desire expressed to revive a bilateral process on sovereignty side-by-side with the trilateral process on co-operation.

Britain had been steadfast during those years but subsequently took a more conciliatory attitude to democratic Spain in an effort to forge alliances and was more willing to compromise over Gibraltar. It led to an agreement to discuss sovereignty in 1984 and eventually to Britain's acceptance of joint sovereignty that only stalled because of local opposition. Spain found that its presence in the European Community allowed it to influence and obstruct measures in respect of Gibraltar on a regular basis. From air measures to frontier flows, global financial initiatives to international conventions, the breadth of Spanish influence was both specific to Gibraltar and in some cases affected other States too.[19] The Note Spain submitted to the United Kingdom[20] a day after accession typified its general attitude and sent a strong signal on what would follow. Accession for Spain did not affect its view that Gibraltar remained a bilateral dispute to be resolved with the United Kingdom as sole interlocutor. It so happened, though, that accession would provide a firm launching pad for Spain to pursue its policy over Gibraltar.

Bilateralism between Britain and Spain contributed to an impasse over Gibraltar. It was the first and principal democratic deficit faced by Gibraltar. It was in stark contrast to all trends promoting legitimacy and the rights of *demoi*. It also provoked a threefold sub-effect by hampering constitutional reform, affecting internal and external governance and obstructing the pursuit of a decolonised status acceptable to the people of the territory. The deficit manifested itself in different forms at European level. Measures were blocked and Gibraltar simply did not acquire commensurate power, representation and influence that other stateless nations enjoyed. The need to deal with this was clear. The longer these items were unattended the more the hard-won constitutional gains were eroded in practice by insufficient power, representation and influence at European level. Inadequate governance arrangements, fuelled by bilateralism, paradoxically meant that Gibraltar suffered an encroachment of its powers, and resulted in it coming to suffer an erosion of power, representation and influence. This paradox encases the sovereign people of Gibraltar within arrangements of a constitutional or conceptual type that they are unable to change. The paradox spans the field of status as well as governance because the bilateralism stems from the territorial sovereignty dispute and spills over into any attempt to obtain constitutional reform, decolonisation or a long-term resolution of the conflict.

This bilateral policy has been in direct conflict with trends within the European Union that have placed emphasis on multi-level governance, participatory democracy and recognition of pluralism. Promoting democracy, legitimacy and greater cohesion for a Europe of peoples 'united in

[19] Because for example the EC were prevented from pursuing Community-wide initiatives: see ch 6.

[20] ch 2, p 105.

diversity' has been at the centre of those efforts. The Commission has regularly been concerned about the ownership and support of the European project by the citizens of the Union. Without such support there is a lack of connection with the citizen, which results in growing disenchantment with Europe. Realisation of this fostered measures to increase accountability, transparency, access to information, greater consultation, participation, influence, subsidiarity and the increased use of 'soft law'. The debate on promoting inclusion and a culture of greater legitimacy dominated the philosophical debates of the Union and the interface between States, parliaments, sub-State executives and European citizens. Even though this was the philosophical flavour of much of the last two decades, the States and European institutions failed to vigorously promote that same ethos to the Gibraltar dispute. In respect of Gibraltar bilateralism was preferred to pluralism. The Commission exercised whatever discretion it held so as to avoid intervening. It did not take action on anti-competitive action by Spanish telecoms carriers, who were following the instructions of the Spanish State. It failed to give a reasoned opinion on the issue of the franchise to European Parliamentary elections even when this was mandatory. It regularly referred to the dispute as bilateral and that it was 'encouraging' the States to resolve 'their' dispute. The people of Gibraltar's European citizens were mere objects of bilateralism and supra-nationalism. The UN level was little different. Since 1960 the landmark Resolution on Decolonisation required that the central matter to be promoted was the road to self-government by colonial peoples. Instead the colonial people of Gibraltar played second fiddle to the concern the UN felt about the bilateral relations between two of its Member States.[21] That State-centricity remains at European Union level and within the United Nations. These supra-national entities have not assisted in breaking that bilateralism, and there is little evidence that this will change. Attempts in June 2007 by the Chairman of the Special Committee on Decolonisation to fight the Gibraltar and Falkland Islands corner in a more active way[22] ended in failure and in her stating to the Committee of 24 that she had had to 'pay a heavy price' for such support.[23]

While the generally accepted view is that sovereignty is evolving in its meaning and has been driving governance changes in Europe it was the classic view of sovereignty that was applied to Gibraltar. It has been seen how sovereignty has been the stifling environment of this dispute and that this has been fuelled by the oxygen of conflicting nationalism. The tradi-

[21] See for example the UN Resolution of December 1973 cited in ch 2, p 77. The bilateralism continues in the text of annual decisions made over Gibraltar.

[22] When she opposed the suggestion made at a Regional Seminar in 2007 that decolonisation for territories on the List of non-self-governing territories subject to a sovereignty claim should not be resolved by application of the right to self-determination.

[23] 9 July 2007.

tional view that sovereignty was the sole domain of States and that only these were objects of international law, combined with a zealous focussing on territory rather than peoples, encouraged the stranglehold of bilateralism. This led to a resistance of participation by Gibraltar on discussions on sovereignty for fear that ceding influence over the decision-making stage would undermine the exclusivity that could otherwise be enjoyed by the administering and claimant States. The interjection of a populace with a claim for a say in the future of the land or worse still sovereign rights could only inevitably upset this strategy. This clash of seemingly unbridgeable aspirations—Spain to the territory; Gibraltar to a self-governing future without Spain; Britain to any solution[24] that discharged its domestic obligations to Gibraltar and its desire for an *entente* with Spain—spilled over into the European stage with significant effect.

1. THE REDEFINITION OF CONCEPTS AND THE EMERGENCE OF THE STATELESS NATION OF GIBRALTAR AS A SOVEREIGNTY PLAYER

Ultimately it is the conceptual source of the dispute that needs to be reassessed and addressed if there is to be a deep-rooted contextual review of the conflict. As has been seen throughout this work sovereignty *qua* international law/status and sovereignty *qua* governance/power are deeply interrelated in the Gibraltar environment. Indeed it is by allowing these potentially distinct streams to converge that there can be some move towards resolution of this conflict. By doing so non-absolutist solutions emerge at both status and governance level.

The concept of sovereignty has radically evolved in its meaning and its interrelationship with civil society over the last few decades. No longer absolutist in nature, restricted to the State level or in a territorial sense equated to exclusivity and independence, there is a delicate interplay of societal groups, representative institutions and other players in the governance framework. The evolution in the meaning of sovereignty cuts across all areas in which it is present. The forces of democracy, self-determination, legitimacy and civil rights drove a different understanding of sovereignty *qua* power and competence in the governance field. The same principles contributed to the drive towards decolonisation and the understanding of sovereignty *qua* international law and Statehood in the status field. In both dimensions the rise of and respect of peoples and their wishes was central.

Already by 1960 it was clear in the decolonisation resolutions that independence was not the sole avenue to full self-government for a colonial

[24] As long as its military interests were safeguarded.

people. Territories on the list of non-self-governing countries[25] had contingent sovereignty by their mere presence on the List and could even argue that there had been a displacement of sovereignty from the administering power in their favour. A people could be sovereign, in that sense, without being independent.[26] But a people could not be independent without being sovereign. The locus of sovereignty can shift as well as the bodies enjoying the shifting sovereignty can change through time. Stateless nationalism has in many ways responded well to that evolution by dropping pro-active separatist ambitions realising that it was no longer necessary to acquire Statehood as a lever to obtain power and influence. The European dimension introduced mechanisms of subsidiarity, proportionality and greater democracy to cater for these ambitions and a wider wish to obtain the endorsement of citizens to the European project. It was possible to contain national movements through an adjustment of State constitutional arrangements and by accommodating the sub-State executive with greater influence at European level. In that task the State was the Primary Driver and the European Union the Secondary Driver. The predominance of the State level as both contributor to the deficits and instrumental to their unblockage is evident throughout this work.

As plurinationalism, multi-level governance and polycentric constitutionalism became the new drivers of governance and sovereignty within a supra-national entity there are dimensions that have not kept pace with that. The first is the United Nations, decolonisation and status dimension. The criteria for decolonisation were devised around 50 years ago. Many States resist any adjustment of the traditional methods of decolonisation even though there is much to be said in revisiting the criteria or acknowledging the place for a tailor-made fourth option of 'any other status' freely determined by the people of the territory. If the same 50- year period were taken as a retrospective benchmark it is easy to see how much things change over time. 50 years before the 1960 decolonisation resolutions, the League of Nations had not been born, the possibility of self-determination being considered an applicable legal principle was ridiculed, and sovereignty principles excluded non-State entities as mere objects of international law. In the sub-State colonial context 50 years ago most of the now independent commonwealth were colonies and there were still arguments about the unity of the Crown. But this 'settled constitutional doctrine'[27] started to evolve to a position of divisibility and eventual recognition that an 'important constitutional change'[28] had occurred. In that context a

[25] Referred to in the rest of this chapter simply as 'the List'.

[26] This is accurate not only in respect of status but also in respect of governance: see reference to *Mellenger* below.

[27] O Hood Phillips, *Constitutional and Administrative Law*, 8th edn (Sweet & Maxwell, London, 2001) 771.

[28] *R v Secretary of State for Foreign and Commonwealth Affairs, ex p Indian Assocn of Alberta* [1982] 1 QB 892, 917 (Lord Denning MR).

50-year period cannot be ignored, and it is unrealistic to solve matters within the international or European dimension through 1960 looking-glasses. As the International Court observed in the *Namibia* case, it is necessary to consider

> the changes which have occurred in the supervening half-century and its interpretation cannot remain unaffected by the subsequent development of law through the Charter of the United Nations and by way of customary law.[29]

Spain already to its credit recognises the possibility of a so-called fourth option[30] though it maintains such cannot be applied to Gibraltar. At the UN level, there should be a review of decolonisation criteria and categories or at the very least a more flexible application of these to give force to Crawford's belief that there is enough in modes of free association to accommodate the remaining territories.[21]

As has been stated, 'legal theory does not always march alongside political reality',[32] and that is particularly appropriate to describe the lack of connection between the studied resistance to change by the UN and the political reality that current criteria may no longer properly accommodate territories. States devised colonialism and the rules for decolonisation.[33] These remain colonial and State-centric in nature, in that, even if asked by a colonial people to de-list a territory, the UN cannot do so unless it is first asked by the Administering Power.[34] Historically, the UN also demonstrated a resistance to other legitimate acts by colonial peoples.[35] There is as much a need for an emergence of an era of 'late decolonisation' as there was for recognition of the continually important but evolved meaning of sovereignty. Here decolonisation would still be important, but would be seen in the modern global and plural context of polycentric constitutionalism and stateless nationalism. In such a world, traditional status change would be as defunct, as traditional sovereignty and flexibility and interplay of polities would be the key.[36]

[29] *The Legal Consequences for States of the Continued Presence of South Africa in Namibia (South West Africa) Notwithstanding Security Council Resolutions 276 (1970)* [1971] ICJ Rep 31.

[30] Intervention of the Spanish Delegation before the UN Fourth Committee October 1998.

[31] ch 2: presenting a bid for decolonisation under the banner of Free Association seems at first sight potentially easier than the fourth option, as it does not engage the territory in debate about whether such a category exists.

[32] Hood Phillips n 25 above, 64, and *British Coal Corp v The King* [1935] AC 500, 520 (Sankey LJ).

[33] For an interesting analysis see J Tully, 'The Imperialism of Modern Constitutional Democracy' in M Loughlin and N Walker (eds), *The Paradox of Constitutionalism, Constituent Power and Constitutional Form* (Oxford, OUP, 2007) 315–38.

[34] Chairman of C24, cited in *Gibraltar Chronicle* (Gibraltar 6 June 2007).

[35] For example by rejecting the West Indies free association arrangements or the 1967 Gibraltar referendum.

[36] The caveat that should be added to this debate is that it is easy to mistakenly assume decolonisation and de-listing as the ultimate goal. Plainly it is not as it does not necessarily take a territory closer to Statehood or finality unless accompanied by adequate reforms.

The application of modern principles seemed also to run askew in Gibraltar's case. At both UN and European levels this was still dominated by State-centric bilateralism notwithstanding the emerging macro governance tendencies. At the very least, what had occurred had converted the people of Gibraltar into a real sovereignty player that could lay claim to corresponding accommodation at domestic, European and international level. A separate people with a distinct identity had evolved over the last three centuries from a combination of the small residue of an indigenous population, civilian settlers and military garrison. It is on that initial fusion of multi-culturalism leading to the evolution of a single national identity upon which the edifice of sub-State constitutionalism is built. That then seeks respect, recognition and peaceful accommodation. In the post-war period that saw the recognition of self-determination as a legal principle, the creation of a European Community of States and a wave of decolonisation, Gibraltar achieved substantial self-government. The introduction of ministerial government in 1964 then swiftly led to the introduction of a further advanced constitution in 1969. Gibraltar was close to full self-government, and only held back because of the territorial sovereignty dispute with Spain. Accession to the Community by Britain (and with it, Gibraltar) in 1973, Spanish democratisation in 1975, followed by its own accession to the EC in 1986, changed the ground rules and made the Community the growing central theatre of developments for Gibraltar.

In the post-war period there were a number of developments that led initially to a clearly identifiable involvement in decision-making and thereafter to a gradual displacement of sovereignty to the people of Gibraltar.[37] First, Gibraltar was listed as a non-self-governing territory and subject to the application of the principle of self-determination. Second, in the face of Spanish proposals over Gibraltar, Britain organised a referendum in 1967 and asked the people to determine the future of the territory.[38] Thirdly, the Preamble to the 1969 Gibraltar constitution set out a commitment that Gibraltar would not be transferred to another State against the freely expressed wishes of its people. This still fell short of a positive right to self-determination but was at least a right to consent.

Substance is more important than form. The similar observation in the Spanish Government's June 2007 UN speech that it is not the exercise of de-listing that is an end in itself, but rather that substantive decolonisation is achieved, is to that extent correct. The example of New Caledonia given in the previous chapter is relevant. As Crawford has noted (at 358), it is not necessary to acquire 'complete independence' to be considered as having features of Statehood or being classified as a State, and as such the consequence of driving self-government to the edge of non-separatism is that the nation may even acquire international personality but not independence: see classification of 'Territorial Entities Proximate to State', J Crawford, *The Creation of States in International Law*, 2nd edn (Oxford, OUP, 2006) 739. There will inevitably be a very fine line between that status and independence.

[37] To coin a phrase, it was recognition of its 'distinct sovereignty': see reference to *Bancoult* in ch 6.

[38] Albeit with limited options of choice.

Fourthly, in 1972 the Gibraltar Government were given the option to decide whether to join the Community with Britain or not. Fifthly, taken collectively, post-war constitutional development had delivered internal self-government of a nature and extent that the Government of Gibraltar had become 'sovereign within its own sphere of influence.'[39] As the Crown is considered divisible, it has also been expressed as the Crown in right of the particular territory being sovereign for these powers.[40] Sixthly, and conversely, the Anglo-Spanish approximation of the 1980s leading to the 2002 agreement to share sovereignty over Gibraltar was representative of the micro-trend of State-centric bilateralism devoid of sufficient reference to the populace and of the consequent legitimacy which the *demos* could confer. The defeat of the joint-sovereignty proposals was driven by the campaign of opposition promoted by the people of Gibraltar, which culminated in the referendum of November 2002, in which more than 98 per cent of those voting rejected the principle of joint sovereignty. This lay emphasis, if such was necessary, to the fact that support of the people is an essential ingredient to any proposal for fundamental sovereignty change. Seventhly, the 2006 Constitution delivered a package of reforms very close to full self-government and inserted a right to self-determination of its people. Within the important sphere of rights to land such changes support this drift of sovereignty towards the people. By section 75 of the 2006 Constitution the land of the Crown in Gibraltar[41] is held in right of Gibraltar. Decisions concerning such land must be taken 'in accordance with the advice of the Chief Minister.' That provision gives the elected Government of Gibraltar a much clearer mechanism to determine and control rights over the land in Gibraltar. Finally, in November 2006, in a third referendum, a majority of the people supported the adoption of the 2006 Constitution in an 'act of self-determination'.

The constitutions negotiated in 1964, 1969 and 2006 all engaged cross-party political representation with the 2006 Constitution being adopted in referendum.[42] The powers discharged by the elected representatives *qua* Crown in right of Gibraltar demonstrate a constitutional convergence between the people of Gibraltar and the Crown in right of Gibraltar. This convergence spans the fields of governance and status and the domestic[43] and international levels.[44] This fact, which is in perfect synchrony with

[39] *Mellenger v New Brunswick Development Corp* [1971] 1 WLR 604, 608—to such an extent that such a territory is entitled to sovereign immunity.

[40] ibid.

[41] There are comparatively few freeholds in Gibraltar. The vast majority of land is held directly by the Crown or by private entities on leases of varying length from the Crown.

[42] *cf* the change in attitude evident in the UK's description of this as 'democratic, lawful and entirely proper' (letter of 22 January 2007 to UN) with their description of the 2002 referendum as 'eccentric': above.

[43] Through the constitutional advances.

[44] Because of the effect of the right to self-determination.

pluralism and late sovereignty, is deeply relevant to the methodology by which the dispute should be approached and resolved. The displacement of sovereignty in favour of the people of Gibraltar either in terms of the cumulative domestic constitutional changes or the right to self-determination at international law seems beyond reasonable resistance.[45] As Wade highlights 'when sovereignty is relinquished in an atmosphere of harmony, the naked fact of revolution is not so easy to discern beneath its elaborate legal dress.'[46] But the political fact of a subtle sovereignty revolution remains as the explication of these developments in Gibraltar's case. In that way this is classic Bodin in action, with the acquisition of sovereignty by the people and the subsequent and continuing delegation by them to their trustees in governance.[47]

Gibraltar may be sovereign within its spheres of influence but the impact of bilateralism threatens to undermine its constitutional gains and produces that paradox of constitutionalism and governance described earlier. Inadequately addressed, there is a slow but continued erosion of power and insufficient influence within Europe, as well as a paralysed international status. Crucial to tackling the paradox is a sustained end to bilateralism, an application of the modern legal context and a climate of comprehensive all-issue trilateralism. If channelled positively 'sub-state nationalism may come to represent part of a trend towards the reclamation of popular politics; and then the new challenge will be to redefine democratic constitutional models better to accommodate it.'[48]

Spain has denied the participation of Gibraltar in sovereignty talks as much as some in Gibraltar have pretended to blank out Spain as a reality in the conundrum. But the lack of acceptance of Gibraltar as a sovereignty player does not accord with the evolved legal environment. Historically, it has been as unacceptable to Spain for Gibraltar to play a sovereignty part as it has been for Gibraltar to accept Spain as a sovereignty player in its future. At the very least, both Gibraltar and Spain should recognise the fact that each others claims to sovereignty exist[49] and that there is therefore a practical need to engage each other in discussions over them. That does not mean that either party's demands will be acceded to or that in any way this is a concessionary act. It is merely recognition of legal and political realities. For Spain it means embracing Gibraltar as a sovereignty player. This is essential from the perspective of the reality that the *demos* of

[45] See further *Dominion of Canada v Province of Ontario* [1910] AC 637.

[46] W Wade, 'The Basis of Legal Sovereignty' (1955) CLJ 177–97, 191.

[47] In the despatch to the 2006 Constitution the then Foreign Secretary makes the point that 'this constitution does not in any way diminish British sovereignty of Gibraltar': Despatch to 2006 Constitution, para 4. Notwithstanding that, and given the general standing of the Despatch, the conclusions stated above are unaffected because of their cumulative constitutional consequence.

[48] S Tierney, *Constitutional Law and National Pluralism* (Oxford, OUP, 2004) 340.

[49] Without the need for accepting them.

Gibraltar is the constituent power of present and future constitutional form. Equally, Spain has sought to restrict governance reform for Gibraltar or other changes for fear that by acquiring external competences or a presence on the international stage it signalled the actions of independent statehood.[50] This attitude affected not only the UN stage, but also Spain's attitude to constitutional reform and the presence and participation of Gibraltar in the European Community. But even though concern about the potential use of self-determination as a separatist lever is understandable the parties must also be conscious that, in fact, Gibraltar's governance ambitions within Europe and its current decolonisation and status ambitions could be accommodated without the pursuit of separatist options. Obtaining international recognition and lasting political peace can motivate all parties to a more productive all-issue process, but in doing so there is also a need to factor in principles of justice, human rights and Kymlicka's call for greater respect to be injected into the management of complex international, multi-cultural problems.[51]

It is no more possible to forcibly integrate Gibraltar and then grant it devolution within Spain than it would be to repeal the devolution arrangements of the Basque Country and Catalunya. No Spanish Government could seek a mandate to abolish self-government for the historic nations of the Basque Country and Catalunya without provoking a constitutional schism within Spain. It is not a greater leap of constitutional assumption to accept that is similarly impossible to seek integration of Gibraltar. While Spain has offered Gibraltar formulas of generous devolution within the Spanish State those options can never realistically progress because the source and constituent power of that devolution are the civil society of Gibraltar that has made clear its opposition to a constitutional solution with Spain. If the people of Gibraltar wish to choose to share some powers in future cooperative, multi-national arrangements then that is their right to exercise but it would have to follow recognition and respect of its sovereignty. As MacCormick has colourfully noted, the key questions are:

> Is sovereignty like property which can be given up only when another person gains it? Or should we think of it more like virginity, something that can be lost by one without another gaining it—and whose loss in apt circumstances can even be a matter for celebration.[52]

But to continue the analogy, a person cannot celebrate a loss of virginity without knowing that this is held, and it being accepted that this is so. First

[50] Case C-145/04 *Spain v UK* [2006] ECR I-07917.

[51] For a detailed analysis of the role that such principles should play in the resolution of international conflicts see A Buchanan, *Justice, Legitimacy and Self-Determination* (Oxford, OUP, 2006).

[52] N MacCormick, *Questioning Sovereignty: Law, State and Practical Reason* (Oxford, OUP, 1999) 126.

that pre-requisite of implied or express acknowledgment must be met. That may entail a cathartic process for Spain—in some ways more cathartic than legalising the Communist Party in the 1970s or contemplating a Basque right to self-determination, but still a necessary catharsis. Post- the catharsis, new understandings are possible because they are built on the more solid foundations of a plural perspective of mutual acceptance, respect and participation. All three parties in the Gibraltar dispute are, or were at some stage, sovereignty players, and the position of each should be recognised and respected. Spain is the original grantor, Britain the original recipient and the People of Gibraltar the acquirer and possessor, because of constitutional developments and the modern legal context. At the very least and on a *de minimis* basis, it would have to be recognised that Gibraltar is sovereign within its domestic spheres of influence and, as would now be said in Catalunya, because of its 'inalienable right to self-government',[53] which may, because of its own domestic constitutional scene, be the closest Spain could presently come to trumpeting the concept of self-determination.

There is no contradiction when approaching the dilemma from the perspective of late sovereignty to take the correlation of the Gibraltar *demos* to sovereignty as the starting point. As has been seen, sovereignty remains a meaningful concept, full of emotion, and of legal and political relevance to all parties. In that way we are in a re-defined evolved sovereignty environment, and not in an era 'post-sovereignty'. It is entirely appropriate in that environment to recognise the claim of the people of Gibraltar to be the constituent power and sovereign in its own right. Solutions would stem from giving the *demos* a full role and recognising the power of the Crown in right of Gibraltar on behalf of its people, first at any consideration of sovereignty questions, and secondly in the full enjoyment and recognition of its status and governance rights. At that stage the division and combination of powers at regional, State, European and international level, with the full participation of the sub-State level, can be considered. Any agreement in relation to that would stem from liberation of the people that give moral force and legitimacy to the constituent form. Imaginative forms for local, regional, intra-State and multi-national structures can follow as they would be grounded in that necessary respect for sub-State constitutionalism as its constituent polity.

2. ALL-ISSUE TRILATERALISM, THE END OF THE DEFICITS AND THE ACTIVE ACCOMMODATION OF THE STATELESS NATION

Trilateralism should therefore not exclude the dimension of sovereignty, because that necessarily perpetuates the climate of bilateralism and fails to factor in the legal context of the redefined meaning of sovereignty across

[53] *Estatuto de Autonomia*, Catalunya, Preamble.

the relevant spheres. Maintaining bilateralism also retains the consequences of that destructive force and makes it impossible for the conscious realisation and application of the modern legal context. It will continue to lead to friction and misunderstandings if there is insistence on restraining perceived expansion into external competences and manifestations of Statehood. It will regularly give rise to inflammatory language that will heighten emotions and tension rather than follow a policy of neutralising emotions and managing sensitivities.

With a genuine and productive application of the modern legal context what should come first is a departure from bilateralism and the adoption of all-issue trilateralism. That should be followed by confidence-building, which should address language, emotions and tension as a priority. The rounds at the UN, which punctuate relations and give the parties an opportunity to reignite old emotions and arguments, should be replaced or influenced by a consensus trilateral position. It is axiomatic that for such all-issue trilateralism to have any chance of success it must proceed on the basis that all parties participate on an equal footing and have the right to agree or disagree and that agreements can only emerge if all parties agree.[54] Addressing the tensions between the parties should then lead to a greater understanding of Gibraltar's aspirations and the ability to accommodate these so as to achieve more power, representation and influence on the European stage. Productive all-issue trilateralism could facilitate obtaining these reforms if it leads to a dissipation of traditional resistance to governance changes from Spain. These could still be achieved without Spanish co-operation and in a climate of higher tension and bilateralism, but this would be a more tortured process.

In a reform environment Gibraltar could learn much from the federal arrangements in Belgium, Germany or Austria. Equally, the stateless nations co-existing within the Anglo-Spanish constitutional frameworks are both comparators and drivers for internal reform. These may facilitate Gibraltar reforms because of the pressure Britain and Spain face to devolve further powers to these nations. Demands that Gibraltar makes may not seem so radical in the context of wider evolution of State constitutional arrangements.[55] The acquisition of a very full measure of

[54] Unlike the 2001–02 joint sovereignty talks.

[55] See, for example, the Catalan 2006 *Estatuto*, which proclaims that the powers of its government emanate from the Catalan people (Art 2(4)) and produce a modernised package of devolved governance arrangements for Catalunya within Spain and at European level: *Ley Organica 6/2006 de 19 de Julio de Reforma del Estatuto de Autonomia de Cataluna*, BOE, num 172, 20 July 2006. Additionally, for example, the manifestos of both the *Partido Nacionalista Vasco* and *Euskal Alkartasuna* to the Basque elections of March 2009 emphasised the demands made on the Spanish State by moderate and separatist nationalism, from the acquisition of further competences to a right to self-determination. The latter sought a 'sovereignty law' to further its more radical agenda. Basque nationalist parties secured more than 40 per cent of the vote in the Basque elections of 1 March 2009.

self-government by Gibraltar side by side with EU membership has in effect changed the nature of the UK–Gibraltar relationship into a quasi-federal one. In that sense this co-operative federalism must be maximised with supportive governance mechanics to breathe an expansive air into this constitutional environment.

In terms of governance reforms, it is the sub-State executive level that is the most crucial level at which empowerment should be achieved. The reasons for that are simply because this level represents the people of the territory and can acquire the greatest level of influence in prospective measures, because of its capacity for liaison with State and European executive. For example, there is a case for a separate MEP being assigned to Gibraltar and for representation to be granted within the Committee of the Regions or Assembly of the Regions. But in all cases—valuable as they may be —such representation can be engulfed by the pure minority of that participation and in the latter two cases the comparative remoteness from the centre of influence. As such, the sub-State executive can be empowered at different levels. First, the relationship with the United Kingdom at European level and the discharge of its duty under Article 299(4) of the TEC needs to be clarified and demarcated. In the context of the objectives marked out within the 2002 reform proposals, it is clear that Gibraltar would want such relationship to be as close as possible to a political agency. Secondly, an intergovernmental Agreement would have to establish formal liaison arrangements to guarantee influence at all levels of European law-making. Thirdly, there would have to be domestic constitutional reform to clarify and strengthen the provisions touching on the European dimension. Fourthly, the sub-State executive should be empowered to enter into certain international agreements[56] and acquire a special status within certain international bodies.[57] Fifthly, and in conjunction with the Gibraltar legislature, it should acquire greater ability to scrutinise and influence draft legislation. Sixthly, pure sub-State or sub-State/State forums could be established by which Gibraltar could interface with other entities grappling with similar governance challenges. There is no suggestion that Spain should participate in the domestic constitutional panorama of Gibraltar but rather that through a process of all-issue trilateralism misunderstandings will dissipate and objections to these reforms withdrawn.[58] Additionally, the recognition of Gibraltar as a sovereignty player can lead to regional co-operative arrangements where different parties voluntarily pool powers which could acquire momentum at both multi-national and European level.

[56] As is the case already in Belgium or Germany.

[57] Short of full membership perhaps or observer status. eg, it should be possible to confer observer status for Gibraltar at Commonwealth Heads of Government Meetings (CHOGM) and other Commonwealth forums. The Spanish dimension should not be a factor there.

[58] It will be recalled that even reforms as innocuous as giving Gibraltarians the right to vote in European elections have been objected to.

3. STATUS PRO-ACTIVE OR STATUS DRIFT?

As practical self-governance issues are progressed and the European and external governance issues are substantively improved, attention could turn to Gibraltar's status.[59] The manner in which this could be approached will largely depend on the overall practical realities. In this work two possible solutions are presented.[60] The first is that of a so-called European Free Association. The second is a drifting towards an undefined end by a series of conventions or adjustments through time. A fundamental cornerstone of both is the support by expression of the free will of the people of the territory. In fact the position of referenda to underpin agreed arrangements and give them endorsement and necessary legitimacy is crucial. Referenda should not be limited to the people of Gibraltar. If agreements emerge that would touch on the status of Gibraltar and secure arrangements in the European Union this should be put to a referendum of the people of Gibraltar. In parallel, and akin to the Irish example, the withdrawal of the Spanish claim to sovereignty or (to put it less provocatively) the permanent acceptance of any emergent arrangements, should be put to the Spanish people. It may be difficult for Spanish officials or politicians to move away from the historic line over Gibraltar without being accused of reckless abandonment of sovereign rights. If the Spanish people in referendum took such a decision, it would provide the necessary legitimacy and support.[61]

The first and more proactive way of combining all these features is to see whether an agreement or status could emerge from a genuinely purposeful trilateral process. The virtue of that is openness and not secrecy. For years, a deep culture of mistrust has been bred in Gibraltar by the perception that officials have privately been brewing plans over Gibraltar's future behind closed doors. There is much in that, as papers released at the Public Record Office demonstrate the number of ideas considered from time to time by the British Foreign Office. A major virtue of an attempt at a trilateral agreement is that, first, those talks can occur openly and with the necessary mandate of the people of Gibraltar. Secondly, such talks would be entirely safe if the process were on a firmly equal footing. Thirdly, nothing would be finalised at such talks, and would be subject to

[59] Spain recently made clear that it harbours aspirations to also review Gibraltar's relationship with the European Union, *Gibraltar Chronicle* (Gibraltar 27 March 2007).

[60] A third is possible: that a new decolonised status is borne out of confrontation and notwithstanding the Spanish Government's opposition. This is not only unlikely without a fundamental reappraisal of current methodology but even if it did transpire would not provide a permanent and secure end to the dispute.

[61] For some comparative discussion on the use of referenda as a basis for constitutional accommodation see S Tierney, *Constitutional Law and National Pluralism* (Oxford, OUP, 2004) 284–324.

the two referenda alluded to. In such an attempt, the people of Gibraltar would not only be able to ensure that any route mapped out follows their express wishes, but that they were driving an initiative to find a way through the historic conundrum.

Any Agreement could deliver a decolonised and permanent status ratified and endorsed by a new Treaty between the three countries.[62] This would deal with and bypass the State-centricity of the UN and EU. Indeed, it would be quite welcome if in a more pro-active environment both the UN and EU adopted a constructive and involved attitude which could assist in coaxing the States forward or providing the necessary supportive mechanics. An acceptance of statelessness by Gibraltar could be matched by an abandonment of the sovereignty claim by Spain. Both aspirational goals[63] are valuable to the relevant parties in equal measure. A form of Free Association could be developed to maintain the Crown association and give Gibraltarians the element of self-government desired.[64] This would, in effect, confirm the quasi-federal relationship with the United Kingdom. Securing the position within the European Union by providing the President of the European Commission a personal role within the constitutional arrangements might be an imaginative element of any framework. It would ensure more constructive involvement from that quarter and stress the supra-national environment within which Gibraltar cohabits and which is central to its governance. The status is 'European', to reflect the importance of the European dimension to everyday governance and the need to give practical vent to influence at that level. There need not be an EC Treaty amendment itself, as Article 299(4) is flexible enough to accommodate free association.[65] What would be needed are arrangements of a domestic nature, to reposition the manner in which the United Kingdom discharges any external affairs 'responsibility'. Such a status would be a merger between a non-independent form of advanced self-government, vested with democratic legitimacy and the necessary cohabitation within the supra-national environment of interdependence. The new arrangements must also deliver sufficient domestic, State and European mechanisms to secure power, representation and influence within the EU. These would include structures at a different regional level

[62] As for the mechanics of this, see A Aust, *Modern Treaty Law and Practice* (Cambridge, CUP, 2002).

[63] To independence (Gibraltar) and to the integration of Gibraltar into Spain.

[64] The basis for multi-party agreement would lie in neutralising the absolutist aspirations of sovereignty. In that respect, there is no outright sovereignty 'win' for either. Spain does not achieve the integration of Gibraltar and the latter does not acquire independence. The possibility of seeking independence is suspended or abandoned altogether simultaneously with Spain's claim. Gibraltarians might be prepared to drop any prospective claims to independence if Spain drops its claim.

[65] Though amendment may be necessary to endow the European guarantor of the arrangements—if one emerges—with specific legal cover.

for trans-border co-operation so that there was an adequate response to deliver that degree of cohabitive multi-national federalism. The specifics of any possible arrangements cannot be set in stone and would emerge after discussions.[66] The aim of breaking down State-centricity and safeguarding sub-State constitutionalism would be to achieve a 'multi-level constitutional system designed to protect human rights, popular sovereignty and democratic self-government across frontiers.'[67]

Any further constitutional refinements would have to be laid over the fairly settled constitutional framework set out in the 2006 Constitution, as this provides a constitutional patchwork that has the advantage of having received recent legitimacy in a vote of the Gibraltar people.[68] Without attempting an exhaustive list, any further changes would ideally cater for an agency arrangement in external affairs,[69] the right to disassociate after endorsement by referendum,[70] an end to the reserve power of legislation without consent and a right to amend the constitution by domestic process.[71] The opportunity would have to be taken to re-examine the nature and terms of membership of the European Union to see if these, in any way, require revision. A system of free association could provide the necessary radical reconfiguration of relations.[72] It provides that opportunity for a merger between a non-independent form of full self-government and a constructive multi-national, quasi-federal cohabitation within a supra-national environment of interdependence. That interplay of powers might actually, conversely, generate more power rather than less.[73] Given the complexity inherent in the historic sovereignty dispute managing this task is in many ways a more complex challenge than simple secession.[74] There can be no doubt that the challenge is great. But the reward of ending one of the longest-running disputes is also significant. For that to occur, the radical reappraisal that puts active consent of the Gibraltar people at its heart needs to precede such a reconfiguration of relations. Formulae substantively different to the one traced above could be

[66] It may be possible to also deliver a specific EU cross-border funding programme to foster cooperation as the EU did with Ireland-Northern Ireland.

[67] As Petersmann has described in a different context: see Petersmann in N Walker (ed), *Sovereignty in Transition* (Oxford, Hart Publishing, 2003) 163.

[68] The Constitution should also be 'patriated' and entrenched.

[69] Cook Islands-style. The formal devolution of the external affairs responsibility is also a possibility albeit one which may call on human or technical resources. Defence would need to remain the province of the UK within any free association or Treaty arrangements.

[70] Subject to any alternative agreement if it emerges in trilateral talks that, eg, Spain would drop her claim.

[71] See the West Indies Act 1967 for a model of free association arrangements.

[72] S Tierney, 'Reframing Sovereignty? Sub-State National Societies and Contemporary Challenges to the Nation-State' (2005) 54 ICLQ 161–83, 181.

[73] Loughlin in N Walker (ed), *Sovereignty in Transition* (Oxford, Hart Publishing, 2003) 55–86.

[74] Tierney n 70 above, 181.

considered if it remains rooted in an acceptance of the wishes of the sovereign constituent power of the territory—its people.

If traditional mistrust persists and it is impossible to achieve or even attempt such an Agreement, the less pro-active way of proceeding is to allow a drifting into a status that could emerge much more slowly. The substantive objectives might not be dissimilar to a free association model and would entail pursuing domestic reforms with the United Kingdom in three ways: internal constitutional reforms; intergovernmental and European arrangements to secure power, representation and influence within the Union; and United Kingdom legislation to deal with domestic colonial aspects.[75] Recourse could be had to the development of conventions as in the period 1969–2006. Any developments that affect other stateless nations would provide useful guidance.[76] This option offers less adventurous and more conservative progress.[77] The downside is that Gibraltar would continue on the UN List, and the achievement of formal decolonisation in a State-centric UN seems unlikely if only one side pursues this. Additionally, a status would emerge much more slowly and would be subject to significant lack of certainty, political fragility in all three countries, and substantial resistance and obstruction. At European level, this approach would not necessarily resolve the deficits experienced, which would be facilitated by a more productive trilateral attitude. These factors provide an unsatisfactory dimension to the option of simply drifting. Greater clarity would be achieved if the parties were bolder, to try to secure more in the knowledge that any final decision on proposals emerging from a tripartite process would be determined by the people of Gibraltar.

In the emotional, political cauldron that Gibraltar is, sovereignty has not lost its importance to either Spain or Gibraltarians. Any prospect for a solution to this conundrum lies in a more constructive approach that deals head-on with the issue between the parties. The focus has to be on putting the modern legal context first, and accepting an environment of stateless pluralism and that this amounts to sovereignty as redefined. There needs to be an emphasis on co-operative, cohabitive powers rather than on absolutism, and on trilateralism and inclusion rather than bilateralism and

[75] Such as exclusion from the formal definition of colony and legislation, akin to the Statute of Westminster.

[76] This could work if the parties put sovereignty to one side and addressed the issues of external and European governance under an umbrella of statelessness, and then allow time to pass to make wider changes. More radical drivers like Scottish independence and Basque free association will influence that process.

[77] It is quite possible to get to that constitutional destination by this method—see *R v Secretary of State for Foreign and Commonwealth Affairs, ex p Indian Assocn of Alberta* [1982] 1 QB 892, 923; L Zines, *Constitutional Change in the Commonwealth* (Cambridge, CUP, 1991); and P Oliver, *The Development of Constitutional Theory in Australia, Canada and New Zealand* (Oxford, OUP, 2005), cited previously.

exclusion. Sovereignty continues to be important, albeit in an evolved sense. In that evolved context, it relies on different polities interacting with each other—both State and sub-State. In decolonising options short of independence the same issues arise, especially in its interrelationship with a supra-national sphere. Gibraltar's governance and democratic deficit was caused by bilateralism that arose from the continued application of a now spent sovereignty context. It will be dissipated by trilateralism, late sovereignty, pluralism, constitutionalism and an acceptance of the decolonised and sovereign stateless nation of Gibraltar. In that way the collective human rights of the people of Gibraltar will have converged with the sovereignty they hold.

Index